RONALD J. WALDRON
United States Department of Justice

JAGDISH C. UPPAL
National Center for State Courts

CHESTER L. QUARLES
University of Mississippi

R. PAUL McCAULEY
University of Louisville

HILARY HARPER
Marshall University

ROBERT L. FRAZIER
Lamar University

JAMES C. BENSON
University of Houston/Clear Lake

JOHN R. ALTEMOSE
Lamar University

THE CRIMINAL JUSTICE SYSTEM

CONTENTS

List of Figures   xviii

List of Tables   xix

Preface   xxi

PART ONE
OVERVIEW: THE CRIMINAL JUSTICE SYSTEM

CHAPTER ONE
LAW IN SOCIETY   3

Sociology of Law   4

The Evolution of Law • The Nature of Law • A Normative Legal System

General Functions of Law   6

Rule of Law   8

Divisions of Law   9

Substantive and Procedural Law • Civil Law and Criminal Law • Statutory Law
and Common Law

Sources of Law   10

Nature, Formulation, and Development of Criminal Law   11

Controlling Crime in Primitive Societies • Criminal Law in Ancient Greece • Criminal Law in
Ancient Rome • Criminal Law in Medieval England • Criminal Law in Colonial America •
Criminal Law in Post-Revolutionary America • Contemporary Criminal Law in America

Basic Premises of Criminal Law   16

The Principle of Legality • Guilty Act *(Actus Reus)* • Mental State *(Mens Rea)* • Concurrence in
Time • Harm (An Injury or Result) • Causation

Purpose and Object of Criminal Law   18

Prevention • Restraint • Rehabilitation • Education • Retribution

Classification of Crimes   20

Crimes of Social Harm • Felonies and Misdemeanors • Crimes *Mala in Se* and *Mala Prohibita* •
Infamous and Noninfamous Crimes • Crimes of Moral Turpitude • Common Law Crimes and
Statutory Crimes • Major Crimes and Petty Offenses

Discussion Questions   Notes

800593

CHAPTER TWO
THE CRIMINAL JUSTICE SYSTEM   27

Criminal Justice System 1 as a System   29

The Adversary System   31

Due Process of Law   33

Primary Functional Areas   34
Police • Prosecution • Criminal Court System • Probation • Corrections • Parole

Discussion Questions   Notes

CHAPTER THREE
THE CRIMINAL JUSTICE PROCESS:
ADMINISTRATION OF THE CRIMINAL LAW
IN THE UNITED STATES   43

The Criminal Incident   44
Prearrest Investigation • Apprehension

The Arrest   45
Constitutional Protections • Police Discretion

Booking   49

Case Screening   50

Police Interrogation   52

Initial Appearance and Bail   52
Release on Bond • Release on Recognizance • Assigned Counsel

Investigation   55

Preliminary Hearing   55

Characteristics of the Administration of Criminal Law   56

Trial Court Information Systems   57

The Decision to Charge   59

Grand Jury Indictment or Information   60

Arraignment in Court of Trial   62
Exchange Justice • Guilty Plea • A Plea of Not Guilty

Filing a Motion   66

Trial   67
Prosecution Case • Defense Motion • Defense Case and Prosecution Rebuttal • Instructions of
the Court to the Jury • Arguments to the Jury • Charging the Jury • Deliberation and Verdict •
Sentencing

Appeals 70

Habeas Corpus 70

Juvenile Justice System 71

Juvenile Proceedings 72
Preadjudicatory Phase • Adjudicatory Hearing • Dispositional Hearing

The Administration of Criminal Law 74

Discussion Questions   Notes

PART ONE ANNOTATED BIBLIOGRAPHY 77

PART TWO
THE POLICE

CHAPTER FOUR
HISTORY AND DEVELOPMENT OF POLICE 81

Police Development in Anglo-European Societies 83
Early English Development • Frankpledge System (A.D. 800) • Early Foundations of Anglo-
American Police

Origin of Modern Policing 85
Nineteenth Century: A Model for Modern Policing • Twentieth-Century Development in England

Police Development in the United States 88
Municipal and County Law Enforcement • State Law Enforcement • Federal Law Enforcement

Discussion Questions   Notes

CHAPTER FIVE
LAW ENFORCEMENT IN THE UNITED STATES 95

Law Enforcement: A Legal Construct 96

Federal Law Enforcement 97

State Law Enforcement 97

Local Law Enforcement 98
County Law Enforcement • Municipal Law Enforcement • Special and Auxiliary Police

Nongovernmental Police 101

Coordination and Cooperation of Police 103
Uniform Crime Report (UCR) • Office of Justice Assistance, Research and Statistics (OJARS) •
Recent Developments

Discussion Questions   Notes

CHAPTER SIX
POLICE ADMINISTRATION AND OPERATIONS   107

Primary Line Functions   108

Secondary Line Functions   108

Nonline Functions   108
Staff Services • Auxiliary Services

Principles of Organization   109
Homogeneous Assignment (Division of Labor) • Unity of Command • Chain of Command •
Delegation of Responsibility and Authority • Delineation of Responsibility and Authority • Span
of Control • Objective • Coordination • Time • Territory • Clientele

Management Innovations   113
Program Management • Management by Objectives (MBO) • Program Evaluation and
Review Technique (PERT)

Police Operations   116
Patrol • Traffic • Criminal Investigation

Other Administrative and Operational Functions   123

Discussion Questions   Notes

CHAPTER SEVEN
CONTEMPORARY ISSUES IN LAW ENFORCEMENT   127

Role of the Police   128

Personnel   133
Civil Service • Civilians in Law Enforcement • Promotion by Assessment Center • Minority
Recruitment • Personnel Training • Minimum Standards of Quality • Personnel Selection •
Female Police Officers • Executive Training

Lawsuits Against and by Police Officers   141

Interagency Corporation   142

Police Reorganization   143

Productivity   145

Tax Limitation Measures   145

Police Unions   146

Crime Prevention   146

Crime Analysis   148

Change   149

Planning and Research 149
Federally Supported Police Research

Administrative Policy versus Individual Discretion 155

Working in the Community 157
Police-Community Relations • Community Government

Issues in Perspective: An Integrated Solution 158

Discussion Questions   Notes

PART TWO ANNOTATED BIBLIOGRAPHY 161

PART THREE
PROSECUTION AND DEFENSE

CHAPTER EIGHT
HISTORY AND STRUCTURE OF ADVOCACY 165

The Development of the Law Profession 166

The History of Prosecutorial Services 167

Development of Prosecution in America 168
United States Attorney General • State and Local Attorneys General • The Prosecutor Selection
Process • The Rand Study

Influence of the Contemporary Prosecutor 174

Discussion Questions   Notes

CHAPTER NINE
THE STATE'S ADVOCATE 177

Screening and Diversion 178

Decision to Prosecute 180

Preliminary Hearing 180

Indictment and Information 181

Pretrial Negotiations 182

Arraignment 184

Trial 185

Discussion Questions   Notes

CHAPTER TEN
THE DEFENDANT'S ADVOCATE   189

Defense Delivery Services   190

Defense Consultation   193

Role of the Defense   195

Assessing Criminal Defenders   196

Discussion Questions   Notes

CHAPTER ELEVEN
CONTEMPORARY ISSUES IN ADVOCACY   199

Working with the Police   200

Minimizing Discretion   201

Deciding the Charge   202

Suggesting Informal Alternatives to Prosecution   202

Improving the Office of the Prosecutor   203
Status and Pay • Advocacy Training

Examining the Role of the Grand Jury   205

Appointing a Public Defender   205

Controlling the Power of the Advocates   206

Discussion Questions   Notes

Part Three Annotated Bibliography   208

PART FOUR
COURTS

CHAPTER TWELVE
DEVELOPMENTAL HISTORY OF COURTS   211

Chronology of Development   212
Origin of Courts • Courts from Antiquity through the Middle Ages • Development of Modern
Courts • Development of Courts in the United States • Overview of Contemporary Courts

Court Lag, Reform   218
Recognition • Theory • Limitations and Vulnerability • Reforms
Discussion Questions   Notes

CHAPTER THIRTEEN
STRUCTURE OF THE COURTS
IN THE UNITED STATES   229

Federal Court System   230
United States Supreme Court • United States Courts of Appeals • District Courts

Military Court System   235
Grades of Court-Martial • Safeguards • United States Court of Military Appeals

State Court System   237
Variety of State Courts • Levels of State Courts

Juvenile Court System   241

Dual Court System and Unification of State Systems   244
Overlap and Conflict • Court Unification

Discussion Questions   Notes

CHAPTER FOURTEEN
FUNCTIONS OF THE COURTS   249

Pretrial   250
Warrants and Presentment • Bail • Disposition of Misdemeanors • Preliminary Hearing,
Information, Return of Grand Jury Indictment • Arraignment • Pretrial Motions

Trial   258
Petit Jury • Evidence • Witnesses • Closing the Trial

Sentencing   261
Objectives of Sentencing • Sentence Hearing Factors • Sentencing Alternatives and Diversion

Postconviction Remedies   262
Appeal • Appellate Review • Other Postconviction Remedies
Discussion Questions   Notes

CHAPTER FIFTEEN
COURT ISSUES AND PROBLEMS: THE PARTICIPANTS' PERSPECTIVES   267

Active Participants   268
Judges • Adversaries • Jurors • Witnesses

Indirect Participants   272
Peripheral Personnel • The Public

Discussion Questions   Notes

PART FOUR ANNOTATED BIBLIOGRAPHY   275

PART FIVE
CORRECTIONS

CHAPTER SIXTEEN
BACKGROUND AND HISTORY OF CORRECTIONS 279

The European Heritage 280

The American Heritage 280
The Prison System • Women's Reformatories • Juvenile Training School • Work Camps

History of Community-Based Corrections 284
Jails • Juvenile Detention Centers • Halfway Houses and Prerelease Guidance Centers • Programs for Predelinquents • Individual and Group Placement • Special Programs

Discussion Questions   Notes

CHAPTER SEVENTEEN
CORRECTIONAL ORGANIZATIONS 291

Concept of Corrections 292

Types of Correctional Organizations 293

Federal Correctional Organizations 293

Military Correctional Organizations 294

State Correctional Organizations 295
Formal Prison Organizations • Informal Prison Organizations

Local Correctional Organizations 299
Jails • Predelinquent Centers • Foster Homes and Group Homes • Community Prerelease Centers and Halfway Houses

Discussion Questions   Notes

CHAPTER EIGHTEEN
FUNCTIONS OF
CORRECTIONAL ORGANIZATIONS 307

Management and Administration 308
Planning and Policy • Fiscal Operations • Personnel Management • Research and Evaluation

Custody and Control 310
Security • Control Procedures • Reception and Intake • Classification • Food Service • Medical Service • Industry Programs • Discipline

Correctional Treatment 315
Prisoner or Client Services • Counseling, Therapy, and Individual Evaluation • Short-term
Treatment Programs • Work Furlough • Education and Recreation • Prerelease Counseling

Discussion Questions   Notes

CHAPTER NINETEEN
PROBLEMS, CONTROVERSIES,
AND MODERN CONCEPTS IN CORRECTIONS 321

People Involved in Corrections   322
Correctional Workers • Prisoners

Inadequacies in Management and Organization   325
Correctional Management • Correctional Organizations

Institutional and Noninstitutional Corrections   328
Prisons • Jails • Community Corrections

Responsibility   330
The Public • Law Enforcement Agencies • The Courts • The Legislatures

Discussion Questions   Notes

PART FIVE ANNOTATED BIBLIOGRAPHY   332

PART SIX
PROBATION AND PAROLE

CHAPTER TWENTY
HISTORY AND PROCESS OF PROBATION   337

Definition of Probation   338

Philosophy and Objective   338

Historical Perspectives   339

The Probation Process   342

Probation Administration and Organization   342

Probation and Parole Personnel   343

Application and Eligibility   343

Juvenile Probation   344
Intake and Screening • Social Study and Diagnosis • Supervision and Treatment • Auxiliary
Programs • Application and Eligibility

Misdemeanant Probation 346

Presentence Report 347

Revocation of Probation 348

Discussion Questions   Notes

CHAPTER TWENTY-ONE
PROBLEMS AND RECENT
DEVELOPMENTS IN PROBATION 351

Problems 353
Special Issues • Lack of Skilled Personnel • Case Load

Recent Developments 356
Probation Subsidy Programs • Volunteers as Probation Supervisors • Research and Evaluation •
Impact of Public Awareness • Establishment of Standards • Cooperation and
Coordination of Components

Discussion Questions   Notes

CHAPTER TWENTY-TWO
HISTORY AND PROCESS OF PAROLE 363

Definition of Parole 364

Philosophy and Objective 365

Historical Perspectives 366

The Parole Process 368
Parole Eligibility • Parole Selection • Supervision, Control, and Guidance • Conditions of Parole
and Its Revocation • Contract Parole

Discussion Questions   Notes

CHAPTER TWENTY-THREE
PROBLEMS AND
RECENT DEVELOPMENTS IN PAROLE 379

Problems 380
Fragmented System • Lack of Skilled Personnel • Parole Board Members • Individual Rights •
Research

Recent Developments 383
Public Awareness • Determining Sentencing and Abolishing Parole • Establishment of
Standards • Court Intervention • Community Involvement • Ex-offenders as Advisors

Discussion Questions   Notes

PART SIX ANNOTATED BIBLIOGRAPHY 386

PART SEVEN
THE FUTURE OF
THE CRIMINAL JUSTICE SYSTEM

CHAPTER TWENTY-FOUR
SYSTEMS APPROACH
TO CRIMINAL JUSTICE   391

Need for a Systems Approach   392

Basic Elements of the Systems Approach   393
Examining the Whole System and Its Parts • Understanding Goals and Objectives • Stating Goals in Measurable Terms • Developing Alternative Systems and Mathematical Models

Long-range Contributions of the Systems Approach   397
Measuring Effectiveness of Agencies and Programs • Resolving Conflicts Within the System • Setting Priorities: Cost-Benefit Analysis

Short-range Benefits of the Systems Approach   399
Concentrating on Goals • Using a Systems Approach to Criminal Justice Subsystems

Limitations of the Systems Approach   401
Omitting Important Goals of the System • Assuming That Only the System Can Be Changed

Discussion Questions   Notes

CHAPTER TWENTY-FIVE
THE IMPACT OF
SCIENCE AND TECHNOLOGY   405

Technology in the Laboratory   406
Fingerprinting • Voiceprinting • Analyzing Physical Traces

Technology in the Field   408
Communications • Computers

Electronic Data Processing   409

Other Technological Advances   411

Effect of the Behavioral Sciences on Criminal Justice   412
Business Administration • Public Administration • Industrial Psychology • Experimental Psychology • Counseling • Sociology • Probability and Statistics

Science and the Shape of Things to Come   415

Discussion Questions   Notes

CHAPTER TWENTY-SIX
REFORM   419

National Crime Commission Recommendations for Reform   420

Research   420

Personnel   422
Recruiting versus Working Conditions • Recruiting Women • Recruiting College Graduates •
Recruiting Minorities • Standards for Recruiting • Education and Training

Funding   428

Reform and the Future   429

Discussion Questions   Notes

CHAPTER TWENTY-SEVEN
BASIC CHANGE   433

Societal Reform   434

Criminal Justice System as a Cause of Crime   435
"Labeling" Theory • "Labeling" Theory versus Reform • Victimless Crime •
Laws That Cause Crime

Injustice in the Criminal Justice System   438
Discretion • Discrimination

Instituting Changes   439
Social Justice • Change in Criminal Law • Reduction of Discretion • Decentralization of Power

Discussion Questions   Notes

PART SEVEN ANNOTATED BIBLIOGRAPHY   442

APPENDIXES

APPENDIX A
CAREER OPPORTUNITIES IN
THE CRIMINAL JUSTICE SYSTEM

Career Opportunities in Federal Law Enforcement   446
Nature of the Work • Places of Employment • Training, Other Qualifications, and
Advancement • Employment Outlook • Earnings and Working Conditions • Sources of
Additional Information

Career Opportunities in State Law Enforcement   450

Nature of the Work • Places of Employment • Training, Other Qualifications, and Advancement • Employment Outlook • Earnings and Working Conditions • Sources of Additional Information

Career Opportunities in Municipal Law Enforcement   451

Nature of the Work • Places of Employment • Training, Other Qualifications, and Advancement • Employment Outlook • Earnings and Working Conditions • Sources of Additional Information

Career Opportunities in Corrections   453

Nature of the Work • Places of Employment • Training, Other Qualifications, and Advancement • Employment Outlook • Earnings and Working Conditions • Sources of Additional Information

Career Opportunities in the Legal Profession   456

Nature of the Work • Places of Employment • Training, Other Qualifications, and Advancement • Employment Outlook • Earnings and Working Conditions • Sources of Additional Information

Bibliography   458

APPENDIX B
THE UNITED STATES CONSTITUTION   459

APPENDIX C
INDIVIDUAL RIGHTS UNDER THE CONSTITUTION   473

APPENDIX D
SELECTED CRIMINAL LAW CASES   492

APPENDIX E
GLOSSARY   498

INDEX   505

LIST OF FIGURES

1.1 Punishment 19

2.1 Flow Diagram of the Criminal Justice System 30

2.2 A Fighting System of Justice 32

2.3 Primary Functional Areas of the Criminal Justice System 34

3.1 Criminal Justice Highway 46

3.2 Pretrial Case Screening 51

3.3 Criminal Justice Decision Making 58

3.4 The Legal Citation 72

5.1 Law Enforcement Code of Ethics 99

6.1 A Well-Organized Municipal Police Department 110

6.2 Organizational Structure of a Police Operations Bureau 118

6.3 Laboratory Technicians Processing Soil 122

7.1 Recommendations of the National Crime Commission 129

7.2 Recommendations of the National Advisory Commission on Criminal Justice Standards and Goals 130

7.3 The Code of Hammurabi 147

7.4 Formulation and Execution of Police Policy 156

7.5 Apprehension Process 159

8.1 United States Department of Justice 169

8.2 Organizational Chart — Office of the District Attorney 172

9.1 Prosecutorial Encounters in the Justice System 179

13.1 United States Supreme Court 232

13.2 State Court Structure 239

14.1 Felony Case Time Schedule 251

14.2 The Path to Trial in Florida 252

17.1 Organization of the Federal Bureau of Prisons 294

17.2 State Corrections Organization 296

17.3 Maximum Security Unit 297

17.4 Jurisdictional Structure of Criminal Justice Operations at the Community Level 300

18.1 Functional Positions in a Large Prison Unit 309

18.2 Super-Security Institution 311

19.1 Cellblock 324

19.2 Community-based Corrections 329

24.1 Criminal Justice System 394

25.1 Voice Spectograph 407

25.2 National Criminal Justice Information System 411

26.1 Major Recommendations of the National Advisory Commission on Criminal Justice Standards and Goals 426

LIST OF TABLES

6.1 Police Functions: Line and Staff   109

8.1 The Attorney General: Selection and Term   170

9.1 Justice Interrelationships   181

10.1 Relationship Between Type of Attorney and Method of Disposition   191

10.2 Pretrial Custodial Status of Defendants During Trial by Type of Attorney   193

12.1 Judicial and Administrative Personnel of the Federal Courts   218

12.2 Judges in Appellate and Major Trial Courts, by Type of Court and Jurisdiction   220

13.1 United States Judicial Circuits   234

20.1 Number of Offenders on Probation and on Parole or in Institutions   341

20.2 Number of State and Local Agencies Performing Probations and Functions   342

20.3 Number of Personnel in State and Local Probation and Parole Agencies   343

22.1 Prison Population and Number of Releases in State and Federal Institutions   367

22.2 Comparative Data on Inmates Released on Parole from State and Federal Institutions   368

PREFACE

The 1960s brought forth a new era for the American criminal justice system. Rising crime rates and social unrest strained the system to near breaking point, and because of the inadequacies in the system, it began to grind to a halt. It became clear that the American criminal justice system was in need of major repair and reform.

One response was the establishment of criminal justice programs on college campuses. Over the past two decades the number of college programs in criminal justice has grown from a small handful to a point where criminal justice courses are offered on almost every college campus.

To reach this growing audience, the first edition of *The Criminal Justice System: An Introduction* was planned. Because the field of criminal justice broadly encompasses law and law enforcement, the prosecutor, the courts, and corrections, it was decided to bring together a group of specialists from the various areas of criminal justice to write a comprehensive textbook on the criminal justice system. The approach has proved to be viable, and the first edition has been well received.

Since the development of the first edition, however, some major changes have taken place in the criminal justice system. And we have recognized the necessity that both text and illustrations be improved and updated. Thus, the second edition incorporates the latest developments, while retaining the basic organization of the first edition.

TEXTBOOK APPROACH

There are many valid approaches to writing an introductory textbook on the criminal justice system. One could write from a legal, criminal process, or sociological point of view, among others. We chose to write from the criminal justice *system* perspective.

We view the criminal justice system as a whole composed of many subsystems — the police, the prosecutors, the courts, and corrections, including probation and parole. Our task, as we have seen it, is to describe the subsystems of the criminal justice system as we know it to be — not as it should be.

PEDAGOGY

The Criminal Justice System: An Introduction was written primarily for the introductory course in criminal justice. This book is designed to provide students with basic information on the system. The chapters are organized in the sequence in which we suggest they be covered. The first part of the text places the criminal justice system in proper perspective. Students are first introduced to the nature of law and society in general. Then they are presented with a brief overview of criminal justice agencies and the criminal justice process. The criminal justice agencies are discussed in the order in which they are usually encountered when an individual goes through the criminal justice process. Sections on the police, the prosecution and defense, the courts, corrections, and probation and parole all follow a basic pattern. Within these sections the history, present structure, current functions, and contemporary problems of each major area are thoroughly discussed. The final section of the text speculates on what the future will bring for the criminal justice system.

As an aid to students, a *Study Guide* is available. The *Guide* includes objectives, chapter outlines, vocabulary exercises, and multiple-choice and true-or-false questions with answers, so that students can check on their understanding of the subject matter.

ACKNOWLEDGMENTS

The authors would like to express their thanks to the following individuals for their careful reviews of the manuscript: Warren W. Bundy, Schenectady County Community College; Mark L. McDermott, Brevard Community College; Kenneth E. North, Attorney General, Territory of Guam; George D. Schrader, Auburn University at Montgomery; and Fred E. Whitmore, Long Beach City College. The opinions expressed in this book are the authors' and are not necessarily those of the agencies that they represent.

THE AUTHORS

PART ONE

OVERVIEW:
THE CRIMINAL
JUSTICE SYSTEM

CHAPTER ONE

LAW IN SOCIETY

SOCIOLOGY OF LAW

GENERAL FUNCTIONS
OF LAW

RULE OF LAW

DIVISIONS OF LAW

SOURCES OF LAW

NATURE,
FORMULATION, AND
DEVELOPMENT OF
CRIMINAL LAW

BASIC PREMISES OF
CRIMINAL LAW

PURPOSE AND OBJECT
OF CRIMINAL LAW

CLASSIFICATION OF
CRIMES

*Purpose: To develop an understanding of law
and its function in, and relationship to society.*

THE DEVELOPMENT OF a highly organized industrialized society has made possible many of the important technological advances that directly influence the lifestyle and standard of living of every individual in this nation. The average American household now maintains a standard of living unparalleled in any other nation in the world. However, with such technological, scientific, and industrial advances and their attendant benefits for the individual have come many social problems. Vast industrial growth now threatens to outstrip the nation's energy-production capabilities. Increased mobility, while aiding in the development of large industries, has contributed to the deterioration of traditional American institutions, as reflected by an increasing divorce rate and significant levels of criminal activity ranging from street crimes to organized crime and white-collar crimes. The stress of modern industrialized society has led to a substantial increase in alcohol abuse and alcoholism in the average American worker. Industrial wastes have so polluted the atmosphere in some cities that factories must curtail production to protect the health of the residents. The list of social problems goes on.

Although it would be difficult to determine which of these social ills is of greatest concern to the American people as a whole, the fact that the press devotes substantial coverage to the social problem of crime and delinquency indicates America's concern about this menace to society. Traditional means of social control — churches, communities, schools, families, and so on — seem to be losing their position as the primary forces for maintaining order, with the ever-increasing burden of maintaining order falling on a more formal means of social control, the criminal justice system. This ever-increasing burden on the criminal justice system has placed additional emphasis on the role of criminologists in American society. The life work of these individuals is "concerned with the study of the phenomenon of crime and of the factors or circumstances — individual and environmental — which may have an influence on, or be associated with, criminal behavior and the state of crime in general."[1] Their goal is to acquire knowledge about the causes of crime in order to reduce, if not ultimately eliminate, this monumental plague on our society.

In general, modern criminologists approach the study of crime from three directions: (1) the *sociology of law*, an analysis of the origin, development, and definition of criminal law in our society; (2) *criminal etiology*, a scientific analysis of the causes of crime; and (3) *penology*, a study of methods for controlling crime and criminals.[2] Because criminal law is the principal weapon the present system of criminal justice in America uses to combat crime, a discussion of the general nature, development, and functions of law in society, particularly the criminal law, is necessary.

SOCIOLOGY OF LAW

For centuries, legal scholars have struggled with the problem of understanding law. The fact that law is a very complex social institution, varying in nature in different societies and at different stages of historical development, has placed barriers in the way of developing a universally accepted definition of law that would serve as a foundation for future discussion and research. Faced with the complexity of this institution, some scholars have even argued against efforts to define law, expounding the belief that total immersion in a legally based profession will provide each individual with a sound feeling for law. While this observation may hold once people are employed in some aspect of our legal system, the student contemplating a career in one of the criminal justice professions needs an adequate understanding of the essence of law and its relation to society. To this end sociologists have contributed the most research and analysis.

THE EVOLUTION OF LAW

Sociologists view society as a vast social system that is structured or molded by the interactions among members of society, particularly those interactions or contacts that recur with some degree of regularity. The position each member of society holds within this social structure is differentiated by varying sets of obligations collectively called his or her *role* and a set of rights referred to as his or her *status*.[3] These obligations and rights are expressed in the form of rules known as *norms*, which may or may not be clearly articulated. Take, for example, norms that define parental roles and status, which are generally understood or implicit. Family members generally expect fathers to be in charge of their households, to be providers and protectors of their clan with the right to make the final decisions on matters relating to the families' well-being. However, other norms relating to family obligations and rights have been made more explicit over time in the form of statutes or laws, such as those dealing with child abuse and neglect.

The reason for this gradual process of codifying norms, or lawmaking, can be traced to the earliest human efforts at self-preservation. Although people were engulfed by a society that necessitated such combinations as clans and tribes for protection, as well as for social and economic advancement, their individuality led to the development of certain expressed general rights with regard to person and property. Over time, unwritten rules governing social and economic interaction were expanded until they recognized each individual's right to defend himself or herself from injury and to enjoy property without outside interference. While a sufficient standard for primitive societies, unwritten rules of social control were ineffective in a rapidly developing and advancing society. Consequently, an effort was made to clarify and reword them so that all people would know their definitions, limits, and applications. Some of these rules became the laws that later received further breadth and expression through the growth of courts and legislative bodies. For example, the right of defense from personal injury was gradually qualified by the rule that if an individual attempted to injure the person of another, and was personally injured while doing so, the attacker could not claim any compensation. These laws — laws that create, discover, and define the rights and obligations of each person in society — are referred to as *substantive laws*.

THE NATURE OF LAW

The rules of law in society are legal or formalized norms that define how people or institutions "ought" to act and how state officials or sanctioning agents are supposed to act when a rule violator is brought before them. "Every law expresses a valuation. Even the law that commands us to drive on the right-hand side of the street expresses the value choices of order over chaos, of right handedness over left handedness."[4] As such, law is based on a normative system, a value system that represents our social conscience. Some rules of law,

> like the laws against murder, are directed to everyone. Some, like the traffic laws, are addressed only to a particular category of persons (automobile drivers). Others

are pertinent to very specific positions (such as laws which define the role of the President of the United States). Still others are addressed to collectivities (corporation law).[5]

Collectively, the *rules of law* or *law* serves as a means of social control in society. More specifically, law is "a formal means of social control that involves the use of rules that are interpreted and are enforceable by the courts of a political community."[6] Law is that portion of the normative system sustained by state power.

Law, as a means of social control, is but one of the many social institutions that help give order to social life. On a daily basis, the norms or standards of other social institutions, such as church, community, family, and school, influence a person's patterns of social behavior. What differentiates law from these other social-ordering institutions is the formal and general nature of its ordering process. Take, for example, a violation of the social norm dictating that a husband provide his wife and children with adequate support. A husband's failure to fulfill this social obligation will normally activate informal social pressures in the form of public opinion, which may originate from local clergy members, elder family members, or neighbors. If these more personal methods of informal social control fail, then a legal solution to the problem may be sought. Law will be more formal and general in its handling of the violation. Before a court of law, the issues involved will be clearly defined by highly structured, often time-consuming, court procedures. The legal process facilitates an objective decision reflecting a community judgment as opposed to a personal judgment. Law, then, is a special kind of formal ordering process that is characterized by the carefully chosen steps it follows in an effort to create, maintain, or restore social order.

A NORMATIVE LEGAL SYSTEM

As a dynamic process, law involves much more than merely a body of rules. Law encompasses virtually every aspect of state action — the process of law creation, the process of authoritatively defining the content of societies' norms, the settlement of disputes, the sanctioning of the breach of norms, the redistribution of resources — therefore, law is in fact a subsytem of society, a very important element of the state.

As individuals in society make demands upon the state, the demands lead either to the creation of new norms or to a change in the application of existing rules. "Every demand for a change in the rules of law, therefore, is a demand that society be changed to that extent. Every demand for a change in the law reflects the sort of society envisioned by those who demand it; that is, reflects their values and goals."[7]

If a citizen demands that a rule-making institution, such as the legislature, formulate a new legal norm of conduct for its citizenry (for example, Prohibition), then simultaneously a new norm or rule for sanctioning agents will be created, directing them, in their individual or institutional role, to impose a sanction if the new legal norm is breached. This normative system of law or legal system "is a system by which one part of the population uses state power to coerce another segment. It is a system for the exercise of state power."[8]

GENERAL FUNCTIONS OF LAW

In all but the most simplistic societies, a system of law performs social functions that are essential to the maintenance of the society itself.[9] If a society could exist without potential disputes, then there would be no need for formalized procedures to define the rights and obligations of each person. Since this is not the case, *one of the primary functions of law is to reestablish order in society when disputes arise.* The conflict may simply be a quarrel between two neighboring families over the issue of disciplining one another's children without appropriate consent. The dispute may be immediately resolved through the informal pressures of neighborhood families, church, or other social institutions; but if it is not resolved, one of the injured parties may seek a legal remedy for the problem, bringing the social function of law into play. From society's point of view, a legal remedy serves as a means of settling a dispute that might otherwise further deteriorate into acts of personal violence or private revenge.

Inherent in a legal solution is a second major function of law, that *law serves as a means of reaffirming the social norms that may have been violated.* When a dispute arises because one party does not act the way the other party in the dispute expected or wanted, then when the matter comes before a third party, "the principal argument to be made in order to persuade the third party to decide the case in favor of one side or the other is to appeal to commonly held norms to justify the action."[10] The degree to which a court will or will not sanction the breach of a legal norm will be directly determined by whether or not the principal objective of the dispute settlement is compromise, so that future relations may be preserved, or absolute victory, where no further contact between the parties involved is anticipated.

While the law performs this important norm enforcement function when the norms of society have been violated, the primary method for controlling certain patterns of behavior still rests with the social institutions of family, community, church, and school: people base their behavior on calculations of probable reward or punishment for conformity or nonconformity to society's rules. Instilled in each member is knowledge of the consequences of personal actions that violate acceptable patterns of behavior. Although this kind of social control is important, its effectiveness is limited by the complex nature of society and the problems and consequences that can stem from this complexity. As society becomes more diverse, community consensus (the shared belief in basic norms) becomes more difficult to achieve and sustain. The current level of geographic mobility, coupled with urbanization and social evolution, has reduced the effectiveness of community consensus as an element of social order. *Thus, a third major function of law is to reinforce these informal methods of control by further enabling each individual to calculate the consequences of personal actions.* This function makes it possible to predict with more assurance what others will do, adding rationality and efficiency to social interaction. For example, laws perform an important function in governing everyday vehicle traffic in this nation. A driver entering a major highway complex has a legal obligation to yield the right of way to the main flow of traffic. The yield sign provides a driver entering the highway with specific instructions as to what to do and, in turn, provides the motorist speeding down the highway with certain expectations about the conduct of the motorist approaching the entrance ramp. If an auto accident results because a motorist fails to yield, then the dispute settlement function of law is brought into play in an effort to resolve the conflict.

A fourth function of law is its role as an instrument of social change or social engineering. Law emerges not only to codify existing norms but also to modify behavior, to remold moral and legal conceptions, and to convey the emerging attitudes, standards, and beliefs of a rapidly changing society. "Consciousness control over the normative system by man provides a means by which man's intelligence and consciousness can control social processes to structure a better society."[11] To this end the educational function of law, an extremely important function in light of the many social problems plaguing our society, depends on two interrelated processes: the institutionalization and the internalization of patterns of behavior. "In this context, institutionalization of a pattern of behavior means the establishment of a norm with provisions for its enforcement, and internalization of a pattern of behavior means the incorporation of the value or values implicit in a law."[12] Although law can directly affect behavior solely through the institutionalization process, resistance to institutionalization greatly diminishes the successful internalization of attitudes and beliefs. Such was the case with the Volstead Act, which provided for federal enforcement of liquor prohibition as defined by the Eighteenth Amendment of 1919. The law was enacted both to serve as a social control and to fulfill an educational task, but it failed to achieve the latter goal. This failure can be attributed to the fact that people did not believe in the law. The Volstead Act rested upon what modern jurists refer to as *pretended authority,* not authority conjoined with control. Consequently, no internalization of the values implicit or explicit in the Volstead Act took place. For a law to be complete, it must rest on a flow of official or unofficial activities that shows a sizable degree of conformity to prescribed norms and sanctions.

RULE OF LAW

Other societies rely as heavily as American society on well-ordered legal systems to maintain their civilizations, but there are vast differences in the way different systems affect the lives of the people under their control. The United States operates under a legal system that recognizes the *rule of law,* or government under law. These phrases

> describe the willingness of a people to accept and order their behavior according to the rules and procedures which are prescribed by political and social institutions — such as legislatures and universities — and enforced, where necessary, either by those bodies or by other institutions — such as governors, police, and courts. The "rule of law" expresses the idea that people recognize the legitimacy of the law as a means of ordering and controlling the behavior of *all* people in a society, the governors and the governed, the rich and the poor, the contented and the discontented.[13]

This includes sanctioning the use of deadly force by select groups of individuals designated as law enforcement officials in the interest of the safety and welfare of the state's citizenry. Should the orderly and appropriate use of force be abused, under the rule of law, the rules governing the conduct of those in authority will be challenged and most likely changed. *In essence, this constitutes a fifth general function of the law: determining who will maintain the authority to "exercise physical coercion as a socially recognized privilege/right, along with the selection of the most effective forms of physical sanction to achieve the social ends that the law serves."*[14] In short, law functions to make rules for the rulers as well as the ruled, whether they be the president, the Congress, or the judiciary.

While the philosophical notion that "ours

cial security benefits, civil rights, and the like. Case law, the rules announced in the decisions of the various state and federal courts, answers questions not answered by legislative enactments; it determines the proper application of ambiguous statutes; and, most important, it declares unconstitutional those statutes that do not fit the provisions of state and federal constitutions.

In the hierarchy of legal authority, the constitutions of the several states are supreme in their jurisdictions, subject only to those provisions of the United States Constitution made applicable to the states through the Fourteenth Amendment. Next in the hierarchy of legal authority are the statutes, which are subject only to the constitutions; below them are the decisions made in court cases.

Secondary sources of law include commentaries on the three primary sources of law. Here there is no formal hierarchy of authority, as secondary sources of law have no legal authority. Secondary sources include articles such as those found in the *Harvard Law Review,* various legal texts on selected topics, treatises on law, and official comments such as the United States attorney general's opinions on the interpretation of statutes. The value of secondary sources of law lies in the expertise of the authors and in that understanding and clarification their writings may contribute to a fuller knowledge of the law.

NATURE, FORMULATION, AND DEVELOPMENT OF CRIMINAL LAW

The *substantive law of crimes* is the body of law that declares what conduct in a society is criminal and prescribes the punishment to be imposed for such conduct. It is the oldest branch of law; its origins can be traced to

the earliest of ancient civilizations. Edwin Sutherland, a noted criminologist, advances four principal theories regarding the origin of the criminal law as an agency of social control. He proposes that criminal law originated

1. in torts, or wrongs to individuals;
2. in the rational process of unified behavior;
3. in a crystallization of mores; and
4. in conflicts of interests among different groups.[17]

Taken alone, any one of these theories is an inadequate explanation of the development of criminal law. In total, they account for its development at various stages in the growth of a politically organized society.

CONTROLLING CRIME IN PRIMITIVE SOCIETIES

Earliest primitive societies maintained control over human behavior through folkways and mores, not law. Each person's life centered around personal rights rather than property rights. As tribes emerged and governments developed, people took a greater interest in both personal and property rights and protected their interests through personal acts of vengeance.

> The concept of criminal law emerged only when the custom of private vengeance was replaced by the principle that the community as a whole is injured when one of its members is harmed. Thus, the right to act against a wrongdoing was taken out of the hands of the immediate victim and his family and was, instead, granted to the state as the representative of the people.[18]

This new system of criminal justice, however, involved nothing more than substituting public vengeance for private vengeance. Calhoun points out that true criminal law contains several legal concepts that further distinguish it from elementary tort and primitive law:

1. It will recognize the principle that attacks upon the person or property of individuals, or rights thereto annexed, as well as offenses that affect the state directly, may be violations of the public peace and good order.
2. It will provide, as part of the ordinary machinery of government, means by which such violations may be punished by and for the state, and not merely by the individual who may be directly affected.
3. The protection it offers will be readily available to the entire body politic, and not restricted to particular groups or classes of citizens.[19]

These legal concepts of criminal law emerged and developed principally from three different societies of the Western world: Greek, Roman, and English.

CRIMINAL LAW IN ANCIENT GREECE

Richard Quinney states that the turning point in the development of criminal law in the Western world took place in Athens, Greece, around the sixth century B.C. Living under economic and political oppression, the lower classes threatened revolution and were appeased by the ruling aristocrats through legal reforms, which "established popular courts, provided for appeal from the decisions of magistrates, and assured the right of all citizens to initiate prosecutions."[20] Thus, each citizen was protected from the wrongdoings of others as well as from wrongs perpetrated by the government.

CRIMINAL LAW IN ANCIENT ROME

Unlike Greek law, Roman criminal law did not emphasize the protection of the rights of the individual against the state. This was because Roman society placed great emphasis on private legal matters and civil procedure. Early Roman society, a rural community, operated under a system of customary or unwritten law. It was not until 450 B.C. that the Roman Senate ordered that these laws be collected and put into written form so that the injustices they had brought about could be rectified. Under the control of the *Decembri* (the "ten men"), this codification process produced the Twelve Tables, a system of private criminal law that was well received by the plebeians of Roman society.[21] However, as Rome grew rapidly from a rural community to a city-state, the Twelve Tables became inadequate as a means of controlling the internal threats that grew with the development of the Roman state.

> Subsequently, during the third century B.C. and the beginning of the second century, a criminal jurisdiction was established for the control of those engaged in such politically threatening activities as violence, treason, arson, poisoning, and the carrying of weapons, and the theft of state property. Tribunals and courts were instituted to deal with such cases.[22]

CRIMINAL LAW IN MEDIEVAL ENGLAND

At the time of the Norman Conquest in A.D. 1066, the administration of law in England, although well coordinated and long established, lacked a unified national character. There were three main bodies of law — the *Wessex law,* the *Mercian law,* and the *Dane law* — all of which were similar, but greatly influenced by local custom and tradition.[23] Because this was largely a system of tribal justice, long blood feuds often raged among neighboring families and within the same family. The only political consolidation that the peace and safety of society' and to relieve the public from the 'depredations' of 'notorious offenders' and the 'tax levied on the community by . . . privateering' of thieves."[37] The transition to secularized criminal law brought with it a new attitude toward offenders: that they were not fellow sinners, but a separate, distinct lower class of people that must be severely punished and segregated from society. When crime ceased being a sin, forgiveness and reintegration into society ceased being popular functions of the criminal law.

As criminal law and the agencies of the state began playing a larger role in the protection of social order and property, there was growing concern that these very agencies, with their new array of severe penalties, posed a threat to each individual's liberty. This fear prompted postrevolutionary legal scholars to search for safeguards that would prevent the arbitrary use of state power. Questions concerning the degree of protection afforded each individual solely through the auspices of an independent judiciary and jury trial began to be raised, and the rights of the accused became of foremost concern to the legal scholars of this era. Whereas prerevolutionary colonial America was concerned with the fair and impartial exercise of state power, postrevolutionary America showed less reverence for the social value of this exercise of state power. Concluding that the fair and impartial exercise of state power could not always be assured, legal scholars sought the total prohibition of this power in those instances where its fair and impartial exercise could not be guaranteed. For example, the prerevolutionary practice of issuing "'general standing warrants good from the date of issue until six months after the death of the issuing sovereign, which permitted the holder to enter any house by day . . . and their search for smuggled goods

without special application to a court'" was stopped.[38] By the late 1780s, a "search warrant could be granted only upon an oath stating that a felony had been committed, and, in theft cases, that the party complaining thereof had probable cause to suspect that stolen property was in a particular place. The reasons for the suspicion also had to be stated, and any warrant issued had to state the specific places to be searched and the persons to be seized."[39]

CONTEMPORARY CRIMINAL LAW IN AMERICA

While these observations on the postrevolutionary criminal law reform movement in colonial America shed a great deal of light on many criminal law issues today, some comment must be made about the emergence of criminal law in the American West, oriented toward the evolution of criminal law in America. In the early West,

fast-growing settlements developed their own codes to promote local order. For example, local rules were established to regulate the disputes that arose over land and mining rights in the western mining camps. Since there were as yet no territorial or state governments to formulate and administer law, there emerged a "local law" among the miners to regulate their own social and economic interests. These laws spread throughout the western territories, and eventually, when states were formed, many of the local laws were enacted into statute law or were incorporated into court decisions.

With the closing of the frontier, new problems emerged which required new laws for the preservation of domestic order. Once again, as in a former time, a host of laws was enacted for the regulation of morality, although this time more than religion was at stake. Morality, or control of the moral order, became an excuse for the control of the more material aspects of society. Laws bearing on private and public morality reflected the desire to preserve all aspects of life. If the moral base of social and economic life should be threatened, then the social and economic order itself might give way. Thus laws regulating sexual activities, drinking, drug abuse, and the like were enacted to control the total environment, even the most intimate aspects of one's life, so that the existing order would be secured and perpetuated — according to the interests of the established order.[40]

With this pattern of enforcing morality through criminal law repeating itself, the United States in 1980 has more criminal laws and more elaborate law enforcement machinery than at any other time in its history. The rapid growth of criminal sanctions has caused many legal scholars to question the ability of society to discriminate between appropriate and inappropriate use of these sanctions, and to express concern as to the impact of this trend on law as an effective means of social control. "Overcriminalization — the misuse of the criminal sanction — can contribute to disrespect for law, and can damage the ends which law is supposed to serve by criminalizing conduct regarded as legitimate by substantial segments of the society, by initiating patterns of discriminatory enforcement, and by draining resources away from the effort to control more serious misconduct."[41] Nowhere has the impact of this trend been more apparent than in the nation's recent attempts to regulate the use of narcotics through the Harrison Act of 1914 and the use of alcohol through the Volstead Act of 1919. Common to both these pieces of legislation is that "either there is no victim in the usual sense of the word, because the participants in the offense are willing; or the defendant himself is the victim; or the interest of the victim is so insubstantial that it does not justify imposition of the criminal sanction to protect it."[42] The passage of these criminal laws to deter conduct not significantly harmful to persons or to the property of others raises very important questions as to what principles are supposed to guide the formulation of criminal law, and what principles do in fact guide its formulation in society today.

BASIC PREMISES OF CRIMINAL LAW

A closer analysis of the nature of criminal law in America reveals that basic principles "have been more or less strictly observed by courts and legislatures when formulating the substantive law of crimes."[43] They are: (1) legality, (2) act, (3) mental state, (4) concurrence, (5) harm, and (6) causation.

THE PRINCIPLE OF LEGALITY

Essentially, the principle of legality is synonymous with rule of law. Earlier it was stated that rule of law expresses a people's willingness to accept and order their behavior according to the rules prescribed by political and social institutions. As long as the people recognize the legitimacy of the law, it will remain a means of ordering and controlling the behavior of all people. To ensure this legitimacy, certain legal maxims have evolved to govern the definition of a crime in our society: (1) no crime without law, (2) no punishment without law, and (3) no crime without punishment. Together these maxims constitute the principle of legality: the premise that conduct is not criminal unless it is forbidden by a law that provides advance warning that such conduct is criminal. (An example of a violation of this principle is an *ex post facto* law, one which defines a new crime and applies this definition retroactively to an act that was not criminal at the time it was committed.) A crime, then, in our society, "is any social harm defined and made punishable by law." [44] It is also a public injury, an offense against the state, created by the state, punishable only by the state, by either fine or imprisonment.

GUILTY ACT (ACTUS REUS)

A second basic premise of criminal law is that no crime can be committed by bad thoughts alone. Simply thinking about breaking into a friend's house to steal an expensive stereo unit does not constitute a crime if one does not take action to achieve the desired results. If, however, one were in fact to break the lock on the front door of a neighbor's house and enter with the intent to steal the stereo unit, one would have committed a criminal act or *actus reus*, which can give rise to legal action. In addition to protecting each citizen from being prosecuted for his or her thoughts, the principle of *actus reus* minimizes the temptation to create crimes of status.

Definitions of acts that are considered criminal or constitute wrongful conduct vary from one code to another. According to the following definition from the Texas state penal code, the conduct described would constitute the crime of burglary: The offense of burglary is constituted by entering a house by force, threats, or fraud, at night, or in like manner by entering a house at any time, either day or night, and remaining concealed therein, with the intent in either case of committing a felony or the crime of theft. Another state's code might well differ in details.

While this example involves an act of *commission,* an *omission,* or failure to act when there is a legal duty to act, may also constitute a crime. Such would be the case if a motorist involved in an automobile accident failed to stop, or if a taxpaper avoided filing an income tax return each year. In both examples, the criminal statutes impose the duty to act, and breach of the duty constitutes the wrongful act.

MENTAL STATE (MENS REA)

Just as there can be no crime without a guilty act, there can be no crime without a guilty or wrongful purpose in mind. This is often referred to as criminal intent or *mens rea.*

> Since the modern concept of crime assumes the rational ability of the particular violator to undertake an act designed to harm either an individual or property, legal punishment can only be enacted against the violator if his action was "intended" and "apparent" to his mind. While intent presupposes that the individual desires to complete whatever act he originates, *mens rea* assumes that the intent was knowledgeable and intelligible to the person as he undertook his particular action. [45]

For some crimes — burglary, for example — the controlling penal statute defines not only the wrongful act but also the *specific intent* necessary to make the act a crime. In this case, the breaking and entering must be done with the specific intent of committing a felony or theft. Other statutes defining criminal conduct often use such phrases as "knowingly" or "willfully" to indicate the type of mental state required.

Where regulatory offenses, such as traffic laws governing speeding, are involved, often no specific *mens rea* requirement is stated. In such cases, the *mens rea* requirement is understood: the legislature is not expected to make reference to it in all cases, particularly when those offenses that are oriented toward social betterment rather than the punishment of a serious offense are involved.

CONCURRENCE IN TIME

For those crimes whose definitions require both a wrongful act and a guilty mind, no crime is committed unless the mental state concurs 'with the act, in the sense that the guilty mind actuates the wrongful act.[46] Take, for example, John Doe, who decides to visit his next-door neighbor, Mary Roe. Because they are good friends, John Doe simply opens the front door and enters Mary's home with completely innocent intentions. While inside, John decides to steal Mary's expensive stereo system. Has John committed the crime of burglary? No, because by most definitions of the crime of burglary, John would have had to enter Mary's house by means of force, fraud, or threats with the "intention aforehand" of committing a felony or crime of theft.

HARM (AN INJURY OR RESULT)

To be constitutional, a criminal statute must have been enacted to protect the public health, the public morals, or the public safety. If it is determined that there is no real relation between the criminal statute and the protection of the public from some harm or injury, the statute may be declared unconstitutional. Such would be the case if a statute were enacted making a physical state, such as being fat or short or tall, a criminal offense. As an element of crime, and very possibly the most important element, harm or injury resulting from a criminal act determines the statutory penalties affixed to that specific violation.

CAUSATION

An essential element of every crime is that a causal relationship exists between the offender's conduct and the harm or injury sustained by another. In the usual sense, there is very little difficulty in demonstrating this connection. Take, for example, Mary Roe, who has returned home and found her expensive stereo stolen. Questioning of her neighbors reveals that John Doe was seen leaving her house with the stereo set. Taking her pistol, she goes to John's house with the intent to kill him, and does in fact shoot and kill him. Mary not only legally caused John's death but also intended to do so, and therefore is guilty of murder. The definition of the crime of murder specifies that the defendant's act must cause a death.

These basic premises underlie American criminal law and so have been extremely important in shaping the development of the substantive law of crimes. Although the definition of each crime stipulates a different combination of act and state of mind, each major crime has two elements, a *criminal act* and *criminal intent*. Neither alone is sufficient to constitute a major crime; the two must concur to establish criminal responsibility.

The categories of crimes that are punishable without *mens rea* (guilty mind) involve for the most part violations of regulatory statutes punishable by light monetary fines rather than imprisonment. Many of these violations are such that establishing the defendant's state of mind at the time of the violation is particularly difficult, if not impossible. Regulatory offenses like traffic violations or violations of motor vehicle laws fall into this category. Even if intent could be established, the vast number of people who commit such violations would thwart any efforts at enforcement.

PURPOSE AND OBJECT OF CRIMINAL LAW

If the purpose of law is the regulation of an individual's conduct as it relates to society

FIGURE 1.1 PUNISHMENT

How do you feel about punishment, capital and otherwise? Should the criminal offender be punished for committing a crime, or should society attempt to rehabilitate the criminal offender? Can society punish and at the same time rehabilitate the offender? If society is going to punish an offender, how severe should the punishment be for a given crime? Does the threat of punishment actually deter individuals from committing crimes? Does punishment deter offenders from committing further crimes? These are not easy questions to answer, yet if our criminal justice system is to work, answers must be found.

SOURCE: © 1975 Los Angeles Times Syndicate, *The Washington Star,* Oliphant.

as a whole or in part, then from this general purpose originates the primary objective of criminal law: the prevention of certain specified undesirable conduct with resulting protection for various interests of society. Because these results are achieved by punishing the criminal for infractions of the criminal law whenever they occur, some authors have gone so far as to say that the purpose of criminal law is to punish.

The purpose of punishment, however, is not so clearly defined. Various theories have been advanced: prevention, restraint, rehabilitation, deterrence, education, and retri-

bution, any one or all of which may secure the aims of criminal law.[47] Which one of these theories or what combination thereof best achieves the goal of a minimum standard of conduct on the part of each individual in society has yet to be determined.

PREVENTION

The advocates of this theory feel that if the criminal offender is aware of a punishment, such as prison, for a crime, he or she will not wish to endure the punishment and therefore will not commit the crime.

RESTRAINT

This theory is based on the belief that society may protect itself from persons whom it deems dangerous either by executing them or by imprisoning them for life.

REHABILITATION

By far the most popular of the recent concepts of penology to be advanced, this theory emphasizes that criminal behavior is the product of causes that can be identified and treated.

EDUCATION

According to this theory, the criminal justice process itself — from arrest to final punishment — teaches the general public what conduct is or is not socially acceptable. This kind of education is particularly important when the crime committed is relatively unknown or misunderstood.

RETRIBUTION

This is by far the oldest societal theory: society imposes punishment on criminals in order to obtain revenge for the harm one person has inflicted on another person or on his or her property.

CLASSIFICATION OF CRIMES

Crimes can be classified in several ways: the social harm caused; the grade of the offense, whether *mala in se* (wrong in themselves) or *mala prohibita* (wrong because prohibited); crimes of infamy; crimes of moral turpitude; common law crimes or statutory crimes; and with reference to procedure. Regardless of the classification, however, crimes are always offenses against the state and are always prosecuted by the state (at whatever level, federal, state, or local).

CRIMES OF SOCIAL HARM

The following definitions of the seven major offenses of the Federal Bureau of Investigation's *Uniform Crime Reports*[48] make it apparent that crimes are classified according to the protections against harm the criminal law affords to the various interests of society: protection from physical harm to the person (1 through 4), and protection of property from loss, destruction, or damage (5 through 7).

1. *Murder and Nonnegligent Manslaughter:* The willful (nonnegligent) killing of one human being by another.
2. *Forcible Rape:* The carnal knowledge of a female forcibly and against her will.
3. *Robbery:* The taking or attempting to take anything of value from the care, custody, or control of a person or persons by force or threat of force or violence and/or by putting the victim in fear.
4. *Aggravated Assault:* An unlawful attack by one person upon another for the purpose of inflicting severe or aggravated bodily injury.
5. *Burglary:* The unlawful entry of a structure to commit a felony or theft.
6. *Larceny-Theft:* The unlawful taking, carrying, leading, or riding away of property from the possession or constructive possession of another.
7. *Motor Vehicle Theft:* The theft or attempted theft of a motor vehicle.

FELONIES AND MISDEMEANORS

This is the most important classification of crimes presently in use in the United States. A *felony* is generally any crime that is punishable by death or imprisonment in a penitentiary, whether state or federal. Any other crime is a *misdemeanor,* normally punishable by fine or imprisonment in a local jail. Some penal codes distinguish between felonies and misdemeanors according to the length of sentence imposed, a felony being considered a crime punishable by imprisonment for more than one year or by death.

The importance of this distinction for the criminal offender is threefold in nature. First, as far as the substantive criminal law is concerned, certain crimes such as burglary require as an element of the offense the intent to commit a felony, and hence the intent to commit a misdemeanor will not constitute the crime of burglary. Second, this distinction is important to the offender in terms of criminal procedure because a court's jurisdiction over a crime is determined by whether the crime committed is a felony or a misdemeanor. The third effect is in legal consequences, which will generally be different for a convicted felon and for an individual who has sustained a misdemeanor conviction. A felony conviction may constitute grounds for loss of professional license (doctors, lawyers, and so forth), divorce, loss of civil rights, and numerous other penalties.

CRIMES *MALA IN SE* AND *MALA PROHIBITA*

This classification of offenses (one of the most ancient) can be traced back to the common law. A crime *mala in se* at common law was considered to be an offense that was inherently wrong or inherently evil. A crime *mala prohibita* is an offense that is wrong only because it is prohibited by legislation. Most regulatory crimes such as traffic violations fall into the second category, whereas felony offenses are usually crimes *mala in se*. One author has suggested that the distinction between these classifications of offenses can be made by determining whether intent is an

element of the offense.[49] If no criminal intent is required, as in the case of regulatory crime (traffic offenses), then the classification is *mala prohibita*. Where intent is specified as part of the definition of the crime, as it is for burglary, the classification is *mala in se*.

INFAMOUS AND NONINFAMOUS CRIMES

Under the early common law, certain crimes were considered *infamous* because of the shameful status that resulted after conviction for the offense. Initially, infamous crimes included treason, all felonies, offenses involving obstruction of the administration of justice, and any crime included within the scope of the Roman term *crimen fals,* that is, all crimes involving deceit or falsification. In this country, before the adoption of the Constitution, two kinds of infamy were recognized, one based on the mode of punishment to be inflicted and the other related to the future credibility of the defendant. The accepted modern view is that a crime punishable by imprisonment for more than one year in a state penitentiary is an *infamous crime*.

CRIMES OF MORAL TURPITUDE

The distinction between crimes that are crimes of *moral turpitude* and those that are not is similar to the distinction between crimes *mala in se* and crimes *mala prohibita*. Moral turpitude can be defined as an act that goes against the contemporary standards of conduct and decency, a base, depraved act that shocks the conscience of society. Most theft crimes, such as grand larceny and embezzlement, as well as such criminal acts as bigamy and rape, are generally held to involve moral turpitude. Other crimes, such as fornication and adultery, are crimes of moral turpitude in some states but not in others. The importance of this distinction to the criminal offender rests in the extraordinary legal consequences that result from conviction for a crime of moral turpitude. These consequences are similar to those following a felony conviction — disbarment, loss of professional license, and so forth.

COMMON-LAW CRIMES AND STATUTORY CRIMES

The distinction between common-law and statutory crimes was touched on briefly during the discussion of the various divisions of law. Under the common law, many of the definitions of criminal conduct were developed from specific cases. As the power of the legislative branches developed, many of these common-law crimes were redefined by statute, and other definitions of crimes were added. Today all crimes must be defined by statutory law to be constitutional.

MAJOR CRIMES AND PETTY OFFENSES

The final classification to be touched on here involves the distinction between major crimes and petty offenses. A felony is a major crime, while a misdemeanor may be either a major crime or a petty offense according to the punishment allowable. If the criminal violation is deemed a petty offense, then in most jurisdictions the offender is tried by a magistrate through summary procedure. In most states this procedure does not involve the processes peculiar to the trial for a major crime (preliminary hearings, indictments, trial by jury, and so on).

This chapter has briefly explored the relationship between law and society, with particular emphasis on the development of the substantive law of crimes and its nature and function. Criminal law has been described as an important instrument of social control by which organized society defines certain human conduct as criminal and attempts to prohibit or restrain such conduct by a system of procedures and penalties. If a crime is committed, criminal prosecution will begin, governed by the appropriate code of criminal procedure. This operational side of criminal law, greatly influenced by the doctrine of *stare decisis,* determines the nature and extent of criminal liability for each offender. The scope of criminal law, as presented in this chapter, includes substantive criminal law, which declares what conduct in our society is criminal and prescribes the punishment to be imposed for such conduct, and procedural criminal law, which is the formal machinery for enforcing the substantive law of crimes. In the following chapters, the process of the criminal justice system will be discussed as will the administration of the police, courts, and corrections.

DISCUSSION QUESTIONS

1. Can a society exist without law?
2. What are the major differences between common law and statutory law? Which do you prefer?
3. If police officers could maintain order without regard to legality, their short-run difficulties would be considerably diminished. Discuss the merits of this argument.
4. It is often said that swift and certain punishment will deter crime. Is this a true statement? If so, how swift and certain must the punishment be? What is swift and certain punishment?
5. Should a law be general or specific? What are the dangers inherent in each approach?
6. Do all segments of society have an equal opportunity to have their values expressed in law?
7. What steps must be taken to reverse the trend toward overcriminalization?

8. How does the substantive law of crimes differ from the procedural criminal law?
9. Have the principles that have traditionally guided the formulation of criminal law been weakened or discarded in the twentieth century? Give an example.
10. In your opinion, is the criminal justice system or criminal law expected to achieve too many varied objectives? What objective would you eliminate if you had a chance?

NOTES

1. Leon Radzinowicz, *In Search of Criminology* (Cambridge, Mass.: Harvard University Press, 1962), p. 168.
2. Donald R. Cressey and Edwin H. Sutherland, *Criminology,* 8th ed. (Philadelphia: J. B. Lippincott Company, 1966), p. 3.
3. William J. Chambliss and Robert B. Seidman, *Law, Order and Power* (Reading, Mass.: Addison-Wesley Publishing Company, 1971), p. 7.
4. Chambliss and Seidman, *Law, Order and Power,* p. 8.
5. Chambliss and Seidman, *Law, Order and Power,* p. 8.
6. F. James Davis et al., *Society and the Law* (New York: The Free Press of Glencoe, 1962), p. 41.
7. Chambliss and Seidman, *Law, Order and Power,* p. 17.
8. Chambliss and Seidman, *Law, Order and Power,* p. 10.
9. Harold J. Berman and William R. Greiner, *The Nature and Functions of Law* (Brooklyn: Foundation, 1966), pp. 31–34.
10. Chambliss and Seidman, *Law, Order and Power,* pp. 28–29.
11. Chambliss and Seidman, *Law, Order and Power,* p. 9.
12. Jerry D. Rose, *Introduction to Sociology* (Chicago: Rand McNally & Company, 1971), p. 44.
13. *Law and Order Reconsidered: Report of the Task Force on Law and Law Enforcement to the National Commission on the Causes and Prevention of Violence* (Washington, D.C.: U.S. Government Printing Office, 1970), pp. 8–9.
14. Joel B. Grossman and Mary H. Grossman, eds., *Law and Change in Modern America* (Pacific Palisades, Calif.: Goodyear Publishing, 1971), pp. 8–9.
15. Hazel B. Kerper, *Introduction to the Criminal Justice System* (St. Paul, Minn.: West Publishing Company, 1972), p. 27.
16. Bernard F. Cataldo, *Introduction to Law and the Legal Process* (New York: John Wiley & Sons, 1965), pp. 15–16.
17. Cressey and Sutherland, *Criminology,* pp. 10–11.
18. Richard Quinney, *Crime and Justice in Society* (Boston: Little, Brown and Company, 1969), p. 5.
19. George M. Calhoun, *The Growth of Criminal Law in Ancient Greece* (Berkeley: University of California Press, 1927). p. 5.
20. Richard Quinney, *Social Reality of Crime* (Boston: Little, Brown and Company, 1970), p. 46.
21. Frank Day, *Criminal Law and Society* (Springfield, Ill.: Charles C Thomas, 1964), p. 34.
22. Quinney, *Social Reality of Crime,* p. 47.
23. Day, *Criminal Law and Society,* p. 36.
24. Quinney, *Social Reality of Crime,* p. 49.
25. Day, *Criminal Law and Society* p. 37.
26. Day, *Criminal Law and Society,* p. 38.
27. Quinney, *Social Reality of Crime,* p. 49.
28. William J. Chambliss, *Crime and the Legal Process* (New York: McGraw-Hill Book Company, 1969), p. 52.
29. Chambliss, *Crime and the Legal Process,* p. 54.

30. David H. Flaherty, ed., *Essays in the History of Early American Law* (Chapel Hill: The University of North Carolina Press, 1969), p. 122.
31. Flaherty, *Essays in the History of Early American Law,* p. 123.
32. Flaherty, *Essays in the History of Early American Law,* p. 124.
33. Flaherty, *Essays in the History of Early American Law,* pp. 126–127.
34. Richard Quinney, ed., *Criminal Justice in America: A Critical Understanding* (Boston: Little, Brown and Company, 1974), p. 94.
35. William E. Nelson, "Emerging Notions of Modern Criminal Law in the Revolutionary Era: An Historical Perspective," in *Criminal Justice in America,* ed. Richard Quinney (Boston: Little, Brown and Company, 1974), p. 106.
36. Nelson, "Emerging Notions of Criminal Law," p. 108.
37. Nelson, "Emerging Notions of Criminal Law," p. 109.
38. Nelson, "Emerging Notions of Criminal Law," p. 116.
39. Nelson, "Emerging Notions of Criminal Law," p. 123.
40. Nelson, "Emerging Notions of Criminal Law," pp. 96–97.
41. National Commission on the Causes and Prevention of Violence, "The Problem of 'Overcriminalization,'" in *Criminal Justice: Law and Politics,* ed. George F. Cole (North Scituate, Mass.: Duxbury Press, 1976), p. 18.
42. National Commission, "The Problem of 'Overcriminalization,'" p. 19.
43. Wayne R. LaFave and Austin W. Scott, Jr., *Handbook on Criminal Law* (St. Paul, Minn.: West Publishing Company, 1972), p. 1975.
44. Rollin M. Perkins, *Criminal Law* (Brooklyn: Foundation, 1957), p. 5.
45. Richard D. Knudten, *Crime in a Complete Society: An Introduction to Criminology* (Homewood, Ill.: The Dorsey Press, 1970), p. 42.
46. LaFave and Scott, *Handbook on Criminal Law,* p. 238.
47. Herbert L. Packer, *The Limits of the Criminal Sanction* (Stanford, Calif.: Stanford University Press, 1968), pp. 35–62.
48. Federal Bureau of Investigation, U.S. Department of Justice, *Uniform Crime Reports for the United States, 1977* (Washington, D.C.: U.S. Government Printing Office, 1978), pp. 7–32.
49. LaFave and Scott, *Handbook on Criminal Law,* p. 29.

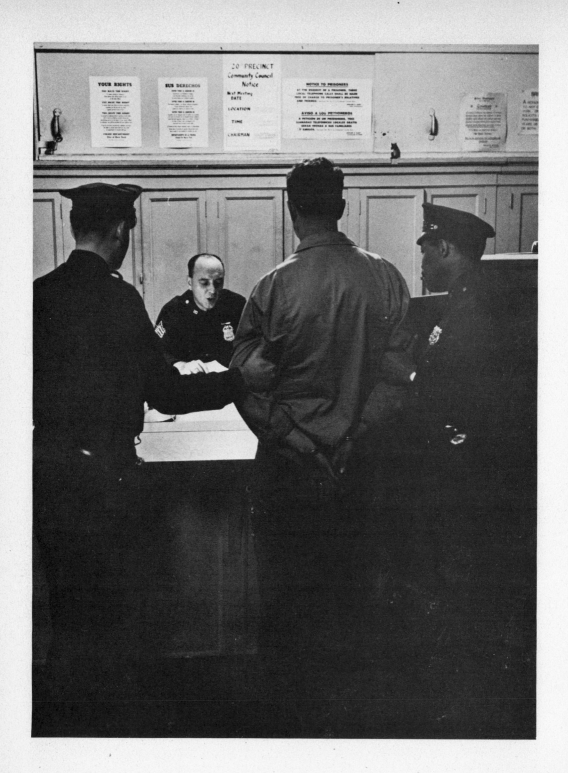

CHAPTER TWO

THE CRIMINAL
JUSTICE SYSTEM

CRIMINAL JUSTICE
SYSTEM 1 AS A SYSTEM

THE ADVERSARY
SYSTEM
DUE PROCESS OF LAW

PRIMARY
FUNCTIONAL AREAS

Purpose: To provide a brief overview of the agencies of the criminal justice system and their relationships. To put the agencies of the criminal justice system in their proper perspective.

THE SYSTEM OF criminal justice in the United States today consists of the many loosely related institutions and procedures through which "society identifies, accuses, tries, convicts, and punishes offenders against the norms of society expressed in law."[1] In the most general sense, our system of criminal justice has three interrelated components staffed by more than 1.0 million people: The *law enforcement community,* consisting of more than 580,000 police personnel, both state and federal (of whom about 80 percent are sworn officers), county sheriffs, marshals, and so forth; the *judicial community,* consisting of over 190,000 people involved in "courts, prosecution and legal services, and indigent defense agencies, including about 28,000 judges and other judicial officers, about 21,000 prosecutors, assistant prosecutors and other attorneys in prosecution and legal services offices, and 4,000 defenders or assistant defenders"; and the *corrections community,* involving more than 220,000 people, including about "70,000 correctional officers in adult facilities, 18,000 child care workers, 23,000 probation and parole officers, and 23,000 treatment and education specialists of all types."[2] Each of these components and its respective personnel in turn contributes to the criminal justice *process,* which is a well-defined legal continuum through which each offender may pass from detection and investigation of the criminal act; to arrest and accusation; to trial, conviction, sentencing, and possible incarceration; to eventual release. As a crime control mechanism, the system of criminal justice strives to achieve three purposes beyond the immediately punitive one: "It removes dangerous people from the community; it deters others from criminal behavior; and it gives society an opportunity to attempt to transform lawbreakers into law-abiding citizens."[3]

Although the three major components of the criminal justice *system* are common to each level of government — village, town, city, and county; state; and federal governments — the criminal justice *process* is tailored to meet the individual needs at each level. Within the governments of some fifty-five states and territories, the process will vary, as will the goals, standards, penal codes, and codes of criminal procedure that govern the operation of the local processes.

Isolating and analyzing any single state reveals that various components of the criminal justice system are controlled by different branches of the state government. For example, state police organizations are part of the executive branch, whereas the court system falls under the control of the judicial branch. Consequently, when a state police officer arrests a suspect, the suspect may in fact become a defendant in the court system, which is controlled by the judicial branch. If convicted and sentenced to incarceration, the defendant moves from the realm of the judicial branch of government back to the executive, which controls the correctional institution. Although one's initial reaction to such a multijurisdictional process may be to question the efficiency and effectiveness of the system, the system and the process that ties the basic system components together were intentionally structured in this manner by our founders to protect the rights of each individual and ensure local government autonomy.

While the criminal justice system just described is visible and generally recognized by the public, there is in fact a second criminal justice system in America that remains generally submerged and unrecognized. Dubbed *Criminal Justice System 2* by the National Advisory Commission on Criminal Justice Standards and Goals in its publication *Criminal Justice System* (1973), this second system encompasses many public and private agencies and citizens outside of police, courts, and corrections whose role in reducing and preventing crime, the Commission felt, has long been overlooked. For example, a state legislature

> becomes part of this larger criminal justice system when it considers and debates any criminal justice activities. So also the executive agencies of the State, educational administrative units, welfare departments, youth service bureaus, recreation departments, and other public offices become a part of Criminal Justice System 2 in many of their decisions and actions. Moving outside the State and local governments, community organizations, union offices, neighborhood action groups, and employers may also be important functionaries in the second system.[4]

As the crime and delinquency prevention role of Criminal Justice System 2 receives more recognition for its decisive role in the prevention, detection, and prosecution of crime; the fair and impartial administration of justice; and the reintegration of offenders into society, the true scope of the criminal justice system in America will become more clearly defined.[5]

We have then what might be called two systems of criminal justice: Criminal Justice System 1, the formal system of criminal justice consisting of the police, prosecutor, courts, and corrections; and Criminal Justice System 2, those persons, groups, and institutions whose formal or informal actions impinge on the operation of Criminal Justice System 1.

CRIMINAL JUSTICE SYSTEM 1 AS A SYSTEM

To refer to anything as a system implies "some unity of purpose and organized interrelationship among the component parts."[6] In Criminal Justice System 1, the police, courts, and corrections components interface with one another, with changes in one directly influencing the operations of the others much as one falling domino in a series of dominoes induces a chain reaction. For example, as the law enforcement community becomes more professional in daily operations, one can anticipate that an increasingly large number and broader range of crimes will be detected and solved. This increased police activity will in turn generate a larger number and greater variety of cases brought before the courts, and possibly more business will in turn be generated for the prisons as the courts attempt to deter further misconduct. If correctional personnel are successful in rehabilitating the offenders, then the offenders will be out of the system and most likely will not have further contact with the law enforcement community. Should correctional officials fail in their rehabilitative efforts, the law enforcement community will again encounter these individuals, further increasing the community crime problem, court case loads, and the number of individuals reincarcerated.

This organized interrelationship becomes more apparent when one examines the *process* of criminal justice administration — the sequence of events from the point of an individual's apprehension, to prosecution, conviction, and sentencing. Figure 2.1 outlines the process of criminal justice administration as it currently operates in most jurisdictions.

Generally, when a crime is reported, the police are notified and an effort is made to determine whether a crime has been committed and who has violated the substantive criminal law. If a suspect is detected and an arrest made, the police bring the suspect before a magistrate as quickly as possible. If

FIGURE 2.1 FLOW DIAGRAM OF THE CRIMINAL JUSTICE SYSTEM

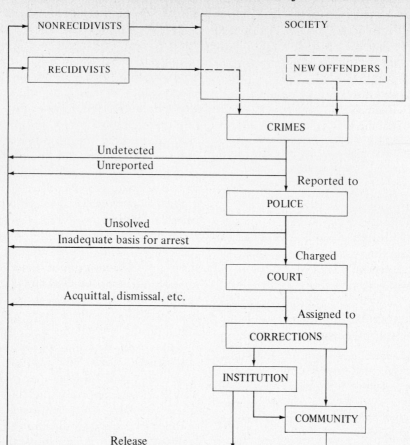

SOURCE: U.S. Department of Justice, *Criminal Justice Models: An Overview* (Washington, D.C.: Government Printing Office, 1976), p. 4.

a petty offense is involved and if the defendant pleads guilty to the offense charged in the complaint, the magistrate normally disposes of the case at once. However, when a more serious offense is involved or when the defendant does not choose to plead guilty, the magistrate files an information in the court where the defendant is to stand trial, and a date for the trial appearance will be set. When a felony offense is involved, the defendant is given a preliminary hearing before a judge in order to review the charge and the evidence that is alleged to support it. In those states requiring an indictment if an accused is to be brought to trial on a felony charge, a grand jury reviews the evidence and the charge and either affirms the charge by delivering it to the judge in the form of an indictment or dismisses it. Once at trial, the state, operating by rules of criminal procedure that govern the criminal justice process, attempts to prove the defendant's guilt beyond a reasonable doubt. Should the state succeed and the jury find the defendant guilty, the defendant is sentenced either by the jury or by the presiding judge. If the sentence is a term of years in the penitentiary, a systematic effort is made to rehabilitate the defendant. Should the sentence be a term of years on probation, the defendant is returned to the community conditional upon good behavior.

While the organized interrelationship characteristic of a true system is quite evident from this brief description of the criminal justice process, the lack of unity of purpose among the system components has led many observers of Criminal Justice System 1 to describe it as a nonsystem. Critics point out that while the officials of each component share a common objective of reducing crime and processing cases,

> each uses different, sometimes conflicting, methods and so focuses frequently on inconsistent objectives. The police role, for example, is focused on deterrence. Most modern correctional thinking, on the other hand, focuses on rehabilitation and argues that placing the offender back into society under a supervised community treatment program provides the best chance for his rehabilitation as a law-abiding citizen. But community treatment may involve some loss of deterrent effect and the ready arrest of marginal offenders, intended to heighten deterrence, may by affixing a criminal label complicate rehabilitation.[7]

These observations, which are in fact valid, do raise serious questions as to the existence of unity of purpose among the system components; however, what most critics fail to realize is that to the extent these value conflicts exist, the multiple objectives of the criminal law remain balanced in society's best interests. For example, to allow the objective of deterrence to totally dominate the criminal justice process might lead to a severe reduction in due process protections, which tend to slow the rapid processing of cases. Or, under the influence of a philosophy of deterrence or crime control, some individuals may go so far as to argue that rehabilitative programs be canceled in favor of 20-year sentences for all offenders, regardless of age or circumstances surrounding the criminal incident, or that trials by jury be eliminated as an unnecessary waste of time. While unity of purpose may serve bureaucratic needs, such as allowing for increased efficiency in processing criminal cases, the overall health of the criminal justice system is maintained by the multiple objectives of the criminal law.

THE ADVERSARY SYSTEM

The conflicting values underlying the various objectives of the criminal law surface as an offender moves through the criminal justice process. From the point of arrest to eventual release, a struggle is in progress, because the American legal system is an adversary system of law. What do we mean by an adversary system of law? We mean the method of dispute settlement underlying the procedural facet of the criminal law, which is grounded in the basic notion that out of a controlled battle or struggle, truth will be discovered. In theory, when a criminal law violation is at issue before a court in our society, a battle ensues — the state on one side and the accused offender as the defendant are locked in battle until the issue before the court is resolved. Sometimes referred to as a "fighting system of justice" (Figure 2.2),

FIGURE 2.2 A FIGHTING SYSTEM OF JUSTICE

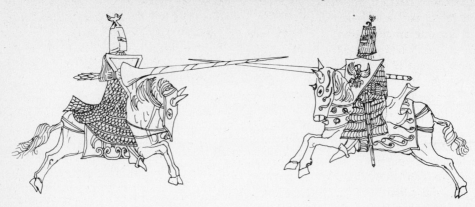

The roots of the adversary philosophy of law underlying the American legal system can be traced to the ancient belief that trial by battle will produce truth. Who are the contemporary knights in combat in the American legal system? How are they trained for combat? What weapons do the knights of the American legal system use? Do you believe that America's adversary process of law produces "truth" during a court battle?

our adversary process of law has its roots in a much earlier practice:

> Once upon a time, before written laws, judges, and courts, the administration of justice in disputed cases was inexpensive and direct. If evidence was inadequate or too evenly balanced or an issue sufficiently hotly contested, the accused was made to undergo some physical peril. His survival or demise was interpreted as the verdict upon him of the all-knowing gods. Did he live? Ah, innocent. Oh, he died? Guilty, obviously! That tidy episode was trial, judgment, and punishment in one. Such was judicial ordeal.[8]

As the spiritual parent of our adversary system of law, judicial ordeal eventually focused on "trial by battle" as the most reliable method of ordeal after perjured testimony prevented lesser forms of ordeal from ferreting out truth in judicial proceedings. In Europe and England, trial by battle even touched witnesses. Between the tenth and thirteenth centuries, if you found yourself involved in a judicial proceeding and your case was going badly, "you simply challenged an inconvenient witness to defend his veracity. If your swordsmanship was good, this generally took care of both the witness and the case. Such tactics quickly became a favorite method of escaping legal condemnation. Witnesses, in fact, were finally required to come into courts armed."[9] These conditions eventually forced authorities to formulate basic rules of battle, which in contemporary terms we refer to as procedural criminal law.

Under such conditions it eventually became popular, around the twelfth and thirteenth centuries, for the wealthier members of European society to seek ways of appointing substitutes to take their place in trial by combat. Eventually a class of professional champions arose that stood in the place of the litigants involved in the dispute. It was their paid and sworn duty to represent their master's truth, no matter how fabricated it might be, and to fight when necessary. Over

OVERVIEW: THE CRIMINAL JUSTICE SYSTEM

time the introduction of oaths and precise language to the nonbattle portions of the ordeal became an additional fact of trial by battle. All trials had various oath-taking ceremonies as part of their governing rules. In addition, the language setting forth the rules of the proceeding, and the language to be used in the proceeding, eventually became very exacting. For example, in the *Legis Actio Sacramenti,* the parent document of all Roman law, "you could not sue for injury to your vines and call them vines, you would fail. You must first call them trees, because the Twelve Tables of Roman Law . . . spoke only of trees." [10]

> Where judicial ordeal was fully developed, its procedural strictures, both physical and verbal, were often as numerous as they were minute. In the days of ordeal's decline, a finicking formalism frequently provided the element of risk that was ordeal's essence: one slip and the victim's race was run. [11]

Today "trial by ordeal" or "trial by battle" is still with us in the form of the *adversary process of law*. Instead of swords, our legal system relies upon *cross examination* to challenge or destroy the veracity of a witness's testimony. Instead of references to the Twelve Tables of Roman Law, we find references to the various codes of criminal procedure that specify the exact language to be followed in the wording of a criminal charge or the filing of an appeal. The rules of combat have been modified, but the basic underlying assumption remains the same: from a struggle, truth will be forthcoming.

DUE PROCESS OF LAW

Just as earlier civilizations had to develop rules to govern their judicial ordeals, so has the American legal system. Underlying our adversary process of law is the basic philosophy expressed in law that "a person may be punished by the government if, and only if, it has been proved by an impartial and deliberate process that he has violated a specific law." [12] For the state or plaintiff to "win" in a criminal proceeding, evidence must be introduced by the state that proves the defendant's guilt "beyond a reasonable doubt." And beyond

> a reasonable doubt means just what it says, a *reasonable* doubt. It does not mean beyond any doubt whatsoever. Thus, it does not require proof amounting to absolute certainty to convict an offender, or to adjudicate a juvenile delinquent. A reasonable doubt is a doubt such as a reasonable man would have after hearing all the evidence in the case and the arguments of counsel, and after applying the law to the case as instructed by the court. [13]

The rules that make this philosophy a reality, the rules that guarantee each individual in society a fair trial or hearing in matters concerning life, liberty, or property, are to be found in the United States Constitution and the Bill of Rights. (See Appendixes B and C.) These include, but are certainly not limited to, the right of each individual to a public trial conducted in an orderly manner before an impartial tribunal; the right to reasonable notice of charges as well as notice of the time and location of the trial; protection against involuntary self-incrimination; the right to counsel; the right to confront and cross-examine hostile witnesses; and the opportunity to speak in one's own defense.

The maintenance of these rights, as contained in the United States Constitution and the constitutions of all the states, is generally summed up in the legal concept known as *due process of law*. Although *due process* has never been defined by the courts of the land, it is generally understood to mean that an individual who has been accused of a crime must be given certain rights and protections as guaranteed by the United States Constitution, and tried according to specified procedures. The state may act against the accused within the limitations of these procedures, thus ensuring that the rights of the accused are maintained. This is a basic assumption underlying the American system of law — that there are limits to the powers of government to investigate, apprehend, and charge persons suspected of committing crimes, and that it is through the concept of due process that the adversary system of law ensures fundamental fairness and acts in keeping with community values as to an individual's guilt or innocence.

PRIMARY FUNCTIONAL AREAS

Within the overall criminal justice process there are six primary functional areas or subsystems of Criminal Justice System 1. Figure 2.3 sets forth these six subsystems — police, prosecution, criminal court system, probation services, corrections, and parole — each of which contributes to the overall criminal justice process.

POLICE

The two primary functions of the police are law enforcement and general community service. As part of their law enforcement function, police assume both a preventive role and a protective role. Through active patrolling, both on foot and in vehicles, the police attempt to provide the general public with a blanket of security that will act as a deterrent to potential criminals, while simultaneously providing means of rapid response to reported criminal activity. To further their efforts at providing the

FIGURE 2.3 PRIMARY FUNCTIONAL AREAS OF THE CRIMINAL JUSTICE SYSTEM

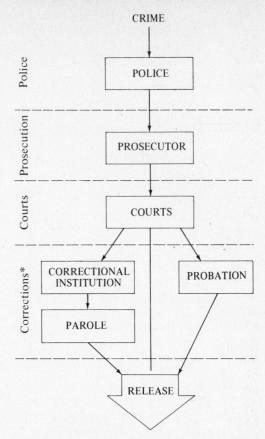

* Though primary functional areas of the criminal justice system, probation and parole are generally considered subsystems of corrections.

community with adequate protection, many police agencies are engaged in community programs that give the public firsthand information about the extent of crime in their neighborhoods; educate them about their roles as responsible citizens in crime prevention; and provide them with up-to-date information on basic security measures available to them that will better protect their persons, homes, and properties. In addition, police may provide such services as driver education programs, which help ensure public order by preventing accidents.

Although these efforts at crime prevention, detection, general public ordering, and security constitute the primary function of police (law enforcement), this function is not easily separated from the other main function of police, community service. The average patrol officer, who is the heart of every police department, spends a disproportionate amount of time in noncriminal situations. These may include finding lost children, settling marital disputes, helping a drunken citizen find the way home, or counseling the lonely citizen who has no family to talk to. Many have argued that this social work or community service aspect of police work should be left to the social agencies designated to handle such problems. Unfortunately, such agencies either are nonexistent, do not operate on a twenty-four-hour basis, or do not cover as wide a geographical area as do the police. *Task Force Report: The Police,* by the President's Commission on Law Enforcement and Administration of Justice (hereafter referred to as the National Crime Commission), views both the law enforcement function of the police and the community service function as inseparable elements of crime control. Citing as an example the numerous cases of drunks who fall victim to criminal attacks while in a stupor, the National Crime Commission points out that although this is a social problem, the only agency currently available to deal with these people and the crime-related aspect of their drinking problems is the police. In a report issued six years later by the National Advisory Commission on Criminal Justice Standards and Goals, the community service role of law enforcement was again emphasized and further rationalized.

Although local government provides many services the police are its most visible representatives. Because they are the agents of the government who are most frequently in contact with the public, and because they are accessible around-the-clock, police are often contacted regarding services provided by other municipal, county, State, and Federal agencies.

Often the public does not differentiate between various elements of local government. An irate citizen is simply concerned that he is not receiving a service to which he feels entitled. If he is bewildered by the profusion of government divisions, he turns to the one most familiar and most recognizable — the police. Because their service to the citizen affects his respect for government in general and the police in particular, police should respond as helpfully as possible, even if the matter is outside their immediate jurisdiction.[14]

A full discussion of whether police officers should or should not be involved in both law enforcement and community service is not appropriate here. Suffice it to say that it is the police officer's law enforcement function that initiates the criminal justice process. To fulfill this obligation, police are given formal authority to invoke the criminal justice process through their power of arrest.

PROSECUTION

The duties of prosecutors in the criminal justice process entail numerous responsibilities. More commonly referred to as district attorneys, these officials and the offices that they represent are charged with the responsibility of seeing that justice is done. This function brings prosecutors into contact with the criminal justice process from arrest to sentencing. It is the district attorney who decides whether to continue the prosecution of a criminal case when an arrest has been made without a warrant. When arrest warrants or other related legal documents such as search warrants are issued, the district attorney participates in the decision about issuing them. When an arrest is made, it is the district attorney who makes the decision to charge, determines the specific criminal offense or offenses with which the individual will be charged, and influences the bail bond process. The district attorney represents the state before the grand jury when seeking an indictment and at the preliminary hearing and arraignment, ready with the evidence gathered by his or her own investigative staff in cooperation with the appropriate law enforcement agencies. Before the trial the district attorney develops still more information and prepares the appropriate legal documents to support the state's position. When appropriate, the district attorney engages in plea negotiations. During the trial phase he or she must prove the defendant's guilt beyond a reasonable doubt with the expertise of a trial lawyer. If the defendant is found guilty, the district attorney is influential in determining the severity of the sentence (within the legally prescribed limits) handed down by the court.

Because of the position district attorneys occupy in the criminal justice system, they and their offices can have a very positive influence on the other participants in the criminal justice process, particularly on police practices and policies. Many prosecutors' offices maintain a staff of police officers who conduct investigations, secure evidence, and initiate prosecutions, and these police officers' practices and conduct, and those of their fellow officers, come under the close scrutiny of the district attorney's office. This vigilance aids police by providing them with up-to-date information concerning the rapidly changing laws that govern arrest practices, search and seizure, and so forth. It has been determined in many jurisdictions that "investigations and prosecutions for crimes such as homicide, consumer fraud, governmental corruption, and organized crime, which typically involve difficult problems of proof and require lengthy and careful investigations, are best conducted under the direct supervision of the prosecutor's office."[15] In this position, the prosecutor is both criminal investigator and initiator of the criminal process. This dual role has led many to consider the district attorney the chief law enforcement agent in the criminal justice process.

CRIMINAL COURT SYSTEM

"The courts are the pivot on which the criminal justice system turns."[16] Although details of organizational structure and jurisdiction vary, the state court systems of the United States are generally structured in the following manner:

- *Lower courts,* such as magistrate's courts, justice of the peace courts, and municipal courts, render judgment when petty offenses are involved and set bail and conduct preliminary hearings in felony cases.
- *Trial courts,* such as county courts and district courts, occupy an intermediate level in the court system. As courts of record, that is, courts in which a written transcript of the trial is kept, trial courts with general jurisdiction handle appeals from the lower courts and try cases outside the jurisdiction of the lower courts, such as felony offenses.
- *Appellate courts* and *supreme courts,* which occupy the highest level in the state court structures, hear appeals from the trial courts and exercise restricted original jurisdiction.

In their formal organization, the courts are concerned with punitive sanctions for violations of the criminal law. This concern is reflected in the activities of the court personnel, as well as in the very trial process itself, a process that has as its goal the determination of the guilt or innocence of the accused.

There is, however, an informal court organization that allows the court a certain degree of discretion about whom it should or should not punish and about the nature and extent of the punishment to be imposed. This informal side has made possible some new approaches to the control of crime, for example, treatment instead of punishment. As the court system now operates, an attempt is being made to be as nonpunitive as possible through the use of such programs as probation and halfway houses, coupled with warnings of punishment if the offender ventures outside the rules of those programs. Further analysis of the formal and informal organization of the criminal court suggests that eventually the conflict between punishment and treatment may lead to the criminal court system having as its sole function the determination of the guilt or innocence of the accused with a separate organizational system evolving to prescribe the appropriate treatment, whether punitive or otherwise, for the offender.

PROBATION

When an individual is convicted of a crime, the criminal court involved must determine what sentence to give the defendant. *Probation* is a court suspension of a prison sentence in order to allow the offender to remain in the community while the sentence continues. To help the courts make this decision, there is a tool known as the *presentence investigation,* which, if thoroughly and professionally done, can furnish the court with a factual basis for granting or refusing probation. If probation is granted, the judge releases the defendant without imprisonment on the basis of a number of conditions, which may include such things as continued good conduct, adequate support of family, and steady employment.

The responsibility for aiding and supervising the offender on probation rests with the court's probation department. Its role or function in the criminal justice system begins with the drafting of the presentence report and continues until those offenders who have been put on probation successfully complete their probationary period. Probation officers aid those offenders who constitute their caseload, providing sound advice on matters ranging from finances to family matters and providing moral support for the offender.

CORRECTIONS

"'Corrections,' America's prisons, jails, juvenile training schools, and probation and parole machinery, is the part of the criminal justice system that the public sees least of and knows the least about."[17] Its isolated nature can be attributed to its normally rural location, its nondramatic activities, and the fact that it is the collection point for many of society's problems and outcasts. So total has this isolation been that only recently have the courts attempted to open correctional institutions to public scrutiny and reform. All this is astounding considering the fact that on any given day there are well over two million people being "corrected" in America, two-thirds on probation and parole, and one-third of them in prisons or jails.[18]

In the history of correctional institutions in the United States, the trend has generally been away from punishment toward treatment and rehabilitation under supervision. Within the crime control process, society expects these correctional institutions or agencies to reform the offender, act as a means of retribution, and simultaneously reduce crime rates. What is readily apparent is that performance of the first task conflicts with performance of the two other objectives. It is generally assumed today that the conditions conducive to reformation of the offender by treatment do not in most cases include the intentional infliction of suffering, while the objectives of retribution and deterrence necessitate conditions punitive in nature. Even a probated sentence can be considered punitive by an offender because of the restrictions on freedom of movement and the standards of conduct it imposes. It is this conflict of objectives with which all correctional officials must deal in the daily administration of their agencies.

PAROLE

The true test of the success of institutional corrections programs, whether the goal is rehabilitation, retribution, or deterrence, comes when the offenders are released to the community. Some offenders are released directly from prison on completion of their sentences, without further supervision. However, growing numbers, now more than 60 percent of adult felons in the nation as a whole, are released on parole before completing their entire prison sentences. With the exception of sentencing, no decision in the criminal process has more impact on the convicted offender than the parole decision. Ironically enough, the parole board, which must make this all-important decision, usually can spend no more than a few minutes with each potential parolee before determining whether to parole or to continue detention.

When an offender is paroled, he or she faces a situation similar to that of a probationer. Under the supervision of a parole officer, the parolee will be required to work at approved jobs, avoid companions who have criminal records, adequately support his or her family, and so forth. If these and other parole conditions are violated, the offender may be returned to the penal institution to serve the remainder of the sentence. The function of the parole officer is to help the parolee return to employment, family life, and the community in general. This period is very critical in the life of the offender, who must once again face the problems from which he or she has been temporarily separated and encounter the additional problems that arise from the new status of ex-offender.

The parole function, then, is at the end of the criminal justice system. The offender has by now been processed by the police, the prosecution, the courts, in some cases probation, and the correctional institution. Theoretically, if these agencies have been effective in carrying out their respective responsibilities, one would expect that the offender on parole would now be ready to assume his or her rightful place in society. It is the responsibility of the paroling authority to ensure that the offender is given every possible chance to assume this law-abiding role.

Briefly then, the adversary system of criminal justice in America today is the apparatus whereby society identifies, accuses, tries, convicts, and punishes offenders for violations of the criminal law. As a sequential crime control process, the system attempts to remove dangerous people from the community, deter others from law violation by punitive sanctions, and make the offender into a law-abiding citizen. To achieve these purposes, the system is divided into three major components — the *law enforcement community,* the *judicial community,* and the *corrections community.* At the various levels of government, the law enforcement community is composed of police officers, sheriffs, state troopers, FBI agents, and other functionaries, who are responsible for enforcing the laws. In addition to enforcing the laws, police officers are responsible for a number of community services such as providing ambulance service, resolving domestic problems, and performing numerous other service functions. The judicial community includes the prosecution and the courts. It is the prosecution's responsibility to represent the government in court and to see that the proper persons are appropriately charged. The courts, which consist of judges, magistrates, juries, and so forth, are responsible for the trial process. The courts must ensure that the law is properly applied to the case at hand and that all parties to the proceedings receive justice. The corrections community comprises probation, prisons, and parole. Probation is a process whereby a convicted offender is released to the community after trial under certain conditions.

A probation officer supervises the offender to ensure that he or she adheres to the conditions of the sentence, and provides the probationer with assistance should it be necessary. The corrections community includes the many institutions that house convicted criminal offenders. Correctional workers are responsible for detaining and rehabilitating the offender. Finally, parole is a process whereby the offender is released from prison to the community under certain conditions. A parole officer supervises the offender to ensure that the specified conditions are met, and also assists the parolee should it be necessary. All of these agencies, the police, the prosecution, the courts, probation, corrections, and parole, are major functional areas of the criminal justice system. They are the agencies that we shall be dealing with in the following chapters.

DISCUSSION QUESTIONS

1. Would you call the police the "catchers" or the "gatekeepers" of the criminal justice system? Why?
2. Does the action of one agency of the criminal justice system affect another agency of the system? How?
3. Recognizing that the agencies of criminal justice are sealed off from one another by boundaries of legal jurisdiction, political jurisdiction, and budgetary responsibility, discuss the feasibility of creating a full-time "criminal justice office" to help alleviate these roadblocks to an effective criminal justice system.
4. The American legal system is an adversary system of law. Discuss alternatives to this adversary system for implementation of the legal processes in America.
5. After a close inspection of Figure 2.1, determine where your local agencies of criminal justice are located in this illustration. Do your local agencies perform the processes indicated in this illustration? How do they differ?
6. Should the police be concerned only with law enforcement? Who should provide the many social services that police officers provide?
7. Probation and parole are similar processes. Should they be performed by one agency, as they are in some locations, or by separate agencies? Why?
8. As you may have noticed, judges wear black robes, the bench or desk is elevated, and some of the court procedure is ritualistic. What psychological effect does this have on the trial process? Is this a good or bad effect?
9. What is the National Advisory Commission on Criminal Justice Standards and Goals referring to when it talks about Criminal Justice System 2 in the United States?
10. Who should have the primary responsibility for crime prevention in the United States, Criminal Justice System 1 or Criminal Justice System 2?
11. Why do you think the fundamental legal concept "due process of law" has never been precisely defined by the nation's courts?

NOTES

1. Hazel B. Kerper, *Introduction to the Criminal Justice System* (St. Paul, Minn.: West Publishing Company, 1972), p. 171.
2. National Institute of Law Enforcement and Criminal Justice, *The Natural Manpower Survey of the Criminal Justice System: Executive Summary* (U.S. Department of Justice: Law Enforcement Assistance Administration, 1978), p. 2.
3. President's Commission on Law Enforcement and Administration of Justice, *The Challenge of Crime in a Free Society* (Washington, D.C.: Government Printing Office, 1967), p. 159.
4. National Advisory Commission on Criminal Justice Standards and Goals, *Criminal Justice System* (Washington, D.C.: U.S. Department of Justice, 1973), p. 1.
5. National Advisory Commission on Criminal Justice Standards and Goals, *Community Crime Prevention* (Washington, D.C.: U.S. Department of Justice, 1973), p. 7.
6. *Law and Order Reconsidered: Report of the Task Force on Law and Law Enforcement to the National Commission on the Causes and Prevention of Violence* (Washington, D.C.: U.S. Government Printing Office, 1970).
7. President's Commission on Law Enforcement and Administration of Justice, *The Task Force Report: Science and Technology* (Washington, D.C.: Government Printing Office, 1967), p. 53.

CHAPTER THREE

THE CRIMINAL JUSTICE PROCESS: ADMINISTRATION OF THE CRIMINAL LAW IN THE UNITED STATES

THE CRIMINAL INCIDENT

THE ARREST

BOOKING

CASE SCREENING

POLICE INTERROGATION

INITIAL APPEARANCE AND BAIL

INVESTIGATION

PRELIMINARY HEARING

CHARACTERISTICS OF THE ADMINISTRATION OF CRIMINAL LAW

TRIAL COURT INFORMATION SYSTEMS

THE DECISION TO CHARGE

GRAND JURY INDICTMENT OR INFORMATION

ARRAIGNMENT IN COURT OF TRIAL

FILING A MOTION

TRIAL

APPEALS

HABEAS CORPUS

JUVENILE JUSTICE SYSTEM

JUVENILE PROCEEDINGS

THE ADMINISTRATION OF CRIMINAL LAW

Purpose: To overview the criminal justice process and place the process in its proper perspective.

ONE OF THE PRIMARY functions of an organized society is to protect its members from the criminal element. In the United States this function is handled through the crime control process known as the *administration of criminal justice*. The entire process involves those agents and agencies of the government that have been assigned crime control functions; those statutes and the case law that define criminal conduct; and, most important of all, the concept of due process, guaranteed to every individual in the society by the federal Constitution.

When a crime is committed, the criminal justice process begins with the police, who have the primary obligation of investigating the criminal act and apprehending the criminal offender. If the police collect sufficient evidence, the prosecutor prepares the formal charges and initiates the court action. The trial proceeding itself assumes the defendant innocent until the state can prove guilt beyond a reasonable doubt. This constitutionally prescribed minimum requirement of proof is ensured not only by the court itself but by the defendant's counsel, whether that counsel is privately retained or assigned by the court. Each step of the process of arrest, evidence gathering, and pleadings is carefully scrutinized by the court so that due process is upheld. If a verdict of guilty is returned against the accused, sentencing approximates as closely as possible the rehabilitative needs of the defendant as outlined in the presentence report and allowed by law. Regardless of whether the sentence is probation or incarceration, each defendant has the right to appeal all lower court decisions to the appropriate court of higher appeal. These courts of appellate jurisdiction may review the case in its entirety and, if the situation warrants it, reverse the decision of the lower court.

In order to explain fully the inner workings of this criminal justice process, the cases of two individuals will be traced through from incident to release. The criminal justice process outlined in this example is typical, but in actuality details would vary from state to state. For the purposes of this chapter, the criminal justice process of a major metropolitan city somewhere in the United States is used. Although the characters are fictitious, as is their armed robbery of a liquor store for $600 in cash, this walk-through is intended to bring the criminal justice process to life. From incident to release, this process is filled with constitutional safeguards, enforced by the procedural law, to protect both the innocent and the guilty so that justice may be served. Although the time lapse between stages varies according to jurisdiction, Figure 3.1 (pp. 46–47) provides a sequential frame of reference for the hypothetical armed robbery.

THE CRIMINAL INCIDENT

Billy B. and his younger brother Mark B. had been riding around for hours in Billy's car within a few miles of their parents' home. Bored and restless from the summer heat, each in turn suggested things they might do for some action while their parents were out for the evening. How they finally arrived at the notion of robbing a liquor store remains difficult for both of them to explain to this day. Possibly it was the fact that they had run out of beer and coincidentally found themselves in front of "Kuick-Sales-Liquor," a dilapidated liquor store just 15 minutes away from closing time. Maybe it was the exciting talk about Billy's new .38 caliber pistol, which he had purchased in a pawn shop earlier that day; it was a symbol of his new-found freedom since he had dropped out of high school. Whatever it was that had molded their actions earlier in the evening, before Billy and Mark knew what was happening, they were speeding away from the flashing lights of "Kuick-Sales-Liquor" with a brown bag stuffed with $600 cash taken at gunpoint from a very frightened store manager. Their actions, coupled with a phone call to police headquarters by the store manager victim, would initiate the criminal justice process and start their journey down the criminal justice highway.

PREARREST INVESTIGATION

A local police patrol unit staffed by Officers Lane and Kean was dispatched to the scene of the crime. Through on-the-scene interviews with witnesses to the crime and the store manager, Officers Lane and Kean were able to piece together a description of the vehicle used by the robbers, a license plate number, and a description of the suspects. This information was dispatched to other patrol units in the district while the officers completed the crime-scene investigation.

Although this is a very common beginning for prearrest investigations, not all police investigations start this way. Some are initiated through a citizen's complaint, perhaps a complaint about a noisy party. Others unfold through the routine police patrol function; that is, a local patrol unit might have detected this robbery and apprehended the robbers at the scene of the crime. All of these are examples of daily police investigations that may or may not lead to an arrest.

Finishing their investigative work, Officers Lane and Kean returned to service patrolling in their district.

APPREHENSION

Very frightened, Billy and Mark drove directly to their parents' home, just a few miles from the scene of the crime. Once at home,

they decided to leave most of the money hidden in their parents' garage along with the pistol. Not wanting to be at home when their parents arrived, Billy and Mark immediately returned to the road as they tried to think of what to do next. In their haste, neither saw the red light they drove through or the traffic patrol unit who observed their traffic violation and quickly signaled them to pull to the side of the road. Armed with information about the recent robbery, the traffic officers notified their dispatcher of the traffic stop they were making and their suspicion that they had stopped the armed robbers of the "Kuick-Sales-Liquor" store. Monitoring the radio transmission were Officers Lane and Kean, who quickly drove to the scene of the traffic stop to assist and confer with the traffic officers.

While waiting for Officers Lane and Kean, the traffic patrol officers had Billy and Mark step from their car while they initiated a *field interrogation*. When both boys gave evasive and conflicting answers as to their whereabouts for the last hour and their reason for speeding through a red light, the traffic officers initiated a pat-down search, or *frisk*, of both Billy and Mark to see if either suspect was carrying a weapon. Finding none, the traffic officers continued their interrogation while issuing a traffic citation to Billy B., who had been driving.

THE ARREST

When Officers Lane and Kean arrived on the scene, the four officers conferred for a few moments. Their conversation focused on whether or not they had sufficient probable cause to take the boys into custody for the armed robbery, *probable cause* being a state of facts, apparently sufficient in themselves to warrant belief by a person of reasonable

FIGURE 3.1 CRIMINAL JUSTICE HIGHWAY

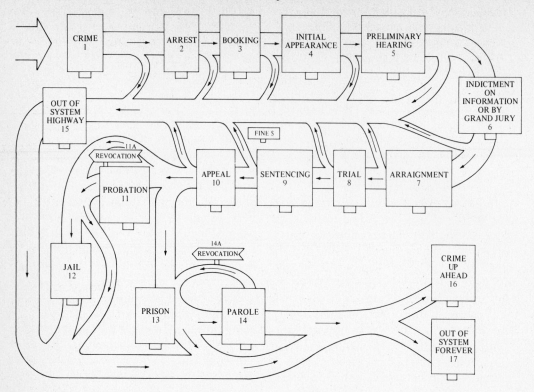

The Criminal Justice Highway represents a simplified version of the criminal justice process. The road signs represent the major points along the highway. As you will note, one can leave the Criminal Justice Highway at almost any point. For the most part, it is a one-way highway.

1. *Crime* is an act committed or omitted in violation of a law forbidding or commanding it, and to which, upon conviction, there is some form of punishment.
2. *Arrest* is the apprehending or detaining of a person in order that he or she may be forthcoming to answer an alleged or suspected crime.
3. *Booking* is the preparation of official police records of the arrest or an administrative record of arrest.

4. *Initial Appearance* is a formal notice of charge and advice of rights. Bail and the date for a further hearing are set. For petty offenses, this may be a summary trial without further processing.
5. *Preliminary Hearing* is an examination before a magistrate of a person charged with a crime to determine whether there is evidence to warrant and require commitment and/or to hold to bail the person accused.
6. *Indictment* is a written statement charging a person with committing a crime. It is arrived at through a grand jury or information. *Grand Jury* is a body of people who listen to charges presented, usually by the prosecutor, and then determine whether to indict or to dismiss the case. *Information* means that on the basis of facts

that the prosecutor has, charges may be filed directly with the court and the case may go to trial.

7. *Arraignment* is the appearance for plea by the defendant, who then elects trial by judge or jury. It is during arraignment that counsel is appointed for those defendants who cannot afford to retain a lawyer. At this point plea bargaining usually begins. The defendant and counsel negotiate with the prosecutor for a lesser charge in exchange for a plea of guilty. Plea bargaining usually brings the defendant a lesser charge, and it removes the case from the trial process.

8. *Trial* refers to an adversary proceeding at which the prosecution tries to prove the defendant's guilt, and the defendant's counsel tries to prove innocence before either a judge or jury.

9. *Sentencing* If found guilty, the defendant may be condemned to a punishment by the judge or, in some states, by a sentencing jury. Sentences may include fines, suspended sentence, probation, jail, prison, or whatever punishment is deemed appropriate. The sentence, of course, must be within procedural guidelines.

10. *Appeal* is the defendant's request to a higher court for a review of the trial. Such a court may reverse the decision, confirm the decision, or remand for a new trial.

11. *Probation* is a sentence of a person for a specified period of time, under supervision of the court, restricted to certain conditions while living in the community. If the conditions are violated, the probationer may have probation revoked (11A) and be sent to jail or prison.

12. *Jail* is usually a facility operated by a local government for short-term misdemeanant offenders. A jail usually holds persons whose sentences are a year or less. Persons awaiting trial are also held in jail when not on bail.

13. *Prison* is usually a state-operated institution that holds offenders who have committed a felony and whose sentence is longer than a year. Offenders may be released to parole or released directly from prison.

14. *Parole* is the offender's release from prison into the community under supervision, under certain conditions, and for a specified length of time. Parole may be revoked (14A) and the parolee returned to prison if the conditions of parole are violated.

15. *Out of System Highway* At almost any point along the way a person can leave the Criminal Justice Highway provided that the legal authorities cannot show cause as to why he or she should continue on the Criminal Justice Highway.

16. *Crime up Ahead* Some people commit new crimes and find themselves back on the Criminal Justice Highway.

17. *Out of System Forever* Some persons and ex-offenders never become involved in the Criminal Justice Highway again.

caution that an offense has been or is being committed. On the basis of matching license plate numbers and the description of the vehicle and the suspects, Officers Lane and Kean felt that they had sufficient probable cause to make an *arrest*. Both Billy and Mark were informed that they were "under arrest," searched a second time but much more thoroughly, handcuffed, read their "rights," and placed in the back of a patrol car.[1] Officers Lane and Kean then searched the front seat area of the youths' car and discovered an envelope containing $200 in cash. The officers then notified the dispatcher of their actions, ordered a police wrecker to come to the scene to impound the youths' vehicle, and headed for the central police station.

CONSTITUTIONAL PROTECTIONS

The act of taking a person into custody is ordinarily known as an *arrest*. Although the situation described may suggest that an arrest is a very simple procedure, in actuality the rules that govern an arrest are complicated. The standards that all law enforcement officials must comply with in order to legally arrest an individual have their foundation in the Fourth Amendment to the federal Constitution, which reads as follows:

FOURTH AMENDMENT

The right of the people to be secure in their persons, houses, papers, and effects, against unreasonable searches and seizures, shall not be violated, and no Warrants shall issue, but upon probable cause, supported by Oath or affirmation, and particularly describing the place to be searched and the persons or things to be seized.

This provision of the federal Constitution has been held by the United States Supreme Court to be applicable to the states via the Fourteenth Amendment, which states that "no state shall . . . deprive any person of life, liberty, or property without due process of law." The right to be free from unreasonable searches and seizures, like other constitutional rights outlined in the Bill of Rights, is considered to be part of the due process requirements incorporated in the Fourteenth Amendment. The key word is *unreasonable*; the Constitution does not prohibit lawful arrests, searches, and seizures. Since the traffic officers making the initial contact with the suspects had a reasonable suspicion that these men had committed armed robbery, they were authorized to conduct a "stop and frisk." A *frisk* is a pat-down search of the person to see whether he or she is carrying a weapon. While the legal rule of thumb is that search and seizures made without a warrant are unlawful,[2] there

are a number of basic exceptions to the warrant requirement, the most notable being search incident to lawful arrest.[3] "An officer is justified in detaining one who he 'reasonably suspects' is committing, has committed, or is about to commit certain specified crimes." Officers may search an individual, as the traffic officers did, to detect concealed weapons that may be used to injure them.[4] When the situation changed from merely detaining the suspect to a lawful arrest, Officers Lane and Kean were authorized to search the area within the arrestee's immediate control (the front seat area of the car) for weapons or evidence that could be destroyed, such as the money they discovered.[5] A search of the trunk of the car in such a situation would have been an unreasonable search, prohibited by the Fourth Amendment and therefore subject to the *exclusionary rule* during criminal proceedings.[6] If the B. brothers had placed the pistol in the trunk of the car, and the trunk had been opened by the arresting officers without the express permission of the brothers or without a search warrant, the discovery of the pistol could be excluded from any criminal proceeding against the boys, subject to a motion to suppress evidence at the request of their defense attorney.

Had Billy and Mark B. confessed their role in the "Kuick-Sales-Liquor" store robbery before the arresting officers had informed them of their rights, their confession of guilt could have been challenged in a criminal proceeding against them as being in violation of their Fifth and Sixth Amendment constitutional rights:

FIFTH AMENDMENT

No person shall be held to answer for a capital, or otherwise infamous crime, unless on a presentment or indictment of the Grand Jury, except in cases arising in the land or naval forces, or in the Militia, when in actual service in time of War or public danger; nor shall any person be subject for the same offense to be twice put in jeopardy of life or limb; nor shall be compelled in any criminal case to be a witness against himself, nor be deprived of life, liberty, or property, without due process of law; nor shall private property be taken from public use, without just compensation.

SIXTH AMENDMENT

In all criminal prosecutions, the accused shall enjoy the right to a speedy and public trial, by an impartial jury of the State and district wherein the crime shall have been committed, which district shall have been previously ascertained by law, and to be informed of the nature and cause of the accusation; to be confronted with the witnesses against him; to have compulsory process for obtaining witnesses in his favor, and to have the assistance of counsel for his defense.

The Supreme Court brought life to these constitutional protections in the case of *Miranda* v. *Arizona,* 384 U.S. 436 (1966), where the court ruled that an individual, while in custody or in some other manner deprived of freedom of action in any way, must, before interrogation, be informed of his or her constitutional rights. More specifically, the Court requires that the following warning be given to an accused or suspect who may be subject to criminal prosecution:

(1) You have the right to have a lawyer present to advise you either prior to any questioning or during any questioning.
(2) If you are unable to employ a lawyer, you have the right to have a lawyer appointed to counsel with you prior to or during any questioning.
(3) You have the right to remain silent and not make any statement at all, and any statement you make may and probably

will be used in evidence against you at your trial.
(4) You have the right to terminate the interview at any time.

Once an accused has received these instructions, he or she may waive these rights. In such situations the Supreme Court has mandated that the burden of proof rests on the prosecution in a criminal proceeding to show that such a waiver was given knowingly and intelligently.

POLICE DISCRETION

If our two traffic officers involved in stopping a vehicle for running a red light had discovered nothing more than two youths out drinking and riding, rather than armed robbers, the course of action they took might have been completely different. They might have talked briefly with the driver of the vehicle and issued a traffic citation, or possibly simply given the driver a verbal warning for carelessness. Had the officers discovered a small amount of marijuana in the youths' possession, they might have issued a summons in lieu of arresting the youths, thereby preventing the youths from penetrating the criminal justice system any further than necessary, in keeping with the contemporary emphasis on diversion practices.[7] In general, police have a vast amount of discretion at their disposal when they come in contact with the general public, particularly in those situations where criminal incidents involved are of a minor nature.[8]

BOOKING

With both suspects in custody, Officers Lane and Kean proceeded to their district station. While making an administrative record of the arrest, formally known as *booking,* the officers discovered that Mark B. was only fifteen years of age. Since a fifteen-year-old is a juvenile, Mark was not taken through the adult booking process with his eighteen-year-old brother. Instead, Mark was handed over to the juvenile officer on duty with the police department to be processed with the appropriate juvenile intake personnel of the county juvenile court.

While this was happening, the booking process for Billy B. continued, with the jail staff making an official arrest record of his name, the offense for which he was arrested, the time and place of the offense, and the nature of the evidence seized. Officers Lane and Kean completed a detailed report on the nature and circumstances of the arrest for later verification of probable cause, because arrest and search warrants had not been issued. To positively establish the arrestee's identity, the jail staff both fingerprinted and photographed Billy while simultaneously checking for any warrants outstanding on him. Before his detention in a cell, Billy was thoroughly searched, a record was made of the personal belongings taken from him, and he was issued a receipt for his valuables. Again he was informed of his right to remain silent, warned that anything he said might be used against him, and advised that he had a right to counsel. This entire procedure was noted in the arrest record. After it was completed, Billy was allowed to notify one individual of his detention in jail — a relative, his lawyer, etc. Billy immediately called home.

CASE SCREENING

While Billy was contacting his family, Officers Lane and Kean proceeded to the district attorney's twenty-four-hour case screening office, located in the building ad-

jacent to the municipal jail. Here the officers briefly conferred with one of the assistant district attorneys assigned to the pretrial screening section about the nature of the arrest they had made, the circumstances under which they had made the arrest, and the specific facts outlined in their arrest report. "Pre-trial screening is an intake and review procedure, whereby the prosecutor or his assistants attempts to determine, based upon information given them by law enforcement agencies, what type of action should be taken with regard to a particular case."[9] This procedural step, although not required by the code of criminal procedure, had been initiated six months earlier by the district attorney's office in an effort to improve the quality of the complaints processed. The district attorney hoped that through this review process, those cases that simply could not be successfully prosecuted because of a lack of evidence to support a particular charge could either be dismissed or the arresting officers instructed as to what information they would need to file a complaint for the purpose of remedial action.

Weighing the merits of the offense report, in conjunction with the comments of the arresting officer, the assistant district attorney reviewing Officers Lane and Kean's offense report determined that a *complaint* should be filed. A complaint is an affidavit charging the commission of an offense. The assistant district attorney also determined that sufficient evidence existed to hold Billy B. on one count of aggravated robbery, defined in the state penal code as follows:

Sec. 11.23 Aggravated Robbery
    (a) An individual commits aggravated robbery if in the course of committing theft with the intent to obtain or maintain control of the property
        (1) he intentionally, knowingly,

or recklessly causes serious bodily injury to another, or
  (2) he intentionally or knowingly threatens or places another in fear of imminent bodily injury or death, or
  (3) he uses a deadly weapon.
(b) Aggravated robbery is a felony of the first degree.

Satisfied with the support they were receiving from the District Attorney's staff, Officers Lane and Kean returned to the booking desk while the assistant district attorney initiated a case file containing the suspect's physical description, record of prior arrest, known as a *rap sheet,* and a current offense report (Figure 3.2).

FIGURE 3.2 PRETRIAL CASE SCREENING

The offense report prepared by the arresting officers is examined by an assistant district attorney. Should a complaint be filed? And for what offense? Have the arresting officers followed the procedural requirements of the law? If an individual is booked into jail and an assistant district attorney determines that sufficient evidence to support the arrest does not exist, have the arresting officers committed a false arrest?

POLICE INTERROGATION

Returning to the booking desk, Officers Lane and Kean conferred with Detective Holmes, a robbery detective who had been checking to see if the individuals the officers had arrested fit the *modus operandi,* or *M.O.,* of two other males who had been robbing liquor stores in the same general area over the past two months. Excited about the prospect that their arrest might have ended a crime spree, Officers Lane and Kean asked to sit in on Detective Holmes's interrogation of Billy B. Joining the detective in one of the police interrogation rooms, the officers observed while Detective Holmes began his questioning of Billy with yet another full reading of the Miranda warning and a reading of the charges. Billy acknowledged that he understood his rights, particularly his right to have an attorney present during questioning and the nature of the charges against him. He informed Detective Holmes that he did not want a lawyer and that his parents were on their way to police headquarters. Billy asked about his brother and was informed that he was being held by county juvenile authorities.

Under questioning, Billy admitted his part in the "Kuick-Sales-Liquor" store robbery. He stated that the money the officers found in the car was part of the stolen money. Further questioning by Detective Holmes revealed the location of the .38 caliber revolver and the rest of the money, both hidden in Billy's parents' garage. When Detective Holmes asked Billy if he would be willing to make a statement, Billy agreed, and Detective Holmes began recording Billy's responses with a tape recorder. On tape, Billy was asked his full name and age, read his rights and the complaint against him, and questioned as to his understanding of both. In addition, Detective Holmes asked Billy if his statements were voluntary, made without coercion or any promise of leniency. Again the question of counsel was presented to Billy, and he again waived his right to counsel during the interrogation. On tape Billy reconfirmed his role in the crime and the sequence of events leading up to, during, and following the incident. At the completion of the taping, Billy was informed that his parents had arrived at the station and that he would be allowed to see them after Pretrial Release Center personnel had finished interviewing him back in jail.

INITIAL APPEARANCE AND BAIL

When a person is arrested, with or without a warrant, both state and federal statutes require that this individual be taken without unnecessary delay before the nearest magistrate or judge.[10] These statutes, of course, do not preclude law enforcement officials from first carrying out such a postarrest process as booking, and the legality of the arrest is not put in jeopardy if a delay occurs because a magistrate is not readily available.

The purpose of this *initial appearance* is twofold. First, the defendant is informed of the charges pending against him or her and is given a written copy of the complaint. In addition, all applicable constitutional rights are reviewed, and the defendant is asked whether he or she understands the charges and knows his or her rights. These rights normally include notice of the defendant's right to remain silent and right to counsel, as well as the right to have a preliminary hearing and to know the date and the time of that hearing. The charge itself, whether it is a felony or a misdemeanor, determines whether the offense is within the legal jurisdiction of that particular magistrate or judge.

Most misdemeanor offenses are within the legal jurisdiction of the magistrate or judge who presided at the initial appearance, which allows the same magistrate or judge to hear the case unless the defendant requests a trial by jury. Felony charges are generally beyond the trial jurisdiction of the lower courts in which the initial appearance is made.

RELEASE ON BOND

The second major purpose of an initial appearance is to allow a magistrate or judge to set bail for the accused. The purpose of bail is to assure that a defendant who is not being held in jail awaiting trial will appear in court at the designated time.[11] *Bail* is a guarantee, usually in the form of money that is forfeited if the defendant does not appear in court as required. The amount is traditionally based on the nature of the offense involved, although magistrates initially have a great deal of flexibility in setting the amount of money. This discretion exists because the procedural criminal law does not specify amounts for each type of crime, with the exception that in some states bail may be legally denied those accused of murder or voluntary manslaughter. In most bail settings, the magistrates will take into consideration other factors concerning the defendant (prior criminal record, employment record, family ties, and so on).

As most defendants do not have the personal funds to offer as surety, they turn to a *bail bondsman* for assistance. Bail bondsmen are individuals whose profession is providing surety for others in return for a fee, usually 10 percent of the surety required by the court. Being private entrepreneurs, outside the legal system, bail bondsmen cannot be ordered by a court to provide surety for a defendant regardless of the amount involved. This fact places bail bondsmen in the very interesting position of being able to nullify court orders indirectly without being members of the judicial community accountable to the court. *Bond forfeitures* occur when the defendant does not appear in court at the designated time; then the presiding judge may order the full amount of the bond to be forfeited. In those cases where a defendant under surety from a bail bondsman fails to appear, the bail bondsman or any appointed representative is legally authorized to retrieve the defendant who has failed to appear.

Returning to our story, Billy B. was escorted by Detective Holmes from the police interrogation room to Criminal Court A in the adjacent municipal building for his *initial appearance* before Magistrate Taylor. The complaint prepared by the assistant district attorney was filed with the clerk of the court and, following an oath affirming the truth of its contents, officially presented to Magistrate Taylor. In the complaint, Billy B. was accused of the crime of armed robbery, and a description of the criminal incident was set forth.

In the presence of Billy and his parents, who had arrived thirty minutes earlier with their family attorney, Magistrate Taylor reviewed the complaint to ensure that sufficient "probable cause" existed to justify the officers' arrest. The lawyer accompanying Billy's parents, Attorney Anderson, informed Magistrate Taylor that she would be the attorney of record representing Billy B. at his parents' request. Turning to Billy, Magistrate Taylor verified Billy's full name, informed him of the charges against him, gave his attorney a copy of the complaint, read Billy his rights, and questioned Billy as to his understanding of the charges and his rights. After completing this procedure, Magistrate Taylor turned to the question of bail. In front of him was a Release-on-Recognizance (ROR) report that had been completed by a Pretrial Release Center interviewer while Billy was in his cell waiting to be called for his initial appearance.

RELEASE ON RECOGNIZANCE

Billy remembered the interview quite well because the Pretrial Release Center representative had been a pretty blonde.[12] Ms. Reed had told Billy that her job was to collect certain background information on him that the magistrate would take into consideration when setting bail. She had explained that it was possible, if Billy met certain minimum standards, to be considered for "release on one's own recognizance," that is, released from jail without posting bond on the basis of a personal promise to appear in court for trial when ordered to do so. The questions that Ms. Reed had asked Billy concerned his employment record, his place of residence, the length of time he had lived in the city, his family ties in the area, and any prior convictions that he might have had. At the time, the questions had seemed rather pointless to Billy, but to Magistrate Taylor the answers provided some insight into the nature of Billy's character and aided him in his decision regarding bail. The *pretrial release report* revealed the following information about Billy, information confirmed by Ms. Reed before its submission to Magistrate Taylor:

- Billy had last worked at Baker Industries three months ago, when he was laid off following production cutbacks; until that point Billy's employment record had been good; he had not worked since.
- Billy resided at home with his parents, who were his only relatives in the community besides his brother.
- Billy had dropped out of high school in his senior year.
- Billy had no prior felony criminal convictions, although he had been issued a $25 summons for possession of marijuana a few months earlier.
- Billy's current offense before the court did not result in physical injury to the store manager.

On the basis of the information before him, Magistrate Taylor asked Billy and his parents some additional questions regarding Billy's background. Given the seriousness of the offense, a first-degree felony punishable by from 5 to 99 years in the penitentiary, Magistrate Taylor felt that release on recognizance was inappropriate. He did feel, however, that setting Billy's bail at $10,000 would be sufficient to ensure his presence at subsequent court hearings. Magistrate Taylor informed Billy of the exact day, time, and place of his *preliminary hearing* and told Billy's parents that as soon as Billy's bond was executed, he would be free to return home with them.

ASSIGNED COUNSEL

In a recent decision, the Supreme Court ruled that without "a knowing and intelligent waiver, no person may be imprisoned for any offense, whether classified as petty, misdemeanor, or felony, unless he was represented by counsel at his trial."[13] Had Billy's parents not been able to retain a private attorney to represent their son, it would have been at this stage of the criminal justice process that the court would determine whether the B. family was indigent and therefore eligible for court-appointed counsel at the taxpayers' expense. A pauper's oath would have to be taken as part of the application for assigned counsel, and the court would then issue an order to carry out the assignment once the financial status of the family had been verified.

INVESTIGATION

On their way home, Attorney Anderson began questioning Billy about exactly what he had told the arresting officers and about the statement Billy had made to the detective. No sooner had the B. family returned home minus their younger son, Mark, than Detective Holmes and his partner arrived at their front door. After identifying themselves, Detective Holmes informed the family that he had been issued a *search warrant* to search the B. home for the weapon the boys had used in the armed robbery and the remainder of the stolen money.

Detective Holmes had made application for the search warrant in Magistrate Johnson's court just a few hours earlier, after taking the taped statement from Billy in the presence of Officers Lane and Kean. In applying for the search warrant, Detective Holmes had had to file with the appropriate judicial authority a deposition or affidavit showing *probable cause* to believe that the items identified in the application were located in a certain place. In this case, probable cause was established by the statement Billy had made to the detective, which included the exact location to be searched, the tool shed in the garage.

Somewhat confused and embarrassed about the prospect of a search of their home, Mr. and Mrs. B. questioned their attorney about the legality of this action. To calm their nerves, Attorney Anderson tried to explain what a search warrant was. She pointed out that although offensive, a *search warrant* was a lawful written order issued by a magistrate in the name of the state, directing an officer of the law to search specific persons or premises, or both, for specific items identified in the application. Attorney Anderson assured Mr. and Mrs. B. that the warrant

looked in order and that they should cooperate with the detective. They led Detective Holmes to the garage, and both the pistol and the money were quickly recovered. Before leaving, Detective Holmes gave Mr. and Mrs. B. a receipt for the items he recovered, then returned to the station after thanking them for their full cooperation.

As soon as Detective Holmes had left, Attorney Anderson began to question Billy B. extensively as to what had transpired at the police station, particularly the statements Billy had made. She explained to Billy that in order to be prepared for the next series of court appearances, she must have Billy's full cooperation. She pointed out that Billy's preliminary hearing was less than 48 hours away and that she needed time to prepare, unless Billy chose to waive the preliminary hearing.

PRELIMINARY HEARING

Although the federal Constitution does not require that an individual have a *preliminary hearing,* the main function of such a hearing is to double check that an unwarranted detention of an accused has not taken place and that sufficient probable cause has been established. (Probable cause is a constitutional requirement.) The burden in such a hearing falls on the prosecution to establish that a crime has been committed and that there exists reasonable ground to believe that the accused did, in fact, commit the crime with which he or she is being charged. This does not mean, however, that the state must prove the case against the defendant beyond a reasonable doubt; in most jurisdictions a *prima facie* case (one good on the surface or face) will suffice at this stage of the criminal proceedings. Failure to establish reasonable belief of guilt results in the discharge of the accused, but this does not bar a grand jury indictment on the same evidence or additional evidence at a later date.

Returning to court, Attorney Anderson listens with Billy and his parents as Billy is once more informed of the charges against him. The arresting officers, Lane and Kean, as well as Detective Holmes, are present. Under questioning from an assistant district attorney, they testify under oath as to their actions in the case to date, and they relate to the court the facts contained in Billy's statement. Through cross-examination of the officers, Attorney Anderson makes further inquiries about the circumstances under which the arrest was made, the basis on which the boys' car was initially stopped, who initially stopped the boys, and whether or not Miranda warnings had been given. In addition, Attorney Anderson questioned Detective Holmes at length about the conditions under which Billy had been interrogated at the police station at the time he had given his statement.

After Attorney Anderson's questioning, the magistrate decided that the prosecution had established sufficient probable cause to hold Billy B. for the *grand jury*. Billy was informed by the magistrate that he could remain free on bail while awaiting further action.

Upset after hearing so much damaging testimony about their son, Mr. and Mrs. B. asked Attorney Anderson why she had not introduced evidence in their son's defense instead of merely questioning the prosecution's witnesses. Attorney Anderson quickly explained that besides ensuring the constitutional requirement of showing probable cause, the preliminary hearing was providing their son with two other safeguards through her cross-examination. Attorney Anderson pointed out out that in order to

establish probable cause, the state must reveal some, but not all, of the evidence it has against Billy, thus often providing valuable information (referred to as *pretrial discovery*) she could use in preparing Billy's defense. Second, because much of this evidence is likely to come in the form of testimony by witnesses for the prosecution, the preliminary hearing provides an ideal opportunity to pin down the testimony of the state's witnesses so that any deviation during the trial itself can be brought to the attention of the jury and used to weaken the credibility of the state's case.[14] This is why, Attorney Anderson explained, she had not wanted to waive the preliminary hearing even though Billy had the right to do so. The record of this proceeding could be referred back to during a trial should the criminal justice process continue past the grand jury phase.

CHARACTERISTICS OF THE ADMINISTRATION OF CRIMINAL LAW

Halting Billy's travels down the criminal justice highway for a moment let us make a closer analysis of some of the more important characteristics of the administration of criminal law in the United States that have been indirectly highlighted to this point. First, it is important to note that while Figure 2.1 may lead one to believe that the various institutions of the criminal justice system handle an individual accused of a crime independently of one another, Billy's contact with the system reveals that institutional handling of an accused overlaps as he or she moves through the criminal justice process. In fact, in Billy's case, within hours of his arrest, he was handled by the law enforcement community in the form of the arresting agency, the courts in two separate appearances, and the correctional community during his temporary stay in the municipal jail. This multiple institutional involvement at each step in the criminal justice process is spelled out in the procedural criminal law, and is characteristic of our system of law, built upon a strong sense of checks and balances.

Another important characteristic of the administration of criminal law revealed by Billy's case is that this administration is a very complex decision-making process punctuated by many critical decision-making activities involving many agencies. Take, for example, the question of bail, release on recognizance, or total release from the system, graphically portrayed in Figure 3.3. We can see in this decision flow diagram that once a decision to effect an arrest is made, the criminal case flow process involves the ongoing collection, evaluation, and reevaluation of information for decision-making purposes. At each decision point the standard of probable cause is applied in an effort to reevaluate whether an accused should remain in the system, how far the accused will penetrate the system, and what the next step to be taken in the process will be. As these questions are being asked and reasked, a third characteristic of the administration of criminal law becomes apparent, the increasing formality of the legal process. Billy's initial appearance before a magistrate, while structured, did not have the same legal requirements or degree of formality as the preliminary hearing. In fact, as Billy passes through subsequent phases of the criminal justice process, a fourth characteristic of the administration of criminal law will become apparent, that an increasing standard of proof is necessary to keep the accused in the system and advance him or her to the next phase in the criminal justice process. A criminal case may start based on *reasonable suspi-*cion that a crime has been committed, but to continue the process to the punishment phase, the state must meet an evidentiary standard of *proof beyond a reasonable doubt.*

These characteristics of the administration of criminal law, which will become clearer as Billy's case penetrates further into the criminal justice system, are often overshadowed by the increasingly large number of cases and voluminous amounts of paperwork that accompany the criminal justice process. Over the last few years, the growing use of computer technology and massive information systems has of necessity become yet another characteristic of the system.

TRIAL COURT INFORMATION SYSTEMS

The same night Billy and Mark were arrested, 179 other individuals were handled by the police department, producing 137 new felony cases for the local courts. As the number of criminal cases has increased, the paperwork involved in processing cases has reached tremendous proportions.

> Since the majority of court actions are matters of public record, the courts have traditionally maintained files containing the original case documents plus other items prescribed by legal dictate or the erstwhile needs of court personnel. The accumulation of such documents usually results in bulky and frequently unmanageable case folders. Documents contained in these folders may vary in size from index cards to legal-size pages, and the same information may consistently reappear on various forms in both typewritten and handwritten versions.[15]

How many documents will eventually be contained in Billy B.'s case folder is difficult to say; however, it is fair to estimate that at

FIGURE 3.3 CRIMINAL JUSTICE DECISION MAKING — BAIL OR RELEASE ON OWN RECOGNIZANCE

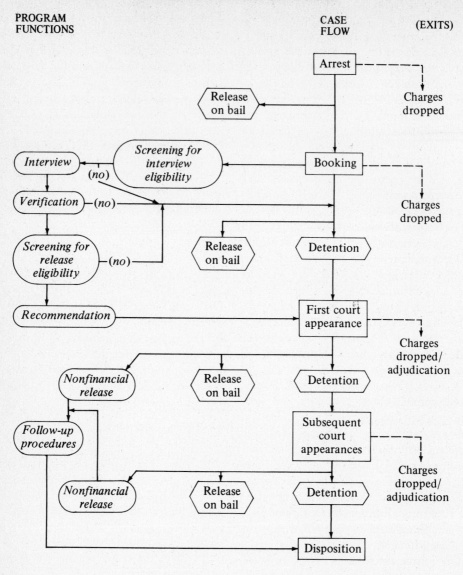

SOURCE: U.S. Department of Justice, *Pre-Trial Release Programs* (Washington, D.C.: Government Printing Office, 1977), p. 85.

OVERVIEW: THE CRIMINAL JUSTICE SYSTEM

least 39 documents will be posted to his case folder, all part of his criminal history file.[16]

When you couple Billy's case folder with those of the other individuals arrested on the same night plus those of all the individuals processed by the courts that year and other years, the problem of maintaining these voluminous records rapidly becomes critical in the areas of storage, indexing, and retrieval. Such conditions tend to threaten the orderly process of justice, as lost or misplaced case folders have at times left individuals sitting in jail cells long after their case should have been called to trial or dismissed.

Feeling the pressures of an ever-increasing case load, the local criminal justice officials in the jurisdiction handling Billy's case have converted their manual case flow system to a computerized trial court information system. Their decision to make such a conversion was prompted by their discovery that in the period between case initiation and final disposition, case files were being scattered throughout the various components of the criminal justice process and were often misplaced or misfiled; even in those cases where the files were in the proper location at the conclusion of a case, access was assured only if the court official making the inquiry happened to know the exact case number that had been assigned. With their new computerized information system, the various justice officials involved in the processing of Billy's case could within minutes know the exact action taken in his case, the date of the last action, the next scheduled action and the date, the name of Billy's attorney, his bail bondsman's name, etc.[17]

THE DECISION TO CHARGE

A quick query of the trial court information system reveals that Billy's case has been bound over to the grand jury. The fact that an accused is to be held or bound over for the grand jury does not necessarily mean that this process will automatically take place, nor is the accused informed during the preliminary hearing exactly when this next step will take place. In fact, between the preliminary hearing and the grand jury indictment, the prosecutor's office has a vast amount of discretion as to whether to continue the case proceedings or cease further prosecution. Stated simply, the prosecutor is in the driver's seat in the criminal justice system at this point. How fast he or she chooses to proceed, if he or she chooses to proceed at all, falls within the realm of professional discretion. Two extreme examples may highlight this point.

Each prosecutor has within his or her discretionary power the lawful authority not to proceed any further with a case, even where there is sufficient evidence to continue the prosecution against the accused.[18] Commonly referred to as *nol pros,* the prosecutor's decision not to proceed may be prompted by any number of circumstances — the reluctance of a key witness to testify; an agreement not to prosecute an accused in a criminal action in exchange for testimony in support of the state's case against others, or, with increased frequency today, a belief that the needs of the accused and of society may be better served through programs operated outside the mainstream of the criminal justice system.[19] For example, a prosecutor may be confronted with a drug addict burglar who is committing his offenses to support his habit, an addiction he incurred while recovering from wounds inflicted during military service in Vietnam. The prosecutor knows of a highly successful community-based drug treatment program that has established close ties with the district attorney's office over the last year. The prosecutor, in such a situation, may elect to divert the accused from the system informally to receive treatment he or she knows the accused would not receive in the penetentiary. In some areas, the prosecutor may simply inform the accused that he or she will not proceed with the prosecution if the accused enrolls in and successfully completes the specified treatment program. In some jurisdictions, this diversionary process is a highly formalized uniform process requiring special legal motions made in open court, supervised by the presiding judge, who orders a form of semiprobation for an accused, to be terminated upon the successful completion of the drug treatment program. Where an accused fails to fulfill his part of the agreement, the prosecutor is at liberty to proceed with full prosecution. From a prosecutor's standpoint, a well-organized diversion program serves to screen out less serious offenders so that scarce resources can be devoted to more serious cases.

> When weak cases and cases which don't warrant prosecution are removed from the docket, it eliminates the need for judges and other court personnel to devote time to them. In this, as in any other profession, time saved is money saved. When civilian witnesses and police officers are not required to appear, it not only translates into savings on witnesses and police overtime, but allows civilians and police alike to use their time in more productive ways.[20]

When prosecutors are not exercising their powers of *nol pros,* they are often found working at an accelerated pace to process serious criminal cases, generally involving recidivists, through the criminal justice process. Faced with increasing evidence over the past few years that a handful of repeat offenders seem to be committing a disproportionately large number of crimes, many prosecutors have begun initiating "career criminal programs" designed to rapidly remove these offenders from society.[21] These programs are highlighted by some of the following characteristics: prosecutors rather than police officers handle the postarrest investigation of repeat offenders in order to build as strong a case as possible; to minimize procedural errors, the case is not passed from one prosecutor to another, but receives attention from one prosecutor; career criminals who are arrested on probation and parole are detained in jail without bond as long as is legally possible while the revocation of their probation or parole is expedited; case processing time, particularly the movement to indict, is rapidly accelerated; criteria for pretrial release have been tightened; and better witness management is being undertaken.[22] In such cases as Billy's, where there is no evidence of prior criminal convictions, the criminal justice process operates at a more leisurely pace through regular caseprocessing channels.

GRAND JURY INDICTMENT OR INFORMATION

After reviewing Billy's case, Assistant District Attorney Jonas, a veteran of ten years in the prosecutor's office, decides to move *to charge.* In this particular state any individual accused of a crime carrying a penalty in excess of one year in the penitentiary must be formally charged through a grand jury *indictment.* As Billy's alleged offense carried a possible sentence of from 5 to 99 years in the state penitentiary, Assistant District Attorney Jonas begins preparing the case for presentation to the grand jury. His first step is to give the accused the mandatory two-week notice of the proceedings as required by the procedural law of the state.

The *grand jury* itself is a body of men and women, numbering between six and twenty-three, who serve terms that may be as long as 18 months reviewing prosecutorial pleadings and conducting investigations. The primary function of a grand jury is to ensure that prosecutorial pleadings follow the statutory requirements of the law and demonstrate that a crime has been committed and there is probable cause to believe that the defendant being charged committed the alleged offense. In theory the grand jury is supposed to act as a semiautonomous unit interposed between the accuser and the accused. If the requisite number of jurors concur with the prosecutorial pleading, they return an *indictment* or *true bill,* a written accusation charging that there is, in the opinion of the grand jurors, probable cause to believe that the person or persons named in the indictment committed the criminal offenses specified. This means that the prosecution of an individual will continue. A *no bill* occurs when an insufficient number of the grand jurors, as specified by law, fail to agree as to the sufficiency of the indictment. Thus the prosecution's case against the defendant, or at least those charges lacking sufficient supporting evidence, will be dropped.

In arriving at its decisions, the grand jury has substantial powers at its disposal. It may compel the testimony of witnesses and provide immunity where necessary. Evidence may be considered without the restrictions of the *exclusionary rule,* and records may be subpoenaed.[23] The grand jury conducts its business in a triallike atmosphere with a presiding judge, although in no way are the proceedings of a grand jury a trial. Members of the jury are sworn to secrecy, and the proceedings themselves are secret and protected by law from public disclosure. The prosecutor calls sworn witnesses who present evidence against the accused, although

neither the accused nor his attorney is entitled to be present.[24] Following the presentation of evidence, the jury retires and deliberates in private. A unanimous decision is not required to indict; usually a minimum of twelve jurors must concur for the signing of a bill of indictment to become a *true bill.*

Assistant District Attorney Jonas had little trouble having a *true bill* returned on his pleading charging Billy B. with the crime of aggravated robbery, a copy of which was immediately forwarded to Billy by the clerk of the court. The ease with which the prosecuting attorney was able to have Billy true billed further added to Billy's frustration. He asked Attorney Anderson why they had not simply waived his right to a grand jury indictment as provided by state law, since his case did not involve murder or voluntary manslaughter. Attorney Anderson explained that there was always the possibility, however remote, that the prosecution might not have been able to establish probable cause, and that it was sometimes possible to challenge grand jury indictments on the basis of improper jury selection or a clerical error in drafting of the charging instrument.[25]

Despite Attorney Anderson's reassurances that the grand jury proceeding should not have been waived, Billy B. could not help feeling that this step in the case processing was nothing more than a legal formality. Sharing Billy's observation are many criminal justice critics, who feel that the grand jury, historically created to defend citizens against the arbitrary exercise of executive power, now functions mostly as a honorary body, rubber-stamping prosecutorial recommendations. This criticism is based on grand jury operations in which the members of the grand jury are put in the position of hearing unchallenged prosecution testimony without the accused or his or her attorney present to cross-examine or present evidence on behalf of the accused. To some observers such conditions raise serious questions as to the effectiveness of the grand jury as a check on possible excesses of the state. Although the grand jury may seem to be nothing more than a tool of the prosecutor when viewed from the perspective of its charging function, the truth is that grand juries have vast statutory powers that they simply fail to use. When not reviewing charges brought before them, grand juries may conduct their own investigations of criminal activities within their jurisdiction that are brought to their attention by the prosecutor, their own members, or any source, whether the information be mere speculation, tips, or rumors.[26] In conducting such investigations the person(s) being investigated are generally not notified that they are the subject of a grand jury inquiry or investigation until or unless a true bill is returned.

Had Billy been accused of a misdemeanor, the grand jury would not have been the charging vehicle selected by the prosecutor. Instead the charging vehicle would have been an *information*. This is a legal document that the prosecutor drafts after receiving a sworn misdemeanor complaint. In substance, an information is no different from an indictment except that it is filed by the prosecutor in the trial court without the approval of a grand jury. Also common to both documents is that they notify the accused of the scheduled time and place for arraignment.

ARRAIGNMENT IN COURT OF TRIAL

Billy B.'s indictment indicated that he was to appear in the 308th District Court on the following Thursday to be *arraigned*. Attorney Anderson explained to Billy that this next step in the criminal justice process marked the beginning of the formal trial process. Billy would once again have to stand before a court and be informed of his rights and the nature of the charges against him; however, this time his statements would be made before a trial court. Confused by what seemed to be undue repetition, Billy questioned Attorney Anderson about the difference between this proceeding and all the others he had been through.

Attorney Anderson patiently explained that unlike the other proceedings, this was the critical stage in the case process where Billy would have his *first* opportunity to officially respond to the allegations against him. Standing in open court, with Attorney Anderson at his side as required by law, Billy would be allowed to enter a plea of *guilty, not guilty,* or *nolo contendere.*[27] Attorney Anderson explained that if Billy elected to plead *guilty,* that would be the equivalent of having been found guilty by a jury, and he would thereby forgo trial and be sentenced by the court. Should Billy choose to plead *not guilty,* the criminal justice process would continue, and a date would immediately be set for trial. Billy would have the right to a trial by jury, but could waive the jury if he chose to do so. Billy's third option, according to Attorney Anderson, was to plead *nolo contendere,* which she explained to Billy meant that he would not contest the charges that had been made against him; he would then be sentenced by the court. Billy was somewhat confused by the difference between a *guilty* plea and a plea of *nolo contendere,* and Attorney Anderson explained to him that a *nolo contendere* plea could not be used against Billy at a later date should the store manager bring a civil suit against him for any mental or physical harm resulting from the robbery.

With his plea options before him, Billy

asked Attorney Anderson to advise him as to his chances of beating the charges against him should he elect to plead *not guilty* at the time of arraignment. Attorney Anderson carefully explained to Billy that she felt that the state's evidence was very strong. Billy had signed a confession that from all appearances had been voluntarily given, the robbery weapon and the stolen money had been recovered, and Attorney Anderson was sure that the police had already matched Billy's fingerprints to those on the weapon. Seeing the total despair in Billy's eyes, she went on to emphasize that while the evidence seemed on its face to give the state a very good chance of winning the case should Billy elect to go to trial, the *burden of proof* remained on the state to prove Billy's guilt beyond a *reasonable doubt,* and that until the state had done so, Billy was innocent. Attorney Anderson went on to explain that the rules of the *adversary process* of law would allow her to challenge every single piece of evidence introduced against Billy by the state through such weapons as cross-examination, all in an effort to counter or weaken the state's efforts to establish Billy's guilt beyond a reasonable doubt. Feeling the need to be more specific, Attorney Anderson pointed out that while Billy had made a confession, state law required that such a confession be voluntary, and that the circumstances under which Billy had given the confession not be coercive or threatening to the suspect. She explained that if she could show that the circumstances surrounding Billy's confession made it less than voluntary, this vital piece of evidence would have to be excluded from the trial. In summary, Attorney Anderson explained that her role was to ensure that each of Billy's rights was protected under the law.

Reflecting on his attorney's comments, Billy asked what kind of sentence he could expect to receive if he were to plead *guilty*. Would this lead to any leniency in sentencing? Attorney Anderson explained that she would have to talk with the prosecuting attorney assigned to try the case before she could tell Billy anything. She left immediately for the district attorney's office.

EXCHANGE JUSTICE

Attorney Anderson hoped that she could initiate a conversation with the prosecuting attorney assigned to try Billy's case that would lead to some leniency for Billy should he decide to plead guilty. Although Billy had been questioned by the police in recent months about some burglaries in his neighborhood, had received a number of speeding tickets, and had been issued a $25 summons for possession of one ounce of marijuana while attending a rock concert, Billy had no prior criminal record that Attorney Anderson felt would hurt her request for leniency. When she arrived at the district attorney's office, it took her only a few minutes to find out that Assistant District Attorney Jonas, who had originally drafted Billy's indictment, would be trying Billy's case. Prosecutor Jonas and Attorney Anderson were not strangers to each other, much to Attorney Anderson's relief. Both had met before in court to do battle. Each respected the other, and on previous occasions they had carried on informal conversations outside the courtroom concerning those cases in which they had a mutual interest. Prosecutor Jonas was expecting Attorney Anderson when she walked into his office.

The conversation that followed the initial exchange of courtesies between the two did not reflect the adversary nature of the criminal proceedings they were both involved in; rather, their conversation reflected a tone of mutual agreement, mutual exchange. Prosecutor Jonas had expected Attorney Anderson and knew exactly what she had come for, a recommendation from him to the court that Billy not be punished to the fullest extent of the law, in exchange for a plea of guilty. This process, known as _plea bargaining,_ which has been held constitutional by the United States Supreme Court,[28] may involve negotiations about the plea as well as the charges, and/or about the sentence recommendation by the prosecuting attorney. In preparation for his anticipated meeting with Billy's attorney, District Attorney Jonas had reviewed Billy's case and knew it to be factually sound. He felt that he could go to trial immediately and convince twelve good citizens that Billy was guilty. He also felt that the mood of the community was so much against crimes of violence that he could get a fairly substantial prison sentence following Billy's conviction. However, even with this position of strength, District Attorney Jonas was still willing to talk with Billy's attorney. Why? The district attorney's office was facing an unprecedented case load. They had a number of major cases pending for trial and were running short of staff to make the necessary trial preparations. A plea of guilty with an appropriate sentence would save the state an enormous amount of valuable time and money when they most needed it. Assistant District Attorney Jonas decided in his mind that he would recommend to the court a 5-year prison sentence in exchange for a plea of guilty to a robbery charge, a second-degree felony carrying a possible penalty of from 5 to 20 years in the penitentiary. That way the store manager would be saved the inconvenience of having to testify, yet would feel vindicated.

On her way to the district attorney's office, Attorney Anderson had decided to ask the prosecuting attorney to recommend _probation,_ a sentence which would allow Billy to remain in his community under the supervision of a probation officer, an officer of the court, for a specific period of time. She hoped to sell this idea to the prosecuting attorney with the argument that Billy was only eighteen, not a real bad kid, and would not benefit from a long prison sentence. Attorney Anderson also hoped to argue that since the store manager had not been physically harmed and all the money had been recovered, punishment to the fullest extent of the law would not serve the ends of justice in this case. She was also relying heavily upon her long-standing relationship with Prosecutor Jonas to help her position.

With their individual interests and hopes clear in their minds, Attorney Anderson and Assistant District Attorney Jonas sat down to discuss Billy's case. After an hour's discussion Assistant District Attorney Jonas was not convinced that Billy B. was as nice an individual as Attorney Anderson portrayed him to be, nor was he convinced that a few years in the penitentiary would not be good for Billy's attitude. Assistant District Attorney Jonas also felt that not to put Billy in the penitentiary, to recommend probation, would be a foolish political decision given the local press campaign calling for all law enforcement agencies to get tough with those offenders who committed violent crimes. Two juries in the last few weeks had handed down thirty-year prison terms for similar offenses, and he felt he had to respect these community pressures. Attorney Anderson was about to cease her plea-bargaining efforts with the prosecutor and advise Billy of the offer of five years in exchange for a plea of guilty to a lesser charge of _robbery_ when she decided to make one more counteroffer.

Attorney Anderson proposed to Prosecutor Jonas that Billy be handled under the state's new _shock probation law,_ which had been enacted one month earlier. Seeing that Prosecutor Jonas was not completely familiar with this law, she briefly reviewed the new statute. She explained that under the provisions of the new law, in those cases where a defendant convicted of a felony of the second degree or higher had used or exhibited a firearm during the commission of the crime, and the defendant is granted probation, the court may still order the defendant confined in the penitentiary for a period not less than 60 and not more than 120 days to convince the offender of the seriousness of his or her actions. The sentencing judge, on his or her own motion or the motion of the defense, may order the defendant released to probation after serving the minimum amount of time. This sentencing procedure, Attorney Anderson emphasized, would serve the prosecutor's needs, prevent Billy B. from becoming a hardened criminal, and meet the public's demand for tougher law enforcement.

Intrigued by this proposal, but hesistant to agree to make such a recommendation until he had personally reviewed this new law, Assistant District Attorney Jonas agreed to consider the proposed alternative only if Billy's *presentence investigation* report was favorable. Attorney Anderson left the district attorney's office prepared to advise Billy that if he were to plead guilty to the lesser charge of robbery, the prosecution would recommend to the trial court that no more than a five-year penitentiary sentence be imposed.

A presentence investigation report is essentially a character report on a defendant prepared by a probation officer, an officer of the court. This report is usually initiated at the request of the trial court following the entering of a plea of guilty by bench or by jury. The purpose of this report is to aid the trial court in carrying out its sentencing function by providing additional detail on a defendant's background, criminal history, family history, employment record, and general overall physical and mental health. Although the report is generally considered confidential, most states allow both the prosecution and the defense to inspect it for errors and to make appropriate clarifying comments that may be brought to the attention of the sentencing judge. In cases where death sentences have been imposed, based in part upon information contained in a presentence investigation report that the defendant never had the opportunity to deny or explain, the Supreme Court has held the sentencing phase to be unconstitutional, in violation of the constitutional guarantee that no person shall be deprived of life without due process of law.[29]

Returning to Billy's case, Billy agreed to Attorney Anderson's suggestion that he plead guilty to the reduced charge of robbery and a recommended sentence of five years. Although Billy's first inclination was to plead innocent and fight his case every step of the way through the remainder of the criminal justice process, he recognized that the case against him was strong and that the risk of a severe sentence by an irate jury was an extremely large gamble. While Billy felt safer with the prosecutor's offer, he asked Attorney Anderson how well he could trust Assistant District Attorney Jonas to carry out his verbal commitment to recommend no more than five years in the penitentiary. She put Billy's mind at ease by pointing out that the rules of criminal procedure had specific safeguards regarding plea-bargaining agreements. More specifically, Attorney Anderson explained that during arraignment the trial court would inquire about the existence of any plea-bargaining agreement between the state and the defendant following the entering of a plea of guilty. When the trial court is informed of the bargain agreement, it must then inform Billy whether it will follow or reject the agreement in open court before any finding on the plea. Should the court reject the agreement, Billy could withdraw his plea of guilty, and no statement or other evidence received during the hearing could be admitted against him on the issue of guilt or punishment in any subsequent criminal proceeding.

GUILTY PLEA

Billy's story draws to a close with his entry of a plea of guilty to armed robbery during arraignment and his sentencing to the state penitentiary for five years. The presentence investigation report compiled on Billy confirmed Attorney Anderson's contention that Billy was basically not a bad kid, although his crime had been quite serious. The nature of the presentence investigation report, coupled with his review of the *shock probation* law, convinced Assistant District Attorney Jonas that after Billy had been *shocked* by 60 days of penitentiary life, he would file a motion with the trial court to have Billy returned to the community to serve the remainder of his sentence on probation. Although Billy's stay in the penitentiary was short, it turned out to be sufficient to prompt him to return to school to finish his high school degree, again seek serious employment, and, most importantly, stay out of trouble.

A PLEA OF NOT GUILTY

It is estimated that in some jurisdictions in the United States, up to 95 percent of all defendants plead guilty, in most cases in exchange for some benefit conferred by the prosecution.[30] The negotiated plea is now considered to be the principal method for disposing of criminal cases in the United States. This process leaves just a few defendants traveling down the remainder of the criminal justice highway. For those who do not find themselves in a plea-bargaining situation, the criminal justice process is filled with other intersections and stopping points. If Billy B. had not pleaded guilty to the reduced charge of robbery offered by the prosecutor, then the entire criminal trial process would have been set in motion, beginning with the setting of a trial date and the filing of pretrial motions where sufficient *good cause* exists.

FILING A MOTION

Before the actual trial stage, a defendant has a number of options that can be explored through the legal procedure known as *filing a motion*. A *motion* is simply a request for a court order. For example, a defendant may file a *motion to suppress evidence* in an effort to prohibit the introduction of certain evidence at trial that the defendant believes to have been seized in violation of his or her Fourth Amendment rights. Other motions that may provide legal relief are a *motion for a change of venue* (to change the place of trial), a *motion for a bill of particulars* (to provide more specific information than is contained in the charging vehicle), a *motion to dismiss* (to dismiss the indictment, information, or complaint on such ground as that the court does not have jurisdiction over the offender or offense), and a *motion of continuance* (a request for additional time to prepare for trial). Such motions, whether filed by the prosecution or defense, are normally heard during a pretrial hearing without the trial jury present. To counter such motions, an affidavit showing why such grounds do not exist may be filed.

TRIAL

When appropriate pretrial motions have been exhausted, a defendant, who has to decide at the time of arraignment whether to have a trial by bench (that is, by the judge alone) or by jury as guaranteed by the Sixth Amendment, must begin to prepare for the trial process. Waiving a jury trial is usually a defendant's option, but not in all states. Should a defendant elect to proceed with a jury trial, the following sequence of events would be encountered:

1. Selection of the jury
2. Opening statements by the prosecution and the defense, in that order
3. Presentation of the government's evidence, including witnesses and exhibits, in an effort to establish proof beyond reasonable doubt. (This entails the direct examination by the prosecution of its witnesses and the cross-examination of these witnesses by the defense.)
4. Presentation and arguments of defense motions
5. Presentation by the defense of evidence that will create a reasonable doubt as to the evidence presented by the prosecution. (This entails the direct examination by the defense of its witnesses and cross-examination by the state.)
6. Presentation of rebuttal evidence by the government if the defense raised affirmative defenses that were not negated by the prosecution in the presentation of its case
7. Instructions of the court to the jury
8. Arguments to the jury by prosecutor and defense counsel
9. Charging of the jury by the judge
10. Jury deliberations and verdict
11. Judgment and posttrial motions
12. Sentencing

How soon after arraignment this trial process will begin depends on many factors: the trial court's caseload, granted pretrial motions, whether the defendant is being held in jail, etc. The Supreme Court recently commented on the constitutional safeguard of speedy trial as set forth in the Sixth Amendment:

> This guarantee is an important safeguard to prevent undue and oppressive incarceration prior to trial, to minimize anxiety and concern accompanying public accusation, and to limit the possibilities that long delays will impair the ability of an accused to defend himself. However, in a large measure because of many procedural safeguards provided to an accused, the ordinary procedures for criminal prosecutions are designed to move at a deliberate pace. A requirement of unreasonable speed would have a deleterious effect, both upon the right of the accused and upon the ability of society to protect itself. Therefore, this court has been consistently of the view that the right of a speedy trial is necessarily relative. It is consistent with delays and depends upon circumstances. It secures rights to a defendant. It does not preclude the rights of public justice.[31]

Some states, for example, Illinois, have enacted statutory provisions that prescribe that an individual must be brought to trial within 120 days if held in custody and within 160 days if out on bail. Motions for continuance can be granted for a period not to exceed 60 days.[32] Failure to comply with this statutory provision may result in the dismissal of the case for want of prosecution, depending on the circumstances of the delay. While other states have followed the speedy trial time frame set by Illinois, the Supreme Court has made it clear in its rulings that there is no constitutional basis for holding that the right to a speedy trial can be quantified into a specific number of days or months. States are free, in the opinion of the Court, to prescribe a reasonable period consistent with constitutional standards.[33]

PROSECUTION CASE

Success for a prosecuting attorney lies in the ability to introduce evidence[34] that will prove the state's case beyond a reasonable doubt. As the burden of proof rests on the plaintiff (the state), the plaintiff is entitled to the first and last word during the evidence-presentation phase of the trial.

A prosecuting attorney begins the state's case by calling witnesses who can establish the elements of the offense, then proceeds to witnesses who will introduce real evidence (physical or demonstrative objects). For example, in our robbery case, the manager of the liquor store on duty the night of the robbery could provide the jury with a detailed account of the criminal act as he saw it. The arresting officers could supplement this testimony with pertinent testimony regarding the money that they seized from the two armed robbers on the night of the crime. To be relevant, evidence must bear some relationship to the contested issues of the case and must have a tendency to prove some fact that is material to the dispute. If the arresting officers had found marijuana in the suspect's vehicle, that fact would not be relevant to the issue at hand, and defense counsel would normally object to such testimony as irrelevant and immaterial. There are *rules of evidence* in statutory law and in case law to protect the defendant from evidence that is irrelevant, immaterial, and incompetent.

The prosecution's direct examination of its witnesses is followed by the cross-examination of the same witnesses by the defense. At this stage, counsel for the defense is restricted to the facts brought out by the prosecution in the direct examination phase, so here the defense attempts to discredit the prosecution's efforts to establish proof beyond a reasonable doubt.

DEFENSE MOTION

At the close of the prosecution's case, the trial judge may dismiss the case from the jury (referred to as a *directed verdict*) if the state has failed to provide enough proof to sustain a conviction. Or the defense may enter a motion to this effect. The granting of such a motion by the trial judge results in the defendant's *acquittal,* which means dismissal of charges against the defendant. He or she is released from custody, with immunity from further prosecution for that specific crime. This motion may also be entered at the conclusion of the introduction of all evidence.

DEFENSE CASE AND PROSECUTION REBUTTAL

Having failed to secure a directed verdict of acquittal, the defense begins its case. Like the prosecution, the defense counsel presents witnesses for direct examination. The state has the option of cross-examination if it sees fit. When the defense has exhausted all its evidence in an attempt to establish the accused's innocence, it will rest its case.

The prosecution may, after the defense's presentation of evidence, feel that various aspects of its case have been weakened and need to be bolstered. Consequently, the prosecution is allowed to rebut the defendant's evidence with new witnesses or the reexamination of those previously called. Rebuttal is not, however, a privilege only of the prosecution. The defense, in an effort to strengthen its case, may also call additional witnesses or reexamine those previously called.

Occasionally, the defense may feel it necessary to have the accused testify on his or her own behalf. This decision involves the waiver of the defendant's privilege against self-incrimination as guaranteed by the Fifth Amendment to the Constitution. A defendant's failure to testify cannot be commented on by either the trial court or the prosecution in the presence of the jury.[35]

INSTRUCTIONS OF
THE COURT TO THE JURY

When the court does not direct or grant a motion for dismissal after the evidentiary stage of the proceedings, the case goes to the jury, and the judge delivers to the jury a written charge that sets forth the law applicable to the case. These instructions are prepared by the judge and the attorneys in the case after all the evidence has been received. In these instructions, the judge is not allowed to express any opinion as to the weight of the evidence presented or to summarize the testimony or discuss any of the facts or arguments that might arouse the sympathy or excite the passions of the jury.

ARGUMENTS TO THE JURY

Usually this segment of the trial proceedings is by far the most dramatic and critical stage for the defense and for the prosecution. It is now that each side attempts to persuade the jury to reach a verdict favorable to its position. They attempt to influence the jury by reviewing the evidence presented, interpreting the instructions to the jury, and condemning the credibility of the opposition's witnesses. Generally, the state is allowed the final argument.

CHARGING THE JURY

On completion of the arguments, the judge instructs the jury as to its responsibility to render a true and just verdict in light of the facts of the case, the instructions of the

court, and the arguments of counsel. The jury is told the possible verdicts it may render according to the statutory provisions governing the case. Possible verdicts may be guilty, not guilty, not guilty by reason of insanity, and so forth.

DELIBERATION AND VERDICT

After being charged by the court, the jurors retire to the jury room, where they deliberate on the issues of the case. One of the duties of the bailiff of the court is to ensure that the deliberations are carried out in complete privacy. Requests for transcripts of the testimony, additional instructions from the court, and other necessary information may be made directly to the presiding judge. Because deliberations very often take more than one day, the bailiff is also in charge of securing food and housing for the jury.

When the jury has reached a decision, it advises the bailiff and returns to the courtroom. The verdict may be returned either orally or in writing by the foreman of the jury. In some cases the verdict in written form is read by the court itself instead of by the foreman. A jury that fails to reach a unanimous verdict is known as a *hung jury*; this results in a *mistrial*. Before the court declares a mistrial, the jurors are normally questioned in open court about their inability to reach a unanimous decision.

If either the state or the defense feels that the verdict rendered does not represent the considered, voluntary judgment of all the jurors, the jury may be polled in open court. Normally the defense makes this request after a guilty verdict has been entered. A declaration by any juror that he or she was pressured to make a verdict unanimous results in a mistrial. A finding of not guilty would result in the immediate release of the defendant. A verdict of guilty initiates the sentencing phase.

SENTENCING

To the defendant who has been found guilty either by bench or by jury, the sentencing phase of the criminal justice process is the most critical. Before issuing the penalty, most judges order a *presentence investigation* report on the defendant's background. Many states stipulate increased sentences for offenders who have repeated the same or similar offenses. For the first offender, such a report may reveal that the defendant can best be rehabilitated by serving a sentence on *probation*. In that case, instead of incarcerating the individual, the court permits him or her to remain free under the conditions set forth by law. Before passing sentence, the judge conducts a hearing, at which time the prosecution and the defense are allowed to advance opinions as to the severity of the sentence that should be imposed.

At present, in all but thirteen states, the sentencing function rests with the trial judge.[36] However, when the crime carries an extremely heavy penalty, as in the case of murder or rape, this responsibility is often turned over to the jury. In some states, the defendant is permitted to choose between judge and jury sentencing. Regardless of who has the authority to decide the penalty, any sentence imposed must be within the limits prescribed by law. Many states utilize *indeterminate sentencing,* which allows the trial judge to sentence for the maximum term allowed by law and gives the parole board authority to determine the exact amount of time to be served. More recently, the trend has been to eliminate the sentencing discretion of trial court judges because of vast disparities in the sentences being handed down to individuals convicted of similar offenses, with similar backgrounds and criminal histories.[37]

APPEALS

After sentence has been pronounced, a defendant may appeal the conviction to a reviewing court. Although there is no constitutional right to appeal, every state and the federal courts grant a convicted person the right to appeal a lower court's decision.[38] The appeal process is set forth in the statutes or judicial rules of the jurisdiction involved. In general, appeals are carried from the lower courts to a court of general jurisdiction, and from this court of general jurisdiction to an intermediate appellate court or the highest state court.

After reviewing the case, the appellate court involved can make any one of a number of decisions. The court may simply *affirm* the lower court's decision, or it may go so far as to *reverse* it. Reversal means that the conviction is nullified and the defendant cannot be retried. A less drastic ruling by the court is to *reverse* and *remand* the decision, which means that the defendant may be retried if the state elects to do so.

Until recently, state prosecutors had the right to appeal a judgment of acquittal when the trial judge had improperly terminated the proceedings before the prosecution had sufficient opportunity to present its evidence. Today, however, the state may appeal only such pretrial orders as motions to dismiss indictments and motions to suppress evidence. Some jurisdictions do allow the government to appeal judgments for the sole purpose of clarifying questions of law to provide guidance for future criminal cases.

HABEAS CORPUS

To a defendant who has been convicted, has exhausted the appeal processes, and is incarcerated in the appropriate state or federal penitentiary, the hope of a reversal of the original court's verdict seems all but lost. In our society, however, the government must always be accountable to the judiciary for the imprisonment of one of its citizens. A petition for a writ of *habeas corpus,* filed by the prisoner, questions the legality of the petitioner's detention by alleging violations of the petitioner's rights during the trial process. Such violations may involve denial of counsel at the preliminary hearing or appeal, use of false evidence by the prosecution, use of an involuntary confession, denial of transcript on appeal, and so on.

Normally, these petitions are filed with the court of general trial jurisdiction, which will conduct a hearing to determine whether legal authority exists to hold the petitioner. But state prisoners may also file for *habeas corpus* relief in the federal district court that has jurisdiction over the penal institution or in the United States Supreme Court. This was made possible by the United States Supreme Court decision in *Brown* v. *Allen,* 344 U.S. 433 (1953), which expanded the scope of federal *habeas corpus* jurisdiction to include state prisoners. Since 1953, in a series of cases the United States Supreme Court has vastly increased the availability of federal *habeas corpus* to state prisoners. In the case of *Townsend* v. *Sain,* 372 U.S. 293 (1963), the Court held that in reviewing a *habeas corpus* petition, a federal court must hold an evidentiary hearing whenever an applicant has not received a "full and fair evidentiary hearing in a state court."[39] This means that every federal court may, if certain conditions are met, "reverse the findings of any state criminal court as to either the law or the facts."[40] This expansion of federal *habeas corpus* is reflected in the increased number of petitions filed in federal district courts since *Townsend*;

in 1960, there were 868 state prisoner *habeas corpus* petitions; in 1964, there were 4243; and in 1970, there were 9063 state prisoner applications.[41] This expanding workload for the federal courts prompted the Supreme Court to suggest that "federal collateral review of a state prisoner's Fourth Amendment claims 'should be confined solely to the question of whether the petitioner was provided a fair opportunity to raise and have adjudicated the question in the state courts.'"[42] Since this comment in *Schneckloth* v. *Bustamonte,* 412 U.S. 218 (1973), the Supreme Court has begun to severely restrict the availability of *habeas corpus* relief (Figure 3.4).[43]

JUVENILE JUSTICE SYSTEM

With Billy B. convicted, sentenced, and in the state's correctional institution, it is time to return to the juvenile member of the criminal team, his brother Mark, whom we left with juvenile officers of the police department. Though Mark may have felt very lonely sitting in the virtually empty juvenile detention area of the police department awaiting transfer to the intake section of the local juvenile probation department, he was, in fact, in good company. Six other juveniles had already been arrested and processed for criminal activities that very same evening, some for crimes far worse than his. In fact, an average of 1 million juveniles are arrested each year and handled by special juvenile courts that have been established by each state.[44]

The juvenile court is not a criminal court, nor is it an ordinary civil court. It is, in fact, a special statutory court that has among its responsibilities the hearing and disposing of cases against juveniles who either offend

FIGURE 3.4 THE LEGAL CITATION

PLAINTIFF	VERSUS	DEFENDENT	VOLUME 372	United States Reports	PAGE 335	VOLUME 83	Supreme Court Reporter	PAGE 792	VOLUME 9	Lawyer's Edition, 2nd	PAGE 799	YEAR OF THE CASE
Gideon	v.	Wainwright	[372	U.S.	335,	83	S.Ct.	792,	9	L. Ed. 2d.	799	(1963)]

Throughout this book you will see legal citations such as *Gideon* v. *Wainwright* [372 U.S. 335 (1963)]. This is the short citation for this particular case. The long citation would be as follows: *Gideon* v. *Wainwright* [372 U.S. 335, 83 S.Ct. 792, 9 L.Ed. 2d. 799 (1963)]. While a legal citation may appear forbidding at first glance, it merely serves as an identification procedure for locating the cited case in the books of law. The insert above shows how the citation would be interpreted. This citation indicates that the *Gideon* v. *Wainwright* case can be found in volume 372 of the *United States Reports* on page 335; or volume 83 of the *Supreme Court Reporter* on page 792; or volume 9 of the *Lawyer's Edition,* 2nd Edition on page 799. The decision was handed down in the year 1963.

Legal research and bibliography is an art in itself. For further information, the student should consult *How to Find the Law,* 6th ed., ed. William R. Roalfe (St. Paul, Minn.: West Publishing Company, 1965).

against the criminal law or transgress against other rules especially set forth for juveniles. Under the juvenile court's philosophy of individualized justice for each child there are two principles that distinguish the juvenile court system from the adult court.

1. A child in a juvenile court is not regarded as responsible for criminal acts until he or she has attained a much greater age.
2. Under the jurisdiction of the juvenile court, a child is never accused of a crime and suffers no conviction or stigma. A child brought before the juvenile court is declared to be a delinquent child needing the care and protection of the court. This is referred to as the court's *delinquency jurisdiction*. It also has *dependency jurisdiction,* the power to hear cases involving dependent and neglected children.

JUVENILE PROCEEDINGS

The juvenile court's philosophy is expressed in civil procedural law through a series of carefully delineated proceedings designed to identify the child's needs and facilitate appropriate corrective action. Juvenile proceedings are generally broken into four phases, beginning with Mark's handling by the police department's juvenile division.[45]

PREADJUDICATORY PHASE

In conjunction with arresting Officers Lane and Kean, members of the police department's juvenile division prepared a complete report on the circumstances surrounding Mark's arrest. The juvenile officers placed a call to Mark's parents, notifying them of his detention and informing them that he would be referred to the *intake section* of the juvenile court. On the basis of the information pro-

DISCUSSION QUESTIONS

1. Refer to Figure 3.1 for a moment. What steps in the felony process would you eliminate in order to improve the administration of justice in America?
2. Can a defendant delay the criminal justice process? Is this to the individual's advantage? To the state's advantage?
3. Many states have discontinued the use of the grand jury as a way of indicting a suspect. Discuss the pros and cons of this decision relative to the criminal justice process.
4. What impact have the following three Supreme Court decisions had on the juvenile justice process?
   a. *In re Gault*, 387 U.S. 1 (1967)
   b. *Kent* v. *U.S.*, 383 U.S. 541 (1966)
   c. *In re Winship*, 397 U.S. 358 (1970)
5. List the major processes involved in the administration of criminal law from arrest to parole. Compare and contrast this with the juvenile justice process.
6. If a defendant voluntarily pleads guilty in exchange for a reduced charge or leniency in sentencing, should that defendant at a later date be allowed to appeal the conviction?
7. Should the victim of a crime have the opportunity to review the plea-bargaining agreement before it is presented to the court for approval? Do victims of crimes have this opportunity now?
8. Juveniles have virtually all the constitutional rights guaranteed adult felons in criminal proceedings. What keeps the two systems from becoming virtually identical processes?
9. Compare and contrast the distinguishing characteristics of the grand jury indictment process with those of the preliminary hearing. Which provides more constitutional safeguards?
10. In your opinion, which phase of the criminal justice process provides the fewest constitutional safeguards for the accused?

NOTES

1. For Officers Lane and Kean to progress from merely detaining these suspects to a lawful arrest, four distinct elements are involved:
   a. the purpose or intention to make an arrest
   b. the communication of this intention to the person to be arrested
   c. the accomplishment of an actual seizure or constructive (implied or expressed) seizure or restraint by the arresting person of the individual to be arrested
   d. the understanding by the arrested person that he or she is being arrested
2. *Katz* v. *United States*, 389 U.S. 347 (1967); *Coolidge* v. *New Hampshire*, 403 U.S. 443 (1971); *Chambers* v. *Maroney*, 399 U.S. 42 (1970).
3. *United States* v. *Robinson*, 414 U.S. 218 (1973).
4. The Supreme Court in *Terry* v. *Ohio*, 392 U.S. 1 (1968), held that "a police officer may in appropriate circumstances and in an appropriate manner approach a person for purposes of investigating possible criminal behavior even though there is no probable cause to make an arrest."
5. *Chimel* v. *California*, 395 U.S. 752 (1969).
6. This is a legal rule that was made applicable to the states via the Fourteenth Amendment in the famous case of *Mapp* v. *Ohio*, 367 U.S. 643 (1961). In this case the Supreme Court ruled that evidence seized in violation of an individual's Fourth Amendment rights may be excluded from use by the state in a criminal proceeding initiated against an individual.
7. See National Institute of Law Enforcement and Criminal Justice, *Cost Analysis of Correctional Standards: Alternatives to Arrest*, Vols. 1 and 2 (Washington, D.C.: U.S. Government Printing Office, 1975).

8. Joseph Goldstein, "Police Discretion Not to Invoke Criminal Process: Low Visibility Decisions in the Administration of Justice," in *Criminal Justice: Law and Politics,* 2nd ed., ed. George F. Cole (North Scituate, Mass.: The Duxbury Press, 1976), pp. 101–107.

9. National Institute of Law Enforcement and Criminal Justice, *The Prosecutor's Charging Decision: A Policy Perspective* (Washington, D.C.: U.S. Government Printing Office, 1977), p. 3.

10. *Mallory* v. *United States,* 354 U.S. 449 (1957).

11. *Stack* v. *Boyle,* 342 U.S. 1 (1952).

12. National Institute of Law Enforcement and Criminal Justice, *Pretrial Release Program* (Washington, D.C.: U.S. Government Printing Office, 1977).

13. *Angersinger* v. *Hamlin,* 407 U.S. 25 (1972).

14. John Henry Coleman and Otis Stephens, *Petitioners* v. *State of Alabama,* 399 U.S. 1 (1970).

15. SEARCH Group Inc., *Proceedings of the Third International Search Symposium on Criminal Justice Information and Statistics Systems* (Philadelphia, Pa.: SEARCH Group, Inc., May 24–26, 1976), p. 34.

16. SEARCH Group Inc., *Proceedings on Criminal Justice,* p. 34.

17. SEARCH Group Inc., *SJIS — State Judicial Information Systems, State of the Art,* Technical Memorandum No. 11 (Sacramento, Calif.: SEARCH Group, Inc., June 1975), p. 71.

18. *Oyler* v. *Boles,* 368 U.S. 448 (1962).

19. National Institute of Law Enforcement and Criminal Justice, *The Prosecutor's Charging Decision,* p. 6.

20. David Rossman and Jan Hoffman, *Intake Screening: A Proposal for Massachusetts District Attorneys,* (Boston: Center for Criminal Justice, Boston University, 1975).

21. In former President Gerald R. Ford's June 19, 1975 "Message on Crime to the Congress of the United States," he reported that in one jurisdiction in the United States 10 persons committed 274 crimes in one year: 200 burglaries, 60 rapes, and 14 murders.

22. Institute for Law and Social Research, *Curbing the Repeat Offender: A Strategy for Prosecutors* (Washington, D.C.: INSLAW, 1977), pp. 19–20.

23. *United States* v. *Calandra,* 414 U.S. 338 (1974); *Kastigar* v. *United States,* 406 U.S. 441 (1972); *United States* v. *Mandujano,* 425 U.S. 564 (1976).

24. *In re Groban,* 352 U.S. 330 (1957).

25. *Alexander* v. *Louisiana,* 405 U.S. 625 (1972).

26. *Costello* v. *United States,* 350 U.S. 359 (1956).

27. *Hamilton* v. *Alabama,* 368 U.S. 52 (1961).

28. *Santobello* v. *New York,* 404 U.S. 257 (1971).

29. *Gardner* v. *Florida,* 430 U.S. 349 (1977).

30. Arthur Rosett and Donald R. Cressey, *Justice by Consent: Plea Bargains in the American Courthouse* (Philadelphia: J. B. Lippincott Company, 1976).

31. *United States* v. *Ewell,* 383 U.S. 116 (1966).

32. Illinois Revised Statutes, Chapter 38, Article 103-5 (1965).

33. *Klopfer* v. *North Carolina,* 386 U.S. 213 (1967).

34. Evidence includes all legally admissible proof, which may be in the form of eyewitness testimony, physical objects of the crime, documents, etc.

35. *Griffin* v. *California,* 380 U.S. 609 (1965).

36. American Bar Association Project on Standards for Criminal Justice, *Standards Relating to Sentencing Alternatives and Procedures* (New York: Office of Criminal Justice Project, Approved Draft, 1967), p. 43.

37. National Institute of Law Enforcement and Criminal Justice, *Sentencing Guidelines: Structuring Judicial Discretion* (Washington, D.C.: Government Printing Office, 1978).

38. The Supreme Court has ruled that where a state has established procedures for appeals, they must be equally available to all defendants. More specifically, the Court states that an indigent defendant must be provided with counsel on appeal plus a free transcript. *Griffin* v. *Illinois*, 351 U.S. 12 (1956).
39. Peter W. Lewis and Kenneth D. Peoples, *The Supreme Court and the Criminal Process: Cases and Comments* (Philadelphia: W. B. Saunders Company, 1978), p. 1043.
40. Lewis and Peoples, *The Supreme Court*, p. 1043.
41. Lewis and Peoples, *The Supreme Court*, p. 1043.
42. Lewis and Peoples, *The Supreme Court*, p. 1044.
43. *Stone* v. *Powell*, 428 U.S. 465 (1975).
44. Federal Bureau of Investigation, *Uniform Crime Reports* (1968–1977) (Washington, D.C.: Government Printing Office).
45. Lewis and Peoples, *The Supreme Court*, p. 703.
46. *Parens patriae* is the doctrine that the juvenile court acts as a kind and loving parent toward the child.
47. *McKeiver* v. *Pennsylvania*, 403 U.S. 441 (1971).

PART ONE ANNOTATED BIBLIOGRAPHY

Casper, Jonathan D. *American Criminal Justice: The Defendant's Perspective.* Englewood Cliffs, N.J.: Prentice-Hall, Inc., 1972.
A text that allows the reader to see the administration of law in the United States from the defendant's point of view. This text is an excellent consumer's guide to criminal justice in America.

Holt, Wythe (ed.). *Essays in Nineteenth Century American Legal History.* Westport, Conn.: Greenwood Press, 1976.
A series of essays on the evolution of American law during the nineteenth century and its impact on contemporary legal principles, institutions, and questions.

Lewis, Peter W., and Kenneth D. Peoples. *The Supreme Court and the Criminal Process — Cases and Comments.* Philadelphia: W. B. Saunders Company, 1978.
A superb case-method analysis of the United States Supreme Court and its influential role in shaping the criminal justice process in America. Significant Supreme Court cases are carefully reviewed, with special attention to the constitutional guarantees in the Fourth, Fifth, Sixth, Eighth, and Fourteenth Amendments. Additional text material deals with the historical development and interpretation of the Bill of Rights, the juvenile justice process, legal rights of the convicted, First Amendment rights in a criminal context, and other key areas of concern to the student of criminal justice.

Quinney, Richard (ed.). *Criminal Justice in America: A Critical Understanding.* Boston: Little, Brown and Company, 1974.
An excellent collection of readings on the nature of crime, the administration of criminal law, the proper role of law in society or the necessity of law itself, ideas about justice, and the agencies of crime control in our society.

Rosett, Arthur, and Donald R. Cressey. *Justice by Consent.* Philadelphia: J. B. Lippincott Company, 1976.
This text carefully explains how the "guilty plea" or "exchange system" of justice operates in most American courthouses. The process of determining guilt and assessing punishment is analyzed from the standpoint of the impact on individual freedom and safety in society. The text is based on the authors' personal experiences and reading concerning a number of jurisdictions in the United States.

Silberman, Charles E. *Criminal Violence, Criminal Justice.* New York: Random House, 1978.

A highly readable essay on crime and the criminal justice system in America.

Strick, Ann. *Injustice for All.* New York: G. P. Putman's Sons, 1977.

A thought-provoking analysis of the evolution of the adversary concept of law in the United States. The author addresses the fundamental question of whether or not truth, and consequently justice, can be attained through a legal system based on trial by combat.

PART TWO

THE POLICE

CHAPTER FOUR

HISTORY
AND DEVELOPMENT
OF POLICE

POLICE DEVELOPMENT
IN ANGLO-EUROPEAN
SOCIETIES

ORIGIN OF MODERN
POLICING

POLICE DEVELOPMENT
IN THE UNITED
STATES

Purpose: To briefly trace the historical development of the police and the origins of the American police force as we know it.

LAW ENFORCEMENT almost certainly had its beginnings in the lost centuries of prehistory. Undoubtedly early people felt the need to protect their territory and crude possessions. It was not, however, until city-states evolved, as exemplified in the Mesopotamian and Egyptian civilizations (3500–700 B.C. and 4500–500 B.C., respectively), that formalized methods of community protection became necessary.

Before then, and as early as 7000 B.C., farming communities like the permanent settlement found at Jarmo, Iraq, had appeared. Although history fails to record much of the culture of such a community, its general protection, as well as the enforcement of its "rules," was probably the responsibility of each individual. Perhaps a community head or clan head was established, but this point is not clear.

Self-policing was probably the first form of law enforcement. The patriarch maintained order in the family or community by putting the responsibility for maintaining order equally on each member. As centuries passed, however, and communities increased in both numbers and sophistication, the concept of self-policing proved inadequate and so deteriorated. The complexities of ever-increasing social systems created the need for social protection. About 3700 B.C., cylinder seals were used to identify ownership of documents and vessels. Formal contracts for land sales were drawn up, written in cuneiform, by approximately 2750 B.C. Implicit in these developments is the effort to combat crimes of theft and land fraud.

Apparently the folkways and mores were not being complied with; thus they became ineffectual as implements of social control. This fact is substantiated by the attempt in 2150 B.C. of Ur-Nammu, a Sumerian, to establish a code defining societal conduct. Scholars attribute to the Babylonian King

Hammurabi (2100 B.C.) the first set of codified laws, commonly known as the Code of Hammurabi.

The development of law is of basic importance to the function of law enforcement. It is the provisions of the law that determine expected conduct and provide for the law's enforcement. Therefore, because Hammurabi's code provided penalties for noncompliance, it is reasonable to assume that it was to be enforced. To ensure that violators of the code were apprehended and punished, the king in all likelihood designated someone to take whatever measures were necessary to deal appropriately with such offenders. Whether this someone was an officer of the king's army or a newly appointed official is unclear. Nevertheless, the Code of Hammurabi can be considered a foundation for the development of law enforcement.

Similar developments occurred in ancient China. About 1500 B.C. the Shang Dynasty established and maintained a loosely organized military authority over the settlements in the Yellow River valley. Although this control was accomplished by military and political power, it illustrates compliance with rules established by a central authority. Later, the Chou Dynasty (1000–221 B.C.) established a written legal code.

Early Greek civilization (800–600 B.C.) gave birth to the coinage of money and the severe legal code of Draco. Solon, a statesman and reformer, prepared a legal code that opposed tyranny and injustice and laid the constitutional foundations of Athenian democracy. Of great importance in Solon's model was the concept of local autonomy. Note, however, that during that period in history the cities of Athens and Attica combined to form a single political unit. In contemporary law enforcement, such mergers have significant effects.

Roman law was codified by the publication of the Laws of the Twelve Tables (450 B.C.); these laws were enforced by units of the Roman legions. Maintaining order in the city, frequently disrupted by the early Christians, was in later years a major task for the Roman centurions.

Before Anglo-European developments are addressed, several factors should be reiterated. Thus far it has been observed that compliance with rules and customs in the early farming communities was a product of self-policing; that is, each person was individually responsible for his or her conduct. Later, as societies became more complex, laws and legal codes were developed. The development of formalized law created a more formal means of enforcement: It delegated enforcement powers to designated officials of the established military, or it simply put the responsibility for social order on a designated individual in the community or on the community as a whole (that is, an entire community might suffer a penalty should a violation occur therein). The point is that responsibility for the enforcement of the law was being delegated to someone or to some group.

At the fall of the Roman Empire (A.D. 395), the enforcement of law by the military was well established, and to this day, the military model prevails in much of continental Europe. This is an important point: The police service in many European countries is in fact part of the military forces. In England and the United States, on the other hand, police services are totally independent of the military organization. They are created by legislative enactments; they are accountable to civilian authority; and their authority, powers, and jurisdiction are defined by the legislature. In spite of this distinction, many police departments in the United States are organized along military lines.

POLICE DEVELOPMENT IN ANGLO-EUROPEAN SOCIETIES

EARLY ENGLISH DEVELOPMENT

After the Roman Empire crumbled, the continent was an array of fragmented peoples attempting to maintain some sort of identity. With the leadership of Rome gone, small nations began to form. Most of them desired additional territory, wealth, and power, and this obsession created conflict — war, death, and misery. To avoid the barbarian invasions and the unbearable civil strife, many families migrated in various directions. The continent of Europe became a scene of bloodshed and suffering.

England, however, prospered during this time. Groups formed in small settlements called *tuns*. For protection the principle of *hue and cry* was originated. This concept required every able-bodied man to help in the chase and apprehension of lawbreakers. Failure to take part could force payment of restitution or punishment equal to that of the lawbreaker. This informal method for maintaining peace and order prevailed until the ninth century.

FRANKPLEDGE SYSTEM (A.D. 800)

The *frankpledge system,* which was the progenitor of the tithing system, required every freeman above the age of twelve years to belong to a group of ten families (*a tithing*) for the purpose of maintaining the peace and harmony of the community. At the head of each tithing was the *chief tithingman,* elected from the ten families. The duties and responsibilities of the chief tithingman were to ensure the protection of the tithing as he deemed necessary.

At this point, reconsider the patriarchal system the farming community employed some nine thousand years earlier. The difference lies not in the duties or responsibilities of the clan head or his counterpart, the chief tithingman, but rather in the formal system that stipulates, in explicit terms, the protective measures that the tithing must employ. The tithing system can be considered one of the earliest attempts to formalize the means by which the community maintains peace and harmony and apprehends and punishes offenders against established customs and laws.

Ten tithings were called a *hundred,* headed by a *reeve.* Several hundreds formed a *shire,* headed by a *shire-reeve* (from which the word *sheriff* was derived). The shire-reeve was given military, judicial, and civil powers, which were frequently exercised inequitably. Although the duties of the shire-reeve were many, enforcing the law and maintaining the peace are of most significance to us. To provide him with the help necessary to adequately meet the demands of the shire or county, the shire-reeve was vested with *posse comitatus,* or "power of the county." This power permitted the shire-reeve to assemble any or all able-bodied men to respond to a hue and cry and to seek out and return the offender for trial and punishment.

With all its failures and imperfections, the frankpledge system endured for some time. As society became more complex and the population more mobile, however, the system became inadequate. Growth of the cities added greatly to the deterioration of the tithing system.

EARLY FOUNDATIONS OF ANGLO-AMERICAN POLICE

With the conquest of England in 1066 by William, Duke of Normandy (William the Conqueror), the pendulum swung away from community responsibility for maintaining peace, as established by the tithing system, toward a concept of "state" responsibility. The Norman Conquest did not remove completely the concepts of the tithing system, but it supplemented and supervised the system through military officers who had defined geographical areas of responsibility. The frankpledge system was in effect reaffirmed by the Assize of Clarendon (1166), which required all citizens to pursue by hue and cry and by "horn and hounds" any offender fleeing from justice.

During this same period the *comes stabuli* (constable) came into being. His duties were actually to assist the shire-reeve in his duties and to maintain the weapons of the shire.

King Edward I made an authentic attempt to establish a bona fide police organization. The Statute of Winchester (1285) provided a form of police for every community in the empire. The Statute of Winchester tried to cope with increasing crime and provide domestic security. It required that city gates be closed between the hours of sunset and sunrise and instituted a night watch. The watchmen, called *bailiffs* (who are today's officers of the court), guarded the city's gates and made tours through the inner city, keeping vigil over all residents and lodgers. The *police des moeurs* was a unit of the night watch responsible for regulating streetwalkers and prostitutes and containing them in the areas of the city where such activities were permitted.

The origin of the word *police* can be traced to either the Greek word *polis,* meaning "city," or to the Roman word *polites,* meaning "citizen." Whatever the case, the Statute of Winchester uses the term *police* in the context of law enforcement, and the genesis of police control and crime prevention through curfews, physical security, and vice control lies with Edward I.

To place these events in proper perspective, note that America had not been discovered — Columbus had not yet been born

— and Asia was in turmoil — Temujin (Genghis Khan) was attempting to unify the Mongol nation. Europe and England, however, were more secure. The University of Paris and University College, Oxford, were established. The European and English atmosphere favored increased urbanization, trade, affluence, and, unfortunately, crime. The need to deal with the increasing crime problem became more apparent.

Edward III created an act establishing the *justice of the peace* in 1361. This official was a peace officer appointed by the crown, and his duties were twofold: first, to replace the shire-reeve as the county peace officer; and second, to act in a judicial capacity. In fact, the justice of the peace was both a law enforcement official and a judge (*magistrate*). Although at first this brought about greater efficiency, it led to the office of the justice of the peace becoming an office of injustice and corruption.

To understand the methods used in selecting persons to occupy the positions of constable, shire-reeve, night watch, and bailiffs is to realize the cause of the system's disintegration. "Citizens who were bound by law to take their turn at police work gradually evaded personal police service by paying others to do the work for them . . . they were usually ill-paid and ignorant men, often too old to be in any sense efficient."[1]

Lack of police efficiency, increasing crime, and public rejection of compulsory police service created a profound dilemma, especially for the city's merchants, who were in dire need of protection for their businesses. Consequently, these merchants began to employ their own private police to protect their establishments and to seek and return stolen goods. This new form of policing was called the *merchant police*.[2]

Cities and towns attempted to combat crime by forming distinct territorial divisions (*parishes*); every member was required to take his turn in the *parochial police*. This system was short lived because of the development of the *paid police*.

England was in a state of lawlessness when her civil war ended in 1655. Oliver Cromwell was in power and had placed the country under military police rule — martial law. Cromwell first divided England and Wales into twelve districts and put each under the direction of a *provost marshall*. The provost marshall acted as the judge in his district and at the same time controlled the civilian population with mounted troops. Military rule was maintained for two years (1655–1657.)

In 1663, Charles II created a new system of night watch for the City of London. "The act provided for 1,000 watchmen or 'bellmen' to be on duty from sunset to sunrise. They were ineffective and bore the brunt of English humor, being called 'Charlies' and the 'Shiver and Shake Watch.'"[3]

It was not until 1737 that any significant advancement was made. King George II authorized town councils to levy taxes for the expressed purpose of providing police protection, the first instance of taxation for police protection.[4] Salaries remained deplorable, however, and this was reflected in the quality of personnel.

ORIGIN OF MODERN POLICING

Many scholars consider the noted novelist and playwright Henry Fielding (author of *Tom Jones*) the father of modern policing. Fielding was appointed justice of the peace for Westminster in 1748, and he and his half-brother, Sir John Fielding, sat at the Bow Street Magistrates Court.

Henry Fielding took his work seriously and devoted much of his energy to reform. His "Inquiry into the Cause of the Late Increase of Robberies, etc." attracted considerable attention in Parliament, and he was granted funds to implement his suggested remedies. He recruited an elite group of constables having the qualities of "champions of character" and paid them a salary sufficient to make it possible for them to withstand bribes.[5] The *crème de la crème* became known as the Bow Street Runners. The Runners were equipped with a tip-staff or hollow baton, handcuffs, and pistol, as well as being smartly uniformed.

Nevertheless, crime increased beyond the remedial capabilities of the Bow Street magistrates' efforts. After the Fieldings, other attempts were made to combat crime — without noticeable results.

NINETEENTH CENTURY: A MODEL FOR MODERN POLICING

By 1800 it was evident that the tithing system, hue and cry, constables, justices of the peace, Bow Street Runners, and other methods of crime control were ineffectual. Crime was increasing at an unprecedented rate. This phenomenon can perhaps be attributed to the overwhelming influx of rural people into the cities. Industrialization, with all its opportunities, also had its consequences — crime — and the Industrial Revolution was upon the British nation.

Sir Robert Peel, then England's Home Secretary, recognized that severe punishment for lawbreakers was in itself not the solution to the crime problem, nor was a mere increase in the number of persons vested with the duties of enforcing the law of any real value. Peel presented to Parliament in 1829 "An Act for Improving the Police in and near the Metropolis," now called the Metropolitan Police Act of 1829. On September 29, 1829, the Metropolitan Police became operational with a strength of 3,000 qualified and trained men. Although

selection of personnel had over the centuries been based on established criteria, it was under the Police Act of 1829 that the selection criteria, along with mandatory training provisions, became formalized.

To appreciate fully the meticulousness, depth, and far-sightedness of Peel's innovations, the following extract from the first *Instruction Book* (1829), a copy of which was given to each member of the "new" Metropolitan Police in October 1829, should be studied.

> It should be understood, at the outset, that the principal object to be attained is "the Prevention of Crime." To this great end every effort of the Police is to be directed. The security of person and property, the preservation of the public tranquility and all the other objects of a Police Establishment, will thus be better effected, than by the detection and punishment of the offender, after he has succeeded in committing the crime. This should constantly be kept in mind by every member of the Police Force, as the guide for his own conduct. Officers and Police Constables should endeavour to distinguish themselves by such vigilance and activity, as may render it extremely difficult for any one to commit a crime within that portion of the town under their charge.
>
> When in any Division offences are frequently committed, there must be reason to suspect, that the Police is not in that Division properly conducted. The absence of crime will be considered the best proof of the complete efficiency of the Police. . . .
>
> He [the Constable] will be civil and attentive to all persons, of every rank and class; insolence or incivility will not be passed over. . . .
>
> He must be particularly cautious, not to interfere idly or unnecessarily; when required to act, he will do so with decision and boldness. . . .

He must remember, that there is no qualification more indispensable to a Police Officer, than a perfect command of temper, never suffering himself to be moved in the slightest degree, by any language or threats that may be used; if he does his duty in a quiet and determined manner, such conduct will probably induce well-disposed by-standers to assist him, should he require it. . . .

But the first duty of a Constable is always to prevent the commission of a crime.[6]

Command of the Metropolitan Police was initially entrusted to two commissioners, Sir Richard Mayne and Sir Charles Rowan, who were *ex officio* justices of the peace. The Metropolitan Police soon replaced the many independent organizations that existed in the city of London.

The first commissioners impressed upon the force that they were public servants and sent them out unarmed and dressed in a uniform resembling the civilian attire of the period — a suit of blue cloth and a stovepipe hat. This was contrary to Fielding's Bow Street Runners, who had been armed with pistols and wore uniforms resembling those of the military. In 1829 the civilian character and traditions of the modern English police were founded.

Headquarters for the Metropolitan Police was finally established at 4 Whitehall Place, along the Thames. The building was adjacent to the courtyard that had accommodated the kings of Scotland centuries before and was commonly called Scotland Yard by the press. (The Metropolitan Police remained there until 1967, when they moved to a modern high-rise, steel and glass structure several blocks away. However, tradition being firmly rooted, the name Scotland Yard moved with them to their twentieth-century skyscraper.)

Experience proved that the number of commissioners should be reduced to one. Nominated by the secretary of state, the commissioner was appointed by the crown and given the title Commissioner of Police of the Metropolis. The London Police Act of 1839 established a separate police force for the city of London, headed by its own commissioner.

The Municipal Corporations Act of 1835 required all boroughs in England, regardless of size, to establish a police force, but some of the smaller boroughs did little if anything to comply with this act until provisions for inspection were introduced by the County and Borough Police Act of 1856. The 1856 act made mandatory the permissive powers of the Municipal Corporation Act of 1835 and the County Police Act of 1839 and required each county and borough to establish a police force. To ensure compliance with the provisions of the act, the appointment of H. M. Inspectors of Constabulary was provided for in the act. It also stipulated that a grant of 25 percent of the approved annual local police expenditure, including pensions, would be paid by the Exchequer. (In 1890 a comprehensive pension plan was introduced.) By the end of the nineteenth century a defined police system had clearly taken shape in England, that is, police forces were established, locally controlled and financed, but with some financial assistance from and some supervision by the central government.[7]

TWENTIETH-CENTURY DEVELOPMENT IN ENGLAND

A committee was created in 1919 to determine what measures, if any, the police should take with regard to methods of recruiting, rates of pay, and conditions of service. Subsequently the Police Act of 1919 addressed these issues. Further, it established the Police Federation for the purpose of affording members of all police forces of England the opportunity to consider all matters affecting their welfare and enabling them to transmit their views as a body to the secretary of state.[8]

As World War II drew to a close and thousands of qualified men returned to the British labor market, a general review of the police services was essential. The Police Post-War Committee, which sat from 1944 to 1949, considered immediate as well as long-term policy questions. The committee issued four reports, which dealt with the following topics: (a) facilities for training members for higher police ranks, which ultimately led to the creation of the Police College, now located at Bramshill; (b) female police officers, qualifying examinations for promotion, recruitment and training, police prosecutions, and the beat system; (c) police buildings and facilities, and police welfare; and (d) responsibilities in the higher police rank, and a special constabulary.[9]

The Police Act of 1946 was directed toward administrative and operational efficiency. It merged each borough police force with its county force and made possible the amalgamation of two or more forces.[10]

Several other committees were convened to consider the state of the service. However, the Royal Commission on the Police, established in 1960, undertook perhaps the most comprehensive and influential study in the twentieth century, issuing several reports between 1960 and 1967. The various acts that resulted from the several reports dealt with such provisions as the appointment and retirement of chief officers, the duties and powers of the police, the strengthening of the Inspectorate of Constabulary, a central planning and research unit, the consolidation and amalgamation of police forces, district training centers, forensic science laboratories, and regional crime squads.[11]

POLICE DEVELOPMENT IN THE UNITED STATES

History produced many police models that the United States might have emulated. But when our founders established police in their new land, perhaps the common language was the primary factor in their adoption of the English system of government and later the English police model. It should be noted, however, that while our police are similar, they are not an exact copy of our British neighbors'. The American political scene and American police systems are unique, and many factors contribute to the nature of our police forces.

An understanding of law enforcement in the United States requires knowledge of the general political and cultural development of the nation as a whole. The English colonists were apprehensive of central authority. Their migration was, in fact, an attempt to flee the king, who had sought to intimidate and suppress political and religious opposition. From such governmental intimidation and suppression of opposition, by means of a formally organized police force, a "police state" evolves. It is obvious, then, that our founders would go to considerable lengths to limit the power of a central government.

As a result of geographical factors, the Atlantic coastal region developed two distinct parts. The Northeast depended chiefly on timber and fishing, and thus small coastal villages and towns matured. On the other hand, the southeastern settlers found fertile soil, and there rural-agrarian communities prevailed. It was logical that the colonies should adopt protective methods known to them from their native England. Therefore, it is not surprising that the New England towns instituted the office of constable and the sparsely populated South relied upon the county sheriff.

Although at least two types of law enforcement existed in Colonial America — the constable (urban) and the sheriff (rural) — as the nation's population, area, and political and cultural base changed, so did the number and types of protective arrangements.

Unlike England, the United States does not have a centralized system or arrangement for regulating the duties, functions, and organization of its police service. The Tenth Amendment to the Constitution reserves this power to the states. In effect, American law enforcement is composed of many semi-independent systems. Every level of government — municipal or local, county, state, and federal — maintains some form of law enforcement function.

MUNICIPAL AND COUNTY LAW ENFORCEMENT

The first "modern" city police organization in the United States was established in 1844 — the New York City Police Department. Before this, many attempts had been made to protect the citizens in every major city. As early as 1636 Boston had a night watch, followed by Philadelphia's in 1700. In 1833 Philadelphia established the first daytime paid police. Five years later Boston followed. Crime problems and subsequent police remedies instituted by our cities were very much like those of England, and they often had equally disturbing results.

Sir Robert Peel's Metropolitan Police provided the model from which New York City and later other major cities molded the first American city police departments. Although the basic Peelian principles led the way, several modifications were made, primarily because of the differences in national governments. In the United States the establishment and administration of each political subdivision's police department are relatively free from any controls by the next higher level of government. (Local identity and community autonomy — "home rule" — have not been compromised in the tradition of American government.)

The major cities could provide some form of law enforcement, although the problems of recruiting qualified personnel, training, obtaining police buildings, establishing policy and procedures, and much more had to be solved. But what about the vast majority of America's citizens? Who was to protect them? Certainly New York City, Philadelphia, Boston, and the other cities could not provide police services to the entire population of the United States. There were no state police agencies at this time. Consequently, the rural population looked to their local governments for police service.

County sheriffs typically provided what service they could. However, because both the county sheriff and the town or municipal constable were elected officials, they were noted for political rather than professional police qualities. Most early state constitutions specifically provided for these offices, making their abolition or even the dismissal of their holders virtually impossible. These constitutional deficiencies still plague law enforcement in many states.

The western expansion brought still other peace officers, ranging from citizen groups (vigilantes) to the frontier sheriff. Many exciting tales are told about the frontier sheriff. His duties were comparable to those of the peace officers in eastern counties, but his methods were often somewhat different, as were those of town marshals. Town marshals were often elected by the people of the community, as was the chief of police in the larger cities. Today, with few exceptions, the chief of police is an appointed official.

STATE LAW ENFORCEMENT

Areas outside the cities were likewise becoming more populated, and the need for

AUGUST VOLLMER
1876–1955

Photo and Biography Courtesy of the Berkeley Police Department, Berkeley, Calif.

August Vollmer was born March 7, 1876, in New Orleans, Louisiana. His father died in 1884, and his mother took August and his younger brother to California, where the family settled in San Francisco in 1888. In 1890, the family moved to North Berkeley, where his mother died in 1938.

While living in New Orleans, August Vollmer attended the New Orleans Academy. His move to California brought an end to his formal education, although anyone who met him later recognized him as a highly educated man.

At the outbreak of the Spanish-American War, Vollmer liquidated a fuel and feed store partnership in North Berkeley and enlisted. He participated in the battle for Manila in 1898 and served as one of ninety volunteers on the gunboat Laguna de Bay, keeping the rivers open to travel, convoying troops, and assisting in the capture of river towns.

Returning to Berkeley from the Philippines in 1899, Vollmer received an appointment as a letter carrier, which he held until his friends, be-lieving that he was the only person qualified to deal with the vice conditions then existing in Berkeley, were successful in convincing him to file for the position of Town Marshal. Despite the objections of his family, who thought that service as a policeman would bring disgrace, he was elected to the position on April 10, 1905, thus crossing the threshold of a law enforcement career that was to last a lifetime.

During Vollmer's four-year term of office as Marshal, the city adopted a new charter and a form of government that provided for a police chief to be appointed by the City Council. On August 13, 1909, he was appointed Berkeley's first police chief, a position he filled with distinction until his retirement on July 1, 1932.

Almost immediately after his election in 1905, Vollmer adopted the first of many innovative practices: he mounted his officers on bicycles, followed in 1910 by mounting them on motorcycles. In 1914, with half of his force in the hospital as a result of injuries received in motorcycle accidents, he placed them all in automobiles.

Late in 1905, Vollmer requested an appropriation from the City Council to install a system of flashing lights throughout the city, to be used in conjunction with telephones conveniently installed in boxes on telephone poles so that his headquarters might summon officers on patrol for dispatch on police calls. The council was reluctant to grant such a large appropriation, but instead put the issue before the voters in a $25,000 bond issue that carried. In 1906, Vollmer had a communication system in operation that enabled the speedy dispatch of bicycle-mounted officers to the scene of action.

In 1919, during the period of crystal radios and headsets, Vollmer experimented with a radio receiver installed in a patrol car.

Vollmer immediately recognized the need for complete and accurate police records and set about developing such a method of record keeping. His system, including a modified British *modus operandi* file, has been widely adopted by other police departments.

In 1907, as president of the California Police Chiefs' Association, he urged the state legislature to create a State Bureau of Criminal Identification. The California State Bureau, created in 1917 after ten years of persistent promotion, has served as a model for many other states in the creation of similar clearinghouses of information relating to crimes and criminals.

On a national level, a uniform system for the classification and collection of crime data was developed by the International Association of Chiefs of Police some years after Vollmer served as its president in 1921.

Vollmer assisted personally in the reorganization or modernization of the operating methods of scores of police departments, including San Diego, Detroit, Chicago, Kansas City, St. Paul, Minneapolis, Portland, Dallas, Syracuse, and a number of other cities. He served as chief of police of Los Angeles while on a year's leave of absence from Berkeley in 1923. He served as a police consultant to the Wickersham Commission on Law Observance and Enforcement.

Children invariably received sympathetic attention from Vollmer. He organized a junior police before the First World War and later organized the School Boy Patrol. Under his leadership, Berkeley organized the first Community Coordinating Council for the Prevention of Delinquency in 1919.

He concerned himself with the treatment accorded convicted criminals; he took an active part in promoting the creation of the Youth and Adult Authorities in California. In 1923 he constructed a minimum security prison in Los Angeles, a superior practice that has spread throughout the country.

An awareness of the need for police training prompted Vollmer to establish a police school in the Berkeley Department. Instruction was principally provided by his friends on the faculty of the University of California. A three-year program was designed; each officer was required to complete the program.

At the same time, he interested his University friends in a plan to offer police and other criminology courses at the summer sessions. The plan was inaugurated in 1916 and such courses were given every year (except 1927) until 1932, when the University offered similar courses during the regular school year. Police officials from all parts of the West Coast attended the summer session courses.

Vollmer was appointed Professor of Police Administration at the University of Chicago in 1929, a position he held until 1931, when he accepted a similar appointment at the University of California. He continued in this capacity until he resigned in 1938.

Nearly a dozen West Coast universities and colleges were strongly influenced by Vollmer to institute police and other criminology courses. The program started at the University of California in 1916 developed into a School of Criminology, offering Bachelor's and Master's degrees in Criminology.

Vollmer wrote numerous articles for technical and scientific journals as well as four books: *Police and Modern Society*; *The Criminal*; *Crime, Crooks and Cops*; and, with A. E. Parker, *Crime and State Police*.

His service as a citizen has been acknowledged by three awards. In 1929 Vollmer received the Harmon Foundation Medal for the most notable contribution to social science in the preceding year. In 1931 he received the Benjamin Ide Wheeler "Distinguished Citizen of Berkeley" award. And in 1934 he received the Academy of Science "Public Welfare Medal," awarded in recognition of the application of scientific principles to police administration.

---

protective services was apparent. Sheriffs could not provide the necessary law enforcement. Thus, the state governments were pressed to provide a remedy. The Texas Rangers were established in 1835 in response to this need; they became the first form of state law enforcement. Massachusetts in 1865 and Connecticut at the turn of the century organized varieties of state law enforcement. In 1905, Pennsylvania established a force that became the model for later state police organizations. Although the official title of Pennsylvania's police force organization has been changed several times in its history, its functions from the beginning have had the essential characteristics of a modern state police unit. The old Pennsylvania State Constabulary today bears the title Pennsylvania State Police.

The need for state law enforcement agencies had been recognized. In 1901 the Arizona Rangers were established, and in 1905 the New Mexico Police were established. A 1917 study by the New Jersey Bureau of State Research recognized that there were a number of statewide police problems.

> The most pressing problems of a statewide nature, which seem to indicate the need for additional protection in New Jersey, are the number of unapprehended criminals, the rural and suburban crime element, the policing of riots, the foreign element, the loss from forest fires, and the enforcement of the road, fish, and game laws.[12]

New Jersey went on to establish a state constabulary in 1921, later to be known as the New Jersey State Police. Other states followed suit, and by 1930 twenty-two states had created state police agencies. By 1939 another twenty-four state police agencies were created. Today, all states have some form of state law enforcement under various names and titles.

FEDERAL LAW ENFORCEMENT

The United States marshal was the first law enforcement officer in the federal government, created by the Judiciary Act of September 14, 1789. The Revenue Cutter Service was also established in 1789 to prevent smuggling along our seacoasts.

In 1865 legislation was passed to create the Secret Service within the Treasury Department. Counterfeiting of currency had reduced public confidence in the country's money, and the Secret Service was to restore this confidence by enforcing the counterfeiting laws. After the assassination of President McKinley in 1901, the Secret Service was assigned, informally, the task of protecting the president, and in 1903 Congress appropriated funds to the Secret Service for the formal assumption of these duties. John F. Kennedy was the first president to be assassinated while under the protection of this specialized branch of the United States Secret Service.

With the passing of time other federal law enforcement agencies evolved. The forerunner of the Federal Bureau of Investigation was organized in 1908. The FBI itself was a product of a reorganization in 1924 under the directorship of J. Edgar Hoover, who held that post until his death in 1972. In addition, the Drug Enforcement Administration, the Internal Revenue Service, the United States Marshals, the Border Patrol, and many other enforcement bodies in the federal government today provide services to the American public.

Early societies used self-policing as their method of law enforcement. Each individual protected property and person. As social groups such as clans and tribes developed, the law enforcement function became less the responsibility of the individual and more the responsibility of the group. As societies became even more complex and city-states developed, the government assumed responsibility for law enforcement. In England, where most of the roots of American law enforcement are found, the frankpledge system evolved, and from this the offices of sheriff and constable developed. Paid police or watchmen were used in the cities of England during this period. In 1829 Sir Robert Peel introduced an act in Parliament that established the Metropolitan Police of London. This police force served as a model for later American police forces. Colonial

Americans adopted the English offices of sheriff and constable. Later in the 1800s city police organizations were created in the large cities. Attempts had been made to create police forces in other cities, but the establishment of the New York City Police in 1844 is considered to be the establishment of the first city police organization. Other cities soon followed. The sheriffs and constables continued to provide law enforcement for the rural areas. The states and the federal government also developed law enforcement agencies. The Texas Rangers were established in 1835, and in 1905 the Pennsylvania State Constabulary was established. The Pennsylvania police force became the model for later state police organizations. The federal government established the United States Marshal and the Revenue Cutter Service in 1789. In 1865 the Secret Service was established, and in 1908 the forerunner of the Federal Bureau of Investigation was organized. In time more than fifty federal law enforcement agencies have evolved.

DISCUSSION QUESTIONS

1. Are police salaries sufficient to make it possible for them (the police) to withstand bribes, as Fielding stated in his "Inquiry into the Cause of the Late Increase of Robberies, etc."?
2. How did Fielding, Peel, and others know crime was increasing? How was it measured and by whom?
3. What are the advantages and disadvantages of maintaining federal, state, and local law enforcement agencies in the United States?
4. Do you find a single police agency for your state a threat? Why or why not?
5. Do we still need the office of sheriff?
6. How, or to what extent, are police agencies in the United States like those of England? Would the English model work in the United States?

NOTES

1. Cecil C. H. Moriarty, *Police Procedures and Administration,* 6th ed. (London: Butterworth & Co., 1955), p. 18.
2. Private police or contract security organizations provide a multimillion dollar service to today's modern industrial firms. This topic will be dealt with in more detail in Chapter 5.
3. A. C. Germann, Frank D. Day, and Robert R. J. Gallati, *Introduction to Law Enforcement* (Springfield, Ill.: Charles C Thomas, 1965), p. 57.
4. Germann, *Introduction to Law Enforcement,* p. 13.
5. Ronald Howe, *The Story of Scotland Yard* (New York: Horizon Press, 1965), p. 18.
6. *Manual of Guidance* (London: Her Majesty's Stationery Office, 1966), para. 1.9.
7. *Manual of Guidance,* 1.13.
8. *Manual of Guidance,* 1.14.
9. *Manual of Guidance,* 1.15.
10. *Manual of Guidance,* 1.16.
11. *Manual of Guidance,* 1.18–1.20.
12. Paul Garrett, *The State Police Problem in America* (Newark, N.J.: New Jersey Bureau of State Research, 1917), p. 181.

CHAPTER FIVE

LAW ENFORCEMENT
IN THE
UNITED STATES

LAW ENFORCEMENT: A LEGAL CONSTRUCT	STATE LAW ENFORCEMENT	NONGOVERNMENTAL POLICE
FEDERAL LAW ENFORCEMENT	LOCAL LAW ENFORCEMENT	COORDINATION AND COOPERATION OF POLICE

Purpose: To provide a description of the various governmental levels of law enforcement in the United States.

ALTHOUGH IT MIGHT be convenient to describe the police department of Kansas City or Seattle because either one would suffice as a typical municipal police department, it would be erroneous to submit either one as typical of the whole of the American police service. This point becomes clear when one considers the broad spectrum of federal, state, local, and private police services. To appreciate the difficulties involved in presenting a profile of the "typical" police department, one should be aware of the vast diversity in size, function, and jurisdiction, as well as role, mission, and other properties inherent in law enforcement.

Today over 500,000 persons are employed in the police service by approximately 40,000 separate law enforcement agencies.[1] The federal government accounts for 50 of these 40,000 agencies, the various states for another 200, and the remaining 39,750 occur at the local level of government (city, township, county).[2] It is therefore apparent not only that law enforcement has diverse jurisdictions, but also that police responsibilities are disproportionately distributed among the three levels of government, the largest portion resting firmly on local government.

Confounding the situation further is the fact that local agencies are created under the provisions afforded by their respective states. Significantly, each of the fifty states provides a distinct and unique model on which its portion of the 39,950 state and local enforcement agencies is fashioned. It is not surprising, then, that our fragmented police service has been referred to as the American Police Nonsystem.

Perhaps the only generalization to be made is that law enforcement is a function of the executive branch, whatever the level of government. The president, the governors of the fifty states, and the mayors, commission chairpersons, and other executive officers of the many local political subdivisions (local governments) share these responsibilities.

LAW ENFORCEMENT: A LEGAL CONSTRUCT

The Constitution of the United States does not provide expressly for the establishment and maintenance of police services, nor does it prohibit such services. The implicit powers of Article I, Section 8, Clause 18, which provides for the common defense and for the promotion of the general welfare of the people, have been interpreted as enabling the federal government to establish federal law enforcement organizations. Therefore, the Constitution is the *basis* for federal law enforcement. This is not, however, to be confused with the concept of *source,* which is the act or instrument by which a specific law enforcement agency is created. For all practical purposes, the source of all federal law enforcement agencies is the Congress. It is the Congress that enacts appropriate legislation for each agency's creation and maintenance (salaries, training, and general operating budgets).

At the state and local levels of government, the majority of law enforcement organizations are also established and maintained by legislative provisions. Several states, however, provide explicitly for such law enforcement officers as sheriffs and constables in their constitutions.

FEDERAL LAW ENFORCEMENT

Distrust of, and the subsequent limitations placed on, the central government by our nation's founders make the absence of a national police force very conspicuous. In the United States there is no single federal agency responsible for enforcing all federal laws. In actuality, responsibility for enforcing federal laws is distributed among some fifty or more federal law enforcement agencies.

When a law enforcement agency is created by a congressional act, that piece of legislation defines the jurisdiction and authority of the agency. For example, the Federal Bureau of Investigation has authority to deal with about 185 federal crimes. Geographically, its authority is restricted to the United States and its possessions. In addition, legislation specifically provides that when a crime such as murder, which as such is not a federal offense and is usually the responsibility of the state or local police authorities, occurs on a military installation, it falls within the jurisdiction of the FBI.

It is not surprising that the average American is unaware that there are approximately fifty law enforcement agencies at the federal level, nor is it surprising that the majority of interested people seeking federal enforcement positions apply to those few agencies with which they are familiar. The Federal Bureau of Investigation, Drug Enforcement Administration, and Secret Service are probably the most visible and the most frequently discussed enforcement units at the federal level. Yet, these three perform less than 1 percent of the federal law enforcement activities. Other federal enforcement and investigative functions are found in these departments:

I. *Department of Justice*
   (a) Immigration and Naturalization Service: Border Patrol
   (b) United States Marshal
   (c) Drug Enforcement Administration
   (d) Federal Bureau of Investigation

II. *Department of the Treasury*
   (a) United States Customs Service
   (b) Internal Revenue Service
   (c) Secret Service
   (d) Treasury Guard Force
   (e) White House Police Force
   (f) Bureau of Alcohol, Tobacco, and Firearms

III. *Department of Defense* (Employing Non-military Personnel)
   (a) Office of Special Intelligency (OSI), United States Air Force
   (b) Office of Naval Intelligency (ONI), United States Navy
   (c) Criminal Investigation Division (CID), United States Army

IV. *United States Postal Service*
   Postal Inspection Service

V. *Department of Transportation*
   United States Coast Guard

Still other law enforcement units are found in the Departments of State; Interior; Labor; Health, Education, and Welfare; Agriculture; and Commerce. In addition, various independent administrative agencies maintain law enforcement units, among them the Nuclear Regulatory Commission (NRC); Civil Aeronautics Board (CAB); Federal Communications Commission (FCC); Interstate Commerce Commission (ICC); and United States Civil Service Commission. This partial list of federal law enforcement agencies or units makes it quite apparent that there are many career opportunities in federal law enforcement.

STATE LAW ENFORCEMENT

Unlike the federal government, many states maintain an enforcement agency that has the responsibility and jurisdiction to enforce all state criminal laws anywhere within the state (general police powers). State law enforcement agencies are the creations of the state legislature. Even when a state law enforcement agency is expressly provided for in the state constitution, supplemental legislation is required to maintain contemporary training, salaries, budget, etc. Usually such agencies are referred to as state police or state highway patrol, but the official designation of a police organization is often misleading. Even if the official title of an organization does not reflect it, that agency may have general police powers. Therefore, it is not the title that should be of concern, but rather the functions performed and the organization, authority, and jurisdiction.

State police organizations can be categorized as having either general police powers or restricted police powers. The Pennsylvania and Michigan State Police are in the first category and enforce "all" laws in their respective states. The North Carolina and California Highway Patrols illustrate the latter category and are restricted to the enforcement of traffic laws, accident investigation, accident prevention, and general highway safety.

Several states maintain more than one state enforcement organization, each having restricted police powers. Florida maintains a state police as well as the Florida Department of Law Enforcement; the former is responsible for traffic and minor criminal offenses, whereas the latter provides specialized investigation and enforcement in the more serious crimes. Similar to this is the North Carolina State Bureau of Investigation, which is the investigating agency in the state and deals with criminal offenses (remember that traffic enforcement is the responsibility of the North Carolina Highway Patrol).

Texas exemplifies another modification. There, the Texas Department of Public Safety has general police powers, which are functionally distributed between two enforcement units: the highway patrol for traffic and criminal enforcement, and the Texas Rangers for specialized investigating assignments. Texas law enforcement is very much like that of Florida. The rather subtle organizational variations, although not necessarily important, are still worth notice.

Various other law enforcement units exist in state government, particularly within the regulatory and administrative bodies. Alcoholic beverage control boards, liquor control boards, public utilities commissions, agriculture commissions, public health services, fire marshals, departments of fish and wildlife, insurance commissions, pollution control boards, and scores of other such governmental bodies maintain law enforcement units. Admittedly, the scope of each of these enforcement functions is greatly limited and highly specialized. However, the combined efforts of all these units are extremely broad and account for a considerable number of law enforcement personnel in the state governments, and all these units are continually seeking qualified personnel.

LOCAL LAW ENFORCEMENT

Law enforcement at the local level has frequently been described and categorized as urban, suburban, or rural. Such terminology portrays the characteristics of the population being served more accurately than it does the formal governmental structure from which it is created, maintained, and regulated. To be more precise, we shall refer to the various local law enforcement agencies as either municipal (city, town, borough, village, township) or county, as determined by their charters or origins and not by demographic properties.

FIGURE 5.1 LAW ENFORCEMENT CODE OF ETHICS

As a law enforcement officer, my fundamental duty is to serve mankind; to safeguard lives and property; to protect the innocent against deception, the weak against oppression or intimidation, and the peaceful against violence or disorder; and to respect the Constitutional rights of all men to liberty, equality and justice.

I will keep my private life unsullied as an example to all; maintain courageous calm in the face of danger, scorn, or ridicule; develop self-restraint; and be constantly mindful of the welfare of others. Honest in thought and deed in both my personal and official life, I will be exemplary in obeying the laws of the land and the regulations of my department. Whatever I see or hear of a confidential nature or that is confided to me in my official capacity will be kept ever secret unless revelation is necessary in the performance of my duty.

I will never act officiously or permit personal feelings, prejudices, animosities or friendships to influence my decisions. With no compromise for crime and with relentless prosecution of criminals, I will enforce the law courteously and appropriately without fear or favor, malice or ill will, never employing unnecessary force or violence and never accepting gratuities.

I recognize the badge of my office as a symbol of public faith, and I accept it as a public trust to be held so long as I am true to the ethics of the police service. I will constantly strive to achieve these objectives and ideals, dedicating myself before God to my chosen profession . . . law enforcement.

COUNTY LAW ENFORCEMENT

County law enforcement, which accounts for 3,050 agencies,[3] is of two major types — the county sheriff and county police. Typically, the county sheriff, a constitutional officer (one provided for by the state constitution), is the chief law enforcement officer of the county. The sheriff is usually an elected official and may or may not possess those qualities considered essential for performing the complex tasks of the office. Deputy sheriffs are appointed by the sheriff and serve at the sheriff's pleasure. However, in some sheriff's departments deputies must meet established selection criteria. For example, the Los Angeles county sheriff's deputies are among the best trained and most respected officers in the nation today.

There is great disparity among the many hundreds of sheriff's departments throughout the United States. In the northeastern states, the county sheriff generally functions as an officer of the court. Traffic enforce-ment and criminal investigations are left to the state or other local agencies. In the western and southern states, it is more common to find sheriff's deputies engaged in both traffic enforcement and criminal investigation duties. The size of a sheriff's staff may range from one to several thousand deputies and civilian personnel. Likewise, the levels of technical sophistication attained by the sheriff's departments vary from no training facilities and minimal equipment (some sheriffs must use their private automobiles to perform their duties) to training academies, crime laboratories, helicopters, and a fleet of vehicles. Such extreme diversity prohibits any attempt to describe the typical or average sheriff's department, and each department must be evaluated individually on its own merits and deficiencies.

County police are not synonymous with the county sheriff's department. Usually they are not provided for by state constitutions, but are created by the county commissioners (the county legislative body). County police units are generally headed by a chief of police, who in turn is directly accountable to a county manager, county prosecutor, county director of public safety, or county commissioner. The county chief of police is normally an appointed officer and traditionally has been promoted from within the ranks of the department. County police for all practical purposes have general *county* police powers. The degree of sophistication and expertise in such departments again varies from meager to excellent.

Another county law enforcement officer, found in Pennsylvania and some other states, is the county detective, who is appointed by and serves directly under the district or county attorney. County detectives may be a special unit of a county police department assigned to the district attorney, although it is more common for the district attorney to maintain a unit of special investigators distinct from either the sheriff's office or the county police department. It is possible for there to be a county sheriff, county police, and a county detective in the district attorney's office in a county simultaneously. Difficulties are likely to arise under such conditions, however, and they can lead to duplication of effort and organizational friction and animosity.

MUNICIPAL LAW ENFORCEMENT

Law enforcement at the municipal level (city, town, borough, village, or township) accounts for 36,700 agencies — clearly a majority of the 40,000 total agencies currently providing public protective services to America.[4] This means there are 36,700 separate jurisdictions, each with its own departmental policies, organization, and police chiefs, as well as pay scales, pension funds, retirement plans, police headquarters, and many other related factors. Perhaps the full impact cannot be appreciated until one considers the variety of guidelines (municipal and state laws) that are applicable to these thousands of agencies.

Because municipalities are creations of the state, the state obviously retains the power to regulate them. Thus, state legislatures establish certain guidelines in the form of charters and codes for cities and towns to follow. The degree of regulation is determined in large measure by the size (population) of the municipality or political subdivision. States commonly classify political subdivisions in accordance with population and provide specific guidelines in the form of codes and charters accordingly. Among these many provisions are those involving law enforcement.

Pennsylvania, for example, categorizes cities by class. Philadelphia is a first-class city; Harrisburg is a third-class city. Towns and townships are also denoted by class. Kentucky classifies cities in a similar way. For each city, town, or township, there is a charter or a code of state regulations that must be met. Almost always included in these codes are requirements related to police civil service commissions, retirement, and pension arrangements. But equally important is the fact that some political subdivisions are not required by law to maintain any law enforcement, while others must establish and maintain police services.

To illustrate the many forms of law enforcement, consider the state of Kentucky. The Kentucky State Police have general police powers. However, until 1976, certain classes of cities could, by law, remove themselves from the jurisdiction of the state police. In effect, these cities had at their discretion the right to keep the state police out of the city.

Another form of law enforcement is seen

in Connecticut. Towns may request the state police to assign a *resident trooper* to provide local law enforcement. Under this arrangement, the town is billed by the state for the salary and other expenses of the resident trooper as agreed upon. The mechanics of this scheme result in a town-state police officer.

Contract law enforcement is similar to the resident trooper concept, and its most extensive application is found in Los Angeles County, California. A municipality in Los Angeles County, rather than maintaining its own police department, may ask the county to provide the required services. The city and the county enter into an agreement whereby the city promises to pay the county for police services. In some cases, the conditions of this agreement may require the county to provide one mobile police officer to patrol between the hours of sunset and sunrise. In others, the conditions may be quite extensive, calling for a comprehensive study of the city and full-time police service, which may require many police officers and even a police building.

SPECIAL AND AUXILIARY POLICE

Many police departments throughout the country maintain a body of officers to serve in a reserve capacity. Although some states make a legal distinction in the duties and authority of special and auxiliary police, they are for all practical purposes a supplemental force that serves at the pleasure of the chief of police. The qualifications required to become a special or auxiliary police officer range from none to a comprehensive selection process and extensive training. Many times these officers volunteer, and receive little or no pay. In other cases, when on duty, they may receive a salary equal to the salary of the regular officers.

NONGOVERNMENTAL POLICE

Law enforcement at the federal, state, and local levels of government covers a variety of police models. Still another segment of protective services exists and increases the milieu of law enforcement: private security or private police agencies.

Early in the developmental stages of British law enforcement, the merchant police were introduced. Likewise, in the United States, the Pinkerton's and Burns's detectives achieved notable productivity and popularity. Apparently the services rendered by these and similar organizations are regarded as assets to the task of public protection. We can derive such a conclusion from the fact that an estimated $6 billion is expended annually for private security services,[5] and the number of private security personnel is estimated at approximately 1 million.[6]

Private security personnel, according to their descriptive title, should have little impact on public law enforcement. If their functions were represented by their titles, they might not be major contributors to contemporary police problems. But their functions do create difficulties and conflicts.

Normally private police have no police powers. Their function is to observe and report to proper authorities any incident detrimental to the safety and security of their employer's property and personnel. However, this is not always the case in practice. In many areas, private security personnel are deputized police officers or sheriffs; others have been appointed special and auxiliary police officers. Another common situation is that in which a regular police officer, with full police powers, is employed part time (moonlighting) as a security officer in industry or elsewhere in the private sector of the community. It becomes impossible to determine what authority a security officer possesses by merely looking at the uniform.

Critical to this issue is the quality of personnel employed in private security, especially when they have the authority to engage in law enforcement functions, regardless of how limited such authority may be. Typically, private security personnel are not adequately trained in the technical aspects of law enforcement. Often they have received no formal instruction about the specific duties they are expected to perform for their employers, let alone general police instruction. Often armed with a weapon and having minimal or no training, they engage in the duties of police officers to the limits prescribed by the laws that permit these organizations to exist and to function.

The role of the private security officer has attracted new attention in many circles, including Office of Justice Assistance, Research and Statistics (OJARS) and the International Association of Chiefs of Police. Arthur Bilek, chairman of the task force on private security, makes some rather significant comments. Bilek states,

> The application of the resources, technology, skills, and knowledge of the private security industry presents the best hope available for protecting the citizen who has witnessed his defenses against crime shrink to a level which leaves him virtually unprotected.
>
> Underutilized by police, all but ignored by the prosecutors and the judiciary, and unknown to corrections officials, the private security professional may be the one person in this society who has the knowledge to effectively prevent crime.
>
> Not represented on the boards or staffs of state planning agencies, rarely used by municipal or county planners, only infrequently consulted by elected officials, these members of a six-billion-dollar-a-year industry have crime prevention answers desperately needed by homes,

school, businesses, neighborhoods, and communities. This report is premised on the belief that the private security industry constitutes a massive resource that holds great promise for aiding the nation in a joint effort to prevent and reduce crime. The purpose of this report is to propose how to upgrade the ability, competence, relationships, and effectiveness of that resource for the anticrime effort.

Up to the present, the anticrime role of private security generally has been ignored. Admittedly, there are important differences between the private security industry and the formal criminal justice system, although the two fields share many of the same goals. The private security industry exists to make a profit in return for the provision of services. It is not supported by public taxes. It is not an arm of the government.

Nonetheless, in serving its clientele, the private security industry serves all of society. Its personnel often are as much "on the line" as our sworn officers. The industry is responsible for the safety and well-being of the public in many locations and situations and for the protection of billions of dollars of assets and property.

The simple truth obscured by the massive anticrime program is that the criminal justice system, by and of itself, cannot and does not prevent crime and criminality. This vital goal can only be achieved by individuals not committing crime because of their respect for law and their acceptance to the ultimate wisdom of that behavior.

The report of the *Private Security Task Force* was developed in the hope that these standards and goals will provide the necessary impact to reduce crime to manageable levels so that this nation's citizens can then rebuild into our society the missing understanding and respect for the law.[7]

The standards and goals that were provided by the Private Security Task Force are of importance not only to the private security industry but to law enforcement in general. Furthermore, students interested in careers in private security should review these standards and goals, because they are guidelines for the future development of the private security industry.

The private security industry, not unlike public law enforcement, has experienced considerable change over the years. Collective bargaining, unions, contracts, arbitration, mediation, advanced training, professional certification, and education are all part of the private security profession. Professional organizations such as the American Society for Industrial Security are representing the security industry much as the International Association of Chiefs of Police represents the police.

The role of industrial security in the fight against crime is one that must not only be looked at but also integrated into an effective strategy against crime. With police administrators trying to increase police productivity and often confronted with increased competition for the tax dollar, the private security industry may be the mechanism by which both public and private interests can be met.

COORDINATION AND COOPERATION OF POLICE

Local autonomy, which has been so basic an element in American government, is a concept of fundamental importance to the study of the fragmented system of policing. Reducing the number of police agencies in this country is a monumental effort, and no significant reduction will probably be achieved in the near future. The fragmentation of the police service was recognized by Raymond B. Fosdick as early as 1921,[8] by the Wickersham Commission's "Report on Police" in 1931, by the National Crime Commission

in 1967,[9] and as recently as 1973 by the National Advisory Commission on Criminal Justice Standards and Goals.[10] Attempts to compromise the principle of home rule have generally failed, however. Thus, instead of consolidating police services, attention has turned to coordination and cooperation, and for this purpose, several important institutions have developed.

UNIFORM CRIME REPORT (UCR)

At the national level the *Uniform Crime Report* was developed to collect, compile, and distribute crime statistics. This program was instituted as early as 1930. The Committee on Uniform Crime Records of the International Association of Chiefs of Police (IACP) acts as an advisory body. The *UCR* is a nationwide index of documented law enforcement information on crime and criminals. It is expected that the extent, fluctuation, and distribution of crime can be measured more meaningfully from these data. Further, such information should be valuable in determining and adjusting police activities, policies, and procedures at *all* levels of government. In January 1967, a separate program for the systematic computerization of active crime information, the National Crime Information Center (NCIC), became operational at FBI headquarters. The *UCR* and NCIC are major contributions, not only to synthesizing crime statistics, but to modifying enforcement operations and strategies based on these data sources.

OFFICE OF JUSTICE ASSISTANCE, RESEARCH AND STATISTICS (OJARS)

As a result of the increasing crime of the 1960s, the President's Commission on Law Enforcement and the Administration of Justice and the Office of Law Enforcement Assistance (OLEA) was established. The name has since been changed twice: the Law Enforcement Assistance Administration (LEAA) and now the Office of Justice Assistance, Research and Statistics (OJARS). Reauthorization legislation passed in 1979 restructured LEAA into three bureaus, coordinated under OJARS. The three bureaus are: the National Institute of Justice, the Bureau of Justice Statistics, and a bureau which will continue to bear the name Law Enforcement Assistance Administration. The duties of these bureaus are, respectively, research, statistics collection and dissemination, and general grant administration.

In the reports of the National Crime Commission, many problems confronting law enforcement were isolated, of which fragmentation was only one. Noting the discrepancies, the federal government provided financial grants, through OJARS, to the states to develop programs in an effort to increase the effectiveness and efficiency of law enforcement. The availability of financial support was the impetus for innovative programs at all levels of government. Local government was enabled to implement such programs as regional training centers and area crime laboratories, thus improving quality and at the same time minimizing unnecessary duplication of effort. Small police departments whose separate budgets were unable to support such high-cost facilities can now in many geographical areas collectively finance and share these common services, which are essential for modern policing.

RECENT DEVELOPMENTS

The creation of a single police force to serve the entire United States (or fifty agencies, each to serve one state) is not probable, and perhaps not desirable. However, local control has been compromised to a degree by state minimum standards acts, which require all police officers in the state to achieve certain levels of proficiency, regardless of their department affiliation. California is an excellent example of a state's establishing minimum police standards in its Police Officers Standards and Training (POST).

As in the past, voluntary interdepartmental cooperation will continue to be a common ingredient by which the police achieve a semblance of unity. Recent police developments commencing at the federal level have flowed to the state and local governments in such a way as to foster a greater degree of cooperation. In the final analysis, these may prove to be the means of perpetuating the fragmented police systems, rather than a stage in the process of reshaping the system into a more comprehensive and unified model.

DISCUSSION QUESTIONS

1. What is (are) the mission(s) of the police? What kinds of organization, personnel, and philosophy are needed to meet the mission(s)?
2. Discuss the concept of home rule. What implications does it have for the police service?
3. Does the disparity of the quality of law enforcement on the American police scene compromise public trust in the police? Should this disparity be reduced?
4. What is the relationship of public police and private police? How can the image of one be affected by the other?
5. Could your city police be consolidated with the neighboring city police or county sheriff's office?
6. Do we need federal, state, and local police forces? Would a national police force be more efficient?

CHAPTER SIX

POLICE ADMINISTRATION AND OPERATIONS

PRIMARY LINE FUNCTIONS	NONLINE FUNCTIONS	POLICE OPERATIONS
SECONDARY LINE FUNCTIONS	PRINCIPLES OF ORGANIZATION	OTHER ADMINISTRATIVE AND OPERATIONAL FUNCTIONS
	MANAGEMENT INNOVATIONS	

Purpose: To provide an introduction to the administrative and operational aspects of contemporary police, including such functions as patrol, traffic, and criminal investigation.

ALL POLICE FUNCTIONS and activities can be categorized as either line or nonline. *Line functions* are those tasks that directly facilitate the accomplishment of organizational goals, whereas *nonline functions* are those tasks that supplement the line in its task performance. Line activities are further broken into subcategories: primary and secondary line functions, both of which are field services.

PRIMARY LINE FUNCTIONS

The primary line function is police patrol; that is, the patrol activities of a police organization are considered basic and of first priority. The patrol division has the initial responsibility for crime prevention and detection and the apprehension of offenders. It also assists in preparing the facts for presentation in a court of law. Theoretically, if the patrol force were 100 percent effective in the execution of its assigned tasks, the need for specialized units (traffic and detective) would be eliminated. The patrol function is accurately called the "backbone" of the police service.

SECONDARY LINE FUNCTIONS

Historically, police departments were established only as police patrols. However, as municipalities increased in population, area, and technology (for example, when the automobile was invented), the burden on these patrols was greatly increased. The departments, unable to provide additional personnel because of budget limitations, were unable to increase the number of officers on a patrol beat in proportion to the rising population and crime rate, and were forced to enlarge each officer's beat.

It soon became evident that traffic control and crime investigation were consuming a great deal of the officers' time and removing them from their primary patrol activities. Further, the sophistication of many police problems was above the level of competence normally expected of patrol officers. The need for specialized, trained units became apparent. As a product of the patrol force's inability to respond adequately to its prescribed tasks, spin-off elements evolved, for example, traffic units and criminal investigation. Although some departments have other units, these two are the major elements, often designated as secondary line functions. The important fact is they are spin-offs of the patrol force. What has resulted is a "rob Peter to pay Paul" situation — a major fault of specialization. The patrol force is depleted to provide the supportive services of specially trained officers with expertise in a given area: traffic, vice, juvenile, narcotics, and so forth. Specialization is a luxury most often enjoyed in larger police departments. It can be abused, however, to the extent of reducing the effectiveness of the patrol force. In smaller departments, generalization prevails: the patrol force has total responsibility for all line services, and the patrol officer is traffic controller, detective, or undercover agent when the situation arises. An absolute formula for the degree of generalization or specialization has not been developed.[1]

NONLINE FUNCTIONS

Simply put, *nonline functions* are those services that support the line. Whereas the line provides services directly to the citizen, nonline activities help the line to accomplish its primary tasks. Traditionally nonline or support activities consist of two major categories: staff and auxiliary services.

STAFF SERVICES

Those activities involving personnel development and departmental management are *staff services*. Personnel development includes recruitment, selection, promotion, training, and supervision. Budget, planning and research, inspection, and similar activities fall under the heading of managerial activities.

AUXILIARY SERVICES

All nonline activities not regarded as staff services are classified as *auxiliary services*. Typically, they provide support services of both a technical and a nontechnical nature to both line and nonline activities. Polygraph examiners, photographers, fingerprint and crime-scene technicians, and the police laboratory are technical auxiliary services that support the line activities. The jail and the communications system are nontechnical auxiliary services that support both line and nonline (staff) activities. Some activities are extremely difficult to classify as either staff or auxiliary. In many instances they perform a dual service. Police-community relations units, although performing secondary line services, may be designated as an auxiliary

or even a staff function. Table 6.1 presents the various functions graphically.

PRINCIPLES OF ORGANIZATION

To understand the organization and operation of police departments, certain general basic principles of organization must be understood. These principles of organization were generated by the experiences of industry, business, and the military services. They have no absolute values, but they do provide a check list against which an organization can be structurally and functionally evaluated. This notion will become more clearly defined as each principle is considered. Figure 6.1 will be referred to frequently in the discussion of principles of organization.

HOMOGENEOUS ASSIGNMENT (DIVISION OF LABOR)

For a police organization to be effective, work assignments must be designed so that similar (homogeneous) tasks, functions, and activities are given to an individual or group for accomplishment. In Figure 6.1 Internal Investigation, Operations Bureau, Services Bureau, Community Relations, Administration Bureau are each assigned their own kind

---

TABLE 6.1 POLICE FUNCTIONS: LINE AND STAFF

LINE FUNCTIONS		NONLINE FUNCTIONS	
PRIMARY	SECONDARY	STAFF	AUXILIARY
Patrol	Criminal investigation	Planning and research	Police records system
	Vice investigation	Inspection	Identification service
	Traffic regulation and control	Personnel administration	Property control
	Crime prevention	Training	Communications
		Budgetary control	Crime laboratory
		Purchasing	Jail
		Public relations	Supply
			Transportation and maintenance

FIGURE 6.1 A WELL-ORGANIZED MUNICIPAL POLICE DEPARTMENT

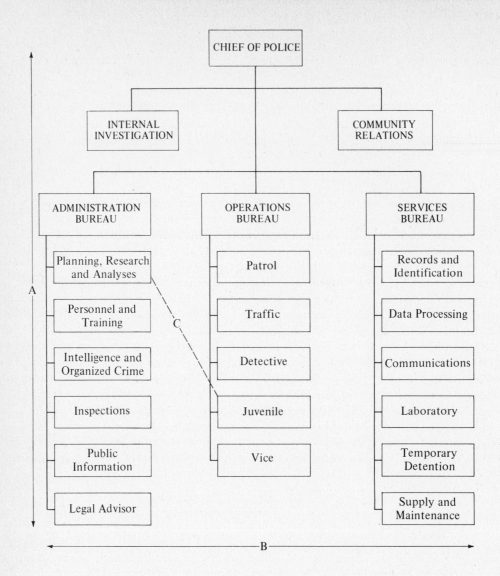

SOURCE: President's Commission on Law Enforcement and Administration of Justice, *Task Force Report: The Police* (Washington, D.C.: Government Printing Office, 1967), p. 47. Lines A, B, and C, added.

of task (for example, the Service Bureau does not engage in patrol operations because this would be a dissimilar task).

Police functions are subdivided into units that are described as follows:

Bureau: usually the largest unit within a municipal, state, or federal department (Richmond Bureau of Police, in the Department of Public Safety; Federal Bureau of Investigation, in the Department of Justice).

Division: part of a bureau having a department-wide function (Detective Division; Traffic Division).

Section: basically one of several functional elements of a division (robbery section of the Detective Division; traffic accident investigation section of the Traffic Division).

UNITY OF COMMAND

Unity of command requires that an individual be directly accountable to only one superior. No one person can effectively serve two superiors at a given time. (It is interesting that Peel's Metropolitan Police violated this principle, because when he established the department, two commissioners, or chiefs of police, were appointed. This dual command arrangement was, however, short-lived.) Note that in Figure 6.1 only one line connects any organizational block with any other block.

CHAIN OF COMMAND

Primarily this principle provides for the vertical movement of authority up and down established channels in the organizational hierarchy. To illustrate this concept, consider a directive originating in the patrol commander's (captain's) office intended for the patrol force (downward movement). Two levels of authority fall between the captain and the patrol officer — lieutenant and

sergeant. Because both levels are held responsible for various aspects of patrol supervision, both must be aware of such directives. If either supervisor is bypassed, that supervisor cannot be held accountable for the lack of knowledge. Further, performance of supervisory duties is greatly hindered, and a potentially serious morale problem is created. Line A in Figure 6.1 represents the chain of command.

DELEGATION OF RESPONSIBILITY AND AUTHORITY

There must be a clear line of formal authority running from top to bottom of every organization. Ultimate authority and responsibility for a police organization lies at the top of the chain of command — with the chief. However, if a subordinate is to be held responsible for accomplishing a given task, he or she must be given the authority to carry out those responsibilities. It is important, also, that the responsibility and the authority be clearly defined. If a patrol officer is given the responsibility for evaluating police response time on a given day or in a specific situation, the officer must be given the authority to procure the communications logs from the communication center. Without this authority, the entire task cannot be accomplished.

DELINEATION OF RESPONSIBILITY AND AUTHORITY

A clear-cut delineation of responsibility and authority is essential to prevent confusion of lines of authority. If responsibility and authority are not clearly defined, conflicts, duplications, and overlaps of functions can occur and lead to confusion and inefficiency. Each officer and each organization segment must clearly understand what is to be done and the extent of authority delegated to accomplish the job.

SPAN OF CONTROL

The number of officers or units reporting directly to a supervisor should not exceed the number that can be feasibly and effectively coordinated and directed. There are innumerable factors that limit the span of control, including distance, time, knowledge, personality, and the complexity of the work to be performed. It is not unusual to find fifty or sixty workers who perform identical functions reporting to one supervisor. On the other hand, as we ascend the chain of command and the diversity of functions increases, the number of individuals that a police executive supervises decreases rapidly. In Figure 6.1 the chief of police has a span of five, as does the commander of operations. However, the commander of the administrative bureau has a span of six.

OBJECTIVE

All organizational elements must contribute, directly or indirectly, to the accomplishment of the objective of the enterprise. Each organizational element should be formed for a definite purpose, and this purpose must be to accomplish the major objective. Any police function or organizational element that is not needed to accomplish the overall objective should be eliminated.

COORDINATION

The organizational structure must facilitate the development of close, friendly, and cooperative relations, especially between line and staff activities. Effective coordination is dependent almost entirely upon adequate communication among all elements of a police organization. Line B in Figure 6.1 represents the horizontal dimension of the organization. Often, it is necessary to function horizontally and diagonally (Line C) within the organization to achieve the objective.

This movement is provided for through departmental orders and regulations.

TIME

The police service is among the few public services that maintain a twenty-four-hour schedule. It is necessary for the department to assign officers in sufficient numbers to meet the demands at any given time. The allocation of personnel is a complex problem. On the surface, it would appear logical to divide the total police complement into three equal parts or shifts. However, for any given city, experience indicates that during certain hours of the day activities requiring police services increase and decrease. For example, on a normal weekday in a city, the vehicular and pedestrian traffic is heaviest from 7:00 to 9:00 A.M. and from 4:00 to 6:00 P.M., when people are going to and coming from work. Therefore, the distribution of personnel of the traffic function must be regulated to take these rush periods into account.

It is important to remember that this principle is applicable to *all functions* of the organization; this is an organizational principle and is not confined only to line units. It may be necessary to increase or decrease the number of people in the records or jail section in accordance with pay periods of local industry. In many small towns where there is a single industry, payday means increased social activity, some of which may necessitate police services. The police administrator must take this timetable into account. Police personnel are assigned during the day in the following manner:

Watch or Shift: a time division of the day to ensure proper allocation of personnel. Shifts are normally eight consecutive hours, five days a week, giving an officer a forty-hour work week. However, longer working hours and work weeks are common. Further, shifts frequently overlap to provide additional personnel during peak periods.

Platoon: personnel assigned to a given shift or watch. A platoon may serve an entire city or only a portion of it. Usually, a platoon is determined by the hours worked rather than its assigned area or task.

TERRITORY

Territorial distribution is necessary to ensure the availability and general suitability of the patrol service throughout a jurisdiction. Geographical or territorial divisions of the department can be described as follows:

Post: a fixed or stationary point or location (e.g., a specific street intersection, a surveillance site, or an assigned desk or office).

Route or Line Beat: a length of street normally assigned to a traffic and patrol officer (whether foot or mobile). The route has the characteristic of being continuous, in a straight line or in line of sight.

Beat: a geographical area, again assigned to a foot or mobile patrol and traffic officer. To illustrate a beat, visualize one square city block and arbitrarily designate this a beat. The patrol officer assigned to this beat is responsible for all patrol activities within it, all the streets, side streets, and alleys, and any specific calls to which he or she may be required to respond. Assume for a moment that a major street is within this beat and that this street requires a major portion of the patrol officer's time and energies. Under these conditions, the major street could feasibly be assigned to another officer, who would devote full attention to this single length of street (a route), while the beat officer would be better able to patrol the now reduced beat. The beat is the basic unit of police organization, and is among the terms most commonly referred to in the police service.

Sector: two or more beats, routes, posts, or any combination thereof.

District or Precinct: a geographical subdivision of the city for police patrol purposes. (A district for a state police department usually consists of several counties.) Typically a district has a station and perhaps other physical facilities.

Area: two or more districts.[2]

CLIENTELE

The distribution of patrol services with respect to the characteristics of the population served must be recognized and dealt with in contemporary law enforcement. The development of specialized functional units expresses the principle of organization by clientele. For example, the juvenile division is important in a young community. In contrast, a police department in a retirement community has less need for a juvenile division, but ambulance service may be a necessary police service and have a great effect on police organization. The development of police-community relations units is, to a great extent, an indication of earlier police failure to comply with this organizational principle.

MANAGEMENT INNOVATIONS

Although the traditonal management styles and concepts described earlier are essential to an understanding of organizational behavior, past and present, there are alternatives to the pyramid organization and to the usual way of thinking about organizations and management. In the last twenty to twenty-five years, both scholars and practitioners have examined the management of complex organizations and have derived some alternatives. More recently, the American police service has found itself engaged in similar activities — ones that only ten years ago were unheard of in policing.

PROGRAM MANAGEMENT

Traditionally the management process has been described as a planning, organizing, and controlling operation. Today, however, emphasis is being placed on other things, and many good organizations have become stagnant because they have failed to change with the times. The railroads are a good example; they failed to see that planning should lead to innovating, and they missed the opportunity to get into the airline business.

In the organizing process, we have developed new techniques directed toward goal attainment instead of assigning tasks by similarity as was done in a traditional, functional organization. The concept of directing has also changed. Previously, the person with power told others what to do, but now, because of unionism and other influences, the boss must think in terms of motivating employees. Even the concept of control has been modified. In the case of a social problem like crime, control means coordinating the efforts of several diverse groups to achieve a goal — crime prevention.

The classic approach toward accomplishing objectives is to set up a pyramid organization with one individual at the top in control and specialized functions in line under him or her. Then in each of the functional areas there are task units doing specialized work. Some organizations can have up to eight layers of authority in their hierarchy. In modern society, these organizations encounter difficulties handling certain situations because the organizational structure is not flexible enough to meet rapid and complex demands. Therefore, to handle these special problems, the concept of situational management has evolved. We organize around a special program or with a project emphasis. Project organization and project management has been developed to cope with these special situations.

There are basically four types of project management organizations. The primary factor distinguishing one type from another is *assigned organic capacity*. What this means will become clear as we examine these four types.

The first type is the individual, in which a person exercises project control even though functional departments will perform the tasks. An example of this would be for a police department to assign one person to keep an eye on personnel turnover in every unit within the department. This person has, or should have, the responsibility, but depends on the functional organization to carry out any plans. This kind of organization is best suited to small endeavors, where one person can supervise a function throughout the other parts of the organization.

The second type, on an increasingly complex scale, is the staff concept of organization. This organization usually has some unique or more complex function, so that one person cannot handle the task. The police organized crime division in a larger department could be this complex. This operation has the ability to plan, direct, and monitor results, but it still depends on the functional organization to carry out tasks.

The intermix project organization is the next level. In the intermix the project manager has some unique functions that require the assignment of some functional personnel to the organization, that is, some of the personnel assigned to the project are from different units. The team policing concept, in which patrol and detective personnel are assigned to a project team, could in a pure sense be an example.

The final type is the aggregate approach, in which the project manager is given all the resources required to perform the objective. An example would be a crime prevention project set up by the chamber of commerce, with the project manager given the specialized police personnel, funds, and equipment necessary. The project manager might be a police officer or a non-police officer specializing in crime prevention.

There are many factors that influence the use of project management, both internal and external to the organization. Our objective is not at this point to teach project management but to inform the serious administrator that there are alternatives to the traditional pyramid organization and to the traditional ways of assigning work.

MANAGEMENT BY OBJECTIVES (MBO)

Management by Objectives is another concept that has found its way into the police service. Shanahan, in his textbook *Patrol Administration: Managing by Objectives,* defines MBO as a means of defining objectives or goals, allocating resources to the defined objectives, allowing all members of the department to completely understand the objectives, developing a parallel path between the organization and the individual toward achieving the defined objectives, providing subgoals for specific components of the organization, establishing short- and long-range goals, designing and implementing programs for achieving the goals, and self-renewal.[3]

Very simply, and at the risk of oversimplifying, management by objectives is a process by which people within the organization participate in establishing goals and objectives. Once these goals and objectives are defined and reduced to statements that can be measured, then the people will pre-scribe their expected level of performance. Perhaps an example would best illustrate the notion of MBO. Traditionally police officers are assigned to a beat, and in the course of their shift they patrol, assuming that they are patrol officers. But what does being on patrol actually mean? Does it mean riding around and putting 100 miles on the patrol car? Does it mean running radar for two hours? Does it mean parking in a parking lot and reading a good book? Management by objectives reduced to the first line of patrol supervision means essentially this: The patrol supervisor and the patrol officers for whom the supervisor is responsible will agree on a set of achievable and measurable objectives which a patrol officer is to perform during a shift. If the patrol officer and the sergeant agree that the patrol officer should run radar for two hours and cruise behind the warehouse district for the remainder of the shift, then that patrol officer has two objectives — run radar for two hours and patrol the warehouse district for the remainder of the shift. These two objectives can be measured by the supervisor. The obvious advantage is that when both the sergeant and the patrol officer achieve those objectives, their performance is deemed acceptable. On the other hand, if the patrol officer does not achieve those objectives, then there is an immediate feedback situation in which the supervisor and the patrol officer can determine what went wrong. Often there will be times when exceptions to the stated objectives have to be accepted. In the case of our patrol officer who was to run radar for two hours and then cruise the warehouse district, suppose that he had no sooner left for his beat than he had to investigate a serious traffic accident, which took eight hours. Obviously he could not run his radar or patrol in the warehouse district as agreed upon. The patrol officer, however, has a legitimate reason in this case, and this performance can still be deemed quite satisfactory. Management by objectives helps establish priorities for accomplishing the mission of the unit or the entire department. It provides for planning, and it improves accountability. One of the major arguments against MBO is this ability to increase individual accountability. People resist accountability, and yet it is the essence of a professional organization and professional management.

Management by objectives is appropriate at all levels of organization. The example given above merely reduced it to its lowest possible level. It is suggested, however, that the concept of managing by objectives and improving accountability in police management become a department-wide phenomenon, not an isolated occurrence.

PROGRAM EVALUATION AND REVIEW TECHNIQUE (PERT)

In the past controlling has been a qualitative aspect of management. Newer techniques such as PERT provide the kind of information not readily available with traditional methods. Therefore, when PERT is used, it is usually in addition to the control devices that are most often discussed in police administration. Specifically, most of the recently developed control techniques emphasize control of time, whereas budgeting, the most important traditional control device, is directed toward the control of money. PERT was developed by the Office of Special Projects of the U.S. Navy in building the Polaris Project in 1958, and within the last decade or so it has infiltrated its way into municipal and state law enforcement.

A similar tool developed about the same time is the critical path method (CPM), again oriented toward achieving better managerial control in respect to time. The purpose of PERT and CPM is to show the relationship between milestones, or the completion of significant phases of a task, with regard to time. Suppose, for example, that a police department wishes to acquire a new fleet of vehicles. A PERT network could be constructed to show all the events and activities necessary to recall the existing fleet; remove radios, red lights, sirens, and other special equipment; draft vehicle specifications for the new fleet; order the new vehicles; receive them; and have specialized equipment installed. It is obvious that some of these things must occur before others; for example, the existing fleet would not be recalled and existing equipment removed before the specifications for the new fleet are drafted and the vehicles contracted for. If we wish to plot only what events have to occur before other events can occur, we might wish to construct a milestone or Gantt chart, a predecessor to PERT. But the Gantt chart would not tell us some important things. For example, if the police administrator were to ask the commander of services, "Can the fleet be replaced within 85 days?" the Gantt chart would be inadequate to make such a decision. The PERT chart, on the other hand, could give a better estimate of that, and it could also indicate whether the fleet could be replaced in a given time even if one or more aspects of the changeover ran into difficulty. Such control precision is edging its way into government operations, not only in law enforcement but in other areas as well. Students are encouraged to review appropriate literature on such new controlling techniques as PERT and CPM.

POLICE OPERATIONS

Another word in the large collection of police service terminology is *operations*. For the most part, operations is synonymous with *line functions.* In accordance with previous definitions, operations includes both primary and secondary line functions.

Although a comprehensive study of police operations is not within the construct of an introductory textbook, it is necessary to examine the major points: patrol, traffic, and criminal investigative functions. Figure 6.2 illustrates the operational structure of a police department. Compare Figures 6.1 and 6.2.

PATROL

Patrol officers are the most important element in the police service. Their reason for being is to *serve.* In their efforts to fulfill this demand, their jobs can become extraordinarily complex. It may be surprising to learn that the patrol officers devote relatively little time to enforcing the law, that is, detecting crime, apprehending criminals, and preparing facts for presentation in court. The primary task of crime prevention is not easy to measure because of the absence of qualitative and quantitative indexes. Traditionally, patrol officers spend the majority of their working hours in nonenforcement or peace maintenance activities: directing traffic, routinely covering the assigned beat, engaging in interpersonal communications with the clientele, and so on. General administrative duties and special assignments further remove patrol officers from the law enforcement function.*

Traditionally patrol officers are responsible for all criminal activity on the beat. It is

* Studies such as the *Kansas City Preventive Patrol Experiment* have attempted to evaluate the effectiveness of patrol. As with many studies, there were as many questions raised as answered. The interested student should see: *The Kansas City Preventive Patrol Experiment* (Washington, D.C.: Police Foundation, 1974); and *Police Chief,* Vol. 17, No. 6, June 1975.

important that they use all resources with optimum efficiency. The most valuable resource is the people with whom the officer has official and casual contact. Ironically, this reservoir of knowledge and assistance often is not developed.

Prudent officers realize that they are unable to cope with every incident independent of the community in which they work. The alternative is to seek the assistance of those persons who have entrusted their protection to the police. In the final analysis, law enforcement and public protection cannot be defined as the sole responsibility of the police; it is a joint venture of both the police and the public. Theoretically the police could reduce its enforcement function by refining and making its peace maintenance function more productive in terms of crime prevention.

Because patrol officers are expected to be "on the street" and always close at hand, it is reasonable that they should be the first to respond to public need. Being the first at the scene places patrol officers in a rather precarious position: What should they prepare for? What special knowledge should they possess? Their obligation to respond to all incidents does not afford them the luxury of selectivity. They must, therefore, be generalists, and must be prepared academically, physically, and emotionally to meet the demands of any given situation. An understanding of human behavior is crucial when confronting the emotionally disturbed, the alcoholic, the juvenile, and the quarreling family. Likewise, a general knowledge of the broad range of police technology must be acquired; patrol officers can make the difference in a criminal investigation simply by providing investigators with accurate and detailed factors. Patrol officers must observe and record the smallest details in the initial investigation. They must protect the crime

FIGURE 6.2 ORGANIZATIONAL STRUCTURE OF A POLICE OPERATIONS BUREAU

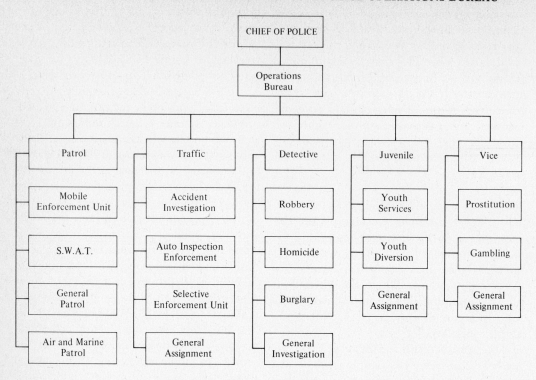

scene to ensure investigators as much first-hand information as possible. Undoubtedly, the patrol function is the foundation on which the department is built.

Directed Patrol Directed patrol is an alternative to traditional patrol and has very strong ties to the concept of management by objectives. Perhaps we could call directed patrol patrol by objectives. Directed patrol as a formal term is a product of a program developed by the Kansas City, Missouri, Police Department. Although the Kansas City Directed Patrol Program was rather sophisticated, it can be simplistically described as a patrol method in which patrol is directed based upon comprehensive crime and management data analysis. Based upon these data, a variety of things are done. Community education programs in which crime

information is distributed are implemented; police attend community meetings, establish crime prevention displays, and publish articles for newspapers and local media. Also, operational identification and residential security surveys are conducted by patrol officers and citizen volunteers as well as by community block watchers. All these activities are designed to prevent crime through police and citizen cooperation and efforts. In addition, these activities are designed to control the patrol work load enough to allow police officers to be assigned to priority calls. This means that when an area in which many priority incidents occur is identified, more patrol officers will be assigned to that area. By employing this systematic allocation and employment technique of directed patrol based on statistical information, many of the inadequacies of random, unstructured patrol may be overcome. Data at this point seem to suggest that citizen satisfaction and crime control efforts increase when patrol is based upon a systematic analysis of crime.[4]

Team Policing Team policing is a modification of both police organization and police operations. Although team policing has been labeled "new," it has origins both in Aberdeen, Scotland, in 1948 and in the police departments and sheriff's departments of small American communities before 1900. Traditional police organization and operations focus on assigning personnel either by time of day — shifts — or by geography — beats. Team policing reduces the rigidity of both concepts — time and geography — by creating a police team of from five to ten or twelve or more officers who have a considerably larger geographical area to police. The team also has the flexibility to assign officers at times appropriate to and in a strength proportional to the need for police services.

The goals of team policing are to improve police-community relations, create a more challenging and attractive work environment for the beat officer, increase crime clearance rates through an exchange of police intelligence information, minimize response time, and use personnel more efficiently and productively by combining resources. These goals are achieved through the following organizational/operational arrangement. Each team is usually assigned a supervisor, who is charged with the supervision and coordination of all the team members. The team would probably also include several officers assigned to vehicles for the purpose of preventive patrol and emergency calls. Other officers would be assigned to either foot beats or joint foot and mobile patrol and would act as generalists in community relations. Also on the team is a detective or criminal investigator who provides investi-

gation and specialist services to the team. A team may have an additional member who is responsible for the collection, analysis, and distribution of crime data information — an analyst.

Team policing cannot be defined in absolute terms because of its many and changing characteristics. And its successes and failures are difficult to measure. Nevertheless, it is a concept that has been put in operation in many departments in the United States. It is a departure from traditional police organization and operations, and it is worthy of serious study.[5]

TRAFFIC

Typically, the traffic function encompasses three tasks: traffic control, accident investigation, and law enforcement. Just who assumes these various tasks is an organizational decision. In smaller departments the patrol division is responsible for all police operations, including traffic. In such situations the total traffic function belongs to the patrol officer. Larger cities, on the other hand, establish specialized functional traffic units, usually at the bureau level. Then traffic control and accident investigation are, for all practical purposes, the responsibility of the traffic bureau, and the enforcement function is shared, at least to the extent of not excluding patrol. Likewise, traffic officers are not totally excluded from the patrol function. Imagine a traffic officer observing a serious crime and not attempting to apprehend the offender because his or her job is directing traffic at a certain intersection. On the other hand, the patrol officer who observes a traffic accident and does not render assistance because patrol is his or her specialty has failed to meet the basic obligation of service.

Traffic Accident Investigation Sound traffic safety programs are a necessary and vital product of the collection and tabulation of facts acquired at the scene of traffic accidents through investigative techniques. Often it has been said, however, that police traffic accident investigation is in fact not investigation but simply reporting. At issue, perhaps, is the lack of agreement on the definitions of investigation and reporting — an issue that cannot be addressed here. Nevertheless, anyone taking notice of the investigative techniques employed by the Civil Aeronautics Board (CAB) to determine the cause of aircraft accidents could become skeptical of the phrase "traffic accident investigation" as it is used in most police departments.

Traffic Control The importance of the traffic control function is twofold: first, it assists in expediting the safe movement of vehicular and pedestrian traffic; second, it is the way in which the police make the most direct contact with the greatest number of the public. Many people have never talked to a police officer, and the chances are that when they do, it will be in a traffic control situation.

Traffic Law Enforcement By definition, traffic law enforcement is the total of those actions taken by the police in dealing with violators of traffic laws and ordinances. Its function is to reduce traffic accidents and encourage voluntary compliance with laws and ordinances. Determining the quantity or quality of the traffic law enforcement function is a difficult task.

The *traffic law enforcement index* is merely a quantitative measure: the ratio of the number of citations, arrests, and subsequent convictions for moving violations to the number of vehicle accidents that involved personal injury or death. A traffic enforcement index of twenty is the accepted norm. Although this figure is not absolute, it is a widely used criterion. Some departments may have an index of eighteen, while others maintain an index of thirty. The index must be formulated on the basis of local conditions and experiences.

Selective enforcement is a quality measure based upon the principle that enforcement efforts must be applied at specific times and places against those violations that appear to be causing accidents. It further maximizes the proper allocation and distribution of personnel. Good traffic law enforcement can provide the police department with considerable information, which when properly analyzed yields significant results concerning the causes of traffic accidents, trends, and so on. The police department, from these data, can and must take remedial steps to further reduce accidents. This remedial process functions in two ways: education and engineering.

Two segments of the community must receive current *traffic enforcement education*: the private citizen and the police officer. Public and police awareness of the many aspects of traffic law enforcement and traffic safety is crucial in the fight against damage and loss of life on the highways. Instances of traffic education are common in the schools, for example, school safety patrols and driver training programs. Auto safety inspection, driver retraining programs, television and radio presentations, and public addresses by police officials are other means by which the public can become and remain informed and knowledgeable in the many areas of traffic law enforcement.

Traffic engineering is a very real part of the total traffic picture. The traffic engineer requires information concerning the flow of traffic, problem areas (dangerous intersections, road surface conditions), and so on. No other unit of government is more qualified to provide this information than are the police. Police officers travel over the majority of the streets, twenty-four hours a day. They are in a prime position to observe and report meaningful traffic information to the traffic engineer for evaluation or implementation of structural change. It is logical to assume that improved engineering reduces traffic accidents. Therefore, increased input to traffic engineering from police accident investigation summaries indicating engineering problems should logically play a significant role in the reduction of traffic accidents.

In conclusion, it is not difficult to justify the traffic function. Annually more than 50,000 Americans lose their lives on our nation's highways. Property damage is calculated at hundreds of millions of dollars. Human agony and personal grief are not measurable, but certainly they exist in abundance.

CRIMINAL INVESTIGATION

Criminal investigation is a line function and traditionally a task for patrol. However, the type and frequency of crimes may necessitate a specialized organization component, commonly referred to as the detective division. Remembering that the criminal investigation division is a secondary line element will help clarify its relation to the patrol function. Normally the patrol officer is the first police representative to arrive at a crime scene. His or her first obligation is to render assistance to injured parties. Second, the crime scene must be protected so that relevant facts can be observed and recorded. This second requirement can be subdivided into two phases: protection and recording.

Crime-scene protection is simply protection. It ensures that the physical properties of the scene are not disturbed or altered until all the facts have been properly noted. The patrol officer, who is usually the first at the scene of a crime, must be trained to protect the crime scene. Whenever a serious crime occurs, it usually attracts a number of spectators. The patrol officer must keep these individuals from removing or possibly destroying evidence. Crimes have been solved by the mere presence of a dropped match or cigarette. (Figure 6.3) Failure to protect the crime scene could easily result in the loss of such valuable clues.

Crime-scene data collection is, as are most aspects of criminal investigation, an art and a science. Because the actual crime scene is a short-term phenomenon, it is imperative that its general characteristics and specific properties be quickly and accurately recorded. Consequently, a detective must be an accurate note taker and have good reporting skills. Only with such information can the crime scene be reconstructed at a future time. Should one investigating officer be removed from the department by retirement, death, or some other reason, the basic facts would be largely lost; they would be available to the newly assigned officer only if the crime scene were carefully recorded.

In the larger police departments, the detective divisions have undertaken further specialization. These specialized sections of the detective division take various forms. One approach is to divide the detective division into specialized units according to specific types of crimes. For example, some large detective divisions have a robbery squad, a homicide squad, a burglary squad, an auto theft squad, and so on. Other detective divisions may be organized by general categories. For example, a detective division may have a crimes against person section, a crimes against property section, and a general assignment section. This type of further specialization usually exists only in the larger police departments. These departments generally believe that this specialization allows

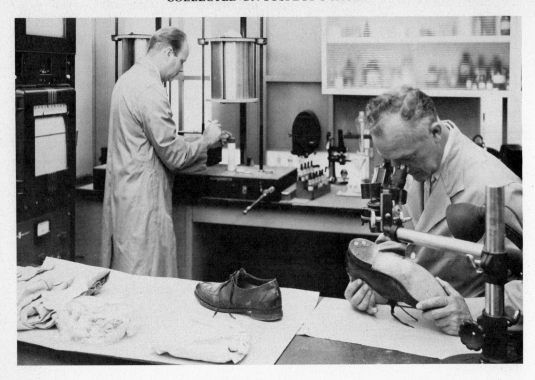

SOURCE: Courtesy of FBI Laboratory, Washington, D.C.

the detective to become familiar with the criminals and the methods associated with a given type of crime. A given criminal's method of operation, for example, may consist of "peeling" a safe with a sledge hammer and a crowbar. A detective who works full time on burglaries is more likely to be familiar with this technique and the individual criminals who use it than is the detective who investigates all types of crimes. Hence, the specialist should be able to solve the crime more quickly than the nonspecialist.

The investigative duties outlined here in a few words may in reality consume hours of the patrol officer's time and seriously detract from the primary responsibility, patrol.

It is precisely for this reason that the specialist — the detective or investigator — is created.

Departmental organization and policies regarding patrol/detective relationships are almost as many as the number of police agencies. The point at which the patrol officer leaves off and the detective takes up an investigation is not always defined. O. W. Wilson, V. A. Leonard, and other scholars in the field of law enforcement have discussed this issue in detail, and the student is encouraged to review this literature.

It should be mentioned that in 1975–1976, criminal investigation operations and management were examined rather carefully, and the results of these examinations were published with different conclusions. The Rand Corporation published a report entitled *The Criminal Investigation Process* that concludes, based on survey data from 156 agencies, that investigation resources as they are commonly managed are not particularly productive. The report strongly challenged the conventional wisdom regarding follow-up criminal investigation by detectives.[6] Other earlier studies, although less known, had drawn similar conclusions. Even if the conclusions drawn by the Rand study are shown to be totally in error, it has opened the subject to legitimate inquiry. As police administrators seek to improve productivity not only in investigations but department-wide, age-old investigative practices and allocation will come under microscopic scrutiny.

The Rochester, New York, Police Department engaged in an experiment in early 1971 called a coordinated team patrol (CTP) concept, which was a variant of neighborhood team policing; its goal was to determine whether the CTP system could improve the department's investigative and apprehension operations. The conclusion of the Rochester study was both contradictory and supportive of the Rand report. The Rochester system concluded that follow-up investigations by detectives were succcessful if they were built on the CTP team's preliminary investigation. The Rochester data support the notion of an integrated patrol investigative effort.[7]

Whether the crime is investigated by a patrol officer or a detective, there can be no doubt that there is a need for some degree of investigative specialization.[8] Today more than ever before the criminal investigator relies on scientific investigative techniques — techniques that require special training to master. Also, the investigator must be familiar with the law as it relates to criminal investigation. Many criminal cases have been lost after months of preparation and investigation because the investigator failed to consider the legality of the evidence that he or she had gathered.

The criminal investigation function is a difficult and important one — difficult because it requires special skills and training, and important because crime can never be stopped or deterred if the police cannot detect, apprehend, and successfully prosecute the criminal offender.

OTHER ADMINISTRATIVE AND OPERATIONAL FUNCTIONS

There are many functions within a police department that we have not discussed. Intelligence, Internal Affairs, Records, Juvenile, Property, and other functions all are part of the total police service. Each of these activities plays a vital interacting role in the total success of the department and the achievement of the department's mission. A brief comment should be made, however, regarding police intelligence in light of the terrorist activities that have besieged continental Europe and South America in the 1970s.

Terrorism, with its several definitions, is a topic of major importance throughout the world in the 1970s and probably will remain so in the 1980s. It has been predicted that the United States will probably experience terrorist activities in increasing numbers and magnitude in the future. It has been stated that the primary line of defense against terrorist activities is adequate police intelligence. Police intelligence, therefore, has an additional function with regard to terrorism, that is, to determine potential terrorist targets and collect and analyze data that might indicate a potential threat to such a target.

This intelligence would then be used in the police manager's decision-making process for planning and implementing counterterrorist activities, which would require appropriate police training in advance. Without appropriate intelligence, the police service will be planning arbitrarily, and it may develop training programs that will teach police officers how to do the wrong thing well.

The role of police intelligence is already complex and sensitive, as is internal affairs. However, much has to be done in a changing political and social world. As the essayist E. B. White once said, "With one thing leading to another I predict a future of complexity." White could have been saying this to a police administrator somewhere, for it is very appropriate.

DISCUSSION QUESTIONS

1. Is contemporary police organization effective? Is it efficient? How would you change it? Why?
2. Is the patrol officer the backbone of the police department? Should this be the case?
3. How can a police organization become more responsive to the community as well as to its own needs?
4. If you had your preference, for what assignment would you volunteer in a police department? Why? How does this task relate to the other units of the department and to the community?
5. Discuss the factors that contribute to determining the span of control in a large police organization.
6. Should a large police organization be administered like a big business? Why or why not?
7. The detective is the police officer most often seen in the movies and on television shows. Why do you suppose this is so?
8. How is your local police department organized? Do you consider this organization a proper one?
9. Can you see a common theme in directed patrol, MBO, PERT, and team policing? What are the reasons for engaging in these "new" activities?

NOTES

1. See *Municipal Police Administration,* ed. George Eastman (Washington, D.C.: International City Management Association, 1969); V. A. Leonard, *Police Organization and Management,* 2nd ed. (Brooklyn: Foundation Press, 1964).
2. Any discussion of territory introduces the question of centralization versus decentralization. Answers to this controversy are extremely complex and by no means absolute. It is suggested that the student refer to texts in business, industrial, public, and police organization and management for in-depth coverage of this material.
3. Donald T. Shanahan, *Patrol Administration: Management by Objectives* 2nd ed. (Boston: Holbrook Press, 1978), p. 5.
4. George J. Sullivan, *Directed Patrol* (Kansas City: Kansas City Police Department, Operations Resource Unit, 1976).
5. William G. Gay et al., *Issues in Team Policing: A Review of the Literature* (Washington, D.C.: U.S. Department of Justice, September 1977), Appendix A.
6. Peter W. Greenwood, Jan Chaiken, and Joan Petersilia, *The Criminal Investigation Process* (Lexington, Mass.: D. C. Heath and Company, 1977).
7. Peter B. Bloch and James Bell, *Managing Investigations: The Rochester System* (Washington, D.C.: The Urban Institute, Police Foundation, 1976).
8. O. W. Wilson and Roy C. McLaren, *Police Administration,* 3rd ed. (New York: McGraw-Hill Book Company, 1972).

CHAPTER SEVEN

CONTEMPORARY ISSUES IN LAW ENFORCEMENT

ROLE OF THE POLICE	PRODUCTIVITY	ADMINISTRATIVE POLICY VS. INDIVIDUAL DISCRETION
PERSONNEL	TAX LIMITATION MEASURES	
LAWSUITS AGAINST AND BY POLICE OFFICERS	POLICE UNIONS	WORKING IN THE COMMUNITY
	CRIME PREVENTION	
INTERAGENCY COOPERATION	CRIME ANALYSIS	ISSUES IN PERSPECTIVE: AN INTEGRATED SOLUTION
	CHANGE	
POLICE REORGANIZATION	PLANNING AND RESEARCH	

Purpose: To provide a discussion of contemporary problems and issues in today's law enforcement community.

THE POLICE SERVICE today is confronted with diverse problems. Attempts are being made at every level of government to identify them, to establish priorities, and then to solve them. However, in many instances, the problems are not new but recurring and age-old. This chapter, then, is a search for contemporary solutions to age-old problems.

As early as 1931, the Wickersham Report discussed an impressive assortment of discrepancies relating to the police service. These shortcomings were further expounded by a variety of scholarly works. In 1967, many of these same issues were reiterated by the National Crime Commission. However, in addition to restating the problems confronting the police service, OJARS (formerly LEAA) made federal money abundantly available in the 1960s, in an effort to study, define, and ultimately remedy many of these complex police issues. In 1973, the National Advisory Commission on Criminal Justice Standards and Goals issued a comprehensive list of standards for police. Many of the same issues covered by the Wickersham Commission (1931) and the National Crime Commission (1967) were covered again by the National Advisory Commission (1973). The comparison of the recommendations of the National Crime Commission (1967) and the National Advisory Commission (1973) in Figures 7.1 and 7.2 clearly illustrates the recurring nature of many of the problems confronting law enforcement. This comprehensive list demonstrates the difficulties of the police role.

ROLE OF THE POLICE

Police administrators, patrol officers, and the community at large are experiencing tremendous difficulties in defining the role of the police service. In recent years the "advances" in law enforcement have been the results of reaction to specific situations; for example the riot-torn 1960s apparently indicated the need for more equipment, for the establishment of police-community relations units, and for stronger police training and educational requirements. Increased crime indicated the need for "better" law enforcement. The community demanded that the police improve, but without suggesting a direction. It failed to put priorities on its demands, and the police in most instances lacked the knowledge necessary to properly evaluate the problems and establish sound priorities themselves. The lack of priorities resulted in the police service operating without direction. It was required to enforce the law more intensely and at the same time establish and maintain the support of the community. Although such a task is realistic in many areas, it would appear that in some minority communities strong enforcement of the law and strong community support are not compatible.

The police role is determined by community priorities. If major emphasis is placed on crime detection and apprehension of lawbreakers (criminal law enforcement), then police public service activities such as directing traffic may become deficient. A basic fallacy in this notion of community-set priorities is the fact that a community is not a homogeneous entity. The suburban and core areas of a city may and normally do have needs peculiar to their location and cultural composition. Even within the confines of a typical suburban or core area, the demands made of the police department may vary greatly within a relatively short distance. The dilemma is one of extreme complexity. For the police to serve any population, they must be aware of and understand the root problems of that culture. Inherent

FIGURE 7.1 RECOMMENDATIONS OF THE NATIONAL CRIME COMMISSION (1967)

Community Relations

Establish community relations units in departments serving substantial minority population.

Establish citizen advisory committees in minority-group neighborhoods.

Recruit more minority-group officers.

Emphasize community relations in training and operations.

Provide adequate procedures for processing citizen grievances against all public officials.

Personnel

Divide functions and personnel entry and promotion lines among three kinds of officers.

Assess manpower needs and provide more personnel if required.

Recruit more actively, especially on college campuses and in inner cities.

Increase police salaries, especially maximums, to competitive levels.

Consider police salaries apart from those of other municipal departments.

Set as goal requirement of baccalaureate degree for general enforcement officers.

Require immediately baccalaureate degrees for supervisory positions.

Improve screening of candidates to determine character and fitness.

Modify inflexible physical, age, and residence recruitment requirements.

Stress ability in promotion.

Encourage lateral entry to specialist and supervisory positions.

Require minimum of 400 hours of training.

Improve training methods and broaden coverage of nontechnical background subjects.

Require one-week yearly minimum of intensive inservice training and encourage continued education.

Require twelve to eighteen months' probation and evaluation of recruits.

Establish police standards commissions.

Organization and Operations

Develop and enunciate policy guidelines for exercises of law enforcement discretion.

Clarify by statute authority of police to stop persons for questioning.

Include police formally in community planning.

Provide state assistance for management surveys.

Employ legal advisers.

Strengthen central staff control.

Create administrative boards of key ranking personnel in larger departments.

Establish strong internal investigation units in all departments to maintain police integrity.

Experiment with team policing combining patrol and investigative duties.

Adopt policy limiting use of firearms by officers.

Pooling of Resources and Services

Provide areawide communications and records coordination.

Pool and coordinate crime laboratories.

Assist smaller departments in major investigations.

Explore pooling or consolidation of law enforcement in all counties or metropolitan areas.

SOURCE: President's Commission on Law Enforcement and Administration of Justice, *The Challenge of Crime in a Free Society* (Washington, D.C.: Government Printing Office, 1967), pp. 294–295.

FIGURE 7.2 RECOMMENDATIONS OF THE NATIONAL ADVISORY COMMISSION ON CRIMINAL JUSTICE STANDARDS AND GOALS (1973)

The Police Role

Formulate policies governing police functions, objectives, and priorities.

Publicize and respect the limits of police authority.

Formalize police use of discretion.

Improve communication and relations with the public.

Enhance police officers' understanding of their role and of the culture of their community.

Publicize police policies and practices.

Promote police relations with the media.

Role Implementation

Develop workable agency goals and objectives.

Establish written policies to help employees attain agency goals and objectives.

Establish a formal police inspection system.

Developing Community Resources

Establish geographic team policing.

Involve the public in neighborhood crime prevention efforts.

Criminal Justice Relations

Coordinate planning and crime-control efforts with other components of the criminal justice system.

Develop cooperative procedures with courts and corrections agencies.

Formalize diversion procedures to ensure equitable treatment.

Utilize alternatives to arrest and pretrial detention.

Develop court followup practices for selected cases.

Divert drug addicts and alcoholics to treatment centers.

Allow telephoned petitions for search warrants.

Enact state legislation prohibiting private surveillance and authorizing court-supervised electronic surveillance.

Planning and Organizing

Establish a police service that meets the needs of the community.

Consolidate police agencies for greater effectiveness and efficiency.

Implement administrative and operational planning methods.

Assign responsibility for agency and jurisdictional planning.

Participate in any community planning that can affect crime.

Assign responsibility for fiscal management of the agency.

Develop fiscal management procedures.

Derive maximum benefit from government funding.

Formalize relationships between public and private police agencies.

Form a National Institute of Law Enforcement and a Criminal Justice Advisory Committee.

Develop standardized measures of agency performance.

Team Policing

Determine the applicability of team policing.

Plan, train for, and publicize implementation of team policing.

Unusual Occurrences

Plan for coordinating activities of relevant agencies during mass disorders and natural disasters.

Delegate to the police chief executive responsibility for resources in unusual occurrences.

Develop an interim control system for use during unusual occurrences.

Develop a procedure for mass processing of arrestees.

Legislate an efficient, constitutionally sound crisis procedure.

Implement training programs for unusual occurrence control procedures.

Patrol

Define the role of patrol officers.

Upgrade the status and salary of patrol officers.

Develop a responsive patrol deployment system.

Operations Specialization

Authorize only essential assignment specialization.

Specify selection criteria for specialist personnel.

Review agency specializations annually.

Provide state specialists to local agencies.

Formulate policies governing delinquents and youth offenders.

Control traffic violations through preventive patrol and enforcement.

Train patrol officers to conduct preliminary investigations.

Create a mobile unit for special crime problems.

Establish policy and capability of vice operations.

Develop agency narcotics and drugs investigative capability.

Develop a statewide intelligence network that has privacy safeguards.

Manpower Alternatives

Employ civilian personnel in supportive positions.

Employ reserve officers.

Professional Assistance

Establish working relationships with outside professionals.

Acquire legal assistance when necessary.

Create a state police management consultation service.

Support Services

Train technicians to gather physical evidence.

Consolidate criminal laboratories to serve local, regional, and state needs.

Establish a secure and efficient filing system for evidential items.

Guarantee adequate jail services and management.

Establish crime laboratory certification standards.

Recruitment and Selection

Actively recruit applicants.

Recruit college-educated personnel.

Ensure nondiscriminatory recruitment practices.

Implement minimum police officer selection standards.

Formalize a nondiscriminatory applicant-screening process.

Encourage the employment of women.

Develop job-related applicant tests.

Develop an applicant scoring system.

Classification and Pay

Maintain salaries competitive with private business.

Establish a merit-based position classification system.

Education

Upgrade entry-level educational requirements.

Implement police officer educational incentives.

Affiliate training programs with academic institution.

Outline police curriculum requirements.

Training

Establish state minimum training standards.

Develop effective training programs.

Provide training prior to work assignment.

Provide interpersonal communications training.

Establish routine inservice training programs.

Develop training quality-control measures.

Develop police training academies and criminal justice training centers.

(Figure 7.2 continued)

Figure 7.2 continued

Development, Promotion, and Advancement

Offer self-development programs for qualified personnel.

Implement formal personnel development programs.

Review personnel periodically for advancements.

Authorize police chief executive control of promotions.

Establish a personnel information system.

Employee Relations

Maintain effective employee regulations.

Formalize policies regulating police employee organizations.

Allow a collective negotiation process.

Prohibit work stoppages by police officers.

Internal Discipline

Formulate internal discipline procedures.

Implement misconduct complaint procedures.

Create a specialized internal discipline investigative unit.

Ensure swift and fair investigation of misconduct.

Authorize police chief executive adjudication of complaints.

Implement positive programs to prevent misconduct.

Study methods of reducing police corruption.

Health Care, Physical Fitness, Retirement, and Employee Services

Require physical and psychological examinations of applicants.

Establish continuing physical fitness standards.

Establish an employee services unit.

Offer a complete health insurance program.

Provide a statewide police retirement system.

Compensate duty-connected injury, death, and disease.

Personal Equipment

Specify apparel and equipment standards.

Require standard firearms, ammunition, and auxiliary equipment.

Provide all uniforms and equipment.

Transportation

Evaluate transportation equipment annually.

Acquire and maintain necessary transportation equipment.

Conduct a fleet safety program.

Test transportation equipment nationally.

Communications

Develop a rapid and accurate telephone system.

Ensure rapid and accurate police communication.

Ensure an efficient radio communications system.

Conduct research on a digital communications system.

Set national communications equipment standards.

Evaluate radio frequency requirements.

Information Systems

Standardize reports of criminal activity.

Establish an accurate, rapid-access record system.

Standardize local information systems.

Coordinate federal, state, and local information systems.

Source: National Commission on Criminal Justice Standards and Goals, *Police* (Washington, D.C.: Government Printing Office, 1973), summary of entire report.

in this concept is the need for a more knowledgeable police officer. Education and training, essential to achieve this level of knowledge, is a financial burden that will be placed directly on the shoulders of the taxpayer. Furthermore, members of the police department are traditionally middle class, and the social disparity between the police and other classes compounds the problem.

Project STAR (System and Training Analysis of Requirements for Criminal Justice Participants), in California, was an attempt to identify police roles, tasks, and performance objectives; determine the knowledge and skill required; formulate educational recommendations; develop training programs; and identify personnel selection criteria for police positions.[1] The project was set up in response to some very basic questions. Before the police can respond to contemporary change, they must determine just what they are doing now; the police must find out where they are before they attempt to decide where they want to go.

PERSONNEL

In any organization, the most valuable resource is its members. For years the typical response to an increase in crime has been to increase the size of the police department. It has become apparent, however, that more officers do not necessarily increase the effectiveness of law enforcement. The emphasis on size changed somewhat in the mid 1960s, after the advent of the Office of Law Enforcement Assistance (OLEA; now OJARS) at the federal level. Quality, rather than quantity, policing became the national interest. Efforts were made to develop personnel allocation plans and to use existing police to greater effect.

Great effort was put into elevating the academic level of the police, and the two-year associate degree and later the baccalaureate degree became the goals. Because many thought that education was the absolute answer to all police problems, college programs in law enforcement grew rapidly; enrollments increased, and ultimately so did the number of graduates. The effects of the increase in degree-holding patrol officers are not yet clear. Although many studies have compared the personalities and performance of noncollege and college officers, the findings of these reports have been less than conclusive.

CIVIL SERVICE

When President Garfield was assassinated in 1881 by an individual who had been rejected for appointment to a federal office, the public responded with the Pendleton Act of 1883, which provided for civil service in the federal government. The Spoils Era, which existed from 1829 to 1883, was confronted with a system that would reduce political interference and favoritism in governmental operations. This move on the part of the federal government led to civil service at the state and local levels of government. Today over 95 percent of all government employees at the federal, state, and local levels, or more than 12 million persons, are covered by civil service.

Civil service has not completely solved the problems of police staffing, but it has provided the impetus for removing political interference and paved the way for merit employment.

The terms *merit system* and *civil service system* are often used synonymously to describe a personnel system in which personal ability is stressed above all other considerations. Merit system is accurate; civil service, however, refers to nonmilitary employment.

The basic emphasis of a merit system is on attracting, selecting, and promoting the most able people available for the available positions and on seeing that they are adequately compensated and treated fairly on the job. To do this, the system must be fair and flexible. An arbitrary or rigid system is destined to abuse and failure. Ideally a civil service law or ordinance will be passed to create an environment in which the merit system can be nourished and in which it can grow and prosper. In some situations, unfortunately, personnel programs get bogged down in procedures, rules, and regulations, and the system becomes an end in itself, not a means to achieve a goal.

Across the United States there is a broad range of police merit systems in operation; some are just, some injust; some are flexible, some rigid. At one extreme, some merit systems are nonfunctional and exist only on paper; and political manipulations occur. At the other extreme, there are merit systems that are so rigid and so lopsided that management has little control and inept employees cannot be removed. Some systems seem to guarantee life tenure in the department and provide an atmosphere of absolute employee protection instead of stressing merit, which the system was designed to emphasize.

At the federal level, civil service laws were recently reformed. The Civil Service Reform Act of 1979 is designed to improve government efficiency and to balance management authority with employee protection. Among the major features of the act are an independent and equitable appeals process, protections against abuse of the merit system, and incentives and rewards for good work and skilled management. Although President Jimmy Carter has high hopes for the act, it remains to be seen how effective it will actually be in reforming the federal civil service system.

CIVILIANS IN LAW ENFORCEMENT

In 1975, the National Institute of Law Enforcement and Criminal Justice (LEAA) published a monograph entitled *Employing Civilians for Police Work*. That piece of research indicated clearly the trend toward employing civilians for many jobs normally performed by sworn officers. The abstract of that study states,

> The use of civilians in jobs normally performed by police officers has increased rapidly in the past 25 years — particularly in larger cities — as police departments have sought to reduce cost and put more men on the beat.
>
> This urban institute study describes the experiences of thirteen police departments in cities of varying size across the country. It should be useful to departments considering whether to hire civilians, to departments already employing civilians but experiencing problems, and to federal, state, and local officials concerned with planning and funding police activities.
>
> The findings are based largely on interviews in thirteen cities with 158 people, including police managers, officers in charge of civilian employees, and the civilians themselves. Two types of activities were surveyed: (1) the employment of civilians on jobs and communication, identification and detention facilities; and (2) the use of civilians in Community Service Officer (CSO) programs. The CSO's are generally 18–20-year-olds who assist police officers on the street.
>
> As a whole, police managers and officers were favorably impressed with the use of civilians because they relieved officers of more critical duties, cut cost, and improved service to the public. Many officers felt that civilians performed some tasks better than police, partly because civilians can concentrate on one job since they are not subject to rotation and special assignment as officers are, and partly because officers tend to consider some of the

civilianized jobs confining, sedentary, a form of punishment and not proper police work. Some problems exist, but most are related to police management practices and can be alleviated by improved training and supervision of civilians. Other problems, described as "personality conflicts," by both officers and civilians, result from blockage in communication which may be overcome with a passage of time.

Officers generally believe the civilians want careers in police work, and a very large portion (86%) recommend that more be hired. Civilians also say that they want to continue police work. Their assessments of benefits and problems closely parallel those of the officers, but they desire improved pay, job security, and training. Also mentioned was the need for more stringent entrance requirements matching the qualifications of civilians for a given job.

The use of civilians reduces overall cost. Salaries average 23% less for civilians than for officers and overhead about 10% less — though in the larger cities, overhead costs tend to be equal for both.

The degree of a program's success depends on the quality of planning, implementation and management. Even in the few unsuccessful efforts — where civilian jobs were terminated — police managers had no doubt that civilians could have fulfilled job requirements.

Thus, the use of civilians in selected roles has been successful. It is likely to be expanded within departments and introduced to others. The variety of jobs for civilians also is likely to increase as its successes and savings are recognized.

The savings due to civilianization are due primarily to lower civilian pay, overhead, and training cost — prime sources of civilian complaint. If additional funds are expected to meet those complaints, the cost incentive may be reduced substantially.

Although each department must make its own assessment of the cost and the benefit trade-offs, it is clear that employing civilians in the jobs described has been substantially beneficial to all departments visited.[2]

Because of cost and productivity factors, police administrators in future will be examining the role of civilians in their departments. If the data presented in the above report present an accurate picture of the police profession across the country, more civilian jobs are likely to become available in the future. Such a development would be important to students of police administration, especially to those students with physical impairments who cannot pursue a career as a sworn police officer. Civilian employment in law enforcement agencies may also be an attractive alternative to those individuals having technical skills in the computer field, mathematics (crime analysis), or operations research.

PROMOTION BY ASSESSMENT CENTER

The police service is becoming very much aware that 20 years service in a police department does not necessarily make an individual a police manager. The traditional promotion criteria of oral interview, written examination, and evaluation of past performance have been found to be of questionable value in producing managers for the future. A technique of the World War I era that has been used by private industry in modified form in recent years is now finding its way into the public sector and police administration. This technique is known as an *assessment center* (AC).

An assessment center is not a physical place but rather a dynamic process, a process whereby a standardized evaluation is made of a person's capacities, capabilities, and behavior habits, based upon an experience involving a variety of tasks and activities.

Assessment center candidates are evaluated in a group setting by a team of trained professional observers. The key ingredient is simulation, which enables the assessor team to measure interpersonal behaviors that are often not brought out during traditional testing routines. At the conclusion of the assessment process, raters use their observational notes of each assessee's performance in an effort to obtain consensus on which ratees have the potential to perform well in the position for which they are being assessed.

Through the assessment center process, the agency is trying to determine whether an individual has the potential to perform in a given position in the future. Police management is attempting to simulate the task the candidate will have to perform and the environment which he or she will face in a future position (promotion or reassignment). In the assessment center, police management is not asking the old traditional questions ("Why do you want to be a sergeant?" or "Why do you want to be a lieutenant?"); they are giving the assessee an opportunity to perform specific tasks and respond to a variety of situations encountered by a sergeant or a lieutenant.

Although the assessment center has weaknesses as well as strengths, it appears that it will continue to gain acceptance in the police service. Gary Brown wrote in the June 1978 edition of *Police Chief* (the official journal of the International Association of Chiefs of Police) an article entitled, "What You Always Wanted to Know About Assessment Centers but Were Afraid to Ask." In concluding his article, Brown presented a bibliography that will give the interested student an excellent background in the development and uses of assessment centers. Since the student may one day be a candidate at an assessment center, either in industry or in the police service, it is suggested that he or she not wait to become familiar with its workings.

MINORITY RECRUITMENT

Minority recruitment is an extremely controversial issue in law enforcement, especially in criminal justice, and public administration in general. Many law enforcement agencies have made considerable achievements in the area of minority recruitment. Some law enforcement organizations have been very active and aggressive in recruiting minorities. On the other hand, some agencies have resisted minority recruiting efforts and have been confronted with court actions. The Office of Justice Assistance, Research and Statistics has twice withheld or withdrawn federal money from law enforcement agencies because of alleged improprieties in the area of minority recruitment and promotion. The U.S. Department of Justice developed a manual entitled "Equal Employment Opportunities Program Development Manual" in 1974 to answer questions regarding minority employment. Most of the states and local governments have prepared formal documents to provide guidelines for compliance with federal and state minority employment–related legislation. The state of Ohio, through the the Office of the Attorney General and the Ohio Peace Officer Training Academy, recently published a manual entitled "Minority Recruitment Manual for Ohio Peace Officers." This manual was distributed to all local police and sheriff's departments.[3]

There are many instances of discrimination in American law enforcement. A civil action was brought before the U.S. District Court for the northern division of Ohio, eastern division civil action, by the shield club of the Cleveland Police Department against the city of Cleveland, Ohio. Judge

— the pool of people possessing the basic attributes necessary for a career in law enforcement — increase when military service personnel return after a major military buildup. This was true immediately after World Wars I and II, the Korean conflict, and Vietnam.

With large numbers of applicants, any organization becomes more stringent in selection procedures. Even when these numbers are reduced, the objectives of the selection program should remain consistent with the needs of the department. The individuals selected will remain, under current retirement plans, in the organization's employ for twenty to thirty years. Twenty years is a long time for a police department and a community to maintain individuals with qualities less than appropriate to fulfill adequately the organization's needs. The vital issue is: What are the personnel qualities necessary to meet the organization goals? In essence the selection process is complex, and its operation is influenced by many variables. The quality of future police personnel is related to the quality of the selection criteria and process.

FEMALE POLICE OFFICERS

The worth of the female in the police service has been greatly underestimated. Female police officers are as much a minority as blacks, Orientals, Mexicans, and other ethnic groups. However, the police are venturing out of traditional bounds and meeting contemporary issues with innovative techniques. For example, the Pennsylvania State Police, the Texas Department of Public Safety, and the New York City Police now have women officers. The women of the Pennsylvania State Police Department perform normal patrol duties and are assigned to both one- and two-officer patrol units. Domestic disturbance teams, police inter-

vention units, and police-court liaison offices are employing women and minorities to a greater degree. The long-range contributions of these practices will be calculated at a later time, but one thing is certain in terms of personnel development: competition by women for advancement in specialized areas of law enforcement will continue to increase.

Since 1972, there has been a considerable amount of research on the performance of women in law enforcement. The controversy continues, however, about whether women perform as well as men in patrol, traffic, criminal investigation, juvenile, and other functions of modern police operations. In the past decade, women have achieved a new status in law enforcement, with women being elected sheriffs and attaining higher ranks in the police services. The provost marshal at Fort Knox, Kentucky, who headed a military police contingent of more than 400 people from 1975 to 1978, was a full colonel — and a woman. Perhaps the most recent study of women in policing was conducted in New York City. The executive summary of that report indicates that the performance of the women officers was compared with that of men who had similar experience and were assigned to the same or similar precincts. The study was restricted to New York City and to the patrol function. The study did not say that the women or the men were absolutely more competent. But the study did say that in certain respects women performed better than men, and in other situations men performed better than women.[4]

EXECUTIVE TRAINING

A chief of police in the United States does not enjoy the prestige and social position that a top executive would expect, and there are many reasons why. One is that the chief of police is traditionally selected from within the ranks of the organization. Thus, the selection of the chief is actually an extension of the police selection process, and the patrol officer who is selected today may in twenty years or so become the chief administrative officer of the department. Perhaps no single problem looms larger than that of executive selection and development.

In the case of elected county sheriffs, it is readily acknowledged that experience in law enforcement or administration is not required to achieve a majority of the popular vote. As a result, qualified personnel are the exception rather than the general rule. Inept sheriffs appoint deputies with equally poor qualifications, further damaging the image of law enforcement. Where qualified sheriffs are elected, they must respond to pressures in order to be reelected. Because some states prohibit sheriffs from succeeding themselves, a qualified person can serve only one term in office. On the other hand, in some counties highly competent sheriffs have had a long tenure and at the same time have elevated law enforcement in many respects.

If minimum standards are intended to elevate the quality of personnel at the entrance levels, shouldn't minimum executive standards also be established? Twenty years of patrol experience does not, in itself, develop those qualities an effective police administrator needs. A great deal of specific knowledge must be acquired if one is to manage a departmental budget and a large contingent of personnel. If a police department or any organization is in fact the reflection of its leader, a serious examination of law enforcement can provide us with an equally serious message concerning the state of the office of the chief of police. Perhaps this problem can be solved by elevating the standards at each supervisory level.

It is generally accepted that to become a police officer, one should first undergo train-ing in a police academy, but where does a police officer undergo training to become a police executive? The answer to this question is of great importance to the future management of law enforcement. The United States military services have, in addition to the various academies, command and staff colleges, the Army War College, and other advanced training centers for senior command officers. The military has recognized that an officer needs to develop special skills in order to perform efficiently and effectively, but we do not have a United States Police Command and Staff College at our disposal.

The Federal Bureau of Investigation provides training for the nation's police personnel at the National Academy, located at Quantico, Virginia, which offers an intensive course in firearms, physical fitness, and classroom studies. This training is not, however, designed to develop executive talent.

At the 1974 annual meeting of the Academy of Criminal Justice Sciences, John Jay College of Criminal Justice, Professor John Stead, former academic dean of probably the most prestigious center of police education in the English law countries, Her Majesty's Police College, Bramshill, stated during a keynote address that the Southern Police Institute is the closest institution the United States has to Bramshill. Because of this similarity of purpose and its objective of providing executive training to the nation's police command, the Southern Police Institute's program should be discussed briefly.

The Southern Police Institute of the School of Police Administration at the University of Louisville is perhaps the command and staff college for the police service. The primary objective of the Southern Police Institute is to develop executive police leadership. The course is open only to active administrative police personnel from anywhere in the world, and since the institute was founded in 1951, Great Britain, Guam, Thailand, and other lands have been represented in the administration course. Student officers are required to submit their applications for admission to the University of Louisville. These officers must meet the same admission standards as any student in the university; this factor alone indicates the level of study one can expect. Students' applications that have been accepted by the office of admissions are forwarded to the director of the Southern Police Institute along with the results of the entrance examination and an evaluation of any college work the students may have. A selection board then determines the students who will be accepted. Five areas of study are required of each student officer, and the courses are intense. In addition to formal class lectures, individual and small group research is required, and group seminars and specialized workshops in contemporary problems of police administration are conducted weekly. On completion of the twelve-week course, the successful student officers have earned fifteen semester hours of college work. Those officers who already hold a four-year degree can enroll in two special courses and receive six semester hours of graduate credit on the successful completion of the program.

States are now beginning to recognize the need for executive development, and several states have initiated special executive development programs and seminars within their general training programs. The larger city and county law enforcement agencies and the state police are beginning to implement career and executive development programs.

The Federal Bureau of Investigation, the International Association of Chiefs of Police, the Traffic Institute, Northwestern University, and some of the larger police academies are also providing management training programs, either in-house or in cooperation with institutions of higher education.

LAWSUITS AGAINST AND BY POLICE OFFICERS

Lawsuits against police officers arising out of the performance of their duties have been common. Police officers have been subject to criminal and civil litigation in both state and federal courts. Violation of civil rights, assault, malfeasance in office, false arrest, reckless driving, and even burglary and homicide charges have been brought against police officers. Unfortunately, some of these charges were warranted, and the police officers were convicted. However, many of the charges were unfounded, brought by citizens (suspects or victims) who for one reason or another found it necessary to strike back at an individual police officer when the officer's performance, although legal and in compliance with department policy, was inconsistent with the citizen's expectations. A citizen may wish to harass a police officer by bringing a false and arbitrary charge with the intent of causing the officer some injury or "getting his badge." Other citizens may be motivated by the prospect of "lucking out" and getting a judgment and some compensation from the government, even if the charge against the individual officer is untrue. Police officers have been subjected to many false legal actions, and have now engaged in a counterattack. Officers who have been falsely accused are now bringing countersuits against the accuser. Recent literature on the subject indicates that police officers are receiving substantial judgments against individuals who have made false accusations that damaged the officers' personal lives and professional careers.

Vicarious liability is a legal concept that, in the context of police service, means that a superior can be held liable for the actions of subordinates if it can be shown that the superior was negligent in providing the subordinate appropriate information and resources to perform adequately. These civil actions have influenced police administration considerably in that police managers and supervisors are responsible not only for providing an atmosphere in which subordinates are employed, work, and retire or get dismissed, but also for providing an environment in which individuals are developed to perform a variety of tasks and are provided with appropriate training and the resources necessary to complete those tasks successfully.

Recently, in Philadelphia, Pennsylvania, the Department of Justice used the approach of holding top city and police officials responsible for alleged police violations of the citizens' constitutional rights. The Justice Department filed a lawsuit against the mayor and 19 other city and police officials. The suit charges the police with using unnecessary deadly force, physically abusing motorists, and pressuring citizens to withdraw complaints of police abuse. The U.S. Attorney in Philadelphia had pursued suits against individual police officers for police brutality. However, the Department of Justice was of the opinion that the practice was institutionalized and that prosecuting individual police officers was not the answer. Therefore, the Justice Department chose to file suit against top department officials. Whether this move will serve to curb alleged practices of police brutality remains to be seen; it has certainly not strengthened the relationships between federal and city law enforcement officials in Philadelphia.[5]

INTERAGENCY COOPERATION

American society is not static, nor are its lawbreakers. Today, more than ever before, we are a mobile nation. Automobiles, airplanes, and assorted other forms of land and water transportation virtually remove jurisdictional boundaries. A police officer or government official is naive to believe that law enforcement for any political subdivision can function exclusively within that subdivision's territorial limits. Not uncommonly lawbreakers come into a city, commit a burglary, for example, and then return to their homes several miles away, perhaps across county or state boundaries. The successful investigation of this violation is greatly inhibited by the jurisdictional limitations.

The primary means of overcoming this blockage has been *voluntary* cooperation between police departments. Such arrangements have been in existence for years; their effectiveness, on the other hand, is difficult to determine. Let us assume that our armed robbers of Chapter 3 return to their home town, where the police department becomes aware of their newly acquired fortunes and excessive spending. The home town police have reason to suspect them, and miles away the "victim's police" could provide the facts necessary to successfully bring these violators before the courts. However, the home town police do not know to which of the other 40,000 police agencies they should make inquiry. Hypothetical indeed. Nevertheless, this instance portrays one of the many problems confronting the police service today.

In an attempt to reduce some of the problems created by jurisdictional boundaries, the National Crime Information Center (NCIC) was established as a national clearinghouse for criminal information. Operated by the Federal Bureau of Investigation, NCIC collects crime data (for example, stolen motor vehicles, wanted persons) and makes them available to state and local authorities. Computerization has made the retrieval of this information reasonably fast; however, there is a fundamental problem: a computer can only provide information that has been fed into it. Crime information is submitted voluntarily to NCIC by state and local police. A police officer in Utah may have stopped an Ohio vehicle for some reason and, requesting data from NCIC, find no record of this vehicle, when in fact it was stolen. The answer is simply that the stolen vehicle information was never submitted to NCIC by the Ohio police.

At the state level, similar centers are maintained, usually by the state police, to collect and distribute state criminal information. With NCIC functioning as the hub, an interstate network of crime data is available — limited by the extent of voluntary participation.

At the local levels and among police departments a variety of staff services have been consolidated under metropolitan or regional agreements. Communications and detention facilities are perhaps the services most commonly amenable to consolidation. Often when several small municipal police departments operate within a county, each municipality will maintain its own communications system. Not surprisingly, each system may be on a different frequency, and communication between departments is impossible. Police vehicles of adjoining towns, where jurisdictions are often separated by a street's width, are unable to communicate by radio with one another even in emergency situations. Likewise, if it is necessary to engage in a joint police operation (such as a narcotics raid or roadblock), the lack of interagency communication is a definite handicap. The need for a better system is evident, and, with federal money available, these situations are being remedied. In many instances, however, the lack of proper planning produces a different but not an improved system — a system that will remain incompatible with the demands placed upon an expanding and changing police.

The Los Angeles City Police, Chicago City Police, and police in other cities have sophisticated communications systems. In August 1973 the New York City Police Department contracted for a law enforcement data communication system, a federally funded project.[6] These systems are departmental systems and are not usually designed to give support to neighboring police departments. The support that the major cities usually provide to neighboring departments is computer terminal linkage with state and federal (NCIC) crime information systems; this is vitally important, and its continuation and expansion are certainly encouraged. The critical lack of communications is apparent at the operational level in situations involving two or more smaller departments; this has led to the concept of regional criminal justice planning as a function of the various state planning agencies.

POLICE REORGANIZATION

There is a great deal of literature on the issue of integration, consolidation, and contract police services. UNI-GOV and metropolitan forms of government have given us examples of alternative forms of law enforcement. Elinor Ostrom, Robert B. Parks, and Gordon P. Whitaker published a document entitled *Policing Metropolitan America* for the National Science Foundation that challenged several assumptions that have been the basis of many proposals for police organization.

Their findings show that the policing of metropolitan areas can be divided among separately organized agencies as well as among the personnel of a single police department. The division can be either geographic or functional; that is, each agency may serve its own separate jurisdiction, or each agency may supply only one or a few related services.

Whether departments should decentralize, consolidate, or remain the same depends on the service needs and the resources of each particular metropolitan area. The erroneous but common picture of metropolitan police agencies is that they are too numerous and too diverse to work together. Since municipal departments producing direct services are most numerous, they are especially under fire. The many separate agencies are seen as isolated from one another, as acting independently, and as limiting the opportunities for pursuing of suspects and for mobilizing large numbers of officers in response to crisis. That picture is largely inaccurate. This study also found that duplication in delivery of police services is not common. Few police agencies serving the same community act in isolation from one another. Instead, agencies patrolling the same area usually alternate their patrols by time of day, type of thoroughfare or public place, or type of clientele. Agencies investigating crimes within the same jurisdiction also rarely act in isolation from one another. Instead, they coordinate their investigations. Police agencies also interact in supplying and using auxiliary services. Most police agencies serving metropolitan areas obtain entry-level training, chemical analysis of evidence, and pretrial detention of suspects from other agencies. This accounts for the great diversity of organizational arrangements within police departments.

Some common assumptions about department size are also erroneous. Small departments are thought to dominate service delivery, "waste" resources by duplicating administrative personnel, and fail to provide complete service to the communities they serve.

The data reported in this study indicate that small departments are indeed numerous, but that they actually supply only 10 percent of the 10:00 P.M. on-street patrol force. The large departments employ most of the police officers and serve most of the residents in metropolitan areas. Small departments seem to be less wasteful. They generally get a higher proportion of their officers out on the street than do the larger departments. We find that the median citizen-to-patrol officer ratio at 10:00 P.M. is less than 2,400 to 1 from municipal departments with five to ten officers, and more than 4,200 to 1 from municipal departments with more than 150 officers. The large departments are also likely to have a higher proportion of personnel in administrative positions. While in many cases small departments do not themselves supply all police services to the communities they serve, a full range of services is available almost without exception. Specialist agencies, larger full-service police departments with overlapping jurisdictions, supply the services that small local agencies do not supply. Ostrom considers the small departments to be "patrol specialists." They may be a useful organizational alternative in some metropolitan areas.

The report findings are not to be interpreted as demonstrating that small departments are more effective at protecting the people they serve. The consequences of increased numbers of officers on patrol remain to be demonstrated.

The significance of this report is that it shows that there are alternative organizational models that can be used in police organization. Furthermore, discussions of consolidation, centralization, decentralization, and integration cannot be based on the assumption that the larger the agency, the better or worse it will be.

PRODUCTIVITY

Today there is an increased interest in improving the quantity and quality of the police. For years industry, military, and government have been aware of the need to improve productivity. However, only since the 1970s has the police service looked at productivity concepts and tried to apply them to the police function. The Police Foundation, the Urban Institute, the National Commission on Productivity, the International City Management Association, the International Association of Chiefs of Police, and other agencies have explored public productivity at length, giving considerable attention to the police. A thread common to most of this literature is that we are not certain what productivity is and we have no absolute method to measure it.

Of course, there are methods for measuring police productivity, depending upon one's definition of productivity. Very simply, *productivity* means the return or output received for a given unit of input. In the late 1960s and the 1970s, the police service had conducted experiments aimed at increasing the police output to the community — improving police productivity. There have been many of these experiments. They include the Kansas City Preventive Patrol Experiment and a variety of modified team policing experiments such as COM-SEC (Community Sector Team Policing) in Cincinnati, Ohio. Studies in community and dispatching techniques to increase efficiency and effectiveness have been examined in de-

tail. In the past, the police response to the increasing crime rate has been to increase personnel. In the mid-1970s we started seeing a decline in the crime rates, and using the past logic of the police, the number of personnel should be decreasing. The so-called tax revolt of 1978 (Proposition 13 in California) and inflation have increased the competition between department heads at the federal, state, and local levels for the government dollar. Cutback management, or managing with a declining or constant budget, continues today. Increased productivity and improving the quality of work and the workplace have been and will continue to be matters of extreme importance at all levels of the American police service.

TAX LIMITATION MEASURES

With the passage of Proposition 13 in California in 1978, the country embarked on a series of tax limitation measures. Basically, tax limitation measures mean that the amount of taxes that citizens have to pay is limited by law. Governments, therefore, are limited in how much money they have to spend. When governments have less money to spend, budgetary cuts must be made and programs must be cancelled. Although the so-called frills of government are usually the first to be eliminated, there comes a time when police budgets, programs, and personnel are threatened. In the absence of adequate justification for continuing all police services, it may be necessary in the near future to plan for smaller police forces that will handle larger workloads. Police officials who wish to continue present levels of service or to expand services should make an effort to impress on the public and the city officials their community's need for police services.[7]

POLICE UNIONS

One of the primary change agents in American law enforcement has been police unions and other employee organizations. It is ironic that during the early history of law enforcement in the United States, strikebreaking was a strong motive for the establishment of organized law enforcement organizations. Today police and firefighters' strikes have dotted the United States, such as the firefighters' strike in Cleveland in July 1978 and the Memphis, Tennessee, police strike in August 1978, which followed shortly after that city's firefighters' strike.

It was not until the American Federation of Labor reversed its position against granting union charters to police employee organizations in 1919 that police rank and file groups developed an influence. At about the same time the Fraternal Order of Police was founded by two Pittsburgh, Pennsylvania, police officers. The Fraternal Order of Police today is an extremely powerful organization in some police agencies, especially on the East Coast of the United States.

The aim of the union, quite simply, is to force police management to recognize the grievances of the rank and file and resolve them. In the private sector, history has shown that the most satisfactory method of arriving at acceptable settlements of these grievances is through the process of collective bargaining. For management to recognize the union and to bargain are the primary initial demands of a police union.

During the 1960s on several occasions city management chose not to recognize a union. When management failed to recognize the fact that the rank and file of the police department had voted overwhelmingly to be represented by a union, it was a safe bet that the city administration was looking for trouble. A common response by the police rank and file has been work stoppages — "blue flu," picketing, and as a less drastic measure, job slowdowns.

Employee organizations varying in influence and organizational strength have been formed in a number of cities, including Boston, Buffalo, Dayton, Detroit, Hartford, New Haven, Rochester, and New York City, and in the Pennsylvania State Police. These organizations view anything associated with wages, hours, or working conditions as a bargainable issue. In some cities beats and shifts are assigned based on a traditional seniority system in which senior officers bid for assignments. In the Pennsylvania State Police, contract troopers get their birthdays off with full pay. Many diverse issues and benefits are seen in contracts across the country, including some areas where there are no unions. It appears that police unionism; collective bargaining; the processes of mediation, arbitration, binding arbitration, and compulsory arbitration; and contracts are firmly a part of today's police scene. The challenge now is for police labor and management to engage in dialogue for their mutual benefit.

CRIME PREVENTION

Crime prevention is not a new concept. Early people undoubtedly blocked passageways to their caves with rocks and logs to prevent people and animals from taking food and other possessions from the dwelling. Perhaps the oldest recorded laws of prevention can be found in the Code of Hammurabi. The translation in Figure 7.3 is from the Code of Hammurabi, 2200 B.C., which regulates building. As we are finding today, the building codes are of primary importance in the prevention of crime. It is ironic that

FIGURE 7.3 THE CODE OF HAMMURABI (2200 B.C.)

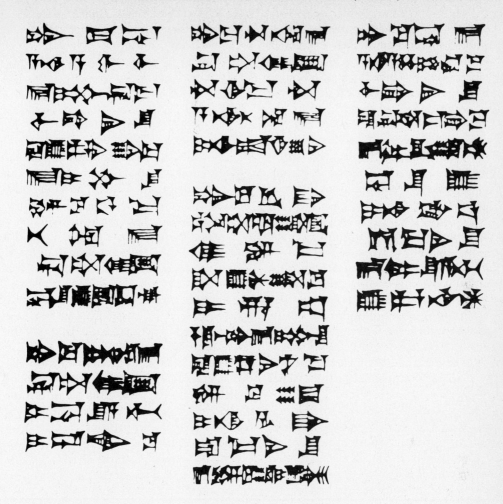

In the translation that follows, each sentence represents one block of characters, starting with the top left block of the code.

If a builder builds a house for a man and does not make its construction firm and the house collapses and causes the death of the owner of the house — that builder shall be put to death.

If it causes the death of a son of the owner — they shall put to death a son of that builder.

If it causes the death of a slave of the owner — he shall give to the owner a slave of equal value.

If it destroys property he shall restore whatever it destroyed and because he did not make the house firm he shall rebuild the house which collapsed at his own expense.

If a builder builds a house and does not make its construction meet the requirements and a wall falls in — that builder shall strengthen the wall at his own expense.

Source: Courtesy of National Crime Prevention Institute, School of Police Administration, University of Louisville, Louisville, Ky.

Hammurabi was aware of this 4,000 years ago.

Although Robert Peel recognized crime prevention as a function of law enforcement in the 1800s, it was not until the 1960s that England formally included crime prevention in a police program. In 1971, the concept of crime prevention was formalized in the United States with the creation of the National Crime Prevention Institute at the University of Louisville. The NCPI was established to provide a national training, technical assistance, and information resource in the field of crime prevention. Since then, the NCPI has presented more than 100 training programs and has trained more than 4,000 people in the principles and practices of crime prevention. These graduates represent more than 1,500 law enforcement jurisdictions at local, state, and federal levels as well as elected government officials and private security personnel. Graduates of NCPI have been instrumental in training other practitioners to develop and administer crime prevention efforts throughout the fifty states and foreign countries.

Crime prevention, according to the National Crime Prevention Institute, involves actions that reduce the opportunity for crimes to occur and increase the likelihood that criminals will be apprehended. It is oriented toward the potential victim and involves collaboration between government, law enforcement agencies, community organizations, individual citizens, and private security. Crime prevention programs have been effective in reducing crime and loss from criminal attacks. Another aspect of crime prevention is target hardening. This concept is rather self-explanatory in that the emphasis is on making the criminal's target as difficult as possible to violate. Targets obviously can be property or individuals, and there is a variety of measures that can be taken to harden the target, whether it is an individual or a building. Building construction and architecture, doors, windows, locks, alarms, lighting, individual habits, and community education are some aspects of crime prevention.

CRIME ANALYSIS

It may come as a surprise that most of the police agencies in the United States do not have a formal process of crime analysis. Although many police departments contribute crime data from their jurisdictions to the Uniform Crime Report, they still do not maintain a formal system of analysis upon which personnel allocation and deployment are based.

Although every police officer is a crime analyst of sorts for that particular beat, the police officer on the street, the detective, the crime prevention officer, and their first-line supervisors need analysis support from police management. This support should include not only breakdowns in terms of time of day, incidence, day of week, and week of the month, and comparisons for the same period of the previous year, but also trend analysis, forecasting, and displacement data should be provided to show changes in crime and to help police administrators make inferences about the efficiency and effectiveness of police operations.

In 1973, the U.S. Department of Justice published a prescriptive package entitled *Police Crime Analysis Unit Handbook*. This book was designed to help police agencies establish a formal crime analysis unit. Although this handbook is not the last word in crime analysis organization, it is very useful and should be reviewed seriously. In 1977, Reinier and others published a monograph entitled *Crime Analysis in Support of Patrol* that investigated the state of the art of crime analysis in support of traditional preventive patrol, team policing, and specialized patrol.

> The survey showed that generally police intuitively believe in the value of crime analysis; however, there is a void in knowledge as to its *actual* value. Crime analysis has not been examined on its own merits, independent of the programs it supports, because analysis is an integral part of the total allocation and employment decision-making processes and it does not lend itself well to classical evaluative measure apart from these programs. Several findings stand out: (1) Allocation decisions are made infrequently and equalized work loads are the most commonly used tools. (2) The more formal the analysis program and separated from the users of the output information the less likely the information will be used, regardless of the background of the analysts. The inverse is also true. (3) Police, at all levels, are suspicious of sophisticated analysis and do not believe it contributes significantly in meeting the ongoing problems of allocation and deployment of patrol resources.[8]

The message of the study is clear: there must be better understanding and cooperation between the analyst and the department management. Also, police management is relatively unsophisticated in its analysis perspective; it does not hold more complex analyses in much regard and therefore does not use the more complex methods in decision making.

CHANGE

Citizens, police practitioners, and observers of law enforcement have expressed a need for change. Since the mid-1960s, there have been changes in law enforcement, and in some instances perhaps these changes have occurred too fast. There is one notable example of the effect of rapid change on a police department, and that is the case of Dallas, Texas.

In 1972, the newly appointed Dallas police chief and the fledgling police foundation sought to make radical changes in the Dallas Police Department's organizational structure. In 1978, the Police Foundation published a report entitled *The Dallas Experiment: Organizational Reform*[9] that discusses the history of their effort in Dallas, the limited success of the project, and the many failures that resulted from an attempt to accomplish too much too quickly. The Dallas experience resulted in the dismissal of the chief and several commanders and a department filled with frustration and reduced morale. Patrick Murphy, president of the Police Foundation and a former police executive, stated in the Preface of the report that it "can help other funding and planning agencies and city and police administrators avoid the pitfalls spelled out in the report and manage improvement more effectively."[10]

It has been said that the only permanent thing in this world is change. We can expect the police service to undergo continued change; however, this change must be directed and carefully managed, for change without direction is like a unguided missile: the result is self-destruction.

PLANNING AND RESEARCH

The whole area of planning and research, important to communications, must be expanded still further. A majority of the nation's police agencies lack the knowledge to research a given problem scientifically and subsequently to plan an effective and responsive program. Although most of the nation's larger police agencies have adequate research capabilities, the small departments do not have formal planning and research units. Research and planning are secondary functions in the small departments, even if these units exist. Admittedly, research is complicated, and its results are more often indications than concrete solutions. However, programs based on the product of these scientific indications are more likely to succeed than are programs instituted to combat a problem that has in fact not been adequately identified. Because law enforcement is frequently unaware of the nature of its problems, corrective measures are too often hit-and-miss propositions. Although their intentions have merit, the results are less valuable.

Urban planning is a matter of great concern to the police service. Unfortunately, police administrators, community leaders, and government officials have not always realized that they should consider the police function when they are developing community plans. For example, the construction of a major highway through a municipality can have a great influence on the police and the community in general. In addition to causing an obvious change in the traffic pattern, this highway may be perceived as a line dividing the town into two distinct territories. On a short-term basis the effects may or may not be discernible; over a period of time distinct characteristics may appear. The socioeconomic distribution of the population may fluctuate — with housing deteriorating or improving, with crime increasing or decreasing. Therefore, the police should be aware of, and act upon any development of new subcultures or subcommunities. Such factors have usually not been considered to lie within the province of the police, because the police service has often failed to provide capable, qualified, and articulate administrators.

The degree of police involvement in urban planning does range from nothing at one extreme to major participation at the other extreme. In the area of crime prevention, however, police are taking an increasing role in urban planning and design.[11] Profiles of crime areas can be developed through collecting data from police crime reports. These profiles in turn may indicate that certain physical characteristics provide criminal opportunities. A classic example of a remedy based on such information is the improvement of street lighting in formerly dark areas experiencing a high rate of crime.

FEDERALLY SUPPORTED POLICE RESEARCH

Much of the progress in police research stems from enactment of the 1968 Safe Streets Act and subsequent federal funding for law enforcement improvement.[12]

But many police science textbooks still rely heavily on professional anecdotes, descriptive experience, and ad hoc rules of thumb. One example is that 10 percent of the force should be composed of detectives and that 2 percent should be on the vice squad — but no one knows why. Textbooks also give scant coverage to such subjects as productivity, corruption, and internal discipline.

Old traditions, however, are being challenged, and the need to increase the present state of knowledge is more keenly felt. To advance police science, the National Institute of OJARS has chosen three major areas as having critical significance for police effectiveness. The first is *police management,* emphasizing research to strengthen program evaluation systems and program direction systems. The second is *police operations,* concentrating on more efficiency and effectiveness in patrol and criminal investigations, and on special problems. The third is an *overview of the law enforcement system,* that is, how police agencies can better meet the needs of society and of the criminal justice system. Research in these areas is directed by the Police Division of the Institute's Office of Research Programs. Indicative of OJARS contribution to police research is the following summary of findings of current police research projects.

Taking Corruption out of the Closet This project is developing materials to help police administrators cope with internal corruption problems. Among the materials being developed are a manual for police administrators on developing and managing an anti-corruption program, research papers that examine different aspects of police corruption, and an extensive bibliography and literature review of police corruption.

The first product will be *Developing and Managing an Anti-Corruption Program: A Manual for Police Administrators.* It will address such issues as defining, locating, and measuring corruption; policy and program development; and program implementation. It is intended to help administrators develop a systematic approach to anticorruption management, one that will involve such activities as cataloguing corruption hazards (tow trucks, bars, construction sites, etc.), specifying indicators of the level of corrupt activity for each hazard, and selecting the appropriate management strategies. Examples of management alternatives are the creation of turnarounds; requiring a proportion of self-initiated investigations by internal affairs units; and the use of field associates. The manual will also help administrators develop a realistic and operationally meaningful definition of corruption that will permit them to focus on specific types of corruption.

Among the monographs to be produced are:
- *The Functional Approach to Police Corruption*
- *Police Socialization and the Psychological Costs of Police Corruption*
- *The Role of the Media in Controlling Corruption*
- *A Police Administrator Looks at Corruption*
- *Police Integrity: The Role of Psychological Screening of Applicants*
- *Developing a Police Anti-Corruption Capability*
- *A Six-City Comparison of Responses to a Questionnaire on Police Corruption*

Developing Procedures for Internal Police Discipline Police officers are regularly exposed to situations that may result in accusations of improper conduct. Effective standards, well administered, may help to reconcile the often conflicting needs for accountability and for procedural protection.

A previous OJARS-supported study, conducted by the International Association of Chiefs of Police, developed a set of prototype rules of conduct and procedures for internal police discipline: Based upon an in-depth study of 17 law enforcement agencies, these rules and procedures were felt to reflect a rational, fair, and legal approach to internal disciplinary action, and will lead to the formulation of model rules of conduct.

Currently, the rules are being subjected to a fifteen-month field evaluation in two cities, Denver, Colorado, and Albuquerque, New Mexico. The objective is to assess their effectiveness in an operational setting.

Performance Measurement System to Be Tested The American Justice Institute is developing a system that police administrators and others can use to better evaluate the effectiveness of police operations.

Program evaluation systems now in use not only measure police program effectiveness poorly, but actually distort police activity. The Uniform Crime Report statistics are an example. Such data are inadequate in that they consider only reported crime; they consider only anticrime activity; and they measure activity resulting from such other factors as luck, social forces, and the activities of other elements of the criminal justice system as well as from police action.

The lack of an effective program performance evaluation system was reported by the 1973 National Advisory Commission on Criminal Justice Standards and Goals. It recommended that "a national study be undertaken to determine methods to evaluate and measure the effectiveness of individual police agencies in performing their crime control functions."

This study first identified and ranked the five basic objectives of police work. Then it developed productivity measures to correspond with these objectives. The resulting performance measurement system tries to solve some of the problems associated with the traditional measures of police work.

The system will be refined and tested in three major cities. Once implemented and validated, it will give public administrators a new tool for evaluating police performance and determining alternative allocation of resources.

Re-evaluating Police Response Time A study of response time, conducted by the Kansas City Police Department, may change our understanding of the significance and nature of response time. The study has implications for the use of communications technology, for citizen reporting, and for patrol allocation.

Using civilian observers — unlike earlier studies of the subject that relied on officer self-reporting — after analyzing the communications center tapes and interviewing victims and witnesses, the Kansas City Police Department collected data on Part I Crime, other crime, potential crime, medical emergencies, and other citizen calls for service. The citizen and police response times were analyzed in terms of such outcomes as arrests, handling of injuries, and citizen satisfaction.

Findings and interpretations from the study include the following:

• For the first time, response time was examined in its broadest context, including the time it takes a citizen to report an incident. This is particularly noteworthy, since citizen mobilization time was found to be longer than any other response time interval.

• Overall, more than 46 percent of the total response-time continuum, from the time the citizen was free to call the police until the field officer began an investigation on the scene, was consumed by citizen reporting. Long citizen reporting delays tended to nullify the impact of rapid police response.

• Citizens were generally very satisfied with police response time. Citizens were satisfied with police response time in 86.8 percent of the cases, and they were very satisfied in 70.2 percent of the cases. Dissatisfaction with police response time occurred in only 13.3 percent of the cases.

• Citizens tended to be more dissatisfied when they thought a faster response could have made a difference in the outcome of the crime.

• Citizens reported problems in reporting crimes to the police in 76 percent of all cases.

• Citizens were responsible for most of the problems that caused delay; 75 percent of these problems stemmed from an exchange of additional information, advice, or instructions with other citizens before the police were called.

- Problems with police communications were the least frequent cause of reporting delays. Problems in communicating with the police dispatcher about the incident occurred in only 7 percent of the cases.

Testing Wilmington's Split-Force Patrol The Wilmington Police Department is now concluding an experiment designed to test and evaluate a selected patrol strategy, *Split-Force Patrol*. A significant byproduct of the research was the development and evaluation of a directed or planned approach for improving preventive patrol.

The experiment was conducted over an eighteen-month period on a citywide basis. Wilmington split its patrol force into two parts. One part responded only to complaints and requests for service; it undertook no preventive patrol activity. The other part was responsible only for preventive patrol; it did not respond to calls for service. Naturally, there were situations in which this distinction could not be maintained, such as extreme emergencies.

As part of the study, Wilmington developed improved approaches for planning and implementing directed preventive patrol activities. Directed preventive patrol in this sense contrasts with the traditional practice of leaving preventive patrol essentially to the discretion of individual officers.

Patrol activities conducted as part of the experiment were evaluated in terms of crime control and service effectiveness. The results of the experiment are now being analyzed, and the findings should be useful for strengthening patrol operations.

Tentatively, the study suggests that specialization, rather than the generalist approach, is useful and feasible, and makes officers more accountable, which contributes significantly to patrol effectiveness. Wilmington intends to continue and further develop the split-force strategy after the experiment ends.

Analyzing the Criminal Investigation Process Rand Corporation conducted a two-year evaluation and analysis of criminal investigation. Its findings question traditional practices in this area.

After surveying the investigative function in some 153 police departments, the researchers concluded:

- The single most important determinant of whether or not a case will be solved is the information the victim supplies to the immediately responding patrol officer. If information that uniquely identifies the perpetrator is not presented when the crime is reported, the perpetrator usually will not be subsequently identified.
- Of those cases that are ultimately cleared but in which the perpetrator is not identified at the time of the initial police incident report, almost all are cleared as a result of routine police procedures.
- Differences in investigative training, staffing, workload, and procedures have no appreciable effect on crime, arrest, or clearance rates.
- The organization of police investigators (i.e., team policing, specialists vs. generalists, patrol officers–investigators) cannot be related to variations in crime, arrest, and clearance rates.
- Substantially more than half of all serious reported crimes receive only superficial attention from investigators.
- The data consistently reveal that most of an investigator's time is spent in reviewing reports, documenting files, and attempting to locate and interview victims on cases

that experience shows will not be solved. For cases that are solved (i.e., in which a suspect is identified), an investigator spends more time in postclearance processing than in identifying the perpetrator.

- Most police departments collect more physical evidence than they can process productively. Allocating more resources to the processing capabilities of the department can lead to more identifications than some other investigative actions.
- In relatively few departments do investigators consistently and thoroughly document the key evidentiary facts so that the prosecutor can be reasonably assured of a conviction on the most serious applicable charges.
- Failure to document a case investigation thoroughly may contribute to a higher dismissal rate and weaken the prosecutor's plea-bargaining position.
- Investigative strike forces are able to increase arrest rates for a few difficult target offenses, provided they concentrate on activities for which they are uniquely qualified; in practice, however, they are frequently diverted elsewhere.

The researchers recommended that police administrators consider the following:

- Reduce follow-up investigation on all cases except those involving the most serious offenses.
- Assign generalist-investigators, those who would handle the obvious leads in routine cases, to the local operations commander.
- Establish a Major Offenders Unit to investigate serious crimes.
- Assign serious-offense investigations to closely supervised teams rather than to individual investigators.
- Strengthen evidence-processing capabilities.

- Increase the use of information processing systems instead of investigators.
- Employ strike forces selectively and judiciously.
- Place postarrest (i.e., suspect in custody) investigations under the authority of the prosecutor.
- Initiate programs to impress on citizens the crucial role they play in crime solution.

Measuring Polygraph Accuracy How useful are polygraphs? To answer that question, a research project conducted two laboratory and six field experiments to investigate:

- the general accuracy and reliability of polygraph tests;
- the utility of various physiological measures;
- the adequacy of current field polygraphists' techniques;
- the validity of the belief that psychopaths could deceive the polygraph.

According to the study, the polygraph can be accurate more than 90 percent of the time in detecting truth or deception in criminal cases.

In cases where the panel and polygraph reached a conclusive decision, the agreement rate was 86 percent. When the actual outcome was compared with the polygraph results, the agreement rate rose to 88 percent.

Although the findings are clear, the policy implications need further explication. The principal investigator believes that polygraph tests should be considered another form of expert testimony. Others would use the polygraph only as an investigative aid. Whatever the outcome, this study has provided a sounder data base for policy decisions.

Guidelines for Police Discretion Police officers, like judges or prosecutors, must make decisions affecting the course of justice — decisions such as arrest, search, and the seizure of evidence. Increasingly, police administrators are under pressure to develop and enunciate policies that will structure this discretionary power. Research, conducted by the Boston Police Department in conjunction with the Boston University School of Law, is examining ways of structuring this discretion.

Major findings include the following:

- Police guidelines are needed to guide police officers in structuring discretion and to assist courts in defining reasonable police practices.
- If guidelines are to be useful to police officers, they must be practical. They must, therefore, be developed with the active participation of police officers.
- It is possible to develop a policy-making process in a police department in which outsiders participate. The method used in this project is not the only one that can be used, but whatever methods are adopted ought to be tailored to a specific police department.
- Guidelines on criminal investigative procedures ought to describe what is permissible, not what is forbidden. Affirmative guidance is more useful than prohibitions.
- Successful implementation of investigative guidelines will require commitment by supervisors and command officers, creative training programs that involve supervisors, clear indicators that the guidelines are in the best interests of patrol officers, and close cooperation with courts and prosecutors.
- Research and development in police policy making continues to be important. Special attention should be given to questions about selective enforcement of the criminal law and enforcement priorities, particularly in sensitive areas.

ADMINISTRATIVE POLICY VS. INDIVIDUAL DISCRETION

Considerable emphasis has been put on the formulation of administrative police policy that will reduce individual discretion at the operational level. Simply stated, the police agencies are being asked, by both citizens and police officers, to formulate a general direction for the agency within which all personnel and activities must operate. The purpose of establishing policies is to prescribe parameters within which individual police officers and units must function. Policy sets limits but does not remove the elements of discretion, initiative, and flexibility. Policies are guidelines that relate to and complement the total objectives of the department.

At the operational level there appears to be a notable lack of developed procedural guidelines. The issue is whether operational guidelines should be established for the individual officer to follow, or whether the existing high degree of discretionary tolerance should continue. Many proponents of the former feel that only such policy guidelines can ensure the responsiveness of the police. They further argue that individual discretion negates the much desired element of "consistent law enforcement." Established guidelines increase uniformity of procedures and consistency of enforcement, and at the same time define a legal area in which the officer can function with certainty. This concept is contradicted by the fact that administrative guidelines cannot adequately account for all possible situations. Guidelines, in order to be generally applicable, must be stated in such broad terms that they become meaningless. If the patrol officers' security rests solely with themselves, then their actions should, but may not, have departmental or community support. Every effort should be made to ensure that every officer knows what is and what is not acceptable police conduct and procedure.

Nevertheless, the broad latitude of discretion the police currently enjoy could in many instances be reduced through established policy without reducing effectiveness. Judicial decisions and procedural law have definitely influenced police policy. Since the *Miranda* decision, the officer is not given a choice as to whether an arrested felon, for example, has the right to counsel during interrogation. Yet the police continue to function despite the formulation of this policy and the curtailed discretion.

Policy formulation is a complex task involving all the resources of the community and the police department. To illustrate the multivariate nature of policy formulation, examine Figure 7.4, where everyone seems to have some part in policy formulation. In essence that is accurate, but there are exceptions. One is the right of police to engage in policy formulation through collective bargaining. Because civilian control over law enforcement is so fundamental to the American form of government, law enforcement policy cannot be subject to collective bargaining. Further, local policy cannot be influenced by a state or national police union.

FIGURE 7.4 FORMULATION AND EXECUTION OF POLICE POLICY

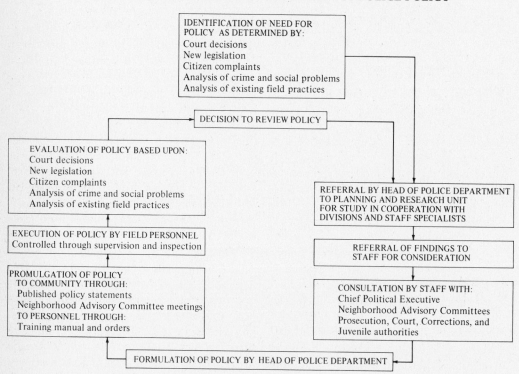

SOURCE: President's Commission on Law Enforcement and Administration of Justice, *Task Force Report: The Police* (Washington, D.C.: Government Printing Office, 1967), p. 26.

THE POLICE

Police policy is formulated in response to local requirements and may, therefore, be inconsistent with the policies prescribed by a state or national police union.

Although the complete removal of police discretion is not within the realm of logic, nor has it been insisted upon, guidelines are essential for the proper exercise of police power and authority. Established guidelines offer the police officer protection from unwarranted personal liability suits and protect the citizen from unwarranted police conduct and activities. Properly formulated and executed, police policy is of benefit to both police and citizens.

WORKING IN THE COMMUNITY

The effective control of crime is not the sole responsibility of the police. On the contrary, law enforcement is a community concern, and the police are merely a formalized supplemental community organization. Bringing this message to the public is undoubtedly a very difficult task for the police service. Surprisingly enough, this principle is frequently not recognized by the police, and consequently, they make little effort to inform and educate the citizenry — and themselves — about their roles and positions in the arena of public protection.

POLICE-COMMUNITY RELATIONS

Within the last decade, many of the nation's police departments have established police-community relations units. However, this vital function must not be restricted to a single specialized unit: police-community relations is a task for every member of the department. Every officer represents the department by his or her mere presence. The public presumes that each officer's actions and general performance of duty represent departmental policy, whether such a policy exists or not.

A police officer is a member of the police department; however, he or she is also a member of the community. Unfortunately, both citizens and police officers often lose sight of this fact. The police officer should have a dynamic role in the integration of community-police relations and problem-solving activities. When law enforcement is motivated to seek community support in response to police and crime problems, solutions are more readily attainable, and it is the simple truth that crime control is best achieved through public knowledge, understanding, and awareness of the crime problem.

The community is a complex entity with which the police must interact constantly. Police-community relations must be more than a block on an organizational chart or a written policy statement; they must actively involve the recruitment of qualified minorities and encourage maximum use of their skills and attributes, create positive relationships with the news media to inform the public about police tasks and problems,[13] and otherwise become an integral part of social organization.

A number of myths, as well as many truisms, have evolved over the years concerning the nature of law enforcement. Fear of the police is common, and history has recorded incidents that warrant such emotions. Certain ethnic groups, for example, have experienced police actions beyond the comprehension of any civilized person. Distressing isolated instances that may or may not have ethnic significance still occur. If it is axiomatic that the community gets the police service it deserves, then change is a future certainty: municipal government is changing, and the police are making the transition with it.

COMMUNITY GOVERNMENT

Municipal law enforcement, in many ways, is influenced greatly by the system of local government in which it must operate. The great majority of the 39,750 local police agencies in the United States function under one of three basic governmental models: the mayor-council, the commission, and the city manager. Each has certain properties that directly or indirectly determine the nature of the police department. More bluntly stated, the degree of police effectiveness and efficiency, whether "good" or "bad," in many cases is not solely dependent on the police department; it is determined by the local government. Undoubtedly, the position of the police department in the administrative pattern of present-day municipal organization is of the greatest importance, for without a sound administrative structure at the top, no police organization can be administered and controlled efficiently and honestly.[14]

ISSUES IN PERSPECTIVE: AN INTEGRATED SOLUTION

It is difficult to understand the nature and extent of police problems, but understanding is a prerequisite to any formulation of solutions. To best illustrate many, but certainly not all, of the problems currently confronting law enforcement, let us reexamine the hypothetical armed robbery of Chapter 3.

Two armed robbers, one of whom was an adult, the other a juvenile, were stopped by a police traffic unit after they had committed a traffic violation. The traffic officers had received the license plate number of the robbery vehicle from the patrol unit investigating the robbery, and they established probable cause by matching the number of the vehicle that committed the traffic violation

and took both suspects into custody, or effected an arrest. The traffic officers searched the suspects and found cash. The adult suspect was then booked, fingerprinted, photographed, and jailed, while the juvenile was referred to proper juvenile authorities. The apprehension process as just described is not so simple as it might seem, and Figure 7.5 shows the various phases in detail.

The above description, although very brief, raises some profound questions that should be discussed because they relate to both police administration and the individual beat officer. Let us assume the role of the two traffic officers stopping the vehicle that carries the license number of two armed robbery suspects. What are they armed with? Guns, knives, chains, starter-pistols? Perhaps they are not armed at all! How should you approach the suspects' vehicle? What does your partner officer think? What is your partner going to do? These questions and scores of others undoubtedly confront you. Each can be answered in one of three ways — individual discretion, formulated police policy, or a combination of both. Radio communication may provide an answer to the first question, how the suspects are armed, if the patrol officer investigating the robbery reported the information. If it was not reported, is the investigating patrol officer available to respond to your radio call? This officer may be involved in the investigation and away from the vehicle radio. The other questions must be answered, but these answers may not be as absolute. In police departments where training is inadequate and policies to guide the officers are not clearly established, it is possible that each officer will approach the situation from a different perspective. A very elementary question these officers will probably ask is, Should we remove our weapons from their holsters? If such a decision is left to the individual's discretion, the option of removing

FIGURE 7.5 APPREHENSION PROCESS

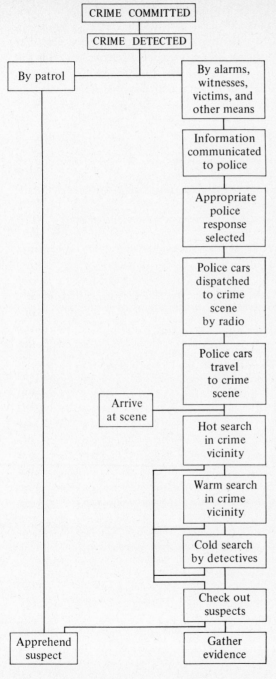

or not removing is present. If, however, established department policy and training requires officers to approach a vehicle suspected of being involved in an armed robbery with weapons unholstered, the option of keeping the weapon in the holster no longer exists. This requirement may increase the element of personal security for both officers, not because unholstered weapons are necessarily safer, but because each officer is aware of the other's actions and state of readiness.

Without becoming involved in a case study of stop and frisk, arrest, evidence search and seizure, and so on, let us recognize here that every phase of the law enforcement function is based on substantive, procedural, and constitutional law. If the two traffic officers had not had the license number of the robbery suspects, they might not have been able to search the two "traffic violators." Furthermore, the cash would have been found during an illegal search, because the traffic violations did not give the police probable cause to search for the results of an armed robbery. A search is conducted incidental to an arrest — a suspect is not arrested incidental to an illegal search.

Subsequently, of course, the booking procedure, fingerprinting, photographing, arrest information, and lineup procedures are all subject to legal safeguards. In many legal areas, court decisions have firmly established the rules under which the police must operate. The police must know, for example, if and when a suspect is required to have legal counsel present. With regard to the juvenile offender in our robbery case, the officers must be aware of and follow the requirements set forth in another body of law, including *Kent* v. *United States* [383 U.S. 541

SOURCE: President's Commission on Law Enforcement and Administration of Justice, *Task Force Report: The Police* (Washington, D.C.: Government Printing Office, 1967), p. 26.

(1966)] and *In re Gault* [387 U.S. 1 (1967)] and related cases, which provide guidelines for police dealing with juvenile offenders.

It is absurd to expect every police officer to also become a legal scholar and social scientist. Nevertheless, a police officer must possess a certain level of expertise in both the law and the social sciences in order to perform his or her duties in today's complex society. Attainment of these required levels of expertise is a responsibility of police administration. Every police department must recognize the need for competent police officers and establish a training program to meet that need. The police have a sworn obligation to provide protection and service to the community, and the community has the right to the best possible police service.

DISCUSSION QUESTIONS

1. How much education does a police officer need? Before you answer, ask, What is a police officer? Keep in mind rank, assignment, and other related factors.
2. How does one determine one's role in an organization? How does one change that role? What are the change agents in a contemporary police agency?
3. Have the police failed? How do you measure success or failure in a police department?
4. Of what value can the police be in total urban planning?
5. Why is it difficult for many police agencies to retain college-educated police officers? What steps can be taken to remedy this problem?
6. Why should efforts be made to define the police role?
7. Have public employee organizations, and more specifically police unions, become more or less influential in the past five years? Do you consider employee organizations to be effective change agents? Why?
8. Who rules the police: the police chief, the rich, the poor, university professors?
9. Discuss the impact the "litigation society" has had on police organization and the police officer.
10. How productive should a police officer be? Who should set productivity standards? How productive are you as a college student? Is the student sitting nearest you more or less productive than you are?

NOTES

1. "Criminal Justice Roles, Tasks, and Performance Objectives: Working Document," in *Systems and Training Analysis of Requirements for Criminal Justice Participants (STAR)* (Sacramento: California Department of Justice Commission on Peace Officer Standards of Training, 1973), p. x.
2. National Institute of Law Enforcement and Criminal Justice, *Employing Civilians for Police Work* (Washington, D.C.: Government Printing Office, 1975), preface.
3. Richard W. Snarr and R. Paul McCauley, *Minority Recruitment Manual for Ohio Peace Officers* (London, Ohio: Ohio Peace Officer Training Academy, January 1978).
4. Joyce L. Sichel, et al., *Women on Patrol: A Pilot Study of Police Performance in New York.* National Institute of Law Enforcement and Criminal Justice (Washington, D.C.: Government Printing Office, January 1978), p. xi.
5. "Philadelphia: Brotherly Excess?" *Newsweek,* August 1979, p. 26. "Philadelphia: The Last Days of the Rizzo Era," *Police Magazine,* July 1979, pp. 26–37.
6. "New York City Police Data Communication System," in *Kriston-Bram* (Chanute, Kan.: Kriston Electronics, Inc., 1973), chap. 4.

7. Waldron, Ronald J., and John R. Altemose, "Determining and Defending Personnel Needs in Criminal Justice Organizations," *Public Administration Review,* July/August 1979, pp. 385–389.
8. G. Holbart Reinier, et al., *Crime Analysis in Support of Patrol,* National Evaluation Program Phase 1 Summary Report (Washington, D.C.: Government Printing Office, August 1977), p. iii.
9. The Police Foundation, *The Dallas Experience: Organizational Reform* (Washington, D.C.: Police Foundation, 1978).
10. Ibid.
11. C. Ray Jeffery, *Crime Prevention Through Environmental Design* (Beverly Hills, Calif.: Sage Publications, 1971).
12. The following sections through "Guidelines for Police Discretion" are adapted and reprinted from the *LEAA Newsletter,* March 1977.
13. American Bar Association Standards for Criminal Justice, *The Urban Police Function* (New York: Institute of Judicial Administration, 1972), p. 17.
14. V. A. Leonard, *Police Organization and Management,* 2nd ed. (Brooklyn: Foundation Press, 1964), pp. 22–31.

PART TWO ANNOTATED BIBLIOGRAPHY

Garmire, Bernard L., ed. *Local Government Police Management.* Washington, D.C.: International City Management Association, 1977.
  A textbook composed of a series of works written independently by police executives and scholars. Gives the student a good cross section of contemporary police thought.

Meir, William Ker, Jr. *Police: Streetcorner Policemen.* Chicago: The University of Chicago Press, 1977.
  A recent study of the police officer on the street and the nature of the officer's power. Provides excellent insight into the nature of the individual officer's role as one who both influences and is influenced.

More, Harry W., Jr., ed. *Critical Issues in Law Enforcement.* Cincinnati: W. H. Anderson, 1972.
  An excellent presentation of current police problems to which students of law enforcement must give careful consideration if law enforcement is to be relevant to contemporary society.

National Advisory Commission on Criminal Justice Standards and Goals. *Police.* Washington, D.C.: Government Printing Office, 1973.
  A list of police problems and of goals toward which the police should strive. Recommendations are offered in an attempt to make the goals more attainable.

President's Commission on Law Enforcement and Administration of Justice. *Task Force Report: The Police.* Washington, D.C.: Government Printing Office, 1967.
  One of ten reports of the President's Commission on Law Enforcement and Administration of Justice. This report presents the research and findings of the Commission's task force on police topics ranging from administrative problems to police field problems.

Reith, Charles. *The Blind Eye of History.* Montclair, N.J.: Patterson Smith, 1975.
  A classic study of the origins of the present police era. A detailed investigation of the roots of modern law enforcement.

Whisenand, Paul M., and R. Fred Ferguson. *The Managing of Police Organizations.* Englewood Cliffs, N.J.: Prentice-Hall, Inc., 1973.
  A nontraditional study of police organization. An excellent text covering changes in police management and organization thought.

Wilson, O. W., and Roy C. McLaren. *Police Administration.* 3rd ed. New York: McGraw-Hill Book Company, 1972.
  A textbook on police administration. An in-depth presentation of police organization and administration.

PART THREE

PROSECUTION
AND
DEFENSE

CHAPTER EIGHT

HISTORY
AND STRUCTURE
OF ADVOCACY

THE DEVELOPMENT OF THE LAW PROFESSION	THE HISTORY OF PROSECUTORIAL SERVICES	INFLUENCE OF THE CONTEMPORARY PROSECUTOR
	DEVELOPMENT OF PROSECUTION IN AMERICA	

Purpose: To trace the historical development of advocacy and describe the present-day structure of prosecutorial agencies.

IN THE ENGLISH-speaking countries, law as a profession traces its beginnings to the late Middle Ages, when many governmental and professional institutions developed. The English bar was much like a professional fraternity. The term *bar* originated because of the first legal training method. Students of law would often meet at public inns or private homes to study together. The common table at which they received their training was often called a bar.

The practice of law in America was significantly affected by the ancient cultures of Greece and Rome as well as by the more contemporary English civilization. The task of law is to adjust relations and order conduct so as to give the most effect to human expectations in a civilized society with a minimum of friction and waste.[1] Skilled advocacy or representation saves the courts both time and expense. The attorney or advocate filters out unnecessary information and puts relevant information into a logical order.

THE DEVELOPMENT OF THE LAW PROFESSION

Greek legal practitioners were called *interpreters*. There were three types of interpreters, the jurisconsult, the scribe, and those who represented others in litigation. The jurisconsult performed judicial duties, and the scribe was a researcher and writer. The advocate who represented others in tribunals was the early lawyer. These men were usually the heads of clans or kinsmen of aggrieved persons.

Some advocates representing government were called *synegoros*. These men spoke in behalf of proposed legislation. The speech writers were called *logographos*. Jurors were called *dikasts,* and juries or dikastries might have over 200 members. The dikasts were judges and jurors at the same time. The speech writers were of great importance to those who needed to defend family members. While the logograph did not present his own speech, his work was invaluable.

The Romans continued to develop a social consciousness. Romans called representatives in litigation *cognitors*. Later a more informal litigation method was developed. The informal litigation agent was called a *procurator*. The judge was a *judex,* or a trier of fact, appointed by the local Roman government.

A trial during the Anglo-Saxon era was not an investigation. The Anglo-Saxons were seeking a device to "reveal God's will or judgment." Oath taking by witnesses and *compurgation* by friends and character witnesses were the rule rather than the exception. Compurgation is a process in which a friendly witness swears before God that he believes another person testifying under oath. Under this trial form, advocacy was not needed.

> By the time of Edward I, the common-law courts had become well established. . . . Under Edward I the [legal] books show a body of lawyers practicing in the courts. There were two types; attorneys and pleaders, called also narratores, counteurs or serjeants-counteurs.[2]

In the thirteenth century, many legalists practiced law in civil and criminal courts of common law as well as in ecclesiastical courts.[3] Sir John Fortescue described the three categories of legal organizationalists in his book *De Laudibus Legum Angliae,* which was written between 1468 and 1471. These categories included (1) the judges and sergeants; (2) the apprentices, including readers or benchers and inner barristers, which eventually became divided into outer barristers or juniors, and inner barristers or students; and (3) the attorneys.[4]

Later a distinction developed between barristers and attorneys. Barristers were directly under the control of the Inn, or original location of training. Attorneys were admitted to practice by specific courts of law. Later *barrister* was used as a synonym for apprentice. *Attorneys* were fully functioning practitioners.

Solicitors were employed by attorneys as local agents of Westminster who kept the attorney fully informed on the progress of cases. The term *solicitor* was later used to describe a country attorney and was associated with the court of the chancery instead of the court of law.

THE HISTORY OF PROSECUTORIAL SERVICES

Prosecution is the process whereby accusations are brought before a court to determine the guilt or innocence of the accused. The *prosecutor* is an officer of the court who is responsible for carrying out this legal process, as required by law. Prosecution is made up of a series of contacts between a government official (who is a lawyer) and criminals and the attorneys representing them, both in and out of legal tribunals or courts of law. From the initial criminal proceedings, through continuances, plea bargainings, habeas corpus hearings, at many different levels of the criminal justice system, and in the trial process itself, the prosecutor is functioning in behalf of the community he or she serves.

Basically, the prosecutor has the responsibility and the obligation to present the government's case in courts of law. If a crime has been committed, it is the prosecutor's task to bring the accused to court. The prosecutor must ensure that there is sufficient reasonable evidence to prove the accused is guilty. He or she must also ensure that the prosecution is conducted according to due process of law. During the trial the prosecutor presents the state's case. The adversary (the defendant's lawyer) is there to protect the defendant's interest and to ensure that the prosecutor does not prosecute unjustly or deprive the defendant of his or her rights. By analogy, the trial is a battle: the prosecutor is the state's champion, the defense attorney is the client's champion, the judge is the referee, and the jury are the deciders of the outcome. The adversary process has many significant precedents from a historical standpoint.

The federal or state prosecutor is usually known as the *attorney general*. The office of attorney general originated hundreds of years ago in the jurisprudential development of the common law of England. Its powers are derived from the common law, federal and state constitutions, federal and state statutes, and the case law of various state and federal courts of appeal. In the Middle Ages, the king had attorneys, sergeants, and solicitors to perform some of the functions of the modern attorney general. Before the thirteenth century, the king appointed special attorneys to prosecute criminal cases.[5] The general term *attornatus* was used in English official documents in the Middle Ages to mean anyone who appeared for another as pleader, attorney, or essoiner.[6]

The earliest laws of England defined crimes as being committed against a particular individual, not against the state or some other governmental body. The original prosecutor was a victim or an individual representing a victim who stepped forward personally to initiate the prosecution of the alleged offender. The fact that the injured or aggrieved were their own advocates quite often caused the prosecution to be motivated by a zealous quest for vengeance.

Originally all crimes were torts; thus, in early common law, any injury, whether to person or property, was a tort. (A tort today is an injury to an individual that is not an offense against the state.) The historical custom of victim-prosecutors led to so much feuding that eventually the English king took over the obligation of punishing each and every offender. The original royal declaration or concept was known as the *king's peace*. From this time on, any conduct that resulted in an injury to person or property was considered an offense against the king's peace. Later, the injury was considered an offense against the state.

One way in which "justice" was effected and punishment meted out was the imposition of fines. The king could be paid, and he could also require that monies be paid to a victim or a victim's family. Before law was codified, the punishments meted out by governmental authorities were quite often on a level that would be considered deplorable, barbaric, and inhumane today. They were, however, quite acceptable by the standards of that period.

Henry V, King of England (1413-1422), required that four specific offenses be classified as felonies, or major offenses, and that all lesser offenses be classified as demeanor offenses. The four felonies were treason, counterfeiting, arson, and murder. (In later years the demeanor offenses came to be known as *misdemeanors*.) At the same time, Henry V provided that all crimes be considered offenses against society. The state or government, representing society, was to bear the burden of law enforcement, prosecution of offenders, and public trials, as well as punishment and incarceration.

There is some disagreement as to who the first attorney general was. However, it was during the reign of Edward IV (1461-1483) that William Husse was appointed attorney general of England, and Husse is recognized by most authorities as the first.[7]

Henry VIII (1509-1547) eliminated the vengeance prosecution system and in its stead provided a system of *sergeants*. Sergeants were required to act as police prosecutors and to enforce penal statutes. They were later to become well trained in the law. Even though sergeants were compensated for their services by the king, they could also practice in civil and criminal courts. Unfortunately, from the outset of this system, prosecutors were able to make much more money from civil pursuits, and so from the very beginning of this publicly funded and supported system, divided interests were a problem. Many prosecutors tended to spend very little time on the less financially rewarding prosecution cases as opposed to their more rewarding private practice.

DEVELOPMENT OF PROSECUTION IN AMERICA

In the United States, the development of the prosecutor's office at the state level was erratic. The majority of the colonies created or continued the office of attorney general in their new state constitutions. Territories generally established this office by law when they were granted statehood, although this was not universal. Hard as it is to imagine a state operating without an attorney general, Virginia did not legislate the office of attorney general until 1904.[8]

The United States attorney general is not a constitutional officer. The office was created by the Judiciary Act of 1789. The attorney general soon became a member of the president's cabinet, but did not head a department until 1870, when the Department of Justice was created by an act of Congress.[9]

The agencies of prosecution that eventually developed are like many other elements of the American criminal justice system in that they exist at federal, state, and local levels. At the federal level, the United States attorney general is the chief law officer. At the state level, the state attorney general is the chief law officer. The chief law officer at the local level (city, county, or municipality) has such titles as district attorney, prosecutor, and city attorney.

UNITED STATES ATTORNEY GENERAL

The chief United States prosecutor is given the title United States attorney general and is a member of the president's cabinet, appointed by the president and confirmed by the Senate. In addition to performing duties related to the job of chief prosecutor, the attorney general renders legal opinions to the head of the various governmental bureaus and administers the work of all personnel under his or her command, including the employees of the federal correctional institutions. Agencies coming under the attorney general's direct supervision and administration are displayed in Figure 8.1.

The attorney general has a tremendous amount of authority and control over many different branches of the criminal justice system. Although the attorney general's direction and that of his or her subordinates in the Justice Department directly affect many different units of federal and state government, most federal prosecutions are handled locally by the United States attorney or the

FIGURE 8.1 UNITED STATES DEPARTMENT OF JUSTICE

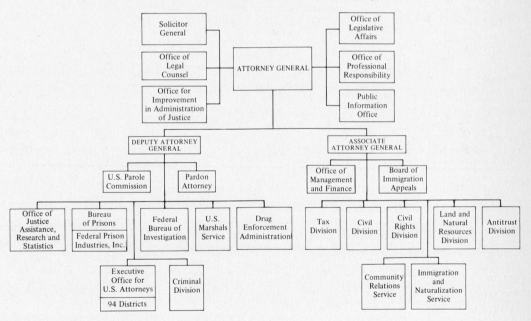

SOURCE: Office of the Federal Register, *United States Government Manual 1978–79* (Washington, D.C.: Government Printing Office, 1978), p. 346.

The authority of the state attorney general differs from state to state. In Connecticut, Florida, Idaho, Illinois, Missouri, Tennessee, Virginia, and West Virginia, the attorney general has no authority over local prosecutors and cannot take over the prosecution of any particular case. All other states have provided constitutional or statutory authority for the state attorney general to initiate local prosecutions. Although this authority is often restricted to extreme conditions, the prosecutor's discretionary power to prosecute those cases over which he or she has authority is usually not limited.

The number of personnel in the state attorney general's office ranges from fewer than four in Montana, Nebraska, and South Dakota to 462 in New York. Overall, the states employ approximately 3,000 lawyers in the offices of their attorneys general.[10]

The prosecuting attorney of a district, county, or municipal area is either chosen by election or appointed by a court or governing body. In the vast majority of cases, however, local prosecutors are elected. Although the prosecutor's office may be found at any level of local government, the county level is the most common. See Figure 8.2 for an example of office structure in a California district.

FIGURE 8.2 ORGANIZATION CHART — OFFICE OF THE DISTRICT ATTORNEY

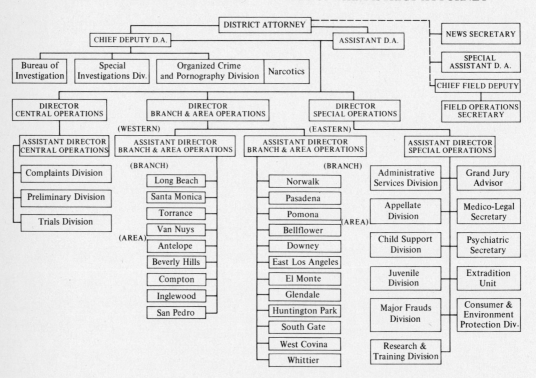

SOURCE: Reprinted by permission of the Publisher, from *Prosecution of Adult Felony Defendants* by Peter W. Greenwood et al. (Lexington, Mass.: Lexington Books, D. C. Heath and Company, Copyright 1974, The Rand Corporation), p. 9.

PROSECUTION AND DEFENSE

THE PROSECUTOR
SELECTION PROCESS

At the state and local levels today, the public prosecutor usually gains office by local election. This makes the prosecutor an independent public official with very little central supervision. While the court may place controls over the prosecutor in the courtroom, the prosecutor can act independently most of the time. The broad discretionary powers of the prosecutor before any court appearance include (1) decisions about which cases should be presented to the grand jury and in which cases the prosecutor will file an information, (2) decisions about which cases will be presented for trial and on which the prosecutor will file nolle prosequi (which is a refusal to prosecute), and (3) decisions made in bargaining with the accused and defense counsel about whether some charges will be dropped to a lesser offense or not prosecuted.

> The district or county attorney in most States is a locally elected official. In larger communities the prosecutor has a staff of assistants, but the great majority of the country's more than 2,700 prosecutors serve in small offices with at most one or two assistants and frequently the prosecutor and his assistants are part-time officials. Their official duties are to prosecute all criminal cases and in most jurisdictions to represent the local government in civil cases, but when not engaged in a case they are free to practice law privately. This pattern of outside practice is common to the rural counties and smaller cities although it may be found in our largest cities.[11]

Because the job is a part-time one in most jurisdictions within the United States, many prosecutors receive extremely low salaries. In addition, crime is not equally distributed, so prosecutors in some locations work much harder for the same amount of money than their colleagues in other places. Since salaries are not based on number of cases, the district or county prosecutor who has only a few cases to prosecute may be very well reimbursed for the time spent, while the prosecutor in an urban or high-crime area may be very poorly paid on an hourly basis. An overburdened system encourages plea bargaining and case manipulation, especially when the prosecutor is poorly paid. Private pressures may encourage the part-time prosecutor to keep prosecutions from interfering with private practice. On occasion this situation may result in a preponderance of negotiated pleas or in poor pretrial preparation.

THE RAND STUDY

In 1976 the Rand Corporation documented the results of a very significant prosecutorial research effort. As a result of these studies, two prosecutorial models were found, a *rigorous model* and a *laissez-faire model.*

> The Rigorous Model implies the following: (1) moderate to low complaint rejection rates if the quality of police investigation is high and if police arrest and charging standards are similar to those of the prosecutor (and high rejection rates if police investigation quality is low and arrest standards are different); (2) low termination rates in Municipal Court and low dismissal rates in Superior Court because complaint filing standards are high; (3) above-average court and jury trial rates; (4) above-average plea rates; (5) high conviction rates, especially for jury and court trials; and (6) more severe sentencing because of prosecutorial participation in probation and sentencing hearings, although sentencing outcomes are mainly products of judicial and Probation Department decisions.
>
> The Laissez-Faire Model essentially embodies the opposite characteristics and would tend to exhibit opposite outcome measures.[12]

After extended studies in Los Angeles and other parts of California, the Rand Corporation came to several significant conclusions and made several recommendations.

In conclusion, Rand found: (1) that there is at present no reasonable set of performance standards for criminal justice agencies;[13] (2) that the performance of criminal justice agencies in Los Angeles County differs considerably from the performance of those in other parts of the state,[14] (3) that the systems offer strong incentives to settle cases without a trial,[15] and (4) that defendants who have secured some form of pretrial release are more likely to be acquitted and less likely to receive a felony sentence if convicted than defendants who have not been released.[16]

These studies are currently being debated by many professionals. Their findings should be carefully considered, however, for it certainly seems that privately funded defense attorneys are securing a substantially higher rate of release, probation, and "not guilty" findings.

INFLUENCE OF THE CONTEMPORARY PROSECUTOR

The prosecutor is one of the most influential officials in the American system of criminal justice. The powers of the public prosecutor exceed those of all others in the criminal justice system, with the possible exception of the judge, and they exceed even those of the judge in the area of discretionary authority, since the prosecutor's authority is less subject to formal review. The prosecutor is entrusted with the basic responsibility of deciding whether or not to charge or prosecute a suspect and determining the nature of the charge, and has the authority to reduce the charge or even, as occasionally happens, recommend the dismissal of an action after it has been filed with the court.

The prosecutor, through this discretionary power, usually determines the direction that law enforcement agencies in his or her jurisdiction will take. Many Americans erroneously believe that the prosecutor functions primarily in the courtroom. Many prosecutors have the right to make arrests and carry weapons, just as a police officer does. Many also have investigatory powers in some areas. Occasionally the prosecutor is the only member of the criminal justice community empowered by legislation to investigate organized crime, gambling, governmental corruption, and ecological problems. In those areas where exceptional prosecution power is granted, the prosecutor may be the initial investigator of an alleged crime as well as the initiator of the criminal process through an arrest or an investigation. The prosecutor may choose to make his or her own investigations in many cases or to supplement the police investigation, especially when the prosecutor perceives the local police or sheriff as inept, poorly trained, or dishonest.

There seems to be very little correlation among practices in different locations. The discretion of the prosecutor and his or her assistants, the qualifications required for the office, and the relationships of police investigators with the prosecutor are not consistent from state to state or city to city.

DISCUSSION QUESTIONS

1. Discuss the primary responsibility of the prosecutor.
2. Recount the development of the attorney general's office in America.
3. Why is the attorney general referred to as the chief law enforcement officer?
4. Is the power of the attorney general conducive to criminal justice efficiency?
5. Should a prosecutor be elected or appointed? Why?
6. Discuss the Rand Study on prosecutors.
7. Do you believe the state attorney general should have the power to take a case away from a local prosecutor? Why or why not?

NOTES

1. Allen Harding, *Social History of the English Law* (Baltimore: Penguin Books, 1966).
2. Hugh C. Bellott, "The Origin of the Attorney," *Law Review Quarterly,* 25 (1909), 400.
3. National Association of Attorneys General on the Office of Attorney General, *The Office of Attorney General* (1971), p. 12.
4. *The Office of Attorney General,* p. 18.
5. Office of the Federal Register, *United States Government Manual,* 1973/1974 (Washington, D.C.: Government Printing Office, 1973), p. 289.
6. *The Office of Attorney General,* pp. 209–211.
7. President's Commission on Law Enforcement and the Administration of Justice, *Task Force Report: The Courts* (Washington, D.C.: Government Printing Office, 1967), p. 73.
8. Peter W. Greenwood, Sorrel Wildhorn, Eugene C. Poggio, Michael J. Strumwasser, and Peter De Leon, *Prosecution of Adult Felony Defendants* (Lexington: D.C. Heath and Company, 1976), p. xxix.
9. *Prosecution of Adult Felony Defendants,* p. 116.
10. *Prosecution of Adult Felony Defendants,* p. 116.
11. *Prosecution of Adult Felony Defendants,* p. 118.
12. *Prosecution of Adult Felony Defendants,* p. 118.

CHAPTER NINE

THE STATE'S ADVOCATE

SCREENING AND DIVERSION	PRELIMINARY HEARING	PRETRIAL NEGOTIATIONS
DECISION TO PROSECUTE	INDICTMENT AND INFORMATION	ARRAIGNMENT TRIAL

Purpose: To provide an introduction to the functions of the prosecutor as they relate to the criminal justice process.

O NCE AN ARREST or a complaint has been made, the prosecutor examines the charge and decides whether or not to initiate prosecution of the accused individual. (In only certain states or localities can a judge throw out the case before a prosecutor becomes involved.) The prosecutor's first step is to examine the information contained in the warrant and commitment papers that come to the prosecutor's office from the lower-court magistrate. After evaluating all the evidence, the prosecutor decides whether or not to initiate prosecution of the person charged with the crime. (See Figure 9.1 for the relationship of the adversaries as a case proceeds through the system.) In this way he or she performs a screening function by reviewing the evidence before initiating the prosecution. This independent exercise provides some additional protection against unwarranted prosecutions or prosecutions based on insufficient, inadequate, or contaminated evidence. The questions asked before prosecution are as follows:

1. Is there sufficient reasonable proof of guilt to warrant subjecting the defendant to a trial and a unit of government to the expense of paying for that trial?
2. If there is sufficient probable cause or probability of guilt, is there any reason that prosecution should not be carried out?
3. If an accused is charged with several offenses, which of the crimes should be pursued in the criminal justice process?
4. Will this particular prosecution be in the best interest of the jurisdiction served?

In deciding whether to prosecute, the prosecutor usually makes an initial determination based on the facts known to the police officers making the arrest at the time they took the action. A decision that probable cause or reasonable belief of guilt does not exist is one of the most common reasons for eliminating a case from court action. The prosecutor thus eliminates cases that are vague, inaccurate, or speculative. Usually these cases have been handled by poorly trained officers or by officers hampered by an overload of cases to investigate. On other occasions, a prosecutor may choose to prosecute an offender whose case has been mishandled because of the nature of the offense or of the intensity of social feeling about the particular offender and the offense.

The prosecutor has the immediate basis for a good case when a police officer makes an arrest for probable cause, with or without a warrant. The case will not be compromised unless there was some investigative ambiguity, or the defendant was coerced or not informed of his or her rights. In some cases, when a police officer merely serves a warrant on the authority of a magistrate, the officer may not have any personal knowledge of probable cause. In such a case, the private citizen making the complaint to a magistrate on oath or affirmation caused the initial decision to arrest, which in turn led to the prosecutor's involvement in the case.

SCREENING AND DIVERSION

Screening usually occurs in any case where the prosecutor doubts that a conviction can be obtained. Occasionally evidence may be insufficient, a primary witness may lack credibility, or the police may have mismanaged a particular situation. In other cases, the intent of a criminal action may be very difficult to prove: domestic disturbances, checks that are drawn on insufficient funds, or juvenile pranks that may have violated the letter of the law quite often fall into this category. The prosecutor realizes that the most outstanding indiscretion of office is the

FIGURE 9.1 PROSECUTORIAL ENCOUNTERS IN THE JUSTICE SYSTEM

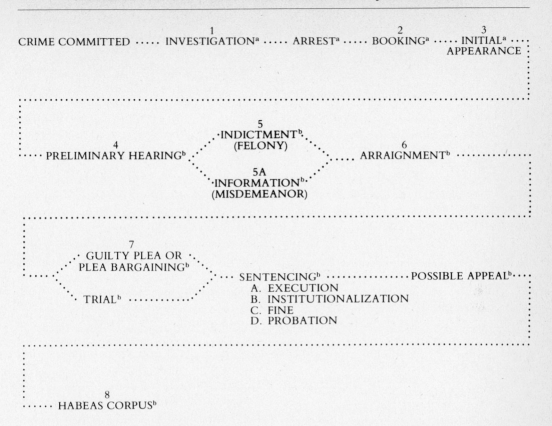

1. Investigation may continue until trial.
2. Booking is a police administrative record of arrest.
3. Initial appearance is before a justice or magistrate, with a formal notification of charge and a formal advice of rights. Bail may be set or summary judgments made for petty offenses.
4. Preliminary testing of evidence. Defense may petition to suppress evidence. Plea negotiations may be made.
5. Grand jury reviews evidence to determine whether sufficient evidence exists to merit a trial.
5A. Charge is filed by prosecutor on basis of affidavits of police or citizens.
6. Arraignment is the appearance before a magistrate for plea. Defendants may elect trial by judge or by judge and jury. States that do not have formal public defender systems will appoint counsel at this stage.
7. It should be noted that the charge may be reduced at any time prior to trial in turn for guilty plea or for other justice aid.
8. Habeas Corpus proceedings, or the challenge to the legality of detention, may be sought at any point in the justice process.

[a] Those stages in which a prosecutor *may* contribute.
[b] Those stages in which a prosecutor *must* participate.

institution of formal charges against all violators of the law, never screening or diverting offenders to other social agencies.

> The prosecutor who institutes . . .
> charges against all defendants arrested by
> the police fails to make the necessary
> choices at this stage of the proceeding.
> . . . [A] prosecutor's failure to screen at
> this level introduces some cases which are
> not important enough to merit full prosecution. By clogging the courts with marginal cases, he is unfortunately ensuring
> that the more serious crimes, which merit
> the full attention of the criminal system
> will not get the scrutiny they deserve.[1]

Whereas *screening* involves the cessation of formal criminal proceedings by the prosecutor and the removal of the individual from the criminal justice system, *diversion* refers to the halting or suspending, before conviction, of the formal criminal proceedings against a person on the condition or assumption that that person will do something in return.

> Diverted cases are those removed from
> court jurisdiction without any decision on
> their merits. This may occur if a particular case is combined with another . . . or
> if the defender is released into the custody
> of another jurisdiction where he has committed a more serious offense.[2]

Usually, when the prosecutor determines that alternative methods are more appropriate than treatment or punishment within the criminal justice system, the prosecutor will offer the defendant the opportunity to choose between the alternative method (join the army, seek psychiatric help, accept informal probation, or the like) and continuation of the criminal justice process. Through the screening and diversion processes the prosecutor eliminates from the criminal justice system many marginal cases that do not warrant full attention.[3]

DECISION TO PROSECUTE

Quite often many statutes are violated in a single criminal encounter, and prosecutors are responsible for selecting the crime for which the offender is to be prosecuted. The prosecutor usually picks an offense that is a little more stringent than the ultimate charge. (See Table 9.1.)

The decision to prosecute is a very serious one. In making it, the prosecutor announces that the offender's freedom must be curtailed for his or her own protection or for the protection of society. The individual charged may lose job, status, prestige, and large sums of money. On the other hand, the prosecutor may decide not to charge on the grounds that prosecution is not in the best interests of the community.

> If the prosecutor is obliged to choose his
> cases, it follows that he can choose his defendants. Therein is the most dangerous
> power of the prosecutor: that he will pick
> people that he thinks he should get, rather
> than pick cases that need to be prosecuted. With the law books filled with a
> great assortment of crimes, a prosecutor
> stands a fair chance of finding at least a
> technical violation of some act on the part
> of almost everyone.[4]

PRELIMINARY HEARING

Having decided to proceed, the prosecutor's next step in a felony case is generally the preliminary hearing. Here the prosecutor introduces evidence and tries to convince the court that there is probable cause for believing the accused guilty. At this hearing, witnesses may be presented and cross-examined, and other aspects of the adversary process are permitted. If the court finds that probable cause exists, it will carry the case

PROSECUTION AND DEFENSE

TABLE 9.1 JUSTICE INTERRELATIONSHIPS

POLICE	PROSECUTION	COURT	DEFENSE
Apparent Corpus Delicti			
Arrest	Decision to endorse arrest		Habeas corpus challenge (at any phase of defense)
Investigation			
	Prosecution–defense plea negotiation		Prosecution–defense plea negotiation
	Screening considered?		Screening recommended?
	Extradition[a]		Extradition[a]
	Initial appearance (Bond consideration)	Initial appearance (Bond consideration)	Initial appearance (Bond consideration)
	Preliminary hearing[b]	Preliminary hearing[b]	Preliminary hearing[b]
	Indictment or information		
	Arraignment	Arraignment	Arraignment
	Plea bargaining		
	Diversion consideration?		Diversion recommended?
	Prosecution goal established		Defense goal specified
	Trial	Trial	Trial — decision of defense on bench or jury trial
	Venire selection	Venire selection	Venire selection
	Prosecution presentation[b]		Defense presentation[b]
		Adjudication	
			Appeal

[a] If apprehended outside of state of jurisdiction and waiver is not obtained.
[b] May be waived by defense.

to the next step in the prosecution. The prosecutor may then take the case before a grand jury or file an information, which is a formal charge leveled against the accused.

INDICTMENT AND INFORMATION

A grand jury is primarily an investigative body composed of people selected from the community. It serves as a buffer between the state and the citizen.

It is one of the more unusual phases of the criminal justice process in that neither the defendant or an attorney is ordinarily allowed before it. In some cases, such as those involving governmental corruption, even the local prosecutor may be substituted or forced into a totally passive role during the grand jury proceedings. In many cases the prosecution brings the evidence gathered on a particular case before the grand jury, which must then decide whether there is sufficient probable cause to hand down an *indictment,* or a formal charge against an accused person written by the prosecutor and submitted to a court by the grand jury. The grand jury has investigative power and full charging authority. After the indictment is issued, the prosecutor can proceed with the arraignment.

The prosecutor might file an information instead of an indictment. The *information* is a formal document filed before the court by the prosecutor indicating that there is sufficient evidence to proceed with the case. In some states and for certain offenses, the prosecutor is bound to use the grand jury. In other states the prosecutor has the option of seeking a grand jury indictment or filing an information. Since the Fifth Amendment holds that "no person shall be held to answer for a capital, or otherwise infamous crime, unless on a presentment or indictment of a Grand Jury," the grand jury system is a vital and necessary element of due process.[5]

PRETRIAL NEGOTIATIONS

Pretrial negotiations may involve plea bargaining or giving defendants incentives to testify or to give the police information about those who conspired with them or about other offenders known to them. These negotiations are much more informal at this stage than at later stages of the criminal justice process. Many prosecutors prefer pretrial interaction and negotiation because there is more opportunity for flexibility and because the situation is not so competitive as it is during the adversary phases of the trial process.

Pretrial negotiations have been greatly expanded in the last few years in order to help the courts keep pace with their extremely overburdened dockets or caseloads, especially in high-crime-rate urban areas. Because the court system as it now exists simply cannot handle the huge influx of cases, pretrial negotiations are almost mandatory. The sheer number of cases pressures many prosecutors into accepting a plea of guilty to a lesser offense even when they would prefer to prosecute for a greater offense.

The consideration a defendant receives in return for a guilty plea might include any of the following prosecutorial agreements:

- To drop some counts
- To accept a plea to a lesser included offense
- To not file prior convictions
- To omit allegedly habitual offender pleadings
- To recommend against consecutive sentences
- To recommend against prison time
- To recommend commitment to the rehabilitation center
- To refrain from opposing probation at the probation and sentencing hearing[6]

Many members of the legal profession are very concerned by the large number of inducements available to the police, the prosecutor, and even the defense attorney to encourage a plea of guilty. The offender has reason to hope that this plea will lead to a particular result. Some specialists believe that the criminal justice process in America today would collapse if substantial inducements to elicit guilty pleas were not continued. While this cannot be easily proven, current statistical studies show that 85 to 90 percent of all prosecutions in many jurisdictions end in "negotiated" pleas of guilty.[7] In many jurisdictions, especially those in which the police are not adequately trained, the only prosecutions initiated are against offenders who were caught red-handed. In other places, an offender who "forces" a trial must have hopes that the penalty will be lessened by the trial process. If the prosecutor agrees to charge a lesser offense, the offender may prefer to take a sure thing rather than risk the much more severe sentence that conviction at a trial might bring.

Many prosecutors who have extremely heavy workloads are more than willing to negotiate. Each case negotiated means less time spent, and the possibility of case complications or appeals is almost totally eliminated. Negotiations may also be quite time consuming, but not to the degree of a trial by jury and the appropriate preparation for the case. Through successful negotiation, the defense attorney also obtains a very tangible result for the client. Defense-prosecutor negotiations are generally approved because the court dockets are crowded.

> The negotiated plea serves important functions. As a practical matter, many courts could not sustain the burden of having to try all cases coming before them. The quality of justice in all cases would suffer if overloaded courts were faced with a great increase in the number of trials. Tremendous investments of time, talent, and money, all of which are in short supply and can be better used elsewhere, would be necessary if all cases were tried. It would be a serious mistake, however, to assume that the guilty plea is no more than a means of disposing the criminal cases at minimal cost. It relieves both the defendant and the prosecution of the inevitable risks and uncertainties of trial. It imparts a degree of certainty and flexibility into a rigid, yet frequently erratic system. The guilty plea is used to mitigate the harshness of mandatory sentencing provisions and to fix a punishment that more accurately reflects the specific circumstances of the case than otherwise would be possible under inadequate penal codes. It is frequently called upon to serve important law enforcement needs by agreements through which leniency is exchanged for information, assist-

ance, and testimony about other serious offenders.[8]

The National Advisory Commission on Criminal Justice Standards and Goals (1973) recommended the total abolition of plea bargaining by 1978. The commission viewed plea negotiation as inherently undesirable and maintained that such negotiations should and can be eliminated.[9] Admitting that negotiations could not be quickly eliminated, the commission suggested that until they were, the court should more carefully evaluate every negotiated plea with the total power of acceptance or rejection. The commission has recommended that the court take into account the following considerations when evaluating a negotiated plea:

1. The impact that a formal trial would have on the offender and those close to him or her, especially the likelihood and seriousness of financial hardship and family disruption;
2. The role that a plea and negotiated agreement may play in rehabilitating the offender;
3. The value of a trial in fostering the community's sense of security and confidence in law enforcement agencies; and
4. The assistance rendered by the offender:
   a. in the apprehension or conviction of other offenders;
   b. in the prevention of crimes by others;
   c. in the reduction of the impact of the offense on the victim; or
   d. in any other socially beneficial activity.[10]

In addition, weaknesses in the prosecution's case should not be considered in determining whether to permit a defendant to plead guilty to any offense other than that charged, and a statement of policies should be made available to the public.[11]

In the prosecution standards and goals, the commission has recommended that no prosecutor should, in connection with plea negotiations, engage in, perform, or condone any of the following:

1. Charging or threatening to charge the defendant with offenses for which the admissible evidence available to the prosecutor is insufficient to support a guilty verdict.
2. Charging or threatening to charge the defendant with a crime not ordinarily charged in the jurisdiction for the conduct the defendant allegedly engaged in.
3. Threatening the defendant that a plea of not guilty may lead to a sentence more severe than that which is ordinarily imposed in the jurisdiction in similar cases on defendants who plead not guilty.
4. Failing to disclose before the disposition negotiations all exculpatory evidence material to guilt or punishment.[12]

ARRAIGNMENT

The prosecutor represents the people and the government. The defense attorney represents a particular defendant or defendants against the resources of governmental prosecution. The arraignment is usually, though not always, the first "formal" opportunity for the defense and prosecutor to meet. Simply defined, the arraignment is the defendant's formal opportunity to answer the charge or charges of which he or she is accused. It is a mandatory appearance for the plea. The defendant may elect a jury trial at this stage, and an indigent defendant may have counsel appointed in areas that do not have public defenders.

The most common options in pleading are: (1) guilty; (2) not guilty; and in some states (3) nolo contendere, which means no contest; (4) non vult, which means to stand mute; and (5) not guilty by reason of insanity. (In some state statutes, the term *nolo contendere* means that the accused simply does not understand the charge.) The primary purpose of nolo contendere is to give the criminal court an indication of the defendant's willingness to accept a conviction and the resultant penalty rather than go to trial. The plea is especially helpful in criminal actions that may later lead to civil litigation, for a guilty plea might possibly be entered into the record of the subsequent civil litigation. Non vult is automatically entered as a plea of not guilty on the transcript in some jurisdictions. Usually the nolo contendere plea is accepted in lieu of trial. This plea will rarely be allowed in strictly criminal cases such as robbery or burglary. On the other hand, it may be allowed in cases involving vehicular crimes, tax liability, or other criminal charges that may ultimately result in tort action.

If the prosecutor's case proves defective or if necessary witnesses do not appear for trial, the prosecutor may request a *nolle prosequi,* generally called a *nol pros.* Simply stated, this means that there will be no prosecution. Generally it is an acknowledgement of the realization that the prosecutor cannot prove the charges. It may indicate that records have been lost or stolen, that witnesses did not appear, or that a primary witness has died.

At the arraignment, the defendant is brought before the court that is to be the trial agency and is asked to plead to the indictment. If the defendant pleads guilty, the judge ascertains that certain precautions have been taken. The judge may ask the defendant if he or she understands the charge or ask the prosecutor to present some of the evidence to assure the court that there are sufficient grounds to continue the criminal justice process. If the defendant pleads not guilty or does not plead, the judge will investigate to see whether there is a basis for the plea. If so, the case is *bound over,* or continued for trial. The prosecutor's role in the arraignment is a limited one. The prosecutor is, if you will, the conductor on the train of the criminal justice process as it moves across the criminal justice system to trial.

TRIAL

Once bound over for trial, the defendant may elect a court, or bench, trial (without a jury) or a jury trial. In the latter, the judge determines the legality of the evidence and its admissibility. The jury determines whether the evidence indicates guilt beyond any reasonable doubt.

After a court has been called into session for a jury trial and the announcement of the case made, the *voir dire* (jury examination) is generally the first order of business. In minor cases the examination may take only an hour or two; in difficult cases, several days or even weeks. The first questions are generally asked by the judge. They are usually of broad application, asking the potential jury members whether any of them know the defendant personally or have previous information that might tend to prejudice them in the case. In some jurisdictions the prosecution and defense attorneys conduct the entire examination; in others they limit themselves to areas not covered by the judge. These examinations are always similar, but the specific circumstances govern their completeness.

When the prosecutor or the defense counsel can show cause during the jury examination, a potential juror can be dismissed. The cause may be a potential juror's preconceived notions of guilt, personal prejudices, or other matters that would tend to influence his or her verdict. Both prosecutor and defense are also entitled to *peremptory challenges,* whereby a potential juror can be dismissed without cause, but the number of peremptory challenges is limited.

With the jury selected, the trial or main event of the adversary process begins. The prosecutor makes an opening statement indicating a tentative course of action for the trial. The defense makes an opening statement. The prosecutor calls witnesses and presents evidence. His or her first questions are called a *direct examination.* The defense attorney's first questions are called a *cross-examination.* Additional questions by the prosecutor are called a *redirect examination.* Additional questions by the defense are called a *recross-examination.*

The defense may present its case after the prosecution rests. It is common for the defense to ask for a directed (court) verdict of not guilty on the basis that the state has not adequately indicated that the defendant did, in fact, commit a crime. If the judge agrees with the defense attorney, he or she can accept this petition, effectively ruling that the case was not acceptable and removing the case from the jury. In some states the judge may direct the jury to return a verdict of not guilty. The inverse of this decision is not allowed in a jury trial. The judge could not enter a conviction judgment at this point in the trial.

After the defense presents its case, the prosecution may refute the evidence presented with a rebuttal of the points under contention. After the prosecutorial rebuttal, some states allow a defense surrebuttal, which is the defense's rebuttal to the prosecution rebuttal.

Following the defense presentation and any related prosecutorial rebuttal, the judge will call a recess and receive written jury instructions from the prosecution and defense attorneys. After considering the points of law presented by both sides, the judge will call court back in session and allow the closing arguments to take place. The order of these arguments is basically the same as the order of the trial. The prosecutor presents a statement first. The defense presents its case second. The adversaries may also be allowed rebuttal opportunities, but procedures differ in different areas of the United States.

The judge charges the jury to render a just and true verdict. The jury deliberates and issues its verdict. While this trial process may call forth images of Perry Mason, the typical criminal trial is far less dramatic than those presented on television series.

The American system of justice is an adversary system. Yet, it is an adversary system based on mutual respect between the prosecutor, the defense attorney, and the court. It is a system which seeks to attain justice, rather than to merely convict. The attainment of this goal may often require a great deal of cooperation between the parties involved. Although it is not the prosecutor's function to represent the defendant, he should cooperate with the defense attorney to the fullest extent possible at all stages of the criminal process to ensure the attainment of justice through the most appropriate disposition of each case. Defense counsel should reciprocate to the extent such cooperation does not conflict with the best interests of his client.[13]

In many cases, the prosecutor's role in the criminal justice process ends with the verdict and the sentencing of the defendant. The defendant goes free or moves on to some form of treatment or punishment. In some cases, the defendant appeals the case, and then the prosecutor appears in a higher court, again to present the state's case.

The prosecutor's complete role is very complex, much more so than can be presented in an introductory text. By deciding which cases to prosecute, the prosecutor sets the law enforcement policies for the community. As an elected official, the prosecutor is a political animal and must engage in the political processes of the community. In short, the prosecution function is a difficult one, requiring skill in law, administration, and political science. It requires a person of great determination and, above all, high moral and ethical principles.

DISCUSSION QUESTIONS

1. What questions does the prosecutor generally consider prior to prosecution?
2. Trace the stages of the justice process in which the prosecutor must participate.
3. For what reasons are cases usually screened or diverted?
4. What agreements might a prosecutor make to induce a defendant to plead guilty to a particular offense?
5. What percentage of the cases in our justice system involve pleas of guilty?
6. What does non vult mean?
7. Describe the uniqueness of a bench trial and state why a defendant may choose this option.
8. What is an adversary system? (Review Chapters 8 and 9 before answering.)

PROSECUTION AND DEFENSE

NOTES

1. National Advisory Commission on Criminal Justice Standards and Goals, *Working Papers* (Washington, D.C.: Government Printing Office, 1973), p. 215.
2. Peter W. Greenwood, Sorrel Wildhorn, Eugene C. Poggio, Michael J. Strumwasser, and Peter De Leon, *Prosecution of Adult Felony Defendants* (Lexington, Mass.: D. C. Heath and Company, 1976), p. 21.
3. National Advisory Commission on Criminal Justice Standards and Goals, *Courts* (Washington, D.C.: Government Printing Office, 1973), pp. 24–38.
4. Livingston Hall et al., *Basic Criminal Procedure* (St. Paul, Minn.: West Publishing, 1969), p. 561.
5. *Courts,* pp. 11–16. *Hurtado* v. *California,* 110 U.S. 516 (1884).
6. *Prosecution of Adult Felony Defendants,* p. 121.
7. President's Commission on Law Enforcement and Administration of Justice, *The Challenge of Crime in a Free Society* (Washington, D.C.: Government Printing Office, 1967), p. 134.
8. *Working Papers,* p. 218.
9. *Courts,* p. 46.
10. *Courts,* p. 52.
11. *Courts,* p. 52.
12. *Courts,* p. 57.
13. American Bar Association of Professional Responsibility, Supra Note 1. DR 4-101. National District Attorneys Association, *National Prosecution Standards* (Chicago: National District Attorneys Association, 1977), pp. 395–396.

CHAPTER TEN

THE DEFENDANT'S ADVOCATE

DEFENSE DELIVERY
SERVICES

DEFENSE
CONSULTATION
ROLE OF THE DEFENSE

ASSESSING CRIMINAL
DEFENDERS

*Purpose: To provide an introduction to the
functions of the defense lawyer as they relate to
the criminal justice process.*

THE ORIENTATION OF the defense attorney is diametrically opposed to that of the prosecutor. This vital participant in the justice process helps maintain the balance sought throughout our system of justice. In many ways the defense enjoys and maintains an enviable position in the adversary process because the defendant continues to be presumed innocent until the judge or judge and jury have pronounced him or her guilty.

While the presumption of innocence is an accepted philosophy, many parts of the criminal justice process are designed to treat a defendant as though he or she were guilty! This reality is indicated in those stages of the adversary process that restrict freedom, maintain incarceration, or encourage large bail bonds.

In 1963 the U.S. Supreme Court significantly increased the number of cases in which indigent offenders had to be provided with legal counsel. The *Gideon* v. *Wainwright* decision [372 U.S. 335 (1963)] emanated from the Florida jurisprudential system and departed significantly from tradition. Prior to *Gideon* indigent offenders were considered constitutionally protected only in *capital* cases, those in which a lifetime of liberty can be retracted or in which a defendant may receive the death penalty.

This landmark decision began a movement that, when extended, was to give the right of counsel to those who committed misdemeanors as well as felonies. *Argersinger* v. *Hamlin* [407 U.S. 25 (1972)] was another step in providing full defense services for all defendants charged with offenses for which they might be imprisoned.

Justice Black, writing for the majority in *Gideon,* had this to say:

> The right of one charged with crime to counsel may not be deemed fundamental and essential to fair trials in some countries; but it is in ours. From the very beginning, our state and national constitution and laws have laid great emphasis on procedural and substantive safeguards designed to assure fair trials before impartial tribunals in which every defendant stands equal before the law. This noble ideal cannot be realized if the poor man charged with crime has to face his accusers without a lawyer to assist him.[1]

In the last few years several other important cases significantly enlarged the scope of full and complete defense arrangements for those without adequate funds. Counsel is required during any interrogation of an accused under *Miranda* v. *Arizona* [384 U.S. 436, 86 S.Ct. 157 (1961)]. The *Wade* decision stated that a formally charged defendant appearing in a police lineup has the right to have an attorney present during this proceeding — *U.S.* v. *Wade* [388 U.S. 218 (1967)]. *Hamilton* v. *Alabama* [368 U.S. 52 (1961)] and *Coleman* v. *Alabama* [399 U.S. 1 (1970)] required the states to provide professional assistance at arraignments and preliminary hearings.

Other cases in the late 1960s and early 1970s extended defense services to almost all legal criminal proceedings. The court has held that probationers' revocation hearings are subject to this defense coverage.[2] In those states that provide for automatic appellate review of convictions, the indigent now has full defense coverage at this stage also.[3]

The courts continue to insist that defendants be adequately represented by counsel, even in those cases in which the defendant waives this right or petitions to represent himself or herself.

DEFENSE DELIVERY SERVICES

Contemporary defense resources include private attorneys endowed by their clients, assigned counsel for indigents, public defender officials, legal services, and mixed counsel systems.

In many venues defense attorneys for indigents are appointed on a rotation basis from a list of practicing attorneys maintained by the magistrate. In large venues, many younger attorneys or those recently admitted to the bar ask judges to let them gain experience this way. Of 3,100 counties in the United States, 2,750 still rely on court-approved counsel to defend the indigent. In many states the defense attorney is paid a modest fixed stipend for such labors. Some states, however, expect attorneys to perform such services on a gratis basis. When providing services for a fixed fee or gratis, the private attorney has a very strong motive to expedite the flow of the case. In some jurisdictions the fixed fee is higher if the case goes to trial, so that an attorney might well choose to proceed in order to increase income. Table 10.1 reflects the 1970 California statistics showing that private attorneys are more likely to have their clients plead guilty and court-appointed attorneys are more likely to have their clients go to trial. Public defenders seem to have less success in getting their cases dismissed.[4] It is to be noted that "SOT" stands for the "submission on the transcript" of the original hearing or trial.

While the appointed defender system has several virtues, its most obvious weaknesses include the fact that the attorney usually does not have defense investigative services available. The fact that the attorney will receive the same fixed fee for persuading a client to plead guilty or for preparing fully for a trial is another strong weakness.

The public defender is a salaried public official. His or her services are free and are tax-supported. The system was first begun in the state of California in 1913. At least 50 percent of the United States now has some form of this system. The strongest merits of the system include full funding of defense preparation and defense investigation. Public agency record keeping now offers system analysts a more elaborate portrayal of the full function of the defense attorney. In addition, policies consistent with good defense practice may be developed. Advocates of the system feel that not having to worry about fees and expenses during contact with the defendant is a strong advantage. Certainly this removes some of the stress in the counseling process. Standard 13.7 of the Standards and Goals stressed that:

> The office of public defender should be a full-time occupation. State or local units of government should create regional public defenders serving more than one local unit of government if this is necessary to create a caseload of sufficient size

TABLE 10.1 RELATIONSHIP BETWEEN TYPE OF ATTORNEY AND METHOD OF DISPOSITION

TYPE OF ATTORNEY	DISPOSITION				
	DIVERTED	DISMISSED	SOT	TRIAL	GUILTY PLEA
Public Defender	5%	5%	31%	8%	51%
Court-appointed attorney	3	9	29	11	48
Private attorney	4	7	27	8	54

SOURCE: Reprinted by permission of the publisher, from *Prosecution of Adult Felony Defendants* by Peter W. Greenwood et al. (Lexington, Mass.: Lexington Books, D. C. Heath and Company, Copyright 1974, The Rand Corporation), p. 52.

to justify a full-time public defender. The public defender should be compensated at a rate not less than that of the presiding judge of the trial court of general jurisdiction.[5]

Critics of the system feel that the courthouse cameraderie between public prosecutors and public defenders is detrimental to the criminal justice system. Many defendants just do not understand the professional relationships between opposing advocates.

Drawbacks to the public defender systems include the massive infusion of clients into the system. Since only about 10 percent of all cases are tried in court today, the public defender soon develops an incentive to encourage negotiations and plea bargaining, preventing a massive infusion of cases and backlogs into the system. On extremely crowded court dockets the public defender, just like the prosecutor, has a very real vested interest in reducing caseloads. The public defender's only real method of reducing the workload is to seek prompt disposition of all cases.

Offender problems persist in "escalator justice" situations. When the attorney is publicly paid, the defendant often views the representative in a hostile, alien, or uncooperative manner. The perception of the public defender as just another bureaucrat is certainly counterproductive.

Roselt and Cressey have characterized the court system as consisting of a productive bureau of prosecution and a counterproductive bureau of defense, both of which are mediated by a bureau of adjudication.[6]

Legal aid services and other utility agencies provide specialized legal services under specific circumstances. The American Civil Liberties Union is just such a unit. This organization has helped Communists, revolutionaries, Ku Klux Klansmen, and black militants over the years in specific cases involving procedural case law.

Legal Aid services are often publicly and privately funded and usually provide general legal services similar in nature to those provided by public defenders.

Mixed counsel systems use both public and private defenders and attorneys. The mixed system attempts to incorporate the strongest points of both systems. The public defenders normally accept cases in urban or metropolitan areas, while rural jurisdictions in the same states may still depend on private defenders.

While the National Advisory Commission on Standards and Goals has recommended a publicly financed defense system as a first priority, it still recognized the need for a mixed system in Standard 13.5.

Method of Delivering Defense Services: Services of a full-time public defender organization, and a coordinated assigned counsel system involving substantial participation of the private bar, should be available in each jurisdiction to supply attorney services to indigents accused of crime. Cases should be divided between the public defender and assigned counsel in a manner that will encourage significant participation by the private bar in the criminal justice system.[7]

Any accused who can afford to employ private counsel is expected to do so. The role of the defense attorney is to manage a client's case in the best interest of the client. In this respect the defense attorney is in a difficult professional position. The client may see the attorney's duty as "getting me off," whether or not the defendant is guilty.

In the process the offender wants his attorney to act in a highly aggressive manner with which he can identify. The "fighting" criminal Lawyer is one who is appreciated by his clients, even when counsel's conduct may antagonize judge and jury and actually result in a more severe sentence. Offenders take literally the ethical admonition given to a lawyer to represent his client's interest "exclusive of all others." Lawyers interpret this to mean "exclusive of all others whose interests may be adverse to those of the client"; the offender insists that it means exclusive of all others — period.[8]

The Rand prosecution study made many significant points on defense interrelationships. It found that public defenders, court-appointed attorneys, and private attorneys had a significant disparity in their ability to gain release for their clients while the case was still pending.

> In a 1970 sample including 2617 theft defendants, it was found that over one-half of all indigent offenders — those defended by the Public Defender or court appointed attorneys, remain in jail during the disposition of their case. Of private attorneys' clients over two-thirds are released on bail and less than one-fifth spend the duration of their case in jail.[9]

The report's authors reflected that private attorneys' clients can ordinarily afford bail, while indigent offenders cannot.[10]

Table 10.2 indicates the pretrial custodial status correlated with type of attorney.

DEFENSE CONSULTATION

All private communications between attorney and client are considered to be privileged. These relationships are protected under the same law that covers conversations between physician and patient and between the priest and the penitent. This very strong point of substantive law means that a private attorney hearing a confidential statement cannot legally be compelled to divulge the nature of the communication. Confessions to even the most heinous offenses are protected.

After extended interviews the defense attorney may make several recommendations to a client. The defense attorney may suggest plea negotiation or extrajudicial compromise. The level of sentencing on a guilty plea would also be of significant importance to the defendant. Depending on the type of case, the defense attorney may recommend a trial by jury or a trial without jury. In some notorious cases the defense attorney may request a nonjury trial for a client, believing that justice may best be obtained in this manner.

A defendant's decision to testify in his or her own behalf is of major strategical importance. While the defendant is never re-

TABLE 10.2 PRETRIAL CUSTODIAL STATUS OF DEFENDANTS DURING TRIAL, BY TYPE OF ATTORNEY

TYPE OF ATTORNEY	CUSTODIAL STATUS		
	RELEASED ON BAIL	RELEASED ON OR	REMAINED IN JAIL
Public Defender	28.0%	18.1%	53.9%
Court-appointed attorney	31.2	16.4	52.4
Private attorney	67.2	14.0	18.8
All defendants	38.3	16.9	44.9

SOURCE: Reprinted by permission of the publisher, from *Prosecution of Adult Felony Defendants* by Peter W. Greenwood et al. (Lexington, Mass.: Lexington Books, D. C. Heath and Company, Copyright 1974, The Rand Corporation), p. 52.

quired to testify in his or her own behalf or contrary to his or her best interests, the defendant should do so in selected cases.

When it has been decided to try the case, defense tactics should be carefully considered. The usual criminal defense will incorporate questions of ability to knowingly commit the crime charged. Jurists usually subdivide this issue into intent and capacity. The primary defenses include questions pertaining to (1) sanity, (2) idiocy, (3) intoxication, (4) consent, (5) entrapment, (6) coercion, (7) justification, (8) double jeopardy, and (9) mistake of fact. Each of these involves mitigating circumstances that may have a significant role in the defense. Basically, legal concepts only require that a sane person of competent mentality knowingly, purposefully, and willingly committed an offense of his or her own volition. The concept does not allow entrapment, coercion, or force by third parties to intrude on the subject's willingness to commit the offense.

Intoxication and narcosis are not ordinarily recognized as defenses regardless of the degree to which the defendant's capacity to knowingly function was diminished. However, in many cases the jury may weigh intoxication and narcosis in considering all the facts. One good example might be the difference between first-degree murder (which requires the ability to plan or premeditate) and involuntary manslaughter. In both cases the defendant would be charged with a death, but the sobriety level may be incorporated as a significant feature of the defense.

Most jurisdictions permit a defense in which the accused person's intent was motivated by a variation in facts, even though a mistake of fact is technically not a defense by strict case law interpretation. An example of a mistake of fact might be a citizen causing the death of a person believed to have just committed a felony. The death occurred, but the citizen's intent could mitigate some of the consequences of the act.

Justification can be a defense in some cases. Normally this plea is made in those cases where the defendant claims to have used force that caused the death or injury of another in self-defense, in defense of other persons, or in defense of property. The law looks very carefully at a petition of this type because it must be reasonably demonstrated that serious injury or death was highly likely or inevitable. Case law mandates the "duty to retreat or avoid" any assault encounter.

Double jeopardy is prevented by the First Amendment. This prevents an offender from being tried for the same offense twice or by separate courts of jurisdiction. Double jeopardy is not involved when a violator appeals a conviction and is retried for the offense.

Probably the most significant skill a defense attorney can bring the actual trial process is skill in the voir dire process. The voir dire is the selection or empaneling of the jury. *Voir dire* simply means "to speak the truth," so when the judge orders the jury selection process, the prosecution and the defense ask questions that might affect the criminal justice process.

Ordinarily *challenges for cause* are made when a potential juror has information that might affect the ability to weigh the evidence without bias or prejudice. Friendship with either of the advocates, the defendant, or a witness is one strong example. A jury member may be dismissed for cause after virtually any admission that might seem to affect the ability to render an impartial decision based solely on the evidence.

Each advocate also has a specified number of *peremptory challenges*. The number of peremptory challenges will vary from state to state. Basically, this allows prosecution or defense to disqualify a prospective juror

CLARENCE SEWARD DARROW
1857–1938

Courtesy of Library of Congress. Photo by Herzog.

The Honorable Clarence Seward Darrow was perhaps the most respected defense attorney of all time. Practicing law from 1878 until his death in 1938, he accumulated an enviable bar record.

He was an outstanding debater and platform speaker. He wrote six legal texts and contributed to many other works on jurisprudence, as well as to works of social and economic importance.

Darrow was very active in the early development of unions in the United States. As early as 1895 he handled cases of national significance. After resigning from a position as the primary legal representative of the Chicago and Northwestern Railway, he defended Eugene V. Debs. Debs was the president of the American Railway Union at the time.

He handled many other criminal cases of significance during his lifetime. He represented the accused bomb murderer of Governor Frank Steunenburg of Idaho in 1907 and the accused bomber of the *Los Angeles Times* in 1911. He received tremendous notoriety for defending an alleged Communist in 1920 under an Illinois Sedition Act.

Perhaps his most celebrated case was the Scopes trial. Scopes was a Tennessee school teacher who taught Darwin's theory of evolution in the Tennessee school system.

Darrow was a colorful courtroom dramatist, widely known for his jury pleas and allusions. He has been widely publicized and memorialized in books, plays, and television dramas about his cases and his life.

without giving a reason. In rare cases the defense attorney may attack the entire venire on the grounds that it was in some way improperly selected.

The ability to subjectively determine which jurors may be most appropriate in deciding the case may be the most important defense art. In small American counties, the prosecutor and the defense attorneys may know almost all the residents of a county. In larger jurisdictions, the advocates may actually investigate the entire group subpoenaed for consideration at trial. Prosecutorial investigators and defense assistants may be well aware of lifestyles, salaries, neighborhoods, churches, and social contacts that might affect the selection process. The process is rarely this selective. However, in many notorious cases, usually involving the very wealthy, the jury selection process may become extremely sophisticated.

ROLE OF THE DEFENSE

The defense attorney should be the primary advocate or champion of the defense. The attorney should be sure to prepare the case in such a way that every legal and ethical procedure is accomplished for the client. It is the defense attorney's responsibility to counsel the defendant and to give the most appropriate advice in plea bargaining and case manipulation.

While American law allows defendants to represent themselves, Standard 13.1 of Standards and Goals concluded that:

> Defendants should be discouraged from conducting their own defense in criminal prosecutions. No defendant should be permitted to defend himself if there is a basis for believing that:
>
> 1. The defendant will not be able to deal effectively with the legal or factual issues likely to be raised;
> 2. The defendant's self-representation is likely to impede the reasonably expeditious processing of the case; or
> 3. The defendant's conduct is likely to be disruptive of the trial process. [12]

There is a very obvious need for competent criminal defense. It can be clearly demonstrated that conviction rates fall by one-half when defendants acquire legal counsel. [13] Without this professional help, the defendant may not be able to fully appreciate the situation. The competent defense attorney can maximize a client's chances of avoiding confinement by negotiating bail or recognizance bond, delaying the trial, requesting a jury trial, refusing to waive any procedural formality, and using the full resources of the system through numerous requests and petitions prior to trial. During the intervening time the defense attorney may carefully analyze case weaknesses and prepare to use them at trial.

Even the mere delay of a "speedy" trial is in the interest of an accused, no matter how guilty he or she may be. In a venue already overburdened numerically, the defense attorney may, in fact, overburden the prosecutor.

The American Bar Association has said that:

> a defendant needs counsel not only to evaluate the risks and advantages of alternative courses of action, such as trial or plea, but also to provide a broad and comprehensive approach to his predicament which will take the most advantage of the protectors and benefits which the law affords him. [14]

ASSESSING CRIMINAL DEFENDERS

Abraham Blumberg[15] and Jack Ladensky[16] have studied the quality of the criminal defense function in selected areas of America. They have generally agreed that the type of attorney selected has a significant impact on the defense. Many attorneys who work with "white-collar law firms" are disdainful of criminal practice. Dealing with unhappy people in unhappy circumstances is more than many attorneys can bear. For many reasons, the "better class" of attorney often stays away from the criminal field entirely and holds those attorneys who continue to practice in the field in contempt.

> Published studies conclude that the minority group member, the ethnic, the individual educated in a part-time law school, the son of a laboring father, and the Jew or Catholic are likely to be engaged in individual practice and end up doing the "dirty work" of the bar; personal injury, divorce, criminal work, collections, title searching, etc." Further, since approximately ninety percent of those who appear in a criminal court are persons of the lower class, their limited resources will furnish them with the least qualified lawyers for their defense. [17]

While the adversary process is based on the presumption of innocence, it is the defense attorney's professional duty to maintain an ethical balance in all due process proceedings. The defense attorney's primary or ultimate goal is to professionally represent a client successfully. A successful defense would be an acquittal. The ordinary defense is a "freedom maintenance program" that postpones incarceration for as long as possible. Since 90 percent of all defendants plead guilty to some level of criminal offense, plea bargaining would certainly seem to be a very desirable skill in most cases.

DISCUSSION QUESTIONS

1. Briefly summarize the *Gideon* v. *Wainwright* case.
2. What defense system is most commonly used in American courts?
3. What is the strongest weakness of the appointive defense system?
4. What does the Rand Study indicate about defendants' expectations toward their legal council?
5. Describe the concept of "privileged communication."
6. What are the usual defenses in American courts?
7. What is a peremptory challenge?
8. Of all the skills appropriate to the defense function, list the most important two and justify your answer.

NOTES

1. *Gideon* v. *Wainwright,* 372 U.S. 335 (1963).
2. *Mempa* v. *Rhay,* 389 U.S. 128 (1967).
3. *Douglas* v. *California,* 9 L.Ed. 2d 811 (1963).
4. Peter W. Greenwood, Sorrel Wildhorn, Eugene C. Poggio, Michael J. Strumwasser, and Peter De Leon, *Prosecution of Adult Felony Defendants* (Lexington, Mass.: D. C. Heath and Company, 1976), p. 53.
5. *Prosecution of Adult Felony Defendants,* p. 53.
6. Arthur Roselt and Donald R. Cressey, *Justice by Consent: Plea Bargains in the American Courthouse* (Philadelphia: Lippincott, 1976), pp. 122–123.
7. President's Commission on Law Enforcement and the Administration of Justice, *Task Force Report: The Courts* (Washington, D.C.: Government Printing Office, 1967), p. 263.
8. Hazel B. Kerper, *Introduction to the Criminal Justice System* (St. Paul, Minn.: West Publishing, 1972), p. 442.
9. *Prosecution of Adult Felony Defendants,* p. 52.
10. *Prosecution of Adult Felony Defendants,* p. 52.
11. *American Law Review* 1158.
12. *Task Force Report: The Courts,* p. 254.
13. Lewis R. Katz, "Municipal Courts — Another Urban Ill," *Case Western Reserve Law Review,* 20 (1968), 87.
14. American Bar Association, *The Administration of Justice: ABA Standards* (Chicago: American Bar Association, 1974), p. 112.
15. Abraham Blumberg, *Criminal Justice* (Chicago: Quadrangle Books, 1967), p. 110.
16. Jack Ladensky, "The Impact of Social Backgrounds of Lawyers on Law Practice and the Law," *Journal of Legal Education,* 16 (1965), 128.
17. Blumberg, *Criminal Justice,* p. 103.

CHAPTER ELEVEN

CONTEMPORARY ISSUES IN ADVOCACY

WORKING WITH THE
POLICE

MINIMIZING
DISCRETION

DECIDING THE
CHARGE

SUGGESTING
INFORMAL
ALTERNATIVES TO
PROSECUTION

IMPROVING THE
OFFICE OF THE
PROSECUTOR

EXAMINING THE ROLE
OF THE GRAND JURY

APPOINTING A PUBLIC
DEFENDER

CONTROLLING THE
POWER OF THE
ADVOCATES

Purpose: To provide insight into the major problem areas of the adversary process, contemporary issues are enumerated and discussed.

MOST CONTEMPORARY ISSUES in the advocacy function involve decisions at the outset of a case: the use of discretion about going to trial and the question of time relate to prompt prosecution. Prosecutors must, and do make every effort to maintain their offices at a high level of efficiency and to use wisely the discretion allowed by law.

> A society that holds, as we do, the belief in law cannot regard with unconcern the fact that prosecuting agencies can exercise so large an influence on dispositions that involve the penal sanction, without reference to any norms but those that they may create for themselves. Whatever one would hold as to the need for discretion of this order in a proper system or exercise, it is quite clear that its existence cannot be accepted as a substitute for sufficient law. Indeed, one of the major consequences of the state of penal law today is that administration has so largely come to dominate the field without effective guidance from the law. This is to say that to a large degree we have, in this important sense, abandoned law and this within an area where our fundamental teaching calls most strongly for its vigorous supremacy.[1]

WORKING WITH THE POLICE

Although it is the police, by making specific arrests, who usually make the initial decision that leads to prosecution, it is the prosecutor who oversees the police in this role and makes the ultimate decision to continue a case in the criminal justice process. While the police must in most instances make a prompt decision to arrest, the prosecutor's decision to charge may come after months of haggling. There seem to be no universal norms for these decisions. Quite often, compassion for a first or youthful offender or a belief that the consequences of a law are much too harsh can influence a prosecutor's decision.

Sometimes the police come to the prosecutor and ask that charges against a person arrested by a member of their department be dropped, perhaps for political reasons, reasons of influence, or because the arrested individual is an informant. Occasionally the reason is a technical or judgmental error made by the arresting officer that will inevitably embarrass the department. In some jurisdictions the prosecutor has such a poor relationship with the local police that he or she would refuse such a request in almost all circumstances. In other situations the prosecutor will generally endorse the decision of the police in matters pertaining to informants.

At times the prosecutor is highly suspicious, as is proper, when an offender confesses to a heinous offense or to multiple offenses. Experienced prosecutors know of the mentally ill person who confesses to someone else's crime. Unless great care is taken in all investigations, the overzealous prosecutor may inadvertently misdirect the process of justice.

News articles sometimes report situations in which young offenders "clear" several hundred burglaries for a police department, making the police investigator and the department look good. However, a meticulous background investigation should be made to make sure that the subject in fact committed each particular offense. In crimes against property, every effort should be made to recover as much of the property as possible so that the "fruits of the crime" may be admitted along with other evidence.

Although some prosecutors want more interaction with the police than they now have, others want a clear-cut separation of

band in jail and possibly causing the children to be added to the welfare roles. In family and neighborhood assaults, complainants often later refuse to charge or are persuaded by the prosecutor to forgive and forget.

In cases of statutory rape, unlawful sexual intercourse with a female minor, in which the victim is well known to the defendant, a prosecutor often counsels marriage when the victim is pregnant. Naturally, the prosecutor does not counsel marriage when a forceful rape has occurred or when the victim has not allowed intercourse with the defendant in the past. In a situation involving two high school students and their parents, a prosecutor may counsel marriage instead of prosecution. If the girl does not want to marry, the prosecutor may choose not to prosecute even though the girl's testimony would probably convict the boy of statutory rape. The girl's parents may demand prosecution even if she wants to marry. If the prosecutor chooses to initiate the criminal process, the boy may be convicted and have to spend time in a state correctional facility. In the meantime, if the girl does not have an abortion, she will have an illegitimate child, and her family or society (through subsistence payments) will be charged with her care and the care of her child. Although there are arguments of substance indicating that such a marriage would have little chance of success and should not take place, the prosecutor, whenever possible, prefers the alternatives to criminal prosecution.

IMPROVING THE OFFICE
OF THE PROSECUTOR

The National Advisory Commission on Criminal Justice Standards and Goals (1973) gave a very high priority to improving the prosecution function in order to improve the criminal justice system. Particular mention was made of improving the quality of the personnel so that each criminal case can be more efficiently and effectively handled.[2] Improving the prosecution function will require significant changes in the entire structure of society, not just in the criminal justice system.

Members of the legal community, as well as the general public, feel a growing concern over the functioning of our criminal justice system. Some of this concern has been created by reports from special study groups and the news media, depicting deplorable conditions and practices in many of our courts and correctional institutions. Some has resulted from unresolved conflict between the deterrence, punishment, and rehabilitation functions of the system. And some has come from distressing statistics showing the widespread failure of criminal justice agencies to significantly reduce crime. The pattern perceived is that most offenders are not arrested, most arrestees are never prosecuted, most convictions are accomplished by accepting guilty pleas to lesser offenses, and most defendants who are sentenced to correctional institutions return to criminal behavior soon after they are released.[3]

STATUS AND PAY

It is evident that society and attorneys themselves do not put career-oriented prosecutors or public defenders on the same status level as attorneys who specialize in torts, tax matters, or international law, even though our entire system of government depends on public respect for law and law enforcement. Because of social attitudes and role concepts, very few of the "best" young attorneys are attracted to the field.

The personnel policies, size, and organization of many prosecutor's offices do not promote an effective response to the complex demands of the criminal justice system. The majority of the Nation's 2,700 prosecutors serve in small offices with one or two assistants. Frequently, the prosecutor and his assistants are part-time officials who also engage in outside law practices. Although the salary level of prosecutors and their assistants has been rising, it remains much lower than the earnings of lawyers of similar experience in private practice.[4]

Not only attitudes must change. Prosecutors and other professionals involved in the government process should be offered reasonable economic rewards. If they are not, many competent people may continue to be attracted to other careers despite the need for them in government service. The National Advisory Commission on Criminal Justice Standards and Goals (1973) recommended that the chief prosecutor of a locality have the same basic salary level as the chief judge of the highest trial court of the local criminal justice system. This research council reasoned that because both positions required autonomy and the exercise of broad discretion in the workings of the office, the compensation for these offices should have the same base.[5] The National Advisory Commission on Criminal Justice Standards and Goals (1973) also recommended that all full-time prosecutors be paid out of state funds.[6]

In referring to the salaries of public defenders, the National Commission recommended that the public defender be compensated at a rate not less than that of the presiding judge of the trial court of general jurisdiction.[7] It was also felt that salaries for public defender staff attorneys should be competitive with those of attorneys in local private law firms.[8]

Assistant prosecutors could have their sta-tus improved if their position were protected through civil service or some other form of merit system.

> The position of assistant prosecutor should be a full time occupation, and assistant prosecutors should be prohibited from engaging in outside law practices. The starting salaries for assistant prosecutors should be no less than those paid by private firms in the jurisdiction, and the prosecutor should have the authority to increase periodically the salaries for assistant prosecutors to a level that will encourage the retention of able and experienced prosecutors, subject to approval of the legislature, city, or county council as appropriate. For the first five years of service, salaries of assistant prosecutors should be comparable to those of attorney associates in local private law firms.[9]

ADVOCACY TRAINING

Law schools do not adequately prepare their graduates for positions as prosecutors and defense attorneys. The belief that any licensed attorney is capable of handling the duties of these offices is not true. The criminal justice process and criminal law are unique and require specialized skills and knowledge. The few criminal law courses that a law student may take are, in most cases, inadequate training for the administrative and law enforcement functions of the prosecutor's or defender's office. The National Advisory Commission on Criminal Justice Standards and Goals (1973) has recommended the following for prosecutors and defenders:

> Education programs should be utilized to assure that prosecutors and their assistants have the highest possible professional competence. All newly appointed or elected prosecutors should attend prosecutor's training courses prior to taking office, and in-house training programs for

new assistant prosecutors should be available in all metropolitan prosecution offices. All prosecutors and assistants should attend a formal prosecutors' training course each year, in addition to the regular in-house training.[10]

The training of public defenders and assigned-counsel panel members should be systematic and comprehensive. Defenders should receive training at least equal to that received by the prosecutor and the judge. An intensive entry-level training program should be established at state and national levels to assure that before they represent the indigent accused, all attorneys have the basic defense skills necessary to represent them effectively.[11]

EXAMINING THE ROLE OF THE GRAND JURY

The grand jury system originated in England in the twelfth century as a buffer between state and citizen. Its duties were to oversee the prosecutor, evaluate the cases that the prosecutor brought before it, and act as an independent investigative body. Over the centuries, however, the grand jury has become a mere rubber stamp of the prosecutor's indictment. In most cities it indicts in 80 percent or more of the cases brought before it. In addition, when a grand jury launches an independent investigation today, it sometimes turns into a witch hunt. As a result, several authorities have recommended the abolition of the grand jury system.[12] The National Advisory Commission on Criminal Justice Standards and Goals (1973) has recommended that the grand jury not be required in criminal prosecution, but that the system remain available for investigation and exceptional cases.[13]

APPOINTING A PUBLIC DEFENDER

At trial the prosecutor's adversary is frequently a public defender, a salaried government employee who provides free legal service to individuals too poor to pay, as many involved in criminal cases are. By law, if the defendant cannot afford counsel, then the court will appoint an attorney if the defendant so desires. A court-appointed lawyer usually has a private practice and generally receives a standard fee. Landmark decisions such as *Gideon* v. *Wainwright* [372 U.S. 335 (1963)] require that all felony offenders have access to court-appointed counsel if they do not have sufficient funds to hire an attorney. A 1972 case, *Argersinger* v. *Hamlin* [407 U.S. 25 (1972)], held that *Gideon* also applies to misdemeanors and that no sentence involving loss of liberty can be imposed when there has been a denial of counsel. In traffic cases and those minor offenses not involving deprivation of liberty, the state usually is not required to provide counsel.

The method of providing counsel varies from state to state. Many states have systems in which the judge appoints counsel from a list of members of the local bar association. Some areas provide compensation, while others simply require this service as a civil responsibility. Several states have created a public defender system. In such a system, the public attorney or public defender is paid a salary from tax revenues and generally has no other income.

At the present time many of the weaknesses evident in the prosecution system are also evident in the public defender system. Many of these men and women are part-time public servants rather than fully employed professionals. Their dual roles quite often cause stress within their own practice, and the offender receives the short end of the bargain. The financial rewards of public defense are not nearly so great as those of a normal successful private law practice. A good salary for those in the office of the public defender, professional employment standards, and a satisfactory workload could eliminate many impediments to the criminal justice system.

CONTROLLING THE POWER OF THE ADVOCATES

The strengths of the prosecution system in America are also its weaknesses, for while prosecutors may make independent value judgments in the interest of the individual defendant or of society, other influences are always present that may lead them to make the prosecutional decision on the basis of their own self-interest. In a high-crime-rate jurisdiction or in cases involving gambling syndication or other so-called victimless criminal activity, prosecutors can become very affluent people in a short time if they choose to accept the available opportunities.

There are both indirect and direct controls over the prosecutor's use or abuse of discretion. Direct controls are those that can force the reversal of a decision to charge. A writ of *mandamus* (a court order to stop a specified practice) to compel prosecution is one form of direct control. At times and in some states, direct control may be taken by the attorney general of the state, the trial judge, or a privately employed attorney directing the prosecution on behalf of the individual victim. Indirect control of a prosecutor persistently unwilling to enforce the law usually takes the form of removal from office through the political process.

Politics may lead to certain ambiguous relationships between the prosecutor or defense attorney and his or her constituents.

Perhaps some of the personnel involved in the criminal justice system should be elected as independent rather than as party members. However, the individual politician is still obligated to the electorate, so separation from political parties may have little or no effect.

Because many local prosecutors and public defense organizations are remote from state offices and administrations, few consistent statewide policies are applied, and the differences among the several states are even greater. Many authorities suggest that a state regional office, whether of the state attorney general, a prosecutors' council, or an assessor, should have final coordinating authority over police implementation. Of course, constitutional or legislative enactments would be necessary before any of these alternative solutions could be inaugurated.

The power to investigate and the power over confidential information that comes to the district attorney from the police and other sources are easily abused and represent a constant threat to the rights of the individual. Prosecutors are also free to manipulate charges as they see fit, insofar as judicial and public pressure is concerned. In this way they can maintain control over the decision-making processes of the police. When this power is used as it was statutorily intended, it will enhance the probability of justice; if it is used otherwise, it may leave the door open for abuse and corruption.

It is not suggested that prosecuting attorneys become rubber stamps, constantly endorsing the recommendations of a police unit. The prosecutor's office is not and should not be automatically cooperative, for our system of criminal justice is founded on the principle of a balance as well as a separation of powers. To amalgamate any two or more parts may cause the system to function unjustly.

The Public Defender (too), by the very necessity of protecting those charged with crime is likely to become unpopular in exact proportion to his diligence in performing his duties because the defense of the indigent accused is rarely likely to be popular.[14]

The attempt to limit the influence of the public defender is a very real one, encompassing the entire defense role, no matter whether it is publicly or privately funded. Professionals necessarily blend and merge the necessity of client loyalty with their dedication and responsibility to their profession.

The members of each part of the system have to exercise considerable amounts of discretion and judgment and do so efficiently. Each subsystem is a small but vital unit of the whole, and only when each subsystem works correctly and well can our system of justice function as intended. To accomplish the desired end, each section of the criminal justice system must instill respect for the law and must maintain the highest standards. It is to this end that the prosecutor and defense must proceed. Advocacy demands professionalism, impartiality, fair play, and justice.

DISCUSSION QUESTIONS

1. Should we keep the grand jury for our contemporary justice system? Why or why not?
2. Discuss the alternatives of prosecutorial review.
3. Should we limit the prosecutor's discretionary powers? If so, to what extent? If not, why?
4. What alternatives to prosecution are available today?
5. What system improvements should be made for prosecutors and defense attorneys?
6. In what ways could prosecution be made more effective?
7. Discuss the prosecutor's power to influence police discretion. Is this power justified either philosophically or in actuality? Justify your answer.
8. Examine advocacy training and itemize its weaknesses.

NOTES

1. Herbert Wechsler, "Challenge of a Model Code," *Harvard Law Review,* 65 (1952), 1102.
2. National Advisory Commission on Criminal Justice Standards and Goals, *Courts* (Washington, D.C.: Government Printing Office, 1973), chaps. 1, 2, 3, 12, and 15.3.
3. Peter W. Greenwood, Sorrel Wildhorn, Eugene C. Poggio, Michael J. Strumwasser, and Peter De Leon, *Prosecution of Adult Felony Defendants* (Lexington, Mass.: D. C. Heath and Company, 1976), p. 1.
4. *Courts,* p. 227.
5. *Courts,* p. 229.
6. *Courts,* p. 230.
7. *Courts,* p. 267.
8. *Courts,* p. 275.
9. American Bar Association, *Project on Standards for Criminal Justice: Standards Relating to the Prosecution Function* (Washington, D.C.: American Bar Association, 1970), Standard 3.1(B).
10. *Courts,* p. 239.
11. *Courts,* p. 284.

12. *Courts,* pp. 74–76.
13. *Courts,* p. 74.
14. *Courts,* p. 271.

PART THREE ANNOTATED BIBLIOGRAPHY

American Bar Association. *The Prosecution and the Defense Function: A Report Prepared by the Advisory Committee on the Prosecution and Defense Functions of the Project on Standards of Criminal Justice.* New York: Institute of Judicial Administration, 1971.
Contemporary research worth careful study. The manuscript is a guide manual and should serve as a standard bearer for the prosecutor in contemporary America. This expository manual was a direct result of research directed to prosecutors throughout the United States. It is replete with "philosophy of prosecution" materials and deserves consideration.

Greenwood, Peter W., Sorrel Wildhorn, Eugene C. Poggio, Michael J. Strumwasser, and Peter De Leon. *Prosecution of Adult Felony Defendants.* Lexington, Mass.: D. C. Heath and Company, 1976.
A comprehensive survey of prosecution in central California. The study was funded by the National Institute of Law Enforcement and Criminal Justice. The text is unique although controversial. Many of the expository statistics are prima facie, however, insofar as the research populations are concerned. The text should be considered a must for those who want depth and breadth in their study of prosecution and defense methods.

Finkelstein, Marvin M., Ellyn Weiso, and Stuart Cohen. *Prosecution in the Juvenile Courts: Guidelines for the Future.* Washington: Government Printing Office, 1973.
This document will help the researcher understand juvenile justice prosecutions. The guidelines delineate the direction of trends and philosophies in the juvenile justice field.

Grossman, Brian A. *The Prosecutor.* Toronto: University of Toronto Press, 1967.
Written by a former prosecutor, this text deals with the sociology of the prosecution function. It indicates the political, social, and monetary pressures, along with giving a scholarly analysis of the use and abuse of the negotiated plea.

Miller, Frank E. *Prosecution.* Boston: Little, Brown and Company, 1969.
A most persuasive text on the positive and negative effects of plea negotiation and the philosophy of the American prosecution format currently in use.

National Association of Attorneys General, Committee on the Office of Attorney General. *The Office of Attorney General,* 1971.
The most comprehensive contemporary report on the present status of state attorneys general, district attorneys, and county or city prosecutors. While much of the text is purely descriptive, it is of the utmost importance in any survey of the prosecution system.

National District Attorneys Association. *National Prosecution Standards.* Chicago: National District Attorneys Association, 1977.
This text is the National District Attorneys Association's response to an in-depth challenge of standards and goals. This organization did not formally participate as a group in the Standards and Goals studies of 1973. This extensive document presents the perspective of professional prosecutors.

National District Attorneys Association, *The Prosecutors Deskbook.* 2nd ed. Chicago: National District Attorneys Association, 1977.
The text contains an edited compilation of documents in most of the areas of law a prosecutor is likely to come in contact with. It also includes articles on policy formulation, management practices, and unique prosecutorial problems. The book is encyclopedic but totally appropriate and practically oriented.

PART FOUR

COURTS

CHAPTER TWELVE

DEVELOPMENTAL HISTORY OF COURTS

CHRONOLOGY OF
DEVELOPMENT
COURT LAG, REFORM

Purpose: To trace the development from the courts of antiquity to the present-day courts of the United States.

A USEFUL HISTORY OF courts cannot be just a collection of names and dates. It must be a narrative of changes that have transformed the courts into what they are today. It must be an account of how the courts have developed. And it should point toward the directions of their future development. Some basic definitions are needed, however, before the history can be told. Then the history of the courts can be put into the larger framework of sociology so that the deeper significance of the courts and their development can be appreciated.

Although *court* is a commonly understood word, it is used in several ways: A court may be a person — the judge — or persons — the entire judicial assembly. A court may be a building or room in which cases are heard and determined. A court may be a session of a judicial assembly. A court may be a regular organization that does not have to be in session in order to be a court.

The judicial business of a criminal court is essentially to determine whether an accused is guilty and, if so, to pass sentence. Courts are said to enforce the law and are therefore a necessary complement of the law. Indeed, they are sometimes included in the definition of law. An important aspect of courts is that they are a formal, nonviolent means of settling disputes.

A *tribunal* may be a place where judges sit or a court, or it may have a meaning broader than court, as in, for example, "the tribunal of public opinion."

A *court system* involves a group or groups of interrelated courts. These groupings are based on the kinds of offenses with which the courts deal (from least serious to the more serious) and by the stage of a case that they handle (for example, the initial appearance before a *justice of peace court,* a trial before a *trial court,* an appeal of a conviction before an *appellate court*). These interrelationships are defined by statutory law. Each state has its own statutes and is regarded as having its own separate court system. There is enough distinction between the states and the federal government to warrant the concept of a dual court system in the United States: the states have one court system, the federal government has another. The *court system of the United States* is a phrase used to distinguish United States courts from the courts of another nation.

A *judge* is the official who presides over a court, and may be called a *justice* in some kinds of courts. A *magistrate* is a judge who handles judicial matters other than jury trials or appeals. A magistrate may be limited by law to certain duties or may be a fully empowered judge who is performing the duties of a magistrate in a given instance.

CHRONOLOGY OF DEVELOPMENT

A chronological history of the courts' development has its beginning in the forgotten past and ends with a picture of the courts as they are today.

ORIGIN OF COURTS

To appreciate the origins of courts, one must view the court concept in relation to society. The sociological perspective is closely allied to the historical perspective, as is evident in any elaboration of the definitions of courts. One reason this nation has not been wracked by unrelenting conflicts at the interpersonal level is that the courts provide a way to contain or control conflicts by their acceptance as formal or official means for the settlement of disputes. Social control is necessary if social order is to be maintained.

Informal means of social control exist in families and groups of families (clans, tribes); these are based on the strong desire of members to stay in good standing with their fellows. These kinds of groups of people are called *primary groups*. You and your friends form a primary group. In very large primary groups or in cultures in which primary groups continue to predominate — even though the primary group ties may be weakened by the existence of specialized secondary groups (hunters, craftsmen, farmers, merchants, and so on) — elders or other rulers may listen to disputes and arbitrarily decide how they are to be resolved. These tribunals may become fairly involved. They are sometimes referred to as courts governed by customs.

With the advent of codes of law, genuine courts of law came into being. All cultures too complex and too large for the informal means of social control exercised by primary groups have doubtless evolved a code of law and a corresponding court system. The culture's standards or norms can then be partially maintained by impersonal and formal force. The first courts, therefore, may predate recorded history. The dividing line between courts of custom and true courts is not clear-cut in the history of all cultures.

Courts are units of government or, more accurately, units of a political community, such as the United States. The significance of this is that the courts are supported by the overwhelming physical and moral force that rests in the political community. This is the fundamental source of the courts' social power, although the power that judges wield in a community is a product of many other factors as well.

It should be clear that the courts are part of society. They are not merely instruments of law, as they have sometimes been described. It has been said that a society's degree of civilization can be gauged by the quality of justice its courts mete out. The wavering development of the quality of courtroom justice can be traced through history.

COURTS FROM ANTIQUITY THROUGH THE MIDDLE AGES

From a rudimentary form of court, ancient Greece developed a tribunal in which there might be hundreds of "judges" or "jurors." In 300 B.C. the Jewish nation had a supreme council called the Great Sanhedrin, composed of seventy-one members and having a chief justice, that interpreted Hebrew law and enacted decrees of religious observance. Today, Israel's courts are still closely tied to religion. Rome also began with a rudimentary form of court, but by 300 B.C. it had developed the mature form of Roman law (a comprehensive law code) and a correspondingly sophisticated court system.

In the early part of the Middle Ages, ancient codes of law continued to have some effect. The idea of a law above people, even above sovereigns, continued to lurk in the minds of a few Europeans. Nonetheless the kings and nobles, or their designates, held court and made binding decisions that suited their whims. The word *court* comes from this time. Originally, *court* meant a kind of enclosure or partial enclosure, usually without a roof, and it retains this meaning in the lexicon of the architect.

Along with the ancient codes and the practices of the nobility, religion played a role in European criminal justice. The Roman Catholic Church was a growing force in court activity. It provided priests who officiated at many criminal trials, and it provided, too, a legal framework for judicial activity.

By contemporary standards these early medieval courts were lacking in sensitive, systematic law. They were riddled with superstition, and their processes and sentences produced what would today be called atrocities. Criminal trials were frequently by ordeal, with the Church officiating. Some of the ordeals probably worked as primitive lie detectors; for example, bread held in the mouth of a guilty person would remain dry because one physical result of fear is the cessation of salivation. Many of the ordeals, however, would have required miraculous intervention to prove innocence; for example, an accused person might be required to walk into fire, with the idea that an innocent person would remain unscathed. If people died without confessing, they might be exonerated in memory and a small compensation allotted the family. People were held totally responsible for their actions, and even minor theft might be punishable by death. From time to time, children and animals were likewise held to be totally responsible, and a small child or a pig could be hanged for a minor offense.

These courts were neither in form or in philosophy like the courts of today. They were governed completely by custom, whereas today's courts of law pay only token homage to custom. Nevertheless, they were the forerunners of the modern courts. As time passed, the body of legal practitioners not directly connected with the king and the nobles would grow, and with it a highly complicated body of legal practices would develop.

DEVELOPMENT OF MODERN COURTS

England and continental Europe gradually evolved different court and legal systems, and these two systems had a profound influence on courts virtually the world over.

England The courts of the United States can be traced to the courts of England, which did not begin to come into their own until the eleventh century. The centuries of Roman rule apparently had little influence on England's courts. The Norse invaders in the succeeding six centuries did not alter the system of custom-governed law and local magistrates. It was the Norman conquerors of the eleventh century who began to gather the various laws and the informal and private tribunals into a central system. Henry II (1154–1189), often called the Father of Common Law, declared that no man could be denied a freehold (inheritable land) without a royal writ (written order bearing the king's signature). Centralized control of the courts became inevitable. The power of feudal courts, both Anglo-Saxon and Norman, lessened. Records were kept, and consequently the concept of precedent came to be firmly established.

By 1178 the King's Court could no longer handle cases brought to it. Five judges were appointed, and circuits were established for some of them. The term *circuit court* originally meant that a judge traveled from town to town, holding court in each, until he had circled back to his headquarters. *Circuit* is Latin for "circle."

In England, in June of 1215, King John's nobles forced him to sign Magna Charta. This charter was reactionary in that it was a blow to the development of the courts into a unified system. Its intent was to return the power of the nobles to where it had been before the arrival of the Norman kings, and in time Magna Charta came to mark the subordination of the king to law and thereby to the people. By the fourteenth century, however, the English courts had stabilized, and the unification of the British courts continued until this century.

In 1215, there occurred another major event: at the Fourth Lateran Council, Pope Innocent III forbade the clergy to officiate at trials. As a result, laymen, already important, became still more important in England's judicial process. One body of laymen used their own knowledge of the investigations of the royal coroner to level formal accusations against suspects, and over time this body became the grand jury. A second body of laymen was charged with deciding whether the accusation was true, and this body became the petit jury.

During the fourteenth century, courts that handled only criminal cases came into existence. These courts were run by local landowners. In another development, people who claimed they had not received justice from a court could appeal from the king or his chief administrative officer, the chancellor, for help; between the fourteenth and the seventeenth centuries, this process of appeals evolved into an appeals court. This court also established the branch of law known as *equity,* which means to fairly settle conflicts that are not covered by other law. Other courts answered other needs, notably the admiralty courts, which dealt with ships and sailors, and the church courts, which continued to govern matrimonial cases and the estates of the deceased. Vestiges of these and other courts remain in the courts of the United States, including the Supreme Court.

For the most part, the courts made their own law and attempted to maintain consistency by keeping new decisions in close agreement with decisions made in the past in similar cases. These legal processes, identified as common law, case law, or the doctrine of *stare decisis,* were to become the distinguishing characteristics of Anglo-American law and courts. Knowledgeable lawyers tried to win cases for their clients through the use of *writs.* These lawyers were very sensitive to court procedure; although they were not alarmed by a public hanging, if the procedure leading to the hanging was not proper as they understood it, they were vociferous in their complaints. The confrontation between the courts with their "proper methods" and the king with his royal whims could not be altogether prevented. This conflict led to the development of the concept of *due process of law.*

Lord Chief Justice Edwin A. Coke probably did more than any other single person to establish due process. When, early in the seventeenth century, he informed his monarch, King James I, that the law was above any king, James had Coke supplanted by Sir Francis Bacon. In fact, during the Tudor and Stuart dynasties there were other setbacks to the development of due process of law. For example, a maverick court controlled by the king called the Star Chamber that ostensibly dealt with traitors was much feared. It was sometimes convened in the middle of the night, and might execute individuals far from their homes and neighborhoods, without their friends' and relatives' knowledge of their whereabouts. In the end, though, the traditions of the courts as well as their autonomy prevailed.

Europe In continental Europe the evolution of the courts followed different lines. Pope Innocent's ruling prevented clergy from officiating here too, and in addition the use of laymen declined. The governing bodies of the cities, the city councils, established an inquisitorial procedure in which the accused was questioned about the truth of the accusations prior to the trial. The inquisition may have been largely responsible for the maintenance of police state methods in which confessions were routinely obtained through torture. If the accused denied guilt at the formalistic trial, a witness who had been present at the confession was produced, and the case was closed. In the early sixteenth century, the demand for reform brought about change but no relief. The change burdened the courts with a heavy weight of procedure, rendered the trial nonpublic, and kept the same inquisitorial methods. Only with the revolutions that wracked Europe in the eighteenth and nineteenth centuries was modern continental law established. European courts do not make their own law through precedent-setting decisions, but they do retain the responsibility to question the defendant at length before trial.

Other Continents Curiously, Western civilization has been the chief repository for the concepts of individual liberty (or equal rights) and of law transcending the sovereign. In much of Africa and Asia, the courts were ruled by custom, and other means of social control were heavily relied upon, until colonialization brought courts modeled upon those of Britain and continental Europe. The Russian courts in the days of the czar were sophisticated and contributed to his downfall. Today, the communist countries claim a different development from that of Britain and the rest of Europe.

DEVELOPMENT OF COURTS IN THE UNITED STATES

The original thirteen colonies were British, and the court system that worked in England served in America. The populace was particularly familiar with the lower levels of the court system. With independence, however, there came a renunciation of things British and a common recognition of the legislature, rather than the courts, as the lawmaking body.

With the adoption of the Articles of Confederation in 1779, the Continental Congress established the Court of Appeals in Cases of Capture, the country's first official court. Both Congress and the new court tried cases, a total of 109 cases. On June 20, 1788, the Constitution was ratified, and state courts immediately became subordinate to the United States, although they continued to exercise a high degree of independence.

The sole constitutional basis for the Supreme Court is found in the brief clause popularly called the "judiciary clause," Article III of the Constitution. The clause was too brief, and an act of Congress was required to fill in the details necessary to establish a federal judiciary, the famous Judiciary Act of 1789. It formalized the Supreme Court by (1) defining its authority and limitations (jurisdiction) within the guidelines provided by the Constitution, (2) establishing the number of judges, and (3) establishing a system of "inferior" or "lower" federal courts. Many of the details of the original act have been modified by subsequent acts of Congress, but the Judiciary Act of 1789 has set a pattern that remains essentially unchanged. The Congress could have insisted that all cases be tried in the states' courts before going to the federal courts, as indeed it was urged to do. (Later, in Canada, Australia, and the German Empire, federal court systems were established to hear only cases that had already been tried in provincial courts.) Had Congress limited the federal courts in this way, it would have changed the essential pattern. It is clear that the legislative branch of government can take away what it has given and make other changes, but because the checks and balances of the Constitution, sometimes regarded as a myth, do have a force that is real, it is unlikely that Congress will ever abolish all "lower" federal courts. The Federalists and Antifederalists (States Rightists) in Congress fought and compromised from 1789 to 1911, at which time the Federalists won with the version of the lower federal courts that exists today.

In the 1800s the popular conception of the lawmaking body shifted from the Congress to the courts. The British model was firmly entrenched, the lower court system of England was already in effect, and it seemed inevitable that the British system would prevail. Other countries' systems did have some influence, however. Traces of the Dutch remain in New York's legal system and of the Spanish in the southwestern states. Louisiana, because of its French settlers, was pronouncedly affected by the legal system of continental Europe, and its courts are the only ones significantly different from the courts of other states. None of the varied peoples who have come to the United States since these early times have radically altered the model provided by the British.

OVERVIEW OF
CONTEMPORARY COURTS

The functions of the states' courts are very similar from state to state, but the structure of the courts differs widely. Because of gaps in statutory law, the courts occasionally rely on the old common law of England, though rarely in criminal cases. Indeed, the direction seems to be increasingly toward reliance on statutory law. Political science textbooks commonly consider only the federal system in any detail, thereby implying that the states have miniaturized replicas. The state systems may bear some resemblance to the federal system, but they are not closely patterned on it. Although the Supreme Court of the United States has long been the subject of intense attention, it is in the states' courts that nearly all criminal cases begin and end. Within the states the number of rural courts, like justice of the peace courts, has decreased and there has been a proportionally huge increase in municipal courts, such as magistrates courts and traffic courts.

Because of the diversity and autonomy of the courts, there has been no centralized record keeping in the past. With their antiquated methods, many courts have kept little statistical information or have so buried it in a crude filing system that it is inaccessible. There were no readily available data on the total number of judiciary personnel in the states at the level of local government as late as 1970. In October 1975, there were the equivalent of 124,712 employed full time in the states' judiciary, with 99,132 or 79 percent of these being employed by counties or cities![1] Add 10,082 (see Table 12.1) in federal judiciary, and the total figure is 134,794. This includes the relatively small number of judiciary employees who are judges. The rapid growth of the ratio of supportive personnel to judges is also suggested by Table 12.1.

The dual court system of the United States appears clear-cut: there is a federal system and a state system (composed of 50 state systems). The court systems of some metropolitan areas, however, are more extensive than the court systems of some states. It is estimated that there are more than one hundred systems of major size.[2] Some authorities use the term *metropolitan courts* to describe patterns of courts in urban areas where there may be several cities and towns and one or more counties.

How many criminal cases are tried in the courts of the United States each year? No one knows the actual number, although it is in the millions. Likewise, nationwide figures on the number of courts are not readily available, as existing lists do not include county and city courts of limited jurisdiction.

Each year the *American Law Journal* publishes an issue containing court statistics. The *U.S. Abstracts* and the *Book of the States,* found in most college libraries, also contain information on the courts in statistical form. The National Center for State Courts in Williamsburg, Virginia, also collects and publishes statistics on state courts. Table 12.2 gives a breakdown of the number of judges in the various courts in the state system. This illustration provides a feeling for the number and the different kinds of higher-level courts and the number of judges associated with them.

TABLE 12.1 PERSONNEL IN THE FEDERAL JUDICIARY

PERSONNEL	1977	1978
Judges:		
Circuit	87	95
District	373	381
Special courts	19	20
Territorial courts	3	3
Retired — resigned	181	179
Total	663	678
Circuit	87	95
Staff to circuit executives	11	15
Secretaries to judges	510	544
Secretary-law clerks to judges	1	—
Secretaries to retired judges	153	140
Court (staff) secretaries	56	62
Law clerks to judges	598	689
Law clerks to retired judges	148	160
Senior law clerks	11	11
Court (staff) law clerks	80	73
Total personnel for clerks' offices	2,788	2,917
Total	4,366	4,621
Members of probation staffs:		
Probation officers	1,632	1,673
Probation officer assistants	30	30
Pretrial services officers	86	91
Clerks	1,105	1,108
Total	2,853	2,902

COURT LAG, REFORM

The biggest problem area in today's courts is primarily developmental, although it is manifested in structural problems, administrative problems, and so on. The courts are not static; they are always changing. The courts of the United States form a vast system in which delicate, vital decisions that affect us all, directly or indirectly, are made continuously. It is a complicated system. The problem is that some of the complication is needless and that the pace of developmental change has been too slow.

RECOGNITION

This facet of development is given its character by sociology and by philosophy. Around the turn of the century sociology was becoming accepted as a new discipline using scientific methodology. Roscoe Pound, the dean of Harvard Law School, was an enthusiastic advocate of the application of sociology to law. In his extensive writings and speeches, he noted that law was taught and practiced as though it were a pure form of logic based on premises that had been established for all time.[3] In other words, like Latin, law was unchangeable, a

Table 12.1 *continued*

PERSONNEL	1977	1978
Members of bankruptcy staffs:		
Referees	228	232
Clerks	1,077	1,018
Total	1,305	1,250
United States magistrates	454	455
Staff to United States magistrates	298	325
Federal public defenders & assistants	124	136
Staff to federal public defenders	121	139
Court criers (including court crier-law clerks)	411	436
Court reporters	403	443
Court reporter — secretaries	1	1
Supporting personnel of the special courts	222	219
Miscellaneous personnel in the District of Columbia	24	20
Messengers	8	7
Librarians	48	48
Nurses	3	3
Interpreters	12	13
Temporary emergency Court of Appeals		35
Members of the staff of the Administrative Office	408	444
Members of the staff of the Federal Judicial Center	98	117
Members of the Judicial Panel on Multidistrict Litigation		11
Jury Commissioner's staff		4
Speedy Trial Planning Groups Reporters		2
Total	11,825	12,279

SOURCE: Administrative Offices of the U.S. Courts, *1978 Annual Report of the Director,* Washington, D.C., 1979, pp. 18–19.

dead language. Pound felt that the courts and the laws that had been established in the agrarian past had helped usher in the industrial age, but that in their old forms the courts and the laws were a hindrance to the functioning of modern society. He called the courts archaic and described the ways in which they were antiquated.

For a generation Pound had the company of great jurists, including Chief Justice Oliver Wendell Holmes, Justice Benjamin Cardozo, and Justice Louis Brandeis, all of whom shared the belief that legal justice should give way to social justice. The bench no longer reigns over the sociology of law. Although the courts were affected by this intellectual ferment, the judiciary has not embraced Pound's thinking or acted on his suggestions. On August 10, 1970, Chief Justice Warren Burger addressed the American Bar Association:

[Pound] said that the work of the courts in the twentieth century could not be carried on with the machinery of the nineteenth century. If you will read Pound's speech (to the ABA, 1906), you'll see at once that we did not heed his warning, and today, in the final third of this cen-

TABLE 12.2 JUDGES AND TERMS FOR APPELLATE COURTS AND MAJOR TRIAL COURTS

STATE OR OTHER JURISDICTION	APPELLATE COURTS						MAJOR TRIAL COURTS		
	COURT OF LAST RESORT	NO. OF JUDGES	TERM (IN YEARS)	INTERMEDIATE APPELLATE COURT	NO. OF JUDGES	TERM (IN YEARS)	COURTS	NO. OF JUDGES	TERM (IN YEARS)
Alabama	Supreme Court	9	6	Court of Criminal Appeals	5	6	Circuit courts	108	6
				Court of Civil Appeals	3	6			
Alaska	Supreme Court	5	10				Superior courts	20	6
Arizona	Supreme Court	5	6	Court of Appeals	12	6	Superior courts	73	4
Arkansas	Supreme Court	7	8				Chancery & probate courts	27	6
California	Supreme Court	7	12	Courts of Appeal	56	12	Circuit courts	29	4
Colorado	Supreme Court	7	10	Court of Appeals	10	8	Superior courts	542	6
Connecticut	Supreme Court	6[a]	8				District Court	99	6
Delaware	Supreme Court	3	12				Superior Court	112[a]	8
							Court of Chancery	3	12
Florida	Supreme Court	7	6	District courts of appeal	28	6	Superior Court	11	12
							Circuit courts	287	6
Georgia	Supreme Court	7	6	Court of Appeals	9	6	Superior courts	86	4–8
Hawaii	Supreme Court	5	10				Circuit courts	18	10
Idaho	Supreme Court	5	6				District courts	27	4
Illinois	Supreme Court	7	10	Appellate Court	34[b]	10	Circuit courts	650[c]	6[c]
Indiana	Supreme Court	5	10	Court of Appeals	9	10	Circuit courts	88	6
							Superior courts	80	6
							Criminal courts	4	4
Iowa	Supreme Court	9	8	Court of Appeals	5	6	District Court	299[d]	6[d]
Kansas	Supreme Court	7	6	Court of Appeals	7	4	District courts	209[e]	4
Kentucky	Supreme Court	7	8	Court of Appeals	14	8	Circuit courts	87	8
Louisiana	Supreme Court	7	10	Courts of appeals	32	10	District courts	143	6
Maine	Supreme Judicial Court	7	7				Superior Court	14	7
Maryland	Court of Appeals	7	10	Court of Special Appeals	13	10	Circuit courts of counties	68	15
							Courts of Supreme Bench of Baltimore City	22	15
Massachusetts	Supreme Judicial Court	7	To age 70	Appeals Court	6	To age 70	Superior Court	46	To age 70

Michigan	Supreme Court	7	8	Court of Appeals	18	6f	Circuit courts	147	6f
							Recorder's Court (Detroit)	23	6f
Minnesota	Supreme Court	9	6	…	…	…	District courts	72	6
Mississippi	Supreme Court	9	8	…	…	…	Chancery courts	36	4
							Circuit courts	30	4
Missouri	Supreme Court	7	12	Court of Appeals	24	12	Circuit courts	116	6
Montana	Supreme Court	5	8	…	…	…	District courts	29	6
Nebraska	Supreme Court	7	6	…	…	…	District courts	45	6
Nevada	Supreme Court	5	6	…	…	…	District courts	26	6g
New Hampshire	Supreme Court	5	To age 70	…	…	…	Superior Court	13	To age 70
New Jersey	Supreme Court	7	7h	Appellate division of Superior Court	22	7h	Superior Court	120	7h
							County courts	108	5
New Mexico	Supreme Court	5	8	Court of Appeals	5	8	District courts	40	6
New York	Court of Appeals	7	14i	Appellate divisions of Supreme Court	24k	5l	Supreme Court	257	14
North Carolina	Supreme Court	7	8	Court of Appeals	12	8	Superior Court	66	8
North Dakota	Supreme Court	5	10	…	…	…	District courts	19	6
Ohio	Supreme Court	7	6	Courts of appeals	44	6	Courts of common pleas	313	6m
Oklahoma	Supreme Court	9	6	Court of Appeals	6	6	District courts	189	4n
	Court of Criminal Appeals	3	6						
Oregon	Supreme Court	7	6	Court of Appeals	10	6	Circuit courts	75	6
Pennsylvania	Supreme Court	7	10	Superior Court	7	10	Courts of common pleas	285	10
				Commonwealth Court	7	10			
Rhode Island	Supreme Court	5	Life	…	…	…	Superior Court	17	Life
South Carolina	Supreme Court	5	10	…	…	…	Circuit Court	25	6
South Dakota	Supreme Court	5	8	…	…	…	Circuit courts	36	8
Tennessee	Supreme Court	5	8	Court of Appeals	9	8	Chancery courts	27	8
				Court of Criminal Appeals	9	8	Circuit courts	58	8
							Criminal courts	25	8
							Law-equity courts	4	8
Texas	Supreme Court	9	6	Court of Civil Appeals	42	6	District courts	305	4
	Court of Criminal Appeals	5	6						
Utah	Supreme Court	5	10	…	…	…	District courts	24	6

Table continued on next page

Table 12.2 *continued*

| STATE OR OTHER JURISDICTION | APPELLATE COURTS | | | | | | MAJOR TRIAL COURTS | | |
	COURT OF LAST RESORT	NO. OF JUDGES	TERM (IN YEARS)	INTERMEDIATE APPELLATE COURT	NO. OF JUDGES	TERM (IN YEARS)	COURTS	NO. OF JUDGES	TERM (IN YEARS)
Vermont	Supreme Court	5	6	...	...	...	Superior courts	8	6°
							District courts	11	6
Virginia	Supreme Court	7	12	...	...	...	Circuit courts	107	8
Washington	Supreme Court	9	6	Court of Appeals	16	6	Superior courts	111	4
West Virginia	Supreme Court of Appeals	5	12	...	...	...	Circuit courts	58	8
Wisconsin	Supreme Court	7	10	...	...	...	Circuit courts	53	6
							County courts	128	6
Wyoming	Supreme Court	5	8	...	...	...	District courts	15	6
District of Columbia	Court of Appeals	9	15	...	...	...	Superior Court	44	15
American Samoa	High Court: Appellate	8ᵖ	q	...	...	...	High Court: Trial	8ᵖ	q
Guamʳ	Supreme Court	3	5	...	...	...	Superior Court	5	5
Puerto Rico	Supreme Court	8	To age 70	...	...	...	Superior Court	89	12

ᵃ Does not include senior judges, i.e., judges between the ages of 65 and 70 who are eligible for assignment to judicial duties but who have retired from full-time service as a judge.

ᵇ Elective judgeships. Retired and sitting circuit judges are assigned full time to appellate court as needed.

ᶜ Composed of circuit and associate judges who have full jurisdiction of circuit court. Associate judges serve 4 years.

ᵈ A unified system with 92 district court judges who possess full jurisdiction of the court. An additional 16 district associate judges, 23 full-time judicial magistrates, and 299 part-time judicial magistrates have limited jurisdiction. District associate judges and full-time judicial magistrates serve 4 years; part-time magistrates, 2 years.

ᵉ Sixty-nine district judges, 62 associate district judges, and 78 district magistrate judges.

ᶠ Terms for new judgeships are for 10, 8, or 6 years; elected thereafter for 6-year terms.

ᵍ Effective January 1979.

ʰ With reappointment to age 70.

ⁱ To age 70; judges may be certificated thereafter as supreme court judges (intermediate appellate court) for 2-year terms up to age 76.

ʲ The appellate divisions may establish appellate terms to hear appeals from local courts. County courts, although basically trial courts, may hear appeals from certain local courts.

ᵏ Twenty-four justices permanently authorized; in addition, as of December 31, 1976, 20 justices and certificated retired justices had been temporarily assigned.

ˡ To age 70; judges may be certificated thereafter for 2-year terms up to age 76.

ᵐ Presided over by county judge (court of limited jurisdiction) who serves term of 4 years.

ⁿ Special district judges serve at pleasure of district judges by whom they are appointed.

ᵒ Six years for superior judges; 4 years for assistant judges.

ᵖ Chief justice and associate justice sit in all divisions as well as court of last resort except in matai cases; trial court judges sit in all divisions of the High Court by designation of the chief justice.

q Appointed.

ʳ Reflects 1976 survey.

SOURCE: *The Book of the States, 1978–79* (Lexington, Ky.: The Council of State Governments, 1978), pp. 86–87.

tury, we are still trying to operate the courts with fundamentally the same basic methods, the same procedures, and the same machinery he said were not good enough in 1906.[4]

THEORY

In 1922, William Ogburn developed the idea of *cultural lag*.[5] He held that the material aspects of culture (such as the products of technological advances) would be followed by economic changes, followed by changes in social institutions (such as government or religion), and followed, lastly, by important changes in the values of the culture. Changes in the material culture coexisting with *status quo* social structure and values create an incongruency that is experienced as conflict and problems. These problems will continue as long as changes in the nonmaterial culture lag behind the changes in material culture.

The fundamentals of this theory of social change can be readily applied to the courts' failure to develop properly and rapidly. Technological advances in medicine, agriculture, and so on have made possible the increase in the population of the United States from 76 million in 1900 to approximately 218 million in 1980, with a concomitant rise in the standard of living. There is a huge corresponding increase in court caseload. Technological advances have resulted in a shift from a culture in 1900 based on the small farmer who owned a plot of land to the culture of 1980 based on the employee who lives in an urban area and is neither farmer nor industrial worker. The courts have grown in number, but their methods and their very structure go back to the nineteenth century, when they were rural courts, governed by traditions that are centuries old.

The old method, used by the courts and by the legislatures, of producing more laws

to solve problems, produces still more cases. Technological advances result in new kinds of offenses being added to the books and create a welter of difficult new kinds of cases with which the courts must deal, ranging from stolen credit cards to skyjacking. These new laws are cumulative, for old laws are seldom removed from the books. Even an increase in police efficiency is likely to mean that there will be more people arrested who must be processed by the courts. The time lapse between arrest and trial in felony cases doubled between 1960 and 1970.

The courts' lagging behind has had many unsavory effects. Here are some of the most important: The jails burgeon with untried defendants who cannot muster the necessary bail to buy their freedom. The rate of cases dismissed increases because during the years that may pass before defendants reach trial, witnesses move away or die or their memories become untrustworthy, other evidence is lost, juries regard the cases as past history and no longer important, and so forth. The plea-bargaining system is informal and often covert, and puts the responsibility for a case largely in the hands of the prosecutor; it has replaced the unworkable slow trial in the majority of felony cases. Due process is disregarded in misdemeanor cases as the courts try a new case every fifteen minutes in order to handle the increased volume.

The courts, of course, are only one part of the criminal justice system, and the other parts are also responsible for lag because they have not met the demands stemming from various technological changes. The courts' lag is a bottleneck, however, whereas if their decision-making power were not restricted by obsolescent values, they could be a powerful modernizing force in criminal justice.

The courts lag because they adhere to the venerable value of individual courts' autonomy, which has been guarded as the source

OLIVER WENDELL HOLMES, JR.
1841–1935

Courtesy of the Library of Congress

Oliver Wendell Holmes, Jr. was born in Boston in 1841, the son of a noted American novelist and poet. After attending T. R. Sullivan's Latin School, Holmes entered Harvard and graduated with an A.B. in 1861. In that year he joined the Union Army and subsequently fought in the Civil War. Holmes was wounded quite seriously three times and was eventually mustered out of the service in 1864 as a lieutenant colonel. Holmes then entered Harvard Law School and two years later received his law degree. After a brief sojourn in Europe, he entered into the practice of law in Boston in 1867. During this time he also taught at Harvard Law School in various capacities. For three years (1870–1873) he was editor of the *American Law Review.* Holmes made numerous contributions in articles, re-

views, and editorials, and in 1881 he wrote *The Common Law,* which brought him considerable recognition as a legal scholar.

In 1882 Holmes was appointed to the Massachusetts Supreme Court. After twenty years of distinguished service on this court, Theodore Roosevelt appointed him to the United States Supreme Court as an associate justice. While on the United States Supreme Court, Holmes wrote more than 1,000 opinions; while he concurred with 90 percent of the cases before the Court, Holmes became best known for his brilliantly written dissents. In *Abrams* v. *United States* [250 U.S. 616 (1909)], Holmes wrote one of his more famous dissents. Jacob Abrams had been sentenced to twenty years in prison for distributing pamphlets objecting to American policies. The majority of the Supreme Court affirmed the judgment, but Holmes dissented. In his dissent Holmes wrote,

But when men have realized that time has upset many fighting faiths, they may come to believe even more than they believe the very foundations of their own conduct that the ultimate good desired is better reached by free trade in ideas — that the best test of truth is the power of the thought to get itself accepted in the competition of the market, and that truth is the only ground upon which their wishes safely can be carried out.

Holmes has been called the "Great Dissenter"; yet his major dissents were to become law in later years.

Holmes served on the Supreme Court for thirty years before resigning at the age of ninety-one. He died shortly after resigning, with, as he once said, "the secret isolated joy of the thinker, who knows that, a hundred years after he is dead and forgotten, men who never heard of him will be moving to the measure of his thought."

---

of their impartiality. But unless they are unified into administrative systems, they cannot begin to meet the demands placed on them. Slowly, but with gathering momentum, they have begun to respond to the in-

creased demands. Law journals emphasize the need for unification and for better methods of selecting and training judges to make the courts responsive to the public. State constitutions are being revised with court unification in mind; forty-one states have established court administrators at the state level in recent years; several states have abolished their lower courts; and so on. Money is being poured into the courts for research into their problems and to initiate new programs, primarily as a result of the Omnibus Crime Bill of 1968. At last, in the late 1970s and the 1980s, research reports, books, and university courses are addressing the courts' problems.

LIMITATIONS AND VULNERABILITY

Not all changes in the courts have a cumulative or developmental character. The phrase "developmental history" implies an unfolding, a maturation, a certain progress. The progress of the courts can be reversed. Setbacks such as the Court of the Star Chamber and Coke's banishment occurred long ago, but vulnerability to regression always exists.

Vulnerability to error also exists, particularly when change is being made. For example, before he became chief justice, Warren Burger called the "criminal law revolution" of the 1960s haphazard and ragged. Burger would have had the Supreme Court deliberately establish a model guideline to ensure the consistency of case-by-case decisions and to help in the selection of cases that would receive the Court's official attention. Others in turn have said that Burger's method would have been slow, cumbersome, and negative. Another example of possible error is described by Judge Jerome Frank, who criticized Holmes, Cardozo, Pound, and others who had accented the need for a change in the laws. Frank claimed that the courts' inability to ascertain the correct facts is the problem to which these jurists should have devoted their energies. Still another example may be the effect of *Miranda* on investigatory procedures in the United States, an effect that has been com-

pared unfavorably with the investigating magistrate procedures defined in continental law. In the same vein, perhaps Canada's "federal" court system is better than the federal system established for the United States by the Judiciary Act of 1789. The choices have been made in these instances, and there is no way of being sure that the choices were the best.

If the courts continue to lag, the old ideals of populists and, alarmingly, radicals may be rekindled. As the Colonies achieved statehood, many of them forbade lawyers to sit in legislatures or on the bench. They attempted to restrict judicial authority as much as possible. Their intent was to return control of the courts to the people. Later, in the nineteenth century, radical Jacksonian Democrats wanted a cheap, simple, easily available, speedy judicial process that would ensure equality with only a minimum of contact with the legal profession. They argued for more courts and lower qualifications for judges. The complexities of the twentieth century have resulted in specialized courts and confused court systems. Elements of the Progressive movement responded to Pound's plea for reform by advocating popular electoral recall of judges and judicial decisions so that control of the courts would be more difficult for the few and easier for the many. Pound, of course, wanted better qualified judges, not a downplaying of their role. The Progressives did succeed in establishing legal aid societies and small claims courts (with laymen for judges). Currently, radical groups, identified with Marxism and, in some cases, terrorism, claim that justice is denied the poor while the rich go free. They, too, advocate "people's courts" that would be staffed and run by lay people.

The failure of social institutions to deal with lag has sometimes led to radical change, and unless the courts recognize and deal with court lag, court reform may be replaced by radical change. Former United States Attorney General Herbert Brownell is quoted as saying, "All of the great administrative improvements in New York in recent years came through the efforts of laymen. Citizens forced judges and lawyers to make changes."[6] If professionals do not respond to the problems in their field, the people eventually will — sometimes with overdue reforms; sometimes, unfortunately, with sudden, drastic, ill-conceived changes that wreak havoc and may not work.

REFORMS

The major problems in the judiciary stem from the lag in court administration, not judicial business. Three broad problem areas can be identified: state court unification, case flow, and the need for the judiciary to take a more active role in reform efforts that affect them and the rest of the criminal justice system.

The reforms often suggested for these areas further define the problems. In the area of court unification, it has been recommended that overlapping and conflicting jurisdictional boundaries be eliminated. It has been recommended that state court systems be more tightly organized administratively. Statewide financing for the courts has been recommended. A separate system run by a state court administrator has been recommended. Finally, it has been recommended that the selection and termination of judges be improved.

In the area of case flow, the following are often urged: speedy processing of cases, bail reform, pretrial intervention, reduction or elimination of plea bargaining, comprehensive defense counsel, and due process measures.

It is much harder to specify the recommendations for reforming the courts' role in modernizing the criminal justice system. They might include such items as the judiciary supporting legislation eliminating laws against victimless crimes and creating certain community-based corrections services.

The courts are in serious difficulties; they have begun to respond with reforms, and time will indicate whether the adopted remedies or reforms are good. As institutions, courts cannot change with every change that is introduced into the society; institutions, in a sense, help maintain balance. Court lag, then, will never be completely eliminated, nor is its complete elimination desirable. The expression *court lag* explains nothing by itself. It is a concept that helps to organize and focus attention on the developmental problem of the courts. In the next chapters specific attributes of this problem will become evident.

DISCUSSION QUESTIONS

1. What are some examples of the different meanings of *court* and *tribunal*? How well are the meanings of these words established by their context?
2. What similarities are there between the development of courts and the development of law?
3. Discuss the relationship of the development of courts in America to American society. What might our society be like if it was reflected in our courts, and if they had followed various other lines of development that you can name?
4. Discuss the limitations of the courts.
5. Describe what is meant by court lag. Where are the lag's effects felt most keenly?
6. What direction do you believe the courts will take in their future development — reform or radical change? Which do you believe to be the better direction? Why?

NOTES

1. U.S. Department of Justice, Law Enforcement Assistance Administration, and U.S. Bureau of the Census, *Trends in Expenditure and Employment Data for the Criminal Justice System, 1971-75* (Washington, D.C.: Government Printing Office, 1977), pp. 55-62.
2. Maxine B. Vertue, *Survey of Metropolitan Courts* (Ann Arbor: University of Michigan Press, 1962).
3. Roscoe Pound, "The Need of a Sociological Jurisprudence," in *The Sociology of Law: Interdisciplinary Readings,* ed. Rita James Simon (San Francisco: Chandler Publishing, 1968), pp. 9-18.
   Roscoe Pound, *The Spirit of the Common Law* (Boston: Beacon Press, 1963).
   Roscoe Pound, *Organization of Courts* (Boston: Little, Brown and Company, 1940).
   Roscoe Pound, *The Development of Constitutional Guarantees of Liberty* (New Haven: Yale University Press, 1957).
4. Chief Justice Warren Burger, "Remarks on the State of the Federal Judiciary," an address delivered to the American Bar Association, St. Louis, Missouri, August 1970.
5. William F. Ogburn, *Social Change with Respect to Cultural and Original Nature* (New York: Dell, 1966; originally published 1922).
6. Howard James, *Crisis in the Courts* (New York: David McKay, 1971), p. 209.

CHAPTER THIRTEEN

STRUCTURE OF THE COURTS IN THE UNITED STATES

FEDERAL COURT
SYSTEM

MILITARY COURT
SYSTEM

STATE COURT SYSTEM

JUVENILE COURT
SYSTEM

DUAL COURT SYSTEM
AND UNIFICATION OF
STATE SYSTEMS

---

*Purpose: To describe the structure of the
federal, state, and local court systems and their
relationships to one another.*

COURTS ARE DEFINED, basically, in terms of their structure, the relatively stable framework within which action takes place. The courts in the United States are frequently described as consisting of a "federal" system and a "state" system. This chapter will examine this dualism and the need for unification. The different kinds of federal courts will be treated individually, as will be the different levels of the state courts. The military court system and the juvenile courts will be singled out for special attention. Before these court systems can be considered, however, it is necessary to understand the meaning of *jurisdiction, venue,* and other terms.

Court structure is determined largely by the legal limitations imposed on the court's ability to deal with a case — and a court's authority as described by these limitations is defined as *jurisdiction.* Different sets of limitations or kinds of authority are frequently identified by an adjective preceding the word jurisdiction. Thus, *original jurisdiction* means that a court has the right to try a case, while *appellate jurisdiction* means that a court has the right to hear a defendant's appeal that it set aside a conviction. A court with original jurisdiction may also have appellate jurisdiction. An example of this would be the United States Supreme Court. A court with *special jurisdiction* is a court of special original jurisdiction. An example of a special original jurisdiction court is a magistrate's court that has original jurisdiction over civil and criminal matters when the amount in controversy, or fine, does not exceed $200. The jurisdiction is original but special because the cases the court may try are limited by a dollar amount. Special jurisdiction courts are sometimes referred to as *limited jurisdiction* courts. A *general jurisdiction* court is one that has the power to try a wide variety of cases. Whereas the special jurisdiction court is limited to trying cases involving less than a prescribed sum or trying a limited class of cases, the general jurisdiction court is not. Jurisdiction is frequently used to identify a geographical area in which a court has the authority to hear a case, although technically this is not considered proper usage. Jurisdiction should not be mistaken for the concept of *venue,* the requirement that the trial for an offense be held in the same area in which the offense occurred. The point to remember is that jurisdiction refers to a court's authority to take notice of and decide a case (see Figure 13.2, p. 239).

The courts are frequently divided into higher, or superior, and lower, or inferior, courts. This division reflects a hierarchy of prestige that has been attached to the courts, ranging from the courts of limited jurisdiction at the bottom (the lower courts) to the courts with appellate jurisdiction at the top (the higher courts). Sometimes the trial courts, the courts that can engage in a jury trial, are included in the higher courts, and sometimes they are included in the lower courts. *Court of last resort* means the highest court to which a case can be appealed. The trial courts used to be the first level of court to keep a record of court activity in a case, and *court of record* is an expression used to separate them from the courts with limited jurisdiction. Any court, however, that hears an appeal of a case on the record of the trial in the court below, without calling for a new trial, has identified the court below as a court of record.

FEDERAL COURT SYSTEM

The federal judiciary was set up on the basis of two sources in the law. These two sources are reflected in the terms *constitutional courts* and *legislative courts.* Constitutional courts are the Supreme Court and "such inferior Courts as the Congress may from time to time ordain and establish" (Article III, Section 1), that is, the courts of appeals, the district courts, and various specialized courts. Legislative courts are based on the "legislative article," Article I of the Constitution, which states, "The Congress shall have the power . . . to constitute tribunals inferior to the Supreme Court . . . ." Legislative courts have included trial courts in the U.S. territories, the Military Court of Appeals, and some specialized courts. Because they were created under a different clause than the constitutional courts, it has been argued that they are not subject to the administrative or even the judicial authority of the Supreme Court. Through legislative action and Court decisions, these old distinctions have been largely removed.

UNITED STATES SUPREME COURT

The United States Supreme Court — or "the Court," as it is often called — is composed of nine justices (judges), one of whom is the chief justice, who acts in the capacity of chairperson. The chief justice has no formal authority to make the other justices do anything, although in practice the chief justice determines who will write decisions and do certain other work. These nine people are appointed by the president of the United States, subject to confirmation by the Senate. The president also names the person who will be the chief justice. It is not necessary for the justices to have a background in law, and they may have attracted the attention of the president by their activity in politics. Nonetheless, most of the members have been lawyers, and since 1946 they have generally had the approval of the American Bar Association. If the Senate feels that an individual lacks the stature for the position or has something distasteful in his or her back-

ground, it may refuse to confirm the president's choice, and another choice must be made. The Constitution establishes tenure for "life or good behavior." The only ways to remove a justice are through impeachment and by securing voluntary retirement. The Constitution does not permit Congress (which controls the budget) to reduce the justices' salaries once they start receiving them.

Besides the justices, there are six other regular officers of the Court: the clerk, the chief deputy clerk, the deputy clerk, the marshal, the reporter of decisions, and a librarian. The functions of clerk, reporter, and bailiff (whose functions parallel those of the marshal) are described elsewhere. Each justice usually selects one or two recent law school graduates to serve for a year as a legal aide or law clerk. The Court has its own law library.

The term of the Court is required by statutory law to begin each year on the first Monday in October. It continues as long as there is business before it, usually until the middle of June. A quorum consists of six members. The caseload has increased until more than 3,000 cases are being passed upon in each term.

Despite its appearance of stability and power, the Supreme Court has undergone many changes since it was founded. President Washington had trouble filling the positions, and of the first justices some were out-of-work politicians, some left the position for other jobs, and one justice never attended any of the sessions. Chief Justice John Jay declared on his resignation that the Court would always be weak, of little consequence, lacking the stature it should have to be ranked with Congress and the executive branch. Each justice faced the possibility of a yearly ride on horseback through the wilderness to preside over the circuit courts (now called courts of appeals), one reason for the early lack of interest in serving on the Court.

It was not until 1815 that the Court formally established its authority over the states in case law. A number of strong justices were to add to the Court's status, with the most crucial role being played by Chief Justice John Marshall. Marshall was successful in his legal fight with President Jefferson in *Marbury* v. *Madison* [1 Cranch 137 (1803)] and thereby established the authority of the Constitution (as interpreted by the Court) over the laws passed by Congress. The Court is thus said to possess the "power of judicial review" of legislative law. The list of other famous justices includes Brandeis, Cardozo, Holmes, and Warren. (A number of justices have described Chief Justice

Hughes as the most effective administrator.) (See Figure 13.1 for the present makeup of the Court.) The Court has on a number of occasions been under attack by either the executive branch or Congress.

With the expansion of the federal judiciary and the states' judiciaries, the Supreme Court's workload has increased. It gets most of its cases from these other courts and has not itself expanded. In 1978, for example, the federal judiciary was enlarged by the addition of 117 judges, but the Supreme Court continues unchanged. This has led to a proposal for a National Appeals Court to supplement the Supreme Court, a proposal that gained the support of the American Bar Association in 1974. The new court would handle federal cases that would otherwise go to the Supreme Court.

FIGURE 13.1 UNITED STATES SUPREME COURT

Standing (left to right): William H. Rehnquist, Harry A. Blackmun, Lewis F. Powell, John P. Stevens. Seated (left to right): Byron R. White, William J. Brennan, Chief Justice Warren E. Burger, Potter Stewart, Thurgood Marshall.
Source: Supreme Court Historical Society, Washington, D.C.

COURTS

The jurisdiction of the Supreme Court is limited, as is the jurisdiction of every other court. "I will fight it all the way to the Supreme Court" may be impossible because of the restrictions imposed by the Constitution and the Congress. The Constitution is remarkably concise in its passage on the Court's jurisdiction:

> The Judicial power shall extend to all Cases in Law and Equity, arising under this Constitution, the Laws of the United States, and Treaties, made, or which shall be made, under their Authority; — to all Cases affecting Ambassadors, other public Ministers, and Consuls; — to all Cases of admirality and maritime Jurisdiction; — to Controversies to which the United States shall be a Party; — to Controversies between two or more States; — between Citizens of Different States; — between Citizens of the same State claiming Lands under Grants of different States, and between a State, or the Citizens thereof, and foreign States, Citizens, or Subjects.
>
> In all Cases affecting Ambassadors, other public Ministers and Consuls, and those in which a State shall be Party, the Supreme Court shall have original Jurisdiction. In all the other cases before mentioned the Supreme Court shall have appellate Jurisdiction, both as to Law and Fact, with such Exceptions, and under such Regulations as the Congress shall make.[1]

Congress has conferred appellate jurisdiction upon the Supreme Court, but has no authority to change its original jurisdiction as set up in the Constitution. Actually, cases of original jurisdiction account for less than 1 percent of the cases the Court hears in a term. Congress has granted the Supreme Court the power to prescribe rules of procedure to be followed by the federal courts of appeal, district courts, and other specific federal courts. And the Court has established rules to govern various procedures, including criminal cases in district courts, appellate proceedings in criminal cases, and criminal petty offense proceedings before United States magistrates.

UNITED STATES COURTS OF APPEALS

All federal courts other than the Supreme Court are sometimes called the *lower federal courts.* The highest of these are the United States courts of appeals, also referred to as *intermediate appellate courts,* for they are intermediate between the Supreme Court and the district courts. They were created in 1891 to relieve the Supreme Court of hearing all appeals of cases decided by the federal district courts. The courts of appeals can review all final decisions and some interlocutory or temporary decisions of the district courts, except for the few cases that are appealed directly to the Supreme Court. Like the district courts, they have responsibility for reviewing and enforcing decisions by certain quasi-judicial tribunals — nineteen of them, in fact; examples are the National Labor Relations Board and the Securities and Exchange Commission. The decisions of the courts of appeals are final unless the Supreme Court chooses to review them or unless they are heard on appeal to the Court.

The United States courts of appeals were known as the United States circuit courts of appeals until 1948. The United States is divided into eleven areas known as judicial circuits, and there is one court of appeals in each circuit. Each court has from three to nine permanent judgeships, depending on the amount of work required of the court. Ten of the circuits are identified by number, and each state and territory is assigned to one of them. The eleventh circuit is the one in which the District of Columbia alone is located. (See Table 13.1 for the circuits.)

TABLE 13.1 UNITED STATES JUDICIAL CIRCUITS

IDENTIFYING NO.	STATES	IDENTIFYING NO.	STATES
First Circuit	Maine	Seventh Circuit	Wisconsin
	New Hampshire		Illinois
	Massachusetts		Indiana
	Rhode Island	Eighth Circuit	North Dakota
	Puerto Rico		South Dakota
Second Circuit	New York		Nebraska
	Vermont		Missouri
	Connecticut		Arkansas
Third Circuit	Pennsylvania		Iowa
	New Jersey		Minnesota
	Delaware	Ninth Circuit	Washington
Fourth Circuit	West Virginia		Oregon
	North Carolina		California
	South Carolina		Nevada
	Maryland		Arizona
Fifth Circuit	Texas		Idaho
	Louisiana		Montana
	Mississippi		Alaska
	Alabama		Hawaii
	Georgia	Tenth Circuit	Wyoming
	Florida		Utah
	(Panama) Canal Zone		Colorado
Sixth Circuit	Ohio		New Mexico
	Kentucky		Kansas
	Tennessee		Oklahoma
	Michigan	Eleventh Circuit	District of Columbia

The member of a court of appeals who has been a judge for the longest period of time and who has not yet reached seventy is the chief judge of the court. One of the Supreme Court justices is assigned as circuit judge for each circuit, but is seldom active in this role. Three to nine judges may sit to hear a case, but usually only three sit because of their heavy workloads; two is a quorum. The judges are appointed for "life or good behavior." Each circuit has a judicial council to handle administrative business.

DISTRICT COURTS

The district courts are the lowest in the hierarchy of the Supreme Court, appellate courts, and district courts. The district courts are the trial courts with general federal jurisdiction. There is at least one United States district court in each state, and some states have as many as four. Each district court has from one to twenty-four federal district judges. A single judge presides over a trial except in a few kinds of cases, when three judges are called together to form a court. The purpose of the district courts is to relieve the Supreme Court of conducting jury trials (an activity in which it was sometimes engaged in its early history).

The district court in the District of Columbia has jurisdiction over local matters (those usually heard in state courts) along with its other duties. This is in keeping with the exclusive sovereignty that Congress has over the District of Columbia. In Puerto Rico the district court is called a United States district court, and Puerto Rico's local cases are controlled by the country's system of local courts. The territorial district courts are located in the territories of Guam, the Virgin Islands, and the Canal Zone, and they have federal jurisdiction. The territorial district courts' judges are appointed for terms of eight years except in the Commonwealth of Puerto Rico, where they are appointed for "life or good behavior."

The original jurisdiction possessed by district courts is fourfold: They have jurisdiction in all cases in which a federal criminal law has been broken. They have jurisdiction in cases that give rise to a federal question and in which the amount in controversy exceeds $10,000. They have jurisdiction in suits between citizens of different states in which the amount in controversy exceeds $10,000. They have jurisdiction in suits between a citizen(s) of one state and other states when the amount in controversy exceeds $10,000. The repeated $10,000 limitation was established to limit cases to serious ones; that figure has been waived in special circumstances.

Historically, the district courts made their own law rather than following the conflicting laws of the many states. They were forced to renounce this authority before the 1900s, and now they apply the law of the appropriate states in given cases. The district courts are empowered to review and enforce actions of certain quasi-judicial agencies (five of them), and they handle tort claims against the United States. Most of the cases they deal with are civil, not criminal, cases. The federal crimes with which they are concerned are offenses against the national revenue, postal, patent, copyright, trademark, bankruptcy, and civil rights laws. Kidnaping, killing a president, crossing a state line in a stolen vehicle, and so on, are federal crimes. Crimes, such as murder, robbery, theft, burglary, and so on, that are committed on federal reservations also fall under the jurisdiction of the federal courts.

Each district court has a clerk, a United States attorney, a United States marshal, referees in bankruptcy, probation officers, court reporters, and assistants. The district court judges appoint other judges, called United States magistrates (formerly called United States commissioners), who handle preliminaries, issue warrants for arrest, decide whether an arrested person should be held over for the attention of a grand jury, set bail, and so on. The magistrates are appointed to serve for a term of eight years.

Cases from the district courts are reviewed by the United States courts of appeals. Certain criminal decisions, however, along with certain decisions holding acts of Congress unconstitutional and injunction orders of the special three-judge district courts, may be appealed directly to the Supreme Court.

MILITARY COURT SYSTEM

The military courts have a unique structure and a different procedure from civilian courts. Military justice extends to many kinds of cases besides those involving military personnel on active duty. Their jurisdiction even extends to civilians in certain circumstances. These courts, though not limited to criminal cases, do handle many and deserve special attention.

The military courts for the most part exist within the Department of Defense. Congress is, of course, the major policy-making body for both organizations. In 1952 the Congress approved the Uniform Code of Military Justice (UCMJ), the authority for the courts and judicial procedures, which are the same for each branch of the service.

GRADES OF COURT-MARTIAL

A person in the armed forces who would ordinarily be punished for some kinds of offenses by his or her commanding officer can request and receive a trial by a *summary court-martial*. This is the lowest of three grades of court-martial. Usually the court is convened at the discretion and by the authority of any one of a number of officers. The court does not exist until convened, and the officer or panel of officers appointed to hold court may vary from trial to trial. Large military bases, however, frequently have a regular summary court-martial. The accused is investigated by the commanding officer, who may then send a report to the convening authority for that area. This officer may choose to investigate the charges still further before convening a court or may send the investigatory reports to a convening officer of the next higher court, the *special court-martial*. This officer is higher in rank and may also have the authority to convene a *general court-martial*, the highest court. If he or she does not have the authority but deems such a trial necessary, the material will be sent to a still higher ranking officer, who will convene the highest grade of court-martial. Of course, most cases go directly to the correct convening authority.

The grades of the court-martial are not defined by the seriousness of the offense, as is the case in civilian court systems. They are determined by the seriousness of the penalty. The summary court is limited to cases dealing with enlisted personnel, and the maximum penalty that it may impose is one month's confinement and loss of two-thirds of a month's pay. The maximum penalty a special court-martial can impose is six months' confinement and loss of two-thirds of six months' pay. Both courts would seem to correspond to civilian courts that are limited to trying misdemeanor cases. The general court is reserved for cases involving the penalties for serious offenses. The offenses are given in the UCMJ, but the president of the United States establishes the penalties. Offenses are described as either military or criminal. Death, imprisonment, and various forms of discharge, rank reduction, and pay reduction are included among the more serious penalties.

The president of the court-martial is similar to the chief judge in a civilian court, although the president lacks the authority over the minimum of five other officers impaneled on the court that a civilian judge has over a jury. Military judges are highly qualified. Officer lawyers present at the trial for either the defense or the prosecution must be approved by the judge-advocate general of whichever branch of the military is involved. They, like the military judges, are highly qualified. The judge-advocate general, similar to a prosecutor, is the highest ranking legal authority within the service. Civilian lawyers may serve as defense attorneys at the defendant's request and expense.

SAFEGUARDS

The military system has been criticized because of the investigatory power granted to a commissioned officer who is a fellow of the military judge. This power may be abused, not necessarily deliberately, because at one stage the investigating officer is the accused's commanding officer. These investigations tend to have negative psychological effects on the military judges and may lead them to feel that the accused must be guilty or he or she would not have been charged. A safeguard that enhances judicial impartiality lies in the rigid rules on the conduct of the military judges; failure to follow these rules can result in the military judge being court-martialed.

Another safeguard rests in the review system. Every court-martial is automatically reviewed, sometimes as many as three times, by trained legal staffs for the sole purpose of examining verdicts of guilty. The reviewing staff or board may include the accused's own civilian defense counsel. The number of verdicts modified by these boards suggests that they are not perfunctory. Nonetheless, they are controlled by military officers and therefore are not always above suspicion. In 1950, Congress created the United States Court of Military Appeals, one of the reforms in military justice subsequently reflected in UCMJ.

UNITED STATES COURT OF MILITARY APPEALS

The United States Court of Military Appeals operates for administrative purposes as part of the Department of Defense, but is judicially independent. It is composed of three civilian judges appointed by the president for fifteen-year terms with the approval of the Senate. The court was designed to be the final appellate tribunal in court-martial convictions, although cases can go to the Supreme Court. The court can review only matters of law (did the trial adhere to due process of law), not of fact (did the facts presented at the trial prove guilt). It receives only cases that have been to a board of review. The judge-advocate general may forward the case, or the accused may attempt to obtain review by petitioning the court. The general counsel for the Department of Transportation may certify a case to the court on behalf of a defendant who is a member of the Coast Guard. Cases automatically appealed to the court are those in which a general or flag officer has been convicted and those in which the maximum possible sentence is death.

Boards of review are limited by the UCMJ. The Court of Military Appeals, however, has the power to interpret the code, thereby creating law, and solving some of the problems that arise because of statutory law's inability to cover all possible contingencies. The court's value for criminal justice may be special, for it is not bound by centuries of tradition as are civilian courts, and it faces problems requiring innovative approaches. Its actions may suggest to civilian courts new approaches for handling criminal cases.

STATE COURT SYSTEM

The structure of the courts in any given state is established by that state's constitution and by its statutory law. As a result, the court systems of the various states contain a bewildering variety of court names and a varying number of levels in the case hierarchy.

VARIETY OF STATE COURTS

As an example of the possible variety of courts, until Pennsylvania had its court system streamlined recently, it had common pleas courts (usually for civil cases involving $5,000 or more), oyer and terminer courts (criminal courts for capital crimes and other felonies), quarter sessions courts (predominantly criminal courts meeting periodically and sometimes consisting of the same judges as oyer and terminer courts), orphans courts (for cases involving orphans), equity courts (for equity cases), probate courts (for cases concerning wills and estates), domestic relations courts (for family legal problems such as divorce), surrogate courts (similar to probate courts), chancery courts (which specialize in equity), and juvenile courts. Other states have courts that correspond closely or correspond roughly or do not correspond at all. These courts will have the same names or different names, but similarity of name does not guarantee similarity of function. Confusing the matter still more is the fact that people in the criminal justice field commonly use a name as though its meaning were fixed and universal; thus, they speak of a justice of peace court, county court, or superior court as though everyone knew exactly what they meant.

The word *court* is also confusing to the nonprofessional because the inexperienced associate one court with one judge. The fact is that a particular kind of court located in a specified area may be represented by several judges. For example, a county courthouse may contain offices (called *chambers*) and courtrooms for both the county court and a state district court, and the county court may involve one county judge while the district court involves six district judges. In another county the numbers may be just the reverse.

Criminal courts are not generally distinguished from civil courts, but if they happen to be, the distinction is more likely to be made in the lower courts. All courts that handle criminal cases usually fall into one of two categories, determined by the basic kinds of offenses they try: misdemeanors (drunkenness, traffic violations, simple assaults, petty theft, disorderly conduct, prostitution, homosexual acts, possession of certain drugs, and countless other minor infractions of the law) and felonies (murder, arson, kidnaping, robbery, burglary, rape and other serious assaults, and so on). Courts that are restricted to dealing with misdemeanor cases are police courts, justice of the peace courts, special sessions courts, and the like. Courts that are concerned with trying felony cases are county courts, superior courts, district courts, circuit courts, and so forth. Too much weight should not be attached to the name of the court, however; for example, the county courts of many states do not try felony cases. In addition, the definitions of felony and misdemeanor vary from state to state; for example, as late as 1973 possession of any quantity of marijuana in Texas was a felony with a sentence of from two years to life, whereas it was a misdemeanor in Ann Arbor, Michigan, where a person caught smoking marijuana was fined five dollars, payable by mail.

LEVELS OF STATE COURTS

Some of this confusion is easily resolved by ranking the courts in a three- or four-tiered hierarchy based on jurisdiction, as is shown in Figure 13.2.

Court of Last Resort Each state has a court, usually known as the supreme court, that is the *court of last resort,* or *of ultimate review,* for there is no other court to hear the case on further appeal or petition (except a federal court when certain conditions are present). These courts hear appeals from lower state trial courts or courts of intermediate appeals (depending on the structure of the court system in a particular state). These courts, not the Supreme Court, generally have ultimate jurisdiction over controversies involving interpretation of a state's constitution and its statutes. The number of justices who are members of the court of last resort ranges from three to nine, depending on the state.

FIGURE 13.2 STATE COURT STRUCTURE

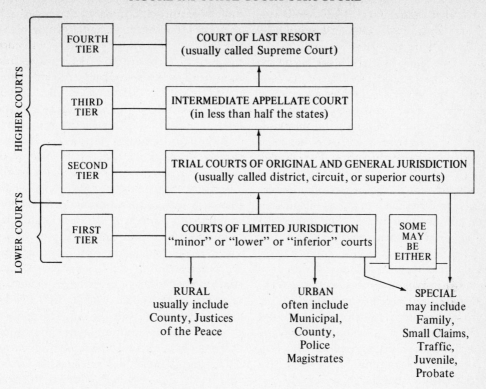

Intermediate Appellate Courts Between the court of last resort and the trial courts, *intermediate appellate courts* have been established to handle appeals. These courts exist in all the larger states, and they relieve courts of last resort of some of their ever-increasing burdens. They are often known as courts of appeal.

Courts of appeals have original jurisdiction in some kinds of cases in some states, but they are generally limited to appellate jurisdiction. The defendant generally has the right to appeal regardless of whether or not the court of appeal wants to hear the appeal. Although most states allow the court of last resort extensive rights to review cases that have been heard or tried by another court, most cases that get as far as the court of appeals end there. States without this level or tier in their court system have a three-tiered court system rather than a four-tiered one.

Trial Courts of Original and General Jurisdictions The courts in which cases may be tried to the fullest extent of the law are frequently called simply *trial courts*. They can and sometimes must use juries. Some states have separate criminal courts at this level; they may also have separate courts for civil litigation, equity suits, probate cases, and other matters. The jurisdiction of some of the larger trial courts overlaps with that of the courts of limited jurisdiction (concurrent jurisdiction). The jurisdiction of any one trial court may be difficult to ascertain without reference to the state constitution and the statutory law that lies behind it. Many court systems are remarkably complex at this level and the level below. In some states a defendant may have to carry what he or she believes to be a single case to more than one court because of the fragmented jurisdiction of the courts. These courts try felony cases and all significant civil cases, and they usually hear appeals from such lower courts as the justice of the peace courts. The number of judges may be restricted by the state's constitution, but in most states the legislature has increased the number as the number of the population increases. See Table 12.2 for the typical number of judges at this level for the different states.

Trial courts within a state may be assigned districts that include several counties. The early trial courts tended to be county courts, housed in the county courthouse, because of the limited mobility of a small population scattered over a wide geographical area. Today, however, a regional system of trial courts is more practical.

Courts of Limited Jurisdiction Historically the courts of special or limited jurisdiction in the United States were courts held by justices of the peace (J.P.). Then, early in the 1800s, different kinds of limited courts began to appear. In many areas, county courts were given concurrent jurisdiction with J.P. courts, and cities developed city courts, magistrate courts, and so on. J.P. courts are still important, although by 1973 seventeen states had abolished them entirely, and in at least four more states they have been replaced in many of the cities.

Typically, the J.P. court is the lowest state court. It is usually a *court of nonrecord*. Indeed, the duties of the office frequently make the name *court* questionable; notary work, the performance of marriages, and other non-judicial duties done for a fee reveal its quasi-judicial character. Calling a J.P. a magistrate does not alter this character. In some places the J.P. is called squire, a title that reflects the history of the office and its origin in fourteenth-century England, where then as now its function was to aid in the administration of justice in minor matters at the local level.

Although the J.P.'s jurisdiction usually extends throughout the county, the court may be restricted to the town in which the J.P. is elected. The term of office is generally from two to six years. In some cities the J.P. is appointed by the city administration. Pay is low as a rule, but inasmuch as it is frequently collected in the form of a fee paid by a defendant or by a person seeking a service, the office can be extremely lucrative in some locales. Backgrounds of J.P.s are extremely varied, and the J.P. often has a "regular" job in addition to holding office. Apparently inherent in the structure that includes and defines the J.P. court are factors that result in a very high conviction rate in criminal cases. The witticism that *J.P.* means "justice for the plaintiff" is as much to the point as it is pointed.

The minor or lower courts in which the justices of the peace have been replaced with magistrates do much the same kind of work: issuing warrants, presentments, setting bail, holding preliminary hearings in felony cases, settling petty misdemeanor cases, and other matters (to be discussed in the next chapter). It is important to note, however, that in one state J.P.s may be so limited that they do not even perform magistrate duties, whereas in another state they may be the equivalent of a higher level court. In addition, courts of limited jurisdiction include many specialized courts — traffic courts, juvenile courts (in many places), and so on. These lowest level courts do not make an official transcript of court proceedings; they are not, therefore, courts of record, and, on appeal, a case will be retried — a procedure known as *trial de novo*.

Trial courts have been called the workhorses of the court system. Certainly most of the people who appear before a court charged with an offense against the law appear before a court of limited jurisdiction. In the huge bulk of these cases, the case begins here and ends here. These courts are often *inferior* courts in the common sense of the word. The National Crime Commission in 1967 echoed the Wickersham Commission's recommendation, made forty years earlier, that the lower courts be abolished in an effort to do away with a dual system of justice that treats alleged petty offenders with less regard than alleged felons. Illinois was the first state to do so.

JUVENILE COURT SYSTEM

Juvenile courts are in a special class, neither civil nor criminal, but with characteristics of both. Juvenile courts are statutorily defined. They have less basis in common law than do many other courts. Seemingly their relation to criminal justice is close, for they deal with delinquency, but is delinquency equivalent to criminal behavior?

In medieval England the Church declared that a child not yet seven could not be guilty of a sin, and the king's court concurred. Children over seven who fell into the hands of the law were treated as adults: they were arrested for the same offenses, tried in the same courts, given the same sentences, and assigned to the same prisons. The prisons were the first to be differentiated; one kind for adults, another kind for children. It was not until 1899 that, with the support of the Chicago Bar Association, the women of the

Chicago Settlement Houses managed to have the first juvenile court in the United States established in Cook County, Illinois. It was twenty-five years before any other state followed suit, and two of the states continued to hold out for many more years.

The Supreme Court upheld the unique character of juvenile courts in a case in which it set forth the idea of the courts as kind and loving parents — to replace genetic parents, if need be — which is the famous doctrine of *parens patriae*. The object of the court's attention in this philosophy is to rehabilitate, not to punish.

Juvenile courts do not convict children; they declare some children to be delinquents and some merely dependents of the court. Dependency jurisdiction is not of direct interest to criminal justice professionals, but cases in which children are labeled delinquent are of direct concern. What is delinquency in the eyes of the court? Perhaps the working definition used by the Children's Bureau of the Department of Health, Education and Welfare best describes the relationship between the court and delinquency:

> Juvenile delinquency cases are those referred to courts for acts defined in the statutes of the State as the violation of a state law or municipal ordinance by children or youth of juvenile court age, or for conduct so seriously antisocial as to interfere with the rights of others or to menace the welfare of the delinquent himself or the community. This broad definition of delinquency includes conduct which violates the law only when committed by children, e.g., truancy, ungovernable behavior, and running away. Also included, but reported separately are traffic violations whenever a juvenile court has jurisdiction in such cases.[2]

As a consequence of the doctrine of *parens patriae*, the structure of the juvenile court approached that of a social welfare agency, with social workers, social workers' language rather than legal language, and an informal model in which due process was not regarded as necessary. The court all too often failed to live up to its ideal of being a loving parent, and the child and the parents were at the mercy of a court with totalitarian powers. In a number of famous decisions in the late sixties and seventies the Supreme Court demanded that due process be followed in juvenile courts.[3]

Another criticism of the juvenile court is that it cannot possibly meet all the needs of the juvenile in trouble because of the structural nature of courts as instruments of law. A clear example is the school truant, or the child who is claimed by the parents to be unmanageable; both are treated as criminals to be punished. The child whose freedom is abridged for such a problem may feel that the punishment would be no different for robbery, murder, or rape. Whatever the value of "training school," for example, the child is aware of locked doors, guards, and insistence on certain forms of behavior "or else" additional detention. Others — parents, teachers, peers, and prospective employers — are inclined to see the child who appears in court as a little criminal. All this is true even though in a few months or perhaps weeks the child would have been old enough to play truant or run away from home with impunity. The National Council on Crime and Delinquency has taken the position that juveniles should not be brought before the courts and sentenced for "status offenses," that is, for offenses that would not be considered criminal for an adult.

For these kinds of reasons, it has been urged that youth service bureaus replace juvenile courts as the chief agencies to help children who might otherwise be classified as delinquents. The National Crime Commission (1967) stated that juvenile courts had failed and should be used only as a last resort. In many instances they have been of genuine benefit to children, but their original purpose is not being achieved.

"Juvenile court age" varies widely. It may begin with birth or age seven, ten, eleven, or twelve, and it may end anytime from age sixteen through age eighteen (formerly twenty-one), depending on the court in question. Juvenile court age may differ with the sex of the juvenile. Moreover, the state-defined juvenile court age does not need to bear any relation to other statutory age limitations, such as those for marriage, consent, drinking, driving, or executing a will. The age of criminal responsibility, the age at which one becomes subject to adult court procedures for certain criminal acts, is independent of juvenile court age.

Chicago, New York, Philadelphia, and other large cities have *youth courts* as well as juvenile courts. These courts are adult courts, but they use the techniques of juvenile courts. They exist for youths from sixteen to nineteen or twenty-one who have committed specified kinds of misdemeanors — and, rarely, felonies. Because youth courts lack exclusive jurisdictions, older boys and girls are frequently tried in the regular criminal courts.

The structural organization of juvenile courts varies enormously from state to state. A model structure and pattern of responsibilities have not yet crystallized. At present there are two broad directions in which juvenile courts are moving: (1) toward placing juvenile jurisdiction within the highest level of trial court, but retaining its specialized character as a juvenile or family division of that court; and (2) toward independent juvenile and/or family courts, usually at general jurisdiction level. These directions are in conflict, and the first one will probably become dominant in the long run because it fits in best with the emphasis on court unification. The District of Columbia's separate juvenile court and the Florida juvenile courts became divisions of general trial courts in the seventies, as did the juvenile courts of several other states. Yet Massachusetts, Kansas, and Delaware have switched to or added new, separate juvenile courts in the seventies.

The structure of the juvenile courts also reflects a wide variety of patterns of responsibility. Whether the courts control probation departments, detention facilities, juvenile aftercare units, etc., depends on the state. The judge's decision in one state may be the police officer's, probation worker's, district attorney's, or welfare worker's decision in another state.

To illustrate the different possibilities, one has only to try to examine the case flow in juvenile cases. In a Texas city, police who arrest a juvenile may take him or her before any magistrate for a decision on detention. In Boston the juvenile is taken before a juvenile court judge, or after hours a probation officer will make the decision. In most states the juvenile is simply taken to a juvenile detention center and automatically admitted. A jail census will show that juveniles are often detained in local jails, even though this is illegal. The detention facility, often called a *juvenile hall,* is administered by a juvenile court in many cities, by a probation department in many counties, by the state in Florida and Georgia, and by welfare departments or county commissioners in other areas. Some areas have no juvenile halls.

Courts handling juvenile cases frequently hold daily detention hearings to review detention decisions. A probation officer is generally present to make recommendations. The probation staff generally decides whether or not to file a formal charge. There are various procedures for involving the prosecutor in this decision-making. In at least one city, the clerk of the court decides whether there are sufficient legal grounds to file. Legal grounds have often been ignored in the past. By statutory law, by court policy, or simply because "it has always been done that way," the child may be placed under informal supervision, instead of being formally filed against or having the case dismissed. In some states the judge ratifies informal supervision by signing a *consent decree.*

The sentence hearing is called a *disposition hearing.* The juvenile and parents, a probation officer, and sometimes lawyers for the defense and prosecution will be present. Euphemistic language is used instead of the familiar terms heard in criminal court (described in the next chapter). A juvenile who is institutionalized and then while on parole (or aftercare) commits technical or minor violations may have to go through the juvenile court intake process again. In most states, however, the parole or aftercare worker will decide what to do in this case.

As can be seen, the role of the juvenile court is inseparable from the correction function. But it is not fixed. Further changes in the court's role may reduce its control over corrections. Florida provides a model in which juvenile probation and detention services are administered by the state. The roles of court and corrections will probably be reduced and the prosecutor's role expanded as the prosecutor takes over more of the functions of the intake workers who now decide whether to file formal petitions (charges).

The improved staffing of juvenile court-controlled probation departments, the elevation of the juvenile courts to general trial court level, the creation of family courts, and the introduction of legal due process standards are some of the features that have led to a general improvement in juvenile courts over the past decade.

The anticipated changes narrowing the role of the juvenile court will hopefully also strengthen and improve it. The effect of possible new statutes requiring juvenile felony cases to be processed and sentenced in adult criminal court fashion is hard to assess at this time.

DUAL COURT SYSTEM AND UNIFICATION OF STATE SYSTEMS

The federal court system is maintained to prosecute federal crimes, and the state system, to prosecute state crimes. Unfortunately, this dual court system contains overlapping jurisdictions that give rise to conflicts, confusion, inefficiency, and injustice. Furthermore, within a state court system there is frequently an overlap of jurisdictions that can only add to the problems. A unified court system within each state would reduce the problems of overlapping jurisdiction.

OVERLAP AND CONFLICT

Congress created the federal court system, even though it could have allowed the states to retain all original jurisdiction in their trial courts. On the other hand, when they ceased being colonies, the states could have given up their courts just as they gave up so many of their other rights and privileges to the new federal government. They chose, however, to retain their already established court systems.

The bulk of criminal cases, perhaps 85 percent, are handled by the state courts because most crimes are defined by state law. A single crime, however, may be both a federal and a state crime. Whenever Con-

gress creates a federal law, the state laws dealing with the same offenses remain untouched. Offenses against federal laws cannot be prosecuted as such in a state court. A single act, however, may be prosecuted by both federal and state governments independent of one another. For example, if a national bank is robbed and the bank robber is convicted and sentenced by a state court, he may later be convicted by a federal court, and vice versa. Double jeopardy applies within court systems, not across court systems.

Although there are federal district courts in all states, neither their number nor their location means that they have authority over the states' courts or the states. Cases involving state crimes get into federal courts through the back door, so to speak, as when they are heard on a writ of *habeas corpus,* described in the next chapter. No state court is bound to regard the decisions of a federal district court as a precedent to be followed. The federal district courts and the federal court of appeals in any one circuit, oddly enough, are not bound by the decisions made in other circuits. If a state court disregards federal law in prosecuting a case, the defendant may obtain the aid of the federal courts, which are empowered to dictate the state court's behavior or reverse its decisions. The federal courts may also intervene if the defendant is a federal officer or a foreign official. Whenever state courts have declared a federal law unconstitutional, the Supreme Court has reacted quickly by reviewing the case and, usually, by striking down the state court's decision.

In the early 1970s the federal court system was being swamped with petitions by defendants who wanted their cases to be heard, largely because of the liberalization of petition requirements in the federal courts. Because states that have strong appeals systems do not have nearly so many cases reaching the federal courts, the federal courts have urged the states to adopt specific appeals measures.

COURT UNIFICATION

The independence of each court has led to its maintaining absolute control over hours, scheduling, and other aspects of administration, and along with autonomy goes the absence of fixed responsibility for court management. The specific results are inept, quixotic, or archaic methods of administration in some courts. The generalized results include structural disorganization of entire court systems.

It is true that there is a hierarchy in a state court system (or in any court system). Classically, however, the hierarchy is based on jurisdiction and does not extend to administration. No one is in charge; there is no administrative authority independent of the individual judge; there is a lack of centralization. Even the courts within a county may have no coordinated administration.

The resulting disorganization is experienced in many ways. The National Crime Commission refers to the confusion and illegal practices exemplified by one state. Only three of more than two hundred city courts had jurisdiction to imprison offenders; the rest were limited to levying fines. Yet a study of ninety-nine city court judges showed that forty-eight of them believed that they had the power to imprison violators of city ordinances. In another instance a practicing attorney was also a city judge, a two-hat role that is unethical and in this case not legal. Also, a fragmented court system does not speed up the communication of precedent-setting decisions. In one state a number of justices of the peace were unaware of changes made in their power to apply contempt rulings, and two-thirds ap-

parently continued to neglect to inform defendants of their right to be silent.[4] A Texas study indicated that a goodly percentage of judges handling juvenile cases were unaware of the revolutionary Supreme Court decision *In re Gault* [387 U.S. 1 (1967)] two years after the decision.[5]

Lower courts frequently lack the wherewithal to support the probation officers, social workers, and clinical psychologists that enable larger and higher courts to mitigate the charge of arbitrariness in judicial decisions. A city court, a county court, and a district court may all have the jurisdiction to handle a given offense, such as petty larceny. The handling of the case, and all too often its outcome, is likely to be affected by the differences in the various courts' administrations. They may have different rules, policies, and traditions. In one court, the docket may be so overloaded that the case would never reach the trial stage; in another court, the case could be tried without great delay; and in a third court the judge might have too much time. The quantity and quality of support personnel (probation officers, social workers, etc.) will depend on the court. The arresting police officer or the prosecutor may select a court to deliberately govern the outcome of the case, as, of course, may the defense. The result is delayed justice and an overabundance of guilty pleas.

The public, of course, pays for this wasteful disorganization, just as it pays for an appeal system that is not only inefficient but frequently overly time-consuming and thus unfair to the innocent defendant. The entire system is also unfair to police, witnesses, and jurors, who must give up their valuable time and submit to a needlessly unpleasant experience.

The framework necessary for good administration is a court system within each state that is unified administratively. Generally, unification requires more than administrative decisions; it requires change at the policy-making level. Legislatures have to pass laws, constitutions have to be changed. State constitutions frequently last a hundred years, and major changes in the state courts are seldom made between times. It is surprising, therefore, to find that a number of states have made great strides toward unification. Model constitutional provisions have been developed by the National Municipal League and also by the American Bar Association's affiliated American Judicature Society. Most important is *The Model State Judicial Article,* approved by the American Bar Association in 1962 and revised in 1973. Furthermore, the National Advisory Commission on Criminal Justice Standards and Goals developed model standards in 1973.[6]

Typical of the unification that has taken place is the consolidation of courts at the same level and the strengthening of the states' hierarchies. Frequently the venerable county court units are superseded by district trial courts that encompass several counties. Courts that have been sources of town or city income (and it is not uncommon for cities to regard courts as sources of income) are transformed by having the fines and fees paid to the state. Courts that could not afford a probation officer or that did not have access to a competent prosecution office find their problems alleviated by districting. Many other benefits occur.

The earliest unification of a state court system occurred in 1947, when the people of New Jersey, over the local bar association's objections, approved a new state constitution. It established a supreme court, a su-

perior court, county courts, and courts of limited jurisdiction. Justice of the peace courts were abolished, as were a few other courts. The supreme court was given a free hand to administer and make rules governing the other courts of the state. It is noteworthy that most states — like New Jersey — have given to the courts some policy-making power that formerly belonged to the legislative branch.

In 1973, Florida streamlined its court system. In 1972 it had 110 different courts. After the change it had four. Of course, many of the courts that had been officially eliminated actually remained as divisions of one of the four courts. The major change was in the court administration.

Typically in such reforms the administrative responsibility ultimately belongs to the state supreme court and its chief justice. They work closely with a state court administrator, who in turn works closely with the chief judge of the trial court and — if there is one — the trial court administrator. The top administrative judge may create and enforce rules concerning jury selection, case processing time standards, collection of statistics, or monitoring techniques; he or she may assign the presiding judges of trial courts. Other employees of the judiciary fall under his or her personnel administration responsibility. The administrator's authority rests primarily on a change in court financing from a patchwork of local, state, and private sources to a single statewide system under the administrator's control. This quiet but profound movement toward administrative unification of state courts may affect all the states before it ends.

DISCUSSION QUESTIONS

1. What examples of court lag can be discerned in the court structure?
2. How are the federal court system and the state court system different?
3. Discuss ideal court structure for federal and state systems. How far are present courts from this ideal?
4. Compare and contrast the military justice system with the federal and state systems. What might be the advantages of the military model? The disadvantages? Should military and civilian models be the same?
5. What is the structure of the courts in your state? How could the state system be improved?

NOTES

1. United States Constitution, Article III, section 2.
2. Children's Bureau, *Juvenile Court Statistics, 1966,* Statistical Series 90 (Washington, D.C.: Government Printing Office, 1967).
3. These cases are among those identified as part of the "criminal law revolution" of the 1960s and include such major cases as *Kent* v. *U.S.,* 383 U.S. 541 (1966); *In re Gault,* 387 U.S. 1 (1967); and *In the Matter of Winship,* 90 S.Ct. 268 (1970).
4. President's Commission on Law Enforcement and Administration of Justice, *Task Force Report: The Courts* (Washington, D.C.: Government Printing Office, 1967), p. 82.
5. Sarah Holden, "A Pre-Post Analysis of the Effect of *Gault* on the Juvenile Court of Harris County, Texas: The Juvenile Probation of Harris County," unpublished master's thesis, Sam Houston State University, Huntsville, Texas, 1969.
6. National Advisory Commission on Criminal Justice Standards and Goals, *Courts* (Washington, D.C.: Government Printing Office, 1973), Standard 8.1, pp. 132–136.

*Geoff Winningham, and The Seagram County Court
House Archives, Library of Congress.*

CHAPTER FOURTEEN

FUNCTIONS
OF THE COURTS

PRETRIAL
TRIAL
SENTENCING
POSTCONVICTION
REMEDIES

Purpose: To describe the functions of the court in the criminal justice process from the court's point of view.

COURT FUNCTION REFERS to the judicial work the courts do; it is the procedure peculiar to the courts that gives them their life, their flavor. The basic process described here is fairly similar throughout the states, the variations being responses to statutory law and to location, rural or urban.

The basic process is reductionary, that is, it begins with a large number and ends with a few. It begins with the huge number of people temporarily detained by the police, progresses through the smaller number of those who have an initial appearance before a magistrate and those who are tried for misdemeanors, through the much smaller number who, charged with a felony, have a preliminary hearing, through the still smaller number who pass through arraignment and pretrial motions and reach trial, to the still smaller number who are sentenced and who are not granted appeal or some other postconviction remedy. Figure 14.1 is a flowchart of the various court functions. It also gives the ideal time-lapse maximums formulated by the National Advisory Commission on Criminal Justice Standards and Goals (1973). Each of the functions is discussed in this chapter.

The flowchart illustrates something else that is important: the way the courts are related to the rest of the criminal justice system by their functions. The criminal justice process follows its well-defined path, but the court's role begins to blend with and shift to other segments of the criminal justice system at either end. The role of the prosecution is intricately interwoven with the rest of the court procedure. The courts are dependent on the police at one end of the process and on corrections at the other end, but because they are vested with decision-making authority and responsibility, the courts are pivotal in the criminal justice process.

A number of well-specified court functions culminate in either a trial or the release of the accused. The National Advisory Commission on Criminal Justice Standards and Goals (1973) states that the time lapse from arrest to trial generally should not be more than 60 days in felony cases and not more than 30 days in misdemeanor cases.[1] Florida's highly regarded 1973 speedy-trial law sets a maximum time lapse of 180 days in felony cases and 90 days in misdemeanors. The order of functions presented here varies slightly from state to state; Figure 14.2 shows the order in one state as an example.

Typical of speedy trial acts is the one that the federal government passed in 1974, which required U.S. District courts to limit the time period between arrest and indictment to 60 days and that between arraignment and trial to 180 days by July 1976. However, the federal law went on to establish permanent time limits, effective July 1979, of arrest to indictment, 30 days; indictment to arraignment, 10 days; arraignment to trial, 60 days.

Courts indirectly influence police behavior by defining what is permissible in court as evidence against a defendant (although it is to be noted that the police may be guided by statutory codes of evidence also) and by insisting that due process be observed in developing cases before adjudication. The courts are bound to these considerations by constitutional and statutory law. Particularly in the 1960s, the Supreme Court, using various Bill of Rights amendments in conjunction with the due process clause of the Fourteenth Amendment, arrived at a number of decisions that seem to be directly intended to control the methods of the police.[2] The Court, therefore, was accused of functioning

FIGURE 14.1 FELONY CASE TIME SCHEDULE

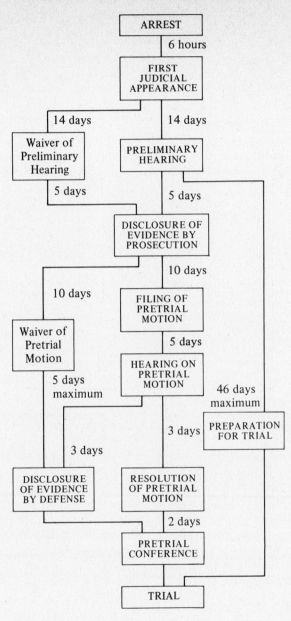

The flow chart depicts the recommended time limits for processing a felony case.
Source: National Advisory Commission on Criminal Justice Standards and Goals, *Courts* (Washington, D.C.: Government Printing Office, 1973), pp. xx–xxi.

FIGURE 14.2 THE PATH TO TRIAL IN FLORIDA

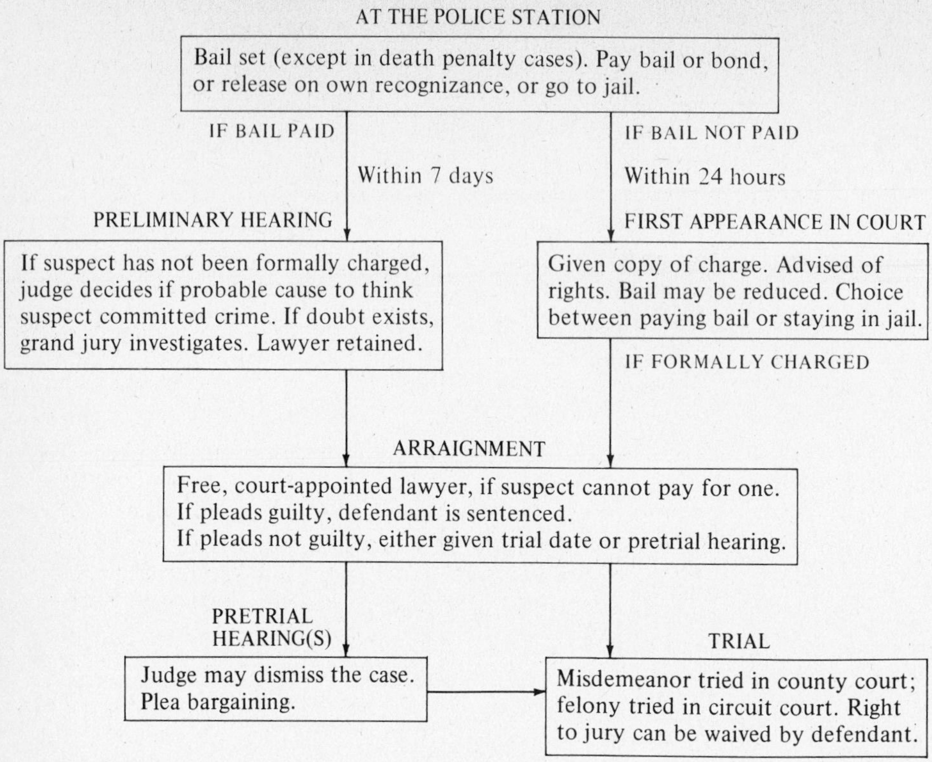

AT THE POLICE STATION

Bail set (except in death penalty cases). Pay bail or bond, or release on own recognizance, or go to jail.

IF BAIL PAID

Within 7 days

IF BAIL NOT PAID

Within 24 hours

PRELIMINARY HEARING

If suspect has not been formally charged, judge decides if probable cause to think suspect committed crime. If doubt exists, grand jury investigates. Lawyer retained.

FIRST APPEARANCE IN COURT

Given copy of charge. Advised of rights. Bail may be reduced. Choice between paying bail or staying in jail.

IF FORMALLY CHARGED

ARRAIGNMENT

Free, court-appointed lawyer, if suspect cannot pay for one.
If pleads guilty, defendant is sentenced.
If pleads not guilty, either given trial date or pretrial hearing.

PRETRIAL HEARING(S)

Judge may dismiss the case.
Plea bargaining.

TRIAL

Misdemeanor tried in county court; felony tried in circuit court. Right to jury can be waived by defendant.

SOURCE: Adapted from a chart prepared by the League of Women Voters of Florida, 1973.

as a police administrator, a role that it could not have wanted or handled. From prearrest investigations through the initial appearance of the defendant before a magistrate, the criminal justice air echoes with such phrases as "Miranda warning" and "exclusionary rule," referring to these famous decisions. The emphasis in these decisions has been on safeguarding the rights of the suspect.

WARRANTS AND PRESENTMENT

The decision to issue a warrant is a judicial decision, although in practice this fact is not always obvious. Police searches are common; but as they usually are "reasonable" limited searches of persons or automobiles, or are preceded by arrest, or are consented to by the person who is searched, search warrants are used infrequently. The Constitution conveys the idea that search warrants are generally required, but they are not. A *search warrant* is a written demand by a magistrate that a peace officer search the premises (which are described) of a person (who is named) for certain goods (which are listed). The reason for the search must be specified, and it must be based on probable cause, a reasonable belief on the part of the magistrate that criminal evidence can be found. A formal affidavit, the *complaint,* must be signed and sworn by the person who has the information leading to the request for the warrant. The search warrant may be combined with an *arrest warrant.* To protect the identity of informers, the person with the necessary information for the warrant may be called a "credible person" and the warrant sworn to by the police officer.

Once a complaint charging the suspect with a violation of criminal law has been signed by an officer or a complaining witness (depending on the nature of the alleged offense), a magistrate usually issues an arrest warrant. The purpose of the arrest warrant is to provide official sanction for arresting the alleged offender. The warrant declares that, in the name of the state, any person with official authority to do so is to place a named person in custody and to accompany that individual to court to answer to the charge specified. The arrest date is noted on the back of the form, and it is then returned to the magistrate as a permanent record of the arrest.

One other kind of warrant needs to be mentioned. A *bench warrant,* also called a *capias,* is an order for someone to be brought into custody although that person is not being arrested for committing a crime. For example, a person who was previously arrested and is perhaps out on bail or a witness may be brought before a court on a *capias.*

The arresting police officer, the desk sergeant, and the prosecutor all possess considerable discretion to let a detained person go without bringing him or her before a magistrate. This "judicial" authority is sometimes exercised with an accompanying stern warning.

At the federal level and in most states, the initial appearance before the magistrate is called "presentment." In all states an initial appearance is required if a person is to continue to be detained. The time lapse between

arrest and initial appearance varies, but it may be unconscionably long. The reasons for delay include the desire of detectives to interrogate the suspect, an arrest occurring on Sunday or a holiday, and the sheer numbers of people being processed by the police. The maximum delay recommended by the National Crime Commission (1967) is one day.[3]

At the initial appearance the magistrate establishes the defendant's identity and informs him or her of the charge(s) and of his or her constitutional rights. If the defendant is indigent, in many states a defense lawyer is appointed at this time. (In at least one state, a defendant able to post bail is declared not to be indigent.) If the defendant is charged with a felony, he or she is notified of the right to a preliminary hearing. If the arrest was made without a warrant, the complaint and the warrant may be handled at this time. Usually, the prosecutor or an assistant prosecutor is present, if the prosecutor's office is large enough to permit it, and the decision whether to proceed with the prosecution may be made. If the offense is a petty misdemeanor, it is usually disposed (that is, the case is concluded) at the initial appearance. In a more serious misdemeanor case, or a case with a plea of not guilty, or a felony case in which the defendant waives the right to a preliminary hearing, an information may be filed. In some places the case may go to a grand jury instead of a preliminary hearing. One of the magistrate's most important functions is the setting of bail.

BAIL

Bail is a term for the assurance sought by the court that an accused not being held in jail will appear for trial. It is a word that is equated with a sum of money. The magistrate's court holds the bail money (or a bond in lieu of money) until the accused appears for trial, at which time the bail money (or bond) is returned. The magistrate generally decides the amount of bail by using a table or schedule listing various amounts for various offenses; these amounts are sometimes fixed by statute. In some instances, the police may determine proper bail at the police station. Bail may be denied to a defendant who is likely not to appear in court if not detained. It is often denied to murder suspects.

A *bail bond* is a document signed by the defendant and by others on his or her behalf guaranteeing that the defendant will appear in court for trial. Those who "go the bond" are called the *sureties,* and they are supposed to show that they have property as great or greater in value than the bail. If the accused cannot raise the bail or get a friend to go his or her bond, it may be possible to get a bond from a *bail bondsman* or *bondsman,* a person who is in the business of acting as a surety in return for a fee, generally between 10 and 20 percent of the amount of bail. The law frequently gives the bondsman unusual powers to take into custody a defendant who has "jumped bail," that is, has failed to appear in court for trial. The hold bondsmen may have over clients and the power they have to bring in nonpaying clients can lead to abuses of this service. Clients have been known to commit crimes to get money for the bondsman! Bondsmen are poorly regulated in many states and may use a piece of property of small value as collateral for large amounts of bail set for several defendants. On the other hand, some courts do not always demand that bondsmen make good a bond when a defendant fails to appear in court.

If a person has bail set at $500 and is required to pay $50 to obtain a bail bond but does not have the $50, he or she may be left in jail until the trial. The trial may be months away, and the person may be innocent. Many people who must pay $50 or more to obtain a bond are unable to do so.

Studies have shown that many people unable to make bail would have appeared for trial had they been released. In one project during the 1960s, case workers obtained brief information from jailed defendants and had the court release certain categories of defendants on their own *recognizance,* their word that they would appear in court. (Release on own recognizance is often abbreviated ROR.) The project was successful and is being emulated in many areas of the country. But because of the misgivings of the judiciary, pressures from the public, and perhaps the influence of bail bondsmen, ROR programs have not been universally accepted. Indeed, the success rate of ROR varies over time and in different locales and is highly dependent on the category of criminal offense involved. Nonetheless, it has been seriously proposed that the money bail system be eliminated altogether.

Extremely high bail intended to keep dangerous offenders locked up and unable to commit crimes while awaiting trial is called *preventive bail.* Well-to-do burglars and criminals with connections to organized crime, however, simply buy their way out. It is frequently difficult to properly define a *dangerous offender,* and preventive bail is technically unconstitutional. *Preventive detention* is a term sometimes used instead of preventive bail, but it is a broader term and does not necessarily have anything to do with bail.

The Eighth Amendment of the Constitution states, "Excessive bail shall not be required, nor excessive fines imposed, nor cruel and unusual punishment inflicted." Yet thousands of poor people, some of them innocent, are in foul, dangerous jails, with no consideration given to their families' needs or their job requirements, their trials weeks and months away, locked up because they cannot buy their freedom. This condition exists even though it has been shown that many of them would not commit another crime and would appear for trial if they were to sign their own bonds and be released. The direct cost to the taxpayers of maintaining this many people in jail is enormous; the indirect cost to society in terms of human suffering and the criminalization of accused persons are far more enormous. Two means of alleviating this problem are (1) greater use of releasing a defendant on his or her own recognizance, with no money bail required and (2) speedy trial laws.

The first opportunity to secure release from custody may come at the initial appearance, when bail is set. If the police have set bail immediately following arrest, as is possible in some states, the magistrate may reduce bail. Or if the bail is excessive, the accused may be able to have it reduced through a *habeas corpus* action, although most accused persons are ignorant of this fact, do not know the procedures, and cannot afford a lawyer to pursue this action. Bail is reset at the preliminary hearing and at the arraignment. A person appealing conviction may secure release on an appeal bond.

DISPOSITION OF MISDEMEANORS

Cases of petty offenses or misdemeanors are usually settled at the initial appearance of the accused before the magistrate. This is the "trial" that most people have experienced. Serious misdemeanors, higher misdemeanor cases, are also settled in the magistrate's court, although they may not be disposed at the initial appearance. The lower court may have the power to hear cases in which the fine does not exceed $200 or some other amount; it may have jurisdiction that overlaps with that of higher courts; or petty of-

fenses may be handled by specialized courts in cities, such as traffic courts.

The incidence of misdemeanor cases is unknown. Studies of certain courts are revealing. In one year's time three judges in Atlanta disposed of more than 70,000 cases. In one year's time, the District of Columbia Court of General Sessions had four judges to process 1,500 felony cases and to hear and determine 7,500 serious misdemeanor cases, 38,000 petty misdemeanors, and about 38,000 traffic violation cases.

Traffic violations are sometimes considered misdemeanors. Nationally, the number is in the millions each year. It is estimated that prosecutors dismiss about 5 percent, as many as 85 percent plead guilty, as many as 25 percent of those tried will be acquitted, and more than 75 percent of those convicted (including those who plead guilty and those who are tried) will be fined, placed on probation, or released.[4]

A person charged with a misdemeanor who can afford a defense attorney tends to be released on bond to prepare for trial at a later date or to engage in plea bargaining. However, the overwhelming majority are without legal representation, and when asked how they plead, reply "guilty." Some of them are aware that they may be returned to jail to await a later trial date if they plead otherwise. Rules of evidence are sometimes ignored in misdemeanor trials; there is seldom a court reporter present; the "due process" safeguards present at felony trials are, at best, strained. The emphasis in many of these lower courts, particularly those in the cities, is on speed. Trials typically last from five to fifteen minutes and, despite complexities, are unlikely to exceed an hour. The defendant is seldom allowed to talk at any length and may not be allowed to offer any defense. Trial records are incomplete or nonexistent.

Jail sentences of several months are common in misdemeanor cases. Probation services and presentence investigations are rare. Fines are the usual result. If a fine could not be paid, the "$30 or 30 days" rule was once applied, but a Supreme Court ruling officially ended this practice. Sentencing is based on the charge and the defendant's appearance and what little of his or her manner the judge may ascertain. Trial and sentencing are affected by the quality of personnel and a multitude of administrative problems, not the least of which is the volume of cases a relatively few judges must process.

PRELIMINARY HEARING, INFORMATION, RETURN OF GRAND JURY INDICTMENT

Following the initial appearance, a felony case is typically scheduled for a *preliminary hearing,* also called *examining trial* and *preliminary examination.* The purpose of the preliminary hearing is to protect the accused from an unjustified prosecution. The prosecutor must produce enough evidence to enable the magistrate before whom the hearing is held to decide whether there is probable cause for believing that a felony was committed by the accused. Proof of guilt is not necessary. In all but a few cases the defendant is "bound over" by the magistrate for trial before a court of general jurisdiction.

In many jurisdictions, not all defendants in felony cases are given a preliminary hearing. Defendants frequently waive it, and in jurisdictions in which the grand jury procedure is used, there may or may not be a preliminary hearing. If the preliminary hearing has been waived, an *information* is usually prepared, often by the prosecutor. An information is like an indictment in that it is a formal charge. Defendants who have lawyers often want preliminary hearings, because these hearings allow defense attorneys

to "discover" the state's case against the defendant. (Until recently, the adversary system in criminal cases has been marked by an absence of formal means by which the defense can discover the prosecution's case against the defendant.)

The time between presentment and preliminary hearing, information, or indictment is ideally from three to seven days. In actuality weeks and even months may elapse.

ARRAIGNMENT

The day the information is filed, the defendant is generally arraigned, but several days may elapse between an indictment and arraignment. Any formal appearance before a magistrate prior to a trial is loosely referred to as an *arraignment.* More strictly, arraignment refers to the appearance of the defendant in a felony case before a magistrate who takes the defendant's plea. Arraignments are plea sessions. The arraignment takes place in the court in which the case would be tried. This means that if the magistrate processing the case has a lower-court jurisdiction, as is nearly always true, the defendant appears before a different magistrate. Counsel must be present, and counsel will be appointed for an indigent defendant at this time if the appointment has not been made earlier. The plea may be guilty, not guilty, or, in some states, *nolo contendere,* a Latin phrase meaning "no contest." There is no plea of innocent. Other pleas, such as former jeopardy and not guilty by reason of insanity, are permitted in some states. Also, at the arraignment the formal charge is read to the defendant.

Before the court can accept a plea of guilty, the judge is required by law to endeavor to determine that the plea is voluntary, that it is made with full awareness of its implications, and that it is accurate. A guilty plea is usually equated with a verdict of guilty, although the judge does follow certain guidelines before accepting a guilty plea. The plea is entered on the back of the information or indictment form, and the defendant is sentenced or a date is set for the sentencing. The court treats a plea of *nolo contendere* the same as a guilty plea. The only benefit that accrues from a *nolo contendere* plea is that certain civil penalties that accompany a guilty plea may not be attached. A plea of not guilty places the burden on the state to prove beyond a reasonable doubt that the defendant is guilty. The plea is entered on the back of the information or the indictment form, and a trial date is set. Federal and state law requires a "speedy trial," but unless "speedy" is specifically defined, this law is flouted.

Nearly all the convictions obtained in felony cases in many jurisdictions result from guilty pleas; in roughly 70 to 80 percent of the felony cases that reach this point, the plea is guilty. These fantastic figures reflect the pervasiveness of plea bargaining. Although it has been denied that judges are a part of the plea bargaining process, they are indirectly involved at the very least because communications regarding the bargain must be good if the bargain is to be kept. The National Advisory Commission (1973) would have the courts abandon plea bargaining.

PRETRIAL MOTIONS

The court's functions are referred to as the *judicial process*. The centerpiece of the judicial process is the trial.

If the plea has been not guilty, much time will be spent in preparation for trial. The National Crime Commission recommends that the maximum amount of time be nine weeks, but frequently the elapsed time is measured in months, and sometimes even in years. Defendants who would rather spend

a year in jail than five or more years in prison frequently seek long delays; the more time elapses between the occurrence of the crime and the trial, the more likely there is to be a dismissal or acquittal because witnesses and evidence have faded or disappeared. However, long delays are not always desired: In 1972, the inmates of the Washington, D.C., jail seized a number of hostages, including the Director of Corrections, and released them only after being promised immediate court hearings.

The defense counsel seeks to win the case, or to at least delay the trial, by pretrial motions. Plea bargaining may be going on during delays. The National Crime Commission recommends that ten days be allowed for filing motions with the court, up to seven days before a court hearing is held on the plea motions, and up to twenty-one days before the court makes its decisions whether to sustain the heard motions. The actual times, of course, are frequently much longer.

Even before the plea is entered, the defense counsel will generally raise an objection to the sufficiency of the indictment or information. Objections based on the statute of limitations, double jeopardy, and improper composition or irregular procedures of the grand jury may be made before the plea is entered. Each of these is a motion to dismiss.

Following the plea, a request for a change of venue may be made. Change of venue is usually requested if it is felt that the emotions of citizens in the area where the offense occurred might prejudice the case against the defendant. When there are codefendants, a request may be made for separate trials. These two motions are made in only a small percentage of cases.

Motions requesting information that the state has against the defendant are more common. Called a *motion for a bill of particulars,* this is a chief means of "discovery." Motions to suppress evidence because it has been illegally obtained result in a high dismissal rate, particularly in cases involving narcotics. A motion for continuance may be granted for a number of reasons; this results in a postponement of the trial. Motions for continuance may be made by the defense simply to improve the odds on winning the case by delaying the trial, but in itself this reason is not grounds for sustaining the motion.

TRIAL

The trials, the sentencing, perhaps some of the pretrial motions, and the system of appeals are what people tend to associate with the word *court.* Final responsibility for the way a person is treated by the criminal justice system classically depends on the judges' decisions at these levels.

The percentage of criminal cases that reach the trial stage is small, but the total number of trials each year is large, and trials require much of the courts' time, with civil cases requiring much more than criminal cases. Major factors distinguishing criminal trials from civil trials include the presumption of innocence, the requirement of proof of guilt beyond a reasonable doubt, the defendant's right not to testify, the exclusion of evidence obtained in an illegal manner, and the frequent use of the defendant's admissions. The case is always the *state* versus the *defendant.* The rate of acquittal in felony cases in large cities is likely to be less than one-third, regardless of whether the trial was by jury (jury trial) or judge (bench trial).

Felony cases and often serious misdemeanor cases will be tried by jury unless the defendant waives the jury, as is done in a large number of cases. In capital cases, statutory law may require a jury.

PETIT JURY

A *petit jury* is a trial jury, the jury everyone thinks of when the word *jury* is mentioned. It is used in civil as well as criminal cases. In felony cases it is usually composed of twelve people; in serious misdemeanor cases, in which it is sometimes used, the number may be less. Until recently a unanimous verdict was required in every state for a verdict of guilty, but now, in some states, a majority vote is sufficient.

Originally jurors were knowledgeable witnesses. Today, they are supposed to be impartial and without opinions about the case at hand. The methods of selecting the *array,* or the *venire* (people who might become jurors), may be made from a list of voters or by some other method. The veniremen answer general questions posed by the prosecutor in the courtroom; for example, "Have you ever been convicted of a felony?" "Can you understand and read English?" From the group who survives this questioning, the judge hears any requests to be relieved from serving and excuses some people from jury duty. The names of the resulting panel of jurors are typically written on pieces of paper and drawn by chance, one at a time. Then both prosecutor and defense examine each individual and may seek to have the judge disqualify the person "for cause," for example, because he or she is related to the defendant or has already formed an opinion about the case. Once the jury box is full, the prosecutor and the defense attorney are each allowed to request that the judge excuse from duty a certain number of specified jurors, without giving any reason. These requests are called *peremp-*

tory challenges. For each juror excused, another is selected to fill the vacant seat. An alternate juror may be selected to take the place of a regular juror if need be.

EVIDENCE

Trial procedure is largely governed by rules of evidence, some of which are defined by state law and some by court-made law. *Law of evidence* has its complexities and is offered as a separate course in law schools. The objective of the rules of evidence is to enable the adversary system to reveal the truth in a case. *Evidence* is defined as the legal proofs presented through records, witnesses, objects, or any other vehicle, intended to sway the beliefs of judge or jurors toward the prosecutor's side of the case or toward the defendant's side. *Real evidence* is the term for concrete objects; *testimony* is the term for the statements of sworn witnesses; *direct evidence* is evidence observed at first hand; *circumstantial evidence* refers to a web of facts that form a tendency toward accepting or refuting a point. The court will not accept anything as evidence unless it is relevant, material, and competent, and the adversaries frequently raise objections to material offered as evidence for the court to sustain.

The order in which evidence is presented during a trial differs from state to state, but it always follows a legally established procedure. For example, once the jury is selected, the prosecution makes an opening statement, stating what the case is about. The defense may follow with a statement or make its statement later in the trial. Typically, the prosecution follows its opening statement with a presentation of witnesses for the state, and the defense follows its statement with a presentation of witnesses for the defense. The defense may argue for various motions following the prosecution's presentation. In rebuttal to the defense, the state may counter with another presentation of witnesses, and the defense in turn may counter the state with another presentation of witnesses. The state and the defense then present their final arguments before the jury.

Privileged communications and confidentiality are aspects of evidence that are often confused with one another by the public. *Privileged communications* are communications that the person who is the receiver cannot be legally made to divulge. *Confidentiality* has no legal protection in a court of law. For example, a social worker may be legally and ethically bound by the principle of confidentiality to keep communications obtained from a client private, but these communications are not privileged by law, and a court could command the social worker to tell what he or she heard.

WITNESSES

Persons who are ordered or subpeonaed by a court to appear as witnesses for the state or who volunteer to do so are "examined" by the prosecutor and then cross-examined by the defense attorney. The witnesses, like the defendant, are guaranteed constitutional rights during the trial. Witnesses called by the defense may be cross-examined by the prosecutor. The examination is a question-and-answer method of eliciting information. The cross-examination is a question-and-answer method of challenging the veracity of the witnesses' accounts. Leading questions ("Have you stopped beating your wife?") and other abrasive techniques are allowed during cross-examinations, and they make the cross-examination a psychological tool for trying (ostensibly) to get at the truth. Witnesses may be impeached, that is, their testimony discredited, by cross-examination. They may also be impeached by using other witnesses to show that the testimony was wrong.

Witnesses are generally limited by a rule of evidence to testifying to what they have observed. Lay witnesses (*lay* means anybody not an expert) can express opinions if they are supported by factual material that is recognized as being in the realm of common experience. An opinion that the defendant was sleeping, for example, may be supported by information that he was lying down at night, snoring, after having fought a fire all day. Expert witnesses may give opinions and support them without having observed the defendant at the time of the criminal action. Police officers who are crime lab technicians or ballistics experts or professional investigators may act as expert witnesses. Any person who can be shown to have relevant expertise may act as an expert witness. Psychiatrists who try to define the mental state of defendants, particularly at the time of their criminal behavior, have become fairly common expert witnesses, although controversy about legal insanity rages in the criminal justice field.

Hearsay evidence is information that witnesses have obtained second-hand. It is not acceptable as evidence because there is no opportunity to determine the veracity of the information through cross-examination. Exceptions to the rule against hearsay evidence includes *res gestae,* "things done," which means that things said that are closely tied to an account of the event are allowed as evidence. For example, in an investigation of a homicide, if the victim's wife at the scene of the crime sobs, "My son didn't mean to do it," her words would be included in the testimony. Admissions against the interest of a defendant may be accepted also; for example, the above-mentioned son may say, "I was there when the murder took place." A confession is also permitted; for example, "Yes, I hit him and his head struck the corner of the table and he died." The judge, however, would try to determine the circumstances surrounding the confession before allowing it to be admitted as evidence. The prosecution wants a written confession because, under the rules of evidence, the defendant cannot be required to testify; the Constitution provides protection against demands for self-incrimination.

CLOSING THE TRIAL

At the close of the evidence, the judge in a jury trial gives the jury written instructions regarding the law as it applies to the facts in a case. The jury is to decide what the facts may truly be. The arguments by the prosecution and defense counsel to the jury follow. The procedure is prescribed by law and varies from state to state.

The judge then charges the jury to consider the merits of the case and return a just verdict on the written forms supplied. The foreman or forewoman is to sign the verdict the jurors agree on and return it to the judge. The jury is isolated (*sequestered* is the word commonly used) from other people and put in the custody of the bailiff to deliberate (that is, discuss the case) and vote on a verdict of guilty or not guilty. In some states the jury must decide on the type of homicide of which the defendant is guilty, and it may have to decide what the sentence is to be. In some trials the jury vote need not be unanimous for a conviction to be obtained. In other instances, if all the jurors do not finally vote the same way, then the jury may be called a *hung jury,* and the trial will be declared a mistrial. The defendant will have to be tried again with a new jury, unless the prosecutor elects not to prosecute. The court then renders the official judgment as to guilt based on the jury's verdict. The judge usually imposes sentence at a later date, but not long after the verdict or the plea of guilty.

If the defendant has been convicted (found guilty), the conviction may be appealed. The use of posttrial motions to try to alter the impact of a conviction is becoming popular.

SENTENCING

A *sentence* is an official judgment declaring the penalty in an individual case in which there has been a conviction for a criminal offense. In some states the legislature fixes only the maximum penalty, allowing the judge to sentence the defendant for any amount of time less than or equal to the maximum. In some states maximum and minimums are established for each offense. The judge must then sentence between the minimum amount and the maximum amount.

Offenders who repeat an offense or who have previously committed a similar one may receive a more severe sentence if the state has *enhancement* or *habitual criminal statutes*. The more severe sentence is called an *enhanced sentence*. The repeater is usually eager to engage in plea bargaining in order to get a reduced sentence. A *fixed* or *definite sentence* is one in which the number of years it is to be in effect is specified. An *indeterminate sentence* specifies a range of years, for example, one to twenty. A high minimum can prevent early parole, and indeterminate sentences tend to result in confinement for the maximum figure, although the proponents of indeterminate sentences did not anticipate this. A *concurrent sentence* is one in which a defendant convicted for more than one offense during the same trial is sentenced

for each offense but serves the sentences simultaneously. The alternative is *consecutive*; the defendant serves the sentences one after the other.

OBJECTIVES OF SENTENCING

The general function of the court is to determine whether the accused has broken the law and, if so, to decide what should be done to or for the convicted person. The objective of sentencing is not clear, either in the general sense or in individual cases. Objectives include revenge, incapacitation, general deterrence and individual deterrence, and rehabilitation. Rehabilitation goals may be constructed either to include or to exclude punishment. It is clear, however, that the circumstances surrounding cases in which the offense is the same may differ so markedly that justice requires individualized sentences. By smoking cigarettes in secret behind a haystack, two boys might set the haystack on fire in a game of "I dare you." A man might burn down an apartment building to try to collect insurance money. A woman might burn a house to get rid of her husband. The boys, the man, and the woman may be found guilty of arson, but to sentence all parties who set fire to people's property to life imprisonment for arson would be unconscionable. Although carefully composed and ordered statutes can eliminate much of the present need for sentencing discretion, discretion cannot be eliminated completely if sentencing is to be fair.

SENTENCE HEARING FACTORS

In a sentence hearing following conviction, a judge typically pronounces that an individual shall be incarcerated for a given amount of time (or range of time), or be placed on probation, or be sentenced to imprisonment but have the sentence suspended. The factors that go into the decision include the legal factors, of course; but there are many more, some of which may be determined by presentence investigation reports. Important factors have been shown to include the nature of the offense, the number of offenses for which the person was tried, and the person's previous criminal record. Other factors include whether the defendant pleaded guilty or was found guilty by verdict, whether he or she was represented by a defense attorney, and whether sentencing alternatives were available and known to the judge. Factors such as the defendant's race, age, sex, and social status are closely linked to the prejudices of the judge.

These last factors are hotly argued as the source of unfair individualized sentencing, called *sentencing disparity*. There is no question that sentencing disparities occur, for sentencing is a difficult decision-making process that is highly subjective, and judges are human and, therefore, prone to err according to their biases. Carefully done studies would seem to indicate that there is less sentencing disparity in felony cases than many social critics believe.[5] If the sentence itself, as distinguished from the verdict, could be appealed (and in most states it cannot be), many people think that sentencing would become more certain to be fair. Probably appellate review of sentences will become standard procedure in all the states in years to come. Some states now have automatic review of death and life sentences. Judges' conferences on sentencing and regular visits by judges to correctional facilities have already become common.

SENTENCING ALTERNATIVES AND DIVERSION

Judges are often in a quandary when they must pass sentence, for in many instances their only choices are to lock up the convicted person or, in essence, to let him or her go. Neither choice may be desirable. In some places, a growing number of sentencing alternatives are available to the judge, for example, halfway houses and schools for drunk drivers.

Diversion programs have been developed with the court's help. For example, rather than being incarcerated for assaulting a relative, a youth may be allowed or directed to begin therapy with a psychiatrist. The National Advisory Commission on Criminal Justice Standards and Goals (1973) states that in appropriate cases, offenders should be diverted into noncriminal justice programs before formal trial or conviction. Diversion programs are usually informal, and there is generally no provision for them in statutory law. This fact gives the court discretion to make unusual demands of offenders. When ongoing programs are established, however, the diversion is apt to take place before the offender becomes a court's responsibility. Police or juvenile probation officers may refer juveniles picked up for minor offenses to youth service bureaus instead of processing them through the courts. Police may take a public drunk directly to a detoxification center instead of booking him. A prosecutor's office may have a fraud division that frequently allows restitution instead of seeking imprisonment through the courts. There are many other programs; they are local, however, and not available in every jurisdiction.

POSTCONVICTION REMEDIES

APPEAL

Defendants who wish to do so may ask a higher court to overturn their convictions. They can do this through the right to appeal (although this is not a right guaranteed by the Constitution) and through the right to seek writs of *certiorari* and *habeas corpus*. An *appeal* is a limited review of a case; that is, the appellate court restricts itself to examining identified points of law in the record of the trial and does not hear testimony on matters of fact. If a convicted offender wants to appeal and cannot afford to pay for a transcript of the trial proceedings or for counsel, it will be provided free by the court. In some states, the prosecution has a limited right to appeal some lower-court decisions that favored the defendant. Appeals within the states are time-consuming; six months to two years may elapse before they are heard.

An appeal may result in the appellate court's agreeing with the trial court's decision in the case, in a reversal of the decision (that is, finding not guilty a defendant whom the lower court had found guilty), or in a remand of the case back to the trial court for a new trial based on guidelines set by the appellate court. Because of the expense and difficulties associated with a new trial, it may not be held, and the once convicted offender is then released. Appellate court decisions are frequently expressed in what is called an *opinion*. The best known of these opinions and dissenting opinions come from the Supreme Court justices and are scholarly works of some literary merit.

APPELLATE REVIEW

As commonly used, the phrase *unified appellate review* is a broader term than appeal. An attempt is being made to get the states to adopt a unified review proceeding that would give every convicted offender the opportunity to obtain one comprehensive judicial review of the conviction and sentence by a court other than the court of trial. The review would extend to all matters of legality in the proceedings leading to the conviction and the legality and appropriateness of the sentence. It would also extend to errors not apparent in the trial record that might otherwise be used in efforts other than appeal to overturn a conviction or change a sentence. For example, if a juror later testified to something that a judge said "off the record" during a trial and the judge's comments were contrary to due process of law, the conviction could be overturned. The courts are not now set up to handle such a unified review proceeding, but it is believed that it would be worth the effort it would take to implement it. (It works in England.) It would streamline a creaky, bureaucratic system and probably reduce procedural time and enhance justice. In special circumstances a second review could be granted.

The National Advisory Commission on Criminal Justice Standards and Goals (1973) worked out details for a proposed unified review procedure. It declared that the dispositional time in a reviewing court should range from sixty days after sentence for insubstantial issues to ninety days in complicated cases. Initial action should begin within thirty days following the sentencing.[6]

OTHER POSTCONVICTION REMEDIES

The most famous of the other remedies is the *writ of habeas corpus,* "you have the body." It is a court order demanding that a person who is restraining the body produce it in court and explain why the body should continue to be restrained. Almost any judge at the trial court level or the appellate court level can issue this writ. The writ of *habeas corpus* has been described as the single most important distinction between a free democracy and a tyrannical country: in a democracy anyone can petition a court or judge to issue a writ seeking to obtain the release of anyone whose freedom is in any way physically restricted. As a logical consequence, prisoners deluge the courts with their petitions.

Also commonly used is the *writ of certiorari*. This is a court order asking that an issue raised in the writ be made certain or clear by a higher court. It permits such a court to review a case, but the court is not obligated to do so (as it is with an appeal). Most petitions for the writs are simply stamped "*certiorari* denied." Most of the cases heard by the United States Supreme Court are heard on writs of *certiorari*, not on appeal. Another use of this writ, at any level, involves a challenge to a trial court's jurisdiction on a particular case. Such a challenge forestalls trial while it is examined by a higher court.

DISCUSSION QUESTIONS

1. What examples of court lag can be discerned in the functions of the courts?
2. Is sentencing fair? How could it be improved?
3. Discuss the importance of the court's functions prior to trial relative to the importance of the trial.
4. Discuss the ways in which courts function to protect the innocent. In what ways do they fail to protect the innocent?
5. Describe the abuses of bail. What can be done about them?

NOTES

1. National Advisory Commission on Criminal Justice Standards and Goals, *Courts* (Washington, D.C.: Government Printing Office, 1973), Standard 4.1, p. 65.
2. These cases are among those identified as part of the "criminal law revolution" of the sixties and include such major cases as *Mapp* v. *Ohio,* 367 U.S. 478 (1964); *Miranda* v. *Arizona,* 384 U.S. 436 (1966); *Terry* v. *Ohio,* 392 U.S. 1 (1968); *Chimel* v. *California,* 395 U.S. 752 (1969).
3. President's Commission on Law Enforcement and Administration of Justice, *The Challenge of Crime in a Free Society* (Washington, D.C.: Government Printing Office, 1967), p. 258.
4. President's Commission on Law Enforcement and Administration of Justice, *Task Force Report: The Courts* (Washington, D.C.: Government Printing Office, 1967), p. 31.
5. The best-known study is Edward Green, *Judicial Attitudes in Sentencing: A Study of the Factors Underlying the Sentencing Practices of the Court of Philadelphia* (London: Macmillan, 1961).
6. *Task Force Report: The Courts,* Standard 6.4, pp. 101–108.

CHAPTER FIFTEEN

COURT ISSUES AND PROBLEMS: THE PARTICIPANTS' PERSPECTIVES

ACTIVE PARTICIPANTS
INDIRECT
PARTICIPANTS

Purpose: To describe the roles of various participants in the courts and to present the problem areas of the court as related to these participants.

"THIS COURT LOOKS with disfavor . . . ." In a statement that begins thus, there can be no question that a judge is speaking and referring to himself or herself as "the court." The judge is the chief figure of the court and embodies it — even when the judicial role appears to be reduced to that of a referee for two nonjudicial adversaries.

The adversaries are the prosecutor and the defense attorney, and their prestige is second only to that of the judge. The jury may be of key importance, particularly in more serious felony cases. The same is true of witnesses, regardless of whether they are for the state or for the defense. There is the "administrative" staff — bailiffs, chief clerks, and so on — who can be crucial, yet their roles are often overlooked by people concerned about the condition of the courts.

The list is by no means exhausted; there are grand juries, probation officers, social workers, researchers, psychiatrists and psychologists, secretaries and bookkeepers, and an endless stream of others — all in the direct employ of the courts or supervised by them. It is sometimes doubtful that the defendant is a participant, although there have been spectacular exceptions.[1]

The courtroom is a public place, despite the frequent closed-door hearings found particularly in quasi-judicial settings. This means that there is an audience, and by its presence it exercises influence. The audience, therefore, is a participant, however passive it may be. In this audience are news media people, and by their participation they bring the court out of the courtroom and into the living rooms of the public. The public, then, by its reaction and potential for reaction, becomes a participant.

If folk wisdom is correct, any organization is only as good as its participants. Who, then, are these court participants, and what are the ground rules by which they abide?

ACTIVE PARTICIPANTS

Some of the participants are active within the courtroom, judges, adversaries, witnesses, and jurors among them.

JUDGES

Crucial questions about the operation and success of the courts center on the judges. What qualifications they possess, how they are selected, what their duties and powers are, and how they may be terminated are all questions that must be answered one way or another.

Qualifications and Training Most kinds of courts are presided over by judges who are lawyers, although many justices of the peace, city judges, and judges of county courts who handle only misdemeanors are not. The value of a law degree in some of the lower courts has been questioned because lawyers are not trained to be judges. On the other hand, an intimate knowledge of law, particularly the law of evidence and how to find material in the law, is generally recognized as necessary in the higher courts, and a law degree is often advocated as a prerequisite for *all* judgeships. Still, unless a judge has been a prosecutor, he or she is unlikely to have had any experience in handling criminal cases and may or may not have had a single course in criminal law in law school. Some of the nonlawyers who are justices of the peace, who routinely sentence people to six months in jail, are unintelligent, easily dominated by police officers and prosecutors, and preoccupied with their regular businesses — which might be anything from being a mechanic to being a homemaker. In short, they seem singularly unfit to be judges.

In many countries people who wish to become judges enter a standard program of training at a recognized school and later become apprentices before becoming fully empowered judges. In the United States, however, the background of judges reflects a startling lack of standards. There is no training for a judgeship, no necessary course in criminal law, no apprenticeship, and, frequently, no standards whatsoever.

In recent years various forms of judicial conferences have been developed that provide some specialized training, and new judges have been given particular attention. For the most part, however, judges do not observe other judges at work. The conferences usually are not limited to criminal cases, but give most of their attention to civil cases. There is no organized system to ensure that judges acquire updated information. (By way of contrast, physicians specializing in family medicine must pass a test every three years to continue to qualify as specialists.)

Selection There is a wide variety of procedures for selecting judges, but they fall into three basic categories: (1) elected, (2) appointed, and (3) mixed. Judges at the state level may be appointed either by the governor or by the legislature. They may be appointed from a selected list of names developed by a professional, "nonpartisan" team. They may be appointed and then have to run for election on their records. They may be elected, rather than appointed, either with political party labels or without them. If they have been appointed, they may be screened by a professional team before they take office.

For the most part, judges are actually selected by the dominant political party in private deals, and the spoils system poses a constant threat to ideal selection. There is danger, too, that the judiciary may be to some extent dominated or controlled by bar associations. A carefully selected nominating team helps to lessen the selection biases arising from these two factors.

A merit system called the Missouri Plan, because it was first adopted by Missouri, is advocated by many jurists, and at least ten states have adopted a similar system. The Missouri Plan requires that judges be nominated by a nonpartisan commission. The judge becomes a judge when appointed by the governor. Then, in a general election, the public is asked for a vote of confidence to keep the judge in office. He or she does not run against anyone. At the end of each term another vote is taken, and at least 50 percent of the votes must be for the judge if he or she is to continue.

Role The duties of the judge of a criminal court have already been largely defined, although they vary enormously with the kind and size of the court. Judges must have a good knowledge of law, skill in court procedure, and the necessary toughness to control the court and to make the taxing decisions demanded of them. As a group, judges probably have more power to bring about major changes in the criminal justice system than any other group. High prestige is associated with the higher judicial positions. Good lawyers, however, can generally make more money and may have an easier professional life if they do not become judges. Judges' salaries range from token sums to amounts equivalent to the salaries of well-paid executives. Retirement systems are generally attractive. In addition, retired judges may be recalled to preside over time-consuming cases and thus relieve regular judges of heavy caseloads.

Termination Until recently, the only ways of removing judges were impeachment and persuasion to retire. This is one reason for good retirement systems, and many states are now able to use a "forced retirement" method. *Impeachment* is a formal procedure for removing a public servant from office. As a means of eliminating bad or poor judges, it is cumbersome and all but unworkable. A judge cannot be removed by impeachment without being touched by scandal (regardless of the truth or falsity of the charge).

In New York, a Court of the Judiciary has been established to hear complaints of judicial misconduct. For smaller states, a court administrator or other special officer has been suggested as a possible disciplinarian. New Jersey, which has a unified court system, apparently has had success with an informal method in which the state's chief justice initially talks with the errant judge. Perhaps the best system that has evolved is the commission plan adopted by California in 1960, by Texas in 1965, and by many other states since then. The Commission on Judicial Qualifications is a permanent body of judges, lawyers, and others that receives complaints about judicial behavior, makes investigations, and can recommend to the supreme court of the state that judges be removed or retired. The commission does *not* make periodic, irregular, unannounced inspections like those used by the military as a form of quality control of personnel practices.

ADVERSARIES

The opposing lawyers in a case make for many an exciting television drama. Since their actual duties and responsibilities have already been discussed, they will be treated only briefly in this section.

Prosecutor Suffice it to say here that prosecutors often wield informal power that dwarfs the power of the other participants. Prosecutors may be held in check by the judge's ability to place them in contempt, but they nonetheless may be tremendously influential in the court. By controlling guilty pleas, they can swamp a judge's docket with trial cases if they wish to put a judge "in his place." By their plea bargaining, they determine verdicts and sentencing. They can, by exercising their discretionary power, dismiss cases by refusing to prosecute. If a grand jury is used, it is generally a weighty rubber stamp of approval that the prosecutor can apply at will to obtain indictments. In the past prosecutors often had a great deal more trial experience in criminal cases and much greater knowledge of criminal law than did public defense attorneys. Prosecutors are not always well paid and may have political ambitions, sometimes with the result that persons of inferior quality with ulterior motives can apply a great deal of power in unjust prosecutions. Bad prosecutors denigrate the very real value of the many dedicated prosecutors of high personal integrity. It is generally a tough, able, honest prosecutor who brings powerful, corrupt public officials to justice.

Defense Attorney Defense attorneys, or defense lawyers, or counsel, or, sometimes, "the defense," represent the defendant's interests during a criminal case. In a typical medium-sized city, only a few lawyers will handle defense cases. The requirement that every defendant who may face incarceration has a right to counsel has resulted in a few lawyers who accept appointments by judges to indigent cases as a form of lawyer welfare. Other cities have arrangements, usually made through the local bar association, by which every lawyer will serve a turn as an appointee to the defense in a criminal case.

Government-sponsored offices of defense lawyers have been created in some places. These "public defender" agencies often have a social work flavor and may even work closely with the prosecutor on the defendant's behalf. They have been accused of not always working on the defendant's behalf. The potential for an increasingly professional, growing body of defense lawyers is now being realized.

JURORS

The grand jury is a body of lay people who determine whether there is enough evidence to justify a formal charge that an accused person has committed an alleged crime. The evidence is provided by the prosecutor. (The grand jury's nature and function was described in Part Three.) Popular opinion frequently equates an indictment with a conviction by a trial court, but newspaper headlines stating that someone has been indicted do not prove guilt, whatever the public may think.

The role of the petit or petty jury or trial jury has been increasingly studied. The jury listens to the trial. Regardless of how long the trial takes, and it may be weeks or months, in many states the jury is not allowed to take notes. The jurors may be isolated from other people all during the trial, or they may be isolated only at the closing of the presentation of evidence. They may be paid as little as $5 a day. The court shows little concern for the requirements jurors must meet in their daily work and domestic lives — other than to excuse a wide range of competent people from jury duty. Conscientious citizens are sometimes soured on jury duty by this lack of regard and by the court's poor handling of a case.

Either the jurors elect a foreman or the first member of the jury automatically becomes the foreman. This role is somewhat similar to that of a committee chairperson. The deliberations of jurors are supposed to be secret, but the accounts of some jurors' behavior during this period have been shocking in their indifference to the trial and to the defendant's lot. The jury may also ignore the law in making its decisions of guilt or innocence. It may render sentences (when it has this responsibility) without regard to the usual considerations. For example, a first offender may be sentenced to twenty years, while a "three-time loser" in similar circumstances is sentenced to five years' imprisonment. Studies have indicated, however, that the verdicts rendered by juries appear to be about the same overall as would have been expected in cases where the jury trial has been waived.[2]

WITNESSES

A witness is a person who swears an oath or affirmation to tell the truth, sits in the *witness stand* beside the judge, and provides testimony for either the state or the defense, who will either examine or cross-examine the witness. In United States courts, much reliance is placed on witnesses. The oath is traditional, but it also serves to make perjury (lying by witnesses) appear more serious and therefore less likely to occur. Perjury laws do not, however, make witnesses paragons of truthfulness. The laws cannot prevent the coaching of witnesses by lawyers, exaggerated pleading by witnesses, or the deliberate omission of essential facts. Furthermore, a case may reach the trial stage years after the person witnessed a crime, and the vagaries of human memory and perception over time are well documented. The witness may find the form of taking testimony during a trial so alien that he or she is unable to give information. If the prosecutor or defense attorney is at all skilled, the witness can be made to appear to say something totally different from what he or she knows to be true.

Some witnesses may feel used and abused by the judge and lawyers. They may also be dismayed by the lack of regard for their time. Witnesses may be requested or subpoenaed to appear on a certain date, only to find that they were not needed on that date but can be expected to be called again. In many instances, there are no facilities or services to meet their simple needs for comfort. Some people, however, make money by being frequent expert witnesses, for example, psychiatrists whose specialty in forensic psychiatry has made them sought-after expert witnesses.

The most common witness in criminal trials is the police officer, who usually appears as a state's witness. Police officers report what they observed at the time of arrest. Other police witnesses are frequently expert witnesses: ballistics experts, police photographers, polygraph operators, and so forth. Special treatment, legal and quasi-legal, has evolved to protect the police informer who becomes a witness, and in many instances a police officer acts as a witness in place of the informer. "Turning state's evidence" means that a defendant has decided to act as a witness for the state and provide testimony against codefendants, usually in return for the prosecution's word that charges will be dropped or reduced or that the sentence will be light.

INDIRECT PARTICIPANTS

The people behind the scenes, as it were, in every trial include the people who work for the court — the peripheral personnel — and the public — the people for whom the court is supposed to work.

PERIPHERAL PERSONNEL
The clerk of court, the bailiff, and the court reporter are adjuncts to all higher courts and many lower ones. They are sometimes erroneously referred to as *court administrators*.

Their work *is* administrative rather than judicial, but they are not to be confused with court administrators, professional executives who handle courts' administrative problems.

The Clerk of Court The clerk of court is an elected official at the county level. In a federal court or an appellate court, the clerk of court is appointed by the federal judge. In many places the clerk of court has an additional job as county clerk and also does work unrelated to the courts. In such cases there may be an assistant, a deputy clerk, who is responsible for the work of the courts. There may be many clerks of court, each with a specific role, such as processing appeals. The clerks usually have no particular qualifications for obtaining the job, and tend to stay in office term after term. Professional associations of clerks are working toward standardization of their procedures.

Clerks of court take care of all court records. They keep on file indictments and informations, pleadings from prosecutors and defense, instructions to the jury, verdicts, and sentences. Such documents are bound into huge books or records. Clerks of court also handle warrants. Docketing and scheduling tend to fall on the shoulders of the clerk of court. During the trial the clerk swears in witnesses and provides records requested by the judge. Their duties are not limited to criminal cases; they are responsible for a number of procedures related to civil cases as well.

An elected clerk not directly responsible to a judge can slow a court's handling of cases to a virtual standstill by either incompetence or dislike of the judge.

Court Administrators The nature of court activity is twofold in that it is either judicial or administrative. The court administrator manages the administrative operations of the court. There are budgets to manage, personnel to handle, facilities and equipment to maintain, cases to be scheduled, juries and witnesses to be seen to, and so on. By tending to the administrative needs of the court, the court administrator gives the judge more time for the judicial operations of the court.

In the past, court administration was the province of the judge. However, with the increase in workload and judicial responsibility, it became apparent in many courts that administrative assistance was necessary. The Administrative Office of the United States Courts was created in 1932. In the state and local courts, however, much of the growth in court administration occurred during the sixties. By 1970 approximately 80 percent of the court administrators held jobs that had come into existence during the previous decade. Their presence has enhanced the efficiency of the court, and, as a result, the judicial operations of the court.

Court Reporters Court reporters are also record keepers, but their specific duty is to record accurately the trial or other court procedures. Court reporters are well paid, for they are highly skilled. They must listen to witnesses mumble and at the same time write the correct dialogue in shorthand or with a stenotype machine. Obviously, they must be accurate and fast. In cases that are appealed, they may be required to prepare a narrative record, or transcript, of the trial.

Because some court reporters have other jobs and do not give as much time to court reporting as they should, they may interfere with the proper recording of trials and particularly with appeal procedure. Efforts to replace court reporters with tape recorders have not yet been successful, but some people anticipate that court reporters will be replaced as technology advances.

Bailiffs Bailiffs perform duties similar to those of a security guard in a bank. During trials they protect the court from dangerous or unseemly behavior. In less active courts,

they may be paid by the trial. They may be hired by the judge, but in metropolitan areas, they are usually employees of the sheriff's office. The bailiff has custody of the defendant in the courtroom, summons witnesses to the witness stand, has custody of the jury, and assists the judge in maintaining order.

Interrelationships There may be many other people employed by a court, but whatever the number, interrelationships are important. Police tend to feel that courts are too lenient and do not have enough respect for the demands and nature of police work. Prosecutors and judges frequently work harmoniously, although prosecutors may feel that judges do not side with them as often as is merited. Lawyers, in general, respect the office of the judge. Sometimes conflicts develop between judges and those elected personnel over whom the judges have little authority. And jurors and witnesses may feel mistreated by the court if interrelationships are ignored.

THE PUBLIC

The public is involved with the courts in more ways than are immediately apparent, sometimes in the courtroom, sometimes in its homes, sometimes in the media.

The Audience Attending trials was once a traditional pastime in America. The audience sitting in the courtroom contained many faces that over time came to be familiar to the judge. They may have exerted a certain pressure on the judge to be consistent and impartial; certainly, their presence demanded that the judge share understanding about a case with members of the community whose judgments he or she could not control. Today, people still attend trials out of curiosity, but the faces in the back of the courtroom are likely to be fewer and transient, usually the faces of family and friends of the defendants. Consequently, the judge has greater control over the courtroom and may, for example, be more likely to angrily jail a spectator for contempt of court if the spectator fails to speedily obey a no-smoking order.

The Media Even as the audiences grow smaller, television or newspapers may transform a trial from a judicial proceeding geared to judge or jury, who must decide on a verdict, into a proceeding geared to the vague but massive influence of the uninstructed public. Although television cameras are banned in the courtroom in most states and what is seen on television sets are sketches by artists accompanied by a narrative, the conflict between the news media and the courts continues. For example, in the 1950s, the trial of Dr. Sam Sheppard for the murder of his wife was heavily covered by a newspaper that assumed that Sheppard was guilty and strongly advocated capital punishment. In 1966 the Supreme Court overturned the verdict in an 8 to 1 decision because "virulent publicity" deprived Dr. Sheppard of a fair trial.[3] Sensationalism sells newspapers, but the problem is often complicated by elected officials — sheriffs, prosecutors, and even judges — who try to get free news coverage in order to further their own careers. This is what happened in the Sheppard case — both the newspaper and some public officials were at fault. In such cases, it is, of course, difficult to find competent jurors unexposed to the prejudicial news. Changing the location of the trial may help, but there may be nationwide coverage that evokes strong emotional responses.

Spectacular displays of the abuse of free speech by the press and by criminal justice officials have led various agencies to suggest or establish rules and guidelines. Police officers may receive formal instructions from their chief about what they can say to the press. The Department of Justice has issued guidelines. The American Bar Association's Project on Minimum Standards and the American Newspaper Publishers Association have conducted studies leading to the identification of the pertinent elements of the controversy. The National Crime Commission recommended that the various agencies and bar associations issue standards concerning the release of information about criminal cases to the media. The National Advisory Commission (1973) recommended that courts establish public information offices. On the other hand, there are a number of examples of restrictive, even repressive, measures courts have taken to limit news coverage. And the news media have made some effort to police themselves in order to avoid being unduly censored by the courts. (In England the media have established a toothless yet somehow very effective control over the handling of court cases.)

Society Ultimately, however, the public controls the media and the courts as much as it is controlled or shaped by either of them. Lynch mobs and vigilante groups did not have to be stirred by the news media to take criminal cases from the courts and exercise their own illegitimate tribunal powers. Changes in the nature of Supreme Court decisions over the decades reflect changes in the attitudes, beliefs, and values of the public. The Supreme Court that upheld slavery at one point gave way to a Supreme Court that abhorred the idea of slavery, and so on. Just as crime itself has in some respects been tolerated and encouraged by the public, so have the outdated characteristics of the courts. And other changes in the public have resulted in more demands being made on the courts. Population increases, new technology, and a more complicated society have brought about new laws and more laws, new crimes and more crimes, new cases and more cases. The courts are changing in response to these changes, and it is likely that they will change very rapidly in the near future.

DISCUSSION QUESTIONS

1. How could we tell a bad judge from a good judge?
2. How could we eliminate *heavy* reliance on the testimony of witnesses? Or could we?
3. Discuss the qualifications and selection procedures for judges in the United States. How could they be improved? In your state?
4. Discuss the relative weight of the general public and the media in influencing the way courts operate.
5. Who are the participants in a court? What should the role of the public be in a sensational criminal trial?

NOTES

1. The actions of the "Chicago 7" in the courtroom of Judge Julius Hoffman in Chicago, 1969–70, made national headlines for months. The defendants were on trial for conspiracy to incite a riot at the 1968 Democratic Convention in Chicago. In 1973 they were charged with a total of 38 contempt of court charges, most of which the court threw out.
2. The argument against jury sentencing is strongly supported by a study reported in Atlanta Commission on Crime and Juvenile Delinquency, *Opportunity for Urban Excellence 72* (1962), Appendix D-6. Judicial conferences have treated the subject of jury versus bench trials. The FBI's *Uniform Crime Reports* show roughly equal numbers of felons being convicted in the two forms of trials — in proportion to the different figures for those pleading not guilty in the two.
3. *Sheppard* v. *Maxwell*, 384 U.S. 333 (1966).

PART FOUR ANNOTATED BIBLIOGRAPHY

James, Howard. *Crisis in the Courts*. Rev. ed. New York: David McKay, 1969.
   A skilled journalist gives his first-hand impressions of courts across the nation. Frequently indignant in tone, the book is always highly readable. James makes numerous recommendations for improving the courts.

Meyers, Lewis B. *The American Legal System*. Rev. ed. New York: Harper & Row, 1964.
   An excellent book on the courts and the law. Although this book is scholarly, it reads well. It is the only book in which information on the courts is well synthesized.

National Advisory Commission on Criminal Justice Standards and Goals. *Courts*. Washington, D.C.: Government Printing Office, 1973.
   The report recommends a major restructuring and streamlining of procedures and practices in processing criminal cases at state and local levels. Recommendations, standards, and goals of the commission are included.

President's Commission on Law Enforcement and Administration of Justice. *Task Force Report: The Courts*. Washington, D.C.: Government Printing Office, 1967.
   Still the best general report on the problems in the courts and what should be done about them. Comprehensive research and analysis of courts and court problems.

PART FIVE

CORRECTIONS

CHAPTER SIXTEEN

BACKGROUND AND HISTORY OF CORRECTIONS

THE EUROPEAN
HERITAGE

THE AMERICAN
HERITAGE

HISTORY OF
COMMUNITY-BASED
CORRECTIONS

Purpose: To trace the historical development of corrections, including early practices and theories.

THE TERM *CORRECTIONS* as it is used in criminal justice is only now becoming familiar to the general public.

Many people equate corrections with the penitentiary system. Corrections does include the agencies and people involved in our systems of prisons, jails, and juvenile facilities, but today it also includes probation and parole and a variety of supporting programs in the community. Because of their importance, probation and parole are discussed separately in Part Six. Historically, corrections in the United States developed around the prisons, and in fact, the penitentiary as we know it today was developed primarily in America. For this reason, the history of corrections in the United States centers on the development of the penitentiary. Nonetheless, corrections in the United States did receive its impetus from European ideas.

THE EUROPEAN HERITAGE

In a previous section of the text there was a discussion of early means of controlling crime. Blood revenge was a method that prevailed for centuries. Later theories tied punishment to an appeasement of the gods and made the apprehension and punishment of offenders a matter of general social concern.[1] The development of the theory of deterrence followed at a later date, as did the theory of reformation, which was strongly influenced by the Roman Catholic Church in the Middle Ages.[2]

Early penal methods, which continued until the 1600s, stressed harsh and cruel punishment and relied to a large degree on the theory of deterrence and on the belief that crime was a sin that required that the offender be punished to protect the public. Some of the punishments used were flog-

ging, the stock and pillory, mutilation, and branding.[3] A number of these methods were not discontinued until the 1800s. From the 1600s to the 1800s, the European countries transported their prisoners to the colonies. Over time, using prison for incarceration came to be preferred to whipping, killing, and banishment to the colonies.

On the Continent a major development of the 1600s was the workhouse, which was known to early reformers in America.[4] In 1779, with the passing of the Hard Labour Act in England, it seemed that a major change in penal methods was at hand. This act, which called for the establishment of penitentiaries, came at a time when England could no longer deport its criminals to the New World.[5] Although reformers in England developed such ideas as separation of prisoners, it was left to America to put these ideas into practice. It was not until the 1800s that incarceration in a system of prisons became the primary means of dealing with the criminal, but England and the Continent were to follow the lead of the New World in this innovation.

THE AMERICAN HERITAGE

THE PRISON SYSTEM

Early Development (1600-1830) In the 1600s the Pennsylvania Quakers, under the guidance of William Penn, passed a criminal code that was less severe than the codes originally brought to this country. Prior to this time, the jails and workhouses had primarily housed paupers, beggars, and persons awaiting trial. Punishment after the trial took the form of a fine, public whipping, confinement to the stocks, or hanging. Because long-term imprisonment was not an accepted sentence, jails were not required to

JOHN HOWARD
1726–1790

Courtesy: Federal Bureau of Prisons

John Howard was one of the leading pioneers in prison reform and the founder of the early English prison system. Howard visited early prisons all over Europe as well as every county jail in England. He recorded the things he saw and proposed a system to "correct" rather than punish. His influence on prison design and programs is still felt today.

Philadelphia in 1790, is considered the first prison in America, even though the Quakers had opened prisons earlier. The prisons of the 1790s were in houses or buildings in the cities. Prison labor, evolving from the workhouse idea, was introduced during this period as a means of reducing the cost of housing criminals. By the 1820s the prisons were recognized as complete failures in everything except as training grounds for more crimes.

As a result of these failures, the Auburn (1819) and Pennsylvania (1829) systems were introduced. These two systems were actually quite similar in that they were both based on the theory that separation and work would bring about rehabilitation. The major difference between the two was the use of congregate labor under the Auburn system and the Pennsylvania requirement that prisoners remain segregated in separate cells. The idea of separation was based on the assumption that the opportunity to reflect on past sins in solitude would bring about rehabilitation. Under the Pennsylvania system, only a selected small group of persons were allowed to see the prisoner, to take care of personal needs. The Auburn system also demanded complete silence at all times, but its use of congregate labor gave it a financial advantage over the Pennsylvania system.[6]

The Systems of the 1800s Until about 1870, the Auburn system of silence, penitence, and productive labor was the standard in the United States. Although many people endorsed the Pennsylvania system, it did not allow inmates to congregate for any purpose. As a result, the more economical Auburn system of bringing prisoners out of their cells to work in prison shops during the day prevailed. Some treatment was initiated before 1870, but it was limited mostly to the use of religion. Harsh punishment was frequently used to enforce the rule of silence.

hold convicted criminals. The Quakers changed this and introduced imprisonment at "hard labor" as a punishment for most serious crimes. As a result, prisons were built in Massachusetts and Pennsylvania, although they produced little rehabilitation and even less deterrence of crime. However, this system was abolished the day after Penn's death, and fulfillment of his ideas was to wait for another 150 years.

The period from 1790 to 1830 is the developmental stage in the penal system. A cellblock in the Walnut Street Jail, opened in

Also, the abuse of prison labor for profit was common.

The model of long, hard daily labor was not without a theoretical base, because failure to observe the protestant work ethic was thought to be a causative factor in criminality. This theoretical base made the practice of contracting with private firms and establishing long work schedules the proper method of reforming criminals. These practices also helped offset the cost of the system.[7]

The Golden Age The so-called "Golden Age of Penology" was introduced with the opening of the Elmira reformatory in New York in 1876. This effort used mass education and religion, parole, indeterminate sentences, and separation of youthful offenders. However, the anticipated result was never fully achieved, and most institutions continued to rely on security rather than rehabilitation. The prisons faced one dilemma after another, most ending in a reinforcement of the custodial model. The Auburn and Pennsylvania systems had no requirement for classifying prisoners according to how hardened, skilled, or dangerous they were, because the rules of silence and solitude met the need of keeping prisoners from influencing each other. Subsequently, overcrowding, with the resultant breaking of the rule of silence, allowed prisoners once again to influence each other. Conditions deteriorated and prisons became ideal places for the hardened criminal to influence the younger prisoner not yet committed to a life of crime. The reform efforts disappeared completely during this period. Prison officials lost all interest in reform and ran the prisons strictly as places to house and punish convicted felons.

A significant accomplishment of this period was the development in 1870 of the Declaration of Principles by the American Prison Association (now the American Correctional Association).[8] These principles, which have had only minor revision and are still applicable today, indicate the foresight of early correctional thinkers.

The Industrial Era The period 1900–1935 was characterized by the expanded use of prison labor for profit in the form of several "systems" of prison labor. These systems included the contract system, the lease system, the public accounts system, the state use system, and the public works system. Prominent during this period was the establishment of meaningful educational, vocational, and medical programs. Emphasis was also placed on improving living conditions and on controlling brutality, and productive labor was recognized as therapeutic treatment.

Despite this seeming progress, the prisons of the early 1900s seemed to be in a holding pattern. They made little attempt to further develop means of correction or rehabilitation. Wardens changed frequently, and the persons charged with running prisons had little or no background for this type of responsibility. Wardens were likely to be political appointees, selected without regard to minimum standards. Firm discipline, continued use of the silence rule, and close security were the typical patterns. The prisons were considered to be failures. The Wickersham Commission concluded in 1931 that the responsibility for the failure of the prison system had to be laid in part to the failure of the wardens to administer their units effectively.[9]

Recent Prison Development Modern concepts in penology have come about largely as a result of the reorganization of the federal prison system. This reorganization, which was started by Sanford Bates in the 1930s, is considered to be the beginning of the modern era in corrections. State prisons followed the lead of the federal prison system both in building new facilities and in introducing treatment programs.

Different methods of classifying inmates for treatment have been developed, as have methods for treatment on an individual and group basis.

Recent developments have caused great uncertainty in corrections. While many people still believe firmly in the rehabilitation and correction role of prisons, there has been strong pressure to abandon these goals. Research concerning the effects of prison programs on recidivism has not been encouraging. Prison populations have exploded in some states, and there are those who advocate eliminating parole and indeterminate sentencing. As the system progresses into the 1980s, significant changes may be made, or the system may simply return to an earlier cycle.

WOMEN'S REFORMATORIES

Although separation of prisoners by sex was initiated between 1790 and 1830, separate institutions for women waited for the reform movement following 1870. In 1930 over half the states still maintained women prisoners in the men's prison under the care of the warden.[10]

The recent history of women's reformatories has been called an exception to the rule in corrections. A national survey in the 1930s indicated that substantial progress and foresight were shown in construction, health, and education programs and in efforts to prepare inmates for release. A national survey in the 1960s did not report on the women's reformatories, probably because of the belief in their significant progress relative to the rest of the corrections field and because of the relatively small number of women in prison. The recent attention given to equal rights for women has pointed up the fact that programs for women prisoners may not be as well developed as has been

thought. Overcrowding has caused states to expand to new facilities. Significant increases in the number of women in prison may result in a long overdue study of the purpose of prison programs for women.

JUVENILE TRAINING SCHOOL

The reformatory, or training school as it is commonly called, was introduced to remove the younger prisoners from the adult prison setting. It was intended to concentrate on building the younger prisoner's character, removal from the influence of the older prisoner, and preparation for successful reintegration into society. The first public training facilities exclusively for juveniles probably were established in Massachusetts (1846), New York (1849), and Maine (1853). By the end of the nineteenth century thirty-six states had established separate juvenile training facilities.[11]

By 1930, however, it was concluded that the reformatory was little different in practice from the prison. The similarities extended to number of inmates, size, and type of construction. The reformatories handled education without regard for individual differences, and many of the teachers actually had been hired as guards and did extra duty as teachers. The vocational and industrial programs were deficient because they were not related to any need of the inmate following release. As a result of these shortcomings, the Wickersham Commission (1931) concluded that the reformatory movement was for the most part a complete failure.[12]

Contrary to the working philosophy of the reformatory, the National Crime Commission's Task Force on Corrections found that in 1965 corporal punishment was still authorized in ten states. Most training schools did not segregate offenders according to a rehabilitation design but maintained a custodial concept contrary to the theory of rehabilitation.[13]

During the first half of the 1970s, the number of detention and correctional facilities for juveniles increased by 15 percent, to 829. During the same period of time, the number of juveniles held in these public facilities decreased by 18 percent. However, most of this decrease was in the first two years. The number of juveniles in training schools and shelters decreased 22 percent during this period, while halfway houses and group homes showed the only increase.[14] These figures demonstrate a change in the methods of handling juveniles, largely influenced by the courts, and a trend toward deincarceration of juvenile offenders. Cost, methods, facilities, length of sentence, program, staff, etc., vary greatly from state to state, indicating that there are wide differences in applying theory to practice. The effectiveness of training schools is still a much debated matter, with the emphasis shifting to community-based programs.

WORK CAMPS

Assigning men to work camps was common before the penitentiary came into being. Contractors in early colonial times paid the state for the use of criminals. The contractor was expected to be responsible for housing and feeding the inmates, and in return was allowed to use them or to hire them out to others. The restrictive laws of the 1930s limited prison labor to state needs and put an end to what had come to be considered a form of slavery.

Nevada used prison camps before 1900, and several other states started them before World War I. Between the wars, several more states initiated camp programs, and after World War II this rapidly expanded. Although it has been suggested that this expansion was the result of far-sighted administrators, reduced cost must have also been a factor.

Industry and the labor unions had brought an end to the hard labor that was common prior to 1900. The Hawes-Cooper Act in 1934 and the Ashurst-Summer Act of 1935 excluded prison-made goods from interstate commerce, and to reduce the pressure from industry and labor, many states further restricted the sale of prison-made goods. Even today, when camps are used under the state works system to relieve prisoners of the burden of idleness and the states of the cost, the problem of how to use prison labor ethically is a major one for many prison and jail administrators.

HISTORY OF COMMUNITY-BASED CORRECTIONS

The term *community-based corrections,* as currently used, refers to those correctional programs and institutions that are close to the centers of population and depend on this closeness for their operation. The classification of an institution, agency, or program as community-based does not refer to the level of government that operates the program. The United States Bureau of Prisons and other federal agencies are leaders in the establishment of this type of program, and many states operate, or support by funding, such programs. In addition, certain prisons can be classified as long-term community institutions under certain conditions, and jails can be classified as short-term community institutions. For the purpose of this text, jails and juvenile detention centers are discussed under the heading of community corrections, even though few are currently operated as correctional centers.

JAILS

Centralized control of our system of jails was recommended in 1930 and again in 1967 as a result of the deplorable conditions in most of them. The 1973 report of the National Commission on Criminal Justice Standards and Goals set state control of jails as a specific goal for corrections. It has been generally agreed, in every study of corrections, that the jail systems are the worst evil of corrections. There are a large number of jails being constructed at present across the country. Some of these represent an improved concept of design and program, but many are little different than jails of one hundred years ago.

The use of the jail to detain accused persons can be traced back thousands of years. Its use as a workhouse was developed in the sixteenth century to deal with minor offenses, and this concept came to the United States during the seventeenth century. The reform movement of the nineteenth century led to general changes in the corrections field for everything but the jail. However, the fact that the jail is in essence the "reception center" for correctional institutions and has considerable impact on the persons processed is beginning to have an impact on correctional thinking. The National Jail Census of 1978 indicated that our 3,493 jails housing inmates longer than forty-eight hours contained 158,000 inmates, an average of forty-five inmates per jail. California housed the largest number (26,000).[15]

A national survey in 1965 found that only 3 percent of our jail employees can be identified as professionals. Many of the local administrators are county sheriffs who stand for reelection every two years, and this tends to hinder any effort to build effective programs. In 1965 only 8 percent of the local jails required the administrator to have a college degree, and only 56 percent were under a merit or civil service system. In 53 percent of the counties there were no minimum education requirements for custodial officers,

and only 1 percent required a college degree.[16]

In many departments, the jail is used as a "holding" position for persons hired to work in regular law enforcement positions within a sheriff's department.

As might be expected, salaries, in-service training, and inmate programs in jails have been at the bottom of the corrections totem pole. It is difficult to imagine significant change in this area, short of a major reduction in the number of persons put in jails and some consolidation for administrative and financial efficiency.

Of particular importance in the findings in the jail census is the fact that on average more than 36 percent of the jail population was in pretrial confinement. Studies done in a number of states in 1974 show that little progress has been made in reducing the number of people in pretrial status. This statistic indicates clearly the role that the courts and the prosecution must play in solving the problem of overcrowded jails. Additional problems indicated in the 1972 census were overcrowding, lack of medical assistance, and lack of areas for recreation and visitation. Meaningful vocational and educational programs were almost nonexistent.[17] Many jails are so old and badly deteriorated that even the most hardened of law enforcement personnel hesitate to use them for human habitation. They are so poorly designed that even basic control and protection of inmates are impossible. Yet, many of these jails house juveniles in different stages of judicial processing as well as housing adults.

Also of importance, when considering jails, is the estimate that in many states up to 80 to 90 percent of them cannot meet the minimum standards for health and safety. There is a cost factor of many millions of dollars at stake in deciding how to solve the problem. Although it is possible that relief will come from the judiciary, which could reduce the number of persons in pretrial confinement, there is still an urgent need to replace many jails. Modern penal reformers are calling for extensive use of community programs as an alternative to the building of new jails. These reformers point out that building new jails simply tends to hide the problems behind bigger and newer walls. Also, because of the cost factor, a number of states, including Vermont, Iowa, and Connecticut, have initiated regional systems with primary emphasis on programs within the community. In any case, it appears that any significant progress in improving our system of corrections will revolve around solutions to our age-old jail problems.

JUVENILE DETENTION CENTERS

After the establishment of the first juvenile court in Chicago in 1899, state after state made provisions for separate detention of juveniles. However, by 1915 only three jurisdictions had constructed special facilities for detention of accused juveniles prior to trial, and as late as 1945 only a few specially designed facilities were available for this purpose. Major construction and program development have occurred only since the 1960s. The 1965 survey of corrections found that 93 percent of the country's juvenile court jurisdictions, covering 44 percent of the population, had no place for pretrial detention of juveniles other than a county jail or police lockup, and most did not detain enough children to justify establishing a detention home.[18]

The National Crime Commission's Task Force on Corrections found in 1965 that it was routine in some jurisdictions to detain all arrested children, whether they were referred to court or not. The total number of juveniles detained in 1965 amounted to 409,218. In one county, two-thirds of the detained children were later placed on probation in their homes. An estimated 100,000 juveniles were still detained in facilities for adults, and only three jurisdictions could claim that youngsters were never detained in jails.

The National Crime Commission did, however, report a number of small model programs for detention of children.[19] These model programs have slowly expanded to the point where most states have one or more advanced concepts in operation. Currently there are attempts to create working relationships with school districts in order to offer a full range of programs in combined detention/community corrections centers, although there is a problem in combining the adjudicated persons with those in need of supervision.

HALFWAY HOUSES AND PRERELEASE GUIDANCE CENTERS

The halfway house concept has been around for many years and has been known by several other names. Many of the early halfway houses and prerelease guidance centers were operated by private, voluntary organizations, and they usually were located close to the prison rather than in the urban area to which the ex-inmate would return. Their primary function was to provide food and lodging to released inmates. The federal government began to enter the halfway-house field in 1960, and several federal and state programs were initiated over the next twenty years.

The distinction between a halfway house and a prerelease center is that the prerelease center is normally administered by, and located in, the institution. It is a program designed to ease the change from institution life to life in the community. The halfway house, on the other hand, is designed to be located in the community and provide not only food and shelter but counseling and other services. Persons residing in the halfway houses are allowed to leave the facility to seek and engage in employment. Florida's program requires residents to pay room and board and has provision for restitution to the offender's victim.

PROGRAMS FOR PREDELINQUENTS

There have been many attempts over the years to reach youths before they commit offenses serious enough to require placement in an institution. The youth-services concept that came into being in the late 1960s was based on the idea that since the system "labeled" a youth, we should offer alternative, noncriminal justice services for predelinquents and minor offenders.

The youth-services concept calls for focusing all the resources of the community on youths who show signs of becoming delinquent. The concept is still evident today in the use of "diversion" programs, but more use is being made of probation staff (contrary to the youth services concept), and also existing social services are rightfully being utilized. It will be a number of years before these concepts are evaluated to the point that standard approaches are identified and implemented on a broad scale.

INDIVIDUAL AND GROUP PLACEMENT

Foster homes, essentially a placement service, have been used for a number of years in the welfare service area, but are relatively new as employed on a large scale in corrections. The National Crime Commission's Task Force on Corrections found that 42 percent of 233 probation offices studied used foster-home placement. Minnesota was using seven group homes, and the Wisconsin Division of Corrections was operating thirty-three.[20] Even today, however, many states are far behind in establishing this type

of alternative to incarceration, but recent studies indicate that this placement concept, along with halfway houses, is growing in use, while all other programs for housing youth have declined in total population.[21]

SPECIAL PROGRAMS

The history of corrections would not be complete unless the agencies using special programs, such as guided group interaction, were mentioned. The best known of the early guided group interaction programs was the Highfields project, established in New Jersey in 1950. Follow-on programs were established at Essexfields, New Jersey, and at Pinehills in Provo, Utah. Basically, these programs involved school or work in the community during the day and special interaction sessions at the home facility in the evening. The idea behind them was that the individual needed to be resocialized in a community program rather than in an institutional environment. Their results are still debated because, like most other correctional programs, they were not adequately evaluated.

A number of drug programs such as Synanon and Narcanon have been developed to deal with drug addiction. Innovative features and unique approaches have been the hallmark of these programs, but they have either lacked adequate evaluation or not had success in demonstrating positive outcomes in most cases.

Currently, there is much debate about the future direction of corrections. Some people have pointed out that rather than building new large prisons, we should establish small community facilities and programs. Others have insisted that we must build new prisons because so many of our present ones are outdated and in need of replacement. Some have argued that correctional treatment does not work. And some have argued that prisons are for punishment, not treatment. We have also heard the argument that only dangerous offenders should be sent to prison, while nondangerous offenders should receive supervision from community programs. Others argue that the sanction of prison is necessary for the nondangerous offender and that prisons are needed in order to make less punitive sanctions function. The direction that corrections will take is not yet clear. There are valid points to the various sides of the argument that are much more complex than can be presented here.

While the 1960s and early 1970s were periods of attempts to follow theories of rehabilitation and correction, during the late 1970s a backlash developed, and some correctional leaders returned to the concept of prisons as primarily a place of punishment. It is clear that today's student of corrections will have an opportunity to contribute to the ultimate solution to this age-old problem.

The development of correctional institutions in the United States, that is, prisons, jails, and juvenile facilities, can find its impetus in Europe. However, corrections as we know it is primarily an American invention. Its early development began with the Quakers, who established jails and workhouses. The early 1800s saw the development of the Auburn system (congregate labor) and the Pennsylvania system (separate cell labor). In 1876 the Elmira (New York) reformatory opened with programs for religion, education, parole, indeterminate sentences, and separation of youthful offenders. The period of 1900 through the 1930s was characterized by the widespread use of prison labor. The reorganization of the Federal Prison System in the 1930s led to similar reorganization and reform in the states' prison systems. With the advent of separate courts for juveniles, separate juvenile detention facilities developed. Also separate institutions for women were established.

While jails were the forerunners of our state and federal prison systems, they have in many cases remained static in their development and improvements. Through the years special programs such as halfway houses, prerelease centers, youth service bureaus, and other unique institutions have been developed. In the late 1960s and the early 1970s corrections embarked on a program of reform and innovation, largely as a result of federal funding from the Office of Justice Assistance, Research and Statistics.

The late 1970s has brought out advocates of the idea that rehabilitation does not work. Other reformers are stressing determinate sentences and abolition of parole, while others stress diversion to community programs. It remains to be seen where this new era in corrections will lead us.

DISCUSSION QUESTIONS

1. What is wrong with our system of jails?
2. What is meant by the phrase *community-based corrections*?
3. Why did a system of prisons develop?
4. Discuss whether prison architecture can make a significant difference in the probability of success of rehabilitation programs.
5. Discuss the pros and cons of state or local control of jails.
6. What does the future hold for corrections?

7. Where is the state prison located in your state? Is it properly located? If not, where should it be?
8. Can we ever have correctional systems that do not, either implicitly or explicity, punish the criminal offender?

NOTES

1. W. Davis Lewis, *From Newgate to Dannemora* (Ithaca: Cornell University Press, 1965), p. 7.
2. Lewis, *From Newgate*, p. 7.
3. Harry Elmer Barnes, *The Story of Punishment* (Boston: The Stratford Company, 1930), pp. 62–64.
4. Lewis, *From Newgate*, p. 12.
5. Lewis, *From Newgate*, p. 23.
6. David J. Rothman, *The Discovery of the Asylum* (Boston: Little, Brown and Company, 1971), p. 82.
7. Rothman, *Discovery of the Asylum*, p. 103.
8. American Correctional Association, *Manual of Correctional Standards* (Washington, D.C.: American Correctional Association, 1959), p. xix.
9. U.S. National Commission on Law Observance and Enforcement, *Wickersham Commission Reports: No. 9, Report on Penal Institutions, Probation and Parole* (Montclair, N.J.: Patterson Smith Reprint, 1968), pp. 19–41.
10. *Wickersham Commission Reports*, p. 55.
11. President's Commission on Law Enforcement and Administration of Justice, *Task Force Report: Corrections* (Washington, D.C.: Government Printing Office, 1967), p. 141.
12. *Wickersham Commission Reports*, p. 51.
13. *Task Force Report: Corrections*, pp. 142–144.
14. Law Enforcement Assistance Administration, *Children in Custody* (Washington, D.C.: Government Printing Office, 1977), pp. 2–3.
15. U.S. Department of Justice, *Census of Jails and Survey of Jail Inmates, 1978,* Preliminary Report February 1979.
16. *Task Force Report: Corrections*, pp. 162–165.
17. U.S. Department of Justice, *Survey of Inmates in Local Jails* (Washington, D.C.: Government Printing Office, 1974), pp. 18–19.
18. *Task Force Report: Corrections*, pp. 119–121.
19. *Task Force Report: Corrections*, pp. 23–24.
20. *Task Force Report: Corrections*, p. 40.
21. *Children in Custody*, p. 3.

CHAPTER SEVENTEEN

CORRECTIONAL ORGANIZATIONS

CONCEPT OF
CORRECTIONS

TYPES OF
CORRECTIONAL
ORGANIZATIONS

FEDERAL
CORRECTIONAL
ORGANIZATIONS

MILITARY
CORRECTIONAL
ORGANIZATIONS

STATE CORRECTIONAL
ORGANIZATIONS

LOCAL
CORRECTIONAL
ORGANIZATIONS

Purpose: To describe the various levels of correctional organizations, including federal, state, military, and local correctional agencies.

THERE ARE SEVERAL perspectives that can provide a focus for a study of corrections. One of these, history, was used in the previous chapter, which also mentioned several others: (1) functions, (2) organizations, (3) theory, (4) facilities, (5) corrections population (inmates, clients, and so forth), (6) treatment programs, and (7) research. The focus of this chapter is organization.

Organization, as related to corrections, can itself be discussed from several perspectives. For example, it is possible to discuss corrections organizations as institutional or noninstitutional. Or corrections organizations can be introduced as community-based and noncommunity-based. Here the perspective is federal, state, and local corrections, but let us first clarify some organization concepts.

CONCEPT OF CORRECTIONS

The word *correction* implies the act or process of correcting. It can include punishment as a tool in the process, but it does not seriously apply to the theories of revenge and retribution. The word has some meaning within the theory of deterrence, but it reaches its full potential only in the theory that the public can best be protected through rehabilitation of offenders and their careful reintegration into the community. However, the void between theory, concept, and actual practice remains great.

There is a legal basis for corrections also. The laws of the United States, of each state, and of local governments provide for apprehension, trial, and correction of offenders. And laws are specific in the requirement that correctional organizations and facilities be established. Probation and parole laws and the formal organizations associated with those laws, for example, are not consistent

with a theory of corrections that does not stress rehabilitation. In addition to the organizations established by law, there are voluntary organizations that function directly, or play supporting roles, in the area of corrections. Such organizations include Alcholics Anonymous and crisis counseling centers.

TYPES OF CORRECTIONAL ORGANIZATIONS

Correctional organizations can be generally classified into three types, or levels. The first type is the planning or policy organization. As the name indicates, this type of organization is primarily concerned with corrections planning and policy (standards and general procedures) on a broad scale. An example is the Board of Corrections in Texas, an organization that does not operate any functional element of the system, but rather sets general policy for the Texas Department of Corrections, which in turn operates the state's adult prison system.

The second type of organization is the central or administrative agency. The director and central administrative staff of the United States Bureau of Prisons or of the California Youth Authority fall into this category. These organizations perform the same functions as the policy and planning agencies, but on a more detailed level. In addition, they are responsible for directing, coordinating, and monitoring the operation of a number of line institutions or agencies. Personnel at this level, like those of the policy and planning agency, normally do not work directly with the inmates or clients.

The third type of level of organization is the *line agency* or *institution*. These agencies might also be called operational agencies because they "operate" the system. They include such prisons as the Glades Correctional Institution in western Palm Beach County, Florida, and the Attica prison in New York, and such community-based agencies as the model system in Des Moines, Iowa. The "operating agency" category of organization works directly with the inmate or client and is responsible for the broadest range of correctional functions, limited only by the assigned goal or mission of the particular agency. For example, the Federal Community Treatment Center in Chicago, Illinois could be concerned with custody and control, as is the maximum security prison, but its facilities and methods of carrying out this function are different from those of the typical prison.

These three levels of organization will appear at each level of government in our discussion of correctional agencies.

FEDERAL CORRECTIONAL ORGANIZATIONS

There are a number of organizations at the federal level that can be classified as policy organizations. Most of them work within the broad framework of the criminal justice system instead of concentrating only on corrections. Although the legislature (establishing laws) and the court (interpreting laws) are agencies that establish corrections policy, our concern here is primarily with the agencies that fall under the executive branch of the government. Within this category are such agencies as the Office of Justice Assistance, Research and Statistics (OJARS) of the Justice Department. Portions of this agency are directly concerned with promulgating corrections policy and planning for corrections improvement on a grand scale. This is accomplished by requiring that minimum

standards be met as a condition for obtaining federal funds.

The major administrative and operational corrections agencies in the federal government are assigned to the Federal Bureau of Prisons. The Federal Bureau of Prisons, like OJARS, is a part of the Department of Justice. The administrative office of the Federal Bureau of Prisons is located in Washington, and its director reports to the Deputy Attorney General on a level comparable to the director of the Federal Bureau of Investigation. The bureau exercises general supervision over the operations of penitentiaries, federal correctional institutions, metropolitan correctional centers, federal prison camps, and community treatment facilities. It also supervises the commitment and management of federal inmates and contracts with local institutions (jails) for confinement and support of federal prisoners being held for trial. Its central office is composed of several divisions plus the Federal Prison Industries, Inc., an office of general counsel, and regional support offices, located in Philadeladelphia, Atlanta, Kansas City, Dallas, and San Francisco. The divisions and offices assigned to the bureau are shown in Figure 17.1.

That section of the bureau called Federal Prison Industries, Inc., is unique. It is responsible for industrial operations in more than thirty institutions across the country, and it provides a variety of goods and services that are sold to federal agencies. The number of operating units in the Federal Prison Industries, Inc., is continually expanding.

The Federal Bureau of Prisons is composed of more than fifty penal and correctional institutions, camps, and medical and treatment centers. McNeil Island, in the state of Washington, was the site of the first federal penitentiary for men. This prison was

FIGURE 17.1 ORGANIZATION OF THE FEDERAL BUREAU OF PRISONS

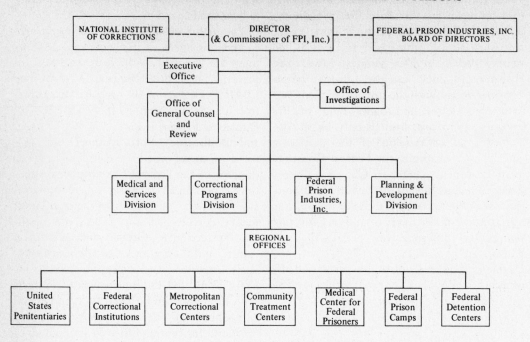

SOURCE: Federal Bureau of Prisons, Washington, D.C.

taken over by the federal government in 1890, although it was constructed approximately twenty years earlier as a territorial prison. It is interesting to note that McNeil Island is still in operation, though present planning calls for its closure by 1982. Prior to 1938 there were no special provisions for juveniles. This changed with the Juvenile Delinquency Act of 1938 and the transfer to the Bureau of the National Training School for Boys in 1939. The first facility for women was the Federal Reformatory for Women at Alderson, West Virginia, opened in 1927. The bureau is responsible for an inmate population larger than that of any state and one that continues to grow. Two recent facility additions are Federal Correctional Institutions located in Otisville, New York, and in Talladega, Alabama.

MILITARY CORRECTIONAL ORGANIZATIONS

The military corrections system is actually made up of three systems; corrections in the Army, Navy, and Air Force is the overall responsibility of the secretary of each department. The corrections policy element in the Department of the Air Force is under the Chief of Security Police, who reports in turn to the Inspector General. Corrections policy in the Navy is the responsibility of the corrections division of the Bureau of Naval Personnel. In the Army also, corrections policy is assigned to a corrections division, but the division reports to the office of the Provost Marshal General.

The administrative-level organization in the Air Force is the Air Training Command.

The organization supervises the 3320th Corrections and Rehabilitation Squadron, which is located at Lowry Air Force Base, Colorado. In the Air Force, all persons worldwide who are considered good candidates for return to Air Force duty are assigned to the 3320th squadron. Base stockades (operational units) in the Air Force are used only for short-term purposes, for example, for individuals pending further legal or administrative action. The administrative-level organization in the Navy is the United States Naval Disciplinary Command, located at the naval base in Portsmouth, New Hampshire.

The administrative activities in the Army are more extensive than those in the other branches of the military service because of the Army's larger size. The Disciplinary Barracks at Fort Leavenworth, Kansas, has the task of providing correctional treatment, care, and custodial supervision. The Disciplinary Command is under the supervision of an official called the commandant. Directors of administration, classification, training, custody, mental hygiene, and logistic support assist the commandant in supervising a Correctional Holding Detachment and the Disciplinary Barracks.

The Army also operates the United States Army Correctional Training Facility at Fort Riley, Kansas. This facility is used for those who can respond to correctional treatment and for those who have completed a sentence but require additional training before reassignment. Persons who cannot or will not respond to correctional treatment are transferred to the Disciplinary Barracks. The personnel in the Correctional Training Facility supervise and furnish technical guidance to a correctional training battalion, which in turn supervises one or more lower level operational units.

The Army also operates a number of United States Army stockades. Twenty-four of these are in the United States and several overseas in such places as West Germany, Korea, and Panama.[1] The stockade provides pretrial and posttrial confinement for persons who have actions pending and confines prisoners serving short sentences. In this respect, the stockade serves a purpose closely related to that of the city or county jail.

STATE CORRECTIONAL ORGANIZATIONS

There are several policy agencies in the corrections organization at the state level. One of these is the state criminal justice planning agency. This agency, commonly called the Criminal Justice Council or Crime Commission, reports to the governor of the state. These agencies came about as a result of funding by the Office of Justice Assistance, Research and Statistics. This agency provided for block grants to be given to the states to fund improvements in law enforcement and the criminal justice system. A state planning agency is organized to work out programs and administer the allocation of these block grants and all other funds for criminal justice components, not just corrections.

Most states also have policy agencies to which the juvenile and adult correctional institutions report, while in a few states the institution directors are responsible to the governor. In Florida, for example, the Division of Corrections (adult) is a branch of the Department of Health and Rehabilitative Service. Sometimes both the juvenile and adult organizations report to one policy agency (commonly called a board), and in other cases there are two separate agencies, each reporting to a separate board. The members of a state board of corrections are usually appointed by the governor, and the board appoints the institution directors.

Administrative-level organizations in the state corrections system are essentially the central offices of the youth and adult penal systems. In some instances, they may include the probation and parole function as well as homes for dependent children and certain welfare and education functions. Generally, the smaller the state, the more functions there are consolidated under one central organization, but the trend is toward a single state agency controlling all corrective elements. These administrative agencies are organized in a manner similar to the central office of the Federal Bureau of Prisons, with the principal exception that juvenile agencies do not normally have extensive agricultural or industrial programs.

Adult prison central offices also vary to some extent, reflecting different perspectives on correction of inmates and differences in state funding support. Texas, for example, has extensive agricultural and industrial programs, and inmates in the Texas system are required to work. In California state prisons, such as San Quentin, on the other hand,

inmates may choose not to work. The central office organization is different in these two states, reflecting the different approach to corrections. An example of a typical organization for corrections at the state level is shown in Figure 17.2. Included in this illustration are all three types of correctional organizations.

Operational or line agencies at the state level are primarily separate penal institutions and training schools that report to the adult or juvenile system's central office, but they may include the jail system, as they do in Vermont, and they commonly include community-based agencies. Small states may have only one adult and one juvenile penal institution. Other states have a few large institutions, and a few states have dozens of small, specialized institutions. The layout of a recently constructed maximum security unit that houses approximately 1,500 men is shown in Figure 17.3. Small institutions (up to 400 inmates) are generally recognized to be preferable to the large units. However, even the smaller institutions tend to be located in rural rather than urban areas, despite the fact that urban areas are preferable be-

FIGURE 17.2 STATE CORRECTIONS ORGANIZATION

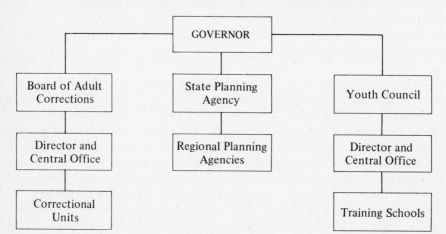

FIGURE 17.3 MAXIMUM SECURITY UNIT

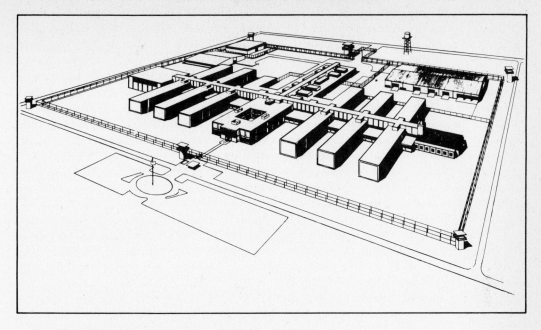

Source: Texas Department of Corrections, Huntsville, Tex.

cause they can support more community-oriented programs and medical services.

The following paragraphs introduce formal and informal organization of an adult institution. The formal organization of the training school for juveniles is similar except that more personnel are assigned to education, vocational training, and casework functions instead of farming, external (perimeters and field) security, and industrial programs.

FORMAL PRISON ORGANIZATIONS

The wardens of prison units are usually the chief executive officers. They are responsible for all the affairs of the unit as defined in policy statements provided by the director and assistant directors of the central office. Among their responsibilities are custody, treatment, training, and discipline of inmates

and the administrative duties involved in supervising all employees.

Classification and discipline committees are appointed by the wardens. These committees, which usually have five or fewer members, have representatives from a cross-section of the unit staff.

The purpose of the classification committee is to determine the total program for each inmate, including job assignment, education, training, and cell-block assignment. Unfortunately, often these committees do not function in actual practice, and the primary needs considered may be those of the units rather than the individual. In other cases, the committees are active, but the units may lack sufficient programs.

The discipline committees may be semi-permanent organizations, or they may be organized as the need arises. Their purpose is to consider the more serious breaches of discipline by inmates. Normally, certain punishments, such as solitary confinement, can be meted out only by the discipline committee.

Security sections are usually supervised by correctional officers, who have several shift supervisors under their control. Each shift supervisor is responsible for assigning guards to permanent posts in cell blocks and on the perimeter, perhaps in three shifts of eight hours each. The shift supervisor is also responsible for coordinating with the other sections to determine their requirements for shop and field guards. A limited number of guards are held in reserve for special details such as transfer of inmates and supervision of inmates during meals or recreation periods. The security personnel are helped in their function by the classification effort, which predetermines, to a degree, the risk potential of each inmate. The security classification given to each inmate helps guide the security element in making special work assignments.

Vocational training sections are identified as separate elements only in the large systems. Otherwise, vocational training is identified as an element of the industrial or farm enterprises or as an element of the education program. The organization of these elements is critical in determining the relative importance of the different functions. Many times, political considerations influence organization; for example, funds for adult vocational training may be harder to obtain than funds for an industrial program emphasizing profit. Actually, vocational training for a large number of inmates can be adequately achieved through industrial programs when the classification committee is active. Problems under this setup exist primarily because profit-making enterprises for a prison (mop-and-broom or license-plate factories, for ex-

ample) do not always match opportunities for employment in the free world, although much can be said for the emphasis on teaching inmates how to work, no matter what the work.

Education programs are common in prisons, and are becoming adequate. Of particular interest is the fact that education programs are one of the few prison programs that may have an effect on recidivism. In addition to the organization elements discussed above, this includes such elements as food service, maintenance, supply, counseling, and a chaplain section. The extent of all these elements depends on the size of the unit, the functions stressed, and the funding support given the prison.

INFORMAL PRISON ORGANIZATIONS

Prisons, like all institutions, have informal organizations. Informal organization is just as potent as formal organization in rule making and controlling behavior.

> The prison runs neither by force nor the threat of force alone, but largely by virtue of acceptance on the part of the inmates and their voluntary adherence to rules. These rules are partly the official rules of the prison, partly the mores of the inmate culture developed in the adaptation of many generations of convicts to the official code.[2]

Informal inmate organization or subculture has a historical base and is built on the power held by those inmates serving long sentences. It is difficult for treatment personnel to influence individuals once they have been influenced by the inmate subculture and have assumed their roles in that culture. This is a basic reason for the belief that rehabilitation is difficult, if not nearly impossible, in the environment of a large prison.

The inmate social organization . . . is a . . . formidable obstacle to any basic change of character among inmates, for this organization produces, in response to their psychological needs, precisely the conditions that make identification with non-criminal values highly improbable.[3]

The custodial staff also has an informal organization. Guards, like inmates, must protect themselves from the "establishment." Their job is to maintain control among the inmates, and so they require the cooperation of the power factions in the inmate subculture. In reward for cooperation with the guards and as a part of this informal agreement, inmates may be allowed to break certain established rules. Although these relationships help maintain control in the prison, they are also counterproductive if the guards attempt to act as agents of change through treatment.

LOCAL CORRECTIONAL ORGANIZATIONS

At the local level there are many organizations that influence the policy under which correctional units operate. Criminal justice coordinators in the regional planning councils (a multicounty or metroarea planning agency) have some effect on policy through their efforts to plan on a broad basis. One of the functions of the criminal justice coordinators is to provide data that support the state criminal justice plan required yearly by OJARS as a condition for obtaining federal funding under OJARS. The city council is also a policy organization, as would be such agencies as the church or social and business clubs that sponsor corrections programs. Many of these agencies play important supporting roles to correctional agencies.

At the local level, it is often difficult to distinguish clearly between the policy, administrative, and operational levels of organizations. A county jail, for example, may receive funding, guidance, and planning support from the administrative organization of the sheriff's department of which it is a part. In a small county, the sheriff may be the only full-time person in the organization. In this example, as in the case of the chief of police, it would help to think of the individual as wearing several hats. At one time, the sheriff wears the law enforcement hat; at other times, the sheriff is an administrator or operator of a correctional institution and performs the functions normal to that job. The same may be said for the chief of police, who is responsible for the police lockup. (Technically, pretrial detention and lockup are not correctional functions.) A typical organization for corrections at the local level is shown in Figure 17.4.

In the paragraphs below, the organizations of several community agencies are presented. With the exception of jails, which are fairly standard, these are only examples of how the corrections functions may be organized in a specific local community. The primary difference between local communities is in the number of staff members (resulting in more or less specialization) and the administrative organization that supports the particular operational unit. These organizations are all classified as community-based, but they may be operated by agencies at levels of government above the city or county.

JAILS

The jail was originally established as a place to detain persons awaiting trial. Over the centuries it has taken on the additional function of housing persons serving short sentences. The jail system as it has developed in America has three parts or general classes:

FIGURE 17.4 JURISDICTIONAL STRUCTURE OF CRIMINAL JUSTICE OPERATIONS AT THE COMMUNITY LEVEL

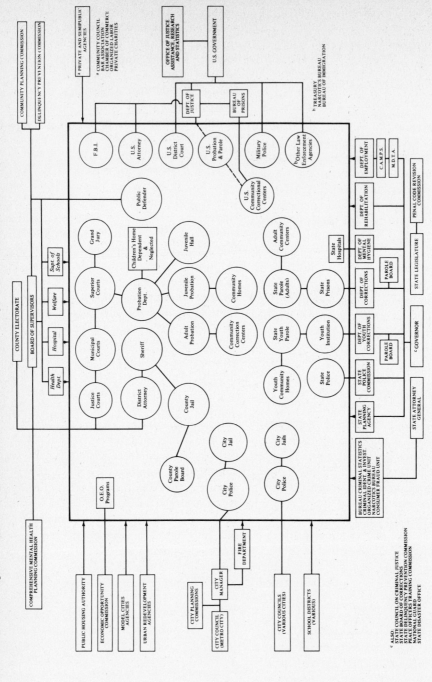

SOURCE: Mark S. Richmond, ed., *Roles for Jails; Guidelines for Planning* (Washington, D.C.: Federal Prison System, 1969), p. 11.

(1) the lockup; (2) the jail; and (3) the workhouse, jail farm, or camp.[4] The lockup is used to hold persons for investigation or for preliminary hearing purposes for up to seventy-two hours. It is usually operated by, and located in the same building as, the local law enforcement agency. The workhouse, jail farm, or camp is often used to house minimum custody offenders who are serving short sentences. They may be operated by the city, by the county sheriff, or by a separate correctional agency under the city or the county.

Jails are facilities under the control of the police or city or county authorities; they house both persons awaiting trial and persons serving short sentences. Some jails house both adults and juveniles and, where adequate facilities are not available to provide for separate care, the noncriminally insane. Most jails also serve as lockups for the law enforcement agency operating the facility. A built-in advantage of the jail is that it is normally located in the center of the community, so that a full range of community services is within reach. Unfortunately, few jails are administered by professional correctional personnel who utilize the services available, nor are they adequately supported financially so that the staff of the jail can provide the needed services. In other cases the laws allowing certain programs, such as work release, have not been enacted.

Organizationally and functionally, the jail would be much like the prison if the inmate population were the same size and if it held prisoners for the same period of time. Most jails, however, have traditionally been given little financial support, and county jails are usually under the control of a sheriff who stands for election every two to four years. Even given these handicaps, however, there are a number of very progressive jails. The jail in Ingham County, Michigan, is an example. It has a complete school program, including vocational training, as well as programs for drug offenders and a work release and a school release program. Also available are extensive medical and dental care, arts and crafts, and a closed circuit television network so that inmates under tight security can go to school in their own cells. The staff of this jail includes five professional psychologists in addition to the normal administrative and custodial staff. A jailer in this system is paid more than the deputy sheriffs who work only in law enforcement.

Although the majority of inmates are housed in large city jails, most jails are in rural areas. The typical small jail is in the care of one person on the staff of the county sheriff's department. Often a police dispatcher is responsible for the jail at night as an extra duty. It is common for a man and wife team to work in the jail, with enough duties combined to justify a salary large enough to attract two people. In the husband and wife team, the husband handles the administrative duties and oversees custody of the male prisoners, while the wife acts as both cook and matron; they may live in the jail. One particular jail in Arkansas that is operated in this manner has a population of ten to twenty inmates.

The jail in the medium-sized county (up to 300 inmates) is large enough to support shift supervisors under the head jailer. The head jailer is typically responsible for all administrative duties, including such functions as preparing the menu. In jails of this size, the kitchen is commonly operated by inmates, while in small jails meals are often provided by a local cafe under contract. One such medium-size jail located in southeast Texas is under the control of a jailer who has been given the title of captain; and the staff is composed of approximately forty-five employees, who are divided into three eight-hour shifts.

Today, most county jails serve as lockup

facilities and pretrial detention facilities and in addition house convicted offenders for one to two years. There are cases where inmates who are appealing convictions have stayed in local jails for years. Jails have historically provided little treatment and, in fact, are not constructed to allow even adequate control or adequate visitation and recreation. This state of affairs, together with general deterioration with age and problems of overcrowding, has resulted in the need to replace a large number of jails.

The regional jail concept has been proposed as an alternative to building bigger traditional jails. The regional concept calls for using holding facilities (lockups) in various locations in a large city or a multicounty area with a central jail to serve the entire region, the central facility being built around the programs required by the particular area. For example, it might have provisions for diagnostic services, education, vocational training, work and school release, and alcohol and drug detoxification. Or, depending on the area and the size of the inmate population, these activities might be housed in separate facilities, with the detoxification activity, for example, in a local hospital.

The regional concept has been slow to be implemented for a number of reasons. One has been a general lack of funding. Jails, like hospitals, are costly to build. Probably the most difficult of the problems to be overcome is that regionalization requires extensive planning and close cooperation between political subdivisions that have not historically been able to cooperate.

PREDELINQUENT CENTERS

The National Crime Commission's Task Force on Corrections reported on several variations of the youth services bureau as a form of predelinquent center.[5] Several of these have sprung up in the past few years

on a demonstration basis. Now, with assistance from federal grants, many of the larger cities and counties have established their own agencies.

One concept is the establishment of an agency that is primarily concerned with coordinating the services already available in the community. This type of agency is staffed primarily by persons who perform intake and case-summary functions; that is, they are primarily concerned with identifying the problem and referring the individual (or the individual case) to the appropriate agency. Most of this agency's responsibility is administrative, although professionals in counseling and therapy may be available when these services are not available in other agencies to fulfill specialized needs.

Another type of bureau provides facilities for youth on a live-in basis. In some areas of the country, several counties have pooled their resources to establish juvenile delinquency prevention projects that take potential delinquents from their environment and provide them with a full range of education, training, and counseling services. What distinguishes this project from the typical training school is that participation is voluntary; the youngsters may not have been officially designated as delinquents, and they are allowed to go home on weekends. They are usually controlled by some form of reward structure, rather than by guards in locked or barred facilities. Referrals to these projects could come from a variety of sources, including the family, the schools, the police, and the juvenile court. One such project located in the Southwest has facilities for housing and feeding up to 250 boys. It has full-time teachers who operate a regular accredited school program, and it has a diversified vocational program that leads to apprentice status in one of several labor unions closely associated with the project. The counties that operate this center for boys also operate a similar project for girls.

A third type of bureau is one that has some of the programs of each of the other two approaches. Many projects in this category are under the general control of the juvenile court. They may employ a director, intake workers, caseworkers, a psychologist, and an individual whose responsibility is divided between research and coordination of other community programs. This agency, like the coordinating bureau, maintains close contact with other local social service agencies. In addition, one of its intake workers may be located at the juvenile court and have the authority to divert individuals directly to the project before juvenile court action. The project maintains close coordination with the police, has daily contact with them, and gives talks during police training programs. Not primarily a referral service, this type of bureau depends more on its own resources but does not provide live-in facilities for clients.

One theory on which these agencies operate is that a juvenile delinquent can be assisted toward a behavior change if community services are brought to bear at an early stage. Whether these youths are diverted from a life of crime depends to a great extent on the validity of the theory that many of these youths are less likely to continue criminal behavior if they are kept out of the formal justice system processing and in the community.

FOSTER HOMES AND GROUP HOMES

Foster homes and group homes are alternatives to state schools for dependent or delinquent children. They are more often used for the dependent and neglected than for youngsters who have committed crimes. Both of these programs basically offer a substitute home for a youngster when the former home environment is believed to be unsuitable. Although the use of foster homes is controversial because it takes children away from their natural home setting in the community, there are cases in which this approach is justified.

Group homes are more often used where the alternative is incarceration. They are generally less expensive than an institution and offer the advantages of such community services as the schools. The basic organization of the foster or group home is the family structure, and the influence that the "parents" can exert on the child is expected to produce rehabilitation. The adults who operate these homes are carefully selected to ensure that they have the proper traits. The child who goes to a foster or group home is also selected carefully on the basis of expectation that he or she can benefit from this type of treatment or care.

COMMUNITY PRERELEASE CENTERS AND HALFWAY HOUSES

The community-based prerelease guidance center or halfway house is normally established to house from ten to twenty-five persons. Since the function of these agencies is to help the inmate through a phased reintegration into the community, a variety of services are required. In addition to providing housing and meals, they provide the important services of counseling and employment assistance.

The typical agency is supervised by a director and, in a large agency, an assistant director. A counselor is available for each ten to twelve persons, and a caseworker or psychologist may be available to oversee the work of the counselors and perform such specialized duties as group therapy. It is also usual practice to employ college students for counseling and control duties during the night hours. A staff cook is available either half or full time to prepare meals. In the larger agency, there is also an employment counselor, who helps those living in the house to find and hold employment and who is also active in the community, finding job opportunities and providing funds for tools and equipment that residents may need in order to obtain jobs in specialized fields. Halfway houses are used most often as a step toward the community after a prison sentence, but they are also used as alternatives to probation or prison.

There are essentially four major systems of corrections in the United States: the federal system, the military system, the state system, and the local system. Within these four major systems, there are planning and policy-making organizations, administrative agencies, and line agencies. Planning and policy-making agencies include Office of Justice Assistance, Research and Statistics (federal), criminal justice commissions (state), and regional criminal justice planning agencies (local). Administrative and line agencies are concerned with the actual operation of correctional systems. The Federal Bureau of Prisons serves this function in the federal system. It supervises the treatment and commitment of federal prisoners, that is, individuals who have committed federal crimes. The military prison system consists of the correctional systems of the Army, Navy, and Air Force. Each has its own system for treatment and commitment of military personnel who have committed acts in violation of the Uniform Code of Military Justice. In the state system of prisons each state has its own unique prison system, ranging from systems with as many as 25,000 inmates in the largest states to as few as 200 inmates in smaller states. Each state provides for the treatment and commitment of individuals who have violated the state's laws. The local level encompasses the many correctional facilities of the cities, counties, and regional government organizations. At this level we find the police detention cells, the county jails, and the regional correctional centers. These facilities generally hold individuals who have received a short-term sentence or those individuals who are awaiting some form of adjudication.

Many other correctional services are also available at the community level, including halfway houses and foster homes. Coordination of these organizations under a unified crime control theory is yet to be realized.

DISCUSSION QUESTIONS

1. What role should a research and evaluation unit play in the central administrative organization of a prison system?
2. Should corrections be a state or local function?
3. Discuss the education and training needs of a prison warden and prison guards.
4. Describe how to determine the size and program requirements for a new jail.
5. Should an inmate receive benefits, such as a free college education, while in prison?
6. Describe your local correctional organizations. Are they adequate?

NOTES

1. *Report of the Special Civilian Committee for the Study of the U.S. Army Confinement System* (Washington, D.C.: Department of the Army, 1970).

2. George H. Grosser, "External Setting and Internal Relations of the Prison," in *Prison Within Society,* ed. Lawrence Hazelrigg (New York: Doubleday, 1969), p. 18.

3. Grosser, "External Setting," p. 20.

4. American Correctional Association, *Manual of Correctional Standards* (Washington, D.C.: American Correctional Association, 1959), pp. 43–44.

5. President's Commission on Law Enforcement and Administration of Justice, *Task Force Report: Corrections* (Washington, D.C.: Government Printing Office, 1967), pp. 22–23.

CHAPTER EIGHTEEN

FUNCTIONS
OF CORRECTIONAL
ORGANIZATIONS

MANAGEMENT AND
ADMINISTRATION

CUSTODY AND
CONTROL

CORRECTIONAL
TREATMENT

*Purpose: To provide a description of the
functions of correctional organizations, including
administration, custody, treatment, personnel,
and research.*

MODERN CORRECTIONAL organizations can be categorized as dealing primarily with the function of *treatment* or with the function of *custody and control*. For example, such institutions as the police lockup, housing only persons in short-term, pretrial confinement, are concerned primarily with custody and control. Many community-based predelinquent centers, on the other hand, are concerned primarily with treatment. Prisons, jails, and reformatories generally fall between the two extremes in that they may stress both of these functions.

It is almost impossible to explain our modern system of corrections only in terms of these two primary functions. Justifying extensive recreational facilities and legal assistance in a prison, for example, on the basis of their direct relationship to either major function is difficult; probably some programs are justified on moral or other grounds as basic human needs. The presence of these programs (prison employment, education, recreation, adequate food, and so on) may not significantly enhance the treatment or custody and control functions, but their lack may hinder the successful implementation of other programs specifically designed to rehabilitate an inmate. Viewing the functions from this perspective can help explain how the methods used in custody and control can adversely affect treatment. If custody and control methods tend to destroy an individual's basic psychological needs, treatment has little chance of modifying that individual's behavior. In the prison environment, this conflict between control and rehabilitation is not easily overcome.

Historically, corrections organizations have been poorly managed. A complicating factor is the obligation of public officials to operate at a minimum cost consistent with adequate performance. The importance of the cost factor introduces another major function called management and administration. Although all organizations need proper management and administration, their historic neglect in corrections gives them special significance. For this reason the *management and administration function* will be introduced in this chapter along with the functions of *treatment* and *custody and control*.

MANAGEMENT AND ADMINISTRATION

The management and administration function is common to all correctional organizations. Obviously, these organizations are composed of more than guards and caseworkers. Many technical and professional skills are required. This is shown in Figure 18.1. And in planning and policy agencies, the management and administration function is everything in that the personnel are not directly involved in treatment and custody functions.

PLANNING AND POLICY

Planning and policy as a part of the management and administration function refer to the establishment of guidelines for performing all the programs of an agency or institution, including, for example, setting goals and determining how the success or failure of different programs is measured. Planning and policy are the primary job of the manager, and the job is done at each organization level. The primary difference between levels is in the length of time on which a particular plan is based. For example, the policy agency normally operates on a planning basis of five years or more, whereas the line agency is normally concerned with periods up to one year.

Planning and policy are extremely impor-

FIGURE 18.1 FUNCTIONAL POSITIONS IN A LARGE PRISON UNIT

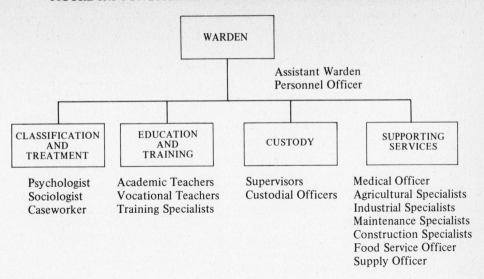

WARDEN

Assistant Warden
Personnel Officer

CLASSIFICATION AND TREATMENT	EDUCATION AND TRAINING	CUSTODY	SUPPORTING SERVICES

Psychologist
Sociologist
Caseworker

Academic Teachers
Vocational Teachers
Training Specialists

Supervisors
Custodial Officers

Medical Officer
Agricultural Specialists
Industrial Specialists
Maintenance Specialists
Construction Specialists
Food Service Officer
Supply Officer

tant functions. For example, the current change in emphasis of some prisons from treatment (medical model) to custody is determined to a large extent by planning accomplished by the director and carried out through fiscal and personnel functions.

FISCAL OPERATIONS

Fiscal operations include consolidating and monitoring the budget, cost control, accountability for property, and internal auditing. In a small operation, such as a community service project, these responsibilities may be carried out by the project director; whereas, in a large prison, fiscal responsibilities are assigned to the staff.

The fiscal officer has all subordinate agencies submit their monetary needs for the coming year. It is then his or her responsibility, along with the manager, to "sell the product," so to speak, to the funding agency. The funding agency in the case of a state prison system, for example, is the state legislature. A community project may

require funding from the city government, a state planning agency, or a district office of the Office of Justice Assistance, Research and Statistics. (These funding agencies also have fiscal officers.) Once funds are received, the fiscal officer is responsible for proper distribution of funds and strict accounting of expenditures.

PERSONNEL MANAGEMENT

The personnel manager is responsible for hiring the number and type of persons previously determined by organization's planning and fiscal functions. The personnel manager works closely with the financial support operation. In small agencies such as halfway houses, these jobs may be combined and done by the director. The personnel officer may be assigned responsibility for recruitment, records of employees, the retirement plan, job specifications, management development, promotion and selection criteria, and the administration of the staff mail system. The manager is also commonly assigned responsibility for the training of employees and for employee evaluation.

RESEARCH AND EVALUATION

The correctional administrator is the important person in any research or evaluation effort. The administrator is responsible for ensuring that every phase of the agency or institution's work is directed toward the achievement of a common goal or mission. To accomplish this task, the administrator must depend on research and evaluation to measure progress toward the objective. Research and evaluation are fundamental elements of effective management.

The scope of research and evaluation in corrections ranges from investigation of the reasons why individuals act as they do and whether a treatment design modifies behavior, to methods for improving training and operating procedures.

CUSTODY AND CONTROL

The custody and control functions of institutions and agencies in corrections are primarily those dealing with secure housing, safety of the facility and persons, and maintenance of a controlled environment. In some cases, these may be the only functions required of an institution by law. Many of the functions classified as treatment activities in a prison can also help to control the inmate; classification is an example. For this reason, it is often difficult, if not impossible, to categorize an activity as one and not the other. The activities identified in this section as belonging to custody or control are traditionally more concerned with custody and control than with treatment. But several could just as well be put in the treatment category, depending on the emphasis, which varies from one organization to another.

SECURITY

For discussion purposes, *security* is defined as the layout or design of a prison, reformatory, or jail and the programs designed to prevent escape from these institutions. For this purpose, prisons can be described as either *maximum, medium,* or *minimum security.* These terms should not be confused with those used to grade inmates as to security risk, because the modern prison may have facilities suitable for any inmate custody grade.

The maximum security prison is an outgrowth of the Auburn architecture of the last century. Many prisons still in use today were built in the 1800s and thus fall into this category. Their chief characteristic is the high, thick wall surrounding all buildings and activities. The "walls unit" in Huntsville, Texas, is an example. Originally constructed in the 1850s, this unit now houses the older first offenders and the persons moved "up" from one of the other prison units. There are still a number of "super security" institutions in use (Figure 18.2), but most new prisons today are medium security.

Probably the greatest number of adult prisons today would be classified as medium security. The major differences between this type and the older maximum security prison are the absence of the wall and the fact that some facilities and activities are handled outside the main enclosure. Characteristically, the medium-security prison is smaller than the maximum-security unit, and the primary facilities are enclosed by two rows of chain-link fence. In many ways, the medium-security classification is a misnomer, because such a unit may be more escape-proof than the older maximum-security unit. Its smaller size and the use of electronic devices to detect escape attempts are effective. Also, most internal doors are electronically controlled

FIGURE 18.2 SUPER-SECURITY INSTITUTION

Federal prison, Alcatraz Island, San Francisco Bay, California. Alcatraz was an army prison taken over by the Federal Bureau of Prisons in 1934. It was used as a "super-security" prison to house the worst offenders. Alcatraz was closed because of its high operating cost and because the facility had deteriorated.
SOURCE: Federal Bureau of Prisons, Washington, D.C.

from a remote, secure room, and external doors can be unlocked only electronically by a guard in a tower removed from the enclosure. Because of the effectiveness of these devices, today most escapes from prisons are likely to be "walk-aways" rather than "breakouts." Walk-aways occur when inmates are allowed to work outside the enclosure.

The minimum-security classification unit is found primarily in the juvenile training schools, although the federal government and several states operate minimum-security units for adults. These units do not have fences, and the inmates are free to travel from the dormitory to school, recreation center, or mess hall. Security is provided at night by locking outside doors. The mini-

mum-security unit is used primarily for juveniles or for those adults with short sentences or a short time to go to complete a sentence. An adult felon prerelease center may be of this design.

Classifying jails for security is even more difficult than classifying prisons. The national jail survey of 1970 indicated that 25 percent of the nation's jails were more than fifty years old, and that many did not provide the minimum essentials for health and safety.[1] Many of these old structures do not have the security devices common in the better prisons, and they lack competently trained staff and the basic programs needed to reduce tension and anxiety.

The security functions, as they have been defined for our purposes, are of relatively minor importance in halfway houses and most other community-based projects. There the emphasis is on voluntary control of oneself, and the secure facility in this sense depends on the individual.

CONTROL PROCEDURES

Another function of custody and control personnel is developing procedures for the orderly and safe conduct of the institution or agency, those to be followed by inmates or clients and those to be followed by custodial and control personnel. All essential elements of the institution should be involved in developing these procedures so that they represent the best mix of custody and control with the other functions of the institution. In this area of rule making, custody and control commonly conflict with treatment.

Safety procedures are of paramount importance in controlling the environment and should encompass all areas of the unit. These include work safety, fire prevention, and the proper storage, control, and issue of firearms and other potentially dangerous material. In the modern prison, for example, firearms are maintained only in outside guardhouses (by the pickets) and are issued only when potentially dangerous inmates are escorted to another facility or to work in the field.

Rules and regulations concerning custody and control are established for all phases of inmate processing, work control, and recreation time. Because of the large concentration of inmates in most prisons and jails, there are rules concerning the personal habits and actions of inmates. Rules generally limit the areas in which an inmate is allowed. Rules also limit loud talking and gathering in groups. Although most of these rules are legitimate requirements for maintaining control, in some prison and jail situations they are also used as a means of repression and punishment in the mistaken belief that control demands complete regimentation in all areas of prison life. Recent federal court decisions have limited this abuse by requiring that prisoners be given a formal disciplinary hearing.

RECEPTION AND INTAKE

The initial reception of individuals into the corrections system may be the most critical period in determining their future actions. At this point attitudes toward the corrections system are initiated, and these attitudes, to a large degree, control inmates' reactions throughout their stay. *Reception* is used in two senses. In the first, the jails can be considered the "reception centers" of the corrections system, and so the attitudes developed in jail have a great influence on how inmates act in later contacts with the criminal justice system. *Reception* is also used to refer to the processing that individuals receive when they first come in contact with a particular agency or institution, such as a state's adult felony reception center.

Institutional Reception The "reception center" concept has been devised to help control the influences operating on individuals during the critical initial phase of their introduction to a penal institution. This concept is common in our prison and reformatory systems but not in our jails. The center may be operated in conjunction with the diagnostic center used for classification; if so, maximum benefit is gained. In addition to studying the background and behavior of the inmate, the reception center may have a program of orientation to remove some of the fear and apprehension all individuals have. Programs of reading, recreation, and religious training may be available, and special work assignments can be provided to lessen tensions and hostilities.

In some cases today and typically in the past, the reception center was a shock treatment used to indoctrinate inmates. An inmate, for example a youth of seventeen or even younger, might be forced to undress, after which his body was inspected, his head shaved, and his personal belongings taken from him. He would then go through an endless session of days and nights filled with regimentation, forced silence, and loneliness in the middle of a crowd. This treatment forced an inmate to seek relief, and one way was to become an active participant in the inmate subculture. Certainly careful attention is required during the reception process to reduce the possibility of introducing weapons, drugs, or physical disease, but it is becoming less common to believe that harsh treatment is necessary to establish control.

Reception in Community-based Corrections In the setting of the community "helping" agency, the reception process is referred to as *intake*. Here an individual's first contact is with the intake worker, who tries to find out what problems the individual has; records basic data concerning age, sex, family situation, and so forth; and determines which particular specialists, either within or outside the organization, are best equipped to work with the client. Essentially, the intake worker handles both the activities associated with intake and many of the activities associated with determining suitable treatment for the individual (classification).

Reception, or intake, is very important in the community helping agency as well as in the institution. Because many of the helping agencies are dependent on the voluntary participation of the client for a successful program, many agencies use their most capable personnel for intake.

CLASSIFICATION

Classification, in the institutional setting, became popular when the emphasis was placed on treatment using the medical model. It is now recognized as an important element of any institutional program. First, classification supports the overall custody and control function in that an inmate is "classified" according to the amount of custodial control required. Secondly, classification determines a treatment plan for the person based on individual needs. A third use of classification is that of supporting the administrative needs of the institution by placing a person with a particular skill or aptitude in the proper program. Classification in the community helping agency setting, on the other hand, is concerned primarily with designing a treatment plan, which may include deciding whether to place an individual under a caseworker who will offer intensive supervision or under a caseworker who will provide only minimum supervision.

However, the mere presence of a system of classification indicates little about what it is actually accomplishing. For example, an inmate may be assigned to work in an office or on a farm because that assignment best meets his or her needs or because the institution has a need for labor. Or a juvenile may be put under minimum supervision because all the agency's casework loads were too high to offer close supervision. Classification is a strong tool, and its use must be closely monitored.

FOOD SERVICE

The food-service function in an institution like a prison or jail can be extremely complicated and costly. Many institutions must get all the necessary food items from outside sources. A few prison systems, however, operate large farms that provide most of the prison's daily needs. And, in some cases, a prison may make excess food available to other governmental institutions, thereby reducing their costs of operation. The prison in Mississippi is an example of a system that has land for extensive agricultural programs.

An effective food-service program combines the essentials of sanitation, menu planning, proper facilities for storage and preparation, and a system of distribution and serving. These specialized activities make professional food service personnel necessary in all but the smallest institutions. From the inmates' point of view, food service probably ranks with mail and visits as the most important functions of the prison, reformatory, or jail. The effect on inmate morale of a poorly run food-service program is significant and can be a major factor in the success of custody and treatment programs.

MEDICAL SERVICE

The medical service operates from reception of an individual into corrections to release. In the community agency, the medical condition of a client is one of the first treatment considerations. In the institution, medical services must be available as a part of rehabilitation, but they must also be available for humanitarian and health safety reasons. Usually, a complete medical checkup is one of the first steps in processing an inmate into an institution. Minor health problems are corrected immediately, and more costly or time-consuming treatments may be attempted, depending on their seriousness or their potential for encouraging rehabilitation.

Most large prisons maintain a permanent professional staff for medical and dental health purposes. It is difficult to conceive of a more terrifying experience than to be locked in a cell and sick, and to know that medical assistance is not readily available. Unfortunately, however, this is the case in some prisons and in many jails, both large and small.

INDUSTRY PROGRAMS

Although industry programs can be classified under the treatment function, consideration of their cost/savings aspect probably outweighs the treatment aspect in most adult prisons for males. The reverse may be true in juvenile or women's facilities, where the training and work benefits may take precedence over the financial advantage. A properly managed prison industry program can save taxpayers millions of dollars each year while offering job training for many inmates.

Prison industries include such programs as furniture repair and manufacture, license-plate manufacture, cattle and horse operations, farming, building, and road construction. The possible diversification of prison industry is limited only by the effect of law (selling for state use only) and the influence of private industry. Although in theory full employment of inmates is possible, in practice it has been achieved in very few prison systems and probably in no large jails. Prison industry, however, does offer the multiple advantages of providing the opportunity for proper placement for treatment, reducing discipline problems by the release of tension through productive employment, and reducing costs by a self-supporting operation.

The Federal Bureau of Prisons operates varied industry programs, as do most states, but methods are different. For example, federal inmates are paid at a daily rate. In Texas state prisons, on the other hand, inmates are not paid. In both cases, these shops provide opportunities for inmates to learn good work habits and job skills.

DISCIPLINE

Strict discipline has been a tradition in penal institutions, including juvenile facilities, since the development of the Auburn system. However, many changes have been made during the 1970s as a result of review by federal judges and a revision of thinking on the part of some administrators. The common practice today is for an inmate to receive a "hearing" for any offense that might carry more than minor punishment. Even conditions in solitary confinement have changed to restrict "bread and water" diets and to limit the time of total darkness. Sound discipline procedures not only help to ensure adequate control but also act to protect inmates from other inmates and protect the staff.

CORRECTIONAL TREATMENT

The treatment program for an individual in prison can actually be thought of as encompassing most correctional functions. In a properly designed and implemented program, all an inmate's work, training, education, and custody assignments are part of treatment. Even though not designed specifically to aid in treatment, a function may have an effect on the treatment programs; that is, the lack of recreation, medical care, or the like can negate an otherwise successful program.

It is probably in the area of integration of functions that overall institution management fails most often. A few primary goals have to be the target for all elements of the institution or agency, and treatment may be the one area that can properly integrate all other functions to develop a realistic and meaningful plan for an individual.

If rehabilitation or treatment is not a goal, then the situation is different. This has caused many problems in the past when rehabilitation was said to be a goal but was not seriously pursued. The following sections cover some of the current functions normally considered to be primarily treatment oriented. They include both a discussion of treatment approaches and a discussion of some programs established in an attempt to avoid the pitfalls inherent in the institutional approach to rehabilitation. The fact that many of these functions can also be categorized as control or custody should not be disregarded.

PRISONER OR CLIENT SERVICES

In the institutional setting, the prisoner services category includes those services provided to inmates in the areas of welfare, morale, and daily comfort. Some of these activities, such as providing clothing, may be required by law. Other services, such as visitation privileges, commissaries, pay, vocational rehabilitation, and welfare counseling, may not be required by law, but they may be justified because they help to maintain basic human dignity or are real tools for treatment and rehabilitation.

In many prisons and jails, visitation, commissaries, and certain other activities, including recreation, have been considered to be privileges. As such, the inmate had to earn the privilege of using them. In other instances, notably the jails, some of these basic services are completely missing. For example, checkers and cards may be the extent of recreation for an inmate serving a year in jail. Most criminologists today feel that all these services are essential for basic health and welfare and that their lack can contribute significantly to the failure of both the treatment and the custody and control functions.

In the setting of the helping agency, client services become a significant activity. Most of these agencies exist in order to provide a specific service or act as a referral source to the proper service. Some predelinquent control agencies, for example, exist for the sole purpose of seeing that juveniles and their families are channeled to the service organization best able to satisfy their need. These agencies may not perform any specific treatment activity; rather, they refer the client to another agency that specializes in the required service. Among the agencies or programs to which a client or his family might be referred are welfare organizations, employment counseling agencies, remedial reading centers, drug programs, vocational training programs, and individual or group counseling programs.

COUNSELING, THERAPY, AND INDIVIDUAL EVALUATION

Professional evaluation of the individual is an essential element in any corrections program. Whether in a community agency or an institution, the experience should begin with an adequate evaluation so that plans for appropriate treatment and control can be made. In the prison setting, this evaluation is begun by interviewers who are skilled in developing a case history. In the agency setting, this is done by the intake worker. After this processing, a case worker or counselor may be assigned, or the individual may be assigned or referred to a program or agency designed to help him or her toward rehabilitation. These decisions are often made in conference or with the advice of professional psychologists or others who are trained in behavior modification programs. Day-to-day counseling may be provided by the caseworker, counselor, or correctional officer, who in turn seeks advice from the staff psychologist.

Although many methods and types of counseling and therapy have been attempted in the institutional setting, the success of these programs has been doubtful, to say the least. This can be explained in part by the difficulty of measuring success. Many reasons have been advanced for this apparent failure to measure adequately, but we probably have never had both the proper setting and adequate research controls to come to a proper conclusion. It has not been proven that rehabilitation does not work in a prison setting, but it also has not been proven that it does or can work.

In the community setting, counseling and individual evaluation activities assume a more all-encompassing role than is usual in the institution. Because these programs are not custodial, behavior change through casework and counseling is of primary importance.

SHORT-TERM TREATMENT PROGRAMS

Several states have special short-term treatment programs. California and Florida have had extensive experience with such programs. One such program involves screening all juveniles who have been committed to an institution by the juvenile court to see if they are eligible for immediate release from a reception center on parole or for release after a short treatment program. Those selected may be placed in foster homes or halfway houses, or they may be paroled to a parole officer as part of his or her normal or intensive casework load.

This type of program for juveniles is in striking contrast to the normal process for adults. Adults (normally 17 to 18 and older), when sentenced to a prison term, must usually wait until they have completed a specified portion of the sentence before they are eligible for parole. A rigid system of parole eligibility does not recognize that some individuals could be released in a short time and have a high probability of success in staying out of the criminal justice system.

Our success record in predicting who will be less likely to return to prison, however, has not been good. This and a general rise in the crime rate have caused several states to consider abandoning parole for those committed to prison. They would emphasize community treatment where possible. Once sent to prison, an inmate would serve a specified time regardless of future conduct.

WORK FURLOUGH

Work furlough or work release is the practice of releasing an inmate from a prison or jail to work in the community. A number of states have initiated such programs in their prison systems, but few jails have tried them (despite the fact that work release was initiated in a few jails several decades ago. The normal procedure is for the inmate to be driven to work each day and returned to the prison or jail each night. Part of the inmate's wages may go toward paying room and board, making restitution, and providing family support, or into a savings account. In the jail situation, the jail's chief administrator operates the program in a similar manner.

Work release, as a concept, is potentially a self-supporting treatment program. It has been strongly advocated by criminologists but meets with considerable resistance from prison and jail authorities, not so much because they cannot see the benefits as because of their rightful fear of public opinion in the wake of a failure. Logically, a person on work release is less likely to commit a crime because of the high probability of being caught and the swiftness of the resulting punishment. The problem lies in the fact that the prison or jail administrator has a direct hand in choosing the person for work release and may therefore be held directly accountable for any failures. Also, failures in a work-release setting are more visible to the public than are failures within the institution. Nevertheless, the fact that probably 98 percent of all inmates will eventually return to the community is sufficient reason to greatly expand this type of reintegration program.

EDUCATION AND RECREATION

Education programs, both academic and vocational, and recreation programs are the backbone of the treatment function in most prisons. Many individuals seem to need only this type of "treatment." The absence of these programs in most jails means that there is no treatment program at all. Like many of the other programs in the treatment category, there is very little evidence that these are significantly effective tools in rehabilitation. Most criminologists and administrators feel, however, that they are justified on other grounds and that in combination with other treatment programs they offer much promise as the foundation for treatment. These programs have become so entrenched that they probably will stay and be improved even if there is a shift further away from treatment.

The major problem with education programs, where they exist, is their quality. In some instances, academic classes have been conducted on a voluntary basis by off-duty guards. In some cases, they are poorly supported by funding agencies, and teaching materials are limited. There are, however, excellent education programs in several prisons and in many juvenile institutions. Those institutions with quality education programs employ qualified teachers and are certified by the state, so that they can issue high school diplomas.

A number of prisons and jails offer college courses for inmates through arrangements with local colleges. Correspondence courses are another common means of gaining college credit. There are also programs where instructors come to the prison, and in some places, like the Federal Correctional Center in Fort Worth, Texas, groups of inmates go to the college itself.

Vocational training programs, like academic education programs, are used more in juvenile facilities than in adult institutions, partly because in adult prisons there are industry and agriculture programs that relieve some of the need and reduce costs. Because many of the industry programs are not related to employment opportunities outside the prison, much effort is being directed to obtaining funds for realistic vocational programs. Common among these are automotive, radio, and television repair, and programs in such areas as meat cutting, metal work, and other specialized skills.

Recreation by itself is only marginally a treatment program, but it is important as a way of providing a climate for other programs, including the custody and control activities. Recreation programs can range from libraries and books to sports like baseball and rodeo. Several states have regular league play between prison units in baseball and basketball. Organized sports activities are, however, concerned primarily with overall morale building and do not directly involve many inmates. For many jail inmates, there are no facilities for recreation or exercise of any kind. This situation is changing because of court orders as a result of suits by inmates.

PRERELEASE COUNSELING

Prerelease counseling includes those activities that take place shortly before an inmate is released from a penal institution and are designed to assist his or her reintegration into the community. A prerelease program is distinguished from a halfway house in that it is normally conducted by the institution and usually within the institution. The other obvious distinction is that it is conducted prior to release from custody, whereas the halfway house usually has ex-inmates, those who have been released on parole or, in some cases, those who have completed their sentence.

The typical prerelease program is little more than a series of lectures on such topics as general financial management, how to buy major products, the cost of items on the outside, and how to get along with a parole officer. Most prisons operate some type of prerelease program; this can range from a few talks given by custodial personnel to a full-scale program, several weeks long, with visiting speakers. Inmates may also be allowed limited freedom in the community as a part of the program and can obtain their driver's license.

Few jails operate any type of prerelease program, which is unfortunate because jails, like prisons, can hold inmates long enough to justify a need for careful reintegration into the community. An advantage to the prerelease concept, as opposed to the halfway house, is that it can be operated from the institution and so is a reasonable program for jails to operate. Also, an institutional prerelease program can handle much larger numbers of people than can the halfway house.

DISCUSSION QUESTIONS

1. Can treatment and control measures exist together?
2. What does *cost/effective corrections* mean?
3. Is the corrections system in agreement concerning the purpose or goal of corrections?
4. Discuss your concept of the goal of corrections.

5. Is time spent serving a sentence a continuation of punishment, or is it the first phase of a rehabilitation program?
6. Discuss whether one of the major penal functions could encompass the other functions.
7. Discuss how security or control measures can influence the rehabilitation process.

NOTE

1. U.S. Department of Justice, *1970 Jail Census* (Washington, D.C.: Government Printing Office, 1971), p. 1.

CHAPTER NINETEEN

PROBLEMS, CONTROVERSIES, AND MODERN CONCEPTS IN CORRECTIONS

PEOPLE INVOLVED IN
CORRECTIONS

INADEQUACIES IN
MANAGEMENT AND
ORGANIZATION

INSTITUTIONAL AND
NONINSTITUTIONAL
CORRECTIONS

RESPONSIBILITY

Purpose: To provide an overview of the major problem areas in corrections with a discussion of their effects.

THE MANY PROBLEMS in corrections are well documented and seem almost insurmountable. After hundreds of years of applying the techniques of punishment and retribution in a system of jails and prisons, we have devoted a few years to the idea of treatment and rehabilitation in prison. Some correctional leaders have dropped the goal of rehabilitation, while others say it has not been adequately developed. Another group would concentrate on keeping people out of prison and on successfully reintegrating into society offenders who do go to prison.

The negative results are many and the successes are few. The task now is to learn from past mistakes and modern technology and then apply this knowledge to finding better solutions. The overriding problem is that of determining the best way to ensure the protection of society at the price in money and involvement that society is willing to pay. According to one authority "[we are] going to need 2,000 new cells every year just to catch up."[1] Since one cell can cost as much as $50,000, it is unlikely the taxpayers will pay for new cells. Alternatives will have to be sought.

This chapter is concerned with where corrections stands today in contrast to where it could be. It explores a number of areas: the people who work in corrections, the population being corrected, the tools with which correctional personnel must work, and certain factors influencing the corrections system over which correctional personnel have little control.

PEOPLE INVOLVED IN CORRECTIONS

The people in corrections are both the people being corrected and the people attempting to do the correcting. Each group has its char-

acteristics and its problems. The inmate population has been referred to as "the captive society."[2] In many ways, the rehabilitation potential of the captive is dependent on improvements in the basic corrections system and on improvements affecting the people who are attempting to accomplish the goals of corrections. That is, the inadequate training of corrections workers, among other things, can be counterproductive and actually be a factor in causing more crime rather than diverting people from a life of crime. For this reason it is important to understand the problems and characteristics of both the captors and the captives.

CORRECTIONAL WORKERS

According to recent studies, there are more than 239,000 correctional workers at the federal, state, and local levels in the United States. Of these, 134,420 or 56.2 percent are at the state level. Approximately 39,000 persons are full-time employees in juvenile detention and correctional facilities. There are 22,767 full-time employees in long-term training schools for juveniles (187 long-term facilities at state and local levels, out of a total of 767 juvenile facilities). Of the total full-time personnel in juvenile detention and correctional facilities, 11,143 are treatment and educational personnel, while 15,975 are individual custody personnel.[3] For adults, at the state level there are 592 institutions, of which 401 are prisons and the remainder classification centers, medical centers, or community centers. In these institutions approximately 38,000 persons are engaged in performing custody functions. In most institutions, the staff consists largely of custodial personnel. The number of custodial staff ranges from an average of 7 to 153 in different size institutions. Twenty-two institutions contain 500 or more total staff positions.[4]

In the approximately 3,900 jails, there were more than 44,000 employees, according to a recent survey. The average number of employees per jail was eleven. California, Florida, New York, Pennsylvania, and Texas had more than 2,000 jail employees. (New York led with 5,468). Vermont had only 21 jail employees, followed by Alaska with 53. The national ratio of inmates to jail employees was 3.2 to 1, while California and Arizona had a 5 to 1 ratio. A severe problem in jails is the lack of specialized staff members. Only 19 percent of jails had a medical doctor on the staff, and 6 percent employed nurses. Even large jails often do not hire psychiatrists, psychologists, social workers, or teachers.[5]

The criminal justice system has suffered from a lack of funding throughout its history, and corrections has had the lowest priority within the system. This low priority has affected the pay and the training of correctional workers. Prison and jail employees as a whole are probably one of the lowest paid groups in the economy. Many prisons and jails do not have education standards for employees, and the pay for correctional workers reflects this lack of standards. Low pay, combined with other factors, makes attracting and keeping qualified workers a difficult task. It is common for prison and jail employees to be paid a starting salary of $600 to $700 per month; and although the standards for noninstitutional workers in the community (probation, parole, and so on) are often higher (a college degree or more), their pay does not always reflect this higher standard.

Lack of adequate training is also a serious problem. Those persons hired to work directly with the inmates in our institutions are often inadequately prepared by either education or other preservice training to undertake a corrections role. Where in-service training is available, it is primarily concerned with security and administration. Although the National Institute of Corrections of the Federal Bureau of Prisons sponsors a training program for local jailers, its impact is necessarily low because of the number of jails and the rapid turnover of jail employees. More and more states are realizing that it is necessary to have centrally administered organizations to set correctional standards and offer training. The National Advisory Commission on Criminal Justice Standards and Goals (1973) has recommended the creation of comprehensive training programs for correctional employees, to be administered by the states.

Another serious problem for correctional workers is the role dilemma or conflict. Are correctional workers police officers and custodians, or are they primarily concerned with rehabilitation? This role conflict is a product of both inadequate training and lack of agreement on the goals of corrections. When correctional officers are asked about their role, some will concentrate their replies on the supervisory aspect of the job and others will concentrate on the rehabilitation role.

The custody and control goal may demand a minimum of conversation with inmates, whereas the treatment or rehabilitation goal may call for interaction. When treatment experts explain acting out by inmates in terms of human behavior change, corrections workers understand, but they also understand that promotion within the custodial system is based on how well they function in the custody and control role, where such acting out may be a threat to the institution. Correctional workers must be able to strike a balance between control measures and rehabilitation so that other employees and inmates are not threatened with harm while these goals are served. This dilemma, common to all correctional workers, has not been solved in practice and is not adequately explained in theory.

PRISONERS

There were approximately 500,000 individuals confined in our correctional institutions on any given day in 1979. There was a total average daily population of 1,550,000 in all phases of corrections (including probation and parole).[6]

During the mid-1970s, prison populations went up in some states and down in others. In the late 1970s there was a rapid increase in the prison population in many states. Prison populations had doubled in several states over one decade.

Consequently, many state institutions were severely overcrowded. Some were so jammed that conditions were declared unconstitutional by federal courts (Figure 19.1).[7] Changes in laws, sentencing policy of the courts, added use of alternatives to incarceration, and improved law enforcement can combine in different ways to cause increases or decreases. A decrease in the prison population in California was attributed in part to a comprehensive probation subsidy program. At the other extreme, the Texas system showed significant increases in population. Texas only recently initiated a coordinated statewide probation subsidy system for adults, and the percentage of people released on parole in Texas is one of the lowest in the country.

The jail population is also influenced by a number of other factors. For example, California's probation subsidy program, while decreasing the prison population, in some cases had the opposite effect on the jail population. As another example, the trend toward reducing drug offenses from felonies to misdemeanors can decrease the prison population and increase the jail population.

FIGURE 19.1 CELLBLOCK

A prison guard monitors one-half of a three-tiered cellblock. The other half of the cellblock backs on this portion and is identical. The complete cellblock can house up to 228 inmates, with two inmates per cell. All doors are remotely controlled by the guard.

SOURCE: Texas Department of Corrections, Huntsville, Texas.

Probably the greatest influence on the jail population is delay in the judicial system. Recent speedy trial laws will have an impact in this area. The jail population across the country is made up to a large extent of those awaiting trial, or some other form of adjudication. In this respect overcrowding is caused to a large extent by inadequate pretrial release procedures and the overload and inefficiency in the court system. Not uncommonly there is a delay of one year or more between arrest and trial. Our money bail practices obviously discriminate against the poor and in large measure account for the jail population being composed of the poor and uneducated. Drunks are another primary group in the jail population, even though modern correctional concepts call for drug (including alcohol) users to be handled outside the criminal justice system. Some researchers have described the jail population as being composed of the failures of the public school system. There may be some truth in this statement, but the problem is more complicated than that and not all the blame can be laid on the schools.

Much emphasis has been placed on correction of youth in the community. Federal court decisions have had a significant impact in this area. Closing of juvenile institutions in Massachusetts in the 1970s also started a trend toward deinstitutionalization of juvenile offenders. However, there are still large populations in our long-term juvenile institutions. The number of long-term state-administered juvenile training schools increased 16 percent between two recent study periods, a time lapse of only two years. During this same period the population of all juvenile facilities decreased from 616,766 to 600,960.[8] Are we winning or losing in our attempts to correct youth? As yet, no one is sure.

The most significant increase in corrections populations has occurred in probation. Is this a problem? It can be if probation is used as an unsuitable alternative to other community programs rather than as an alternative to prison or reform school. Where probation department funds are based on the number of probationers, there is a natural pressure to maintain a high probation population instead of using more appropriate methods or ending a term of probation.

Other problems directly affecting the captive society and indirectly affecting society at large include inadequate programs, unnatural living conditions, and abnormal sexual behavior. These problems are primarily identified with life in an institution as opposed to life in the community. Institutional existence seems to lead naturally to segregation of the sexes, suppression of decision making, and no provision for continuation of normal marital affairs. As punishment, these conditions are effective, but as training for reintegration into society, they are counterproductive. Modern concepts call for inmates to be exposed to the community as much as possible.

Lack of adequate rehabilitation programs is also a problem, but it is characteristic of the goal conflict in corrections. Correctional leaders cannot agree on what programs should be mandatory, and research has given them little information on which to base their decisions. As a result, inmates leaving institutions are scarcely prepared to assume responsibility in society. They have been separated from society; they have not been given basic skills related to work on the outside, and they have not even been fully relieved of the "debt" they owed society. This situation leaves little hope that they will not recidivate.

INADEQUACIES IN MANAGEMENT AND ORGANIZATION

Although corrections is often referred to as a "system," it is actually composed of a number of systems that seem to be only loosely related. Just as a change in the police or courts can cause changes in corrections, so changes in correctional elements affect one another. For example, a planned reduction in the state prison population puts increased pressure on the local jail system. Talking about a system implies that a number of processes are linked together in pursuit of a common goal. At times, dedication to a common goal in corrections is difficult to find, and this is reflected in inadequacies in correctional management and organization.

CORRECTIONAL MANAGEMENT

Inadequate management in corrections has been documented from a historical perspective. The recent attention given to corrections both in national surveys and in court cases indicates how little progress has been made. It is a fact that many correctional managers have mishandled their efforts to correct inmates and clients, but they have also mismanaged the resources they were given. It is common to hear cries for more funds and more employees as the solution to problems in institutional and noninstitutional programs alike. However, some correctional leaders are convinced that proper use of existing resources would be more productive. Through better training, correctional officers can be more effectively used, and improved financial management can decrease the cost of operating institutions while providing meaningful work for inmates. Pressures applied by reformers and federal courts have had various effects. In some cases significant improvements have been made. In other cases, correctional managers have reacted by abandoning valid correctional concepts.

Community agencies often stress a reduction in caseload as a solution to supervision problems, although actually little attention is given to classifying the proper clients into the proper supervision categories. The great majority of clients of these community agencies (youth service bureaus, probation and parole, and so on) would do well with little or no supervision.

Institutional management of inmates is undoubtedly worse than noninstitutional management. Though elaborate classification systems exist in some areas, they are typically poorly managed and little utilized. Most prisons and reformatories have diagnostic programs whereby incoming inmates are processed through a testing and case-history procedure, but this information is more often used to classify inmates for security purposes than to plan for long-range programs.

Another problem associated with management is the lack of adequate planning, research, evaluation, and theory. Large correctional organizations have only recently introduced an integrated planning function. There is a need for planning, both long and short range, to define the goals and objectives and to ensure that all elements of the organization are working as a team to reach these goals and objectives. Like the treatment function, planning is often not properly used to bring about an integration of purpose. Research and evaluation are closely associated with planning in that they provide the manager with information about progress toward planned goals. Planning, research, and evaluation are integral parts of effective management.

It has been said that significant, long-term improvement in corrections can be made only within the framework of theory. Theory can provide direction. Theory brings diversified plans together into an understandable network of required actions. To date, however, the results of research raise troublesome questions about the adequacy of our theories of behavior change. Just as troublesome are questions about the adequacy of a theory to guide methods of research and evaluation. Attempts to evaluate those programs that are operating in the community have pointed up the problems associated with traditional research techniques, and controlling the experimental situation in the community setting is all but impossible.

Another problem related to research is the use of traditional indicators as measures of success. For example, although recidivism is a common measure of the success of a program, a number of programs can be justified on humanitarian grounds even if it is not demonstrated that they have a direct effect on recidivism.

There is little reason to doubt that prisons will always be needed, that a small percentage of criminals will always require long-term incarceration for the protection of society. However, research indicates that corrections should move away from the institutional concept in most cases. One of the reasons for the slow progress in developing such alternatives as halfway houses, probation, parole, and work release lies in our inability to distinguish between good and bad risks. Most parole boards use a complicated checklist of items that are thought to be predictors of behavior on the outside, but there is little if any research that supports these criteria. Prediction criteria are vital to the success of rehabilitative efforts, and our inability to develop such predictive techniques could lead to the elimination of valid correctional devices and organizations. Another reason why corrections has not moved toward community alternatives is that they are viewed as nonpunitive by the public, and the public still demands its pound of flesh.

CORRECTIONAL ORGANIZATIONS

Organizational problems in corrections could be discussed from several perspectives. For example, most correctional organizations can be classified as "functional" organizations, whereas modern correctional concepts often call for a "team" or "project" approach to treatment. A functional organization is one that is designed around the important functions. A review of the chapter on corrections organizations will show that many rehabilitation activities do not seem to be important from an organizational perspective. The unit team or project approach to organization calls for mixing skills or functions within one component. Because organizational structure change has not kept pace with modern theory and improved techniques in corrections, problems have developed.

The major problem is that correctional organizations do not work as a cohesive system. There is a federal correctional system, a state correctional system, and a local correctional system. And within these systems there often are separate systems for probation, parole, adult prison, juvenile reformatories, jails, juvenile detention, *ad infinitum*. Not only is there a lack of coordination between these correctional components, but there is a lack of agreement as to whether they are all a part of corrections and what level of government has responsibility.

In the federal system and the systems of several states, probation is administered by the courts. Youth service bureaus are often administered by the juvenile court as an extension of juvenile probation. It will also be remembered that the Federal Bureau of Prisons operates community treatment centers, as do several states. In other states, community treatment is totally the responsibility of the local community. Jails are also commonly the responsibility of local government. Under a "system" of corrections that has little central planning or control, it is not difficult to see why progress has been slow and painful. Significant further progress will depend to a large extent on some consolidation of administration. Many of our failures in treatment and rehabilitation could very well be related to ineffective structure and lack of ability to coordinate the goals of various organizations.

INSTITUTIONAL AND NONINSTITUTIONAL CORRECTIONS

Modern correctional concepts call for more treatment of convicted offenders in the community or careful reintegration into the community; thus the jails could assume an even more important role than in the past. The jail system of the future, however, will be different in many respects from the present system. In the past, jails and prisons were built to house the correctional population in a custody and control condition; correctional facilities in the future will be built around the needs of that population. Modern concepts call for confinement only in the most extreme circumstances. A review of some of the problems of the present system will help to focus attention on future needs.

PRISONS

Most prisons were designed to house large numbers of inmates. They are typically located in rural areas; thus reintegration programs are most difficult. Large institutions are characterized by regimentation of all areas of daily life under close supervision, which is contrary to the ideal of allowing a person to exercise responsibility in an atmosphere like that in which he or she must ultimately live. Prison architecture also detracts from rehabilitation. The Auburn concept of cellblock construction is still in use today, approximately a hundred and fifty years after its invention. In crowded conditions, with inadequate recreation and rehabilitation programs, with no opportunity for productive employment, and lacking normal sexual relations, prisoners have shown a ten-dency to riot that is not difficult to understand.

Incarceration is also costly. Prison expenses often exceed $30 per day per person, while the cost of probation, by comparison, is commonly less than one-tenth that. The cost of prison construction is another matter. It is estimated that the traditional jail or prison costs between $30,000 and $50,000 per bed to build, not including adequate provision for rehabilitation programs. When prison populations are reduced, cost per inmate rises drastically, presenting a dilemma: while large populations result in less cost, they are not believed to improve the protection of society.

JAILS

Persons coming into the criminal justice system enter through the jail. Most are detained for only short periods of time. Over 50 percent of those detained are drunks, and over 36 percent are pretrial detainees. Jails may house both male and female, adult and juvenile, sane and insane, first offender and habitual criminal. All these types of offenders are typically housed in cells that were constructed years ago. Plumbing has rusted to the point where it cannot be used. Lighting is inadequate, recreation and education are almost nonexistent, and services like visitation are usually inadequate to maintain any sort of normal family existence.

Inmates housed in prisons and jails are a burden to society. The taxpayer commonly supports the inmate's family while also supporting the inmate. The jail system is also a burden to society in that all the evidence points to the jail as a breeding ground for more crime. What is the alternative to the present system? Many believe that it is to be found in a community corrections concept that places emphasis on a combination of coordinated institutional and noninstitutional programs. While the problems associated with this concept have not yet been solved, much attention has been given to such systems.

COMMUNITY CORRECTIONS

Millions of dollars are being spent each year to construct new prisons, jails, and reformatories. The problem of our aging institutions has been known for years, but several organizations and individuals have indicated that more new construction can create or perpetuate facility problems. A number of cities and counties have built new jails, only to find that the jail population expanded to fill both the old and the new facility. Walls are being built around the expanding population as a substitute for taking action to reduce the population. Some also believe that funds used to build institutions rather than create community programs are wasted funds. The National Council on Crime and Delinquency has recommended that construction be stopped until adequate community programs have been established in an attempt to reduce institution population. It is possible that more new facilities have been built than necessary if other reform measures were in effect.

The failure of the old system has led to a concept of corrections that keeps the client within or close to the community to which he or she will return. For reasons previously stated, the regional corrections concept has developed. Figure 19.2 is a pictorial description of a regional corrections program based in a large city. Under this concept, a diagnostic center is the primary receiving institution and the jail is only one of many alternatives.

An alternative design, also a form of regional corrections, might be a grouping of

FIGURE 19.2 COMMUNITY-BASED CORRECTIONS

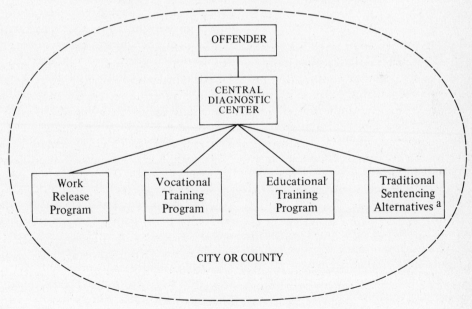

a Probation, jail, suspended sentence, etc.

rural counties. Each county would operate a short-term holding facility. Persons being held longer than forty-eight to seventy-two hours would be transferred to a single regional correctional facility. This facility would have extensive internal diagnostic and program capability and would serve as the focal point for all corrections activities in the region, housing both law enforcement and court functions as well.

Not only do current community corrections concepts attack the problems of institutional corrections, they also tend to force the issue of organization problems. Regional correctional facilities or regional corrections programs require city, county, and state governments to cooperate in planning of facilities and programs. They also require cooperation in funding for both construction and operation. Regional councils of government were established to help gain this cooperation, but progress has been slow. One reason for this has been the failure of state governments to establish standards for facilities and programs.

RESPONSIBILITY

Groups seemingly outside the corrections community have a direct influence on and some responsibility for the problems in corrections, and some solutions rest with these groups: (1) the public, (2) the law enforcement agencies, (3) the courts, and (4) the legislature of each state.

THE PUBLIC

Public apathy toward corrections is evident. The very fact that foul and overcrowded jails are allowed to continue to house human beings is a prime example. The difficulty of organizing and funding community corrections programs requiring cooperation between elements of government is another example. Many people pay lip service to correctional programs, but the difficulties that arise during the establishment of such facilities as halfway houses show that apparent support tends to fade when action is required. A halfway house or other correctional facility is a great idea as long as it is in some other neighborhood. If the public cannot be led to believe that public protection measures require new methods, then our current efforts will be meaningless. It is, nonetheless, encouraging to see many private service organizations initiate and operate correctional programs.

LAW ENFORCEMENT AGENCIES

Law enforcement agencies have traditionally called for longer jail and prison sentences and been quick to point out probation and parole failure. Education programs over the past few years have done much to alleviate this situation, but it still exists.

Law enforcement officers believe correctional goals are in conflict with law enforcement goals. On the other hand, some correctional personnel believe that law enforcement goals are antagonistic to correctional goals. In the final analysis, however, the overall goals of both these subsystems of the criminal justice system are the same. Each element has a distinct part to play, and each must understand the other's roles.

THE COURTS

Most of the inmates and clients in corrections are products of the activity, or inactivity, of the courts. When the courts perform their function effectively and efficiently, they are not in conflict with corrections. Next to our system of jails, however, the court system in many states suffers the most from failure to keep up with the times. Court backlogs make effective prosecution impossible, which results in the overcrowding of the jails. Many prominent persons have expressed the belief that it is the swiftness and sureness of justice that results in deterrence. Until the court system is streamlined, there is little hope that jail problems will be solved.

The role of our federal judges as "managers" must be mentioned because of the great and controversial impact this has had on corrections. Stephen Gettinger has outlined some of the major attempts of federal judges to supervise jails, prisons, and reformatories in an article called "Cruel and Unusual Prisons." Judges have not only ordered the closing of complete prison systems but have dictated the size of rooms, amount of mail, color of clothes, medical services, outside recreation, etc., in large numbers of institutions from Rhode Island to Alabama.[9]

THE LEGISLATURES

Although corrections, which is primarily an executive function, is responsible for planning and administering correctional programs, it is the legislatures that must provide the legal basis and the money. The legal basis is primarily the establishment of modern standards, and these standards are needed for facilities and programs at both the state and the local level. Correctional agencies and associations must adequately plan the standards, and the legislatures must recognize their responsibility in this area.

Standards for jails are a typical example. Local communities, with state and federal aid, are spending millions of dollars on jail facilities. However, in many cases these facilities are not adequate to support current correctional needs because the standards to which they are constructed or refurnished are inadequate. Most jail standards (if any are available at all) cover only the existence of utilities and the size of cells. If the legislatures fail to pass adequate measures or to assign responsibility for standard setting and inspection, these omissions will perpetuate correctional problems, because jails and prisons, once built, will be used for years to come.

If the criminal justice system is to work, it must actually become a network of coordinated subsystems, not just a group of loosely related agencies. In addition, it must have the understanding of the public and the support of the legislature.

DISCUSSION QUESTIONS

1. Under what conditions should incarceration be used?
2. How are community correctional programs coordinated in your area?
3. Should certain classes of offenders be given long prison sentences with little chance of parole?
4. Discuss the advantages and disadvantages of community-based corrections programs.
5. What is in store for corrections in the future?
6. Should federal judges direct and supervise administrative matters?

NOTES

1. W. J. Estelle, "Processing the Offender," *Texas Journal of Corrections,* July/August 1978, pp. 14–15.
2. Gresham M. Sykes, *The Society of Captives* (Princeton, N.J.: Princeton University Press, 1958).
3. U.S. Department of Justice, *Children in Custody* (Washington, D.C.: Government Printing Office, 1976), pp. 22–25.
4. U.S. Department of Justice, *Census of State Correctional Facilities 1974* (Washington, D.C.: Government Printing Office, 1975), pp. 6–7.
5. U.S. Department of Justice, *The Nation's Jails* (Washington, D.C.: Government Printing Office, 1975), pp. 8–11.
6. U.S. Department of Justice, *State and Local Probation and Parole Systems* (Washington, D.C.: Government Printing Office, 1978), p. 1; Administrative Office of the U.S. Courts, *Annual Report, 1978* (Washington, D.C.: Administrative Office of the U.S. Courts, 1979; U.S. Bureau of Prisons' data obtained from computer printouts.
7. U.S. Department of Justice, *Prisoners in State and Federal Institutions* (Washington, D.C.: Government Printing Office, 1978), p. 32.
8. *Children in Custody,* pp. 2–8.
9. Stephen Gettinger, "Cruel and Unusual Prisons," *Corrections Magazine,* 3, No. 4 (1977), 3–16.

PART FIVE ANNOTATED BIBLIOGRAPHY

Morris, Norval. *The Future of Imprisonment.* Chicago: University of Chicago Press, 1974.
An excellent sketch of current problem areas in corrections. The author outlines what he considers to be the direction of and trends in corrections.

National Advisory Commission on Criminal Justice Standards and Goals. *Corrections.* Washington, D.C.: Government Printing Office, 1973.
Presents the recommendations and standards and goals established by the commission for corrections. If they are adopted by the states, these standards and goals should have considerable impact on corrections in the United States.

National Commission on Law Observance and Enforcement. *Wickersham Commission Reports, No. 9, Report on Penal Institutions, Probation, and Parole, 1931.* Montclair, New Jersey: Patterson Smith, 1968.
The Wickersham Reports total fourteen volumes and are named for the chairman of the commission. Report No. 9 provides an in-depth review of the conditions of the prisons during the 1920s as well as an analysis of the problems uncovered. These reports are presented in a simple style and are easily read by the beginning student in criminal justice.

President's Commission on Law Enforcement and Administration of Justice. *Task Force Report: Corrections.* Washington, D.C.: Government Printing Office, 1967.
A detailed account of the status of corrections in the 1960s with recommendations for improvements that are valid today.
Rothman, David J. *Discovery of the Asylum.* Boston: Little, Brown and Company, 1971.
One of the better reference books concerning the early history of prisons. The author presents material on theory and practice in the early years of prison development.

PART SIX

PROBATION
AND PAROLE

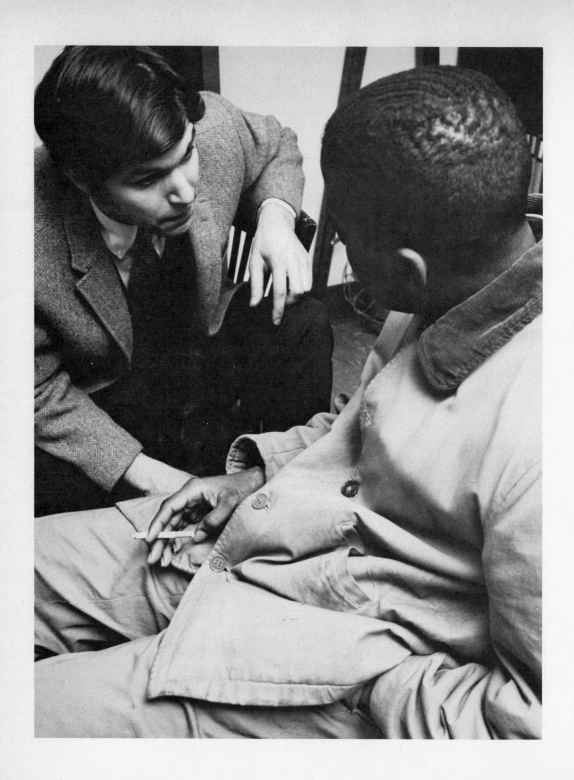

CHAPTER TWENTY

HISTORY
AND PROCESS
OF PROBATION

DEFINITION OF PROBATION	THE PROBATION PROCESS	JUVENILE PROBATION
PHILOSOPHY AND OBJECTIVE	PROBATION ADMINISTRATION AND ORGANIZATION	MISDEMEANANT PROBATION
HISTORICAL PERSPECTIVES	PROBATION AND PAROLE PERSONNEL	PRESENTENCE REPORT
	APPLICATION AND ELIGIBILITY	REVOCATION OF PROBATION

Purpose: To provide a discussion of the historical precedents for probation and a description of the probation process.

PROBATION AND PAROLE are a very significant part of the correctional process. While they are similar in their overall objective, rehabilitating offenders, the distinctions are important. Probation has evolved as an alternative to imprisonment, whereas parole has evolved as an alternative to continued imprisonment. Probation is usually administered at the local level and as a component of the judicial system. Parole, on the other hand, is usually administered at the state level and by an administrative agency that is part of the executive branch. Within statutory limitations, probation rather than a prison term is generally given to those who have committed less serious offenses when there are indications that they are not likely to commit further offenses.

DEFINITION OF PROBATION

The meaning of the term *probation* can be divided into three components: the sentence, the organization, and the process. As a sentence, probation generally means a judicial disposition in which a defendant is allowed to remain "free" in the community subject to certain conditions imposed by the court. As an organization, it is the agency that conducts the operation of probation. As a process, it involves a presentence investigation report of each person before the court and supervision of each person, casework for each individual, program management, and guidance for each person the court places on probation.[1]

The special Task Force on Corrections appointed by the President's Commission on Law Enforcement and Administration of Justice defines probation as "A legal status granted by a court whereby a convicted person is permitted to remain in the community subject to conditions specified by the court.[2]

The National Council on Crime and Delinquency (NCCD) Standards, in Article 1 section 2 (a), defines probation as follows: "Probation is a procedure under which a defendant, found guilty of a crime upon verdict or plea, is released by the court and subject to the conditions imposed by the court and subject to the supervision of the probation service."[3]

The American Bar Association Project on Standards for Criminal Justice defines probation as "Probation means a sentence not involving confinement which imposes conditions and retains authority in the sentencing court to modify the conditions of the sentence or to resentence the offender if he violates the conditions. Such a sentence should not involve or require suspension of the imposition or the execution of any other sentence."[4]

These definitions demonstrate how professional emphasis and orientation can differ. In essence, however, probation is the release of a convicted person by a court, under specified conditions.

The word *probation* comes from the Latin *probare,* which means "to test" or "to prove." Probation is really one of the modern methods for the treatment of offenders, and as such, it is rooted in the broader social and cultural trends of the modern age.[5]

PHILOSOPHY AND OBJECTIVE

The dominant purpose of the entire correctional process is to promote the general welfare of society. Probation, created by laws and an integral part of the correctional process, furthers this objective by providing for the security and protection of the community. Although traditionally imprisonment was used indiscriminately to reach this objective, research has shown that in most instances it is ineffective and harmful to society, including the offender, and also more expensive.[6]

Probation proceeds on the basic notion that taking people out of the community in which they live and work is not the best way to help them learn to live in it. The general premise underlying the new objective of integration or reintegration into society is that crime and delinquency are symptoms of failure and disorganization in the society as well as failure of the individual offender.[7]

This approach marks a shift from the traditional narrow explanation of crime as the act of an individual. The treatment of those lawbreakers who are placed on probation involves a number of different public and private agencies, which, besides providing support, service, and supervision, help the probationers to strengthen their social skills. Confinement, a form of punishment and a method of segregation, deprives convicted persons of their freedom and breaks their ties with family, friends, and employers. Probation, on the other hand, gives them an opportunity to maintain social contacts in a firmer but more helpful environment.

Probation is not intended to be an "easy sentence" or "leniency." It is a positive and firm method of permitting certain offenders to continue functioning in society under specified conditions. These conditions are primarily designed to prevent further violations of the law. If probation is used as a preventative and a corrective tool, society can obtain maximum benefit without unnecessarily jeopardizing the family and social obligations of an individual and allowing that individual to operate as a productive member of society. It is believed that people who are well integrated with the community are less likely to commit other crimes, particularly when they have the help and guidance of probation officers and others. Probation, then, offers a positive approach to the attainment of socially and legally acceptable behavior.

HISTORICAL PERSPECTIVES

Probation had its early origin in such practices as right to clergy (*privilegium clericale*), dating back to the thirteenth century; securing sanctuary; judicial reprieve; and recognizance (a bond stipulating an action for a given period). The English common law practice of suspending sentences with certain restrictions is also a forerunner of probation. However, these early informal practices, sometimes called quasi-probationary measures, though similar in some respects, are not in the strict sense probation.[8]

Massachusetts has the distinction of having given the probation system to the world. During the first half of the nineteenth century, Massachusetts judges tried a variety of measures to make the administration of justice more humane, and a favorable judicial climate was thus established for the development of rudimentary probation practices.[9] In 1841, John Augustus, a shoemaker, used probation for the first time in the United States when he secured the release of a drunkard from a Boston police court. The court allowed the release with the condition that the defendant be brought back in three weeks for sentencing and that the defendant show signs of reform when he reappeared. Encouraged by his first experience, Augustus continued his probation work for almost eighteen years until his death in 1859. During these years he worked with men, women, and juveniles charged with a wide variety of offenses.[10]

Augustus established many of the present-day features of probation. When he undertook the responsibility for offenders, he

JOHN AUGUSTUS
1785–1859

Probation, both as a concept and in its development, is the United States' distinctive contribution to progressive methods of handling law offenders. The name of John Augustus stands out for his unique contribution of first using probation to rehabilitate men, women, and boys and girls.

John Augustus was born in Benbrighton, Massachusetts, in 1785. He operated a shoe manufactory in Boston. It was in his shop at 5 Franklin Avenue, near the police court, that Augustus received frequent calls from those who sought his help. It was Augustus's practice to bail an offender after his or her conviction if there was hope for reformation. The person would be required to appear before the court at a specified time. Augustus would accompany the offender to the court, and if the judge was satisfied with Augustus's account of the individual's behavior, the offender would be fined one cent and costs, which was usually paid by Augustus.

Writing about his first probationer, a common drunkard, Augustus states, "The case was clearly made out, but before sentence had been passed, I conversed with him a few moments — although his looks precluded a belief in the minds of others that he would ever become a *man* again. He told me that if he could be saved from the House of Corrections, he never again would taste intoxicating liquors; there was such an earnestness in that tone, and a look expressive of firm resolve, that I determined to aid him, I bailed him, by permission of the court." [*]

In spite of the problems of opposition, misunderstanding, and even physical abuse from the public, he continued this work from 1841 until his death in 1859. During these years he maintained careful records and took great pride in exhibiting the list. Up to 1858 he had bailed 1,946 persons, 1,152 males and 794 women and girls. [†]

Augustus's work with offenders was characterized by his careful selection of fit subjects for probation. His approach to his critics varied. To some he said that for each person bailed to him, a commitment to a house of corrections was prevented. To those who understood social progress and justice in terms of dollars saved, he pointed out that the public was saved the greater expense of caring for the person in prison. To some others, he replied that his form of treatment was more effective; that it saved offenders for their families and for society and did not disgrace them forever as incarceration would.

---

[*] John Augustus, *First Probation Officer* (reprint of Report of John Augustus, Boston, 1852), National Probation Association, 1939, p. 4.
[†] *Probation & Parole Progress*, Yearbook, National Probation Association, New York, 1941, p. 6.

PROBATION AND PAROLE

agreed to "note their general conduct" and to see that "they were sent to school or supplied with some honest employment." In addition, he very often provided or arranged for accommodation. The register that he kept of all cases handled shows that he supervised more than two thousand persons. Augustus's systematic work was to be the foundation of modern probation.

In 1878 Massachusetts passed its first law regulating probation and authorized the mayor of Boston to appoint a paid probation officer. It is significant to note that this pioneer statute specifically contrasts probation with punishment by directing that "such persons as may reasonably be expected to be reformed without punishment" should be selected for probation. The criteria for selection were much broader than those in some recent laws. In 1880 appointment of probation officers was extended to all cities and towns in Massachusetts; and in 1890, it was extended to the whole state.[11] By 1900 Vermont, Illinois, Minnesota, Rhode Island, and New Jersey had also introduced laws on probation.

In 1899 the first juvenile court was established in Chicago. This was the beginning of the juvenile court movement, which in turn accelerated the spread of juvenile probation. By 1910, thirty-seven states and the District of Columbia had established juvenile courts and probation for juveniles. By 1925 probation for juveniles was available in every state, whereas adult probation was not available in every state until 1956.[12]

In many states the types of agencies that handle probation are as varied as their philosophies. However, probation is usually under the judicial branch of government. Some states do not authorize paid probation officers, and in only fifteen states may probation be granted regardless of the type of crime committed. In some places probation is administered only by the courts in cities and counties, and in others it is administered by the state. Some of the statutory restrictions indicate a conflict between the punitive and treatment reactions to crime.[13]

The importance of probation, nationwide, can easily be ascertained from the figures provided in Table 20.1. On September 1, 1976, there were more than 1.25 million (1,251,918) men, women, and children under state and local probation supervision in the United States. This is almost 66 percent of all (1,918,987) the offenders sentenced to correctional treatment.[14] The figures given in Table 20.1 also show the expansion of probation in recent years. This expansion is noteworthy; the number of offenders on probation continues to increase at a greater rate than the total number of offenders sentenced to correctional treatment.

TABLE 20.1 OFFENDERS ON PROBATION AND ON PAROLE OR IN INSTITUTIONS, 1965 AND SEPTEMBER 1, 1976

LOCATION OF OFFENDER	NO. OF 1965 OFFENDERS		NO. OF 1976 OFFENDERS	
Probation	684,088	53%	1,251,918	66%
Parole or Institution	598,298	47	667,069	34
Total	1,282,386	100	1,918,987	100

SOURCE: U.S. Department of Justice, *State and Local Probation and Parole Systems* (Washington, D.C.: Government Printing Office, 1978), p. 1; other data provided by the Federal Prison System, Washington, D.C., and LEAA National Prisoner Statistics, Washington, D.C.

THE PROBATION PROCESS

Over the years probation has developed into a process that does not vary greatly from state to state, although specific rules, regulations, and practices may vary to suit local conditions. Generally the probation process operates in the following way: After the defendant is found guilty by the court, either following a verdict or a plea of guilty, the court has a number of sentencing choices — suspend the sentence, impose a fine, give a term of imprisonment, place on probation, and so on. There are, however, restrictions in most states as to who may or may not be placed on probation. For example, in some states individuals who commit certain serious crimes and those who have previously been convicted of crimes are not eligible. Such restrictions vary from state to state, but where the defendant is eligible for probation, the court has discretionary power to probate the sentence.

When the judge determines an individual to be suitable for probation, a *probation order* is issued. This order carries a set of obligatory conditions requiring the probationer to act in a certain way and/or restraining him or her from doing certain things. A requirement might be that he or she attend school or college, and a restriction might prohibit his or her association with known criminals or visiting a certain area for a period of time. The person's probation officer is responsible for seeing that the probationer adheres to the conditions. The officer also provides assistance, counseling, and guidance. If the probationer violates the conditions of probation or any law, the court may remove him or her from probation and force him or her to complete the sentence in a correctional institution.

This is a typical probation process. There are, however, some differences and variations from state to state as a result of differences in laws, historical development, and prevailing societal attitudes.

PROBATION ADMINISTRATION AND ORGANIZATION

Because each level of government — city, county, state, and federal — has its own basic probation law, there is very little that might be considered standard procedure in every jurisdiction. There are, however, definite patterns in each aspect of probation. In the main, as Table 20.2 shows, the responsibility for probation appears to be almost equally divided between state and local governments, with state governments having slightly more agencies for adult probation and local governments for juvenile probation. Of the 1,929 agencies having adult probation as a function, 1,087 or 56 percent were state-level agencies, and 842 or 44 percent were at the county or municipal level. The 2,126 juvenile probation agencies include 1,210 local agencies or 57 percent, and 916 or 43 percent state agencies.

In thirty-two states, juvenile courts ad-

TABLE 20.2 STATE AND LOCAL AGENCIES' PERFORMING PROBATION FUNCTIONS, SEPTEMBER 1, 1976

LEVEL OF GOVERN-MENT	NO. OF PROBATION AGENCIES			
	FOR ADULTS		FOR JUVENILES	
State	1,087	56%	916	43%
County	788	41	1,167	55
Municipal	54	3	43	2
State-local total	1,929	100	2,126	100

Source: U.S. Department of Justice, *State and Local Probation and Parole Systems* (Washington, D.C.: Government Printing Office, 1978), p. 2.

PROBATION AND PAROLE

minister probation services. Elsewhere, juvenile services are operated by state correctional agencies in five states, by the state welfare department in seven, and by other state or local agencies in the rest. In thirty states, adult probation is combined with parole services. In the others, probation services are administered by a separate state board or agency or are under local jurisdiction. This diversity is largely the result of historical accident. Because juvenile probation services were developed in the juvenile courts, which were operated by cities or counties, they were administered locally. Services for adults, in most states, were grafted onto existing statewide parole supervision services.[15]

PROBATION AND PAROLE PERSONNEL

Table 20.3 shows there are 55,807 employees working in the 3,868 state and local probation and parole agencies. No separate probation and parole figures are available. This number includes 51,633 full-time employees, 2,779 part-time employees, and 1,395 employees shared with other agencies.

More than half of those employees, 33,248 or 60 percent, were engaged in direct counseling and supervision of probation and parole clients. Another 10 percent were serving in an administrative capacity, and the remainder, 17,252 or 31 percent, were reported in the clerical or "other" category. Of the probation and parole agencies, 72 percent had less than 10 employees, and 88 percent had less than 25 employees. Only 2 percent of the agencies had more than 100 employees.[16]

APPLICATION AND ELIGIBILITY

Probation is available to juveniles and adults, males and females, felons and misdemeanants. Over 4.5 million arrests were made in 1971 for offenses that would be misdemeanors in most jurisdictions.[17] Yet eleven states have no probation service whatever for adult misdemeanants, six have practically none, and most states furnish service of some kind, but on an irregular basis.[18]

The use of probation is greatly influenced by the requirements imposed by statute or sentencing courts. Its use in juvenile cases is rarely restricted by statute, but the court may have a degree of practical restraint, generally influenced by the prevailing custom or community feeling about certain offenses. Theoretically, the courts are free to probate

TABLE 20.3 PERSONNEL IN STATE AND LOCAL PROBATION AND PAROLE AGENCIES BY TYPE OF FUNCTION, SEPTEMBER 1, 1976

TYPE OF POSITION	NO. OF EMPLOYEES							
	TOTAL		FULL-TIME		PART-TIME		SHARED	
Administrative	5,307	10%	4,992	10%	254	9%	61	4%
Counseling	33,248	60	30,761	60	1,484	54	1,003	73
Clinical	15,459	27	14,366	27	811	29	282	20
Other	1,793	3	1,514	3	230	8	49	3
Total	55,807	100	51,633	100	2,779	100	1,395	100

SOURCE: U.S. Department of Justice, *State and Local Probation and Parole Systems* (Washington, D.C.: Government Printing Office, 1978), p. 2.

any juvenile. The statutory limitations, on the other hand, make grant of probation for adults less flexible.

Only fifteen states have no statutory restrictions on who may be granted probation in felony cases. In the remaining thirty-five states, probation is limited by such factors as type of offense, prior convictions, or whether the defendant was armed at the time of the offense(s). The type of offense is the device most commonly used to restrict probation, otherwise there is little consistency among the states.

The National Crime Commission advocated the general reduction of the various outright prohibitions and restrictions on probation and, in their place, the provision of statutory standards to guide the courts in using their discretion in decision making. This approach is considered logical in that probation legislation cannot take into account all the possible extenuating circumstances of particular offenders. Inflexible restrictions based on narrow criteria may defeat the goals of differential treatment by limiting the options from which a judge may choose. The National Advisory Commission on Criminal Justice Standards and Goals (1973) also recommended that barriers confronting probation be reduced.

JUVENILE PROBATION

Juvenile probation, which permits a child or young person to remain in the community under the supervision and guidance of a probation officer, is a legal status created by a court of juvenile jurisdiction.[19] It usually involves: (a) a judicial finding that the behavior of the child or the youth has been such as to come within the purview of the court; (b) the imposition of conditions upon his or her continued freedom; and (c) the provision of means for helping him or her meet these conditions and for determining the degree to which the conditions can be met. Probation thus implies much more than just giving the youth "another chance." Its central thrust is to give him or her some positive assistance in adjusting in the "free" community.

Within the broad goals of welfare and protection of society and of the young people who violate the laws, juvenile probation has the following specific assignments: (a) preventing a repetition of the youth's delinquent behavior; (b) preventing long-term deviance or criminal careers; and (c) assisting the youth, through measures feasible to the probation service, to achieve his or her potential as a productive citizen.

While probation service is primarily aimed toward the young persons found delinquent by the court, it often extends its responsibility to helping the family and undertaking other, broader delinquency prevention programs.

In the main, the modern probation department performs similar functions for adult and juvenile probationers. Juvenile probation, however, is more consequential in the sense that those juveniles who fail on probation tend to become repeaters in the criminal justice system, generally for a longer time than adults. Therefore, probation services for juveniles are also more encompassing.

The modern juvenile probation department performs three central functions, and sometimes several auxiliary functions will be involved. Its central services are: (a) juvenile court, probation department, and detention intake and screening; (b) social study and screening; and (c) supervision and treatment.

INTAKE AND SCREENING

The scope of jurisdiction of the juvenile court and the probation department is defined and limited by law. The intake limitations imposed by law are not always fully understood. Court intervention, on the other hand, is not effective in all types of cases. The probation staff has to examine the cases referred by those agencies that do not fully appreciate the limitations to determine whether the problem can be resolved by referring the case to some other community resource.

Frequently the probation department must also decide or participate in deciding whether the child or the youth should be admitted to, continue in, or be released from detention pending court disposition of the case. Removing a child from home and family and holding him or her in a detention facility, even for a temporary period, is a major intervention in the person's life as well as the family's. For some young people, this may be necessary and perhaps helpful; for others it may be deeply damaging and may contribute to alienation from the conforming society and its institutions. The problem is complicated by the fact that in many jurisdictions the facilities for juvenile detention criminalize, degrade, and brutalize rather than rehabilitate.

SOCIAL STUDY AND DIAGNOSIS

The juvenile court has great power to make authoritative decisions about many vital aspects of the lives of the children and young people and their families within its jurisdiction. Delinquent children may be returned to their homes and families without further intervention, they may be placed on probation, or they may be removed from the families' control for any period ranging from a few weeks to several years.

Such decisions have a great influence on the individuals involved, both at the time the decisions are made and in their later lives. It is recognized that making decisions of this nature implies taking on the difficult task of predicting human behavior. For this reason and because of their impact on human lives, such decisions must be made only on the basis of very careful and competent diagnostic study. The focal concern is the nature of young people's response to the conforming demands of society. Will they or will they not offend again? Important questions like this require skilled analysis of the child's perceptions of and feelings about the violations, personal problems, and life situations. The study of such problems must consider the value systems that influence behavior, the degree of motivation, and the problem-solving techniques that often produce deviant behavior. Physical, intellectual, and emotional capacities are also important to the analysis, as are the influences of family members, friends, and the neighborhood.

All this information must be brought together in a meaningful picture of a complex whole composed of the personality, the problem, and the environment. The total situation must then be considered in relation to the alternatives available to the court. From these considerations a constructive treatment plan must be developed.

SUPERVISION AND TREATMENT

The three interrelated elements of effective supervision are surveillance, service, and counseling. Surveillance, in essence, is keeping in touch with the child or the youth with a view to carrying out the probation plan. It provides individualized treatment and the support and assurance that society, represented by the court and the court officer, is aware of and interested in the probationer's new confrontation with reality. It is also concerned that he or she not engage in future criminal and self-defeating behavior.

Service involves ascertaining what other community services the probationer and the family need are available, for example, employment information or vocational training. The probation officer can coordinate with other agencies so that the probationer and the family can use these services effectively.

Counseling, the third aspect of the probation officer's task, makes it possible to perform the other two aspects more effectively because of systematic contact with the probationer. Everyone concerned, including the child or the youth, must be helped to understand and face the personal or environmental problems that produced the delinquency. The probation officer may be asked to listen, respond, and sometimes counsel in situations not strictly related to the probation work, but such attention can win the trust and confidence necessary for a meaningful relationship.

AUXILIARY PROGRAMS

In addition to these three central functions, probation departments, both for adults and juveniles, frequently perform auxiliary tasks. Large departments often operate mental health clinics and administer other treatment services such as foster homes, forestry camps, group homes, and other residential or nonresidential facilities. Some also engage in community planning and organization efforts on behalf of children, youth, and adults.

APPLICATION AND ELIGIBILITY

Juvenile probation service is authorized by statute in each of the fifty states and Puerto Rico. In a recent year some 192,000 social studies were conducted and put in writing on behalf of young people and children referred to the courts, of whom 189,000 were placed on probation. There were approximately 223,800 children and youth under supervision.

The upper age limit for eligibility for the services of juvenile probation is determined by the statute establishing the jurisdictional limits of the juvenile court. The Standard Juvenile Court Act, which was sponsored by the National Council on Crime and Delinquency, the National Council of Juvenile Court Judges, and the United States Children's Bureau, provides that the court shall have jurisdiction over a youth alleged to have committed an offense "prior to having become eighteen years of age."

MISDEMEANANT PROBATION

Orginally probation was primarily concerned with the handling of the misdemeanant offender. As the practice and the use of probation grew, a change took place. The emphasis of probation moved, for some unclear reason, from the misdemeanant offender to the felony offender, and today, probation for the misdemeanant, the minor or petty offender, is relatively little used. For example, only an estimated 300,440 persons were placed on misdemeanant probation in 1965 out of a total of over 2.5 million arrested misdemeanants. Reliable data on disposition of misdemeanors are not always available, but for all those convicted in all cities for which data are available, probation, with a range of 2.5 percent to nearly 20 percent, is the least frequently used disposition.[20] These figures are low in spite of the fact that probation costs about one-tenth, in direct costs, of the expense of keeping a person in jail. The indirect costs of family support, loss of taxes, and productivity loss are considerably higher. Over and above the monetary costs are the human costs. Logically, it could be assumed that misdemeanant offenders would be the best risks for probation. Usually the nature of their crimes is such that they do not present a serious threat to society. Furthermore, the misdemeanant offenders are often just getting initiated into criminal careers, and perhaps probation could help them live more law-abiding lives. The *Task Force Report: Corrections,* in its recommended standards, states: "The statute should authorize the court to use probation at its discretion, following adjudication or conviction, for the best interests of the offender and society."[21]

PRESENTENCE REPORT

The presentence investigation report is a basic working document in judicial and correctional administration. Such an investigation is often called a social history or social investigation when it is conducted for a juvenile. It performs the following functions:

(1) aids the court in determining the appropriate sentence;

(2) presentence report when available can be helpful to institutions in their classification and treatment programs;

(3) it helps in the release planning of offenders by way of prerelease programs, day-parole, work furloughs, and full parole;

(4) aids the probation officer in his rehabilitative efforts during the probation supervision; and

(5) serves as a source of pertinent information for systematic research.[22]

The primary objective of presentence reports is to obtain as much information as is relevant and available about offenders and their social background, family, friends, school, and employment history. They also assess strengths, weaknesses, and potentials with a view to working out probation plans. During the calendar year 1975, almost 1 million (997,514) presentence investigations

covering adults and juveniles were conducted.

The content of the presentence report is obtained by interviewing offenders, some family members, and sometimes neighbors. Information also comes from previous employers, schools, social agencies, and social control agencies like the police and courts.

The presentence report generally follows a set format, beginning with identification details and circumstances and details of the offense(s), both the official version and the probationer's version. It also contains a brief social history describing significant events relating to behavior and attitudes, and information about previous disciplinary and/or criminal involvements. This section briefly reports significant family members, information on education, employment record, and general behavior patterns in terms of work habits and leisure-time pursuits. Another important factor generally included is an assessment of community attitudes toward the offender and the offense, and the kind of community reaction to be expected if the offender were to be placed on probation. An unfavorable community attitude can lead to difficulties in social functioning. Support from the more significant social institutions like family, police, school, and employers is frequently vital for rehabilitation. Other things being equal, letters offering help from friends, neighbors, and so on are often evidence of available community support.

Thus, the presentence report usually contains a rough diagnosis of the problem, whether it is based in the family, the gang (peer group), the individual, or whatever the probation officer believes are the important factors that contributed to the offense. An assessment of the strengths available within the family, within the individual, within the community, or elsewhere is of assistance in developing a treatment program. Finally, because most courts expect a specific recommendation regarding court disposition, the presentence report includes such a recommendation to the judge.[23]

There is a growing appreciation in the United States of what psychiatric and psychological consultation can do to help the courts and the probation staff cope with problems that arise in the course of investigation. Professional psychiatric and psychological advice has its role at the time of sentence and also during the period of supervision.[24] Psychiatric and psychological evaluations and psychometric testing are being included increasingly in presentence reports, particularly in the more difficult cases.

The basic function of the presentence investigation is to help the courts decide whether to use probation in a given case. Over the years, however, many new and important uses have been found for the information in the report. Now it is used for the entire range of correctional programs — from the appropriate disposition by the court, to the correctional institution's developing treatment programs, to the consideration of a parole application.

REVOCATION OF PROBATION

Every probation statute requires that probationers adhere to certain conditions. Any violations may result in revocation of probation by the court. There are technical conditions imposed by the court (for example, requiring the probationer to report at a given time, to avoid drinking, and so on). And there are legal conditions (for example, no new criminal violations). If a probationer does break a law, then he or she can be ordered to complete the sentence in an institution. The offender whose sentence is suspended or who is placed on probation is given a guarantee by law that unless certain defined conditions are violated, he or she will not be placed under more severe restrictions. A few states explicitly allow revocation without advance notice or a hearing. In half the states and in the federal system, statutes stipulate that a probationer whose case is being considered for revocation must be given a court hearing.

Some courts, interpreting statutory guarantees of a revocation hearing, have held that the defendant has a right to be represented by counsel. The Supreme Court decision in *Mempa* v. *Rhay* [389 U.S. 128 (1967)] has confirmed the probationer's right to counsel at a revocation hearing. In most cases, however, probation revocation is based on a prerevocation report prepared by the probation officer. Revocation is considered an administrative decision; therefore, if it is undertaken in accordance with established rules and regulations, it is not subject to judicial review. Concern for the protection of individual rights and general social awareness are some of the factors influencing the trend toward formalizing revocation procedures.

DISCUSSION QUESTIONS

1. Who was John Augustus?
2. How would you define probation?
3. Discuss probation as an alternative to imprisonment. What are some of the problems and implications involved?

4. Discuss the psychological and sociological consequences of probation as compared with imprisonment.
5. What are the purposes of a presentence report?
6. Do you believe that probation is a "better" alternative than imprisonment? Justify your opinion.
7. Should a probationer be entitled to a probation revocation hearing with full due process in effect? If you believe the probationer should have full due process, who should bear the cost?

NOTES

1. American Correctional Association, *Manual of Correctional Standards* (Washington, D.C.: American Correctional Asociation, 1969), p. 98.
2. President's Commission on Law Enforcement and Administration of Justice, *Task Force Report: Corrections* (Washington, D.C.: Government Printing Office, 1967), p. 206.
3. *Standard Probation and Parole Act,* 1955 rev. (New York: National Council on Crime and Delinquency, 1964).
4. American Bar Association Project on Standards for Criminal Justice, *Standards Relating to Probation* (New York: ABA, 1970), p. 9.
5. Robert M. Carter and Leslie T. Wilkins, *Probation and Parole: Selected Readings* (New York: John Wiley, 1970), p. 3.
6. Edwin H. Sutherland and Donald R. Cressey, *Criminology* (New York: J. B. Lippincott, 1970), p. 517.
7. *Task Force Report: Corrections,* p. 7.
8. Sutherland and Cressey, *Criminology,* p. 463.
9. Carter and Wilkins, *Probation and Parole: Selected Readings,* p. 11.
10. David Dressler, *Practice and Theory of Probation and Parole* (New York: Columbia University Press, 1969), pp. 26–27.
11. Carter and Wilkins, *Probation and Parole: Selected Readings,* pp. 12–13.
12. *Task Force Report: Corrections,* p. 27.
13. Sutherland and Cressey, *Criminology,* p. 27.
14. Department of Justice, *State and Local Probation and Parole Systems* (Washington, D.C.: Government Printing Office, 1978), p. 1.
15. *Task Force Report: Corrections,* p. 27.
16. *Task Force Report: Corrections,* p. 35.
17. Federal Bureau of Investigation, Department of Justice, *Uniform Crime Reports for the U.S. 1971* (Washington, D.C.: Government Printing Office, 1972), p. 115.
18. President's Commission on Law Enforcement and Administration of Justice, *The Challenge of Crime in a Free Society* (Washington, D.C.: Government Printing Office, 1967), p.. ix.
19. *Task Force Report: Corrections,* pp. 130–141.
20. *Task Force Report: Corrections,* p. 156.
21. *Task Force Report: Corrections,* p. 206.
22. Division of Probation, Administrative Office of the United States Courts, *Presentence Investigation Report* (Washington, D.C.: Government Printing Office, 1965), p. 1.
23. Vernon Fox, *Introduction to Corrections* (Englewood Cliffs, N.J.: Prentice-Hall, Inc., 1972), p. 107.
24. United States Bureau of Prisons, *Trends in the Administration of Justice and Correctional Programs in the United States* (Washington, D.C.: Bureau of Prisons, Department of Justice, 1965).

CHAPTER TWENTY-ONE

PROBLEMS AND RECENT
DEVELOPMENTS
IN PROBATION

PROBLEMS
RECENT
DEVELOPMENTS

---

*Purpose: To provide a brief discussion of the
major issues and problems in probation.*

A PRINCIPLE OF THE American Bar Association Project on Standards for Criminal Justice states: "The legislature should authorize the sentencing court in every case to impose a sentence of probation. Exceptions to this principle are not favored, and if made, should be limited to the most serious offenses."[1] This recommendation can be realistically assessed and the advantages of probation determined on the basis of experience with probation in the United States and other countries and by scientific research.

The growing emphasis on community treatment is supported by several kinds of considerations.[2] The main advantage is that the correctional strategy that presently seems to hold the greatest promise, based on social science theory and limited research, is the reintegration of the offender into the community. A key element in this strategy is dealing with problems in their local context, and this means avoiding as much as possible the isolating and labeling effects of commitment to an institution. The question of whether confinement under inhumane conditions violates the constitutional ban on cruel and unusual punishment is a separate one.

These justifications seem to be borne out by the record of probation services themselves. Although probation services have characteristically been poorly staffed and often poorly administered, the success rate of those placed on probation, as measured by not having probation revoked, has been high. One summary analysis of the outcomes observed in eleven probation studies indicates a success rate of between 60 and 90 percent. A survey of probation effectiveness in such states as Massachusetts and New York and in a variety of foreign countries provides similar results, with a success rate of about 75 percent.

The Cambridge Study, published in England in 1958, found that 79 percent of the adults and 73 percent of the juveniles in the research sample successfully completed their periods of probation. A study in Pennsylvania found that 82 percent of a group of 490 probationers were not recommitted within a period of six to twelve years after completion of their probation.[3] More recent figures for the United States federal probation system show success rates in terms of nonviolation while on probation of about 88 percent for nineteen United States district courts. Two recent studies of receptions into California penal institutions support the view that probation might be used more liberally in preference to institutional treatment.[4]

The second advantage is that while on probation the probationer can live a relatively normal life in the community and have an opportunity to become, in many instances once again, a responsible and useful person. Probation makes possible the experience of personal and family life, satisfying and gainful employment, and support of the family. It is also possible to preserve the unity of the family.

The third advantage is that probation inspires self-worth and self-respect, without which it is very difficult to make a good social adjustment. Probation permits changes in attitudes and outlook through the counsel and guidance of a probation officer.

In addition to the social advantages inherent in community supervision, probation is economically sound. Excellent probation services, with all their advantages, cost much less than imprisonment. The National Crime Commission indicated that the average state spends more a year (excluding capital costs) to keep a youth in a state training school than to keep a youth on probation.

Objections can be raised about the validity of such comparisons because expenditures for probation services are now much too meager. However, with the 1 to 10 cost ratio prevailing, probation expenditures can clearly be increased sevenfold and still cost less than institutional programs. This is especially true when construction costs, which now add up to $30,000 to $50,000 per bed in a correctional institution, are included. The difference becomes even greater if the cost of welfare assistance for the families of the incarcerated and the loss in taxable income are considered.[5] In a recent Texas study comparing probation cost and imprisonment cost per person per year in a model probation system, including the cost of facilities and equipment, $274 was spent for probation as against $2,179 for incarceration.[6]

The experience of the European countries has been well summed up by Dr. Roger Hood in the Council of Europe Report entitled *The Effectiveness of Punishment and Other Measures of Treatment* (1967): some offenders can be dealt with in a way that avoids institutional contamination for the offender, offers the public equal protection, saves the time of those engaged in treatment so that they can concentrate on more difficult cases, and saves public money.[7]

It seems important to keep all the advantages of probation and the pragmatic considerations in mind, especially when the more recent figures for the number of persons on probation are reviewed. The National Crime Commission (1967) estimated a 5 to 6 percent yearly increase in the use of both adult and juvenile probation. This rate of growth exceeds the rate of growth of the United States population as a whole.[8]

PROBLEMS

It must be recognized that probation has its critics. Some criticisms and negative attitudes toward probation are the product of genuine failings and therefore understandable. Even though there are no widely agreed upon scientific criteria for what is or is not a failure on probation, probation failures can generally be attributed to any one, or a combination, of several factors. They can result, for example, from improper selection, the limitations of the predictability of human behavior, and other problems like the lack of suitably trained staff and adequate resources.

Criticisms resulting from such factors can be constructive and can produce favorable and sometimes innovative changes, but when criticism represents the negative, hostile, and punitive attitudes of communities, the problems become much more complex. These negative attitudes are exemplified by outright public apathy to the practices and policies of hiring former offenders. Certain segments of society have even formalized these unfavorable attitudes toward the likelihood of offender rehabilitation by incorporating legal restrictions against offenders. Such restrictions are particularly noticeable in the area of bonding or licensing.

SPECIAL ISSUES

Imprisonment as one of the basic sanctions of criminal justice cannot be abandoned until scientific research positively demonstrates that the alternatives have a greater social value. Even then, incarceration may be the only effective solution for some types of offenders. The views of certain experts, including some who think that imprisonment has failed, often conflict with those of law enforcement and prison personnel, causing wasteful conflicts and controversies. It is possible that the prevailing pessimism regarding imprisonment "may be due to the demise of exaggerated hopes and frustration of ideals."[9]

The Advisory Commission on Intergovernment Relations (ACIR) recognizes the importance of institutional confinement as a means of controlling and deterring certain types of offenders, particularly the estimated 15 to 20 percent who are "hardened criminals"[10] and cannot be handled successfully on probation, parole, or similar types of community-oriented programs.

A report by the ACIR aptly summarizes some major problems facing corrections, including probation and parole. The commission concluded that corrections is the stepchild of the criminal justice system, and that it is essential that more public attention and funds be directed to this field.

In one year, the total state, local, and federal expenditures for police were $9.7 billion, whereas corrections expenditures were $3.8 billion. The police employed 669,518 people, whereas corrections employed 232,009.[11]

The amount of Office of Justice Assistance, Research and Statistics funds used for corrections reflects this low priority, and even these funds have been decreasing. In FY 1976 and 1977, Part E funds decreased by approximately 15 percent. In 1976, only $47 million of OJARS' $405 million was directed toward corrections.[12] As a consequence, probation and parole programs received an inadequate share of federal funds.

The National Crime Commission (1967), in one of its seven basic recommendations, stated that "correctional agencies will require substantially more money if they are to better control crime."[13]

The new priorities that OJARS, for example, has established in its commitment of funds and effort to corrections are also generally reflected in the state plans. The emphasis throughout is on community-based programs as alternatives, whenever possible, to the use of institutional facilities.

Another major and frequently encountered hurdle is the generally unfavorable, and at times even hostile, attitude of the public, which is well represented in the press and in some of the law enforcement agencies. As Clarence Schrag put it, "Although the threat of retaliation may have lessened during the ensuing years, there is little doubt that the motive of revenge still plays some part in the public endorsement of repressive measures."[14] The offender deserves punishment for wrongdoing, and the traditional and well-known form of punishment is a sentence to an institution. Probation is not really punishment; and how can law and order be maintained if lawbreakers, or "criminals," are not properly punished? Such concerns can be seen in the way people are continually shocked by sentences that they regard as too lenient. This can be particularly observed in the not-too-uncommon situation of "upper class" citizens stealing substantial amounts of public or private funds, or committing other crimes, and having their sentences probated. In addition, the media and the police often cite a few examples of probationers who sensationally violate their probation and do not mention the majority who are leading useful lives.

LACK OF SKILLED PERSONNEL

The need for trained probation personnel is likely to increase: (1) as probation services expand; (2) if the official crime rate is not reduced (there are indications that the rate is declining, although the overall number of crimes continues to increase); and (3) when probation comes to be viewed as a better and more economical alternative to incarceration.[15] "The real crisis in social welfare is manpower not merely quantity but quality; not merely filling jobs but rendering a valuable professional service; not merely being employed in any agency but working in soundly managed agencies in which professional skills are utilized to their fullest extent."[16]

The problem of skilled personnel is not

only complex and multifaceted but also closely linked to some of the other basic problem areas already mentioned. But there are other problems in probation.

Generally accepted standards for achieving specified goals have not been developed. The Social Defense Section of the United Nations, the President's Task Force on Corrections, and professional organizations like the American Bar Association and the American Correctional Association have recommended standards for probation. Essentially, standard setting in probation agencies means that there are guidelines to follow to bring their services to more acceptable levels. Unlike the army and the regulatory agencies, where standards are more likely to be enforced, probation agencies are not obligated to meet many standards. Standard review procedure to ensure that probation officers or administrators are meeting minimum standards is virtually nonexistent, though the American Correctional Association has initiated a Commission of Accreditation, which is establishing procedures for assessing standard compliance.

Probation agency standards are often merely decorative. There are many historical and value-oriented reasons why standards are not or cannot be accepted or implemented. And there are other reasons within the probation departments. Lack of qualified supervisory personnel and training officers is a problem, as is the lack of educational and training facilities. The Pilot Study of Correctional Training and Manpower in 1967 indicated that 17,800, or 67 percent, more probation and parole personnel were required than were actually employed in 1966.[17]

In spite of all these limitations, the number of probationers has been increasing. The courts are demanding more and fuller presentence reports. Activities like probation officers' involvement in community programs, in schools, and so forth are imposing heavier demands on mostly overburdened, understaffed, and unsystematically organized probation departments. Under such circumstances, quality is often reluctantly sacrificed, with the result that more serious cases are given greater and sometimes undue attention and seemingly minor matters are neglected. Perhaps a probationer who is progressing well may get involved in problems because the probation officer does not have the time to help.

Probation, like many other social welfare systems, deals disproportionately with large numbers of minority groups (for example, blacks, Mexican-Americans, and Puerto Ricans) who are culturally different from the majority.[18] Sometimes there are conflicts between the goals of probation agencies, which often represent the value system of the majority, and the goals of their minority-group clientele. If not enough care is exercised, complex problems can arise because the programs and the people instituting and running them do not take the minority cultural factors into account.

Some people also see the cultural differences within the majority group as causing problems. For example, the probation officer usually represents a social milieu and value system different from those of the clients, who are generally from "lower" socioeconomic groups. Greater understanding among different groups, and greater representation of minorities and minority groups within the majority, may or may not be the answer, but it would be a step in the right direction.

CASE LOAD

The effectiveness of probation depends to a large degree on what is done with probationers after they are put under supervision. There are two major areas of concern, the type and intensity of supervision and the extent of case load. These are significant because the number of cases to be supervised will influence the kind of supervision provided to the probationer, assuming that the probation officer is skilled and competent.

There are divergent views about the ideal case-load size. There is no magic number. Many variables influence the number of cases a probation officer can effectively handle, for example, the policy and size of the probation agency, the quality and the quantity of expectations for probation officers, and the type of probationers. The ideal case load is also influenced by other services available in the community and whether it is urban or rural.

There are, however, ways to reduce case loads. One, the obvious, is to obtain more probation staff, if this is justified and the resources are available. The second is to systematically provide differential supervision according to the real need, particularly for cases in which it is obvious that extensive supervision will not be particularly beneficial. The third method is through discharging probationers by court order when they have derived the maximum benefit from supervision.

RECENT DEVELOPMENTS

New priorities have put additional emphasis on the need for alternatives to incarceration for most offenders, and advocates of this new emphasis contend that it is self-evident because two-thirds of the offenders are already being handled through probation and parole.[19] The increasing amount of money being devoted to corrections is likewise indicative. Rehabilitation by community-based treatment programs, rather than through incarceration and isolation, is generally considered a more effective means of controlling crime.

PROBATION SUBSIDY PROGRAMS

State subsidy programs for locally operated corrections services are not a particularly new idea. This method of financial support dates back to the 1940s, when programs were initiated in California and Virginia. But the state of California took a significant step forward in 1965 by enacting a law subsidizing probation supervision on a performance basis. It recognized quality probation as the most suitable alternative to state incarceration. This was generally viewed as a profitable alternative because of the many human and economic benefits derived from maintaining offenders in society as functioning individuals. The act gave to local probation departments an incentive to improve service by providing a substantial financial reward to those who voluntarily participated in the program and reduced their rate of commitment to prison.

The California experience shows that probation subsidy programs have not only encouraged "more even administration of justice," but have strengthened the view that probation is as effective, if not more so, as most institutional forms of correctional care. Also, probation is less costly than institutional corrections.[20]

The National Advisory Commission on Criminal Justice Standards and Goals recommends that the purpose of an effective probation subsidy program should be to upgrade local probation services as well as to reduce commitment to institutions. This means that the state should set standards that local agencies must meet to be eligible for reimbursement. The state should also give local agencies technical assistance, audit their programs, and withhold funds when there is noncompliance.[21]

Prior to 1960, there were five corrections subsidy programs operating in five states. Since 1977, the number of programs has increased to 41 in 23 states. In addition to California, Minnesota, Pennsylvania, and the State of Washington have probation subsidy programs.[22]

VOLUNTEERS AS PROBATION SUPERVISORS

Another significant development has been the use of volunteers to supervise and be friends with probationers. This innovation was followed by conflicts, strains, and differences of opinion, mostly stemming from negative attitudes and skepticism about lay people working with "criminals." In spite of the difficulties involved, the use of local volunteers in court probation programs had spread from a few courts in 1961 to a few thousand courts by the middle of the 1970s. According to one report on volunteer programs, ten thousand court volunteers work in many different capacities. There are volunteers in all types of communities, in all sections of the United States.[23]

Volunteers, who are generally local citizens working without pay and usually on a part-time basis, are used to supplement and amplify probation services, and they function under the guidance of a trained probation officer. They are selected on the basis of their interest, willingness, and background rather than their performance in special volunteer training, which is rarely given. Volunteers have contributed new and uninhibited ideas and services and have brought the community closer to the offender.

RESEARCH AND EVALUATION

Another noticeable trend, one receiving increasing emphasis, is measuring the effectiveness of treatment programs. There are two reasons for this, one related to value received for the taxpayers' dollars and the other to the technology and tools for evaluation now available. This new systematic and more scientific approach has resulted in additional funds being made available for research and for the evaluation of programs.

The setting up of the National Institute of Law Enforcement and Criminal Justice Information Center by OJARS to disseminate research and results proven to be effective in improving the different components of the criminal justice system is an example of these efforts at the national level. At the local levels, in addition to closer working cooperation between universities and criminal justice agencies, autonomous research organizations are being created to exchange and disseminate information and make use of all the existing research resources. In short, more and more studies are being conducted to evaluate the outcome of probation and its effectiveness as a corrective tool.

IMPACT OF PUBLIC AWARENESS

Another recent development, referred to earlier, which has many practical implications is the public's concern about individuals and civil rights. The public is interested in knowing how officials make decisions affecting the lives of many people and in knowing what constitutional rights they themselves have as the government and public institutions seek to extend their aid and apply sanctions. The result is a strong impact not only on the policy and procedures of public agencies, but also on the organizational structure. Most of the direct and indirect influences have come from one of the more significant social development agencies — the courts. The court decisions relating to law enforcement, welfare, and corrections reflect greater social awareness of the fundamental principle of fairness in decision making.

Judicial activity concerning the rights of those juveniles and adults under the care of the criminal justice agencies, for instance, has some obvious message for probation departments. One important decision is *In re Gault* [387 U.S. 1 (1967)], in which the Supreme Court ruled that juveniles had the right to receive notice of charges, the right to counsel, the right to confrontation and cross-examination, and the protection of their privileges against self-incrimination. Probation, like some of the other criminal justice elements, has policy and criteria governing the "grant, the supervisory period, revocation, and termination." However, these are areas that need clearer and more precise definition.[24]

Judicial decisions also reflect the concerns of citizens as well as those of victims. In a recent case the Supreme Court of California, in a 4 to 3 decision, reversed a trial court order granting probation to a criminal defendant. The trial court had sentenced the defendant, who had pleaded guilty to criminal acts of oral copulation upon children under the age of fourteen years, for the term prescribed by law. It had then suspended the execution of the sentence as recommended by the presentence investigation, and ordered the defendant placed on probation for five years under strict conditions. In reversing the trial court for abusing its discretion by granting probation, the court stated: "The paramount concern in sentencing must be the protection of society. The interests of the defendant are of legitimate but secondary concern."[25]

ESTABLISHMENT OF STANDARDS

The introduction of standards, previously discussed in more detail, is another major trend. More and more probation departments are joining hands with other criminal justice agencies to set up, implement, and evaluate standards relating to programs and personnel. In this regard, professional organizations like the American Bar Association (ABA), the American Correctional Association (ACA), The National Council on Crime and Delinquency (NCCD), and the various state correctional associations have contributed a great deal. The role of the National Advisory Commission on Criminal Justice Standards and Goals (1973), consisting of about 200 national experts representing different areas of the criminal justice system, which met in January 1973, cannot be overemphasized. The proposed standards not only relate to the education and training of personnel but also set out ethical guidelines for probation employees.

COOPERATION AND COORDINATION OF COMPONENTS

Last but not least, the old rhetoric of coordination of efforts among the parts of the criminal justice system is gradually being translated into practice. Rather than each subsystem working on its own and following its individual direction (sometimes nonexistent and often inconsistent with the greater goals), most of the subsystems are now making a greater and a more deliberate effort to consider the offender and his or her environment as pivotal. Many of the new policies, programs, and services that probation and other criminal justice components are providing or planning reflect the new directions being taken. The reorganization of the services and facilities in the court systems (for example, psychiatric clinics, referral services) demonstrates the slow but sure movement toward a more planned system. The establishment of criminal justice councils in every state, under the Omnibus Crime Control Act of 1968, is another definite step toward a more coordinated and planned approach to the whole system. The impact of these and other measures will not be properly felt until the new techniques have been in operation for some time.

Programs are being implemented that combine and coordinate police, prosecutor, defense attorney, diagnostic service, probation, and other court personnel to provide all the relevant information at the decision-making point as each unit of the subsystem deals with a case. For example, the court administration systems are instituting programs to combine and accumulate all the relevant information about the defendants before they are brought to trial. That way, not only does the judge have a more rational basis for disposition but also the defendant does not need to wait or be detained in jail, usually unproductively, while the court orders piecemeal reports and information to decide a case.

To sum up, from the foregoing considerations, both negative and positive, regarding the value and the future of probation, one can conclude that it is one of the more efficient, humane, and economical methods of handling offenders in the community. It is believed that while concerted efforts can resolve some of the problems, some problems will remain, and some will be created because organizations are living organisms, particularly those that function with and for human beings.

DISCUSSION QUESTIONS

1. What do you see as the major contemporary problem of probation?
2. Should probation departments recruit lay persons as probationers?
3. Discuss some of the merits and limitations of a state probation agency. Compare it with locally controlled probation departments.
4. How can the individual rights of probationers be balanced with the notion of a higher social goal pertaining to the protection of society?

NOTES

1. The American Bar Association Project on Standards for Probation, *Standards Relating to Probation* (New York: ABA, 1970), p. 9.
2. President's Commission on Law Enforcement and Administration of Justice, *Task Force Report: Corrections* (Washington, D.C.: Government Printing Office, 1967), p. 28.
3. R. W. England, "A Study of Post-Probation Recidivism among 500 Federal Offenders," *Federal Probation,* 19 (1955), 10.
4. R. F. Sparks, "The Effectiveness of Probation," in *The Criminal in Confinement,* vol. 3, ed. Leon Razinowicz and Marvin E. Wolfgang (New York: Basic Books, 1971), pp. 211-212.
5. *Task Force Report: Corrections,* p. 28.
6. Robert L. Frazier, "Incarceration and Adult Felon Probation in Texas: A Cost Comparison," thesis, May 1972, Sam Houston State University, Huntsville, Texas, p. 47.
7. Roger Hood, *The Effectiveness of Punishment and Other Measures of Treatment* (Strasbourg, France: Council of Europe, 1967).
8. *Task Force Report: Corrections,* p. 215.
9. Norval Morris and Gordon Hawkins, *The Honest Politician's Guide to Crime Control* (Chicago: University of Chicago Press, 1970), p. 116.
10. Advisory Commission on Inter-Governmental Relations (ACIR), *State-Local Relations in the Criminal Justice System* (Washington, D.C.: Government Printing Office, 1971), p. 54.
11. Bureau of Census, *Trends in Expenditures and Employment Data for the Criminal Justice System: 1972-73* (Washington, D.C.: Government Printing Office, 1975), p. 17.
12. A Report of the National Conference of State Criminal Justice Planning Administrators, *State of the States: On Crime and Justice* (Washington, D.C.: Government Printing Office, 1976), pp. 37-38.
13. President's Commission on Law Enforcement and Administration of Justice, *The Challenge of Crime in a Free Society* (Washington, D.C.: Government Printing Office, 1967), Summary X.
14. Clarence Schrag, *Crime and Justice: American Style, Crime and Delinquency Issues* (Washington, D.C.: Government Printing Office, 1971), p. 10.
15. Herman Piven and Abraham Alcabes, *Probation/Parole: Vol. 1, The Crisis of Qualified Manpower for Criminal Justice: An Analytic Assessment with Guidelines for New Policy* (Washington, D.C.: Department of Health, Education, and Welfare, 1969), p. 37.
16. Joseph Weber, "Manpower: The Real Crisis in Social Welfare," *Personnel Information,* 11 (January 1968), 1.
17. Piven and Alcabes, *Probation/Parole.*
18. *State-Local Relations in the Criminal Justice System,* p. 1.
19. *State-Local Relations in the Criminal Justice System,* p. 238.
20. Robert L. Smith, *A Quiet Revolution: Probation Subsidy* (Washington, D.C.: Government Printing Office, 1971), p. 5.

21. National Advisory Commission on Criminal Justice Standards and Goals, *National Conference on Criminal Justice* (Washington, D.C.: Department of Justice, 1973), p. C-176.
22. The Council of State Governments, *State Subsidies to Local Corrections* (Lexington, Ky.: Council of State Governments, 1977), pp. 1–3.
23. *Volunteer Programs in Courts: Collected Papers on Productive Programs* (Washington, D.C.: Government Printing Office, 1969), p. 204.
24. Fred Cohen, *Legal Challenge to Corrections* (Washington, D.C.: Government Printing Office, 1969).
25. *People* v. *Warner,* Criminal 19662, Supreme Court of California, San Francisco, March 1, 1978.

CHAPTER TWENTY-TWO

HISTORY AND PROCESS OF PAROLE

DEFINITION OF
PAROLE

PHILOSOPHY AND
OBJECTIVE

HISTORICAL
PERSPECTIVES

THE PAROLE
PROCESS

*Purpose: To describe the historical background of
parole and to outline the process of parole.*

THE WORD *PAROLE* is derived from the French expression *parole d'honneur,* which means "formal promise," or "a word of honor given or pledged." In the French military, it was a promise given by a prisoner of war that he would not try to escape or, if freed, would return to custody under some stated condition, or would not take up arms against his captors for a stated period.[1] The French corrections system, however, uses the term *libération conditionnelle* rather than parole, which literally means "conditional release."

DEFINITION OF PAROLE

Robert M. Carter and Leslie T. Wilkins define parole as a procedure by which prisoners are selected for release and a service by which they are given the necessary controls, assistance, and guidance as they serve the remainder of their sentences in the free community.[2] Harry E. Barnes and Nagley K. Teeters consider parole a form of conditional release granted after a prisoner has served a portion of his or her sentence in a correctional institution.[3]

The National Workshop for Correctional and Parole Administrators, held in New Orleans in early 1972 under the auspices of the American Correctional Association (ACA), defined parole as:

a decision — by an authority constituted according to statute to determine the portion of the sentence which the inmate can complete outside of the institution, and

a status — the serving of the remainder of the sentence in the community, according to the rules and regulations set up by the Parole Board.[4]

To reiterate briefly the difference between probation and parole: probation involves serving a term in the community without going to a correctional institution, whereas the release on parole follows a specific period in confinement, depending upon the rules of parole eligibility.

There are different procedures for releasing a person from a correctional institution. Not only are these methods different procedurely and governed by different rules, but they also affect those to be released differently in terms of each person's obligation to report and to fulfill the conditions. Therefore, their distinctions should be clearly understood. The methods are:

1. Executive clemency or pardon
2. Mandatory release
3. Release at the expiration of sentence
4. Temporary release programs, and
5. Parole

Executive clemency or *pardon* is granting a person a release with or without conditions and/or supervision under an executive order. This method is used sparingly and only in special circumstances. Richard M. Nixon was granted pardon by President Gerald R. Ford for the former's involvement in the Watergate coverup crimes. The power to grant a pardon is usually vested in the chief executive, the governor of a state, or the president of the country.

Mandatory release, statutory release, or *conditional release* provides for the release of all prisoners or some prisoners before the end of their sentences. There are no selection criteria in this type of release. The basic notion behind mandatory release is that persons who are released under this system can have the benefit of supervision until the original date of discharge.

Release at the expiration of sentence or *discharge* involves none of the selection or supervision that characterizes the other methods of release. Discharge occurs after a person has completed the lawful sentence.

Temporary release programs (like prerelease centers), study release (particularly for juveniles), work release, and release based on immediate family needs are more fully discussed in the section on corrections. The objective of these and other release programs is to enhance the offender's opportunities for rehabilitation, often gradually and under some supervision.

In brief, *parole* is the release of an incarcerated offender to the community, under the supervision of a parole officer and with certain restrictions and requirements, after he or she has completed a portion of the sentence in a correctional institution. Generally, a person becomes eligible for parole consideration after serving one-third of the sentence, although some laws permit parole at any time during the sentence.

Parole is primarily concerned with helping the committed offender make the difficult transition from prison to an acceptable adjustment in society. The dual purpose of parole is protection of society and rehabilitation of the offender. Society is protected more effectively when an offender is diverted from his or her criminal patterns, and successful diversion is more likely to occur within the community than in the artificial environment of prison.

PHILOSOPHY AND OBJECTIVE

Parole, like the rest of corrections and the whole criminal justice system itself, lacks a generally agreed-upon philosophy and objective. Like many other aspects of our society, parole is viewed differently depending on the perspective of the particular observer and the level of observation. In other words, an average American's reaction to parole varies depending on whether he or she is supposed to respond at the intellectual level or is involved in personal interaction. Even among correctional personnel there are markedly divergent approaches to parole, what it is expected to accomplish, and how. The holders of traditional views about methods of handling offenders sometimes question the concept of parole. For a variety of reasons, the value of parole has been increasingly questioned since the early 1970s. This subject will be further discussed in Chapter 23, Problems and Recent Developments in Parole.

There is, however, less disagreement with the notion that parole represents a changing point of view toward crime and punishment generally and toward offenders and their rehabilitation particularly. Some marked changes can be observed in society's beliefs regarding the causes and the control of criminal behavior, and these changes are reflected in the new developments in the field of corrections and in the system of justice.

The new approaches dealing with offenders have diverged widely — "eye for an eye," or revenge; punishment; segregation or isolation; and rehabilitation or reintegration into the community. The late nineteenth and early twentieth centuries saw the offender as more often sick and disadvantaged rather than "wicked." Therefore, treatment and training, rather than punishment, became the method of handling offenders. Parole is an outgrowth of the belief that a person can be "redeemed" by a more helping and humane attitude.

From society's point of view, it must protect itself. "But it is obvious that the most profitable way of obtaining this protection is by turning the 'criminal' into a useful citizen. Parole is a means to that end."[5]

No one who is serving a sentence has an absolute right to parole. Generally, the courts have maintained the rule of noninterference, leaving the matter of granting parole solely to the discretion of the paroling authority. In *Tarlton* v. *Clark* [491 F. 2d 384 (5th Cir. 1971)] the court ruled that it is not the function of the courts to review the discretion of the parole board when it denies an application for parole. Who has and who has not the right to be considered for parole is one of today's actively debated issues. The National Crime Commission, in its Standards for Parole, states that the law should empower the parole authority to consider all prisoners for parole regardless of the nature of the offense committed.[6]

In keeping with the aim of protecting society and the fact that over 90 percent of the offenders eventually return to the community, there are several reasons why parole is a better alternative.

1. Parole, as a service, aids the released offender during the very difficult time of adjusting to the environment of the community after a period in prison.
2. By providing supervision and control, parole makes reversion to criminal activity more difficult, and there are more chances that this can be prevented.
3. Parole provides an opportunity to return a parolee to prison if he or she shows signs of unacceptable and illegal behavior.
4. The parole restrictions provide legal authority to compel an ex-offender to live up to certain acceptable standards of conduct.
5. Parole is much less expensive than keeping a person in a correctional institution.

The success of any parole system, however well designed and well intended, depends on how it is administered with the resources made available.

HISTORICAL PERSPECTIVES

Parole as an individualized form of treatment is not new. The scriptures from India, written more than four thousand years ago, and Plato's writings, over two thousand years old, referred to individual study, classification, and reform of the deviant individual.

More recently, parole began to develop when British criminals were transported to the American colonies and to Australia in the sixteenth century. Initially, convicted persons who were fit enough to work in the colonies were given a reprieve or pardon if they did not return to England during the term of their sentence. A number of them, however, did return to England without permission before their sentence had expired. The result was that more conditions were added to such a pardon, which became known as a ticket of leave. "This ticket of leave was merely a declaration signed by the governor or his secretary, dispensing a convict from attendance at government work and enabling him, on condition of supporting himself, to seek employment within a specified district."[7]

By the early nineteenth century ticket-of-leave laws reflected the idea of selection rather than the earlier indiscriminate use, and prisoners were required to serve a certain portion of their sentences before being granted a ticket of leave. The English Penal Servitude Act of 1853 related to conditional release and gave legal status to the system of ticket of leave.

The development of parole in the United States contains the same three basic concepts: (1) the principle of shortening the term of imprisonment as a reward for good conduct; (2) the indeterminate sentence; and (3) supervision.

The first concept was recognized in 1817

by New York's "good-time" law. Today every state and the federal jurisdiction have good-time laws of some kind. The indeterminate sentence was first introduced in the latter half of the nineteenth century with the establishment of the houses of refuge for children.

The concept of parole as related to supervision first began with the use of volunteers. The master of an indentured child from a house of refuge was also the child's guardian and supervisor. As early as 1851 the Quakers' Society for Alleviating the Miseries of Public Prison appointed two agents to work with discharged prisoners from the Philadelphia county prison and the penitentiary.

It appears that supervision by a paid public employee was first provided in Massachusetts in 1845, when the state appointed an agent to help released prisoners obtain employment, clothing, and other publicly funded aid. This was far from what supervision provides today, but at least a parolee could obtain some material support during the very difficult and critical parole period.

Although parole began in Europe, it is now more fully developed and used in the United States. Today there are fifty-three parole agencies, one in each of the 50 states, the federal system, the District of Columbia, and the California Woman's Board of Terms and Paroles. In twenty-five of the fifty-three jurisdictions, the paroling agency is known as the parole board or board of parole (or paroles); in nine jurisdictions, it is known as the board of paroles and pardons; in eight jurisdictions, as the board of probation and parole; and in the remaining eleven jurisdictions by different names.[8]

The first attempt to apply parole in the United States came in conjunction with the opening of the Elmira Reformatory in 1876. Thus, the first parole statute in the United States was enacted only two years before the first probation law was passed in 1878. By 1900, twenty states had provisions for parole, and by 1944, all states had parole laws.

The provisions for parole vary considerably from state to state, and no one statement applies generally to the administration of parole. There is considerable variation in the extent to which the different states use parole and the efficiency with which the parole functions are carried out.

Table 22.1 represents releases on parole in relation to all releases in 1975 by regions.

TABLE 22.1 PRISON POPULATION AND NUMBER OF RELEASES FROM STATE AND FEDERAL INSTITUTIONS, 1975

REGION	PRISON POPULATION	UNCONDITIONAL RELEASE	CONDITIONAL RELEASE	
			PAROLE	TOTAL
Northeast	34,699	2,384	13,382	15,990
North Central	48,731	2,563	16,179	19,106
South	102,967	17,347	26,805	30,200
West	32,222	2,125	16,575	17,027
Federal institutions	24,131	6,275	5,783	7,485
Total	242,750	30,694	78,724	89,808

SOURCE: U.S. Department of Justice, *Prisoners in State and Federal Institutions* (Washington, D.C.: Government Printing Office, 1977), Tables 1 and 7.

TABLE 22.2 COMPARATIVE DATA ON INMATES RELEASED ON PAROLE FROM STATE AND FEDERAL INSTITUTIONS (Includes Conditional Releases under Mandatory Supervision)

STATE	1966		1975		
	TOTAL RELEASES	PERCENTAGE OF TOTAL RELEASES ON PAROLE	TOTAL RELEASES	PERCENTAGE OF TOTAL RELEASES ON PAROLE	TOTAL ON PAROLE & MANDATORY RELEASES
Idaho	241	63.5	474	48.9	232
Louisiana	1,741	63.1	778	100	778
Iowa	1,085	61.4	429	100	429
Montana	435	59.8	276	88	243
Georgia	2,728	51.3	2,368	73.4	1,740
New Mexico	475	51.2	535	99.8	534
Arizona	633	50.1	550	86.3	475
Alabama	2,198	47.5	1,418	100	1,418
Virginia	1,827	47.3	1,435	100	1,435
Mississippi	863	45.0	710	100	710
North Carolina	2,722	44.5	4,391	100	4,391
Rhode Island	127	44.1	226	97.3	220
Florida	2,899	42.5	2,749	64.2	1,794
Kentucky	1,340	42.3	1,970	68.2	1,345
South Dakota	411	41.8	178	100	178
Delaware	204	39.7	204	100	204
Oregon	1,030	38.7	713	100	713
Tennessee	1,558	37.2	1,592	100	1,592
Texas	5,824	35.7	4,674	100	4,674
Maryland	4,190	35.5	3,267	99.9	3,265
Missouri	1,955	35.5	908	96.8	879
South Carolina	1,323	32.8	665	100	665
Nebraska	780	27.7	493	99.4	490
Oklahoma	1,822	17.3	1,034	95.5	988
Wyoming	187	12.3	51	58.8	30
Alaska	Not available		98	100	98
New Hampshire	117	100	189	99.4	188

During the year 1974–1975 about 38,700 persons were employed full time in the United States in probation, parole, and pardon. And during the same period the state governments alone spent a total of $271 million on probation, parole, and pardon.[9]

THE PAROLE PROCESS

Parole is an executive function and is generally granted by an administrative board or an agency. (Probation, on the other hand, is a function of the courts.) Parole entails supervision and is granted on the basis of such factors as an offender's prior history, the sentence served, his or her readiness and suitability for such release, the need for supervision and assistance in the community before the sentence expires, and the community's reaction to an offender's release under supervision.

Of those released from state and federal prisons, approximately two-thirds are re-

PROBATION AND PAROLE

Table 22.2 *continued*

STATE	1966		1975		
	TOTAL RELEASES	PERCENTAGE OF TOTAL RELEASES ON PAROLE	TOTAL RELEASES	PERCENTAGE OF TOTAL RELEASES ON PAROLE	TOTAL ON PAROLE & MANDATORY RELEASES
Washington	1,391	100	1,411	99.8	1,408
Kansas	1,199	98.2	1,205	65.1	784
Utah	337	93.5	207	100	207
Ohio	4,642	93.4	5,608	72.8	4,081
California	7,766	90.7	10,864	100	10,864
Wisconsin	1,866	89.0	1,129	100	1,129
Hawaii	168	88.7	103	96.1	99
New York	7,602	87.3	6,151	68.8	4,237
Michigan	4,108	85.2	3,279	99.6	3,267
Pennsylvania	2,633	84.7	3,988	84.6	3,377
Nevada	234	84.2	392	100	392
New Jersey	2,918	83.1	3,087	100	3,087
Connecticut	1,114	80.7	926	100	926
Indiana	2,186	78.8	1,381	81.4	1,125
Maine	587	78.5	595	87.2	519
Vermont	277	78.5	120	100	120
North Dakota	152	78.3	89	100	89
Colorado	1,612	76.5	1,353	94.6	1,280
West Virginia	678	76.0	258	93.4	241
Illinois	3,396	73.9	3,782	100	3,782
Minnesota	974	72.5	625	97.7	611
Arkansas	1,123	71.0	1,536	100	1,536
Massachusetts	1,327	66.6	705	100	705
United States	3,129	65.8	7,485	77.2	5,783
District of Columbia	693	65.7	1,151	70.5	812

SOURCE: Bureau of Prisons, *Prisoners in State and Federal Institutions,* Washington, D.C., Bureau of Prisons, 1968, pp. 28–29; U.S. Department of Justice, *Prisoners in State and Federal Institutions* (Washington, D.C.: Government Printing Office, 1977), Table 7.

leased by parole or some other type of conditional release. There were 175,280 persons released on parole in the United States in 1966. As Table 22.2 indicates, in 1966 only two states, New Hampshire and Washington, provided parole or conditional release for all persons leaving the prisons. In twenty-three states, more than 70 percent of releases are by parole or conditional release; and in ten states, it is less than 40 percent.

These statistics clearly demonstrate the wide use of discretion in paroling of offenders.

In comparison, however, in 1975 twenty-four states provided parole or conditional release for all persons leaving prisons, as against only two states in 1966. In 1975, only Idaho released less than half of its prisoners on parole, as compared with eighteen states in 1966. It is noteworthy that in 1975 forty states released more than three-quarters of their prisoners on parole and mandatory supervision, as compared with twenty states in 1966.[10]

Parole is an integral part of the correctional process. As such and as a rehabilitation method it continues the treatment started in the institution, under supervised guidance, in the normal society. The importance of supervision is further highlighted when it is considered that the period immediately following release from prison is most crucial for acceptable social adjustment and integration in the community. An equally important function of parole is to provide assistance and guidance in finding solutions to many of the problems an "ex-con" faces on his or her return to society.

To fulfill these functions, the parole process has several essential elements. All of them presuppose that there is a duly constituted agency, usually called the parole board, with authority to administer parole. A parole board, established under a statutory authority, usually consists of from three to nine or more members. Its functional responsibilities include the grant or denial of parole and its revocation. A parole board is assisted by staff, generally divided into three broad categories: personnel for carrying out the administrative duties, personnel for supervising parolees, and staff stationed in institutions to interview prospective parolees.

The following are considered essential elements in the parole process:

1. Part of the sentence served in an institution in order to gain what is referred to as parole eligibility
2. Selection for parole
3. Supervision, control, and guidance of parolees according to the conditions of parole until discharge from parole
4. Parole revocation when parole conditions are violated

PAROLE ELIGIBILITY

The legal authority within which parole decisions are made varies widely from one jurisdiction to another. Basically, the parole decision for adult offenders may depend on statutes enacted by the legislature, on the sentence imposed by the court, on the determination of correctional authorities, or on independent parole board action. Some statutes require that an offender serve a certain minimum amount of time before parole can be considered. Some statutes prohibit parole for certain types of offenses. Because such restrictions allow no consideration of the individual or the special circumstances, correctional authorities have consistently found that they interfere with effective decision making, at times cause unnecessary confinement, and at times result in substantial inequities.

With respect to parole for juveniles, a number of legal issues are involved in their commitment and subsequent release. Those that most directly affect parole practice are the restrictions on when a juvenile can be released. Of these the most important are the stipulated period of time a youth is required to stay in a training school and the necessary approval from the committing judge before release can be authorized. As with adults, rules of parole eligibility for juveniles vary from jurisdiction to jurisdiction.

PAROLE SELECTION

The parole selection criteria, which also vary from one jurisdiction to another, can be divided into: (1) statutory requirements, (2) type of sentence, (3) institutional recommendations, and (4) parole board policy.

Statutory Requirements The statutory requirements set the limits for the paroling agency with regard to the types of offender who can or, often, cannot be considered for parole and the length of time an offender must serve before becoming eligible. In some places the laws prohibit parole of offenders who have committed serious crimes. The rules in most cases specify the minimum time, the maximum, or both before a person can become eligible for parole consideration, but usually a person becomes eligible after completing one-third of the sentence.

In general, the longer the time a person has served, the greater the possibility that he or she will be considered favorably for parole. Some people believe that serving a longer period in an institution corresponds to society's idea of punishment, and others interpret it as an inmate benefiting from the institutional programs. Reality is perhaps somewhere in between the two. Some inmates merely pay lip service to the rehabilitative programs and appear to cooperate because they know that doing this will increase their chances for an early parole.

Type of Sentence The type of sentence influences parole selection. The sentencing judge may impose a special condition requiring the offender to follow a certain course or prohibiting him or her from doing certain things. The judge may also order a specific treatment plan, though this does not happen often. Parole boards take such considerations seriously, particularly when they are viewed as practical and beneficial to the offender.

Some judges impose longer sentences because they feel that the community expects some offenders to be confined for a longer period, especially those who have committed crimes particularly unacceptable at the time. Naturally, these sentences result in longer confinement before consideration for parole. Perhaps a parole board has full control over a convicted person only when a court imposes a truly indeterminate sentence, with neither a minimum nor a maximum being set.

A few applicants cannot seriously be considered because their behavior, their attitude, and almost every aspect about the case are negative or there are other indications that they will not succeed on parole but will further violate the law. Occasionally, inmates write to say that they are not interested in parole, and such cases are not processed by the parole agency staff.

The cases in which detainers have been lodged, either for violation of a previous parole or for another offense, are handled by parole boards in various ways. (A *detainer* is a legal order to hold a person who is wanted for another crime or for whom a summons has been issued.) Some boards postpone considering such applicants until the detainer is lifted, some consider detainers but decide the case on its own merits, and others disregard detainers.

Institutional Recommendations Some of the parole laws provide that the paroling agency must consider recommendations from the institution. Many paroling authorities not only like to have reports and recommendations but view them as a necessary part of the case preparation, because the institutional personnel usually know the inmates, their attitudes and motivations, and their capabilities for functioning with others. They also have a better appraisal of the programs in which the inmates may have participated. The kind of consideration given to reports from institutional personnel depends upon the board's view of the writer's attitude, whether in favor of or against parole, and the objectivity of the information.

Parole Board Policy Parole board selection criteria revolve around two basic concepts: (1) the community is ready and willing to receive a parolee, and (2) the offender is ready and willing to lead a law-abiding life. These are considerations over and above the legal requirements and the institutional assessment. An individual's suitability for parole and the community's readiness to accept him or her hinge on a number of sociological, psychological, and educational factors. Sometimes a specific factor like the availability of employment or the details of a political or deportation case is taken into consideration. In the political category, most often a specific situation may make it politically imprudent to release an inmate even though he or she is otherwise suitable for release at that time. When nationals of other countries are committed to correctional institutions, they may be granted parole for deportation to their countries after they fulfill certain requirements.

Many parole agencies have a standard form for preparing parole reports and recommendations. Generally these reports provide information regarding the offender's social history and background. The depth and the breadth of information about a potential parolee's personal, family, marital, education, and employment history differ from case to case. The more severe the offense committed, the greater the amount of information expected, and often required, for making a sound judgment.

In addition to a thorough social history, which has been prepared by the parole agency staff in institutions and outside, most parole boards have information concerning the criminal record. The previous criminal history not only includes the present sentence and details about the type and circumstances of the offense; it also includes any previous offense patterns. Information may refer to the use of a weapon, whether an injury was involved, and so on. Parole reports often contain information obtained from the institutional files, including their recommendations, if any, concerning the

process and conduct of the inmate. There may be other special reports, perhaps a medical report, and letters of recommendations from interested citizens (sometimes expressing opposition to parole). More recently there may be such selection aids as parole hearings and statistical prediction tables. Parole hearings are used in most jurisdictions. Usually a team of two parole board members visits institutions to interview inmates. The new prediction aids are mostly "unproven" from the scientific point of view, but more and more experiments are being undertaken to improve the techniques used to predict the outcome of parole.

The proportion of those released on parole as against those discharged has been rising steadily during the past few years. Occasionally, when a parolee is involved in a bizarre or well-publicized offense that generates unfavorable community reaction, parole boards are inclined to enforce stricter selection procedures, for a while anyway. For the most part, however, the use of parole in those states where it is employed has been increasing because of its lower cost and because of the overall trend toward community-based corrections.

Statutes in most jurisdictions allow parole agencies to adopt their own rules and regulations for selection provided there is no conflict with the statutes. Only a few agencies have written criteria for parole selection, supervision, and technical revocation, and those written criteria are generally considered very broad and vague. Some paroling authorities consider the lack of precise written criteria helpful because it allows flexibility and individual treatment. In decisions against parole and parole revocation cases, however, persons whose paroles are denied or revoked want to know exactly why, so that they can improve themselves in the deficient areas, and some consider this information their right.

In one case, the United States Supreme Court ordered the chairman of the United States Board of Parole to meet with lawyers to discuss and spell out parole selection criteria.[11] The courts have begun to take a more active interest in corrections, including parole, and to rule in areas that were once considered strictly administrative. For example, in a recent case, *Morrissey* v. *Brewer* [408 U.S. 471 (1972)], the Supreme Court unanimously ruled that a parolee is entitled to a full due process hearing prior to parole revocation.

The present approach to parole revocation is a significant change from the earlier stand that parole was a privilege that could be taken away almost arbitrarily. The new approach is not only evidence of growing concern for the rights of persons under correctional control; it also recognizes that the correctional system must impress on those working in the system that due process operates fairly and equally for the protection of *all* society.

SUPERVISION, CONTROL, AND GUIDANCE

The principles, concepts, and methods of probation supervision apply equally to the supervision of parolees. One way of looking at what the supervision, control, and guidance functions entail is to relate them to the definition and objective of parole. The task of parole supervision is to provide favorable opportunities and a conducive environment for parolees so that they can readjust their life patterns to societal demands, within the limits set by the community, through the parole board.

Although parolees have had the benefit of correctional treatment programs, in general they are more difficult to supervise than probationers. This is so partly because parolees usually have a long history of criminal careers and serious offenses, whereas probationers have not had the inmate indoctrination of the correctional institution. Adjustment in the community after prison indoctrination is often made difficult by the community itself and takes special effort and time. Parole supervision, like probation supervision, entails working with the parolee and his or her family, if there is one. It involves establishing a professional working relationship with the police department and the sheriff in the area, an awareness of the social services in the community, and a good knowledge of all the potential employees in the area who will hire parolees.

The case load of parole officers varies greatly. Sometimes probationers and parolees are supervised by the same officer. One state reported a probation-parole case load of 314 for each parole officer.[12] Views about the ideal size of a case load differ; the most frequently recommended case load is between thirty-five and fifty, but most parole systems have more than that under the supervision of one parole officer. The type and the intensity of supervision also vary depending on a number of factors: the type of parolees, the social environment, supervision case load, the ratio of parole officers to parolees, and other workload.

Once parole is granted, satisfactory completion of the parole period is related to variations in the regulation and supervision of parole. Nationally, the average parole period for offenders is twenty-nine months. The state averages for parole period range from fewer than twelve months to more than eighty-four months.[13]

If the parole board feels that a particular parolee has had all the assistance available under parole supervision and can function in the community in a socially and legally acceptable manner without supervision, he or she may be discharged gradually from parole obligation. A discharge from parole means a lifting of parole restrictions in accordance with the parolee's ability to integrate into the community. Once a person has demonstrated that he or she does not present any risk, the discharge can be complete.

CONDITIONS OF PAROLE AND ITS REVOCATION

When an applicant is granted parole, it contains conditions that he or she must agree with and abide by. Any violation of these conditions, either by disregarding them (which is referred to as a technical violation of parole) or by breaking any laws or statues, can result in the revocation of parole. In case of violation of a condition of parole, the supervisor may recommend to the parole board that the parolee be returned to prison, either because a parole restriction has been violated or because he or she is likely to commit a crime.

Conditions of parole have a threefold purpose: they represent the expectations of the community; they test a parolee's serious intention of leading a law-abiding life; and they offer the parolee an opportunity for self-improvement.

If a parolee is arrested and charged with a new offense, there is little if any problem about declaring him or her a parole violator; this is also the case if the parolee absconds. In both these situations, the decision to revoke parole does not present any dilemma. However, not all cases are so clear cut. This is one of the criticisms of parole policies: there are no definite criteria. Judicial intervention, previously mentioned, is likely to change this, however.

The decisions of parole supervisors have an important effect on parolees and their families. When supervisors recommend revocation, everything that has been accomplished in terms of treatment, finding employment, and making adjustment in the community more feasible is usually negated.

Should supervisors be more understanding and more flexible in their control duties? Or should they emphasize performing in accordance with the conditions the parolee agreed to? These are some of the important considerations that parole supervisors have to deliberate in almost every revocation case.

Different conditions of parole are used in different jurisdictions, and the diversity of emphasis is considerable. Yet all inmates granted parole have to sign such an agreement and abide by the conditions listed on their parole certificates. Not only are there divergent views about the number and type of conditions, but there is little agreement on what constitutes a realistic approach to enforceability. Some experts believe that it is better to give the parole supervisor greater flexibility in assisting parolees, and others believe that the conditions should be more specific, so that persons charged with their violation know where they faulted, rather than being told in generalities that their attitudes are uncooperative or that they present risks and that it will therefore be safer to send them back to prison.

The courts, on the other hand, have become more concerned, reflecting the interest of the public, with the rights of prisoners, probationers, and parolees. Indications are that the number of parole rules and regulations is increasing, to deal with many special situations, and that such regulations are also tending to be more specific.

CONTRACT PAROLE

Contract parole is also known as Mutual Agreement Programming (MAP). Under contract parole or MAP, the inmate, the parole board, and the correctional institution sign a contract at the beginning of the inmate's sentence. If the inmate fulfills his or her obligations under the contract, he or she will be paroled on an agreed-upon date. If the inmate does not fulfill his or her obligations, the contract becomes void and a new contract may be negotiated. The basic elements of contract parole are:

- A written, legally enforceable contract between the inmate, the institution, and the parole authority;
- A target date, which becomes the parole date if the inmate meets all contract provisions;
- Face-to-face negotiations between the inmate (often helped by an advocate), the institution, and the parole authority;
- The involvement of an outside party who independently determines whether the contract has been fulfilled;
- Contract provisions spelling out measurable goals for inmates in the areas of education, training, counseling and institutional behavior, and a guarantee from the correctional system that programs and services to fulfill these goals will be available as needed.[14]

In some states the target date for parole under the contract system is negotiable, in others it is set by law. Other variations also exist from state to state. Basically, however, under the contract parole system the inmate enters into the contract voluntarily and may withdraw from the contract at any time. Those inmates who withdraw from or fail to fulfill the contract revert to the regular parole process. Those inmates who remain in MAP have the advantage of a definite parole date, specific program objectives, and, in some cases, the possibility of an early release.

DISCUSSION QUESTIONS

1. How would you define parole?
2. Where did the parole concept develop?
3. Discuss the pros and cons of parole for every prisoner, regardless of the type of offense or offenses committed.
4. Some people believe that parole is just an incentive for good behavior during the imprisonment period, and others believe that it does help parolees not to revert to crime. Discuss the implications, particularly from the point of view of an administrator.
5. What are the criteria that a parole board generally uses for parole consideration? Are they valid?
6. Is a parolee entitled to full due process during a parole revocation process? What is your opinion?
7. Discuss the importance of the supervision and counseling skills the parole supervisor requires. What are some of the problem areas?
8. Discuss and outline the rights of prisoners, as they relate to the parole process. Is parole a right or privilege?
9. Who protects the rights of prisoners and why? What is the "hands off" doctrine?

NOTES

1. *Oxford English Dictionary* (London: Clarendon Press, 1933), VII, 489.
2. Robert M. Carter and Leslie T. Wilkins, *Probation and Parole* (New York: John Wiley, 1970), p. 180.
3. Harry E. Barnes and Nagley K. Teeters, *New Horizons in Criminology* (Englewood Cliffs, N.J.: Prentice-Hall, Inc., 1959), p. 566.

4. William Parker, *Parole: Origins, Development, Current Practices and Statutes,* American Correctional Association Resource Document No. 1, 1972, p. 5.

5. G.I. Giardini, *The Parole Process* (Springfield, Ill.: Charles C Thomas, 1959), p. 19.

6. President's Commission on Law Enforcement and Administration of Justice, *Task Force Report: Corrections* (Washington, D.C.: Government Printing Office, 1967), p. 208.

7. Parker, *Parole,* p. 13.

8. Parker, *Parole,* p. 38.

9. Bureau of Census, *Expenditure and Employment Data for the Criminal Justice System, 1975* (Washington, D.C.: Government Printing Office, 1978), pp. 13, 276, 301.

10. "Corrections in the United States," *Crime and Delinquency,* 13, No. 1 (January 1967), 213. Data for 1975 are taken from Table 7, *Prisoners in State and Federal Institutions* on December 31, 1975, U.S. Department of Justice, Washington, D.C., 1977.

11. Parker, *Parole.*

12. Vernon Fox, *Introduction to Corrections* (Englewood Cliffs, N.J.: Prentice-Hall, Inc., 1972), p. 274.

13. Richard Quinney, *The Social Reality of Crime* (Boston: Little, Brown and Company, 1970), p. 194.

14. "Parole Contracts: A New Way Out," *Corrections Magazine,* 2, No. 1 (September/October 1975), 4.

CHAPTER TWENTY-THREE

PROBLEMS AND RECENT
DEVELOPMENTS
IN PAROLE

PROBLEMS
RECENT
DEVELOPMENTS

---

*Purpose: To discuss the problem areas in parole
as well as current developments and trends.*

$\mathbf{A}$NY PROBLEM IN the area of parole takes on a different magnitude depending on who is observing it and why. It is possible to make an objective and realistic review of some of the problems, however, not to blame but in order to better understand the system, as is necessary before any improvements can be effectively incorporated.

PROBLEMS

Many of the fundamental problems that beset parole are not peculiar to parole; they are the problems of our almost goalless, unsystematic, and fragmented system of criminal justice. Therefore, working for solutions, however well designed and well intended, at only one point in the system means fighting half the battle or fighting it half-heartedly.

One of the shortcomings of parole is best stated in the words of a former chairman of the United States Board of Parole: "It is important that our goals be better defined and our definitions of terms clarified."[1] The National Crime Commission (1967) listed the following objectives of a parole system:

1. Release of each person from confinement at the most favorable time, with appropriate consideration to requirements of justice, expectations of subsequent behavior, and the cost.
2. The largest possible number of successful parole completions.
3. The smallest possible number of new crimes committed by released offenders.
4. The smallest possible number of violent acts committed by released offenders.
5. An increase of general community confidence in parole administration.

The methods by which these objectives can be achieved must include the following:

1. A process for selecting persons who should be given parole and for determining the time of release.
2. A system of prerelease planning, both inside the institution with the offender and outside the institution with others in the community at large.
3. A system for supervision and assistance in the community.
4. A set of policies, procedures, and guidelines for situations in which the question of reimprisonment must be decided.[2]

These methods, recommended by the National Crime Commission (1967), bring out some of the other problems facing parole. Not all parole agencies have all the same problems — the extent and intensity of the problems vary from one agency to another.

FRAGMENTED SYSTEM

Tradition is partly responsible for the fragmentation in the criminal justice system, and the result most often has been the single-minded pursuit of organizational philosophies, programs, and procedures, with little regard for what happens to the offender for whom the programs are set up. A change in the attitude of the handling agencies is long overdue, particularly because the actions of one component of the criminal justice system have a direct bearing on the other components.

In terms of parole, this lack of any systematic approach makes finding a correctional institution and a parole agency effectively coordinating and planning together a treatment program for offenders the exception rather than the law, this despite the fact that the correctional literature emphasizes the importance of initiating release plans as soon as a person is admitted to an institution. Cooperation, when it does exist, is more theoretical than actual. Not infrequently organizational rivalries and accusations operate at the expense of the persons who are supposed to be helped, and, of course, at the cost of the taxpayer's dollar.

Difficulties between the courts and the paroling authorities arise from lack of dialogue and lack of communication about the aims and procedures of parole. Some courts, like some law enforcement agencies, feel that parole is contrary to the aims of law enforcement and the judiciary. Community reactions, particularly in smaller rural communities where practically everyone knows everyone else, can be unfavorable and make problems for a parolee trying to adjust. The community must be prepared and its readiness thoroughly investigated.

Unless social services organizations, particularly the police, and potential employers are carefully made aware of some of the problems that ex-offenders face when they are released, parolees can have a hard time finding employment. Until parolees have legitimate sources of income, they are likely to find comfort and support from people who understand them better, and more often than not, these "buddies" will have criminal records. Any association with "undesirables" is in many cases a technical violation of parole and can cause the parolee to be returned to prison.

LACK OF SKILLED PERSONNEL

Given all the functions and responsibilities of parole, it is essential that the staff be sufficient, professionally skilled, and properly trained. Parole officers are expected to supervise, guide, and control parolees, the major functions of their job. They are expected to maintain professional contacts with other criminal justice and welfare agencies. They are expected to be knowledgeable

about the job market, have time for parolees' families, write reports, and perform other administrative chores. Given all these demands, they cannot be expected to be productive and effective when they must look after large case loads. One study indicated that 97 percent of all officers handling adults have case loads above the recommended average.[3]

The shortage of parole officers is even more acute today than in 1967, when the National Crime Commission (1967) reported an immediate need for almost three times the number of parole officers than were employed at the time. As the population increases in the coming years, the total requirements will be even greater.[4]

The parole officer's authority to exercise sanctions sometimes creates conflicts not only with the parolee but also within the parole supervisor. Some people believe that the policing functions of control on the one hand and the helping rehabilitative services on the other are necessarily in conflict. Whether or not such a conflict exists often depends on the orientation and professional training of an individual parole officer and on a particular situation. But a skilled parole officer should have no problem reconciling these apparently conflicting duties.

PAROLE BOARD MEMBERS

In forty-three of the fifty-three jurisdictions, state governors appoint parole board members. In almost three-fourths of the jurisdictions, either there are no qualification requirements for the board members, or qualifications are stated in broad terms.[5] If the board members lack any demonstrable knowledge of human behavior, this will restrict the effectiveness of their parole decisions. In addition, their effectiveness is further limited by the fact that in one-half of the jurisdictions, all or part of the parole board serves only on a part-time basis, which means they must usually give time to another job.

INDIVIDUAL RIGHTS

Another problem relates to the constitutional issues of due process of law and the rights of individuals concerning matters of parole. Traditionally, parolees have been given few rights concerning matters of parole. Parole has been and still is considered a privilege, not a right, extended to the parolee by a sovereign. As such the sovereign or state can grant or revoke parole at its discretion, without due process of law. Recent court decisions, however, have indicated that parolees are entitled to at least some rights in the parole process.

In *Morrissey* v. *Brewer* [408 U.S. 471 (1972)], the Supreme Court held that a parolee is entitled to two separate and distinct hearings before parole is revoked. At the first hearing, the one to determine whether to remove the parolee from the street, the parolee is entitled to present relevant information and to question adverse witnesses. At the second hearing, the revocation hearing, the parolee is entitled to: (1) written notice of the claimed violation of parole, (2) disclosure of evidence, (3) the opportunity to be heard in person and to present witnesses and evidence, (4) the right to confront and cross-examine witnesses, (5) an impartial board, and (6) a written statement of the facts and findings of the board. The Court declined to consider the issue concerning the right to counsel in this particular case, but did so in *Gagon* v. *Scarpelli* [411 U.S. 778 (1973)].

In *Gagon* v. *Scarpelli* the Supreme Court held that in some cases the government must provide parolees with counsel at the revocation hearing. The decision as to whether counsel is needed in a specific case is left essentially in the hands of the parole board. The Court did not make a blanket decision; therefore, the need for counsel must be determined on a case-by-case basis.

Another recent decision related to the application of the due process clause to parole release proceedings. Addressing this question, the U.S. Court of Appeals for the Fourth Circuit ruled that not only does the due process clause of the Fourteenth Amendment apply to parole release proceedings, it requires the following: (1) that a parole board make its parole criteria readily available to all prisoners; (2) that prisoners be allowed access to their files; and (3) that prisoners be allowed to present documentary evidence and witnesses in support of their applications for parole (*Franklin* v. *Shields*, September 19, 1977, No. 75-2056).

In the past few years the parolee's rights have been expanded. There are, however, many issues concerning the rights of individuals in matters related to parole that are still unresolved. The trend now appears to be toward expanding these rights.

RESEARCH

Lastly, there is the problem of lack of research into the different aspects of parole. It is recognized that intensified criminological research has helped to formulate predictive factors for success or failure of parole, but parole prediction is somewhat special in that it has to concern itself with violation of parole agreements. There is a need for reliable information regarding the parole officer's method and techniques of handling parolees. There is a need for an inventory of the factors related to the stresses and strains that parolees experience; for a realistic investigation of the factors that help or hinder their community integration; and for a procedure to establish classes of offenders who are more amenable to treatment and rehabilitation.

RECENT DEVELOPMENTS

PUBLIC AWARENESS

An overall trend among the public and among criminal justice agencies is toward greater awareness and understanding of parole as a rehabilitative technique. Greater numbers of people are recognizing the advantages and the risks involved in releasing offenders on parole. With two-thirds of the total corrections case load under probation or parole supervision today, the central question is no longer whether to handle offenders in the community, but how to do so safely and successfully.[6]

DETERMINATE SENTENCING AND ABOLISHING PAROLE

A little more than a decade after the 1967 Report of the President's Commission on Law Enforcement and the Administration of Justice, different questions are being raised by the public. The legislatures in this country, which pass most of the laws, are particularly receptive to calls for a "crackdown" on crime. One result of this hardening attitude toward "criminals" has been new laws restricting or abolishing parole and eliminating indeterminate sentences or introducing determinate sentences.

The rationale is that having the legislatures fix penalties for offenses would eliminate discretion by parole boards and judges. Under such a system, a person found guilty of a specific offense would be given a definite sentence determined by statute. Whatever the long-term impact on rehabilitation via parole and on the discretionary practices, a number of states have abolished indeterminate sentences and/or parole, or are considering doing so. These states include Alabama, California, Illinois, Indiana, Maine, Virginia, and the District of Columbia. In jurisdictions where determinate sentence laws have been passed, prisoners' sentences can be reduced by only "good time" provisions. A *Time* article, reporting news trends, pointed out, "it is time we realized that prisons are for punishment."[7]

ESTABLISHMENT OF STANDARDS

Another overall trend is toward clarifying standards. An increasing number of parole agencies have set up standards of some kind for parole selection, supervision, and reporting and standards for the qualifications and training of parole officers. There is a greater recognition of the need for board members to have appropriate qualifications and skills. Many parole administrators are aware of these deficiencies and would like, if they had the resources and the public's support, to bring about the much needed improvements and changes in the present system.

As standards are incorporated into parole administration and as more resources are available for research, more evaluative facilities will also become available. Today, however, most parole systems not only lack devices for evaluating either the quality or the quantity of work, they are not even certain what needs to be evaluated. The only criterion presently used in most places is the number of successes and failures on parole, but even success and failure are defined and interpreted in many ways.

COURT INTERVENTION

A definite development can be seen in the courts' attitude. During the later 1960s the courts discarded the "hands off" attitude toward problems in corrections. Now they are intervening to protect the constitutional rights of individuals against the "caprice and whim" of the administrative agencies, such as prisons and parole boards. For instance, the United States Board of Parole has been required to set more precise criteria for parole selection and intervention in specific cases. Overall, courts are increasingly becoming involved in decisions that affect correctional administrators and correctional agencies; for instance, they are requiring that a variety of standards be met. In this regard it should be noted that courts have also imposed standards on themselves.

A good example is a recent Administrative Order of the Court of Appeals of Maryland, the state's highest court, which declared that all judges who serve in the trial courts should furnish to the Maryland Parole Commission the reasons why a particular sentence of incarceration is imposed upon a defendant in a case where imprisonment is for three years or more.[8] This kind of procedure not only provides more explicit reasons for certain paroling decisions, it also helps in maintaining parity.

COMMUNITY INVOLVEMENT

One of the more significant developments in probation and parole has been community involvement at different levels of the rehabilitation process. Community participation is noticeable in the expanded use of nonprofessionals, more commonly known as volunteers. A number of new projects involve opportunities for individual citizens to volunteer, as well as projects for civic organizations. For example, young lawyers in Los Angeles, Sacramento, and Santa Clara counties work as volunteers with the California Youth Authority (CYA) to help CYA parolees in a new, nationally sponsored program. The project in California is part of the National Volunteer Parole Aide Program, sponsored by the American Bar Association

Young Lawyers Section, its Commission on Correctional Facilities and Service, and the Federal Bar Association. This program involves more than one-third of the states. The basic purpose of the program is to provide case-load relief and treatment flexibility.[9]

More recent innovations involve the indigenous nonprofessional in corrections. "Most professional corrections workers agree that a large segment of their clientele are, by virtue of their norms, values, and life styles, alienated from the mainstream — middle class professionals. . . . The indigenous worker, conversely, has often experienced situations and problems similar to those that beset certain clients."[10]

With the increasing acceptance and popularity of treatment within the community, there is wider use of the work-release programs, or, as they are sometimes known, day parole and work furlough. One of the objectives of such programs is to develop a greater sense of responsibility in the parolees by giving them responsibility gradually. The other objectives of work release or work furlough are to involve parolees in employment, education, and vocational programs. In some jurisdictions, work release programs are solely administered either by the institutional or by the parole agency staff; in others, they are jointly administered. The trend, however, is toward increasingly coordinated efforts in program planning.

EX-OFFENDERS AS ADVISORS

Another recent development, which is viewed with great caution and sometimes with skepticism, concerns the idea that ex-offenders might be hired to act in advisory capacities, helping to plan new programs and to make existing ones more effective. Ex-offenders might also be members of reviewing committees and assist legislative committees, the rationale here being the use of an existing source of experience at little cost.

Finally, parole agencies and the other correctional components are becoming more aggressive, competing for their fair share of the resources and support required to carry out the changes that have been neglected or postponed for too long.

Parole, not unlike other agencies of the criminal justice system, is beset by a number of problems. The fragmented nature of the criminal justice system, unskilled parole personnel, unqualified parole board members, issues of parolees' rights, and lack of research hamper the effective and efficient operation of parole. However, recent developments in parole standards, community awareness and involvement, court intervention, and the use of ex-offenders offer some hope for the future of parole.

DISCUSSION QUESTIONS

1. Are there any differences between mandatory release, conditional release, and parole? If so, what are they?
2. Do you believe the courts have the right to tell correctional administrators how to administrate parole?
3. Discuss some of the techniques for tackling public apathy relating to parole and the parolee.
4. Do you believe that ex-offenders have a role to play in the criminal justice system? What should their role be, if any?
5. What is the purpose of judges giving reasons for a sentence of incarceration?

NOTES

1. George J. Reed and William E. Amos, "Improved Parole Decision-Making," *Federal Probation* (March 1972), p. 16.
2. President's Commission on Law Enforcement and Administration of Justice, *Task Force Report: Corrections* (Washington, D.C.: Government Printing Office, 1967), p. 185.
3. President's Commission on Law Enforcement and Administration of Justice, *The Challenge of Crime in a Free Society* (Washington, D.C.: Government Printing Office, 1967), p. 12.
4. *The Challenge of Crime in a Free Society,* p. 167.
5. William Parker, *Parole: Origins, Development, Current Practices and Statutes,* American Correctional Association Resource Document No. 1, 1972.
6. *The Challenge of Crime in a Free Society,* p. 165.
7. "Fixed Sentences Gain Favor," *Time,* December 12, 1977, pp. 98–99.
8. Administrative Order Requiring Trial Judges to Furnish to the Maryland Parole Commission the Reasons for which a Particular Sentence of Incarceration Is Imposed. Signed Robert C. Murphy, Chief Justice, Court of Appeals of Maryland, June 2, 1978.
9. National Council on Crime and Delinquency, *NCCD News,* vol. 53-3 (May–June 1972).
10. Donald W. Belass, William S. Pilcher, and Ellen J. Ryan, "Use of Indigenous Non-professionals in Probation and Parole," *Federal Probation* (March 1972), p. 10.

PART SIX ANNOTATED BIBLIOGRAPHY

Carter, Robert M., and Leslie T. Wilkins. *Probation and Parole: Selected Readings.* New York: John Wiley, 1970.

This can be considered an all-purpose text on probation and parole, both for university study, particularly by those who are beyond the introductory stages, and for practitioners. The articles deal with the philosophy, scope, process, and problems of probation and parole.

Dawson, Robert. *Sentencing: The Report of the American Bar Foundation's Survey of the Administration of Criminal Justice in the United States.* Boston: Little, Brown and Company, 1969.

This book is a good reference for the range of sentencing possibilities, including the granting and revocation of probation and parole. Although its title is somewhat deceptive, it takes a systems approach to the specific processes in the total criminal justice system.

Dressler, David. *Practice and Theory of Probation and Parole.* 2nd ed. New York: Columbia University Press, 1969.

An excellent second book on probation and parole. It contains the current theoretical approaches to correctional functions, particularly those relating to probation and parole. The concern for the individual's treatment and the role of the community in rehabilitation are explained. There is a good deal of case-work detail both to support the theoretical orientation and as a heuristic device insofar as the potential probation and parole officers are concerned.

National Advisory Commission on Criminal Justice Standards and Goals. *Corrections.* Washington, D.C.: Government Printing Office, 1973.

This report presents the commission's work on corrections and, therefore, probation and parole. Standards and goals for probation and parole are covered.

President's Commission on Law Enforcement and Administration of Justice. *Task Force Report: Corrections.* Washington, D.C.: Government Printing Office, 1967.

The research and findings of the commission on probation and parole are presented in this report.

PART SEVEN

THE FUTURE OF
THE CRIMINAL
JUSTICE SYSTEM

CHAPTER TWENTY-FOUR

SYSTEMS APPROACH TO CRIMINAL JUSTICE

NEED FOR A SYSTEMS APPROACH

BASIC ELEMENTS OF THE SYSTEMS APPROACH

LONG-RANGE CONTRIBUTIONS OF THE SYSTEMS APPROACH

SHORT-RANGE BENEFITS OF THE SYSTEMS APPROACH

LIMITATIONS OF THE SYSTEMS APPROACH

Purpose: To explore the concept and application of systems analysis, in lay terms, as it relates to the criminal justice system.

THE CRIMINAL JUSTICE system is just beginning to make use of a powerful tool for data analysis and decision making — the *systems approach,* sometimes called *systems analysis* or *operations research.* This tool has proved so effective in other governmental operations, especially national defense, that there can be little doubt that the criminal justice system of the future will be affected profoundly by its concepts.

NEED FOR A SYSTEMS APPROACH

The possible benefits of the systems approach are numerous. Perhaps its most important contribution will be to reduce conflict between the components of the criminal justice system — the police, the courts, and corrections.

The most visible conflict in the criminal justice system is that between the police and the courts. During the turbulent 1960s, the Supreme Court under Chief Justice Earl Warren handed down a number of controversial decisions concerning police practices. The *Miranda* decision was only one of a series of cases in which the Court held that several long-accepted police procedures violated the rights of suspects. Cries of "handcuffing the police" were common, and the relationship between the courts and the police hit what may have been an all-time low.[1] This police dissatisfaction with the Supreme Court has lessened somewhat in the years since *Miranda.* Many police, however, still regard the courts as an institution working against them, not with them.

If the 1960s was a decade of conflict between the courts and the police, the 1970s saw increasing conflict between the federal courts and corrections. Federal judges found conditions in some prisons so shocking that they held that entire prisons and even entire state correctional systems violated the Constitution.[2] Judicial intervention in the running of prisons has gone much further than intervention in police practices. Judges have not only ruled that certain correctional practices are unconstitutional, they have gone on to specify exactly how the prisons in question must be run. If the prisons should fail to adhere to the very detailed and specific guidelines mandated by the courts, they would have to cease operations. Although the dissatisfaction of correctional officials with what many consider judicial interference has received much less publicity than the police discontent, it is no less real.

Like the relationships between the police and the courts and between the courts and corrections, the relationship between the police and corrections seems to be one of conflict. The police have accused prison officials of releasing dangerous felons to prey upon the community, making the police task more difficult. Prison officials, in turn, have accused the police of harassing parolees, a practice, they say, that may well counteract the rehabilitative effect of parole. Police and probation and parole officers need information and assistance from one another, information and assistance they are not likely to get while they are working at cross-purposes.

All this conflict might seem to indicate that the police, the courts, and corrections do work at cross-purposes, that their goals are basically different and often antagonistic. It might seem that the three parts of the criminal justice system have little in common beyond the fact that they all deal with criminals. However, if it is to be at all effective, the criminal justice system of the future must not be fragmented in this way. The criminal justice system, now as well as in the future, is indeed a *system,* in the sense that all the parts are interrelated and dependent on one another. The courts cannot arrive at just decisions, or for that matter any decisions at all, if the police do not make arrests. If the police arrest the wrong people, if the courts convict the innocent, corrections cannot perform its functions, for how can it correct people who by definition do not need correction? On the other hand, if the courts do not convict the guilty, there is no one to correct. And if corrections does not rehabilitate, the police and the courts will deal with the same individuals over and over again.

Because the criminal justice system is interdependent, a change in one part of the system necessarily affects the operation of the other parts. If the police make more arrests, the courts and corrections have to work faster, expand, or be overwhelmed with cases. If the courts extend their scrutiny to areas that they had previously ignored, police and corrections must alter their operating procedures. A great increase in correctional effectiveness would leave the police and courts with less to do; a decrease in correctional effectiveness would complicate their jobs. Even small changes in one part of the system, such as a change in police patrol procedures, change the criminal justice system as a whole. Because the system is so interdependent, it simply cannot function effectively when its component parts are working at cross-purposes and pursuing independent and conflicting goals. Before examining how the systems approach can help deal with this confusion of goals, it is necessary to examine the important elements of the systems approach itself.

BASIC ELEMENTS OF THE SYSTEMS APPROACH

The systems approach comes with good credentials. Its use in such diverse fields as national defense, medicine, and business management has enabled researchers in these areas to make quantum jumps in their knowledge.[3] In the popular mind, the systems approach is a complicated and confusing method using giant computers, incomprehensible flowcharts, and indecipherable jargon. Its basic principles, however, are not difficult to grasp (Figure 24.1).

EXAMINING THE WHOLE SYSTEM AND ITS PARTS

The systems approach is based on the principle that the whole is often more than the sum of its parts and that it is impossible to get an accurate picture of phenomena without examining the relations between the separate parts and the whole. In terms of criminal justice, this means that the operation of the criminal justice system as a unified whole must be studied and that the overall objectives of the system, rather than the objectives of the police, or the courts, or corrections, must be examined. The systems approach holds that since all parts of a true system are interdependent, it is not only inefficient but often counterproductive to study or advocate changes in any one part of the system without examining the effect these changes will have on the whole system.

Perhaps the clearest example of the need to examine systems as a whole is in the fields of medicine and biology. Common sense agrees with systems analysis that an individual organism, such as the human body, should be studied as a whole. It would be a poor physician indeed who cured a diseased stomach with a treatment that stopped the heart. It is easy to forget, however, that until the modern era the human body was viewed as a fragmented collection of separate bones, muscles, and glands, much as many people now tend to view the criminal justice system as a collection of police agencies, courts, and

FIGURE 24.1 CRIMINAL JUSTICE SYSTEM

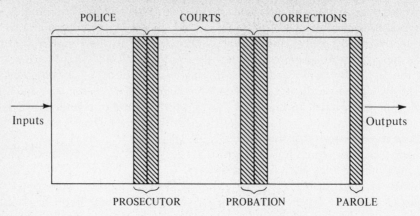

A "black box" illustration is often used to illustrate a system. The criminal justice system is represented above as though it were a box with inputs and outputs. A simple analysis of a system through the black-box approach often provides insight into the system's problems. As an example, consider an offender as an input when arrested, then later consider this same offender as an output when released from prison. If you were to examine the offender at the input and output sides and find that his or her attitudes were essentially the same, you could assume that the criminal justice system had had no effect on this individual. This is, of course, an oversimplification but it does illustrate some of the methods of systems analysis.

prisons. However, no real progress toward either understanding the body or treating its illnesses was made until researchers began to study the body as an integrated system containing functionally related subsystems, the respiratory system, the digestive system, and so on.[4]

If it was difficult to conceive of an individual organism as a system, it is even harder to think of the air defense system of the United States or the Bell Telephone Company as an organism to be studied as a whole. However, viewing the system as a whole is the first requirement of a systems approach to criminal justice.

UNDERSTANDING GOALS AND OBJECTIVES

The second requirement of the systems approach is a clear understanding of goals and objectives, both of the entire system and of its component parts. The usual method of examining the criminal justice system is to analyze separately the goals of police, courts, and corrections. Writers on police tend to emphasize goals that affect only the police, such as crime-solving, patrol efficiency, and professionalization of police personnel. Other police writers emphasize goals that are so general they are almost meaningless, such as protecting the public or serving the community. The goals of the court system, too, are usually stated in broad, general terms: justice, protecting the individual, protecting society. The goals of corrections, as usually stated, are not quite so broad, but are specific to corrections: rehabilitation, deterrence, incapacitation. The goals of the criminal justice system as a whole are rarely considered.

A systems approach to analyzing goals attacks the problem from exactly the opposite direction. The first question to be decided is "What is the purpose of the system as a whole?" Once this question is answered, the goals of the police, courts, and corrections can be analyzed in terms of how well they accomplish the overall goals of the system. The importance of this distinction cannot be overemphasized. Assume that it is decided that the primary purpose of the whole criminal justice system is to reduce crime. Let us further assume that a given objective of one part of the criminal justice system does not further that overall objective. To take a most unlikely example, let us assume that future research demonstrates that providing police with higher education does nothing to reduce crime or accomplish any of the other objectives of the system as a whole. It merely provides the community with educated police. In that unlikely event, the criminal justice system of the future, if it is operating on the basis of a systems analysis, will deny that educating police is a legitimate goal of the criminal justice system.

This insistence on an overall objective does not mean that the police cannot have specific goals the other parts of the system do not share. They can and must. However, the acid test of what the police, courts, and corrections do must be whether the goals of the overall system are accomplished. When analyzing individual goals, police administrators, judges, and correctional officials must ask themselves, "If we accomplish this goal, will crime be reduced? Will other objectives of the system be accomplished?"

STATING GOALS IN MEASURABLE TERMS

Since the systems approach is based on a clear understanding of goals and objectives, there must be ways of determining whether or not a given objective is being accomplished, whether or not there is progress toward the goal that is being sought. The third requirement for a systems approach, therefore, is that goals be stated in such a way that they can be measured. In essence, a systems approach requires that goals and objectives be translated, as much as possible, from words like "serving the public" to numbers.

This is an extremely difficult requirement. It is made necessary, however, by the nature of digital computers as well as by the nature of the scientific method. Although up to this point the description of systems analysis has not mentioned computers, the interested student will find that almost all the literature in the field of systems is heavily computer-oriented. The reason is that a systems approach to a complex subject like the criminal justice system requires and generates such an enormous amount of information that data-processing systems that include computers are needed to avoid drowning in the data. Computers, with their speed and the amount of information they can process, are impressive instruments, but they have their limitations. Basically, they can only add, subtract, multiply, divide, and make simple yes-no decisions. Most information fed into them must be in the form of commands and numbers. Perhaps a police administrator knows what "serving the public" means, perhaps a judge knows what "justice" is, but a computer definitely does not. Computers must be told what to do in the only language they understand, and this fact means that criminal justice officials have to translate the complex concepts they work with into simple, specific statements that are compatible with some system of measurement.

To illustrate the difficulty and the importance of stating goals in terms that make it possible to measure accomplishment, it is useful to examine the concept of reducing crime as a principal objective of the criminal justice system. The reduction of crime is certainly one of the basic functions of the system, and it seems that it should be one of the easiest to measure. For many years the Federal Bureau of Investigation has published annually *Crime in the United States: Uniform Crime Reports.* When the news media report that homicide is up 2 percent in a certain city or that crime in the nation is up 8 percent, this refers to data published in the *Uniform Crime Reports.*

Before it is possible to determine whether the criminal justice system or any of its parts is reducing crime, it is necessary to know how much crime there is, and hence accurate information on the amount of crime, the types of crime, who is committing it, and so on is vitally important. Without such information it is impossible to determine to what extent, or even whether, the criminal justice system is meeting its goal of reducing crime. The *Uniform Crime Reports* are the best available statistics, but they are not accurate enough to serve as the measure of crime.

The difficulty with these reports is twofold. First, the FBI is dependent on data supplied by local police agencies. Any change in a department's method of recording or reporting crime can lead to gross errors in statistics. More important, however, police agencies can report only crime they know about. The National Crime Commission has documented what criminologists have long suspected: the majority — and a very large majority — of crimes never come to the attention of the police.[5] In fact, the amount of serious crime that does come to police attention can be compared with the tip of an iceberg; the vast bulk is submerged. This means that the increase in crime in recent years as reported by the *Uniform Crime Reports* may reflect a real increase in the amount of crime, or it may reflect greater reporting of a lesser amount of crime. This defect of

the *Reports* makes it very difficult to judge police performance. If a city reported a large increase in crime, this might mean that their police had declined in effectiveness and were no longer doing their job in a manner that reduced crime. On the other hand, the very same statistics could mean that the police were much more effective and had gained the confidence of the public, and therefore were receiving more reports of criminal activity despite the fact that crime was decreasing.

In recent years several attempts have been made to develop a set of criminal statistics more accurate than the *Uniform Crime Reports.*[6] Perhaps the most far-reaching attempt has been an effort by the Office of Justice Assistance, Research and Statistics to use census techniques to measure crime. The OJARS survey was based on a National Crime Panel consisting of 60,000 homes and 39,000 businesses, randomly selected to represent all the nation's households and businesses. Individuals in the panel are interviewed monthly to determine the nature and extent of criminal activity to which they have been subjected. It was hoped that surveying victims would avoid some of the drawbacks associated with the reliance on police statistics to measure crime. Unfortunately, surveys are expensive and difficult to perform properly. In fact, the methods the OJARS used to survey crime victims have been criticized sharply by some experts in survey research. Perhaps some new combination of victimization surveys and measures of reported crime will provide the criminal justice system with what it needs so badly: a reliable and valid measure of crime.

This method of measuring crime is only one of the indicators of performance that the criminal justice system of the future will use. After all, a long-term decrease in the amount of crime in a city does not tell us by itself

THE FUTURE OF THE CRIMINAL JUSTICE SYSTEM

whether the decrease can be credited to better police performance, more efficient courts, a more effective correctional system, or factors outside the criminal justice process. Each segment of the system has to have its own methods of measuring effective performance. The importance of the overall measure of the amount of crime is that it will be used as a yardstick to evaluate the individual performance measures the police, the courts, and corrections use. For example, it is relatively easy for the police to measure the number of arrests. Is such a measure a valid performance indicator for police? To put the question another way, do arrest rates for offenses have anything to do with reducing crime? The criminal justice system of the future, equipped with a more accurate measure of crime, should be better able to determine by experiment whether arrest rates correlate with crime reduction. If they do correlate positively, they are a valid measure of police effectiveness; if they do not, other measures will have to be developed.

DEVELOPING ALTERNATIVE SYSTEMS AND MATHEMATICAL MODELS

Once the goals of the system are stated in mathematical terms and a large body of information on the operations of the system has been collected, it is possible to undertake experiments that would otherwise be impossible. An operating system, such as the criminal justice system, is difficult and expensive to change. Experimenting with the actual system can sometimes entail unacceptable risks, as for example, an experiment in eliminating all prisons or in disarming the police. Once the groundwork necessary for the systems approach has been laid, however, it is possible to do these experiments without much expense and completely without risk. A mathematical model of how the system actually operates is developed, a model that serves as a baseline for experiments. Alternative methods of operating the system, for example, doing without prisons or doubling the number of police officers, are examined and transformed into mathematical models. These models are run through a computer to determine how well each alternative operating method achieves the objectives of the system. If enough data are available, if enough is known about how the criminal justice system actually operates, it is possible to determine in advance the results of major changes in operations and to compare the results of one suggested change with those of another.

LONG-RANGE CONTRIBUTIONS OF THE SYSTEMS APPROACH

The systems approach can make several contributions to the criminal justice system of the future. Most of these result from the very nature of the approach.

MEASURING EFFECTIVENESS OF AGENCIES AND PROGRAMS

The systems approach requires the criminal justice system of the future to develop a variety of performance indicators, that is, measures of effectiveness, and the resulting ability to measure effectiveness will be perhaps the most important contribution of the systems approach. It will improve the decision-making process throughout the system. Are one-person patrol cars better than two-person cars? Who should be put on probation, who should be imprisoned? Which correctional treatment is most effective for a given prisoner? Criminal justice officials must make thousands of such decisions every day. Without reliable performance measures and an objective way of determining what works and what does not, these decisions must be made on the basis of hunch and intuition. The measures of performance available to the criminal justice system of the future will lead to a better decision-making process. All the different methods of accomplishing a goal can be tried theoretically and the outcomes measured to determine which works best. Decisions about the most effective procedures can be made on the basis of facts, not guesses.

RESOLVING CONFLICTS WITHIN THE SYSTEM

The ability to measure performance accurately and in terms of the goals of the whole system will not be the only contribution of systems analysis. This chapter began with a discussion of conflicts between the various elements of the system. At present, there is no satisfactory basis for resolving these conflicts. The police pursue police goals, the judiciary has quite different goals, and the correctional system pursues its correctional aims. When these objectives conflict, it is not possible now to determine which should take precedence in order to accomplish overall goals. When there is no rational means of choosing between conflicting objectives, the decision generally depends on which part of the system has the power to enforce its position. When there is more or less equal power, an impasse results that benefits no one.

In the system of the future, with its accurate measures and adequate means for judging performance in terms of larger goals such as reducing crime, there will be a rational way of settling many conflicts. For example, if the police and corrections differ on the best method of handling certain first-time offenders, research will be able to determine whether the "get tough" approach or the liberal use of probation reduces crime

more effectively. This does not mean that there will be no conflict. The system has more than one major objective, and these large-scale objectives, such as reducing crime and protecting the rights of individuals, may conflict. Systems analysis has no technique for deciding cases in which basic goals are antagonistic to one another. It can, however, reduce conflict in those situations in which the problem is simply determining the best way to achieve an agreed-upon goal.

SETTING PRIORITIES: COST-BENEFIT ANALYSIS

A third contribution of systems analysis to the criminal justice system of the future is its ability to set priorities and allocate money effectively. Which is more important, to increase the number of police or to upgrade parole? What is the better crime-fighting technique, speeding criminal trials or providing halfway houses for convicted offenders? Will an individual police force fight crime better if it has more patrol cars, or should it concentrate on training its detectives? If the federal government has a given number of dollars to spend on reducing crime, should it invest in an experimental narcotics treatment program? On scholarships to enable police to attend college? On upgrading prison systems? Which does the best job of reducing crime for the money?

At the present time, there is no rational method of answering such questions. We cannot measure how much a given program reduces crime, so we cannot compare one program with another in terms of crime reduction. The system of the future, however, using performance measures in conjunction with relevant research, will have a basis on which to make decisions about which program should have the higher priority. Using a technique known as cost-benefit analysis, it should be possible to make a good estimate of how much crime is reduced per dollar when the dollar is spent, for example, on a certain probation project, and compare it with crime reduction per dollar spent on patrol cars. Within a given police department, the chief will be better able to judge which of the many possible ways of spending the budget has the most crime-reducing potential. Money can be allocated rationally rather than by hunch and political influence.

SHORT-RANGE BENEFITS OF THE SYSTEMS APPROACH

Despite its many benefits, a systems approach to the whole criminal justice system, the approach discussed so far, is not just around the corner. There is simply not enough information about how the present system operates. The accurate measure of crime that the system so desperately needs will take years to develop. Until this is perfected, it will be extremely difficult to develop performance indicators that can determine what is working well and what is not. Without information about what the system is actually doing, a full-scale systems approach is not possible.

Luckily, however, some of the benefits of the systems approach are available, right now, not just in the far future when the information necessary to analyze the whole system will be available.

CONCENTRATING ON GOALS

Even a small-scale and tentative attempt to examine the criminal justice system in terms of the systems approach forces criminal justice officials to concentrate on goals. Criminal justice officials, whether police officers, judges, or correctional officers, are busy people. They are fully occupied with day-to-day problems and have little time or en-

ergy for reflecting on the big picture, on what it is they are trying to do. They must, however, reflect on this. If we forget what we are trying to do, if we do not think about our goals hard enough to express them in useful terms, we will not be able to improve our operations significantly or cope with the changes the future will bring. The very first step in a systems approach forces the people working within the system to tell the systems analysts exactly what the system is trying to accomplish. Experts in systems analysis are not experts in criminal justice, and they must rely on the people in the system to explain goals and objectives. If this does nothing more than force criminal justice officials to examine their goals, it will have made a significant contribution to the system of the future.

USING A SYSTEMS APPROACH TO CRIMINAL JUSTICE SUBSYSTEMS

Although a systems approach to the entire criminal justice process is now impossible because of the lack of the necessary factual information, an analysis of smaller and less complicated subsystems will be possible in the immediate future. Systems principles and techniques can be applied, for example, to scheduling cases for a single criminal court, or to the improvement of dispatching procedures for a police department. The use of the systems approach in analyzing subsystems has already led to some surprising and useful conclusions. For example, a great deal of research has been done on ways to decrease response time, that is, the amount of time from the police receipt of a call for assistance to the arrival of a squad car. Earlier research has simply assumed that decreased response time would result in more arrests and better public service. A study in Kansas City using the systems approach, however, determined that police response time was not as important as had been assumed.[7] By examining the whole system involved in reporting and responding to a crime, rather than just the police response, the researchers discovered that citizens typically delayed calling for police assistance for so long that knocking a few seconds off response time would rarely make much difference in performance. Since in most departments decreasing response time by even a few seconds would require large expenditures, the significance of a systems approach to the study of the problem should be apparent.

The benefits of systems analysis of small systems is not limited to police work. A number of court systems are already using the systems approach to deal with their growing case loads. In addition, software packages consisting of computer programs designed for the legal profession are being developed. For example, PROMIS is a software package that can serve as a management system for a prosecutor's office, and Lexis and Westlaw allow for computer-assisted searches of the rapidly growing body of law.

The systems approach is perhaps not as extensively used in corrections as in the other two parts of the system. However, it is easy to imagine an example of how useful such an application could be. In our correctional subsystem example, consideration will be given to correctional *inputs, outputs,* and *feedback.* Inputs are those things that move into a system, outputs are those things that move out of a system, and feedback is information about the outputs reported back to the system.[8]

Inputs There are a number of inputs into a correctional system that can affect the system. These include money, employees, materials, and inmates. Inmates are one of the more important inputs. For example, if

court systems continue to divert the less dangerous offenders to community programs, inmates in institutions can be expected to be more dangerous. Consequently, greater security and control of inmates in institutions may be necessary. Every input into the system must be taken into consideration in the day-to-day operation of the correctional system.

Outputs As with inputs, the inmate is one of the more important outputs of the correctional system. Theoretically, the correctional institution must rehabilitate the inmate while he or she is in the correctional system. The criminal offender is supposed to be rehabilitated when he or she leaves the correctional system, although this is often not the case. It becomes the correctional system's responsibility to effect a change in the inmate from input to output. Therefore, it becomes necessary to measure the inmate as an input and as an output, to ascertain whether some change in the direction of socially acceptable behavior has occurred. If not, we may consider our correctional institution a failure in some respects.

Feedback Once the inmate has left the institution, the real test of its effectiveness begins. If the ex-inmate reverts to criminal behavior, then in some respects our correctional institution has failed. If not, then perhaps our correctional institution has succeeded. The correctional system must know (have feedback information) where it failed or succeeded, and why. If authorities at the correctional institution do not have this information, they cannot possibly know what programs affect the success or failure of ex-inmates.

This brief exercise in "systems thinking" illustrates the utility of the systems approach as applied to a criminal justice subsystem.

LIMITATIONS OF
THE SYSTEMS APPROACH

The lack of concrete information on the criminal justice process has already been mentioned as a limitation of the use of the systems approach. This limitation is quite obvious, but it is likely to be overcome as more research is done on criminal justice. There are two other limitations, however, that are much more serious precisely because they are much less obvious and therefore much more likely to be overlooked.

OMITTING IMPORTANT GOALS
OF THE SYSTEM

Determining the goals of the criminal justice system or of its subsystems — the police, courts, or corrections — is not an easy task. Some goals, such as reducing crime, are obvious, but others are not and still others are a matter of dispute. For example, justice is surely a goal of the system, but it is hard to define, difficult to measure, and easy to omit. A further difficulty is that, although the systems model itself is rigidly scientific and objective, goals are determined by value judgments and therefore are subject to error. The assumption that the criminal justice system should reduce crime is a value judgment. The assumption that the system should preserve the rights of the people it handles is also a value judgment, but our system of criminal justice would be far different if it did not include the preservation of individual rights among its goals. Systems analysis is particularly susceptible to this mistake of ignoring important goals because it is so much easier to analyze systems that have only one major objective. This problem is not completely soluble, for systems analysis, by its very nature, must ignore some aspects of the system it is studying. Systems analysis, like the scientific method

itself, must simplify complex reality in order to deal with it.

Perhaps the best rule of thumb for dealing with this limitation is to be very suspicious of any attempt to measure a complex criminal justice function with a single measuring instrument or to proclaim that one particular goal, whatever it may be, is *the* objective of the criminal justice system or *the* objective of the police, the courts, or corrections. The criminal justice system is an extremely complex set of relationships between people and institutions; concentrating on any one objective or trying to measure complex performance with a single measuring instrument can only distort the results.

ASSUMING THAT ONLY THE SYSTEM
CAN BE CHANGED

The other limitation of a systems approach is perhaps even more serious. It is easy to fall into the trap of assuming that only the system can be changed, and all other factors outside the particular system being studied must remain constant.[9] This mistake is particularly easy to make because preoccupation with what is necessary in order to introduce a systems approach makes it all too easy to ignore factors outside the system. For example, a medical systems analysis would analyze a bullet entering a soldier's body as a disruptive outside influence, one that must be handled with whatever success is possible within the system. This is a logical approach, and whatever success in coping with a bullet might well be enhanced by a systematic approach to medicine. However, there might be far better solutions involving changes outside the system that no one who was preoccupied with the system itself would consider. In this case, a change might be made in military tactics to prevent bullets from entering so many soldiers' bodies; a yet broader viewpoint might suggest the desirability of ending the war. This is not to argue that the systematic medical viewpoint is not of value in such a case; given certain assumptions as to the desirability of a particular military tactic and the necessity of a particular war, the medical approach may be the only one possible. The danger is that these broader assumptions may no longer be questioned.

The present criminal justice system is already preoccupied with itself; officials already tend to confine their thinking to improving the system and ignore factors outside of it. The criminal justice system of the future, influenced as it will be by the systems approach, may well go even further in this direction and assume that factors outside the system are given and therefore cannot be changed. To be sure, given the present criminal law, given an economic structure in which a sizable minority of the population lives in poverty while surrounded by luxury, given a value structure that emphasizes competitiveness and material possessions, the question of how the criminal justice system can be made to work better to reduce crime may sound logical. However, the criminal justice system is a subsystem of a much larger and more important system: society. Concentrating on reducing crime by improving the criminal justice system and ignoring other social institutions and processes may well be to make exactly the same mistake made by concentrating on the police, or the courts, or corrections and ignoring the rest of the criminal justice system. Emphasis on the criminal justice system alone may be valuable for certain purposes; in the long run, however, it may be counterproductive.

DISCUSSION QUESTIONS

1. What is a system? Does systems analysis offer any hope for the criminal justice system? Why?
2. Is the criminal justice system a system or a nonsystem?
3. Discuss the possible contributions of the systems approach to improving police efficiency.
4. Draw up a set of goals for the local police department. How would you measure the attainment of these goals?

NOTES

1. Herman Goldstein, "Trial Judges and the Police," *Crime and Delinquency*, 24 (January 1968), 14.
2. Stephen Gettinger, "Cruel and Unusual Prisons," *Corrections Magazine*, 3-4 (December 1977), 3-16.
3. Richard J. Hopeman, *Systems Analysis and Operations Management* (Columbus: Charles E. Merrill, 1969), 65-76.
4. Hopeman, *Systems Analysis*, p. 74.
5. President's Commission on Law Enforcement and Administration of Justice, *Task Force Report: Assessment of Crime* (Washington, D.C.: Government Printing Office, 1967), pp. 17-19.
6. Thorsten Sellin and Marvin Wolfgang, *The Measurement of Delinquency* (New York: John Wiley, 1974).
7. George L. Kelling et al., *Patrol Experiment: A Summary Report and a Technical Report* (Washington, D.C.: The Police Foundation, 1974).
8. Ronald J. Waldron, "A Systems Approach to Corrections," *Federal Probation*, March 1974, pp. 51-54.
9. Robert Boguslaw, *The New Utopians: A Study of Systems Design and Social Change* (Englewood Cliffs, N.J.: Prentice-Hall, Inc., 1965).

CHAPTER TWENTY-FIVE

THE IMPACT
OF SCIENCE
AND TECHNOLOGY

TECHNOLOGY IN THE LABORATORY

TECHNOLOGY IN THE FIELD

ELECTRONIC DATA PROCESSING

OTHER TECHNOLOGICAL ADVANCES

EFFECT OF THE BEHAVIORAL SCIENCES ON CRIMINAL JUSTICE

SCIENCE AND THE SHAPE OF THINGS TO COME

Purpose: To provide an analysis of the possible contributions of science and technology to the criminal justice system of the future.

THERE CAN BE little doubt that the criminal justice system of the future will be tremendously affected by the application of scientific and technological advances to the problem of crime. Much of the scientific brainpower and resources that went into the space program and the development of military hardware have been focused on the criminal justice system. The results of this application of science and technology have already been felt; the outlook for the future is even more promising.

TECHNOLOGY IN THE LABORATORY

The oldest, and still the most common, application of science to crime is in the area of the crime laboratory and its use in solving individual crimes. The capabilities of today's police laboratory are tremendous.[1] By analyzing a single hair, the criminalist working in the laboratory can determine whether it is animal or human, from what part of the body it was taken, whether or not it fell out naturally or was forcibly removed, and other information useful in investigations. Fibers from clothing can be analyzed to determine from what material they came. A blood spot can be analyzed to determine its type and age, the height from which the drop fell and its direction of travel, and sometimes even the part of the body from which the blood came. Recent research has even made it possible to determine the race and sex of an individual from a single dried bloodstain. The use of fingerprints to identify individuals is well known. Impressive as the crime lab of today may be, it has its limitations, which are gradually being overcome by advances in physics, chemistry, biology, and computer technology.

FINGERPRINTING

Movies, television, and detective novels have immortalized the use of fingerprints in criminal investigations. In a typical plot, the alert investigator finds a single fingerprint at the scene of the crime. By comparing the print with the FBI files or the files of the local police department, the hero is able to identify the culprit and justice is triumphant.

In real life, unfortunately, it does not work that way. True enough, if the police have a suspect in mind, a single print or even a partial print is sufficient for identification, but the absence of a particular suspect makes the police task quite different. The FBI maintains more than 200 million identification and fingerprint files, but the system presently used for classification is based on the prints of all ten fingers. Searching through the millions of files for a match-up with a crime-scene fingerprint is a mind-boggling task. Individual police departments maintain single-fingerprint files, but until very recently these files had to be searched manually, a task so difficult and time-consuming that single-fingerprint files are limited to a few thousand prints at most. Therefore, a latent print left at the crime scene was of little value to police other than as additional evidence if the criminal was caught by other means.

All this is changing with the use of automated fingerprint identification systems. The heart of these systems is a computer that searches fingerprint files automatically and compares single prints in the files with latent prints. Since this search is done automatically, the prints of far more individuals can be stored in the computer's memory. The system now used in Houston, for example, can compare a latent print with the fingerprints of 350,000 individuals.

VOICEPRINTING

Fingerprint-retrieval systems will not be the only contribution of technology to criminal identification. Another system now in use is the technique called *voiceprinting*,[2] based on the principle that each person's voice, as well as his or her fingerprints, is unique (Figure 25.1). When the sound waves produced by human speech are fed into the voiceprinting machine, they are transformed into voice spectrograms or prints. The print of even a single word is sufficient to identify the speaker with a high degree of accuracy, despite attempts to disguise the voice by whispering, talking through a handkerchief, and so on. The value of such a technique is considerable in crimes involving the telephone, such as bomb threats and obscene phone calls.

Voiceprints are well on their way to becoming accepted as scientific evidence in courts, giving the criminal justice system of the future another useful technological tool.

FIGURE 25.1 VOICE SPECTROGRAPH

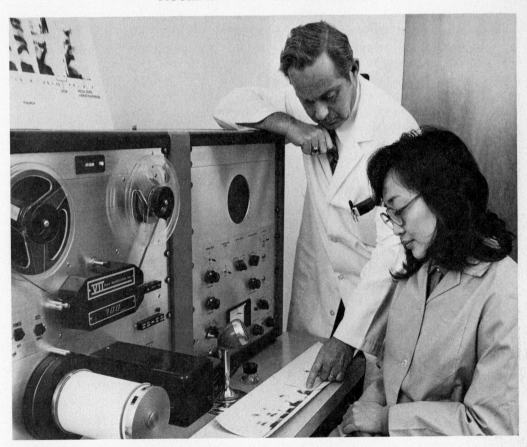

A Voice Spectrograph supplies voiceprints that identify characteristics of an individual's voice patterns.
SOURCE: Courtesy of Los Angeles Police Department.

ANALYZING PHYSICAL TRACES

The analysis of very small amounts of material left at a crime scene can be very useful to police. The criminalist of the future will have sophisticated tools to help in this analysis of physical traces: neutron activation analysis, electron microscopes, and other marvels of science.

Without using recently developed techniques, it is not possible for the criminalist to state that a certain hair or group of hairs is from a particular person. Nor is it possible to determine whether or not a given spot of blood is from a particular individual, even if the blood can be typed, which dried blood usually cannot be. A ballistics expert can determine that a bullet was fired by a given gun only when the bullet is fairly intact. Neuron activation analysis may well be able to make all these determinations, and more.[3]

Neutron activation analysis is based on the fact that many chemical elements not radioactive in their natural state can be made radioactive by bombarding them with neutrons. These elements then give off distinctive radiation, which can be analyzed to determine the type and amount of the elements present in an object, even when a particular element is present in such a small quantity that it cannot be detected by any other method.

Once the physical evidence found at the scene of the crime is analyzed by neutron activation, the results can be compared with an analysis of the hair, clothing, weapon, or blood of the suspect. Comparisons can be made that could not even be attempted without neutron activation analysis.

Another aid in trace identification is the use of *scanning electron microscopes,* instruments so advanced that they can magnify up to 100,000 times. When equipped with energy-dispersive x-ray apparatus, they can not only locate extremely small physical traces such as gunpowder residue, but also determine exactly what chemical elements and how much of each are present. Similarly, a gas chromatograph–mass spectrometer, using a different process, can separate and identify the components of a mixture in quantities so minute as to almost stagger the imagination. The one in use at the F B I laboratory can analyze 0.000000000001 gram of liquid.

TECHNOLOGY IN THE FIELD

Technological advances will not be limited to the crime laboratory. Right now, many police departments are benefiting from the use of space-age technology in patrol work.

COMMUNICATIONS

Effective radio communications are important to police; they enhance both the effectiveness and the safety of officers. The two-way car radio has been a fixture of police work for nearly half a century, but the car radio does the officer little good when he or she is out of the car. Lightweight but powerful radios have been developed that are so small that an officer can carry one on the belt; OJARS funding has spread these hand-held radios to departments across the nation. In the future, nearly all police departments will be equipped with these devices.

A second communication problem results from the fragmentation of law enforcement into many small departments. The number of radio channels is strictly limited. If there are many departments in a small area, some must share a single channel. The resulting confusion and interference is easy to imagine. In addition, some departments cannot communicate with other departments in their immediate area, a situation that makes coordination in tactical situations difficult.

THE FUTURE OF THE CRIMINAL JUSTICE SYSTEM

These problems are rapidly being alleviated by *regional police communications systems,* which take a systems approach to the communication needs of a whole region instead of a single department. A typical regional communication system will include a number of local boosters together with a signal selection and switching capacity to allow multiple use of channels without interference. Technology, therefore, provides the best of both worlds: neighboring departments can communicate when they wish but otherwise do not interfere with each other. In addition, some regional systems include a frequency switching apparatus that alternates between channels during the conversation, making it very difficult for outsiders to monitor calls.[4]

COMPUTERS

The computer too will be used to increase the effectiveness of patrol. A growing number of departments are installing computer terminals in squad cars. For example, the system used in Palm Beach County, Florida, consists of a computer terminal, which looks like a typewriter keyboard, connected to a radio transmitter inside the car.[5] This squad-car terminal can communicate directly with the computer at headquarters and through it with the computers at the Florida Crime Information Center and the National Crime Information Center. Using the computer instead of voice radio communications cuts the transmission time for a dispatch signal from one minute to less than a second. In addition, the message remains on the display screen in the car as long as necessary and cannot be intercepted by criminal elements. Since the terminal in the squad car can communicate directly with computers without human intermediaries, the time required to search the records for stolen car license numbers, for example, is cut from three minutes to less

than six seconds. In addition to these advantages, the system used in Oakland, California, includes an electronic map of the city mounted inside the squad car and connected electronically with a larger map at headquarters. By touching a finger to the spot on the map where the car is located, the patrol officer can notify the dispatcher's office of his or her exact location and so can keep the map at headquarters up to date.

ELECTRONIC DATA PROCESSING

The use of computers in solving criminal justice problems goes far beyond installing terminals in squad cars. One of the most pressing needs of the people in the criminal justice system is information. The police need to know whether or not the man they have stopped for a routine traffic violation is wanted in another state on a felony charge. Judges need to know a suspect's criminal record in order to make decisions involving bail and sentencing. Court administrators need to know at exactly what point the flow of offenders through the judicial system is bogging down. Correctional officials need to know everything possible not only about the individuals they are trying to correct, but also about successful and not so successful correctional programs used in other jurisdictions. Most of this information is recorded somewhere in the criminal justice system, but the problem of getting it to the decision makers quickly remains. The solution to this problem is within the capabilities of present technology, and efforts are already being made in this direction.

A good small-scale example of the use of computers in data retrieval and analysis is the PATRIC system in use in Los Angeles. The Los Angeles police, like any major police department, have a tremendous amount of data available in their standardized police reports. Unfortunately, quantity itself has made the task of manually going through reports to determine patterns of crime and the methods of operation of individual criminals all but impossible, so the information is less than helpful. In a small department, a police officer can keep much of this information in his or her head, using it to determine who is likely to have committed a particular crime and where a criminal is likely to strike next. In a city the size of Los Angeles, of course, no officer can possibly remember all the important facts. The computer can. The PATRIC computer contains data from standardized reports from all over the city. Officers can query the computer not only about specific facts, such as the description of a suspect or the license number of a stolen car, but also about patterns of criminal activity.

On a much larger scale, the FBI's National Crime Information Center (NCIC) has been in operation since early 1967. Tied in with computers in each of the states and in some of the larger local law enforcement agencies, NCIC's computer is a national repository of information on stolen cars, weapons, securities, and other property, as well as on wanted persons. Through local or state computers, police can check on stolen property or fugitives from anywhere in the United States. In addition, the FBI has computerized a master file of over 25 million criminal case histories, sometimes known as *rap sheets*. These criminal histories are available to federal, state, and local criminal justice agencies that need the information to help make decisions on parole, bail, arrest, and other important matters.

All the information in the FBI data files is available almost instantaneously to a criminal justice agency with access to a state or local computer system that can interface with NCIC. More and more agencies have access to such a computer. Once in the system, through a process called *message switching,* local computers could easily exchange information with all computers in the network. At present, not all state and local computers are part of the network, and message switching has encountered resistance from individuals and groups concerned that message switching is a giant step toward a nationwide data bank.

A nationwide data bank would not be technologically difficult. It has been estimated that a 2,000-page dossier on every man, woman, and child in the nation could be coded and stored in a ten-by-twelve-foot room, with any given dossier available in five minutes.[6] In addition, there is no technological reason why such information must be limited to criminal histories. Other government agencies have computerized information on military records, school files, credit, income tax forms, bank records, and so on; it would not be difficult to interface computers and have all this information and more available merely by entering a social security number into a computer. In fact, such an interface of all federal government computers, to be called FEDNET, has been proposed by the federal government's General Services Administration. While some experts, such as the National Advisory Commission on Criminal Justice Standards and Goals, are strongly in favor of a nationwide criminal justice data bank (see their proposal for a National Criminal Justice Information Center in Figure 25.2), other experts point to the possible abuses of such a system. Indeed, a number of abuses of criminal case history files have already occurred.

Any limitations on the use of computer technology will come from political, not technological sources. For example, Congress refused to consider FEDNET because

FIGURE 25.2 NATIONAL CRIMINAL JUSTICE INFORMATION SYSTEM

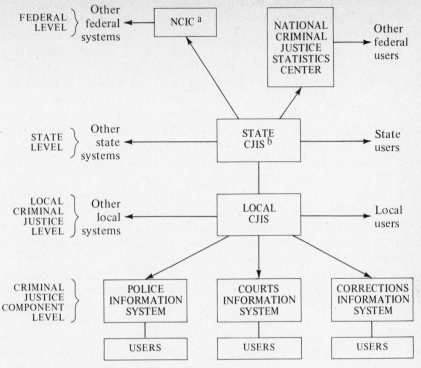

a NCIC = National Crime Information Center
b CJIS = Criminal Justice Information System

SOURCE: National Advisory Commission on Criminal Justice Standards and Goals, *Criminal Justice System* (Washington, D.C.: Government Printing Office, 1973), p. 42.

of the massive invasion of individual privacy that would be an inevitable consequence of such a data bank. The danger is very real: the more technology is used to aid criminal justice in the fight against crime, the more dangers it poses to the rights of citizens. A balance must be struck between the rights of the individual and the effectiveness of criminal justice agencies. In our society, it is the political process that strikes this balance, so the future of computer and other physical science technology in the criminal justice system depends on decisions made in Congress, the state legislatures, and the courts.

OTHER TECHNOLOGICAL ADVANCES

Speculation on other technological inventions that may be available to the police of the future runs the risk of making this text sound like science fiction. Some of the more esoteric electronic devices developed for the Vietnam war are being adapted for police purposes. Although some are secret, a glance at a catalogue of any of the many firms catering to police shows such electronic marvels as viewers that enable the police to see in the dark and surveillance systems that can put large areas of a city under constant police scrutiny. A number of firms are trying to develop useful nonlethal weapons to bridge the gap between the officer's nightstick and handgun. Among the nonlethal weapons proposed are wire guns that release coiled barbed wire, and drugs that rapidly immobilize the victim.

Although by far the greatest amount of federal money for technological improvements has gone to the police, we may also expect other parts of the criminal justice system to profit from technology. For example, courts would benefit from automatic transcription devices for courtroom testimony, and automatic perimeter surveillance systems for prisons are now being installed. These devices sound tame compared with the technological wonderland the police seem to be entering, but they should be useful.

EFFECT OF THE BEHAVIORAL SCIENCES ON CRIMINAL JUSTICE

The impact of the physical sciences and the associated technology on the criminal justice system of the future, though considerable, may well be less than the impact of the social and behavioral sciences. Although criminology or criminal justice is rapidly becoming a scientific discipline in its own right, knowledge and procedures discovered by other behavioral sciences will also be applied to the problems of criminal justice. There is a great deal of overlap in the subject area of the behavioral sciences, but their possible contributions can be more or less arbitrarily divided into seven areas.

BUSINESS ADMINISTRATION

To a great extent, the process of running a police department, a prison, or a parole office is similar to the process of running a business. Personnel must be selected, trained, and paid; supplies and equipment must be ordered; accurate financial records must be kept; and the various activities of many individuals must be managed so that the overall purposes of the organization are accomplished. Insofar as the problems of business and criminal justice agencies are similar, the wealth of information discovered by scholars in the field of business administration can be applied to criminal justice.

This application of the principles of business administration to the problems of criminal justice is already under way. Police chiefs, prison wardens, and court administrators throughout the country are attempting to apply solutions that have worked in industry to the management and administrative situations they encounter. As the educational level of administrators in criminal justice increases, and as more and more criminal justice practitioners are exposed to formal and informal courses in business management, the influence of this discipline will increase.

PUBLIC ADMINISTRATION

Although the administration of a criminal justice agency and of a business are similar in many respects, there are differences caused by the fact that criminal justice agencies are governmental organizations. One of the most important differences is in goals: the major goal of a business organization is to increase profit, whereas the goals of a governmental organization are more complicated and more difficult to measure. If X Corporation doubles its profits under a new set of managers, the new people may justifiably pat themselves on the back. The warden of a prison, a judge, or a police chief has no objective as easily defined and easily measured as profit. In the absence of a well-defined objective, it may be next to impossible to determine whether a criminal justice administrator is doing a good job or not. Another practical difference is that the duties and the areas of discretion of a criminal justice administrator are much more clearly defined by law than are those of a business executive. The management of a company can purchase supplies under any system that appeals to them and may hire and fire personnel with little regard for legal restrictions. The criminal justice administrator, on the other hand, must contend with rigidly specified laws and regulations on such matters as purchases, and civil service regulations usually limit discretion in personnel actions.

Since there are real and important differences between business administration and the administration of a government agency, a separate discipline called *public administration* has become more important. Public administration, as its name implies, is concerned with the problems inherent in the administration of governmental organizations. Because public administration is a much younger field of study than business administration, its contributions to the criminal justice system probably have not been as great. However, because public administration addresses itself to exactly those problems faced by criminal justice administrators, and because criminal justice administrators are showing a real interest in the work of public administration scholars, its future contributions are assured.

INDUSTRIAL PSYCHOLOGY

Industrial psychology is the application of principles of psychology to such problems as the selection, placing, and training of employees, worker efficiency, organizational management, and consumer behavior. Al-though the purchasing behavior of consumers is of little concern to the criminal justice system, the other areas certainly are. The problem of selecting from a group of applicants those who will best fulfill job requirements is in principle the same problem whether the hiring agency is a police selection board or the personnel department of a large industry. There is no reason to think that the psychological principles underlying worker efficiency and job satisfaction in factories do not apply to prisons. Unfortunately, there has been little collaboration between industrial psychology and the criminal justice system. Whether such collaboration will benefit criminal justice is a question for the future to answer.

EXPERIMENTAL PSYCHOLOGY

Experimental psychology is the scientific study of such processes as motivation, perception, and learning. Since individuals involved in the criminal justice system learn, perceive, and are presumably motivated in one way or another, it is reasonable to assume that experimental psychology may well be applicable to the problems of criminal justice. There is some evidence for this. For example, psychologists interested in basic research on perception are now studying the problem of eyewitness testimony in criminal cases. It has long been realized that eyewitness testimony is less than reliable, but police and others have had no information on exactly what variables influence its reliability and how these variables operate. Present research indicates that many of the same variables that influence perception in the laboratory — the significance of the event, the length of observation, the method of questioning, and so on — also influence testimony in criminal cases.[7] When this information is put into a form that police and court officials can use, it may well change the criminal trial of the future drastically.

COUNSELING

Counseling is an attempt to use expert advice and guidance to improve a person's behavior. For a long time psychologists, psychiatrists, social workers, and other behavioral science professionals have tried to change behavior by listening and talking to clients or patients. The use of counseling in criminal justice has a long history, particularly in the field of corrections. Unfortunately, because of the small number of trained counselors and the large number of inmates, probationers, and parolees, traditional counseling methods are not adequate for the task. One attempt to overcome this problem is group counseling, in which the counselor's expertise is available to more than one person at a time.

Perhaps the most promising approach, however, is based on the growing realization that individuals can provide effective counseling without long professional training in the field. Several programs have been initiated that use lay people to aid correctional officials in probation and parole projects. For example, a recent pilot project in Salt Lake City has shown that volunteer helpers can get better results than professional probation officers with some types of probationers. Other studies indicate that under the supervision of trained professionals, homemakers, business people, and other interested members of the community can play an important role in counseling offenders.

In addition, there are indications that the police too have a role in counseling. Police officers have, in fact, long served as informal counselors, since the police are often the first public agency notified when people are in trouble. Today, however, most police officers receive little or no training for this role, and many officers dislike and resent the necessity of intervening in emotionally charged conflict situations like disputes between husband and wife. This resentment is justified: family disturbance calls are a major cause of injuries and fatalities among police. The New York City Police Department has experimented with training officers in counseling and the other behavioral sciences in order to give them the tools they need to handle family crises. In the original study, eighteen officers received an intensive on-campus training course in the application of behavioral sciences to intervention in marital disputes. This initial training was supplemented by a continuing program of consultation with behavioral science experts. These officers returned to their regular patrol function, with the additional duty of handling all family disturbance calls in their precinct. It was determined that the Family Crisis Intervention Unit, as the group was called, was effective in reducing homicides and assaults in the families with which they dealt, as well as preventing injuries to the officers themselves.[8] The New York police feel that the program was of such value that they now include the principles of family crisis intervention in the training program for all officers.

Expanding upon the approach pioneered in New York City, a growing number of police departments are training patrol officers in methods of handling family disputes and other disturbance calls. This long-neglected area of police work, generally called *conflict management,* is now receiving much scholarly as well as police attention. If police and behavioral scientists working together can develop effective strategies for handling disputes between citizens, they may make the most significant contribution of the behavioral sciences to police work.

SOCIOLOGY

Sociology has undoubtedly been the behavioral science most often applied to the crime problem. In the United States, in fact, criminology and juvenile delinquency courses have traditionally been located in university departments of sociology, and much of the information we now have on crime, criminals, and the operation of the criminal justice system has come from the work of sociologists.

Sociology can be expected to contribute to the criminal justice system in at least two areas. The first is the accurate description of exactly what goes on in the criminal justice process. Trained sociological observers will be able to give us a more accurate picture of what really happens in prisons, in police departments, and in the courts. A second contribution will be more precise knowledge about the factors that lead to criminal behavior. Although from past studies sociologists have some familiarity with the effects of poverty, education, housing, family structure, and similar variables on crime, there is. a need to know much more so that the criminal justice system of the future can prevent as well as treat criminal behavior.

PROBABILITY AND STATISTICS

Statistical techniques have long been used in criminal justice to describe data, as in the FBI's *Uniform Crime Reports* describing crime rates and trends. Statistical procedures, however, can help decision making in some situations. Often decisions in criminal justice must be based on an estimation of probable future behavior. In deciding on probation or parole, in determining the type of treatment program best suited to a given offender, in the use of police patrol to deter specific crimes, criminal justice officials must make decisions based on probabilities, not certainties. Usually these decisions are the personal judgments of officials, for example, a parole board will grant or withhold a parole on the basis of an interview with the inmate, or a judge will assign an offender to a certain correctional program on the basis of a "rule of thumb" evolved from personal experience or the experience of other judges. With the proper use of statistical decision-making techniques, however, the process used to arrive at decisions can be formalized, tested, and improved. These statistical techniques can help officials make decisions or, in effect, make the decisions for the officials, as in the use of a parole prediction table to decide whether or not a person should be paroled. Once experimentation has produced reliable statistical decision-making strategies, the data deemed relevant could be fed into a computer to produce decisions without human intervention, eliminating the need for parole boards, judges, and even juries. The extent to which statistical decision making will replace or supplement human decision making in the criminal justice system of the future is not clear; it seems likely that human reluctance to entrust life-and-death decisions to anything but another human may mean that this tool will not be used to its full capacity.

SCIENCE AND THE SHAPE OF THINGS TO COME

Unquestionably the application of science to the problems of criminal justice will make the criminal justice system of the future different from the system of today. This chapter has barely touched on the possible applications of the methods of science to the crime problem. Tomorrow the system may "correct" criminals not by throwing them in prison, but by subjecting them to a brain operation that makes further criminal behavior impossible. Police patrol may decline in importance as a result of technological improvements that allow the police to maintain surveillance of all citizens all the time. These things may not come about, of course, but it would be foolish to bet against them. The history of science has shown that once knowledge makes a new technology possible, that new technology is almost invariably developed. No one has yet said no to a major advance in science, regardless of the possible cost. The hydrogen bomb stands as testimony to the fact that the products of science are ethically neutral: they can be used for good or evil.

It is not difficult to imagine a future in which the criminal justice system, with the help of science, will have succeeded in controlling crime.[9] It is easy to imagine every citizen carrying his or her own police alarm system or a weapon that will immobilize but not harm a potential attacker. It is easy to imagine our police equipped with weapons that can stun or kill an offender; mobile computer terminals that fit into the police officer's pocket; uniforms that are lightweight yet completely bulletproof; electronic "sniffers" that can place a suspect at the scene of a crime or identify contraband drugs; electronic devices that make the telling of a lie virtually impossible; electronic equipment that can monitor the conversation and movement of persons without their knowledge; and police vehicles that can traverse all terrains and carry a sophisticated array of weapons and scientific crime-detection equipment. It is easy to imagine our courts with computers that scientifically select the jurors; recording instruments that transcribe the trial; lie detectors that monitor for perjury during the trial; juries composed not of people but of computers; sentence lengths determined by a computer; or computers that can sustain or overrule an objection through an instant analysis of the law. It is easy to imagine a corrections system where drugs are the major rehabilitative program; where aversion therapy alters criminal behavior; where architects using modern materials build jails and prisons that look like college campuses yet are more secure than present prisons. It is easy to imagine a probation and parole system that can select an offender for probation or parole on the basis of a computer's statistical prediction of success, or in an instant electronically locate all its charges at any time of the day or night. All of these things are within our grasp if this is what we desire.

George Orwell's *1984* is a picture of a society in which crime is all but impossible because freedom is all but unknown. Perhaps the best defense against such a future is a commitment to the second word in the much used phrase "criminal *justice* system."

DISCUSSION QUESTIONS

1. What are some possible future developments in criminalistics?
2. Can science deprive us of our freedoms?
3. Can we have a "1984" in the criminal justice system?
4. How will advances in science and technology affect the police of the future? The courts? Corrections?
5. Discuss the limitations of computer technology and electronic data processing in reducing crime.
6. What recent scientific developments can you think of that may apply to criminal justice?

7. Some states have passed legislation limiting the use of radar, polygraphs, and electronic bugging devices. What does this portend for the future?
8. If science is ethically neutral, how can society protect itself from the misuse of science?

NOTES

1. Richard O. Arther, *The Scientific Investigator* (Springfield, Ill.: Charles C Thomas, 1965), pp. 14–58.
2. William W. Turner, *Invisible Witness* (Indianapolis: Bobbs-Merrill, 1968), pp. 1–29.
3. Jurgen Thorwald, *Crime and Science: The New Frontier in Criminology* (New York: Harcourt, Brace and World, 1967), pp. 417–463.
4. *Target,* 6 (July/August 1977), 1.
5. *Crime Control Digest,* 6 (July 14, 1972), 6–7.
6. Turner, *Invisible Witness,* p. 268.
7. *Behavior Today,* 3 (June 5, 1972), 2.
8. United States Department of Justice, Law Enforcement Assistance Administration, National Institute of Law Enforcement and Criminal Justice, *Training Police as Specialists in Family Crisis Intervention* (Washington, D.C.: Government Printing Office, 1970), pp. 23–33.
9. John R. Altemose, "The Criminal Justice System of the Future," unpublished Ph.D. dissertation, Sam Houston State University, 1973.

CHAPTER TWENTY-SIX

REFORM

NATIONAL CRIME COMMISSION RECOMMENDATIONS FOR REFORM	RESEARCH PERSONNEL	FUNDING REFORM AND THE FUTURE

Purpose: To provide a view of the effects that needed reform would have on the criminal justice system of the future.

IN THE LAST analysis, the shape of the criminal justice system of the future depends on decisions being made today, decisions about what goals to pursue and what changes are most important. Few people involved in the system deny that changes are necessary, but there appears to be basic disagreement on the scope of the change required. On the one hand are those who maintain that reform of the present system is the hope of the future; on the other hand, some insist that more of the same is not enough and that the system must be drastically restructured if we are to achieve the objective of crime control within a free society. Let us examine the position of those who advocate reform within the present system.

NATIONAL CRIME COMMISSION RECOMMENDATIONS FOR REFORM

Reform is the position advocated by the majority, in the sense that most criminal justice practitioners agree with most of the reforms suggested. Perhaps the most comprehensive study of the position of reform was made by the President's Commission on Law Enforcement and the Administration of Justice (the National Crime Commission), which has been mentioned many times throughout this text. The commission presented more than two hundred specific recommendations for reform in its main report and nine task force reports, totaling more than two million words. In the years since, its recommendations have received intensive study and discussion by those interested in criminal justice. While it is doubtful that many students of criminal justice agree with all the commission's recommendations, it is safe to say that most experts agree with most of the recommendations; the commission

report has come to represent the conventional wisdom in the field of criminal justice.

Conventional wisdom holds that the criminal justice system should be revised as it stands, with many changes in procedure and a few in priority, but without any radical changes. Its answer to the crime problem is basically more of the same but better: more police, but more professional police; more courts, but more efficient courts; more corrections that actually correct. This goal is to be achieved through improvement in three broad areas: research, personnel, and funding.

RESEARCH

The commission report is insistent on the need for more research into all aspects of the criminal justice system. The commission members seemed surprised by how little is really known about crime and about the criminal justice system. They call again and again for more data, more knowledge, more information. Their concern is well placed. It is a truism that good people with good information tend to make good decisions, but this truism also reminds us that the best qualified police, judges, and correctional officials cannot perform their functions effectively without information, and that information can come only from research.

Police officials must know what makes a good police officer. They must know what qualities of mind, body, and character separate the good officer from the bad. They must learn how to select officers with the necessary qualifications and how to train them most effectively. They must know what the police should spend their time and effort doing and how to accomplish these tasks more effectively.

Court officials need the information necessary to apply a rapidly growing body of law to a rapidly growing case load. They need a better method of storing and retrieving case law, as well as methods to speed up trials and, more importantly, reduce the delay between arrest and trial. They need information on one of the court's most basic functions: separating the guilty from the innocent. How good a job is done now — how many innocent are convicted and how many guilty are acquitted? By what process is the decision on guilt or innocence made? How can this process be improved? The courts also need research data on another main function, sentencing. Are sentencing decisions really biased by such factors as race or social class? Is a flat sentence such as five years more or less effective in rehabilitation than an indeterminate sentence of one year to life? Who should receive what sentence?

Correctional officials need to know how effective a job correctional agencies are now doing. What programs or approaches increase the probability that an inmate will succeed after release? How is it possible to determine when a prisoner is ready to return to the free world?

These are not academic questions. Criminal justice officials need information of this type in order to make rational and just decisions. All these questions are matters of fact and could be answered by research, but the research has not been done, and the answers are not available.

Indeed, the extent of our ignorance about basic and vital questions concerning the administration of criminal justice is difficult to believe. It is assumed, but it is not known, that more police mean less crime. It is assumed, but it is not known, that solving crime reduces the amount of future crime. It is not known whether probation and parole are effective either in reducing crime or in helping individuals. It is not known whether imprisoning offenders reduces or increases the amount of crime in society.

Imagine the outcry among stockholders if the Ford Motor Company were operating without any idea of what products were being manufactured and without a method of determining whether the company was showing a profit. Imagine taxpayer reaction if the Department of Defense operated with World War I equipment and without any idea of what planes, ships, and troops can or should do, or if NASA decided to send men to the moon without bothering to determine where the moon was located before the rocket was fired. Yet there is little outcry when every year the United States spends billions of dollars, arrests millions of people, and puts hundreds of thousands in prison or jail without the research needed to know what it is we are doing.

For years the Department of Defense allocated about 15 percent of its total budget for research. Research allocations in private industry, particularly in the progressive and competitive industries, have been of similar magnitude. And for years the criminal justice system has allocated, at most, a small fraction of 1 percent of its budget for research. The effects of these years of neglect will be difficult to overcome, but a start was made during the 1970s. Research funded by OJARS began to address some important problems. We have already mentioned some of the contributions of OJARS-funded research, such as the Kansas City study on response time. Other police-related research sponsored by OJARS has included a comprehensive study of the criminal investigation process, published by the Rand Corporation, the development of performance measures for police, and a handbook on police career development. OJARS has also sponsored research of interest to correctional officials, such as an empirically based set of guidelines for parole decisions, a handbook for performing evaluative research in corrections, and a national survey of women's correctional programs. Court-related research has included a study of performance measures suitable for court use, an examination of alternatives to criminal prosecution, and a handbook on the most effective methods of handling jurors.[1]

In addition to the great volume of research funded by OJARS, extremely important studies have been performed by the Police Foundation, a private, nonprofit organization dedicated to the improvement of police work in America. The Police Foundation performed the landmark study on women patrol officers, a study that was instrumental to the acceptance of women on patrol.[2] A Police Foundation study in San Diego may have solved the long-debated question of one-person versus two-person patrol cars; it indicates that not only are one-person cars more cost-effective than two-person cars, they are actually safer.[3] Perhaps the most famous and far-reaching Police Foundation study, however, was the Kansas City Patrol Study, which found that routine preventive patrol in squad cars neither reduces crime nor makes the citizens feel safer.[4] The implications of this study for police work are enormous — so enormous that it may take years of further research to determine what police patrol *should* be doing.

Impressive as this type of research is, the student should not conclude that research alone, no matter how timely and well performed, can solve the many problems of the criminal justice system. Research is of little value unless its conclusions are put into practice. Often they are not. As the National Crime Commission mentions, "Many of the criminal justice system's difficulties stem from its reluctance to change old ways or, to put the same proposition in reverse, its

reluctance to try new ones."[5] This resistance to change, of course, is not limited to criminal justice institutions. Organizational resistance to change is in itself a field of behavioral science study, and one that might prove invaluable to the criminal justice system. However, as the National Crime Commission concludes, the single greatest need in the criminal justice system is the need to know.

PERSONNEL

If the greatest need is the need to know, the second greatest need of a reformed criminal justice system is personnel: more personnel, but especially better personnel. Although the effectiveness of the system is influenced by the level of technology and the equipment available, the most important aspect of the system is the people who work in it. The criminal justice system, both now and in the foreseeable future, is not highly automated; 80 to 90 percent of the total budget is spent on salaries. If the system is to be significantly improved, the people working in it must be significantly improved. There are two distinct but complementary approaches to improving criminal justice personnel. One method is to recruit and hire better people, and the second is to improve the capabilities of the people already there.

RECRUITING VERSUS WORKING CONDITIONS

Perhaps the first and most basic step in attracting qualified people to the criminal justice system is to improve working conditions. The whole system, from the precinct station to the parole office, is characterized by neglect, as reflected in the physical surroundings.[6] Police stations are typically old and run down. Lighting is poor, office equipment inadequate, secretarial help scarce or nonexistent. Courts, particularly the lower courts, are generally overcrowded and frequently squalid. The average municipal or county jail in this country is not a fit place to house stray dogs, let alone human beings.

The difficulty of working in dirty, overcrowded, and ill-designed surroundings is not improved by the salary level. Although many jurisdictions have significantly improved police salaries in recent years, police in many areas would be financially better off if they were to quit and take a job in the local factory. Many do. Prosecutors in many places are paid so little they must maintain a private law practice while attempting to fulfill the demands of their office. It is little wonder that the prosecutor's office is frequently looked upon as a place for young lawyers to get experience to qualify them for a good job. The pay of prison guards is typically so inadequate that attracting high-quality personnel is all but impossible.

Money, of course, is not everything. Many exceptionally capable people are working in the system despite the lack of financial rewards. And it is true that in most areas the pay in the criminal justice system is not as bad as it used to be. Nationwide figures indicate that salaries have increased faster than inflation. But there is a long way to go. It should not be too surprising that in the matter of criminal justice personnel, as in other areas, society gets what it is willing to pay for. To date, we have not been willing to pay for truly professional people.

Pay and physical surroundings are not the only aspects of working in criminal justice that tend to repel qualified people. Hours are long and frequently irregular. The work is often difficult and sometimes dangerous. Police officers, judges, and correctional workers are exposed, day after day, to the least attractive aspects of human behavior. They interact with people who are drunk, enraged, sick, and violent.

Despite their difficulty and importance, jobs in criminal justice are not afforded a high status among the general public. Many police officials are concerned with the low esteem in which police are held by many segments of the community. Nearly every police department in the nation that has tried to recruit qualified minority-group members has experienced grave difficulty. This should surprise no one, considering the reputation of the police in many minority areas. But the police are not the only part of the system with status problems. By and large, the most capable graduates of the best law schools avoid the criminal law.

In corrections few are proud of their positions as prison guards. If the criminal justice system of the future is to attract better-qualified personnel, all these aspects of the job must be improved. It will take time and money, and it will be difficult, but the future of justice in the United States depends upon it.

While working conditions are being improved, the most promising method of getting qualified personnel into the system is to recruit personnel from backgrounds traditionally ignored. Specifically, a reformed system will mount a campaign to recruit and use women, college graduates, and minority-group members.

RECRUITING WOMEN

Contrary to popular belief, women have been used as police officers throughout the twentieth century. However, until recently, women officers were largely limited to those jobs that were considered "women's work": juvenile officer, matron, sex crimes investigator. Despite considerable resistance within the police profession, during the 1970s women were used increasingly in all phases of police work, including patrol. Goaded by lawsuits and court orders, by the end of the decade most of the nation's major metropolitan departments had switched to a "unisex" personnel policy; in these departments the sex of the officer is no longer considered in job assignments. Despite the success of women on patrol in the major metropolitan areas and the research indicating that female patrol officers are as effective as males, most of the nation's police departments still do not use their women officers effectively, nor do they actively recruit more females.

Police work is not the only aspect of criminal justice in which women are underutilized. The proportion of women serving as prosecutors and judges is considerably lower than the proportion of female lawyers. Women in corrections are usually limited to working with other women and juveniles, although women correctional officers in men's prisons is no longer unknown. The resistance to the use of women in jobs traditionally limited to men is intense, particularly in the more rural and conservative parts of the country. Nevertheless, the emergence of women in traditionally male roles is a nationwide trend, a trend that all parts of the criminal justice system are finding increasingly difficult to resist.

RECRUITING COLLEGE GRADUATES

The difficulty experienced by the criminal justice system in interesting college graduates in police and prison work reflects more than the undesirable pay and working conditions. Traditionally, there has been only one place to start in a police department or in a prison system: at the bottom of the ladder. Nearly every police department in the country starts a new officer at the lowest rank, regardless of education or previous experience. In many departments, it is three, four, or even five years before an officer is even eligible for promotion. If Ford Motor Company started college graduates as assembly-line personnel, or the United States Army awarded the rank of private to West Point graduates, the consequent recruiting difficulty would surprise no one. It is not surprising that college graduates avoid jobs in the criminal justice system.

Putting qualified personnel directly into a supervisory position after a period of training is known among police as *lateral entry*. Lateral entry has been discussed for years, recommended by the National Crime Commission, and tried on a very limited basis. The people who now occupy supervisory positions in police departments have come up through the ranks, and most of them think that their successors should, too. Whether police departments and prisons will make more extensive use of lateral entry in the future depends on the willingness of present criminal justice officials to change.

RECRUITING MINORITIES

The third group now underrepresented in the criminal justice system is members of minority groups other than women. The lack of minority-group personnel may well be the most dangerous failing of the system's personnel selection. The police can get along without women in patrol cars; the police and corrections have been doing without college graduates for years; however, it is becoming more unlikely that a police force or a prison staff with a proportion of whites far in excess of that in the population served can do an effective job of serving all the people. To truly serve the community, the police must understand and be able to communicate with all sections of that community. A police force without the trust and respect of the people is quickly seen as an army of occupation, not a source of help. To expect a lily-white police force to effectively serve

THE FUTURE OF THE CRIMINAL JUSTICE SYSTEM

the minority community in times of increasing racial division is to expect the impossible.

The police departments of the United States are not generally lily-white, though some are nearly so. Few departments in the nation reflect the racial proportions of the people they serve, and no single major department comes close. The situation in corrections is, if anything, worse. At Attica State Penitentiary at the time of the 1972 tragedy, the inmates were 85 percent black and Puerto Rican, the correctional staff over 99 percent white.

Interesting minority-group members in jobs in criminal justice is not easy. Although many departments have attempted vigorous recruiting programs in minority neighborhoods, by and large these programs have not been totally successful. However, some progress in recruiting blacks and Hispanics has been made in the last decade. The bright spot in the picture is that most police departments and correctional agencies are aware of the need for minority personnel; in the future the criminal justice system will almost certainly be far less dominated by white males.

Recruiting better qualified personnel is only one part of the task of providing the system with effective workers. An equally important consideration for the criminal justice system of the future is upgrading the skills of the people already working. The two major tools for upgrading personnel are standards and education.

STANDARDS FOR RECRUITING

Standards can be either suggested or mandatory. A standard is suggested when a prestigious organization such as the American Correctional Association recommends that probation and parole officers have master's degrees. Suggested standards give local au-

thorities a goal toward which to work. A standard is mandatory when the organization announcing the standard has the authority to force compliance, as when a state law requires justices of the peace to be lawyers or when a state accreditation agency requires local police to have a specified number of hours of instruction before they can serve.

The criminal justice system does not lack sets of standards. Scores of different organizations have published hundreds of sets of standards in criminal justice matters. The American Correctional Association and the National Council on Crime and Delinquency have been active in setting standards. Unfortunately, most of the standards relate to only one aspect of the criminal justice process and make little or no attempt to view the system as a whole. A giant step toward creating a set of standards for the whole criminal justice system has been taken by the National Advisory Commission on Criminal Justice Standards and Goals (1973).[7] The commission used the systems approach, examining goals and objectives in detail before suggesting methods of accomplishing the goals. The result is a report of such scope and quality that, although many criminal justice professionals disagree violently with some of the suggested standards, the report (Figure 26.1) may well bring about needed change in the criminal justice system.

EDUCATION AND TRAINING

The second method of improving the skills of those already in the system is education and training. The police probably lead the other subsystems in the attempt to train their personnel. The time when a police officer was hired one day and put on the street the next is fast drawing to a close; almost all departments have at least some academy training for officers. Police are also coming

GOALS AND PRIORITIES

Goals for Crime Reduction

The Commission proposes as a goal for the American people a 50% reduction in high-fear crimes by 1983. It further proposes that crime reduction efforts be concentrated on five crimes. The goals for the reduction of these crimes should be:

- Homicide: Reduced by at least 25% by 1983
- Forcible rape: Reduced by at least 25% by 1983
- Aggravated assault: Reduced by at least 25% by 1983
- Robbery: Reduced by at least 50% by 1983
- Burglary: Reduced by at least 50% by 1983

Priorities for Action

The Commission proposes four areas for priority action in reducing the five target crimes:

- Juvenile Delinquency: The highest attention must be given to preventing juvenile delinquency and to minimizing the involvement of young offenders in the juvenile and criminal justice system, and to reintegrating juvenile offenders into the community.
- Delivery of Social Services: Public and private service agencies should direct their actions to improve the delivery of all social services to citizens, particularly to groups that contribute higher than average proportions of their numbers to crime statistics.
- Prompt Determination of Guilt or Innocence: Delays in the adjudication and disposition of criminal cases must be greatly reduced.
- Citizen Action: Increased citizen participation in activities to control crime in their community must be generated, with active encouragement and support by criminal justice agencies.

KEY COMMISSION PROPOSALS

Criminal Justice System

The Commission proposes broad reforms and improvements in the criminal justice system at the State and local levels. Key recommendations include:

- Development by States of integrated multiyear criminal justice planning.
- Establishment of criminal justice coordinating councils by all major cities and counties.
- Establishment by each State of a Security and Privacy Council to develop procedures and recommendations for legislation to assure security and privacy of information contained in criminal justice information systems.
- Creation by each State of an organizational structure for coordinating the development of criminal justice information systems.

The Commission proposes that all Americans make a personal contribution to the reduction of crime, and that all Americans support the crime prevention efforts of their State and local governments. Key recommendations include:

- Increased citizen contribution to crime prevention by making homes and businesses more secure, by participating in police-community programs, and by working with youth.
- Expanded public and private employment opportunities and elimination of unnecessary restrictions on hiring ex-offenders.
- Establishment of and citizen support for youth services bureaus to improve the delivery of social services to young people.
- Provision of individualized treatment for drug offenders and abusers.
- Provision of statewide capability for overseeing and investigating financing of political campaigns.
- Establishment of a statewide investigation and prosecution capability to deal with corruption in government.

Police

The Commission proposes that the delivery of police services be greatly improved at the municipal level. Key recommendations include:

- Consolidation of all police departments with fewer than 10 sworn officers.

Figure 26.1 continued

- Enhancement of the role of the patrolman.
- Increased crime prevention efforts by police working in and with the community.
- Affirmative police action to divert public drunks and mental patients from the criminal justice system.
- Increased employment and utilization of women, minorities, and civilians in police work.
- Enactment of legislation authorizing police to obtain search warrants by telephone.

Courts

The Commission proposes major restructuring and streamlining of procedures and practices in processing criminal cases at the State and local levels, in order to speed the determination of guilt or innocence. Key recommendations include:

- Trying all cases within 60 days of arrest.
- Requiring judges to hold full days in court.
- Unification within the State of all courts.
- Allowing only one review on appeal.
- Elimination of plea bargaining.
- Screening of all criminal cases coming to the attention of the prosecutor to determine if further processing is appropriate.
- Diverting out of the system all cases in which further processing by the prosecutor is not appropriate, based on such factors as the age of the individual, his psychological needs, the nature of the crime, and the availability of treatment programs.
- Elimination of grand juries and arraignments.

Corrections

The Commission proposes fundamental changes in the system of corrections that exists in States, counties, and cities in America — changes based on the belief that correctional systems usually are little more than "schools of crime." Key recommendations include:

- Restricting construction of major State institutions for adult offenders.
- Phasing out of all major juvenile offender institutions.
- Elimination of disparate sentencing practices.
- Establishment of community-based correctional programs and facilities.
- Unification of all correctional functions within the State.
- Increased and expanded salary, education, and training levels for corrections personnel.

Criminal Code Reform and Revision

The Commission proposes that all States reexamine their criminal codes with the view to improving and updating them. Key recommendations include:

- Establishment of permanent criminal code revision commissions at the State level.
- Decriminalization of vagrancy and drunkenness.

Handguns in American Society

The Commission proposes nationwide action at the State level to eliminate the dangers posed by widespread possession of handguns. The key recommendation is:

- Elimination of importation, manufacture, sale, and private possession of handguns by January 1, 1983.

Source: National Advisory Commission on Criminal Justice Standards and Goals, *A National Strategy to Reduce Crime* (Washington, D.C.: Government Printing Office, 1973).

to realize the value of academic education. In 1965, only twenty states had colleges that offered police science courses. Today, junior colleges, four-year colleges, and universities throughout the nation offer education in police science and criminology and grant degrees from the associate to the doctoral level.

Training for court functions has not had the same attention. The effective prosecutor must be knowledgeable in many fields in addition to the law, but there are few training programs for prosecutors. Judges too must know more than the law, particularly in those jurisdictions in which the judge does the sentencing. Unfortunately, the typical judge has received no training whatsoever for the job, beyond the experience picked up in a law practice that all too frequently did not include criminal law. There are signs, however, that the legal profession is recognizing the desirability of training programs for prosecutors and judges, and workshops, courses, and meetings are being held throughout the nation for this purpose. A number of universities now have programs especially designed to educate court administrators, specialists who are trained to take some of the administrative burdens off the judges and free them to concentrate on their judicial duties.

The situation in corrections is similar, and there is a small but increasing effort in higher education programs. Bachelor's and master's degrees in corrections are increasingly common. Although junior colleges tend to emphasize police education, a growing number are including courses in corrections. The experience of colleges located near prisons seems to be that a surprisingly high percentage of prison personnel are eager to continue their academic education.

The effect of higher education on the skills of criminal justice personnel is not yet known. Experience in the fields of law, medicine, and business seems to indicate that the best way to truly professionalize an occupation is to emphasize higher education. There was a time when few lawyers had attended a law school and few doctors had seen the inside of a college. The day may well come when the criminal justice professional without a college degree will be the exception, not the rule.

FUNDING

In addition to research and personnel improvement, most advocates of criminal justice reform emphasize the need for more money. Without the necessary funding, it will be extremely difficult to effect the necessary improvements in research, equipment, or personnel.

Because law enforcement and court functions are basically activities of local government, the bulk of the money for these two operations has come from local taxes. State taxes are the greatest source of correctional funds. Unfortunately for the criminal justice system, state and particularly local taxes are the ones most subject to taxpayer discontent. The increasing movement throughout the country toward limiting local and state taxation threatens the ability of the criminal justice system to pay for reform. Therefore, the system's main hope for additional revenue is the federal government.

The role of federal money in funding the criminal justice system has historically been limited to federal law enforcement, federal courts, and federal prisons. However, during the 1960s it became increasingly obvious that state and local governments could not be expected to raise the funds necessary to improve the criminal justice system significantly. Large cities throughout the country were facing the problem of an increasing demand for services coupled with a decreasing tax base. In 1968 Congress passed the Safe Streets Act, which, among other provisions, set up the Law Enforcement Assistance Administration (LEAA) under the Department of Justice, now called the Office of Justice Assistance, Research and Statistics (OJARS).

Without the billions of dollars OJARS has poured into the criminal justice system in the last decade, most of the improvements already described in this text could not have been financed. However, future federal contributions to the financing of local and state agencies is difficult to predict. OJARS has been under attack from many sources ever since it began. The combination of past mismanagement, internal disagreements, political maneuverings, and a growing taxpayer reluctance to finance government programs may yet lead to the downgrading or even abolition of OJARS. Such an event, if it is not coupled with alternative federal sources of funding, would make it all but impossible for the system to operate at present levels, let alone pay for reform.

Reform of a major institution such as the criminal justice system is expensive, terrifically expensive. "More of the same but better" is costly today; inflation assures that it will be more costly tomorrow. It may very well be that the taxpayer cannot or will not pay the bill. While most people involved with criminal justice look upon this possibility of a taxpayer revolt with dismay, some look upon it as an opportunity. These are the thinkers that maintain that what we need *least* is more of the same, that a radical change in criminal justice will give us not only more justice but perhaps cheaper justice. We will examine this position closely in the next chapter. First, we will take a look at what could be if the nation is willing to work toward and pay for a reformed criminal justice system.

REFORM AND THE FUTURE

It is, of course, impossible to guarantee that the reforms discussed in this chapter will be put into effect. If they are, it is possible to make a guess concerning what the criminal justice system of the year 2000 will be like.

The police patrol officer of our reformed system will be a college graduate, with intensive training in the behavioral sciences as well as in criminology and police science. His or her pay and working conditions will equal or exceed the level of pay and working conditions for college graduates in private industry. If the officer is patrolling one of our major cities, he or she will probably be black, since most of the largest cities will probably have a preponderantly black population by the year 2000. The officer will have available all the technology he or she needs to perform the job effectively — computer-dispatched squad cars and helicopters, mobile crime laboratories, and, through a portable computer terminal, immediate access to the information in national, state, and local files.

The officer's superiors will have advanced degrees in the behavioral sciences and law. The chief will be an expert in management, equal in skills and training to the top management of major industries, and will be assisted by experts in finance, accounting, law, and psychology. The police research department will know what types of crime are being committed throughout the city and where and will have experimented with the best methods of controlling crime. Decisions will be made on the basis of fact, not hunch.

When the police of the future arrest suspects, they will be turned over to a highly sophisticated system for judging guilt or innocence and for sentencing. The trial will take place in a matter of weeks after arrest, depending on how much time the defense attorney needs to prepare the best possible defense. Because of the improvement in the police, guilt will be established much more on the basis of hard physical evidence and much less on the basis of eyewitness testimony and confession.

If defendants are convicted, their fate will

be determined by a judge with intensive training in sentencing. The judge will have available not only the facts about the crime with which the person is charged, but also a presentence report containing the facts from the defendant's life history that are relevant in determining the best possible treatment program. The judge will be aided in this decision by a large body of research on effective treatment for various kinds of offenders. In addition, there will be a variety of sentencing options: a halfway house, a residential treatment center run by charitable or religious organizations, a center for treating drug addicts, an alcoholism treatment center, as well as prison or probation.

The prisons of the future will be much smaller, because all but the most dangerous convicts will be treated in programs outside prison walls. Instead of being located in rural areas, prisons will be close to the major cities from which the offenders come. Prison officials, trained and educated to be experts in human behavior, will have the personnel and physical resources to work individually with each offender. After determining the causes of the individual's criminal behavior, they will design a treatment program for each offender to eradicate whatever caused the individual to turn to crime. Inmates will be released to the community, under parole supervision, at the moment they have received maximum benefit from the correctional experience.

However, in the future emphasis will center on those correctional programs that treat offenders outside of prisons. Research will have determined which are most effective for which offenders and how to improve effectiveness. These programs will be staffed by probation and parole officers with advanced degrees and training in the behavioral sciences, as well as by social workers, psychologists, and psychiatrists.

The people who advocate reform of the criminal justice system are working to make this vision of the future a reality. There are those, however, to whom this vision of the future is a nightmare to be avoided, not a goal to be pursued. It is those advocates of radical change in the system whose views we will examine in the next and final chapter.

DISCUSSION QUESTIONS

1. Can reform work, or is radical change in the criminal justice system needed?
2. What effects will recruitment of women and minorities have on the agencies of the criminal justice system?
3. Discuss various methods of improving criminal justice personnel.
4. Discuss the areas of criminal justice in which the need for research information is particularly acute. What type of research is needed?
5. Is the taxpayer willing to pay the bill for reforming the criminal justice system?
6. If research indicates that raising the educational level of prisoners while they are in prison does nothing to reduce recidivism, should prisoner education programs be terminated? Assuming that the research information is valid and reliable, would you consider such a movement reform?

NOTES

1. Further information on the research mentioned here as well as on other OJARS-funded research can be obtained through the National Criminal Justice Reference Service, a division of the Office

of Justice Assistance, Research and Statistics, U.S. Department of Justice, Washington, D.C. 20531.

2. Peter Bloch and Deborah Anderson, *Policewomen on Patrol: A Final Report* (Washington, D.C.: Police Foundation, 1974).

3. John E. Boydston, Michael E. Sherry, and Nicholas P. Moelter, *Patrol Staffing in San Diego: One- or Two-Officer Units* (Washington, D.C.: Police Foundation, 1977).

4. George Kelling et al., *The Kansas City Preventive Patrol Experiment: A Summary Report* (Washington, D.C.: Police Foundation, 1974).

5. President's Commission on Law Enforcement and Administration of Justice, *Challenge of Crime in a Free Society* (Washington, D.C.: Government Printing Office, 1967), p. 14.

6. Ramsey Clark, *Crime in America* (New York: Simon and Schuster, 1970), pp. 115–238.

7. National Advisory Commission on Criminal Justice Standards and Goals, *Report of National Advisory Commission on Criminal Justice Standards and Goals* (Washington, D.C.: Government Printing Office, 1973).

CHAPTER TWENTY-SEVEN

BASIC CHANGE

SOCIETAL REFORM	CRIMINAL JUSTICE SYSTEM AS A CAUSE OF CRIME	INSTITUTING CHANGES
	INJUSTICE IN THE CRIMINAL JUSTICE SYSTEM	

Purpose: To explore and discuss some of the more provocative suggestions for improving the criminal justice system of the future.

A REFORMED CRIMINAL JUSTICE system as described in the preceding chapter does not satisfy everyone. There are those who maintain that the basic problems of criminal justice are not isolated abuses subject to piecemeal correction but are misconceptions about what the criminal justice system really is and what it should be doing.

SOCIETAL REFORM

The most frequently expressed idea is that reform of the criminal justice system is of secondary importance; society itself must be reformed if we are to have a real chance of reducing crime. The National Crime Commission, which concerned itself primarily with reform of the system as it now stands, has gone on record as stating that "America must translate its well-founded alarm about crime into social action that will prevent crime. To speak of controlling crime only in terms of the work of the police, the courts and the correctional apparatus, is to refuse to face the fact that widespread crime implies a widespread failure of society as a whole." [1] In other words, we need more than reform of the criminal justice system; we need social justice.

Social justice in this context means adequate food, housing, education, and job opportunities for all citizens. It means the end of racial and class prejudice. These goals are seen not only as desirable in themselves, but also as an answer to the crime problem. Perhaps the foremost speaker for this position is former U.S. Attorney General Ramsey Clark,[2] and his approach deserves further investigation.

While Clark admits that no one has the complete answer to the question of why people turn to crime, he states that scholars are familiar with the conditions associated with criminal behavior. Crime flourishes where unemployment is high and where people do not have the skills and training needed to make an honest living. Crime flourishes where education is poorest, where schools are least equipped to teach youngsters, and where most drop out before graduation. Crime flourishes in those areas in which there is inadequate health care, in which the average life expectancy is ten years lower than in the city as a whole.

As Clark points out, people live in areas such as these. Every city has them. The police are very familiar with them; they spend much of their time there. Although they recognize that stating that poverty causes crime is an oversimplification, Clark and others maintain that slums breed crime, because so much human misery concentrated in such a small geographic area cannot help but be explosive and can result in crime.

That human misery leads to all kinds of undesirable behavior should surprise no one. What surprises Clark and the other advocates of social justice is a nation that thinks it cheaper to hire another thousand police officers than to provide its citizens with the education that will enable them to survive without crime, a nation that builds huge prisons while ignoring the housing conditions that breed disrespect for society, a nation that can provide tanks for its police but not decent jobs for its people.

Most people would agree that criminal behavior is caused, that it does not just happen. Most would also agree that the criminal justice system cannot do anything fundamental about any of the causes of crime. Arresting a school dropout does not provide him or her with the education necessary to succeed in a complex society. Bringing an alcoholic before the bar of justice rarely cures the alcoholism. Police, courts, and prisons have proved themselves remarkably ineffective in curing drug addiction. Professional police have created no more jobs for the unemployed than nonprofessional police. The most skilled correctional officials in the nation have not been able to rehabilitate criminals as fast as the slums of the nation turn them out.

For these reasons, Clark is probably correct in insisting that relying totally on the criminal justice system to control crime will not work. People obey laws for one of two reasons: they respect their society and its laws, or they are forced to obey. The criminal justice system stands ready to apply the force, but the use of force without justice only creates the need for more force. Already some of our citizens, because of the conditions under which they must live, have lost faith in America's desire for justice. It is difficult to teach people to respect the law when they have come to believe that the law does not respect them. To rely on the criminal justice system to maintain order while ignoring social justice will be to demonstrate to the disaffected that they are correct, that America cares nothing for its poor and its minorities. This will not be an inviting future for the criminal justice system, for no police force, however strong, has been able to maintain order with force alone.

On the other hand, there is a basic flaw in any approach to crime that limits its concerns to adequate education, housing, job opportunities, and so on. If the slums were eliminated tomorrow, and if all Americans were well-educated, responsible members of the middle and upper classes, there would still be crime. Crime is not limited to the poor; the rich commit crimes, and many of them.

CRIMINAL JUSTICE SYSTEM AS A CAUSE OF CRIME

There are others who reject the reformation of the criminal justice system along present lines not because they think the system is ignoring the causes of crime, but because they believe that the operation of the criminal justice system itself causes crime. That the criminal justice system can cause crime is not a new idea; it has long been recognized that the occasional brutal and unlawful procedures of police and correctional officials may increase the amount of crime by provoking disrespect for the law. It has been suggested, however, that even a well-operated and professional criminal justice system can increase crime by its very operation. There is even some evidence to suggest that the more efficient the system is, the more crime it can create.

"LABELING" THEORY

The theoretical orientation for this position is the sociological theory usually called *"labeling" theory*. The basic tenet of labeling theory has been stated by Howard Becker: "social groups create deviance by making the rules whose infractions constitute deviance, and by applying those rules to particular people and labeling them as outsiders."[3] From this point of view, deviance is not a quality of the act a person commits, but rather a consequence of the application by others of rules and sanctions to an "offender." The deviant is one to whom that label has been successfully applied; deviant behavior is behavior that people so label.

Applied to criminal behavior, this means that society creates crime and criminals in two ways. First, legislators create crime when they pass a law against a certain form of behavior. Without the law, there is no crime, though of course the behavior may still be "objectionable." Second, the criminal justice system creates criminals when it arrests and especially when it convicts individuals for criminal or delinquent behavior. Until the point of arrest and particularly conviction, individuals are not considered criminals by friends, family, and society as a whole. After conviction, they are labeled criminals. If sent to prison, they acquire another label, "con," later modified to "ex-con." At this point, these people are full-fledged criminals, having been so defined by the criminal justice system, the institution in our society entrusted with the task of defining criminals.

The effect of this process on future crime is simple, although this effect has not yet been sufficiently documented by research to be considered a fact. Society expects "criminals" to commit crime, just as society expects people who have been labeled mentally ill to behave in a disordered manner. Once someone has been labeled a criminal or a delinquent, family, friends, peer group, school officials, and the cop on the beat are more likely to expect criminal behavior from that person than from someone who has not acquired the label. Human beings, more often than not, behave in the manner in which they are expected to behave. This phenomenon is known as a *self-fulfilling prophecy*; if the important people in a girl's environment expect her to turn out bad, she will rarely disappoint them. If a boy considers himself a criminal, his fate is almost assured.

If these assumptions are true, it follows that the process of arresting, convicting, and sentencing individuals leads to future crime. Take the case of two youngsters committing their first felony, say burglary. One of the two is caught by the police, taken to court, adjudged delinquent, and placed on probation. The other is never caught. Since the first boy has now been labeled a "juvenile delinquent," those around him, and perhaps he himself, expect him to commit further delinquent acts. Therefore, he is far more likely to commit further offenses than the other boy, who was never caught.

"LABELING" THEORY VERSUS REFORM

It should be noted that reform of the system as proposed in the last chapter would only make matters worse. A professional police force solves more crimes. An efficient judicial system convicts more of the guilty. There is evidence to indicate that professional police tend to handle more juveniles by formal methods; that is, they tend to bring children before the juvenile court rather than reporting them to their parents or lecturing them. The net result, therefore, of a reformed and more efficient criminal justice system in the future may well be that more people will be labeled criminal or delinquent. If the principles of labeling theory are true, and if other factors remain equal, a reformed criminal justice system will experience more crime, not less.

Critics of the labeling approach point out that even if convicting people of robbery makes it more likely that they will commit more criminal acts in the future, *something* must be done about people who steal, kill, and rape. While this is quite true, it is important to note that many people labeled criminal have physically injured no one and stolen no property. The system spends much time and effort arresting and convicting people who have injured no one, except possibly themselves.

VICTIMLESS CRIME

The "crimes without victims" — alcoholism, drug addiction, prostitution, sexual "perversions" with consenting partners, and so on — have received much attention from criminologists in recent years. They have received much attention from the police and courts also; anywhere from one-fourth to one-third of *all* the nontraffic arrests in America are for drunkenness. The policy of using the criminal justice system to suppress behavior that directly injures no other party raises a number of questions that are beyond the scope of this text. One important point, however, is relevant to the future of the criminal justice system, and that is the over-reach of the criminal law.

The variety of behavior presently labeled illegal is staggering. A study in a major city indicated that a normal, law-abiding citizen, in the course of ordinary daily activity, will violate enough laws in one day to merit fines of nearly $3,000 and imprisonment for five years.[4] Many of these laws and ordinances are never enforced, of course; it is not likely that Vermont has arrested many citizens for violation of the statute against whistling underwater. Unfortunately, however, many of these laws are enforced upon occasion.

The problem with having on the books laws that could imprison most of the population is twofold. First, these laws may be enforced. Marijuana laws, for instance, have been on the books of the federal government and the states since the 1930s. Until the 1960s, however, they were rarely enforced, except against occasional blacks, Mexican-Americans, and jazz musicians. Until the 1960s, the use of marijuana was not very common. The causal relationship here is not very clear; it may be that increased use led to increased enforcement, or it may be that increased enforcement led to increased use. One fact, however, is clear: a large number of otherwise satisfactory young men and women have been arrested, convicted, and imprisoned for no other offense than the use of marijuana. If nothing else, this enforcement of marijuana laws gives the researcher an opportunity to subject labeling theory to an empirical test: if the theory is true, many of these young "criminals," on release, should become criminals in fact.

LAWS THAT CAUSE CRIME

It is not necessary to support labeling theory to believe that the enforcement of certain laws directly increases the amount of crime.

Prohibition, of course, is the historical example. It is generally agreed that the attempt to enforce the Volstead Act led to corruption of the criminal justice system, disrespect for the law, and more crime. Laws against other victimless crimes, such as gambling, prostitution, and sales on Sunday, have been blamed for present-day police corruption. The shining example of laws that themselves breed crime are those that make possession of narcotics a criminal offense. Harsh penalties for dealing in addictive drugs have one invariable effect: they drive up the price of drugs. The more effective government action against narcotics is, the higher the cost of drugs. The higher the cost of drugs, the more muggings, holdups, and burglaries that addicts must commit to get the money they need to support their habit. It has been estimated that over half the street crime in our major cities is committed by narcotics addicts, and it cannot be doubted that the need to purchase drugs is a factor in a tremendous number of crimes throughout the nation. Without law enforcement activity driving up the price, narcotics are cheap. The criminal law has created a reason to rob and kill by making what is essentially a sickness into a crime.

The outlook for the future is not good. Although a number of states have reformed their criminal law along the lines suggested by the Model Penal Code, some have not. Even those states that have reformed their laws have found that, little by little, more and more crimes creep into the statutes. In general, legislators have found it more expedient to legislate new crimes than to repeal old ones. If the laws make many varieties of typical human conduct illegal, a reformed criminal justice system might well be dangerous. To put the matter bluntly, it is possible to live under a set of ridiculous laws that make some of the behavior of most citizens illegal only if these laws are not enforced. One hallmark of a reformed and efficient criminal justice system, however, is that it enforces the law. It could hardly be otherwise.

It is by no means unlikely that many of our laws were passed by legislators who thought they would never be enforced. The laws regulating sexual behavior are a case in point; the laws of many states still make almost all forms of sexual activity illegal. If studies by Kinsey and others are to be believed, most of the legislators who passed these laws would be in prison if they were enforced. This was no problem fifty years ago; the police could not have enforced these laws if they had wanted to, because wiretaps, "bugs," and electronic surveillance devices did not exist. The police of tomorrow, armed to the teeth with technology, may well be equipped to seriously enforce the laws against victimless crimes. To the extent to which they are professionals, they *will* enforce the law; after all, it is their job.

The criminal justice system of the future either will or will not have a more reasonable set of laws with which to work. If it does not, society will have to decide whether it really wants a more efficient criminal justice system, whether it really wants better enforcement of the reprehensible laws under which we live. Society's answer to this question is more likely than not to depend on who is arrested.

INJUSTICE IN THE CRIMINAL JUSTICE SYSTEM

It is known who gets arrested now. By and large, the person is disproportionately male, black, young, and, of course, poor. Perhaps the majority of criminals are male, black, young, and poor, or perhaps these arrests are a result of the operation of a factor called *discretion*.

DISCRETION

Discretion means that any police officer gets to pick and choose the persons to be arrested. Our law makes so much illegal that it could not be otherwise; no urban police officer could possibly proceed against everyone seen breaking the law. Discretion also means that the prosecutor gets to pick and choose against whom to proceed, who will be allowed to plead guilty to a lesser charge, and who will be released without trial. Discretion means that the judge gets to pick and choose who will get thirty years for an offense and who will get probation for the same offense. Discretion means that the parole board gets to pick who will serve thirty years on a thirty-year sentence and who will serve ten years of the same thirty-year sentence. Discretion means that probation and parole officers get to pick who will live in the community and who will live behind bars.

The primary result of all this discretion is that we have, contrary to the official rhetoric, a rule of men, not a rule of law. This occurs when legislatures abdicate their responsibility by passing so many laws against so many different types of behavior that the police must decide what type of crime to proceed against, and by making the maximum penalty for law violation so high that courts and corrections must determine which individuals to subject to the full force of the penalty and which to treat more leniently. The principal reason that most legal philosophers prefer the rule of law is that the rule of men tends to be unjust. It tends toward injustice because human beings tend to make decisions not on the basis of the individual's criminal act, but on such extralegal considerations as manner, lifestyle, socio-economic status, or perhaps color of skin.

DISCRIMINATION

The question of discrimination in the criminal justice system is a sensitive one. There can be little doubt that the system tends to be biased toward white, middle-class standards. Upper- and middle-class offenders such as polluters, price fixers, violators of health and safety laws, and owners of criminally substandard housing are treated in a manner far different from lower-class offenders who commit lower-class crimes such as purse snatching, prostitution, or petty theft. Nor is there any doubt that there is a systematic class bias throughout the entire criminal justice system with regard to offenders who commit the same crime. The doctor's children may be just as likely as the black militants to smoke marijuana, but the reaction of the system to the offenders is quite different.

INSTITUTING CHANGES

This chapter has so far concentrated on problems and has all but ignored solutions. However, those advocating more or less radical change in the operation of the criminal justice system have no dearth of proposals for solutions. Taken together, these solutions present a far different vision of the future of the criminal justice system than that presented in the last chapter.

SOCIAL JUSTICE

Although there are many points of disagreement, the advocates of basic change unite on the need for social justice. Social justice is seen as necessary, not only as the only effective way to attack some of the causes of crime, but as a mandatory step to ensure justice within the criminal justice system. Put simply, if the larger society is unjust in its treatment of minorities, it is too much to hope that the criminal justice system can operate fairly. If racial prejudice is prevalent throughout society as a whole, it is unlikely that criminal justice officials will be free of prejudice.

CHANGE IN CRIMINAL LAW

The second basic change in the criminal justice system advocated is a change in the criminal law under which the system operates. Many of the present abuses of the system can be traced to the fact that the criminal law overreaches itself and tries to prevent some conduct that it cannot prevent. It makes criminals of people whose problems injure no one but themselves, and it intrudes into some areas that, to put it bluntly, are none of the government's business.

Of course, to remove public drunkenness, possession of narcotics, and sexual deviation from the scope of the criminal law will not cure alcoholics, reduce drug addiction, or eliminate perversion. Alternative methods of treating these types of behavior must be provided: clinics, hospitals, residential treatment centers, and so on. An example of what can be done is the Montgomery County (Pennsylvania) Emergency Service, a privately operated organization that provides twenty-four-hour emergency care, ambulance service, short-term hospitalization, and referral service for psychiatric, alcohol, and drug emergencies.[5] Working in close cooperation with criminal justice agencies, this service has allowed the local police and courts to concentrate on real crime.

Unfortunately, most areas have no organization similar to the Montgomery County Emergency Service and are not likely to get one as long as local criminal justice agencies are willing to deal with alcoholics, addicts, and mentally disturbed people. Admittedly, attempting to stop these services is difficult for any criminal justice organization. If the police do not haul drunks off the streets, for example, no other agency will. But society has relied on the police to solve all its social problems for too long. Some of these problems are simply beyond the capabilities of the criminal justice system. As long as the criminal justice system spends its time, money, and effort in the futile attempt to cure addiction, prostitution, alcoholism, and gambling by arrest and imprisonment, the facilities and programs needed to really deal with these problems will not be developed.

REDUCTION OF DISCRETION

The third suggestion for basic change is the reduction of official discretion. Once legislators clearly define what actions are criminal and limit the scope of the criminal code to those laws that the public truly wants enforced, it will be possible to insist that the police try to enforce all the laws all the time. Although total enforcement of the law is more a goal than a real possibility, limitation of police discretion and even-handed enforcement of the laws that remain on the books form probably the best method of reform. The reason that there is little public outcry against some of the repressive laws now in effect is that the people who have the ability to make themselves heard, the powerful and the influential, are rarely arrested for violation of these laws. Present practices are so remote from total enforcement of the law that the call for it may sound strange, but the principle seems reasonable: if a law is fair, it should be enforced everytime it is violated; if this enforcement does more harm than good, the law should be repealed or restated. Any other use of the law is inherently discriminatory; any law that is enforced some of the time against

some of the people can far too easily become an instrument of oppression.

The reduction of discretion in the criminal justice system envisioned here is not limited to police discretion. The courts and correctional systems of the United States are used to having tremendous discretion, based on the ideal that has been almost universally accepted for decades: individualized treatment, or "treating the criminal, not the crime." Individualized treatment and the judicial and correctional discretion needed to effect it have become articles of faith; it has been difficult for criminologists to think in any other terms. Yet there is little evidence that the model works, that it reduces crime or, for that matter, helps the offender. There is ample evidence, on the other hand, that the discretion involved in sentencing and in decisions about when an offender is ready for release leads to discriminatory and unjust treatment of individuals.

That individuals who have committed exactly the same crime and have similar criminal records can and do receive different sentences is well documented. It is not unheard of to find one person sentenced to life imprisonment while another gets probation. The varying motives of the judges in sentencing are open to speculation. Did one person receive lenient treatment because he or she looked respectable? Did the other person become the recipient of the full force of the law's wrath because he was poorly dressed? Or was it because the probation officer who made up the presentence report was offended by the way the defendant treated his family? Perhaps the judge quarreled with her husband the morning before sentencing. Maybe the judge decided that it was time to "make an example" of somebody. The motives behind the decisions of parole boards and prison authorities are equally obscure. But when society gives these authorities the mandate to treat the whole person, to treat the criminal, not the crime, it is almost inevitable that, because these people are predominantly white and middle-class, they will judge the offender by white and middle-class standards. Is he respectful to authority? Is she punctual? Does he conform?

Regardless of the motive behind a particular decision, it is typically based on nonlegal considerations. What business is it of the criminal justice system, when deciding a man's punishment for the crime of armed robbery, whether he beats his wife or whether he thinks highly of religion? How is it possible to preserve a government of laws, not men, if a woman's fate is decided on the basis of how officials evaluate her total life history, or whatever portion of her life history they may think relevant?

The answer, of course, is that it is not possible. The alternative is to let the punishment fit the crime, not the criminal. Such a rejection of individualized treatment is nothing less than a revolution in criminological thinking. It is a revolution that is now under way. Maine and California have already abolished indeterminate sentences, relying on fixed sentences based on the crime committed, with relatively little room to change the sentence to fit the individual characteristics of the offender. These same two states have also limited correctional discretion by all but eliminating parole.

In addition, the federal government and several states are moving away from the long-accepted notion that the major purpose of imprisonment is the rehabilitation of the inmate, a theory that has contributed greatly to differential treatment of individuals convicted of the same offense. It appears that limiting discretion in sentencing and corrections is an idea whose time may be coming.

DECENTRALIZATION OF POWER

A final series of proposals advanced by those who advocate basic change in the criminal justice system involve decentralization of criminal justice institutions and community control of these agencies, especially the police. Instead of one police force for a city, they would prefer one for the black community, one for the white community, and perhaps another for another minority area.

The very fact that this division has been proposed tells us much. It tells us that many people in our society doubt that the present police force will do justice. It tells us that many people in minority communities despair of their ability to be heard in the operation of their police department. If the big, predominantly white police department will not listen to them, will not consider their desires, perhaps a smaller force, located in the black community and staffed by black officers, will.

Advocates of decentralization do not limit it to the police. The movement also allows for community control of at least part of the correctional process. To a certain extent, the growing influence of the community crime prevention movement reflects a dissatisfaction with the present criminal justice system and a desire to bring decision making closer to the residents of each neighborhood and community.

In evaluating the movement toward decentralization, it must be remembered that the criminal justice system does not operate in a vacuum; it is affected by all the social trends affecting the larger society. The desire for minority control of the institutions that vitally affect the minority community is not limited to the institutions of the criminal justice system; the movement for minority control of ghetto schools is another example. This desire for decentralization is based on two long-term social trends. The first is the growing desire of the powerless to have some voice in the decisions that affect their lives. The rich hire lobbyists to influence the criminal justice process, the influential help elect politicians. The poor and powerless remain silent. Having their own police department and a community-based correctional system answerable to them instead of to some bureaucrat they never heard of would give them a voice, allow them some control of institutions that directly affect their lives.

The second trend leading to demands for community control of criminal justice institutions is the growing racial polarization in America. The basic conclusion of the 1968 report of the National Advisory Commission on Civil Disorders is that "our nation is moving towards two societies, one black, one white — separate and unequal."[6] Little has happened in the last decade to indicate that this trend has not continued. Unless it is reversed, its effect on the criminal justice system of the future will be profound. Whether the result is minority control of criminal justice institutions, a secret police system to fight social change, or something else is impossible to predict. It is easy to predict, however, that without a firm commitment to justice for all, the criminal justice system of the future could become even more efficient and even less just.

DISCUSSION QUESTIONS

1. Can the criminal justice system be changed, or do bureaucrats have too much invested in the system as it is?
2. Does the criminal justice system actually create crime by processing so-called criminals?
3. What implications does labeling theory have for criminal justice reform?
4. What steps can be taken to prevent injustice?
5. Can you have a free society without abuses of freedom?

NOTES

1. President's Commission on Law Enforcement and Administration of Justice, *Challenge of Crime in a Free Society* (Washington, D.C.: Government Printing Office, 1967), p. 15.
2. Ramsey Clark, *Crime in America* (New York: Simon and Schuster, 1970), pp. 15–114.
3. Howard S. Becker, *Outsiders: Studies in the Sociology of Deviance* (New York: Free Press, 1963), p. 9.
4. L. M. Hussey, "Twenty-four Hours of a Lawbreaker," *Harper's Magazine,* 160 (March 1930), 436–439.
5. Carol Holliday Blew and Paul Cirel, *Montgomery County Emergency Service* (Washington, D.C.: Government Printing Office, 1978).
6. United States National Advisory Commission on Civil Disorders, *Report of the National Advisory Commission on Civil Disorders* (New York: New York Times Co., 1968), p. 1.

PART SEVEN ANNOTATED BIBLIOGRAPHY

American Friends Service Committee. *Struggle for Justice.* New York: Hill and Wang, 1971.
A chilling indictment of the basic philosophy behind our system of criminal justice. This book charges that the problem with the criminal justice system is not that it is ineffective in reducing crime, but rather that it does not, cannot, and will not do justice.

THE FUTURE OF THE CRIMINAL JUSTICE SYSTEM

Boguslaw, Robert. *The New Utopians: A Study of Systems Design and Social Change.* Englewood Cliffs, N.J.: Prentice-Hall, Inc., 1965.

A readable, nontechnical study of both the promise and the peril of the systems approach.

Clark, Ramsey. *Crime in America.* New York: Simon and Schuster, 1970.

Contains both practical suggestions for reform and an eloquent plea for social justice.

President's Commission on Law Enforcement and Administration of Justice. *The Challenge of Crime in a Free Society.* Washington, D.C.: Government Printing Office, 1967.

The most comprehensive study ever made of the operations of the criminal justice system and the need for reform.

Wilson, James Q. *Thinking about Crime.* New York: Basic Books, 1975.

One of the nation's most influential critics of the criminal justice system, Wilson has put together a series of articles of interest both to those who advocate reform and to those who advocate basic change in the system.

APPENDIXES

APPENDIX A

CAREER OPPORTUNITIES IN THE CRIMINAL JUSTICE SYSTEM

The American criminal justice system provides a wide variety of employment opportunities for men and women with varied interests. There are police officers, parole officers, federal law enforcement officers, probation officers, detectives, prison guards, judges, lawyers, forensic scientists, correctional counselors, and public defenders, to name but a few of the many people who make up the criminal justice system. The criminal justice system encompasses many important professional fields open to people with appropriate education, training, and experience. Generally speaking, the employment outlook for the near future appears favorable. Retirement and normal attrition of personnel will continue to provide a number of openings. A national personnel survey of the criminal justice system indicates an average annual growth rate in criminal justice employment of 3 percent through 1985. Employment growth rates in the courts and corrections are projected to be substantially greater than those in law enforcement. In order to provide further information on career opportunities in the criminal justice system, a partial listing of major areas of criminal justice employment appears on the following pages.

CAREER OPPORTUNITIES IN FEDERAL LAW ENFORCEMENT

NATURE OF THE WORK

Federal Bureau of Investigation Federal Bureau of Investigation (FBI) Special Agents investigate many types of violations of federal laws: bank robberies, kidnapings, frauds against the government, thefts of government property, espionage, sabotage, and so forth. The FBI, which is part of the U.S. Department of Justice, has jurisdiction over more than 185 federal investigative matters. Special Agents may be assigned to any type of case, but those with specialized training in accounting are likely to be assigned chiefly to cases involving complex financial records; for example, frauds involving Federal Reserve Bank records. For further information, write

Federal Bureau of Investigation
9th and Pennsylvania N.W.
Washington, D.C. 20531

Drug Enforcement Administration Special Agents with the Department of Justice's Drug Enforcement Administration conduct investigations relating to violations of federal narcotics and drug laws. The work may involve surveillance, raids, interviewing witnesses and suspects, searching for evidence, seizure of contraband goods, arrests, and inspecting records and documents. For further information, write

Drug Enforcement Administration
U.S. Department of Justice
1405 Eye Street N.W.
Washington, D.C. 20537

Immigration and Naturalization Service The Immigration and Naturalization Service, Department of Justice, has officers (Border Patrol Agents) throughout the United States and in Europe, Bermuda, Nassau, Puerto Rico, Canada, Mexico, and the Philippines. Among other duties, they conduct investigations, detect violations of immigration and nationality laws, and determine whether aliens may enter or remain in the United States. They present the government's case at hearings and make recommendations to the courts in such matters as petitions for citizenship. For further information, write

U.S. Department of Justice
Immigration and Naturalization Service
119 D Street N.E.
Washington, D.C. 20536

Alcohol, Tobacco, and Firearms Special Investigators Alcohol, Tobacco, and Firearms Special Investigators (U.S. Treasury Department) work to detect, investigate, and prevent violations of liquor, tobacco, and firearms laws. The duties of a "revenoor" include undercover assignments, investigations of organizations acquiring guns, and much contact with all segments of the American public.

Secret Service Special Agents Secret Service Special Agents (U.S. Treasury Department) have both protective and investigative responsibilities. They guard the president and vice president and their families, the president-elect and vice president-elect, and former presidents upon request for limited periods of time. They also work to prevent the counterfeiting of U.S. currency and investigate forged government checks and bonds.

Internal Security Inspectors Internal Security Inspectors (U.S. Treasury Department) are investigators for the Internal Revenue Service. They check out prospective IRS employees and investigate allegations of serious misconduct or illegal activities on the part of IRS employees, with the aim that only people of unquestionable honesty be employed.

Special Agents, Intelligence Division of IRS Special Agents, Intelligence Division of the Internal Revenue Service (U.S. Treasury Department), perform work unique in the field of criminal investigations. They dig out the facts in tax fraud cases (particularly for income tax, excise tax, and coin-operated gaming devices) and other criminal violations; assist the United States Attorney General in preparing the government's case; and frequently serve as the key witnesses for the prosecution.

U.S. Customs Service Special Agents U.S. Customs Service Special Agents (U.S. Treasury Department) are responsible for making sure that proper duty is paid on goods coming into the country and that narcotics, drugs, and defense materials neither enter nor leave the country illegally.

For information on *all* the above listed agencies of the U.S. Treasury Department, write

Recruitment Coordinator for Law
Enforcement
Department of the Treasury
Internal Revenue Service
Washington, D.C. 20224

Postal Inspectors, Investigators, and Security Force Technicians Postal Inspectors form the criminal investigations arm of the Postal Service. Their cases involve, among others, fraud, burglary, theft, obscenity, and bombs. Investigators assist Postal Inspectors in criminal investigations. Security Force Technicians are a uniformed force providing security at postal installations. For further information, write

Chief Postal Inspector
Post Office Department
Washington, D.C. 20260

PLACES OF EMPLOYMENT

Federal law enforcement agents may be employed anywhere in the United States, depending on the agency they are working for and the type of work they perform. Some federal agencies, such as the Drug Enforcement Administration, have agents assigned in foreign countries. As a condition of federal employment, a person must be willing to serve wherever the agency needs his or her services.

TRAINING, OTHER QUALIFICATIONS, AND ADVANCEMENT

Jobs with the federal government are organized by grades on a general schedule, with each grade (GS-1, GS-2, etc.) having certain general requirements. Salaries correspond to the grades; the higher the grade, the higher the salary. Appointment grades in federal agencies are based on one's qualifications and the hiring levels of that particular agency. Generally, the more education, training, and experience one possesses, the higher the entrance level one can command.

Requirements vary among the agencies. Some federal law enforcement positions have unique requirements. For example, Special Agents (Intelligence, IRS) must have at least twelve hours of college accounting, or equivalent experience. Because of these variations, you should contact the particular federal law enforcement agency in which you are interested in order to learn its specific requirements.

Some federal agencies maintain their own training programs. For example, each newly appointed Special Agent of the FBI is given approximately fourteen weeks of training at the FBI Academy. Many Federal law enforcement officers are trained at the Federal Law Enforcement Training Center in Georgia. The type of training in each agency naturally reflects the specific function of that agency. Narcotics officers can expect to receive training about narcotics, and postal officers can expect to receive training about postal regulations.

Almost all federal law enforcement agents begin their careers at the bottom of the ladder. However, most agencies fill vacancies, whenever possible, by promoting their own employees. Promotion programs in every agency are designed to make sure that promotions go to the employees who are among the best qualified to fill higher positions. How fast employees are promoted depends on openings in the higher grades and on their own ability and effort.

EMPLOYMENT OUTLOOK

Although it is impossible to forecast the personnel requirements for federal law enforcement agencies, employment can be expected to increase with the continued concern over crime in our nation. Also, normal attrition will continue to provide openings over the years.

EARNINGS AND WORKING CONDITIONS

Salaries in the federal service are based on the civil service grade one holds. For example, if you entered the Secret Service as a Special Agent with a grade of GS-7, you would receive the entrance rate currently being paid federal employees at the GS-7 level. In order to keep federal salaries competitive, Congress adjusts the entire salary scale from time to time, based on comparison with salaries in the private sector.

SOURCES OF ADDITIONAL INFORMATION

The above are only a few of the many federal law enforcement agencies. For further general information about law enforcement positions with the United States government, the requirements, the examinations, and the methods of application, the applicant should write the nearest United States Office of Personnel Management *Federal Job Information Center*. If you write to the *Federal Job Information Center,* give a brief description of your education, your work experience, and the kind of job you seek. Telephone numbers of *Job Information Centers* may be found under United States Government listings in the telephone directory in cities where *Federal Job Information Centers* are located. Local State Employment Service Centers can also provide you with information on the location of your nearest *Federal Job Information Center*. For further information about federal law enforcement careers you can also write

United States Office of Personnel Management
1900 E. Street N.W.
Washington, D.C. 20415

Ask for the following pamphlets:

1. "Working for the USA" BRE-37
2. "Law Enforcement and Related Jobs with Federal Agencies" BRE-38

Many federal intelligence and law-enforcement-related jobs are not filled through the Office of Personnel Management. If you are interested in working for any of the agencies listed below, write directly to the address shown.

Central Intelligence Agency (Intelligence)
Director of Personnel
Washington, D.C. 20505

Federal Bureau of Investigation (Special Agents)
9th and Pennsylvania N.W.
Washington, D.C. 20531

National Security Agency (Investigators, Intelligence)
College Relations Branch
Fort Meade, Md. 20755

Department of State (Special Agents, Security Officers)
Executive Office, Office of Security
Room 25513
Washington, D.C. 20520

Atomic Energy Commission (Investigators)
Division of Personnel
Washington, D.C. 20545

U.S. Postal Service (Inspectors, Investigators, Security)
Chief Postal Inspector
Post Office Department
Washington, D.C. 20260

Defense Intelligence Agency (Intelligence)
Civilian Personnel Office
The Pentagon
Washington, D.C. 20301

U.S. Army Security Agency (Intelligence)
Civilian Personnel Office
Arlington, Va. 22212

Naval Intelligence Command (Intelligence)
Washington, D.C. 20350

U.S. Air Force Security Service
(Intelligence)
Kelly Air Force Base
San Antonio, Texas 78240

For law enforcement positions with branches of the United States Armed Services (e.g., Military Police, Air Police), you should contact your nearest Army, Air Force, Navy, or Marine recruiter.

CAREER OPPORTUNITIES IN STATE LAW ENFORCEMENT

NATURE OF THE WORK

State Police/State Highway Patrol State police officers perform general police duties throughout the state. Generally speaking, agencies designated as state police agencies have full law enforcement powers throughout the state, whereas highway patrol agencies have only traffic enforcement powers; however, some highway patrol agencies do have statewide law enforcement duties and powers.

State police duties involve all facets of police work. State police officers are involved in traffic enforcement, traffic control and accident investigation, criminal investigation, and other general police duties. In rural areas the state police may provide all police services, while in urban areas they perform only traffic functions and special investigative assignments, and, when requested, assist the local police forces.

Other State Law Enforcement Agencies Just as the federal government has many specialized law enforcement agencies, so do the various states. There are Liquor Control Boards, Motor Vehicle Agents and Inspectors, Narcotics Agents, Welfare Investigators, Marine Police, and Fish and Game Officers, to name a few.

The number and nature of state law enforcement agencies vary from state to state, and therefore no complete or accurate listing can be provided. You should check with the state civil service commission or the local state employment agency.

PLACES OF EMPLOYMENT

Officers of the various state law enforcement agencies can expect to find work anywhere within the state. The needs of the service come first, and state law enforcement agents must usually be willing to work anywhere in the state.

TRAINING, OTHER QUALIFICATIONS, AND ADVANCEMENT

State Police/State Highway Patrol All state police agencies have vigorous and thorough training programs. State police officers must pass competitive examinations and meet strict physical and personal qualifications. Most require completion of high school. State police agencies are for the most part under civil service regulations, and promotions and advancement adhere to merit concepts.

Other State Law Enforcement Agencies In other state law enforcement agencies, training and qualifications vary with the needs and functions of the agency. You are best advised to check with the particular agency you are interested in, in order to learn of its requirements and training program. Promotions and advancement are usually under state civil service regulations.

EMPLOYMENT OUTLOOK

The employment outlook for state law enforcement agencies through the 1980s is excellent. The interstate highway system will require additional state police/state highway patrol personnel. The continued public emphasis on crime control will create the need for personnel in all areas of state law enforcement. A limited number of openings will also result from normal attrition.

EARNINGS AND WORKING CONDITIONS

State law enforcement salaries vary from state to state, but they are generally competitive within their state. State police/state highway patrol agencies usually furnish officers' uniforms, firearms, and other necessary equipment, or provide special allowances for their purchase. In some state law enforcement agencies, cars are provided. State law enforcement agencies usually provide liberal benefits, such as pension plans; paid vacations; sick leave; and medical, surgical, and life insurance.

In most states, the scheduled work week for state police/state highway patrol officers is forty hours. Since state police/state highway patrol officers must provide protection around the clock, some officers are on duty over weekends, on holidays, and at night.

Like any law enforcement work, the work of state law enforcement officers is sometimes hazardous. They always run the risk of an automobile accident while pursuing speeding motorists or fleeing criminals. Police officers also face the risk of bodily harm while apprehending criminals or controlling disorders.

SOURCES OF ADDITIONAL INFORMATION

For information about state law enforcement agencies, you should write the state law enforcement agency you are interested in. You can also obtain information from the state employment agency or the state civil service commission. For further information, write

National Employment Listing Service
Texas Criminal Justice Center
Sam Houston State University
Huntsville, Tex. 77341

International Association of Chiefs of Police
Eleven Firstfield Road
Gaithersburg, Md. 20760

CAREER OPPORTUNITIES IN MUNICIPAL LAW ENFORCEMENT

NATURE OF THE WORK

The police officer who works in a small community handles many police duties. In the course of a day's work, he or she may direct traffic at the scene of a fire, investigate a housebreaking, and give first aid to an accident victim. In a large police department, officers are usually assigned to a specific type of duty. Most are detailed either to patrol or traffic duty; smaller numbers are assigned to such specialized work as accident prevention or operating communication systems. Some officers are detectives assigned to criminal investigation; others are experts in chemical microscopic analysis, firearms identification, and handwriting and fingerprint identification. In very large cities, a few officers may be trained to work with such special units as mounted and motorcycle police, harbor patrols, helicopter patrols, canine corps, mobile rescue teams, and youth aid services.

An increasing number of city police departments include women. While in the past women officers were generally limited to working with juvenile delinquents and women offenders, or as meter maids, their role in law enforcement is continually expanding. Women officers now perform a wide variety of police functions.

PLACES OF EMPLOYMENT

Municipal police departments range from New York's 30,000 to departments as small as one or two. Almost every city or community of any size has a police force. Local police forces can be found at all levels of local government.

TRAINING, OTHER QUALIFICATIONS, AND ADVANCEMENT

Local civil service regulations govern the appointment of police officers in practically all large cities and in many small ones. Candidates must be United States citizens, usually at least twenty-one years of age, and able to meet other minimum requirements. Eligibility for appointment is also determined by performance on competitive examinations, physical and personal qualifications, and education and experience. In large police departments, where most of the jobs are to be found, applicants usually must have at least a high school education. A few cities require some college credits, and some hire law enforcement students as police interns. Some police departments accept men and women who have less than a high school education as recruits, particularly if they have had work experience in a field related to law enforcement.

Police departments are increasingly emphasizing post-high school training in sociology, psychology, and minority-group relations. As a result, more than 800 colleges and universities now offer major programs in criminal justice.

Before their first assignments, police officers usually go through a period of training. In many small communities, the instruction is given informally as recruits work for about a week or more with experienced officers. In large city police departments, more extensive training may extend over several weeks or a few months. This training includes classroom instruction in constitutional law and civil rights, state laws and local ordinances, and the procedures to be followed in accident investigation, patrol, traffic control, and other police work.

Police officers generally become eligible for promotion after a specified period of service. In a large department, promotion may enable an officer to specialize in one kind of law enforcement activity, perhaps laboratory work, traffic control, communications, or work with juveniles. Promotions to the rank of sergeant are usually made according to each candidate's position on a promotion list, as determined by performance on written examinations and work as a police officer. Advancement opportunities generally are more numerous in large police departments, where separate bureaus work under the direction of administrative officers and their assistants.

EMPLOYMENT OUTLOOK

Police employment is expected to rise moderately during the 1980s as increased population and economic growth create a need for more officers to protect life and property, regulate traffic, and provide other police services. Future police jobs are likely to be affected by changes now occurring in police methods and equipment. Specialists are becoming more essential to the effective operation of city police departments. An increasing number of departments, for example, use electronic data processing to compile administrative, criminal, and identification records and to operate emergency communications systems. Many departments also need officers with specialized training to apply engineering techniques to traffic control and social work techniques to crime prevention. Generally, growth, public concern over law enforcement, and normal job attrition will provide numerous openings in the coming years.

EARNINGS AND WORKING CONDITIONS

In the past, police salaries have been low, but in most cities, salaries and benefits are now becoming competitive with private industry. Most police officers receive regular pay increases during their first few years of employment until they reach a specified maximum. Sergeants, lieutenants, and captains are paid progressively higher basic salaries than patrol officers in the same police departments. Police departments usually provide officers with special allowances for uniforms and furnish revolvers, nightsticks, handcuffs, and other required equipment. Police officers generally are covered by liberal pension plans, enabling many to retire at half pay by the time they reach age fifty-five. Paid vacations; sick leave; and medical, surgical, and life insurance plans are among the benefits frequently provided.

The scheduled work week for police officers is usually forty hours; in localities where the work week is longer, weekly hours are gradually being reduced. Police protection must be provided around the clock; therefore, in all but the very smallest communities, some officers are on duty over weekends, on holidays, and at night. Police officers are subject to call at any time their service may be needed and in emergencies may work overtime. In some departments, overtime is paid at straight time or at time and a half; in others, officers may be given an equal amount of time off on another day of the week.

Police officers may be assigned to work outdoors for long periods in all kinds of weather. The injury rate is higher than in many occupations and reflects the risks police officers take in pursuing speeding motorists, capturing lawbreakers, and dealing with public disorders.

SOURCES OF ADDITIONAL INFORMATION

Information about local entrance requirements may be obtained from local civil service commissions or police departments. Additional information on the occupation of police officers may be obtained from

International Association of Chiefs of Police
Eleven Firstfield Road
Gaithersburg, Md. 20760

Fraternal Order of Police
Pick-Carter Hotel
1012 Prospect Avenue
Cleveland, Ohio 44115

National Employment Listing Service
Texas Criminal Justice Center
Sam Houston State University
Huntsville, Texas 77341

Further information on the salaries and hours of work of police officers in various cities is published by the International City Managers' Association in the *Municipal Yearbook,* which can be found in your local library.

CAREER OPPORTUNITIES IN CORRECTIONS

NATURE OF THE WORK

Correctional operations are administered by federal, state, county, and muficipal governments. The career opportunities within this diverse system are many. Correctional institutions employ people with an array of occupational specialities. There are psychologists, counselors, sociologists, administrators, custodial guards, parole officers, probation officers, teachers, technicians, and people with many other skills employed in the correctional system.

Security is an essential element of prisons, and a considerable number of those employed in the correctional system are employed as custodial guards. Custodial guards maintain a watch over the inmate population to ensure that there are no escapes. They enforce the rules and regulations governing the operation of a correctional institution and oversee the confinement, safety, health, and protection of inmates. They may at times need to resort to using physical effort to subdue recalcitrant inmates who may be armed or assaultive. Custodial guards also supervise the work assignments of inmates and may counsel inmates on personal and family goals and problems. Custodial guards may be used at any location where a guard is needed to maintain a vigil over the inmate population.

Although security is essential in the prison situation, rehabilitation is also considered a goal of the correctional institution. Various occupational specialities work together to develop rehabilitation programs for the prison population. Teachers conduct educational programs to improve the educational level of the inmates. Counselors advise inmates on personal problems and on programs available within the correctional institution. Sociologists and psychologists delve into the social and psychological problems of the inmates and attempt to develop rehabilitation programs that will suit special needs. Correctional administrators develop programs, budgets, personnel plans, and so forth, for the running of the correctional

institution. Vocational instructors provide job training through work programs. All are attempting to rehabilitate the criminal and make possible a return to society and a normal life.

Probation and parole officers assist persons on probation and parole in readjusting to society. Probation officers investigate the social history and background of persons under the jurisdiction of the court and report this information to the court. The judge uses this information in judicial decisions. Parole officers perform this same service for parole boards. Probation and parole officers also counsel and supervise persons on probation or parole, help them secure necessary education or employment, and try to resolve their family problems through counseling or by directing them to other services in the community.

This is only a partial list of the many talents used today in the larger correctional institutions. As in most large institutions, clerks, secretaries, accountants, managers, lawyers, computer operators, research teams, and all the many talents that go to operate a large modern business organization are present in many correctional institutions.

PLACES OF EMPLOYMENT

There are correctional institutions throughout the United States at the federal, state, county, and municipal levels. Correctional facilities are usually located in rural areas; however, there is a trend toward more community-based correctional facilities. The institutional workers in the correctional system are generally employed at prisons, jails, or wherever the inmates are serving their terms. Probation and parole officers generally work out of a local office in the community. Employment in corrections is nationwide, and positions can be found in all fifty states.

TRAINING, OTHER QUALIFICATIONS, AND ADVANCEMENT

There is much variation in the personnel policies of the many correctional systems. However, civil service merit systems cover a majority of correctional systems, with the others most often being smaller, local organizations.

Entrance requirements for jobs in correctional institutions also vary considerably from one jurisdiction to the next. Custodial personnel are usually required to have at least a high school education and to be in good physical condition. The professional staff of correctional institutions — counselors, sociologists, teachers, and the like — are usually required to have a bachelor's degree at a minimum. A number of correctional agencies provide some form of initial training for their personnel.

Although promotions within correctional systems tend to stress seniority, and promotions programs for the most part are rather inflexible, there should be excellent chances for advancement for the well-qualified and dedicated correctional worker in the coming years. Personnel requirements in the correctional systems far exceed the present staffing. The availability of federal funding for correctional systems has given many correctional agencies the impetus to try to meet recommended standards in personnel.

EMPLOYMENT OUTLOOK

Employment opportunities for correctional workers should be excellent in the next decade. The continued concern with crime and criminal offenders has led to the growth and expansion of most correctional agencies. To meet recommended standards, many correctional agencies need to hire additional correctional personnel. As new programs — halfway houses, community-based corrections, work release, and so forth — are initiated, more new personnel will be needed. In addition, normal attrition through retirement and job shifts will continue to provide a steady flow of openings in corrections.

EARNINGS AND WORKING CONDITIONS

Unfortunately, salaries for correctional employees have traditionally been low. Nevertheless, the emphasis on change and improvement in the correctional field should bring about an improvement in salaries. At present, the federal agencies pay higher salaries than the state agencies, and the state agencies usually pay higher salaries than the local agencies.

Prison settings are usually in rural areas. Certain prison services, like security, require twenty-four hour coverage and therefore shift work. Other support services usually work a normal forty-hour week. Correctional agencies are government agencies, and as such they usually supply the liberal job benefits given most government employees.

SOURCES OF ADDITIONAL INFORMATION

Information about local requirements for correctional employees can be obtained from the local correctional agency. Information on state correctional agencies can be acquired from the state civil service commission, the state correctional agency, or the local state employment service office. Information on federal correctional institutions can be obtained from the Federal Office of Personnel Management, or write

United States Department of Justice
Bureau of Prisons
Washington, D.C. 20534

General information on corrections can be obtained by writing

The American Correctional Association
4321 Hartwick Road
College Park, Md. 20740

National Council on Crime and
Delinquency
Continental Plaza
411 Hackensack Avenue
Hackensack, N.J. 07601

National Employment Listing Service
Texas Criminal Justice Center
Sam Houston State University
Huntsville, Texas 77341

CAREER OPPORTUNITIES IN THE LEGAL PROFESSION

NATURE OF THE WORK

Training in law and the legal profession provides many avenues for entrance into various criminal justice positions. Judges are usually lawyers, as are prosecutors and attorneys general. The FBI employs a large number of trained lawyers as Special Agents. Large police departments and some correctional agencies employ lawyers as legal consultants. Criminal justice agencies need expert advice on the law, and the trained lawyer usually provides this service.

Lawyers also provide services to the criminal defendant. Lawyers in private practice represent their clients in criminal matters before the courts. Some, though only a few, specialize in criminal law. Public defenders, who are also lawyers, represent criminal defendants.

A good many lawyers find their way into politics, where they deal with the criminal justice system in many ways. Legislators, many of whom are lawyers, create legislation on substantive and procedural law. Numerous other lawyers serving as elected officials in various capacities deal both directly and indirectly with aspects of the criminal justice system.

PLACES OF EMPLOYMENT

Opportunities for lawyers in the criminal justice system exist mainly in the larger cities. Police departments, district attorney's offices, public defender's offices, and other criminal justice agencies of the larger cities have the need for legal assistance. They also have the size necessary to support the employment of large legal staffs.

The federal government employs a large number of lawyers in the Justice and Treasury departments. Assignments in these agencies could be anywhere in the United States. State and local governments throughout the United States employ lawyers in various positions, for example, as legal assistants to the attorney general or the district attorney.

TRAINING, OTHER QUALIFICATIONS, AND ADVANCEMENT

Before a person can practice law in the court of any state, he or she must be admitted to the bar of the state. In all states, applicants for bar admission must pass a written examination; however, a few states waive this requirement for graduates of their own in-state law schools. Other usual requirements are United States citizenship and good moral character. If a lawyer has been admitted to the bar in one state, he or she can usually be admitted to practice in another state without taking an examination by meeting the state's standards of good moral character and having a specified amount of legal experience.

To qualify for the bar examination in most states, an applicant must have completed a minimum of three years of college work and must in addition be a graduate of a law school approved by the American Bar As-

APPENDIX B

THE UNITED STATES CONSTITUTION

WE THE PEOPLE of the United States, in Order to form a more perfect Union, establish Justice, insure domestic Tranquility, provide for the common defence, promote the general Welfare, and secure the Blessings of Liberty to ourselves and our Posterity, do ordain and establish this CONSTITUTION for the United States of America.

ARTICLE I

SECTION 1. All legislative Powers herein granted shall be vested in a Congress of the United States, which shall consist of a Senate and House of Representatives.

SECTION 2. [1] The House of Representatives shall be composed of Members chosen every second Year by the People of the several States, and the Electors in each State shall have the Qualifications requisite for Electors of the most numerous Branch of the State Legislature.

[2] No Person shall be a Representative who shall not have attained to the Age of twenty-five Years, and been seven Years a Citizen of the United States, and who shall not, when elected, be an Inhabitant of that State in which he shall be chosen.

[3] *[Representatives and direct Taxes shall be apportioned among the several States which may be included within this Union, according to their respective Numbers, which shall be determined by adding to the whole Number of free Persons, including those bound to Service for a Term of Years, and excluding Indians not taxed, three fifths of all other Persons.] The actual Enumeration shall be made within three Years after the first Meeting of the Congress of the United States, and within every subsequent Term of ten Years, in such Manner as they shall by Law direct. The Number of Representatives shall not exceed one for every thirty Thousand, but each State shall have at Least one Representative; and until such enumeration shall be made, the State of New Hampshire shall be entitled to chuse three, Massachusetts eight, Rhode-Island and Providence Plantations one, Connecticut five, New-York six, New Jersey four, Pennsylvania eight, Delaware one, Maryland six, Virginia ten, North Carolina five, South Carolina five, and Georgia three.

[4] When vacancies happen in the Representation from any State, the Executive Authority thereof shall issue Writs of Election to fill such vacancies.

[5] The House of Representatives shall chuse their Speaker and other Officers; and shall have the sole Power of Impeachment.

* The part included in heavy brackets was repealed by section 2 of amendment XIV.

¹ Section 3. **The Senate of the United States shall be composed of two Senators from each State, [chosen by the Legislature] thereof, for six Years; and each Senator shall have one Vote.

² Immediately after they shall be assembled in Consequence of the first Election, they shall be divided as equally as may be into three Classes. The Seats of the Senators of the first Class shall be vacated at the Expiration of the Second Year, of the second Class at the Expiration of the fourth Year, and of the third Class at the Expiration of the sixth Year, so that one-third may be chosen every second Year; [and if Vacancies happen by Resignation, or otherwise, during the Recess of the Legislature of any State, the Executive thereof may make temporary Appointments until the next Meeting of the Legislature, which shall then fill such Vacancies].***

³ No Person shall be a Senator who shall not have attained to the Age of thirty Years, and been nine Years a Citizen of the United States, and who shall not, when elected, be an inhabitant of that State for which he shall be chosen.

⁴ The Vice President of the United States shall be President of the Senate, but shall have no Vote, unless they be equally divided.

⁵ The Senate shall chuse their other Officers, and also a President pro tempore, in the absence of the Vice President, or when he shall exercise the Office of President of the United States.

⁶ The Senate shall have the sole Power to try all Impeachments. When sitting for that Purpose, they shall be on Oath or Affirmation. When the President of the United States is tried, the Chief Justice shall preside: And no Person shall be convicted without the Concurrence of two-thirds of the Members present.

⁷ Judgment in Cases of Impeachment shall not extend further than to removal from Office, and disqualification to hold and enjoy any Office of honor, Trust, or Profit under the United States: but the Party convicted shall nevertheless be liable and subject to Indictment, Trial, Judgment, and Punishment, according to Law.

Section 4. ¹The Times, Places and Manner of holding Elections for Senators and Representatives, shall be prescribed in each State by the Legislature thereof; but the Congress may at any time by Law make or alter such Regulations, except as to the Places of chusing Senators.

² The Congress shall assembly at least once in every Year, and such Meeting shall [be on the first Monday in December,] unless they shall by Law appoint a different Day.*

Section 5. ¹ Each House shall be the Judge of the Elections, Returns, and Qualifications of its own Members, and a Majority of each shall constitute a Quorum to do Business; but a smaller Number may adjourn from day to day, and may be authorized to compel the Attendance of absent Members, in such Manner, and under such Penalties as each House may provide.

² Each House may determine the Rules of its Proceedings, punish its Members for disorderly Behavior, and, with the Concurrence of two thirds, expel a Member.

³ Each House shall keep a Journal of its Proceedings, and from time to time publish the same, excepting such Parts as may in their Judgment require Secrecy; and the Yeas and Nays of the Members of either House on any question shall, at the Desire of one fifth of those Present, be entered on the Journal.

⁴ Neither House, during the Session of Congress, shall, without the Consent of the other, adjourn for more than three days, nor to any other Place than that in which the two Houses shall be sitting.

Section 6. ¹ The Senators and Representatives shall receive a Compensation for their Services, to be ascertained by Law, and paid out of the Treasury of the United States. They shall in all Cases, except Treason, Felony and Breach of the Peace, be privileged from Arrest during their Attendance

** The part included in heavy brackets was repealed by section 1 of amendment XVII.
*** The part included in heavy brackets was changed by clause 2 of amendment XVII.
NOTE.—The superior number preceding the paragraphs designates the number of the clause.
* The part included in heavy brackets was changed by section 2 of amendment XX.

at the Session of their respective Houses, and in going to and returning from the same; and for any Speech or Debate in either House, they shall not be questioned in any other Place.

² No Senator or Representative shall, during the Time for which he was elected, be appointed to any civil Office under the Authority of the United States, which shall have been created, or the Emoluments whereof shall have been encreased during such time; and no Person holding any Office under the United States, shall be a Member of either House during his Continuance in Office.

SECTION 7. ¹ All Bills for raising Revenue shall originate in the House of Representatives; but the Senate may propose or concur with Amendments as on other Bills.

² Every Bill which shall have passed the House of Representatives and the Senate, shall, before it become a Law, be presented to the President of the United States; if he approve he shall sign it, but if not he shall return it, with his Objections to the House in which it shall have originated, who shall enter the Objections at large on their Journal, and proceed to reconsider it. If after such Reconsideration two thirds of that House shall agree to pass the Bill, it shall be sent, together with the Objections, to the other House, by which it shall likewise be reconsidered, and if approved by two thirds of that House, it shall become a Law. But in all such Cases the Votes of both Houses shall be determined by Yeas and Nays, and the Names of the Persons voting for and against the Bill shall be entered on the Journal of each House respectively. If any Bill shall not be returned by the President within ten Days (Sundays excepted) after it shall have been presented to him, the Same shall be a Law, in like Manner as if he had signed it, unless the Congress by their Adjournment prevent its Return, in which Case it shall not be a Law.

³ Every Order, Resolution, or Vote to which the Concurrence of the Senate and House of Representatives may be necessary (except on a question of Adjournment) shall be presented to the President of the United States; and before the Same shall take Effect, shall be approved by him, or being disapproved by him, shall be repassed by two thirds of the Senate and House of Representatives, according to the Rules and Limitations prescribed in the Case of a Bill.

SECTION 8. The Congress shall have Power To lay and collect Taxes, Duties, Imposts and Excises, to pay the Debts and provide for the common Defence and general Welfare of the United States; but all Duties, Imposts and Excises shall be uniform throughout the United States;

² To borrow money on the credit of the United States;

³ To regulate Commerce with foreign Nations, and among the several States, and with the Indian Tribes;

⁴ To establish an uniform Rule of Naturalization, and uniform Laws on the subject of Bankruptcies throughout the United States;

⁵ To coin Money, regulate the Value thereof, and of foreign Coin, and fix the Standard of Weights and Measures;

⁶ To provide for the Punishment of counterfeiting the Securities and current Coin of the United States;

⁷ To Establish Post Offices and post Roads;

⁸ To promote the Progress of Science and useful Arts, by securing for limited Times to Authors and Inventors the exclusive Right to their respective Writings and Discoveries;

⁹ To constitute Tribunals inferior to the supreme Court;

¹⁰ To define and punish Piracies and Felonies committed on the high Seas, and Offenses against the Law of Nations;

¹¹ To declare War, grant Letters of Marque and Reprisal, and make Rules concerning Captures on Land and Water;

¹² To raise and support Armies, but no Appropriation of Money to that Use shall be for a longer Term than two Years;

¹³ To provide and maintain a Navy;

[14] To make Rules for the Government and Regulation of the land and naval Forces;

[15] To provide for calling forth the Militia to execute the Laws of the Union, suppress insurrections and repel Invasions;

[16] To provide for organizing, arming, and disciplining the Militia, and for governing such Part of them as may be employed in the Service of the United States, reserving to the States respectively, the Appointment of the Officers, and the Authority of training the Militia according to the discipline prescribed by Congress;

[17] To exercise exclusive Legislation in all Cases whatsoever, over such District (not exceeding ten Miles square) as may, by Cession of particular States, and the acceptance of Congress, become the Seat of the Government of the United States, and to exercise like Authority over all Places purchased by the Consent of the Legislature of the State in which the Same shall be, for the Erection of Forts, Magazines, Arsenals, dock-Yards, and other needful Buildings; — And

[18] To make all Laws which shall be necessary and proper for carrying into Execution the foregoing Powers, and all other Powers vested by this Constitution in the Government of the United States, or in any Department or Officer thereof.

SECTION 9. [1] The Migration or Importation of Such Persons as any of the States now existing shall think proper to admit, shall not be prohibited by the Congress prior to the Year one thousand eight hundred and eight, but a tax or duty may be imposed on such Importation, not exceeding ten dollars for each Person.

[2] The privilege of the Writ of Habeas Corpus shall not be suspended, unless when in Cases of Rebellion or Invasion the public Safety may require it.

[3] No Bill of Attainder or ex post facto Law shall be passed.

[4] * No capitation, or other direct, Tax shall be laid, unless in Proportion to the Census or Enumeration herein before directed to be taken.

[5] No Tax or Duty shall be laid on Articles exported from any State.

[6] No preference shall be given by any Regulation of Commerce or Revenue to the Ports of one State over those of another: nor shall Vessels bound to, or from, one State be obliged to enter, clear, or pay Duties in another.

[7] No money shall be drawn from the Treasury, but in Consequence of Appropriations made by Law; and a regular Statement and Account of the Receipts and Expenditures of all public Money shall be published from time to time.

[8] No title of Nobility shall be granted by the United States: And no Person holding any Office of Profit or Trust under them, shall, without the Consent of the Congress, accept of any present, Emolument, Office, or Title, of any kind whatever, from any King, Prince, or foreign State.

SECTION 10. [1] No State shall enter into any Treaty, Alliance, or Confederation; grant Letters of Marque and Reprisal; coin Money; emit Bills of Credit; make any Thing but gold and silver Coin a Tender in Payment of Debts; pass any Bill of Attainder, ex post facto Law, or Law impairing the Obligation of Contracts, or grant any Title of Nobility.

[2] No State shall, without the Consent of the Congress, lay any Imposts or Duties on Imports or Exports, except what may be absolutely necessary for executing its inspection Laws; and the net Produce of all Duties and Imposts, laid by any State on Imports or Exports, shall be for the Use of the Treasury of the United States; and all such Laws shall be subject to the Revision and Control of the Congress.

[3] No State shall, without the Consent of Congress, lay any duty of Tonnage, keep Troops, or Ships of War in time of Peace, enter into any Agreement or Compact with another State, or with a foreign Power, or engage in War, unless actually invaded, or in such imminent Danger as will not admit of delay.

---

* See also amendment XVI.

ARTICLE II

SECTION 1. [1]The executive Power shall be vested in a President of the United States of America. He shall hold his Office during the Term of four Years, and, together with the Vice-President, chosen for the same Term, be elected, as follows:

[2] Each State shall appoint, in such Manner as the Legislature thereof may direct, a Number of Electors, equal to the whole Number of Senators and Representatives to which the State may be entitled in the Congress: but no Senator or Representative, or Person holding an Office of Trust or Profit under the United States, shall be appointed an Elector.

* [The Electors shall meet in their respective States, and vote by Ballot for two persons of whom one at least shall not be an Inhabitant of the same State with themselves. And they shall make a list of all the Persons voted for, and of the Number of Votes for each; which List they shall sign and certify, and transmit sealed to the Seat of the Government of the United States, directed to the President of the Senate. The President of the Senate shall, in the Presence of the Senate and House of Representatives, open all the Certificates, and the Votes shall then be counted. The Person having the greatest Number of votes shall be the President, if such Number by a Majority of the whole Number of Electors appointed; and if there be more than one who have such Majority, and have an equal Number of Votes, then the House of Representatives shall immediately chuse by Ballot one of them for President; and if no Person have a Majority, then from the five highest on the List the said House shall in like Manner chuse the President. But in chusing the President, the Votes shall be taken by States, the Representation from each State having one Vote; A quorum for this Purpose shall consist of a Member or Members from two-thirds of the States, and a Majority of all the States shall be necessary to a Choice. In every Case, after the Choice of the President the Person having the greatest Number of Votes of the Electors shall be the Vice President. But if there should remain two or more who have equal Votes, the Senate shall chuse from them by Ballot the Vice-President.]

[3] The Congress may determine the Time of chusing the Electors and the Day on which they shall give their Votes; which Day shall be the same throughout the United States.

[4] No person except a natural born Citizen, or a Citizen of the United States, at the time of the Adoption of this Constitution, shall be eligible to the Office of President; neither shall any Person be eligible to that Office who shall not have attained to the Age of thirty-five Years, and been fourteen Years a Resident within the United States.

[5] In case of the removal of the President from Office, or of his Death, Resignation or Inability to discharge the Powers and Duties of the said Office, the same shall devolve on the Vice President, and the Congress may by Law provide for the Case of Removal, Death, Resignation or Inability, both of the President, and Vice President, declaring what Officer shall then act as President, and such Officer shall act accordingly, until the Disability be removed, or a President shall be elected.

[6] The President shall, at stated Times, receive for his Services, a Compensation, which shall neither be encreased nor diminished during the Period for which he shall have been elected, and he shall not receive within that Period any other Emolument from the United States, or any of them.

[7] Before he enter on the Execution of his Office, he shall take the following Oath or Affirmation: — "I do solemnly swear (or affirm) that I will faithfully execute the Office of President of the United States, and will to the best of my Ability, preserve, protect and defend the Constitution of the United States."

SECTION 2. [1] The President shall be Commander in Chief of the Army and Navy of the United States, and of the Militia of the several States, when called into the actual Service of the United States; he may require the Opinion, in writing, of the principal Officer in each of the executive Departments, upon any subject relating to the Duties of their respective Offices, and he shall have Power to grant Reprieves and Pardons for Offences against the United States, except in Cases of Impeachment.

* This paragraph has been superseded by amendment XII.

[2] He shall have Power, by and with the Advice and Consent of the Senate, to make Treaties, provided two-thirds of the Senators present concur; and he shall nominate, and by and with the Advice and Consent of the Senate, shall appoint Ambassadors, other public Ministers and Consuls, Judge of the supreme Court, and all other Officers of the United States, whose Appointments are not herein otherwise provided for, and which shall be established by Law; but the Congress may by Law vest the Appointment of such inferior Officers, as they think proper, in the President alone, in the Courts of Law, or in the Heads of Departments.

[3] The President shall have Power to fill up all Vacancies that may happen during the Recess of the Senate, by granting Commissions which shall expire at the End of their next Session.

SECTION 3. He shall from time to time give to the Congress Information of the State of the Union, and recommend to their Consideration such Measures as he shall judge necessary and expedient; he may, on extraordinary Occasions, convene both Houses, or either of them, and in Case of Disagreement between them, with Respect to the Time of Adjournment, he may adjourn them to such Time as he shall think proper; he shall receive Ambassadors and other public Ministers; he shall take Care that the Laws be faithfully executed, and shall Commission all the Officers of the United States.

SECTION 4. The President, Vice President and all civil Officers of the United States, shall be removed from Office on Impeachment for, and Conviction of, Treason, Bribery, or other high Crimes and Misdemeanors.

ARTICLE III

SECTION 1. The judicial Power of the United States, shall be vested in one supreme Court, and in such inferior Courts as the Congress may from time to time ordain and establish. The Judges, both of the supreme and inferior Courts, shall hold their Offices during good Behavior, and shall, at stated Times, receive for their Services a Compensation which shall not be diminished during their Continuance in Office.

SECTION 2. [1] The judicial Power shall extend to all Cases, in Law and Equity, arising under this Constitution, the Laws of the United States, and Treaties made, or which shall be made, under their Authority; — to all Cases affecting Ambassadors, other public Ministers and Consuls; — to all Cases of admiralty and maritime Jurisdiction; — to Controversies to which the United States shall be a Party; — to Controversies between two or more States; — between a State and Citizens of another State;* — between Citizens of different States; — between Citizens of the same State claiming Lands under Grants of different States, and between a State, or the Citizens thereof, and foreign States, Citizens or Subjects.

[2] In all Cases affecting Ambassadors, other public Ministers and Consuls, and those in which a State shall be Party, the supreme Court shall have original Jurisdiction. In all the other Cases before mentioned, the supreme Court shall have appellate Jurisdiction, both as to Law and Fact, with such Exceptions, and under such Regulations as the Congress shall make.

[3] The trial of all Crimes except in Cases of Impeachment shall be by Jury; and such Trial shall be held in the State where the said Crimes shall have been committed; but when not committed within any State, the Trial shall be at such Place or Places as the Congress may by Law have directed.

SECTION 3. [1] Treason against the United States shall consist only in levying War against them, or, in adhering to their Enemies, giving them Aid and Comfort. No Person shall be convicted of Treason unless on the Testimony of two Witnesses to the same overt Act, or on Confession in open Court.

[2] The Congress shall have power to declare the Punishment of Treason, but no Attainder of Treason shall work Corruption of Blood, or Forfeiture except during the Life of the Person attainted.

* This clause has been affected by amendment XI.

ARTICLE IV

SECTION 1. Full Faith and Credit shall be given in each State to the public Acts, Records, and judicial Proceedings of every other State. And the Congress may by general Laws prescribe the Manner in which such Acts, Records and Proceedings shall be proved, and the Effect thereof.

SECTION 2. [1] The Citizens of each State shall be entitled to all Privileges and Immunities of Citizens in the several States.

[2] A Person charged in any State with Treason, Felony, or other Crime, who shall flee from Justice, and be found in another State, shall on demand of the executive Authority of the State from which he fled, be delivered up, to be removed to the State having Jurisdiction of the Crime.

[3] * [No person held to Service or Labour in one State, under the Laws thereof, escaping into another, shall, in Consequence of any Law or Regulation therein, be discharged from such Service or Labour, but shall be delivered up on Claim of the Party to whom such Service or Labour may be due.]

SECTION 3. [1] New States may be admitted by the Congress into this Union; but no new State shall be formed or erected within the Jurisdiction of any other State; nor any State be formed by the Junction of two or more States, or parts of States, without the Consent of the Legislatures of the States concerned as well as of the Congress.

[2] The Congress shall have Power to dispose of and make all needful Rules and Regulations respecting the Territory or other Property belonging to the United States; and nothing in this Constitution shall be so construed as to Prejudice any Claims of the United States, or of any particular State.

SECTION 4. The United States shall guarantee to every State in this Union a Republican Form of Government, and shall protect each of them against Invasion; and on Application of the Legislature, or of the Executive (when the Legislature cannot be convened) against domestic Violence.

ARTICLE V

The Congress, whenever two-thirds of both Houses shall deem it necessary, shall propose Amendments to this Constitution, or, on the Application of the Legislatures of two-thirds of the several States, shall call a Convention for proposing Amendments, which, in either Case, shall be valid to all Intents and Purposes, as part of this Constitution when ratified by the Legislatures of three-fourths of the several States, or by Conventions in three-fourths thereof, as the one or the other Mode of Ratification may be proposed by the Congress; Provided that no Amendment which may be made prior to the Year One thousand eight hundred and eight shall in any Manner affect the first and fourth Clauses in the Ninth Section of the first Article; and that no State, without its Consent, shall be deprived of its equal Suffrage in the Senate.

ARTICLE VI

[1] All Debts contracted and Engagements entered into, before the Adoption of this Constitution shall be as valid against the United States under this Constitution, as under the Confederation.

[2] This Constitution, and the Laws of the United States which shall be made in Pursuance thereof; and all Treaties made, or which shall be made, under the Authority of the United States, shall be the supreme Law of the Land; and the Judges in every State shall be bound thereby, any Thing in the Constitution of Laws of any State to the Contrary notwithstanding.

[3] The Senators and Representatives before mentioned, and the Members of the several State Legislatures, and all executive and judicial Officers, both of the United States and of the several States, shall be bound by Oath or Affirmation, to support this Constitution; but no religious Test shall ever be required as a Qualification to any Office or public Trust under the United States.

ARTICLE VII

The Ratification of the Conventions of nine States, shall be sufficient for the Establishment of this Constitution between the States so ratifying the Same.

DONE in Convention by the Unanimous Consent of the States present the Seventeenth Day of September in the Year of our Lord one thousand seven hundred and Eighty seven and of the Independence of the United States of America the Twelfth. IN WITNESS whereof We have hereto subscribed our Names.

a G̱o WASHINGTON—
Presid^t*. and deputy from Virginia.*

[Signed also by the deputies of twelve States.]

New Hampshire
JOHN LANGDON
NICHOLAS GILMAN

Massachusetts
NATHANIEL GORHAM
RUFUS KING

Connecticut
WM. SAML. JOHNSON
ROGER SHERMAN

New York
ALEXANDER HAMILTON

New Jersey
WIL: LIVINGSTON
DAVID BREARLEY
WM. PATERSON
JONA: DAYTON

Pennsylvania
B FRANKLIN
ROBT MORRIS
THOS. FITZSIMONS
JAMES WILSON
THOMAS MIFFLIN
GEO. CLYMER
JARED INGERSOLL
GOUV MORRIS

Delaware
GEO: READ
JOHN DICKINSON
JACO: BROOM
GUNNING BEDFORD, JUN
RICHARD BASSETT

Maryland
JAMES McHENRY
DANL CARROLL
DAN OF ST THOS. JENIFER

Virginia
JOHN BLAIR—
JAMES MADISON JR.

North Carolina
WM. BLOUNT
HU WILLIAMSON
RICH'D DOBBS SPAIGHT

South Carolina
J. RUTLEDGE
CHARLES PINCKNEY
CHARLES COTESWORTH
   PINCKNEY
PIERCE BUTLER

Georgia
WILLIAM FEW, Attest:
ABR BALDWIN
WILLIAM JACKSON,
Secretary

RATIFICATION OF THE CONSTITUTION

The Constitution was adopted by a convention of the States on September 17, 1787, and was subsequently ratified by the several States on the following dates: Delaware, December 7, 1787; Pennsylvania, December 12, 1787; New Jersey, December 18, 1787; Georgia, January 2, 1788; Connecticut, January 9, 1788; Massachusetts, February 6, 1788; Maryland, April 28, 1788; South Carolina, May 23, 1788; New Hampshire, June 21, 1788; Virginia, June 25, 1788; New York, July 26, 1788; North Carolina, November 21, 1789; Rhode Island, May 29, 1790. It was declared in operation September 13, 1788; by a resolution of the Continental Congress.

ARTICLES IN ADDITION TO, AND AMENDMENT OF, THE CONSTITUTION OF THE UNITED STATES OF AMERICA, PROPOSED BY CONGRESS, AND RATIFIED BY THE LEGISLATURES OF THE SEVERAL STATES, PURSUANT TO THE FIFTH ARTICLE OF THE ORIGINAL CONSTITUTION

AMENDMENT I

Congress shall make no law respecting an establishment of religion, or prohibiting the free exercise thereof; or abridging the freedom of speech, or of the press; or the right of the people peaceably to assemble and to petition the Government for a redress of grievances.

AMENDMENT II

A well regulated Militia, being necessary to the security of a free State, the right of the people to keep and bear Arms, shall not be infringed.

AMENDMENT III

No Soldier shall, in time of peace be quartered in any house, without the consent of the Owner, nor in time of war, but in a manner to be prescribed by law.

AMENDMENT IV

The right of the people to be secure in their persons, houses, papers, and effects, against unreasonable searches and seizures, shall not be violated, and no Warrants shall issue, but upon probable cause, supported by Oath or affirmation and particularly describing the place to be searched, and the persons or things to be seized.

AMENDMENT V

No person shall be held to answer for a capital, or otherwise infamous crime, unless on a presentment or indictment of a Grand Jury, except in cases arising in the land or naval forces, or in the Militia, when in actual service in time of War or public danger; nor shall any person be subject for the same offence to be twice put in jeopardy of life or limb; nor shall be compelled in any criminal case to be a witness against himself, nor be deprived of life, liberty, or property, without due process of law; nor shall private property be taken for public use, without just compensation.

AMENDMENT VI

In all criminal prosecutions, the accused shall enjoy the right to a speedy and public trial, by an impartial jury of the State and district wherein the crime shall have been committed, which district shall have been previously ascertained by law, and to be informed of the nature and cause of the accusation: to be confronted with the witnesses against him; to have compulsory process for obtaining witnesses in his favor, and to have the Assistance of Counsel for his defence.

AMENDMENT VII

In suits at common law, where the value in controversy shall exceed twenty dollars, the right of trial by jury shall be preserved, and no fact tried by jury, shall be otherwise reexamined in any Court of the United States, than according to the rules of the common law.

AMENDMENT VIII

Excessive bail shall not be required, nor excessive fines imposed, nor cruel and unusual punishments inflicted.

AMENDMENT IX

The enumeration in the Constitution, of certain rights, shall not be construed to deny or disparage others retained by the people.

AMENDMENT X

The powers not delegated to the United States by the Constitution, nor prohibited by it to the States, are reserved to the States respectively, or to the people.
(Ratification of first ten amendments completed December 15, 1791.)

AMENDMENT XI

The Judicial power of the United States shall not be construed to extend to any suit in law or equity, commenced or prosecuted against one of the United States by Citizens of another State, or by Citizens or Subjects of any Foreign State.
(Declared ratified January 8, 1798.)

AMENDMENT XII

The electors shall meet in their respective states and vote by ballot for President and Vice-President, one of whom, at least, shall not be an inhabitant of the same state with themselves; they shall name in their ballots the person voted for as President, and in distinct ballots the person voted for as Vice-President, and they shall make distinct lists of all persons voted for as President, and of all persons voted for as Vice-President, and of the number of votes for each, which lists they shall sign and certify, and transmit sealed to the seat of the government of the United States, directed to the President of the Senate; — The President of the Senate shall, in presence of the Senate and House of Representatives, open all the certificates and the votes shall than be counted; — The person having the greatest number of votes for President, shall be the President, if such number be a majority of the whole number of Electors appointed; and if no person have such majority, then from the persons having the highest numbers not exceeding three on the list of those voted for as President, the House of Representatives shall choose immediately, by ballot, the President. But in choosing the President, the votes shall be taken by states, the representation from each state having one vote; a quorum for this purpose shall consist of a member or members from two-thirds of the states, and a majority of all the states shall be necessary to a choice. *[and if the House of Representatives shall not choose a President whenever the right of choice shall devolve upon them, before the fourth day of March next following, then the Vice-President shall act as President, as in the case of the death or other constitutional disability of the President.] — The person having the greatest number of votes as Vice-President, shall be the Vice-President, if such number be a majority of the whole number of Electors appointed, and if no person have a majority, then from the two highest numbers on the list, the Senate shall choose the Vice-President; a quorum for the purpose shall consist of two-thirds of the whole number of Senators, and a majority of the whole number shall be necessary to a choice. But no person constitutionally ineligible to the office of President shall be eligible to that of Vice-President of the United States.
(Declared ratified September 25, 1804.)

AMENDMENT XIII

SECTION 1. Neither slavery nor involuntary servitude, except as a punishment for crime whereof the party shall have been duly convicted, shall exist within the United States, or any place subject to their jurisdiction.
SECTION 2. Congress shall have power to enforce this article by appropriate legislation.
(Declared ratified December 18, 1865.)

---

* The part included in heavy brackets has been superseded by section 3 of amendment XX.

AMENDMENT XIV

SECTION 1. All persons born or naturalized in the United States, and subject to the jurisdiction thereof, are citizens of the United States and of the State wherein they reside. No State shall make or enforce any law which shall abridge the privileges or immunities of citizens of the United States; nor shall any State deprive any person of life, liberty, or property, without due process of law; nor deny to any person within its jurisdiction the equal protection of the laws.

SECTION 2. Representatives shall be apportioned among the several States according to their respective numbers, counting the whole number of persons in each State, excluding Indians not taxed. But when the right to vote at any election for the choice of electors for President and Vice-President of the United States, Representatives in Congress, the Executive and Judicial officers of a State, or the members of the Legislature thereof, is denied to any of the male inhabitants of such State, being twenty-one years of age, and citizens of the United States, or in any way abridged, except for participation in rebellion, or other crime, the basis of representation therein shall be reduced in the proportion which the number of such male citizens shall bear to the whole number of male citizens twenty-one years of age in such State.

SECTION 3. No person shall be a Senator or Representative in Congress, or elector of President and Vice-President, or hold any office, civil or military, under the United States, or under any State, who, having previously taken an oath, as a member of Congress, or as an officer of the United States, or as a member of any State legislature, or as an executive or judicial officer of any State, to support the Constitution of the United States, shall have engaged in insurrection or rebellion against the same, or given aid or comfort to the enemies thereof. But Congress may by a vote of two-thirds of each House, remove such disability.

SECTION 4. The validity of the public debt of the United States, authorized by law, including debts incurred for payment of pensions and bounties for services in suppressing insurrection or rebellion, shall not be questioned. But neither the United States nor any State shall assume or pay any debt or obligation incurred in aid of insurrection or rebellion against the United States, or any claim for the loss or emancipation of any slave; but all such debts, obligations and claims shall be held illegal and void.

SECTION 5. The Congress shall have power to enforce, by appropriate legislation, the provisions of this article.

(Declared ratified July 28, 1868.)

AMENDMENT XV

SECTION 1. The right of citizens of the United States to vote shall not be denied or abridged by the United States or by any State on account of race, color, or previous condition of servitude —

SECTION 2. The Congress shall have power to enforce this article by appropriate legislation.

(Declared ratified March 30, 1870.)

AMENDMENT XVI

The Congress shall have power to lay and collect taxes on incomes, from whatever source derived, without apportionment among the several States, and without regard to any census or enumeration.

(Declared ratified February 25, 1913.)

AMENDMENT XVII

The Senate of the United States shall be composed of two Senators from each State, elected by the people thereof, for six years; and each Senator shall have one vote. The electors in each State shall have the qualifications requisite for electors of the most numerous branch of the State legislatures.

When vacancies happen in the representation of any State in the Senate, the executive authority of such State shall issue writs of election to fill such vacancies: *Provided,* That the legislature of any State may empower the executive thereof to make temporary appointments until the people fill the vacancies by election as the legislature may direct.

This amendment shall not be so construed as to affect the election or term of any Senator chosen before it becomes valid as part of the Constitution.

(Declared ratified May 31, 1913.)

AMENDMENT XVIII

[SECTION 1. After one year from the ratification of this article the manufacture, sale, or transportation of intoxicating liquors within, the importation thereof into, or the exportation thereof from the United States and all territory subject to the jurisdiction thereof for beverage purposes is hereby prohibited.

[SECTION 2. The Congress and the several States shall have concurrent power to enforce this article by appropriate legislation.

[SECTION 3. This article shall be inoperative unless it shall have been ratified as an amendment to the Constitution by the legislatures of the several States, as provided in the Constitution, within seven years from the date of the submission hereof to the States by the Congress]*

(Declared ratified January 29, 1919.)

AMENDMENT XIX

The right of citizens of the United States to vote shall not be denied or abridged by the United States or by any State on account of sex.

Congress shall have power to enforce this article by appropriate legislation.

(Declared ratified August 26, 1920).

AMENDMENT XX

SECTION 1. Ther terms of the President and Vice-President shall end at noon on the 20th day of January, and the terms of Senators and Representatives at noon on the 3d day of January, of the years in which such terms would have ended if this article had not been ratified; and the terms of their successors shall then begin.

SECTION 2. The Congress shall assemble at least once in every year, and such meeting shall begin at noon on the 3d day of January, unless they shall by law appoint a different day.

SECTION 3. If, at the time for the beginning of the term of the President, the President elect shall have died, the Vice-President elect shall become President. If a President shall not have been chosen before the time fixed for the beginning of his term, or if the President elect shall have failed to qualify, then the Vice-President elect shall act as President until a President shall have qualified; and the Congress may by law provide for the case wherein neither a President elect nor a Vice-President elect shall have qualified, declaring who shall then act as President, or the manner in which one who is to act shall be selected, and such person shall act accordingly until a President or Vice-President shall have qualified.

SECTION 4. The Congress may by law provide for the case of the death of any of the persons from whom the House of Representatives may choose a President whenever the right of choice shall have devolved upon them and for the case of the death of any of the persons from whom the Senate may choose a Vice-President whenever the right of choice shall have devolved upon them.

* Amendment XVIII was repealed by section 1 of amendment XXI.

SECTION 5. Sections 1 and 2 shall take effect on the 15th day of October following the ratification of this article.

SECTION 6. This article shall be inoperative unless it shall have been ratified as an amendment to the Constitution by the legislatures of three-fourths of the several States within seven years from the date of its submission.

(Declared ratified February 6, 1933.)

AMENDMENT XXI

SECTION 1. The eighteenth article of amendment to the Constitution of the United States is hereby repealed.

SECTION 2. The transportation or importation into any State, Territory, or possession of the United States for delivery or use therein of intoxicating liquors, in violation of the laws thereof, is hereby prohibited.

SECTION 3. This article shall be inoperative unless it shall have been ratified as an amendment to the Constitution by conventions in the several States, as provided in the Constitution, within seven years from the date of the submission hereof to the States by the Congress.

(Declared ratified December 5, 1933.)

AMENDMENT XXII

SECTION 1. No person shall be elected to the office of the President more than twice, and no person who has held the office of President, or acted as President, for more than two years of a term to which some other person was elected President shall be elected to the office of the President more than once. But this article shall not apply to any person holding the office of President when this Article was proposed by the Congress, and shall not prevent any person who may be holding the office of President, or acting as President, during the term within which this Article becomes operative from holding the office of President or acting as President during the remainder of such term.

SECTION 2. This article shall be inoperative unless it shall have been ratified as an amendment to the Constitution by the legislatures of three-fourths of the several States within seven years from the date of its submission to the States by the Congress.

(Declared ratified March 1, 1951.)

AMENDMENT XXIII

SECTION 1. The District constituting the seat of Government of the United States shall appoint in such manner as the Congress may direct:

A number of electors of President and Vice President equal to the whole number of Senators and Representatives in Congress to which the District would be entitled if it were a State, but in no event more than the least populous State; they shall be in addition to those appointed by the States, but they shall be considered, for the purposes of the election of President and Vice President, to be electors appointed by a State; and they shall meet in the District and perform such duties as provided by the twelfth article of amendment.

SECTION 2. The Congress shall have power to enforce this article by appropriate legislation.

(Declared ratified April 3, 1961.)

AMENDMENT XXIV

SECTION 1. The right of citizens of the United States to vote in any primary or other election for President or Vice President, for electors for President or Vice President, or for Senator or Representative in Congress, shall not be denied or abridged by the United States or any State by reason of failure to pay any poll tax or other tax.

SECTION 2. The Congress shall have power to enforce this article by appropriate legislation.

(Declared ratified February 4, 1962.)

AMENDMENT XXV

SECTION 1. In case of the removal of the President from office or of his death or resignation, the Vice President shall become President.

SECTION 2. Whenever there is a vacancy in the office of the Vice President, the President shall nominate a Vice President who shall take office upon confirmation by a majority vote of both Houses of Congress.

SECTION 3. Whenever the President transmits to the President pro tempore of the Senate and the Speaker of the House of Representatives his written declaration that he is unable to discharge the powers and duties of his office, and until he transmits to them a written declaration to the contrary, such powers and duties shall be discharged by the Vice President as Acting President.

SECTION 4. Whenever the Vice President and a majority of either the principal officers of the executive departments or of such other body as Congress may by law provide, transmit to the President pro tempore of the Senate and the Speaker of the House of Representatives their written declaration that the President is unable to discharge the powers and duties of his office, the Vice President shall immediately assume the powers and the duties of the office as Acting President.

Thereafter, when the President transmits to the President pro tempore of the Senate and the Speaker of the House of Representatives his written declaration that no inability exists, he shall resume the powers and duties of his office unless the Vice President and a majority of either the principal officers of the executive department or of such other body as Congress may by law provide, transmit within four days to the President pro tempore of the Senate and the Speaker of the House of Representatives their written declaration that the President is unable to discharge the powers and duties of his office. Thereupon Congress shall decide the issue, assembling within forty-eight hours for that purpose if not in session. If the Congress, within twenty-one days after receipt of the latter written declaration, or, if Congress is not in session, within twenty-one days after Congress is required to assemble, determines by two-thirds vote of both Houses that the President is unable to discharge the powers and duties of his office, the Vice President shall continue to discharge the same as Acting President; otherwise, the President shall resume the powers and duties of his office.

(Declared ratified February 10, 1967.)

AMENDMENT XXVI

SECTION 1. The right of citizens of the United States, who are eighteen years of age or older, to vote shall not be denied or abridged by the United States or by any State on account of age.

SECTION 2. The Congress shall have power to enforce this article by appropriate legislation.

(Declared ratified July 1, 1971.)

PROPOSED AMENDMENT

SECTION 1. Equality of rights under the law shall not be denied or abridged by the United States or by any State on account of sex.

SECTION 2. The Congress shall have the power to enforce, by appropriate legislation, the provisions of this Article.

(Passed Congress March 24, 1972.)

APPENDIX C

INDIVIDUAL RIGHTS UNDER THE CONSTITUTION

The Constitution of 1789 has served as the fundamental instrument of our government for almost all of our country's history as an independent nation. Drawn up at a time when there were only thirteen States, dotted with small towns, farms, and light industry, the Constitution has proved a durable and viable instrument of government despite enormous changes in America's political, social, and economic environment. Whether in a weak country on the Atlantic seaboard, or in a continental nation of fifty States with over 200 million people producing goods and providing services at rates thousands of times faster than in 1789, the framework for democratic government set out in the Constitution has remained workable and progressive.

Similarly, the individual rights listed in the Constitution have also retained an extraordinary vitality despite their application to problems and fact situations which could not have been envisioned by the Founding Fathers.

Each branch of the government — the legislative, judicial, and executive — is charged by the Constitution with the protektion of individual liberties. In this framework, the judiciary has assumed a leading role. Chief Justice John Marshall, speaking for the Supreme Court in the early case of *Marbury* v. *Madison* (1803), declared that it was the duty of the judiciary to say what the law is, including expounding and interpreting that law. The law contained in the Constitution, he declared, was paramount and other laws which were repugnant to its provisions must fall. He concluded that it was the province of the courts to decide when other law was in violation of the basic law of the Constitution and, where this was found to occur, to declare that law null and void. This is the doctrine known as "judicial review" which has become the basis for the courts' application of constitutional guarantees in cases brought before them.

The Congress also has played an important role in the protection of constitutional rights by enacting legislation designed to guarantee and apply these rights in specific contexts. Laws which guarantee the rights of Indians, afford due process to military servicemen, and give effective right to counsel to poor defendants and to the poor in a wide variety of civil cases, are but recent examples of the congressional role.

Finally, the executive branch, which is charged with implementing the laws enacted by Congress, also contributes to the protection of individual rights by devising its own regulations and procedures for administering the law without intruding upon constitutional guarantees.

Before anyone can properly understand the scope of our constitutional rights, he must realize that as a function of our federal system, we Americans live under two governments rather than one — that of the Federal Government itself and that of the State in which we live. The authority of the Federal Government is limited by the Constitution to those powers specified in it; the remainder of governmental powers are reserved to the States. The Federal Government is authorized, for example, to settle disputes between States, to conduct relations with foreign governments, and to act in certain matters of common national concern. States, on the other hand, retain the remainder of governmental power to be exercised within their respective boundaries.

Only a few individual rights were specified in the Constitution when it was ratified in 1788. Shortly after its adoption, however, ten Amendments — called the Bill of Rights — were added to the Constitution to guarantee basic individual liberties. These liberties include freedom of speech, freedom of press, freedom of religion, and freedom to assemble and petition the Government.

The guarantees of the Bill of Rights originally applied only to actions of the Federal Government and did not prevent State and local governments from taking action which might threaten an individual's civil liberty. As a practical matter, States had their own constitutions, some of which contained their own bills of rights guaranteeing the same or similar rights guaranteed by the Bill of Rights against Federal intrusion. These rights, however, were not guaranteed by all the States; and where they did exist, they were subject to varying interpretations. In short, citizens were protected only to the extent that the States themselves recognized their basic rights.

In 1868, the Fourteenth Amendment was added to the Constitution. In part, it provides that no State shall "deprive any person of life, liberty, or property without due process of law." It was not until 1925 in the case of *Gitlow* v. *New York,* that the Supreme Court interpreted the phrase "due process of law" to mean in effect "without abridgement of certain of the rights guaranteed by the Bill of Rights." Since that decision, the Supreme Court has ruled that a denial by a State of certain of the rights contained in the Bill of Rights actually represents a denial of due process of law. While the Court has not ruled that all rights in the Bill of Rights are contained in the notion of "due process," neither has it limited that notion to the rights enumerated in the Bill of Rights. It simply has found that there are concepts in the Bill of Rights so basic to a democratic society that they must be recognized as part of "due process of law" and made applicable to the States as well as the Federal Government.

At present, the following guarantees of the Bill of Rights have been applied to the States under the terms of the Fourteenth Amendment: Amendments I, IV, and VI; the self-incrimination, double jeopardy, and just compensation clauses of Amendment V; and the guarantee against cruel and unusual punishment of Amendment VIII. Only Amendments II and III, the right to indictment by grand jury in Amendment V, the right to jury trial in a civil suit in Amendment VII, and the prohibition against excessive bail or fines in Amendment VIII have not yet been applied to the States.

To place these rights in a broader perspective, one should realize that they make up only the core of what are considered to be our civil rights — those privileges and freedoms that are accorded all Americans by virtue of their citizenship. There are many other "civil" rights which are not specifically mentioned in the Constitution but which nonetheless have been recognized by the courts, guaranteed by statute, and now are embedded in our democratic traditions. The right to buy, sell, own, and bequeath property; the right to enter into contracts; the right to marry and have children; the right to live and work where one desires; and the right to participate in the political, social, and cultural processes of the society in which one lives are a few of those rights that are considered as fundamental to a democratic society as those specified by the Constitution.

Despite the inherent nature of the rights of American citizenship, it should be emphasized that the rights guaranteed by the Constitution or otherwise are not absolute rights in the sense that they entitle a citizen to act in any way he pleases. Rather, he must exercise his rights in such a way that the rights of others are not denied in the process. Thus, as Mr. Justice Holmes has pointed out, "Protection of free speech would not protect a man falsely shouting 'Fire' in a theater and causing a panic." Nor does freedom of speech and press sanction the publication of libel and obscenity. Similarly, rights of free speech and free assembly do not permit one knowingly to engage in conspiracies to overthrow by force the Government of the United States. It is clear, then, that civil liberties carry with them an obligation on the part of all Americans to exercise their rights within a framework of law and mutual respect for the rights of one's fellow citizens.

This obligation implies not only a restraint on the part of those exercising these rights but a tolerance on the part of those who are affected. Citizens may on occasion be subjected to annoying political tirades, or strange dress, or disagreeable entertainment, or noisy demonstrations of protest. They may feel annoyed when a defendant refuses to testify or when they see a seemingly guilty defendant go free because certain evidence was inadmissible in court. But these annoyances or inconveniences are a small price to pay for the freedom we all enjoy. For, indeed, if the rights of one are suppressed, the freedom of all is jeopardized.

Ultimately, a free society is a dynamic society, where thoughts and ideas are forever challenging and being challenged. It is not without the risk that the "wrong" voice will be listened to or the "wrong" plan pursued. But, in the final analysis, a free interplay of ideas in a society produces both a clearer perception and livelier impression of truth.

ARTICLE I, SECTION 9, CLAUSE 2

The Privilege of the Writ of Habeas Corpus shall not be suspended, unless when in Cases of Rebellion or Invasion the public Safety may require it.

HABEAS CORPUS

This clause secures to the Congress the power to suspend, or to authorize the President to suspend, the privilege of the writ upon a declaration of national emergency. A suspension of habeas corpus is probably tenable only when the courts are physically unable to function because of war, invasion, or rebellion.

Originally, the writ of habeas corpus was a pretrial device that enabled a person imprisoned pursuant to executive order to attack the legality of his detention. Subsequently, the concept of the writ has been expanded by the Court so that anyone whose freedom has been officially restrained may now petition a Federal court to test whether that restraint was legally imposed. In this manner of use, it has become an important means of postconviction attacks upon criminal convictions in State and Federal courts. The Court has recently curtailed the availability of this device in State convictions by requiring full compliance with and exhaustion of State remedies before permitting the issuance of a writ of habeas corpus from a Federal court.

Habeas corpus being a vital safeguard against unlawful imprisonment, it is unusual that it is explicitly mentioned only in the context of its suspension; nowhere in the Constitution is this right affirmatively conferred. Nevertheless, there is a long-standing statutory authorization to Federal courts to exercise the habeas corpus power.

ARTICLE I, SECTION 9, CLAUSE 3

*No Bill of Attainder * * * shall be passed [by the Federal Government].*

ARTICLE I, SECTION 10, CLAUSE 1

*No State shall * * * pass any Bill of Attainder.* * * *

BILL OF ATTAINDER

A bill of attainder historically is a special act of a legislature that declares that a person or group of persons has committed a crime and that imposes punishment without a trial by court. Under our system of separation of powers, only courts may try a person for a crime or impose punishment for violation of the law.

Section 9 restrains Congress from passing bills of attainder, and section 10 restrains the States.

ARTICLE I, SECTION 9, CLAUSE 3

No* * * ex post facto law shall be passed [by the Federal Government].

ARTICLE I, SECTION 10, CLAUSE 1

No State shall * * * pass any * * * ex post facto law.* * *

EX POST FACTO LAWS

These two clauses prohibit the states and the federal government from enacting any criminal or penal law which makes unlawful any act which was not a crime when it was committed. They also prevent the imposition of a greater penalty for a crime than that in effect when the crime was committed. However, laws that retroactively determine how a person is to be tried for a crime may be changed so long as no important rights are lost. Laws are not ex post facto if they make the punishment less severe than it was when the crime was committed.

ARTICLE III

THE JUDICIAL SYSTEM

Article III of the Constitution outlines the structure and power of our federal court system and establishes a federal judiciary that helps maintain the rights of American citizens. Article III, section 2, also contains a guarantee that the trial of all federal crimes, except cases of impeachment, shall be by jury. The Supreme Court has interpreted this guarantee as containing exceptions for "trials of petty offenses," cases rightfully tried before court-martial or other military tribunal and some cases where the defendant has voluntarily relinquished his right to jury.

This section also requires that a federal criminal trial be held in a federal court sitting in the state where the crime was committed. Thus, a person is given protection against being tried without his consent in some part of the United States far distant from the place where his alleged violation of federal laws occurred.

ARTICLE III, SECTION 3

Treason against the United States, shall consist only in levying war against them, or, in adhering to their Enemies, giving them Aid and Comfort. No person shall be convicted of Treason unless on the Testimony of two Witnesses to the same overt Act, or on Confession in open Court.

The Congress shall have power to declare the Punishment of Treason, but no Attainder of Treason shall work Corruption of Blood, or Forfeiture except during the Life of the Person attainted.

TREASON

Treason is the only crime defined by the Constitution. The precise description of this offense reflects an awareness by our forefathers of the danger that unpopular views might be branded as traitorous. Recent experience in other countries with prosecutions for conduct loosely labeled "treason" confirms the wisdom of the authors of the Constitution in expressly stating what constitutes this crime and how it shall be proved.

ARTICLE VI, CLAUSE 3

* * * [N]o religious test shall ever be required as a qualification to any office or public trust under the United States.

RELIGIOUS TESTS

Together with the First Amendment, this guarantee expresses the principle that church and government are to remain separate, and that a person's religious beliefs are no indication of his patriotism, his ability, or his right to serve his country. Thus a citizen need not fear that his religious affiliation or convictions may legally bar him from holding office in our country.

THE BILL OF RIGHTS

AMENDMENT I

Congress shall make no law respecting an establishment of religion, or prohibiting the free exercise thereof; or abridging the freedom of speech, or of the press; or the right of the people peaceably to assemble, and to petition the Government for a redress of grievances.

FREEDOM OF RELIGION

Two express guarantees are given to the individual with respect to his religious freedom. First, neither Congress nor a State legislature may "make any law respecting an establishment of religion." This means that no law may be passed that favors one church over another, establishes an official church to which all Americans must subscribe or support, or requires religious belief or religious nonbelief. Second, no law may validly interfere with the "free exercise" of one's religion. This clause assures that each citizen is guaranteed freedom to worship by individual choice.

The Court's modern interpretation of the Establishment Clause has supplied the notions of voluntarism and neutrality as constituting the mortar of this "wall of separation between Church and State." Governmental activity that has the purpose or primary effect of advancing or inhibiting religion or that results in excessive governmental entanglement with religion is proscribed. Moreover, the Establishment Clause guards against measures that would foster political divisiveness on religious grounds in the general community.

While Court decisions in this area are not easily categorized, we have learned that, pursuant to the notion of voluntarism, the Court has been extremely reluctant to permit any governmental involvement with private elementary and secondary schools: it has determined that students there are more impressionable, and thus more liable to be coerced than university level students.

The Establishment Clause, therefore, has been held to prohibit: (1) mandatory religious exercises such as Bible readings, or even nondenominational prayers, in the public elementary and secondary schools; (2) promoting religious creeds through the manipulation of curricula in State-supported schools; and (3) providing financial support through such measures as grants, loans, and tax credits to nonpublic elementary and secondary schools affiliated with religious institutions, even for nonreligious courses of study or for the maintenance of facilities. On the other hand, the clause has been held not to prohibit: (1) providing a neutral service such as bus transportation on an equal basis to children in both religious schools and public schools; (2) loaning secular textbooks to children attending religious schools; (3) making direct general grants to religious-affiliated colleges and universities, depending on the "character" of the college and its ability to separate secular and religious functions; and (4) releasing public school students to attend a religious period of instruction at sites off school premises. Furthermore, the Court has refused to hold that the tax-exempt status accorded church property used exclusively for worship purposes contravenes the Establishment Clause.

In interpreting the Free Exercise Clause, the Court has held that if the purpose or effect of a statute is to impede the observance of religion(s), or to discriminate invidiously among them, then the free exercise of religion is abridged. Indeed, the Court has recently established that only a compelling governmental interest can legitimize a statute restrictive of the free exercise of religion.

In this regard, it is clear that *no* statute can validly impinge upon religious thoughts, that is, religious *belief* devoid of conduct. Moreover, by applying the compelling interest test, the Court has assured that forms of conduct based on religious belief are to receive increasing protection. Thus, when a Seventh-day Adventist was fired for refusing to work on Saturdays (her holy day), the Court ruled that she was fully entitled to unemployment benefits. Similarly, Amish parents were held to be protected in their refusal to send their children beyond the eighth grade to public schools, the State interest in requiring the two years of additional mandatory schooling having failed to outweigh the legitimate devotion of the Amish to their tenets. These forms of conduct based upon religious belief have been held to be protected by the Free Exercise Clause.

Nonetheless, all activity cannot be protected by claims of religious belief. Religious conduct such as polygamy, snake handling, or the ceremonial use of drugs is not protected by the Free Exercise Clause, the Supreme Court having held that the strong societal interests in safety and morality justify the prohibition of such conduct.

One of the most interesting problems posed in this area that the Court will face in the future is the "double-barreled dilemma," when one religion clause "runs up" against the other. Can the State, for example, make a special provision for one religion (an apparent Establishment Clause violation) in order to protect the free exercise of that religion? So far, the Court has not officially recognized this conflict of clauses even though it has explicitly approved special religious State exemptions to protect one's free exercise of religion.

FREEDOM OF SPEECH

Freedom of speech is explicitly established in the First Amendment. While the English common law concept of freedom of speech meant freedom from prior restraint only, the present American theory of freedom of speech generally establishes both freedom from prior restraint and freedom from subsequent punishment for the exercise of these rights. Some justices, in fact, have suggested that freedom of speech is absolute, but a majority of the Court always has maintained that it must be balanced against other legitimate interests: in short, the Court has attempted to preserve the greatest degree of expression consistent with the protection of overriding and compelling governmental interests.

Central to the concept of freedom of speech is the freedom of individual belief. In recognition of this the Court has held that the right to associate with those who hold beliefs compatible to one's own in order to further those beliefs, whether in a political or social context, must receive basic protection from the First Amendment. The State, for example, may procure general membership lists of an organization only where there is a substantial relation between the information sought and a subject of compelling State interest.

The principal way of conveying one's beliefs is through actual expression. Generally, a citizen may speak out freely on any subject. He may exercise this right verbally, by parading, by wearing buttons, by flying flags and banners, and in a variety of other ways. He may, in short, advocate any idea he desires, no matter how unpopular or alien. Even advocacy of the use of force or violation of law may be punished only where it is directed to inciting or producing imminent lawless action and is likely to incite or produce such action. Abusive or profane language also is protected unless it is directed to a specific individual and tends to incite that person to violence.

Engaging in "symbolic speech," such as wearing black armbands or using a flag in certain ways, receives similar First Amendment protection. On the other hand conduct such as burning draft cards may be banned or punished. It is the nature of a particular activity, combined with the factual context and environment in which it is undertaken, that will determine whether it really is "symbolic speech" deserving First Amendment protection. In this determination, the Court will examine whether the conduct is effective enough to constitute "symbolic speech"; is there an intention to communicate, is there an audience, and is the symbolism capable of being understood by the audience? The gravity of the State interest also must be weighed; is the State trying to regulate content (requiring a compelling justification)? Or is it merely attempting to regulate time, place, or manner of speech? These factors will determine whether the activity is protected "speech" or unprotected "conduct."

Parading or picketing in public places is generally protected, although in locations such as military camps or courthouses, restraints may be justified. Permit systems preceding the exercise of such rights are permissible only when official discretion is narrowly bounded and rapid review of denials is assured. Once expression is permitted in a forum, the government may generally regulate only time, place, or manner of that expression. Furthermore, there is an equalitarian guarantee supporting such expression. The First Amendment requires that the arbitrary exclusion of a person or a class of persons from a public forum be subjected to the strictest of scrutiny.

Although at one time the Court required private property dedicated to public use — such as shopping centers — to be treated as public and thus open to expressive activity, it has since overruled these cases, sharply reducing access to private property for purposes of First Amendment expression.

Spending one's own money or contributed money to further one's own candidacy for public office, or to promote one's political and social views, is another protected activity. However, limitations upon how much one may contribute to a candidate for office have been sustained. The Court also has sustained governmental restraints upon the political activities of public employees. Similarly, it has recognized that in cases involving disruption of public business, the government may restrict expression by its employees, though such limitations are subject to careful judicial scrutiny.

Organized institutions, like individuals, are guaranteed freedom of expression, not so much for their own benefit but for their contribution to furthering a free interchange of ideas in our democratic society. That a profit may be derived from, for example, managing a newspaper, does not lessen the guarantee. Furthermore, this protection extends not only to political expression, but to discourse on practically any subject of some serious social value.

However, certain forms of expression — such as obscenity or hard-core pornography — are deemed without "serious" social importance and thus may go unprotected by the First Amendment. Because not all expression dealing with sex is obscene, the Court has held that the First Amendment must determine the procedural and substantive law by which speech may be adjudged obscene. Only that expression which, by the standards of the local community and taken as a whole, appeals to a prurient interest in sex, portrays sexual conduct in a patently offensive way, and does not have serious literary, artistic, political, or scientific value, may be classified as obscene. Even where there has been no official determination as to whether a particular form of expression is actually obscene, ordinances restricting the locations of theaters specializing in films exhibiting "specified sexual activities" or "specified anatomical areas" are permissible. The Court has justified this restriction of expression by claiming that the State's interest in protecting "borderline pornography" is not so great as its interest in planning the use of its property and preventing the clustering of establishments merchandising pornography.

Generally, defamation is another class of expression that has been deemed devoid of any serious social value. There is one basic exception to this classification: because of the importance of comment upon issues affecting government, the Court has carefully restrained State remedies for allegedly defamatory speech in regard to public officials, candidates for public office, and some public figures. In order to recover damages for defamatory comment, public figures must prove that it was uttered with actual malice. Practically all other citizens may recover actual damages for defamatory falsehoods so long as State law establishes a standard higher than strict liability; however, punitive damages are recoverable only upon proof of actual malice.

FREEDOM OF THE PRESS

Freedom of the press and freedom of speech have frequently been treated synonymously by the Court. Nevertheless, it is clear that the press does have a special place in America's heritage. Our own revolution, for example, was ignited by press pamphlets such as Thomas Paine's "Common Sense." Realizing the value of an unrestrained press to American society, the Court has been very reluctant to sanction governmental censorship of the press or management of the news. In fact, prior restraints upon press publications have come to the Court with such a heavy presumption of invalidity that the Supreme Court has *never* upheld them. Even in the Pentagon Papers case, where there was an alleged threat to national security posed by the exposure of secret governmental documents, the Court struck down any form of prior restraint. Only a "grave and irreparable" harm might justify such drastic action.

It must be noted that the recent Court trend indicates a weakening of the guarantee of freedom of the press. Publications' liability for defamation has been broadened. Furthermore, the Court has refused to strike down all prior restraints upon the press in the fair trial context, having admitted the possibility of such circumstances that would justify restraint.

Finally, it should be mentioned that freedom of the press does not insulate the press, as corporations, from those economic regulations applied to all business — such as taxation, equal employment opportunity, labor management, or antitrust laws.

All of the foregoing must be considered within the context of the printed press in the United States, for the broadcast media operate within a different Constitutional framework. Because television and radio station owners are licensees of scarce frequencies, they have been held subject to governmental regulation in a number of areas: they must, for example, guarantee equal time to reply to editorial attacks as well as provide fairness in treatment of issues. Governmental regulation cannot go so far, however, as to require broadcasters to accept paid political or public issues advertising — so long as issues are presented fairly by that station.

FREEDOM OF ASSEMBLY AND PETITION

Freedom of assembly is as fundamental as the freedoms of speech and press, all three freedoms being inseparable parts of freedom of expression. While the assembly clause adds little to the protection of the rights to assemble, picket, or parade that would not already be protected by the speech clause, it does reaffirm the breadth of the rights that are guaranteed.

The right to petition is designed to enable the citizen to communicate with his government without hindrance. It assures his right to present his views both orally and in writing, and also embraces his right to travel to the seat of government.

AMENDMENT II

A well regulated Milita, being necessary to the security of a free State, the right of the people to keep and bear Arms shall not be infringed.

THE RIGHT TO KEEP AND BEAR ARMS

The Second Amendment provides for the freedom of the collective citizenry to protect itself against both disorder in the community and attack from foreign enemies. In America's frontier days, an individual's own arms were vital to our national "Militia" and were "necessary to the security of a free State." But in today's modern, urbanized society, well-trained military and police forces have supplanted the need for individual reliance upon firearms. The Supreme Court, as a result, has upheld

State and Federal laws prohibiting the carrying of concealed weapons, requiring the registration of firearms, and limiting the sale of firearms for other than military uses.

AMENDMENT III

No Soldier shall, in time of peace be quartered in any house, without the consent of the Owner, nor in time of war, but in a manner to be prescribed by law.

QUARTERING OF SOLDIERS

Prior to the Revolution, American colonists had frequently been required to provide lodging and food for British soldiers against their will. The Third Amendment prohibited the continuation of this practice.

AMENDMENT IV

The right of the people to be secure in their persons, houses, papers, and effects, against unreasonable searches and seizures, shall not be violated, and no warrant shall issue, but upon probable cause, supported by Oath or affirmation, and particularly describing the place to be searched, and the persons or things to be seized.

SEARCH AND SEIZURE

The Fourth Amendment protects the individual and his property from unreasonable searches and seizures by generally prohibiting State acts that invade one's reasonable expectation of privacy. This provision applies both to arrests of a person and to searches of his person or property for evidence. In practice, however, the Court treats arrests and searches quite differently.

For example, a police officer may, based upon probable cause, make a warrantless arrest in a public place (including the vestibule of a home) where a person is suspected of committing either a felony or a misdemeanor in the officer's presence. However, the Court has held that, barring exigent circumstances, a search is unreasonable unless preceded by a valid warrant issued upon probable cause. (This also applies to administrative, noncriminal searches, except in specific, heavily regulated areas such as alcohol or firearms.) A strong minority of Justices has argued unsuccessfully for the rule that the proper test should be not whether a search warrant is procured but whether the search under all the circumstances was reasonable.

Despite the dichotomy between arrests and searches, the Court normally encourages warrants in either instance. This reflects the fact that the warrant process is a valuable safeguard of Fourth Amendment rights. For example, a warrant must be issued by a neutral magistrate who is capable of determining for himself whether probable cause exists. This is a practical standard requiring common sense: a warrant may issue only where a reasonably discreet and prudent person would be led to believe by the facts stated that the offense charged was in fact committed and that the individual to be arrested had committed it, or that evidence of a crime would be found on the premises to be searched. Furthermore, a warrant must describe with particularity the person or things to be seized so that broad discretion of the officers executing the warrant is circumscribed. Even with the issuance of a warrant, police generally may not break into a private home without first demanding entrance and stating their purpose.

The circumstances in which searches may be conducted absent a warrant are limited. A search without a warrant may be valid where consent is voluntarily given by the individual whose person or property is to be searched. Under many circumstances, due to their mobility, automobiles may be subject to warrantless searches. Persons lawfully arrested also may be searched without a warrant. If the arrest is effectuated in a home, however, a valid search is limited to the body of the arrestee and the area immediately around him from which he might be able to obtain a weapon. Frisks of persons detained but not arrested are permitted but generally are permissible only to discover weapons endangering the officer. Searches of persons entering the United States are valid only when conducted reasonably proximate to the Nation's borders or points of entry. Finally, searches of open areas and seizures of materials in "plain view" are permissible absent warrants.

After years of adhering to the view that electronic surveillance — such as wiretapping — was neither a search nor a seizure, the Court now holds that the Fourth Amendment requires observance of the warrant requirement in this circumstance. In 1968, Congress buffered this holding by enacting an extensive law on the subject. The subsequent argument of the President that he is permitted to authorize electronic surveillance in national security cases without regard to the Fourth Amendment or the statute has been rejected by the Court in a case involving domestic subversive investigations (though the Court did refrain from addressing this question when applied to the activities of foreign powers within or without this country).

Enforcement of the Fourth Amendment by the courts has generally been effected through the controversial exclusionary rule which provides that no evidence — however reliable — is admissible in court if it has been obtained in violation of the Fourth Amendment. The principal purpose of the rule is to deter violations of the Amendment, although judicial integrity, among other concerns is implicated. Only recently the Court has limited the application of the exclusionary rule. It has held that Federal courts may not set aside State convictions because of illegally seized evidence when they hear pleas for release by State prison inmates. The Court did announce that it will continue to adhere to the rule as applied by State judges in appeals going through State court systems.

AMENDMENT V

No person shall be held to answer for a capital, or otherwise infamous crime, unless on a presentment or indictment of a Grand Jury, except in cases arising in the land or naval forces, or in the Militia, when in actual service in time of War or public danger; nor shall any person be subject for the same offense to be twice put in jeopardy of life or limb; nor shall be compelled in any criminal case to be a witness against himself, or be deprived of life, liberty, or property, without due process of law; nor shall private property be taken for public use, without just compensation.

GRAND JURY

Before a person is tried in Federal court for an "infamous" crime, he must first be indicted by a grand jury. The grand jury's duty is to make sure that there is probable cause to believe that the accused person is guilty. This prevents a person from being subjected to a trial when there is not enough proof that he has committed a crime.

An infamous crime is a felony (a crime for which a sentence of more than 1 year's imprisonment can be given) or a lesser offense which can be punished by confinement in a penitentiary or at hard labor. An indictment is not required for a trial by court-martial or by other military tribunal. Also, the constitutional requirement of grand jury indictment does not apply to trials in State courts. However, where States do use grand juries in their criminal proceedings, such juries must be free of racial bias.

DOUBLE JEOPARDY

This clause prevents the retrial in either State or Federal court of an individual after he already has been placed in "jeopardy." Jeopardy attaches not only after a prior conviction or acquittal but also in jury trials, once the jury is sworn and, in trials without juries, once the introduction of evidence has begun. Thereafter, if for some reason the trial is terminated, a second trial is barred, except in limited circumstances. Such circumstances include the case where a mistrial is declared at defendant's request or with his consent, or in a case of "manifest necessity," such as when the jury deadlocks, or where illness or death prevents continuation of a trial. A second trial also is permissible where an appellate court sets aside a guilty verdict and orders a new trial.

The "double jeopardy" clause will offer no protection where conduct violates both Federal and State law: the offender may be prosecuted in the courts of both jurisdictions. Neither does the clause prevent the multiple prosecution of a suspect for conduct that constitutes more than one offense, though factual issues decided by one jury may prevent relitigation of those factual issues in a subsequent trial. Furthermore, if a defendant obtains a reversal of a conviction and is retried, the clause does not prevent an increase of penalty if he is reconvicted, although due process requires the sentencing judge to demonstrate that the penalty was not increased to penalize the exercise of the defendant's right to appeal.

SELF-INCRIMINATION

The Fifth Amendment also guarantees that no person shall be compelled to be a witness against himself in a criminal proceeding in a Federal court. This right has been extended through the due process clause of the Fourteenth Amendment to apply to criminal proceedings in State courts as well. The basic assumption underlying the self-incrimination clause is that no one is obliged to provide answers to questions tending to convict oneself of a crime. The Court's reasoning stems in part from fears of physical or mental coercion when an individual is interrogated in the custody of the police.

The right against self-incrimination is especially important when we consider that custodial interrogation has been held to extend to questions outside the police station, including police questioning of a defendant in his own bed at home.

To insure that the right against self-incrimination is protected, the Court has ruled that an individual must be warned prior to custodial interrogation of his right to remain silent, that what he says may be used against him in court, and that he has a right to counsel (that counsel being furnished by the State if he desires an attorney and is unable to afford one). Failure to give these warnings results in the inadmissibility in later criminal proceedings of any statement obtained during police questioning.

Although an accused may waive his rights under the Fifth Amendment, he generally must know what he is doing and must not be forced to confess, for any confession obtained by use of force or threat will be excluded from the evidence presented at trial. However, the Court has ruled that even where an in-custody defendant initially exercises his right to remain silent, an incriminating statement procured after a significant time lapse and a fresh set of warnings operates as a waiver and is not violative of *Miranda* principles. Furthermore, if a defendant or a witness fails to invoke the Fifth Amendment in response to a question on the witness stand, such a failure may operate as a waiver of the right and he will not be permitted to object later to a court's admitting his statement into evidence on the basis that it was self-incriminating.

Courts have ruled that the guarantee against self-incrimination applies only to "testimonial" actions. Thus, it has been held that obtaining handwriting samples and blood tests are not violative of the Fifth Amendment. Similarly, the guarantee against self-incrimination has been held not to bar requiring an accused to appear in a police lineup and repeat the words used during the commission of the crime.

Courts have also ruled that the Fifth Amendment prohibits both Federal and State prosecutors and judges from commenting on the refusal of a defendant to take the witness stand in his own defense. The refusal of witnesses to testify to matters which could subject them to criminal prosecutions at a later date also has been upheld. However, courts have recognized a limited right of the government to question employees about the performance of official duties and have upheld the dismissals of such employees for their refusal to answer questions so related.

Government regulations which required registration of items such as highly dangerous weapons or narcotics which were a crime to possess also have been invalidated on the grounds that they require information which may be used in criminal prosecution against the person who registers the item in question. However, one is not excused from filing a tax return because it is incriminatory: the privilege must be asserted on the return or it will be waived.

DUE PROCESS

The words "due process of law" express the fundamental ideas of American justice. A due process clause is found in both the Fifth and Fourteenth amendments as a restraint upon the federal and state governments, respectively.

The clause affords protection against arbitrary and unfair procedures in judicial or administrative proceedings that could affect the personal and property rights of a citizen. Notice of a hearing or trial that is timely and adequately informs the accused of the charges against him is a basic concept included in "due process." The opportunity to present evidence in one's own behalf before an impartial judge or jury, to be presumed innocent until proven guilty by legally obtained evidence and to have the verdict supported by the evidence presented are other rights repeatedly recognized within the protection of the due process clause.

The due process clauses of the Fifth and Fourteenth amendments also provide other basic protections whereby the state and federal governments are prevented from adopting arbitrary and unreasonable legislation or other measures which would violate individual rights. Thus, constitutional limitations are imposed on governmental interference with important individual liberties — such as the freedom to enter into contracts, to engage in a lawful occupation, to marry, and to move without unnecessary restraints. Governmental restrictions placed on one's liberties must be reasonable and consistent with due process in order to be valid.

JUST COMPENSATION

The Fifth Amendment requires that, whenever the government takes an individual's property, the property acquired must be taken for public use, and the full value thereof paid to the owner. Thus, property cannot be taken by the federal government from one person simply to give it to another. However, the Supreme Court has held that it is permissible to take private property for such purposes as urban renewal, even though ultimately the property taken will be returned to private ownership, since the taking is really for the benefit of the community as a whole. The property does not have to be physically taken from the owner. If governmental action leads to a lower value of private property, that may also constitute a "taking" and therefore require payment of compensation. Thus, the Supreme Court has held that the disturbance of the egg-laying habits of chickens on a man's poultry farm caused by the noise of low-level flights by military aircraft from a nearby airbase, lessens the value of that farm and that, accordingly, the landowner is entitled to receive compensation equal to his loss.

AMENDMENT VI

In all criminal prosecutions, the accused shall enjoy the right to a speedy and public trial, by an impartial jury of the State and district wherein the crime shall have been committed, which district shall have been previously ascertained by law, and to be informed of the nature and cause of the accusation; to be confronted with the witnesses against him; to have compulsory process for obtaining witnesses in his favor, and to have the Assistance of Counsel for his defense.

This Amendment sets forth specific rights guaranteed to persons facing criminal prosecution. Its guarantees apply to both the federal courts and the state courts by virtue of the Fourteenth Amendment.

The right to speedy and public trial requires that the accused be brought to trial without unnecessary delay, and that the trial be open to the public. Intentional or negligent delay by the prosecution that prejudices the defendant's right to defend himself has been held as grounds for dismissal of the charges. The Supreme Court has ruled that delay in prosecution was not justified by the defendant's confinement on an earlier conviction because he should have temporarily been released for purposes of trial on the later charge.

Trial by an impartial jury supplements the earlier guarantee contained in Article III of the Constitution. The requirement that the jury have 12 members and that these must reach a unanimous verdict were derived from the common law and are not specifically accorded by the Constitution. The Supreme Court has ruled, however, that state juries need not necessarily be composed of 12 members and actually has approved a state statutory scheme providing for only six. Moreover, the Court has ruled that jury verdicts in state courts need not necessarily be unanimous. The right to jury trial does not apply to trials for petty offenses, which the Supreme Court has suggested as those punishable by six months' confinement or less. In all trials where a jury is used it must be impartially selected, and no one can be excluded from jury service merely because of his race, class, or sex.

The Sixth Amendment requirement that a person "be informed of the nature and cause of the accusation" means that an accused person must be given notice in what respects it is claimed he has broken the law, in order that he may have an opportunity to prepare his defense. This also means that the crime must be established by statute before hand so that all persons are aware of what is illegal before they act. The statute must not be so vague or unclear that it does not inform people of the exact nature of the crime. Generally, the accused is entitled to have all witnesses against him present their evidence orally in court; and subject to certain exceptions, hearsay evidence cannot be used in federal criminal trials. Moreover, the accused is entitled to the aid of the court in having compulsory process issued — usually a subpoena — which will order into court as witnesses those persons whose testimony he desires at the trial.

Finally, the Sixth Amendment provides a right to be represented by counsel. For many years, this was interpreted to mean only that the defendant had a right to be represented by a lawyer if he could afford one. The Supreme Court held in 1963, however, that the Amendment imposed an affirmative obligation on the part of the federal and state governments to provide at public expense legal counsel for those who could not afford it, in order that their cases could be adequately represented to the court. The Supreme Court has held that this right extends even to cases involving "petty offenses" if there is a chance that a jail sentence might result. The indigent were held to have such a right at any "critical stage of the adjudicatory process." Thus, courts have accorded this right at initial periods of questioning, at police lineups, and at all stages of the trial process. In addition indigents were given the right to a free copy of their trial transcript for purposes of appeal of their conviction. Congress enacted the Criminal Justice Acts of 1964 and 1970 to implement this right to counsel by establishing a federal defender system to represent those defendants who could not afford legal counsel. Most state legislatures have enacted similar measures.

AMENDMENT VII

In suits at common law, where the value in controversy shall exceed twenty dollars, the right of trial by jury shall be preserved, and no fact tried by a jury, shall be otherwise re-examined in any Court of the United States, then according to the rules of the common law.

The Seventh Amendment applies only to Federal Civil trials and not to civil suits in State courts. Except as provided by local Federal court rules, if a case is brought in a Federal court and a money judgment is sought which exceeds $20, the party bringing the suit and the defendant are entitled to have the controversy decided by the unanimous verdict of a jury.

AMENDMENT VIII

Excessive bail shall not be required, nor excessive fines imposed, nor cruel and unusual punishments inflicted.

BAIL

Bail has traditionally meant payment by the accused of an amount of money specified by the court to insure the presence of the accused at trial. An accused who was released from custody and subsequently failed to appear for trial forfeited his bail to the court.

This Amendment does not specifically provide that all citizens have a "right" to bail, but only that bail will not be excessive. A right to bail has, however, been recognized in common law and by statute since 1791. In 1966, Congress enacted the Bail Reform Act to provide for pretrial release of persons accused of noncapital crimes. Congress thus sought to end pretrial imprisonment of indigent defendants who could not afford to post money bail and who were, in effect, confined only because of their poverty. The Act also discouraged the traditional use of money bail by requiring the judge to seek other means likely to insure that the defendant would appear when his trial was held.

The lack of a specific constitutional guarantee has, nonetheless, indirectly contributed to legislative enactments which have modified the availability of bail. In 1970, Congress provided for a system of pretrial detention in the District of Columbia for those defendants considered to be dangerous and likely to commit additional crimes if released prior to trial. The law was highly controversial and is considered by many to be a violation of the right to bail which they implied in the Eighth Amendment.

Whether bail, where it is available, is excessive or not will depend upon the facts of each particular case. In a few instances, as when a capital offense such as murder is charged, bail may be denied altogether.

CRUEL AND UNUSUAL PUNISHMENT

This clause not only bars government from imposing punishments that are barbarous and inhumane, but as the Supreme Court has announced, it forbids punishments that society's "evolving standards of decency" would mark as excessive. It also bars punishment that is disproportionate to the offense committed, based on the facts of the particular case.

The Court has recently held that the use of the death penalty as a punishment for murder does not necessarily constitute cruel and unusual punishment. Nevertheless, it did strike down mandatory death sentences for certain crimes, requiring that attention be focused on the defendant, the crime itself, and similarly situated defendants. These considerations notwithstanding, the Court's primary emphasis upon the discretion of the jury is somewhat inconsistent with its 1972 landmark decision which had struck down the death penalty because of the arbitrary, capricious, and racist manner in which it was usually applied by juries.

Finally, punishment for narcotics addiction has been held to be cruel and unusual on the grounds that addiction is a status indicative of an illness and therefore cannot be properly categorized as a crime.

AMENDMENT IX

The enumeration in the Constitution, of certain rights, shall not be construed to deny or disparage others retained by the people.

This Amendment reflects the Framers' view that powers of government are limited by the rights of the people and that, by expressly enumerating certain rights of the people in the Constitution, the Framers did not intend to recognize that government had unlimited power to invade other rights. Indeed, in *Griswold* v. *Connecticut* (1965), some Justices sought to change the Amendment's status as a rule of construction to one of positive affirmation and protection of the right to privacy.

AMENDMENT X

The Powers Not Delegated to the United States by the Constitution, Nor Prohibited by It to the States, Are Reserved to the States Respectively, Or to the People.

RESERVED POWERS

The Tenth Amendment embodies the principle of federalism which reserves for the states the residue of powers not granted to the federal government or withheld from the states.

LATER AMENDMENTS DEALING WITH INDIVIDUAL RIGHTS

AMENDMENT XIII

Section 1. Neither slavery nor involuntary servitude, except as a punishment for crime whereof the party shall have been duly convicted, shall exist within the United States, or any place subject to their jurisdiction.
Section 2. Congress shall have power to enforce this article by appropriate legislation.

SLAVERY AND INVOLUNTARY SERVITUDE

This Amendment prohibits slavery in the United States. It has been held that certain State laws were in violation of this Amendment because they had the effect of jailing a debtor who did not perform his financial obligations. The Supreme Court has ruled, however, that selective service laws authorizing the draft for military duty are not prohibited by this Amendment.

The Court has upheld certain civil rights legislation barring private acts of discrimination that did not constitute "State action," on the basis of the authority granted Congress by Section 2 of this Amendment. The Civil Rights Act of 1866, designed to end discrimination in the sale or rental of real or personal property, is one example. The Court has recently ruled that the reach of the 1866 Act was wide enough to forbid racial discrimination in private schools. Title VIII (the Fair Housing Provisions) of the Civil Rights Act of 1968 also was based upon Section 2. Such legislation is appropriate under the provisions of the Thirteenth Amendment because it was designed to erase "badges of servitude."

AMENDMENT XIV

Section 1. All persons born or naturalized in the United States, and subject to the jurisdiction thereof, are citizens of the United States and of the State wherein they reside. No State shall make or enforce any law which shall abridge the privileges or immunities of citizens of the United States; nor shall any State deprive any person of life, liberty or property, without due process of law; nor deny to any person within its jurisdiction the equal protection of the laws.
Section 5. The Congress shall have power to enforce, by appropriate legislation, the provisions of this article.

CITIZENSHIP

The purpose of the first sentence of the Amendment was to overrule the *Dred Scott* decision, which had held that blacks could not be citizens of the United States. The Amendment's ratification clearly established a national rule with regard to citizenship.

The Supreme Court has held pursuant to this clause that an American citizen becomes a citizen of a particular State once he has resided there without the present intent of establishing another domicile.

PRIVILEGES AND IMMUNITIES

Alexander Hamilton proposed in Federalist Paper #80 that "the citizens of each State shall be entitled to all the privileges and immunities of citizens of the several States." In 1873, however, the Supreme Court confined the protection of the Privileges and Immunities Clause to those privileges "which owe their existence to the Federal Government, its National character, its Constitution, or its laws," which the Court deemed to be very few in number. This decision, in effect, severely limited the scope of the Privileges and Immunities Clause.

DUE PROCESS OF LAW

Most of the specific provisions of the Bill of Rights have been applied to the States through this clause. Its real importance, however, goes far beyond this application. For the due process clause also serves as a procedural guarantee in both civil and criminal cases, where it requires government to observe a host of restraints. Before action may be taken to deprive one of a basic liberty, his property or to restrain his exercise of rights over his property, he must be afforded notice and an opportunity to be heard before an impartial tribunal under conditions that enforce fairness. For example, public school teachers who have a reasonable expectation of tenure must be given the opportunity to have a hearing before they are dismissed. The same requirement applies before a public school student may be dismissed or suspended. Also, criminal defendants are protected from prosecution under vague statutes, and every element necessary to establish their culpability must be proved beyond a reasonable doubt. Due process also insures that prosecutors may not conceal evidence favorable to the defendant and material to his case, at least where the defendant has requested a review of the evidence in the prosecution's possession. It protects the rights of convicted persons, requiring fair treatment of them in prison. Revocation of parole and probation also must be carried out with regard to due process. In addition, the Court has begun to apply the notion of due process to those persons committed to or confined in mental institutions. Finally, as a function of due process, juvenile defendants are now afforded procedures tailored both to protect them and to preserve the uniqueness of the system of juvenile justice. Nonetheless, due process does not require a hearing in all cases where it appears that vested rights of property or liberty are affected. For example, in some contexts public employees may be dismissed without any constitutionally-required opportunity for a hearing to protest that move.

This clause has a substantive aspect as well, protecting individuals against deprivation of important property and liberty interests. Substantive due process for a significant period of our history was held to preclude government from regulating many forms of economic activity. While these restraints were abandoned in the 1930's, the Court now accords the protection of substantive due process to certain fundamental personal rights. Foremost among these is the concept of the right to privacy, which to date has been limited largely to matters involving marriage, procreating, and the parental care of children. For example, it appears that at least in the heterosexual context a sexual relationship between consenting adults in private is considered a generally protected privacy interest.

For most of a woman's pregnancy, abortion is also considered a protected privacy interest. In the first trimester the State may impose no restrictions upon abortion, such as conditioning the abortion upon the consent of a spouse, or a parent in the case of an unmarried minor female. In the second trimester only State laws that are merely regulatory and directly promote the health of the mother are tenable. Finally, only in the third trimester may abortions be restricted by the State, but never where in the opinion of appropriate medical judgment the mother's life or health is thought to be in jeopardy.

The Twenty-Sixth Amendment, which lowered the voting age for all Federal elections from twenty-one to eighteen years of age, became law on July 1, 1971. Amendments XV, XIX, and XXVI together with the Fifth and Fourteenth, prohibit any arbitrary attempt to disenfranchise an American citizen.

AMENDMENT XXVII (PROPOSED)

Section 1. Equality of rights under the law shall not be denied or abridged by the United States or by any State on account of sex.

Section 2. The Congress shall have the power to enforce, by appropriate legislation, the provisions of this Article.

EQUAL RIGHTS

This Amendment was proposed by two-thirds of Congress and submitted to the States for ratification on March 22, 1972. As of the date of this printing, it has been ratified by thirty-four States, four short of the three-fourths requirement of Article V.

The object of the proposed Amendment is to abolish unfair or unreasonable discrimination under the law, based upon a person's sex, which the Court has refused to otherwise invalidate under the Equal Protection Clause of the Fourteenth Amendment.

CONCLUSION

In addition to the specific constitutional rights outlined herein, certain safeguards for the individual are inherent in the structure of American government. The separation of powers between legislative, executive, and judicial branches of government is the basis for a system of "checks and balances," which prevents excessive concentration of power — with the inevitable threat to individual liberties that accompanies such concentration. With respect to the legislative power itself, the existence of two Houses of Congress — each chosen by a different process — is itself a protection against ill-advised laws that might threaten constitutional rights. Similarly, our Federal system, which divides authority between the National Government and the governments of the various States, has provided a suitable soil for the nourishment of constitutional rights.

Yet no matter how well a constitution may be written, the rights it guarantees have little meaning unless there is popular support for that constitution and for those rights. Indeed, it is the citizens of this Nation who are the ultimate repository of the democratic spirit and to whom the fate of our noble experiment must be entrusted.

Reprinted from *The Layman's Guide to Individual Rights Under the United States Constitution,* 5th ed. Washington, D.C.: Government Printing Office, 1976.

APPENDIX D

SELECTED CRIMINAL
LAW CASES

The following are major criminal law cases. The highlights of each case are briefly discussed. For a full understanding of the facts and the ruling of each case, it is suggested that each case be read and studied in its entirety.

THE FOURTH AMENDMENT

SEARCH AND SEIZURE

Weeks v. *United States* [232 U.S. 383, 34 S.Ct. 341, 58 L.Ed. 652 (1914)]

The Supreme Court held that the Fourth Amendment prevented the introduction of evidence obtained through an illegal search and seizure in a federal prosecution. It stated in the opinion that the decision was not based on legislation but was a matter of judicial implication.

Carroll v. *United States* [267 U.S. 132, 45 S.Ct. 280, 69 L.Ed. 543 (1925)]

The Supreme Court upheld a warrantless search, incident to arrest, of a vehicle on a road. The Court noted that a vehicle can be stopped and searched based on an officer's knowledge of trustworthy information that an offense had been, or was being committed. The Court also noted the distinction between a dwelling and a movable object, such as a car.

Wolf v. *Colorado* [338 U.S. 25, 69 S.Ct. 1359, 93 L.Ed. 1782 (1949)]

The Supreme Court held that, in a prosecution in a state court for a state crime, the Fourteenth Amendment did not forbid the admission of evidence obtained by an unreasonable search and seizure, but that the Fourth Amendment forbids the admission of such evidence. The Court did not decide to enforce the exclusionary rule constitutionally by banning evidence collected by illegal search and seizure.

Rochin v. *California* [342 U.S. 165, 72 S.Ct. 205, 96 L.Ed. 183 (1952)]

The Supreme Court did not allow the state courts to allow evidence seized unconstitutionally. (Authorities had asked a doctor to force an emetic solution through a tube into Rochin's stomach in order to retrieve "two capsules of morphine.") The police had used "conduct that shocks the conscience" to obtain evidence from the defendant.

Irvine v. *California* [374 U.S. 128, 74 S.Ct. 381, 98 L.Ed. 561 (1954)]

The Supreme Court in this case affirmed and limited the *Rochin* exception to the *Wolf* doctrine in situations involving violence, brutality, or shocking conduct to the defendant. The Court severely criticized the authorities in this case for their behavior, but it did uphold the conviction.

Elkins v. *United States* [364 U.S. 206, 80 S.Ct. 1437, 4 L.Ed. 2d, 1669 (1960)]

The Supreme Court here overturned the so-called silver platter doctrine, which had previously allowed state authorities who discovered evidence of a federal crime in an illegal search to turn the evidence over to federal agencies for prosecution, as long as federal agents did not participate in the search.

Mapp v. *Ohio* [367 U.S. 643, 81 S.Ct. 1684, 6 L.Ed. 2d. 1081 (1961)]

This decision by the Supreme Court overturned the *Wolf* decision and made the Fourth Amendment applicable to states through the due process clause of the Fourteenth Amendment. Evidence obtained through illegal search and seizure could not be used in a state court.

Ker v. *California* [374 U.S. 23, 83 S.Ct. 1623, 10 L.Ed. 2d. 726 (1963)]

The Supreme Court ruled that evidence obtained by state authorities could be used in state courts, in which admissibility is governed by a constitutional standard, even if the evidence would not be admissible in a federal case because it would violate a federal statute.

Preston v. *United States* [376 U.S. 364, 84 S.Ct. 881, 11 L.Ed. 2d. 777 (1964)]

The Supreme Court held that the search of an automobile at the police garage was too remote in time and place and that the automobile must be searched at the time and place of arrest.

Stoner v. *California* [376 U.S. 483, 84 S.Ct. 889, 11 L.Ed. 2d. 856 (1964)]

The Supreme Court held that the defendant's rights were violated when a hotel clerk authorized authorities to search the defendant's room without his permission.

Aguilar v. *Texas* [378 U.S. 108, 84 S.Ct. 1509, 12 L.Ed. 2d. 723 (1964)]

The Supreme Court established that the standard for obtaining a search warrant by state officers is the same as applies under the Fourth and Fourteenth Amendments.

Cooper v. *California* [386 U.S. 58, 87 S.Ct. 788, 17 L.Ed. 2d. 730 (1967)]

The Supreme Court upheld the search of a vehicle without a search warrant by police a week after the car had been impounded. The search was not related to the arrest charge of the defendant.

Warden v. *Hayden* [387 U.S. 294, 87 S.Ct. 1647, 18 L.Ed. 2d. 782 (1967)]

The Supreme Court held that police may enter premises without a warrant and may seize evidence or a suspect under the rule of "hot pursuit." Police officers are not required to delay an investigation if the delay will injure themselves or others gravely.

Schmerber v. *California* [384 U.S. 757, 86 S.Ct. 1826, 16 L.Ed. 2d. 908 (1966)]

The Supreme Court held that the withdrawal of a blood sample by a physician by an order from the police, over the defendant's objection, was performed in a reasonable manner and did not constitute unreasonable search and seizure.

Bumper v. *North Carolina* [391 U.S. 543, 88 S.Ct. 1788, 20 L.Ed. 2d. 797 (1968)]

The Supreme Court held that police cannot claim that the defendant consented to a search when police have stated that they are in possession of a search warrant although no warrant exists.

Davis v. *California* [394 U.S. 721, 89 S.Ct. 1394, 22 L.Ed. 676 (1969)]

The Supreme Court decided that police cannot obtain fingerprints from citizens after an illegal detention at the police station when the sole purpose was to obtain the fingerprints.

Chimel v. *California* [395 U.S. 752, 89 S.Ct. 2034, 23 L.Ed. 2d. 685 (1969)]

The Supreme Court reassessed its position and limited the search of defendants to their person and to areas within their immediate reach or vicinity. The Court further noted that there was no justification for police to search rooms and other areas except where an arrest takes place.

Vale v. *Louisiana* [399 U.S. 30, 90 S.Ct. 1969, 26 L.Ed. 2d. 409 (1970)]

A search may be incident to an arrest only if it is contemporaneous with the arrest and is confined to the immediate area of the arrest.

Chambers v. *Marooney* [399 U.S. 42, 90 S.Ct. 1975, 26 L.Ed. 2d. 419 (1970)]

When there is probable cause to arrest occupants of a vehicle, their car may be searched at the time of arrest, or it may be taken to a police station and searched there.

Coolidge v. *New Hampshire* [403 U.S. 443, 91 S.Ct. 2022, 29 L.Ed. 2d. 564 (1971)]

Police, whenever they have probable cause, may not make a warrantless search entry for the purpose of making an arrest. The seizure and search of an automobile are not reasonable given probable cause alone, and police may not seize a car, remove it, and search it at their leisure. In this case, the search warrant was invalid because it was not issued by a neutral and detached magistrate.

Adams v. *Williams* [407 U.S. 143, 92 S.Ct. 1921, 32 L.Ed. 2d. 612 (1972)]

Police do not have to possess probable cause to arrest a defendant, but must have enough reasonable cause to stop and frisk for an officer's safety. Stop-and-frisk procedures need not be based on an officer's personal observation, but may be based on information supplied by another person.

Schneckloth v. *Bustamonte* [412 U.S. 218, 93 S.Ct. 2041, 36 L.Ed. 2d. 854 (1973)]

Given probable cause to stop a vehicle, the state does not have to prove that rights were given to its occupants before they consented to a search.

INFORMERS

Brineger v. *United States* [338 U.S. 160, 69 S.Ct. 1302, 93 L.Ed. 1879 (1949)]

Probable cause exists when the apparent facts and the circumstances available to officers, combined with reasonably trustworthy information, are sufficient to cause the officers to believe that a crime has been or is being committed.

Draper v. *United States* [358 U.S. 307, 79 S.Ct. 329, 3 L.Ed. 2d. 327 (1959)]

The Supreme Court upheld a conviction in which the basis for arrest was information that had been given to a federal agent by an informant whose information had been reliable and accurate in the past. The informant gave the federal agent a description of the defendant, time of arrival, and other information that was corroborated by the agent, which resulted in the defendant's arrest. The subsequent search uncovered narcotics on the defendant, as reported by the informant.

Jones v. *United States* [362 U.S. 257, 80 S.Ct. 725, 4 L.Ed. 2d. 697 (1960)]

This case upheld a warrant that was based on a reliable informant's specific information, which was corroborated. The Supreme Court upheld the case even though the officer did not state the names of informants nor swear to the results of his corroboration of information from the informants.

Aguilar v. *Texas* [378 U.S. 108, 84 S.Ct. 1509, 12 L.Ed. 2d. 723 (1964)]

A search warrant may be defective when it does not specify any factual basis for the magistrate to form a decision regarding issuance. Officers need to outline a factual basis for a search.

United States v. *Ventresca* [380 U.S. 102, 85 S.Ct. 741, 13 L.Ed. 2d. 684 (1965)]

A warrant should be tested in a nontechnical, common-sense fashion, even though prepared by officers who are pursuing an investigation hurriedly. The warrant was valid in this case, even though it did not list the sources of observations.

McCray v. *Illinois* [386 U.S. 300, 87 S.Ct. 1056, 18 L.Ed. 2d. 62 (1967)]

The specificity of the informant (who had supplied reliable information in about twenty cases over a year), in addition to the corroboration of the officers, caused the Supreme Court to uphold the conviction of the defendant.

Smith v. *Illinois* [390 U.S. 129, 88 S.Ct. 748, 19 L.Ed. 2d. 956 (1968)]

The Supreme Court held that the defendant was deprived of the right to confront witnesses against him when he was denied the right to ask the principal witness his correct name or where he lived.

Spinelli v. *United States* [394 U.S. 410, 89 S.Ct. 584, 21 L.Ed. 2d. 637 (1969)]

A simple assertion of police suspicion is not itself sufficient basis for a magistrate's finding of probable cause and cannot be used to give additional weight to allegations that otherwise would be insufficient.

Adams v. *Williams* [407 U.S. 143, 92, S.Ct. 1921, 32 L.Ed. 2d. 612 (1972)]

The Supreme Court upheld the conviction of the defendant when information was given to an officer by someone known to that officer. This information was the basis for frisking a person driving a vehicle. The informant told the officer that a man seated in the car was carrying narcotics and that he had a gun in his waistband. The officer found the gun where the informant said it would be located, and this was the basis for the arrest, which then revealed narcotics on the defendant.

THE FIFTH AMENDMENT

CONFESSIONS

Brown v. *Mississippi* [297 U.S. 278, 56 S.Ct. 461, 80 L.Ed. 682 (1936)]

The Supreme Court held in this early case that a coerced confession violated the defendant's due process under the Fourteenth Amendment. The case involved a physical beating of the defendant.

McNabb v. *United States* [318 U.S. 332, 63 S.Ct. 608, 87 L.Ed. 819 (1943)]

Incriminating statements were held inadmissible in court because they were obtained during an illegal detention, as the defendant was being held in violation of federal requirements that he be taken as soon as possible to a magistrate.

Ashcraft v. *Tennessee* [322 U.S. 143, 64 S.Ct. 921, 88 L.Ed. 1192 (1944)]

The Supreme Court held that the defendant's confession was not admissible in court because police had interrogated him for thirty-six hours in succession.

Mallory v. *United States* [354 U.S. 449, 77 S.Ct. 1356, 1 L.Ed. 2d. 1479 (1957)]

The confession of the defendant was held inadmissible in court because the police were required to take the arrestee to a magistrate without unnecessary delay, yet they had questioned him for seven hours first.

Massiah v. *United States* [377 U.S. 201, 84 S.Ct. 1199, 12 L.Ed. 2d. 246 (1964)]

The defendant's confession was held inadmissible because it was obtained by federal agents who had elicited the statement by means of a codefendant who carried a hidden radio transmitter.

Escobedo v. *Illinois* [378 U.S. 478, 84 S.Ct. 1758, 12 L.Ed. 2d. 977 (1964)]

The Supreme Court held that when the legal process shifts from investigation to accusation — when the focus is on the accused and the purpose is to elicit a confession — a defendant must be permitted to consult with an attorney.

Miranda v. *Arizona* [384 U.S. 436, 86 S.Ct. 1602, 16 L.Ed. 2d. 694 (1966)]

This monumental decision instituted the so-called *Miranda* warnings, which require that a suspect be advised of certain rights before being questioned by the police. These rights include: the right to remain silent; the right to counsel; the right to free counsel if the suspect cannot afford one; and the right to terminate the questioning at any time.

Orozco v. *Texas* [394 U.S. 324, 89 S.Ct. 1095, 22 L.Ed. 2d. 311 (1969)]

The Supreme Court noted that incriminating statements are invalid without proper warnings, even when a defendant is not in custody at the police station. The officers in this case questioned the defendant at his boarding-house bedroom during the early morning.

Oregon v. *Hass* [420 U.S. 714 (1975)]

Incriminating statements may be admissible in court to impeach the testimony of a defendant even though the *Miranda* warnings were faulty.

THE SIXTH AMENDMENT

RIGHT TO COUNSEL

Powell v. *Alabama* [287 U.S. 45, 53 S.Ct. 55, 77 L.Ed. 158 (1932)]

The Supreme Court held that counsel must be appointed by the states in all capital (life or death issue) trials where the accused is unable to employ counsel and is unable to conduct his or her own defense.

Johnson v. *Zerbst* [304 U.S. 458, 58 S.Ct. 1019, 82 L.Ed. 1461 (1938)]

The Supreme Court ruled that in all *federal* trials of a serious nature, counsel must be appointed for an indigent defendant unless he or she intelligently waives this right.

Betts v. *Brady* [316 U.S. 455, 62 S.Ct. 1252, 86 L.Ed. 1595 (1942)]

In felony cases in which life or death was not an issue, the Supreme Court ruled that the states are not required to furnish counsel in every case. (Many states at this time, however, provided counsel because it was required by their own constitution or by court rulings of state courts.)

Gideon v. *Wainwright* [372 U.S. 335, 83 S.Ct. 792, 9 L.Ed. 2d. 799 (1963)]

The *Gideon* decision required that all states must provide counsel to all indigent defendants in all felony trials.

Argersinger v. *Hamlin* [407 U.S. 25, 92 S.Ct. 2006, 32 L.Ed. 2d (1972)]

The *Gideon* decision was extended by the Supreme Court to include misdeameanor offenses, and no sentence involving the loss of liberty can be imposed where there has been a denial of counsel.

JUVENILES

Kent v. *United States* [383 U.S. 541, 86 S.Ct. 1045, 16 L.Ed. 2d. 84 (1966)]

The Supreme Court held that a full hearing, with assistance of counsel, must be held concerning the question of transferring a juvenile case to an adult court. The child and his or her attorney must have full access to social records used to make the determination, and the judge must state in writing the reasons for the transfer.

In re Gault [387 U.S. 1, 87 S.Ct. 1428, 18 L.Ed. 2d. 527 (1967)]

The Supreme Court ruled that juveniles have the due process right to counsel, protection from self-incrimination, the right to notice of charges, and the right to confront witnesses.

In re Winship [397 U.S. 358, 90 S.Ct. 1068, 25 L.Ed. 2d. 368 (1970)]

The Supreme Court required the standard beyond a reasonable doubt in the adjudicatory stage of a juvenile proceeding.

CORRECTIONS

PROBATION

Mempa v. *Rhay* [389 U.S. 128 (1967)]

The Supreme Court ruled that a probationer has a right to counsel at a probation revocation hearing.

Gagon v. *Scarpelli* [411 U.S. 778, 92 S.Ct. 1756, 36 L.Ed. 2d. 656 (1973)]

Preliminary hearings and revocation hearings are required, and counsel is required in some cases, but not in all. Grounds for refusal of counsel must be provided. Holding also applies to parole revocation.

PRISONERS AND PRISONS

Johnson v. *Avery* [393 U.S. 483, 89 S.Ct. 747, 21 L.Ed. 2d. 718 (1969)]

In the absence of an adequate substitute, inmates should be allowed to use legal assistance of other inmates.

Wolff v. *McDonnell* [418 U.S. 539, 94 S.Ct. 2963, 41 L.Ed. 2d. 935 (1974)]

The Supreme Court ruled that in procedures resulting in loss of good-time or in solitary confinement, due process required the following: advanced written notice of the violation; written statement of fact findings; the right to call witnesses and present evidence where it will not be hazardous to the operation of the institution; mail from attorneys to be opened and inspected in the presence of inmates; and prison records not in accord with required procedures to be expunged.

PAROLE

Morrissey v. *Brewer* [408 U.S. 475, 92 S.Ct. 2593, 33 L.Ed. 484 (1972)]

The Supreme Court held that a parolee has a right to a revocation hearing in which he or she is entitled to the following: written notice of the claimed violation; disclosure of evidence; the opportunity to be heard in person and to present witnesses and evidence; the right to confront and cross-examine witnesses; an impartial board; and a written statement of the facts and findings of the board.

APPENDIX E

GLOSSARY

acquitted* The finding of the court that the accused is not guilty of the crime or crimes charged.

adjudication A judgment by the court.

admiralty courts Courts originated in England centuries ago to handle maritime cases, those involving sailors, ships, and activities on the high seas.

adversary system A legal system that entails a contest between two opposing parties under a judge who acts as an impartial umpire. (In the United States the accused is considered innocent until the pleadings and evidence introduced in court prove guilt beyond a reasonable doubt.)

affidavit A written statement made under oath before one who is authorized to administer an oath.

appeal The act of transferring a case from a lower court to one of higher jurisdiction for a new hearing. The request for such a hearing of a case already tried. A case that has been so transferred.

appellate jurisdiction The authority to rehear cases and alter lower court decisions.

appellate review A comprehensive rehearing of a case in a court other than the one in which it was previously tried.

*Space does not permit a full treatment of all the words specific to the criminal justice system. The student is advised to consult *Black's Law Dictionary*, West Publishing Co., for further reference.

arraignment A calling into court of the defendant to inform him or her of the charge and to ask for the plea.

arrest The act of depriving a person of his or her freedom in a significant way.

arrest warrant A document issued by a court ordering law officers to arrest a specified individual.

bail A guarantee, usually in the form of money, required by a judge or determined by statutes, that an arrested person must provide in exchange for freedom from jail prior to trial or an appellate hearing, to be forfeited if the defendant does not appear for trial or hearing.

bail bondsman One who provides bail for a defendant, usually a businessperson who charges a fee for the service.

bailiff A court guard with various duties, such as taking charge of jurors and maintaining order in a courtroom (not to be confused with the British bailiff, whose duties are more like those of a deputy sheriff or constable).

bench trial A trial in which a judge hears the trial and renders a verdict; a nonjury trial.

bench warrant A document issued by a judge (the bench) and not requested by the police demanding that a specified individual be brought before the court. Also called a *capias*.

beyond a reasonable doubt To establish facts sufficient to fully convince an ordinary person that a defendant has committed the crime charged. (The standard of proof required under America's adversary system of law.)

booking The process of entering in the official arrest record the suspect's name, the offense charged, and the time and place of the occurrence of the event, usually done at a police station by the arresting officer.

calendaring The setting of a date for trial and various other administrative procedures associated with a court's scheduling of a case.

case law Law created by judicial decisions in specific prior cases; as opposed to *statutory law*. (See *stare decisis*.)

case load The number of parolees or probationers under the supervision of a parole or probation officer.

causation That element of a crime that requires a causal relationship to exist between the offender's conduct and the harm or injury sustained.

cellblock A group of individual or multiple-inmate cells within a locked enclosure.

chancery court A court of equity. (See **equity**.)

change of venue A change in the place of trial, usually from one county or district to another.

chief justice The presiding or principal Justice of a court, possessing nominal authority over the other judges.

circuit courts Originally, courts that were held by judges who followed a circular path, hearing cases periodically in various communities; however, it now refers to courts with several counties or districts within their jurisdiction.

circumstantial evidence Evidence of indirect facts, as opposed to evidence of direct facts.

city courts Usually lower courts of special original jurisdiction; its rural counterparts are the justice of the peace courts.

civil courts Courts that handle civil cases, as opposed to criminal cases. (See **civil law, tort**.)

civil law The division of law that adjusts private and civil conflicts and differences between persons, as distinguished from criminal law.

clerk of the court A court official who handles much of the routine paperwork associated with the administration of a court.

common law A body of law originating in England, based on centuries of case decisions. (See **case law** and *stare decisis*.)

common pleas courts Where used in the United States, courts with this title are usually courts of general and original jurisdiction.

complaint An official form completed by a plaintiff or a law officer in registering a formal charge against another person.

concurrent jurisdiction Jurisdiction over a case held in common by two or more courts.

concurrent sentencing More than one sentence handed out on the same occasion to be served during a common time period. (See **consecutive sentencing**.)

consecutive sentencing More than one sentence handed out on the same occasion to be served one sentence after the other. (See **concurrent sentencing**.)

constitutional officer Any law enforcement officer specifically and expressly provided for in either the Constitution of the United States or a state constitution. The sheriff, constable, and coroner are constitutional officers in several states.

county court A court whose jurisdiction is limited to the boundaries of a county. May be either a court of special original jurisdiction or a court of general jurisdiction.

court A tribunal of one or more judges assembled to conduct the affairs of law and justice.

court of last resort The last court that may hear a case. The United States Supreme Court is a court of last resort for many kinds of cases.

court of nonrecord A court that does not make a written record of the trial.

court of record A court that records trial activity.

crime Any act or omission prohibited by law for which there is a specified fine or punishment.

crimen fals Indicates the class of offenses that involve the perpetration of a falsehood, e.g., forgery, perjury, counterfeiting, etc.

criminal courts Courts that handle criminal cases; they may also handle civil cases, and are then called criminal courts only in reference to the criminal cases that they handle.

criminal justice process The series of actions through which each criminal offender may pass: from detection and investigation of the criminal act, to arrest, booking, indictment, arraignment, trial, conviction, sentencing, possible incarceration, and eventual release.

criminal justice system The agencies society entrusts to operate the criminal justice process and the apparatus that identifies, accuses, tries, convicts, and punishes offenders against the norms of society expressed in law. Major subsystems include the police, the prosecution, the courts, probation, corrections, and parole.

criminal law The division of law that deals with crimes and their punishment, as distinguished from civil law.

criminalistics The use of scientific techniques derived from physics, chemistry, and biology to solve crimes. Also known as forensic science.

cross-examination The examination of a witness by the party opposed to the one who produced him or her.

defendant In criminal law, the party charged with a crime; as distinguished from the plaintiff.

deposition A sworn written record of oral testimony.

detainer A hold order filed against a person incarcerated by another jurisdiction, which seeks, upon his or her release from current confinement, to take this individual into custody to answer to another criminal charge.

detention Holding in custody. Usually indicates the period of time between arrest and the preliminary hearing. The jails or holding facilities of the police are often referred to as detention facilities.

discovery The legal method by which a party in a legal proceeding can gain access to information and evidence held by the opposing party.

district courts Trial courts at the state or federal level with general and original jurisdiction. The boundaries of their venue do not conform to standard political unit boundaries, but generally include several counties.

diversion Refers to halting or suspending, before conviction, formal criminal proceedings against a person on the condition or assumption that he or she will do something in return.

diversion programs Programs designed to prevent defendants from being convicted and incarcerated or from reaching the trial state by providing them with specialized treatment resources.

docket A court record of the cases scheduled to appear before the court.

doctrine of parens patriae The principle that the juvenile court was to be a kind and loving parent to juveniles.

domestic relations courts Courts dealing with family problems. (See **family courts.**)

double jeopardy The principle that a person will not be properly tried in a court of law more than once for the same crime by the same sovereign.

dual court system The courts of the United States can be conceptualized as belonging to one of two court systems: state or federal.

due process Those procedures and safeguards necessary to ensure an individual that he or she will have a fair trial or hearing.

equity The concept that the relationships between men, women, and society be just and fair and in accordance with contemporary morality.

essoiner A person who appears in court to present an excuse for the absence of the defendant.

evidence All the materials or means admissible in a court of law to produce in the minds of the court or jury a belief concerning the matter at issue.

examination The initial question and answer session between the defense or the prosecution and a witness during a trial.

exclusionary rule A rule that any evidence obtained through unlawful means is inadmissible in court.

executive branch That segment of government responsible for the administration, direction, control, and performance of government. Examples of executives are the president of the United States, state governors, city mayors. The police and correctional subsystems are under the executive branch. (See **legislative branch** and **judicial branch.**)

executive clemency or pardon The removal of punishment and legal disabilities of a person by order of an executive (usually the governor).

family courts Courts of original jurisdiction

that typically handle the entire range of family problems, from juvenile delinquency to divorce cases. (See **domestic relations courts.**)

felony A crime that is punishable by death, life, or a term of imprisonment of more than a year. (See **misdemeanor.**).

field interrogation An on-the-street stop and questioning of a suspicious person by police.

fixed sentence A sentence for a specified amount of time to be served by a convicted person; also called determined sentence.

forensic Those things related to law and courts. As an adjective it indicates those persons that specialize in the legal aspects of their profession.

frisk A brief search of the person usually limited to a "pat down" of the person's outer clothing.

general court martial The highest level of court in the military, in which the most serious offenses are tried.

general jurisdiction The authority that permits a court to engage in the full range of trial activities in a wide variety of cases; as opposed to special or limited jurisdiction.

"good time" laws Laws that allow a reduction of a portion of a prisoner's sentence for "good behavior" while in prison.

grand jury A body of men and women called together by legal authority to conduct inquiry into matters brought to the attention of the jury.

habeas corpus A written court order to any person, including a law enforcement official who has a person in custody, directing that person or official to bring the named individual before the court so that it can determine if there is adequate cause for continued detention.

hearsay evidence Evidence that is not first-hand but is based on an account given by another.

higher courts Appellate courts and sometimes trial courts of record; as distinguished from lower courts.

hung jury A jury that cannot agree on a verdict.

indeterminate sentence A sentence in which a convicted person is given a range of time (such as one to twenty years) to serve, the actual time served to be at the discretion of the corrections officials, within legal proscriptions.

index crimes See **uniform crime report.**

indictment, bill of An accusation in writing presented by a grand jury, charging the person named therein with a criminal offense; sometimes called a "true bill." A "no bill" indicates that the accused was not indicted.

information A document issued by a prosecutor constituting a formal charge against a defendant.

initial appearance The first appearance of a suspect in court following arrest.

injunction order A written notice by a court to a party, prohibiting that party from committing some act.

interlocutory decision A temporary judgment pending the resolution of the facts at issue.

intermediate appellate courts The third level of state courts; appellate courts between trial courts and courts of last resort.

judge The official who bears primary responsibility for the activity of a court, whether this be performing the duties of a magistrate, deciding a case, sentencing, regulating the adversaries, or instructing the jurors.

judicial branch That segment of government charged with the interpretation of law and the administration of justice. Examples are the United States Supreme Court; state supreme, superior, and appellate courts; county courts; and magistrates' courts. The court subsystem falls under this branch of government. (See **legislative branch** and **executive branch.**)

jurisdiction (court) The extent of a court's right and authority to interpret and apply the law.

jurisdiction (police) The established geographical boundaries in which the police of a political subdivision have authority.

jury panel The list of jurors summoned to serve at a particular court. From the jury panel, the petit jury is selected.

justice A judge, particularly a Supreme Court judge. An ideal concerning the maintenance of right and the correction of wrong in the relations of human beings.

justice of the peace courts A court, usually rural, possessing special original jurisdiction in most instances and certain quasi-judicial powers.

juvenile courts Courts with special original jurisdiction over juvenile cases.

law A formal means of social control involving the use of rules that are interpreted and enforceable by the courts of a political community.

law enforcement officer Any public agency employee empowered and sworn to enforce, full- or part-time, the criminal and/or regulatory laws of the jurisdiction. Also known as peace officer, police officer, and sheriff.

legislative branch That segment of the government responsible for the consideration, drafting, and enactment of the law. Examples are the United States Congress, state legislatures, county commissioners, and city councils. (See **executive branch** and **judicial branch**.)

limited jurisdiction Authority by which the court is limited in the activity it can engage in when trying a case — for example, it may not be able to call a jury; also called special jurisdiction.

lower courts Courts of special original jurisdiction and sometimes trial courts; as opposed to higher courts.

magistrate A judge who handles cases in pretrial stages; usually handles misdemeanor cases. An officer of the lower courts.

magistrate courts Courts of special jurisdiction; usually urban.

mala in se An offense against common law that was considered to be inherently evil or inherently wrong. (See *mala prohibita*.)

mala prohibita An offense that is wrong only because it is prohibited by legislation. (See *mala in se*.)

mandatory release The release of an inmate prior to the full expiration of his or her sentence, usually under supervision.

misdemeanor A crime less serious than a felony punishable by fine or imprisonment usually for less than a year. (See **felony**.)

modus operandi The characteristic method a person uses in the performance of repeated criminal acts.

motion for a bill of particulars An action before a court asking that the details of the state's case against the defendant be made known to the defense.

motion for continuance An action before a court asking that the trial or hearing be postponed.

motion to dismiss The action before a court asking that the court dismiss the case against the defendant — for specified reasons.

municipal courts Courts of special jurisdiction whose jurisdiction follows the political boundaries of a municipality or city.

"nol pros" The withdrawal or dropping of charges against a defendant by the prosecutor.

Office of Justice Assistance, Research and Statistics (OJARS) Federal criminal justice funding agency, comprised of the National Institute of Justice, the Bureau of Justice Statistics, and the Law Enforcement Assistance Administration. Prior to 1979, the agency was known as the Law Enforcement Assistance Administration.

original jurisdiction First authority over a case or cause; as opposed to appellate jurisdiction.

parens patriae The doctrine according to which the juvenile court is expected to treat a child as a kind and loving parent would.

parole The administrative act of releasing an offender from incarceration while retaining the legal custody of the offender. This release prior to completion of sentence is conditional upon the parolee maintaining standards of conduct prescribed by the parole board.

parole revocation The decision of a paroling authority to return a parolee to serve his or her sentence in an institution because he or she did not live up to the conditions of parole.

peremptory challenge An arbitrary challenge, requiring no cause to be shown, that is used to dismiss a potential juror during jury selection.

petit jury A group of lay people selected from the jury panel to hear a trial and decide on a verdict (usually a verdict of guilty or not guilty) and, in some states, to determine sentences or recommend mercy.

plaintiff The person or party who initiates a legal action against someone or some party. (See **defendant**.)

plea bargaining The process of negotiation between the prosecutor and the defendant for a reduction of the penalty. Usually either the charge is reduced (for example, from murder to manslaughter) or the judge agrees to limit sentence time or grant probation in return for the defendant's plea of guilty or cooperation with the state in providing evidence for other cases; circumvents trial time. (Also called "plea negotiation.")

plea of guilty A full confession of guilt to the accusation in open court.

plea of *nolo contendere* A plea of no contest. While it is equal to a plea of guilty in terms of effect, it is not an admission of guilt. Such a plea provides certain protections in other matters involving the defendant that may be brought before the courts.

plea of not guilty A statement by the defendant denying guilt of the offense with which he or she is being charged.

postconviction remedies The various means a convicted person has of seeking redress for his or her incarceration or conviction.

precedent The principle that the way a case was decided previously should serve as a guide for the handling of a similar case currently under consideration. (See **case law** and *stare decisis*.)

preliminary hearing A preindictment hearing in which the prosecution attempts to show the court that there is probable cause for continuation of the criminal justice process.

presentence report A report containing social and historical background information about an offender, usually requested by a court, and usually prepared by a probation officer.

privileged communications Communications between two or more people that are privileged in law, which the court cannot require either to reveal.

probable cause An apparent state of facts sufficient in themselves to warrant a person of reasonable caution to believe that an offense has been or is being committed.

probation The release of a convicted person by a court under specific conditions for a specified length of time. It is an alternative to imprisonment. If the conditions of probation are not adhered to, the probation can be revoked and the offender sent to prison.

procedural law The division of law which sets forth the rules governing the method of enforcing the laws of crime and punishment.

public defender A government officer whose function it is to serve as counsel for indigent defendants.

quarter session courts Originally, courts that met four times a year, usually to try serious cases. Where this old title is still used, it is in connection with a higher or trial court.

reasonable doubt Sufficient facts and circumstances to form a belief in the mind of a reasonable person that an offense was not committed by the accused. Less than the certainty required to convict.

recidivism The number of offenders who return to an institution or are again processed by the criminal justice system. It is used as a measure of the effectiveness of programs or institutions involved in corrections.

rule of law Describes the willingness of a people to accept and order their behavior according to the rules and procedures that are prescribed by political and social institutions.

screening The removal of selected persons from the criminal justice process.

search warrant A written order by a judge, ordering law officers to search a designated place or person for specified materials.

selective enforcement The enforcement by law officers of selected laws, usually those laws applying to crimes the police administrator has determined to be the most serious or most frequent.

sentence The decision of the court (judge or jury), within the framework of statutory law, concerning the judgment to be imposed upon an individual once he or she has been tried and convicted.

sentence hearing A hearing held shortly after conviction in which the judge reviews the circumstances surrounding a case and then renders the sentence.

sentencing alternatives The range of possibilities the judge (or jury) has in sentencing an individual, for example, probation, suspended sentence, prison, etc.

social justice The fair distribution of important goods and services, such as housing, education, and health care.

special court martial The military court that is second in the three grades of court martial in terms of the severity of the penalty that it can impose.

stare decisis The doctrine of precedent. Under

this doctrine, judges are bound by previous court decisions. (See **precedent** and **case law**.)

status offense An offense committed by a juvenile that would not be an offense if committed by an adult, for example, truancy, running away from home.

statute of limitation A period of time after which a crime that has been committed cannot be prosecuted.

statutory rape Sexual intercourse between a man and a woman who is not his wife and is not yet of legal age; the offense may be either with or without the woman's consent. Legal age varies from state to state.

substantive law That body of law that creates, discovers, and defines the rights and obligations of each person in society. Substantive law prescribes behavior, and procedural law prescribes how unlawful behavior is handled.

summary court martial The military court that is the lowest of the three grades of court martial in terms of the severity of the penalty that it can impose.

supreme court The federal court of last resort specified by the United States Constitution; also the court of last resort in most kinds of cases at the state level.

territorial district courts The federal trial courts corresponding to the United States district courts but located in the territories.

testimony The evidence offered in court as declarations or affirmations of the truth or the facts.

tort In civil law, an infraction; parallel to an infraction in criminal law.

trial The formal court process in which all the evidence connected with a case is presented and a decision is made as to the guilt of the accused.

trial *de novo* a retrial that must take place when a case was originally tried in a court that did not record the trial. The retrial takes place on the initial appeal.

tribunal A court; a place where judges sit; a judicial weighing of information leading to a decision.

uniform crime report A statistical compilation of crime in the United States. The report is published annually by the Federal Bureau of Investigation. The main body of the report is limited to several selected crimes, known as index crimes.

United States commissioners See **United States magistrates**.

United States court of military appeals The highest court in the military system; an appellate court.

United States courts of appeals Federal intermediate appellate courts that handle appeals from federal district courts. There are eleven of them, one for each judicial circuit.

United States magistrates Formerly, United States commissioners. Judges who fulfill the pretrial judicial obligations of the federal disrict courts.

venireman One member of a jury panel.

venue The place of trial; the particular city or county in which the court with jurisdiction will hear and determine the case.

verdict The judgment reached by a jury or a judge at the conclusion of a trial.

warrant A writ issued by a court ordering law enforcement officers to carry out specific acts.

youth services bureau A diversion program for juvenile courts that eliminates noncriminal cases and petty first offenses from the courts' consideration by providing a resource to help a young person become less troubled or less troubling.

INDEX

Abrams v. *United States,* 224

Academy of Criminal Justice Sciences, 140

Accountability (individual), *see* Responsibility

Acquitted: and acquittal, 68, 257, 258; appeal of acquittal, 70; defined, 498

Actus reus (guilty act), 17

Adams v. *Williams,* 494, 495

Adjective (procedural) law, 9

Adjudication, 74, 192; and adjudicatory hearing, 73–74; defined, 498

Administration and management, 28–29, 245–246; business, application of principles of, 412; of correctional organizations, 292, 293, 295–299, 304, 308–318, 454, (inadequacies in) 325–328; of court (administrative staff), 268, 272–273; of criminal incident, 44–74; and discretion, 155–157, 200; management by objective (MBO), 115–116, 118; of parole, 338, 343, 368, 370, 383–384; police, 108–116, 123–124, 128–132, 135, 142, 148–157, 420; prison, 284, 297–299; of probation, 338, 341, 342–343, 348, 355–356, 358, 368, 373; public, 412–413; and vicarious liability, 142. *See also* Jurisdiction, court; Jurisdiction, police; Planning; Research

Administrative Office of the United States Courts, 273

Admiralty courts: defined, 498

Adversary system, 31–33, 34, 38–39, 63, 186, 268, 270–271; and defense, 190, 256; defined, 498; historical precedents for, 167–168; rules of evidence in, 259; *See also* Defense; Prosecution

Advisory Commission on Intergovernment Relations (ACIR), 353–354

Advocacy, 166, 167; and advocacy training, 204–205; control over, 206–207. *See also* Defense; Prosecution

Affidavit: defined, 498

Age: "juvenile court," 72, 242, 346. *See also* Juveniles

Aggravated assault, 20

Aggravated robbery, 50–51

Aguilar v. *Texas,* 493, 495

Air Force, U.S., 294–295, 304, 450. *See also* Military, the; Military court system

Alabama: abolishes parole, 383

Alaska: jail employee-inmate ratio, 323

Alcatraz Island, 311

Alcohol, Tobacco, and Firearms, U.S. Bureau of, 97, 447

Alcoholism, *see* Intoxication

America, *see* United States

American Bar Association (ABA), 196, 219, 246, 274, 355, 358, 384, 456–457; Project on Standards for Criminal Justice, 338, 352; and Supreme Court, 231, 232

American Civil Liberties Union, 192

American Correctional Association (ACA), 282, 355, 358, 364, 425, 456

American Federation of Labor, 146

American Judicature Society, 246

American Justice Institute, 151

American Law Journal, 217

American Law Review, 224

American Newspaper Publishers Association, 274

American Prison Association, *see* American Correctional Association (ACA)

American Society for Industrial Security, 103

Anglo-Saxon (medieval) era, *see* England

Appeal(s), 36, 70, 194, 261; and appeal bond, 255; defined, 47, 263, 498; right of, 44, 74, 239, 263; of sentence, 262

Appellate court(s): Court of Civil Appeals, 74; in court system, 36, 212, 231, 244, 245; evolution of, 215, 216; function of, 44, 70, 262–263; intermediate, 233, 238,

239, (defined) 501; judges and terms for, 220–222; of Maryland, 384; Military Court of Appeals, 231, 237, (defined) 504; National Appeals Court proposed, 232; Supreme Court as, 233, 235, 237; U.S. Courts of Appeal, 233–234, 235, 382, (defined) 504

Appellate jurisdiction, 230, 233, 238; defined, 498

Appellate review, 190, 262, 263; defined, 498

Area, police territorial, 113

Argersinger v. *Hamlin,* 190, 205, 496

Arizona: correctional workers, 323

Arizona Rangers, 92

Army, U.S., 294–295, 304, 450; Criminal Investigation (CID) of, 97. *See also* Military, the; Military court system

Arraignment, 62–63, 184–185, 255, 256–257; defined, 47, 256, 498. *See also* Plea(s)

Array, 258. *See also* Jury

Arrest: constitutional protections and, 48–49; defined, 46, 498; in hypothetical criminal incident, 45, 47; power of, 35, 174 (*see also* Authority); and prearrest investigation, 45

Arrest warrant, 35–36, 235, 253; defined, 498. *See also* Warrants

Ashcraft v. *Tennessee,* 495

Ashurst-Summer Act (1935), 284

Assault, aggravated, 20

Assessment center (AC) process in police service, 135–136. *See also* Police

Assessor (in prosecution), 202

Assize of Clarendon, 84

Association of American Law Schools, 457

Atomic Energy Commission, 449

Attica (New York) State Penitentiary, 293, 425

Attorney(s) general: origin of office, 167–168; selection and term, 170–173; state and local, 171–172; United States, 11, 168, 169–171, 293

Auburn prison system, 281, 282, 288, 310, 315, 328

Augustus, John, 339–341

Authority: centralization of (in England), 13, 89; fears of, as "police state," 88; law enforcement, 8–9, 35, 111, 174; not to proceed (*nol pros*), 59–60, 173, 184, 502 (*see also* Discretion); in police chain of command, 111, 114; pretended, 8. *See also* Court system; Law enforcement; Police; Prosecution; Responsibility

Automobile (motor vehicle) theft, 20

Autonomy: community, 89, 103; court, 223, 245; Greek concept of, 82. *See also* Society

Auxiliary police and services, *see* Police

Auxiliary programs (probation), 346. *See also* Probation; Rehabilitation

Bacon, Sir Francis, 215

Bail, 193, 223; and bail bond process (release on), 36, 53–54, 58, 253–254, 255, 324–325; and bail bondsman, 53, 254, (defined) 498; and bond forfeitures, 53; defined, 53, 253, 498; denial of, 53, 254; preventive, 254; purpose of, 53

Bailiff(s), 272; defined, 498; duties of, 69, 260, 273; origin of, 84

Bakke case, 137

Bar: origin of legal term, 166

Barnes, Harry E., 364

Bates, Sanford, 282

Beat system, *see* Police

Becker, Howard, 435

Behavior: and behavioral sciences, 412–415; deviant, 435; "illegal," 437; modification of, 8, 308, 326, 414; probability of, 316–317, 327, 353, 415, 436; and self-fulfilling prophecy, 436; unified, 11 (*see also* Society). *See also* Counseling; Discretion

Bench trial, 67, 185, 258; defined, 498. *See also* Trials(s)

Bench warrant, 253; defined, 498. *See also* Warrants

Betts v. *Brady,* 496

Beyond a reasonable doubt, *see* Reasonable doubt

Bigamy, 21

Bilke, Arthur, 102

Bill of particulars, *see* Motion(s)

Bill of Rights, *see* Constitution, U.S.

Black, Hugo, 190

Blackmun, Harry A., 232 *illus.*

Blumberg, Abraham, 196

Bond, bondsman, *see* Bail

Booking, 49–50, 52, 159; defined, 46, 499

Book of the States, 217

Border Patrol, *see* Immigration and Naturalization Service, U.S.

Boston: early police in, 89

Boston Police Department, 155

Boston University School of Law, 155

"Bound over" case, 185, 256

Bow Street Magistrates Court and Bow Street Runners, 85–86, 87

Brandeis, Louis, 219, 232

Brennan, William J., 232 *illus.*

Brineger v. *United States,* 494

Brown, Gary, 136

Brown v. *Allen,* 71

Brown v. *Mississippi,* 495

Brownell, Herbert, 226

Bumper v. *North Carolina,* 493

Burden of proof, *see* Proof (of guilt)

Bureau (police unit): defined, 111

Burger, Warren, 219, 225, 232 *illus.*

Burglary: defined, 17, 18, 20

Burns Agency, 101

Business administration, principles of, 412. *See also* Administration and management

Calendaring: defined, 499

Calhoun, George M., 11

California: commission plan (judiciary), 270; electronic data processing used by police in, 409–410; Highway Patrol, 98; jail census, 285; parole system, 383; Police Officers Standards and Training (POST), 104; prison system, 296, 316, 323, 324; probation programs, 352, 356, 357; Project STAR in, 133, 137; Proposition 13 (tax revolt) in, 145; public defender system begun in, 191; sentencing practices, 441; State Bureau of Criminal Identification, 90–91; statistics on attorney-case disposition relationship, 191; Supreme Court, 358; Women's Board of Terms and Paroles, 367

California Youth Authority (CYA), 292

Cambridge Study (England), 352

Canada: federal court system, 225

Canal Zone district court, 235

Capias (bench warrant), 253. *See also* Warrants

Capital cases, 190, 258

Cardozo, Benjamin, 219, 225, 232

"Career criminals," 60

Career opportunities in criminal justice system, 446–458

Carroll v. *United States,* 492

Carter, Jimmy, 134

Carter, Robert M., 364

Case law, 10, 11, 192, 194, 215, 421; defined, 499

Case load, 29, 59, 420; defined, 499; and disposition of case, 256, 313, 324; federal court, 71, 244; parole officer, 373, 381, 383, 384; probation staff, 355–356, 373, 383; reduction, 182, 326, 356, 400 (*see also* Plea bargaining); state court, 239; Supreme Court, 231, 232, 234, 235

Case screening, *see* Screening, pretrial

Causation, 18; defined, 498

Cellblock: defined, 499

Central Intelligence Agency, 449

Certiorari, writ of, 263, 264

Chain of command (police), 111. *See also* Administration and management

Challenges: jurisdictional, 264; to jury members, *see* Jury

Chambers v. *Marooney,* 494

Chancery court: defined, 499

Change: of court system, *see* Reform; in law, 6; in social attitudes, *see* Society; of venue, *see* Venue

Charles II, king of England, 85

Charter of Liberties, 13

Chicago: City Police, 143; first juvenile court established in, 286, 341

Chicago Bar Association, 241

"Chicago 7," 275n.1

Chief justice: defined, 499

Chief(s) of police, *see* Police chief(s)

Children, *see* Juveniles

Children's Bureau, U.S. (Department of Health, Education and Welfare), 241, 346

Chimel v. *California,* 494

China, ancient: law enforcement in, 82

Chou Dynasty, 82

Circuit court(s), 214, 231, 233–234, 238, 244; defined, 499

Circumstantial evidence, 259; defined, 499. *See also* Evidence

City courts: defined, 499. *See also* Court(s)

Civil Aeronautics Board (CAB), 97, 120

Civil courts: defined, 499

Civil law, 9–10, 72; defined, 499

Civil Service Commission, U.S., 97

Civil Service Reform Act (1979), 134

Civil service system, 133–134, 285, 452, 455

Clark, Ramsey, 434–435

Classification of prisoner, *see* Security, prison

Clerk of court, 272; defined, 499

Cleveland, Ohio: minority employment in, 136–137

Code(s): Chou Dynasty, 82; Draconian, 82; of ethics, law enforcement, 99; of Hammurabi, 82, 146–148; of law, 213; penal, 9; Roman (Twelve Tables), 12, 14, 33, 83; of 1636 (Plymouth Colony), 13–14

Coke, Edwin A., 215, 224

Coleman v. *Alabama,* 190

Colonial America, *see* United States

Comes stabuli, 84

Commission on Judicial Qualifications, 270

Common law, 13, 22, 215; defined, 499; in England, 10, 166, 167, 214, 217, 339; and *mala in se, mala prohibita* crimes, 21, 502

Common Law, The (Holmes), 224

Common pleas courts: defined, 499. *See also* Jurisdiction, court

Communications, privileged, 193, 259; defined, 503

Communications, technological: planning and research and, 149–150; police, 90, 132, 143, 149–150, 153, 408–409. *See also* Technology

Community, *see* Autonomy; Police; Society

Community-based corrections, 317, 327, 328, 329–331, 354, 356, 430, 441–442; counseling, 316; history of, 284–288; prerelease programs, 303–304, 312, 318; in primitive society, 11–12. *See also* Counseling; Halfway houses; Prerelease guidance; Society

Community Service Officer (CSO) programs, 134

Complaint, 45, 252–253; defined, 50, 499

Compurgation, 166

Computer technology, *see* Technology

COM-SEC (Community Sector Team Policing, Cincinnati, Ohio), 145

Concurrence in time (and criminal act), 18

Concurrent jurisdiction, 239, 240; defined, 499. *See also* Jurisdiction, court

Concurrent sentencing, 261; defined, 499. *See also* Sentencing

Conditional release, *see* Release (of prisoner)

Confessions, 200; constitutional rights (Fifth Amendment) and, 48, 260, 495–496; as evidence, 260; voluntary (vs. coercion), 63. *See also* Self-incrimination

Confidentiality, 259. *See also* Communications, privileged

Confinement, *see* Custody and control, correctional; Detention; Solitary confinement

Conflict: custody/control-rehabilitation, 37, 308, 312, 323–324,

325, 341, 353–354, 381; federal courts-corrections, 331, 392; of interest, among groups, 11; management (by police), 414; police-court, 273, 392–393, 398

Congress, U.S., 96, 235, 473; and court system, 216, 231, 233, 236, 237, 244 (*see also* Judiciary Act of 1789)

Connecticut: regional prison system, 286; state law enforcement, 91, 100–101

Consecutive sentencing, 261; defined, 499. *See also* Sentencing

Consent decree, 243

Constable: origin of office (England and U.S.), 84, 86, 88–89, 92, 93

Constitution, U.S., 9, 10–11, 21, 33, 34, 252, 459–472; Bill of Rights, 33, 48, 250, 474, 477–487; and constitutional rights and protections, *see* Right(s); and court system, 231, 233; individual rights under, 473–491; interpretation of (by Court), 232; and police services, 96; ratification of, 216, 466; and unconstitutionality, 244, 254, 392; First Amendment, 194; Fourth Amendment, 48, 66, 71, 492–495; Fifth Amendment, 48–49, 69, 182, 495–496; Sixth Amendment, 48, 49, 67, 496–497; Eighth Amendment, 254; Tenth Amendment, 89; Fourteenth Amendment, 11, 48, 74, 250, 382; Eighteenth Amendment, 7

Constitutional courts, 230

Constitutional officer: defined, 499

Constitutions, state, 225, 246

Continuance, *see* Motions(s)

Control boards and officers: over defense (justice board), 201; over prosecution (control board, assessor, writ of mandamus), 201, 202, 206

Control procedures, *see* Custody and control, correctional

Coolidge v. *New Hampshire,* 494

Cooperation and coordination, interagency, 358–359, 392–393; lack of, 327–328. *See also* Police

Cooper v. *California,* 493

Coordinated team patrol (CTP), 123. *See also* Team policing

Correctional organizations (federal, military, state, local), 292–304; court intervention in, 331; 392; functions of, 308–318; organizational problems of, 325–329

Correctional workers, *see* Personnel

Corrections, 497; career opportunities in, 453–456; concept of, 292; defined, 280; history of, 280–288. *See also* Community-based corrections

Corrections community, 28, 29, 39; history of (U.S.), 37–38. *See also* Administration and management; Education and training; Jail(s); Law enforcement; Parole; Prison(s); Probation; Rehabilitation

Costs, *see* Fees; Fiscal operations and funding

Counsel: appointed/assigned, 54, 253, 256, 270 (*see also* public defender, *below*); defendant's, 44, 68, 184, 186, 190–197, 253, 256, 268, 270–271; and defense interrelationships, 191; 193; denial of, 205; education of, 204–205, 456–457; fees for, 191; mixed counsel systems, 192; public defender, 191–193, 203–206, 207, 270–271; right to, *see* Right(s). *See also* Legal profession

Counseling, 292, 303, 414; prerelease, 318; prisoner, 316, 318, 454; probationer, 345–346. *See also* Behavior

County and Borough Police Acts (England, 1839, 1856), 87

County court(s), 36, 238, 240, 246; defined, 499

County law enforcement, 99–100, 101, 140, 285, 299; and county jails, 301–302, 330. *See also* District attorney; Sheriff

Court(s): administrative staff of, 268, 272–273; admiralty, 498; of Appeals, *see* Appellate court(s); chancery, 499; circuit, 214, 231, 233–234, 238, 244, 499; city/municipal/metropolitan, 36, 217, 499, 502; common pleas,

499; conflict of, with police, 273, 392–393, 398; constitutional, 230–231; county, 36, 238, 240, 246, 499; criminal, 37, 215, 238, 239, 499; defined, 212, 213, 498–504 *passim*; developmental history of, 212–217; district, *see* District courts; domestic relations or family, 242, 243, 500; functions of, 250–264; as income source, 246; of last resort, 230, 238, 239, 499; legislative, 230, 231; and meaning of word *court*, 238, 240, 258; of nonrecord, 240–241, 255, 499; and parole, 383–384, 385; "people's," 225–226; police, 238; quarter session, 503; of record, 36, 230, 499; rural, 217, 223; special sessions, 238; superior, 230, 238. *See also* Justice of the peace courts; Juvenile courts; Lower courts; Magistrate courts; Supreme Court, U.S.; Traffic courts; Trial courts

Court of the Judiciary (New York), 270

Court reporter, 272, 273

Courts martial, grades of, 236. *See also* Military court system

Court system: criminal, 36–37; defined, 212, 500; development of, in U.S., 214, 215, 216–218, 225; dual, of U.S., 217, 244–246, 500; federal, 230–235, 244–245 (*see also* Appellate court[s]; District courts; Supreme Court, U.S.); judicial community, 28, 38, 39; juvenile, 241–244; lag in and reform of, 218–219, 223, 225–226, 330–331 (*see also* Time lapse); military, 231, 235–237, 304; relationship, under criminal justice system (1), 29–31; state (U.S.), 237–241, 244 (*see also* State courts); structure of, in U.S., 230–246; unification of, 244, 245–246, 263. *See also* Judge(s); Jury; Juvenile courts; Trials(s)

CPM (critical path method), 116

Cressey, Donald R., 192

Crime: analysis of, 148–149; cause of, 434, 435–438; classification of, 20–22; and crime-scene data col-

lection, 121–123; decline in rate of, 145, 354, 395–397, 401, 421; defined, 16–17, 20, 46, 499; federal, 235; federal and state, 244; as individual act, 339 (*see also* Responsibility); infamous and non-infamous, 21; seven major, defined, 20; as "sin," 14–15, 241; victimless, 16, 436–437

Crime Analysis in Support of Patrol (Reinier et al.), 148

Crime in the United States, see Uniform Crime Reports (UCR)

Crimen fals: defined, 499

Crime prevention, *see* Prevention of crime

Criminal courts, 37, 215, 238, 239; defined, 499

Criminal incident (hypothetical), 44–45

Criminal intent (*mens rea*), 17–18; and classification of offense, 21; and defense, 194

Criminal investigation, *see* Investigation

Criminal Investigation Division (CID), U.S. Army, 97. *See also* Military, the

Criminal Investigation Process, The (Rand Corporation report), 123

Criminalistics: defined, 500

Criminal Justice Council (state agency), 295

"Criminal Justice Highway," 46–47, 66, 74

Criminal justice process: defined, 499–500

Criminal justice system: career opportunities in, 446–458; as cause of crime, 435–438; decentralization of power in, 441–442; defined, 500; flow diagrams of, 30, 57, 58; future of, 37, 402, 406–416, 420, 429–430, 437–438, 441–442; injustice in, 438–442; nature and goals of, 28–39, 56–57, 330, 394–402, 426–427; primary functional areas of, 34–39; reform of, 420–430; as system (System 1 and System 2), 29–39; systems approach to, 392–402

Criminal Justice System (National Advisory Commission), 28

Criminal law: basic premises and purpose of, 16–19, 22; change in, 439–440; defined, 9–10; 500; development of, 11–16, 18; procedural, 9, 32, 53, 57. *See also* Law(s)

Criminology, modern, 4, 315, 317, 328, 338–339

Critical path method (CPM), 116

Cromwell, Oliver, 85

Cross examination: by accused, 358, 382; defined, 500; of prosecution, 56, 63; of witnesses, 33, 67, 68, 185, 259, 382

CTP (coordinated team patrol), 123. *See also* Team policing

Culture(s): and cultural lag, 223; root problems (and police awareness) of, 128. *See also* Minority groups(s); Society

Custody and control, correctional, 310–315; conflict of, with rehabilitation, 37–38, 308, 312, 323–324, 325, 341, 353–354, 381; control procedures, 312; and discipline, 298, 312, 314–315; modern concepts of, 328, 338–339. *See also* Pretrial procedures; Punishment; Restraint; Security, prison; Solitary confinement

Customs Service, U.S., 97, 447–448

Dallas Experiment, The: Organizational Reform (Police Foundation report), 149

Dane law, 12

Dangerous offender, 254

Darrow, Clarence Seward, 195

Data bank, 410–411. *See also* Technology

Davis v. *California*, 494

Debs, Eugene V., 195

Decembri, 12

Decentralization of power, 441–442

Defendant: defined, 500

Defense: arraignment of, *see* Arraignment; counsel for, *see* Counsel; and defense motions, 68, 257–258; justification as, 194; multijurisdictional process and, 28; preparation of (and pretrial discovery), 56, 256, 257–258; presentation of case by, 67, 68–69, 185–186, 193–196, 255, 259; public defender and, 191–193, 203–206, 207, 270–271, (defined) 503; right to, 33, 44, 49; role of, 195–196; and testimony of accused, 49, 69, 193–194, 258, 260. *See also* Plea(s); Plea bargaining

Defense, U.S. Department of, 97, 236, 237, 421, 450

Definite sentence, 261. *See also* Sentencing

De Laudibus Legum Angliae (Fortescue), 166

Delaware juvenile court system, 243

Delay, *see* Time lapse

Delinquency: defined, 241; jurisdiction, 72; juvenile, 72–74, 241–242, 302–303, 344–346; and predelinquent agencies, programs, 287, 302–303, 308, 315–316

Deportation, 372

Deposition: defined, 500

Des Moines, Iowa: model community-based correctional system, 293

Detainer (legal order), 371; defined, 500

Detectives: county, 100; and police detective units, 108, 119, 121–123

Detention: defined, 500; pretrial, *see* Pretrial procedures; preventive, 254. *See also* Custody and control, correctional

Detention centers, *see* Jail(s); Juveniles

Detention hearing, 73, 243

Deterrence theory, *see* Prevention of crime

Developing and Managing an Anti-Corruption Program: A Manual for Police Administrators, 151

Directed patrol, 118. *See also* Police

Directed verdict, *see* Verdict(s)

Direct evidence, 259. *See also* Evidence

Direct examination, *see* Witness(es)

Discipline: committees, 297–298; police (conduct), 151; prisoner, 298, 312, 314–315. *See also* Punishment

Discovery; defined, 500; pretrial, *see* Defense

Discretion: court (in sentencing and/or granting parole), 37, 261–262, 342, 344, 347, 366, 383, 440; individual, vs. administrative policy, 155–157, 200; minimizing, 201–202, 383, 415, 440–441; police, 49, 153–159, 201, 438–440; prosecution (decision to charge and/or prosecute), 35–36, 59–60, 173, 178, 180, 200–203, 206–207, 253, 260, 270, 272, 438

Discrimination, 439, 440

Dismissal of cases, 223, 257

Dispositional hearing, *see* Hearing(s)

District, police territorial, 113

District attorney, 35–36, 100, 169, 206; organization of office of (California), 172. *See also* Prosecution

District courts, 36, 238; defined, 500; federal, 71, 231, 233, 234–235, 244, 250; state, 246; territorial, 235, (defined) 504. *See also* Court(s)

District of Columbia: Court of General Sessions, 255; district court, 233, 235; juvenile court, 243, 341; parole system, 367, 383

Diversion: defined, 180, 500; and diversion programs (sentencing alternatives), 60, 262, 287, 288, 303, (defined) 500. *See also* Rehabilitation; Screening, pretrial; Sentencing

Division (police unit); defined, 111

Docket: defined, 500

Doctrine of *parens patriae*, *see* *Parens patriae*, doctrine of

Domestic relations courts: defined, 500. *See also* Family courts

Double jeopardy, 194, 244; defined, 500

Draconian code, 82. *See also* Code(s)

Draper v. *United States*, 494

Drug addiction, 194, 437; programs, 287, 301, 325

Drug Enforcement Administration, 92, 97, 447, 448

Drunkenness, *see* Intoxication

Dual court system, 217, 244–246; defined, 500. *See also* Court system

Due process of law, 31, 33–34, 44; in court-martial convictions, 237; defined, 500; development of concept of, 215, 474; disregard of (in misdemeanor cases), 223, 255; in juvenile courts, 74, 242, 243; in parole proceedings, 373, 382; Supreme Court and, 48, 65, 250

Education and training, 434; advocacy, 204–205; for careers in criminal justice system, 448, 450–457 *passim;* correctional worker, 285, 322, 323, 330, 424, 428, 455; in crime prevention, 118, 148; criminal justice process as, 20; and educational function of law, 8; of judges, 268–269, 428, 430; juvenile, 37, 74, 242, 283–284, 294, 296, 297, 302, 311, 318, 322, 325, 370; lawyer, 204–205, 456–457; police, 88, 91, 131, 133, 137–138, 139–141, 160, 414, 424, 425, 427, 429, 452; prisoner, 298, 317–318, 454; prosecution personnel, 427–428; punishment as, 19; requirements for custodial officers, 285; traffic enforcement, 120

Edward I, king of England, 84, 166

Edward III, king of England, 85

Edward IV, king of England, 168

Effectiveness of Punishment and Other Measures of Treatment, The (Hood), 353

Electronic data processing, 409–411. *See also* Technology

Elkins v. *United States,* 493

Elmira (New York) Reformatory, 282, 288, 367

Embezzlement, 21

Employing Civilians for Police Work (National Institute of Law Enforcement and Criminal Justice), 134

Employment (career opportunities) in criminal justice system, 446–458

England, 216; appellate review system in, 263; Common Law of, 10, 166, 167, 214, 217, 339; law enforcement development in, 83–88, 92, 140, 214–215, 280, 281; medieval, criminal law and courts in, 12–13, 32, 166–168, 204, 214–215, 240, 241; news media in, 274; Norman Conquest of, 10, 12, 84, 214; Police Acts (legislation) in, 86–88; police services in, 83–88, 92; probation study in, 352; vagrancy statute in, 13

English Penal Servitude Act (1853), 366

Enhancement statutes, 261

Equal Employment Opportunity Commission, U.S., 138

Equity: as branch of law, 215; concept of, defined, 500

Escobedo v. *Illinois,* 496

Essoiner: defined, 500

Etiology, criminal, 4

Europe: law enforcement authority in, 83, 85; medieval court system in, 213, 215–216, 217; prison system in, 280, 288; probation study in, 353; "trial by battle" in, 32

Evidence: circumstantial, 259, 499; defined, 259, 500, 501; hearsay, 260, 501; legality of, 123, 260; motion to suppress, 66, 70, 258; protection of (at crime scene), 117–118, 121; rebuttal, 67; rules of, 68, 259, 260; rules of, ignored, 255 (*see also* Due process of law)

Examination: defined, 500; of jury (*voir dire*), 185; preliminary (or examining trial), *see* Hearing(s); of witnesses, *see* Witness(es)

Exchange justice, *see* Plea bargaining

Exclusionary rule, 48, 61, 252, 258; defined, 500

Executive branch (government), 473; defined, 500

Executive clemency, 364; defined, 500. *See also* Pardon

Expert witnesses, *see* Witness(es)

Family courts: defined, 500–501; trend toward, 242, 243

Family Crisis Intervention Unit, 414

Federal Bar Association, 384

Federal Bureau of Investigation (FBI), 92, 93, 97, 143, 293, 408; career opportunities in, 446–447, 448, 449, 456; data files, 410; fingerprint files, 406; training programs, 140, 141. *See also Uniform Crime Reports (UCR)*

Federal Bureau of Prisons, 293–294, 296, 304, 314, 323, 327. *See also* Prisons, U.S. Bureau of

Federal Communications Commission (FCC), 97

Federal Community Treatment Center (Chicago), 293

Federal correctional organizations, 293–294, 304, 327

Federal court system, *see* Court system

Federal Job Information Centers, 449

Federal law enforcement, *see* Law enforcement

Federal Law Enforcement Center (Georgia), 448

Federal Office of Personnel Management, 455

Federal Prison Industries, Inc., 293

Federal Prison System, 288

FEDNET (proposed), 410

Feedback (in correctional system), 400

Fees: bondsman, 254; lawyer, 191. *See also* Bail; Indigence

Felony(ies), 22, 30, 47; courts dealing with, 238, 240; defined, 20–21, 238, 501; four, under Henry V, 168; and jurisdiction, 21, 53; and jury trial, 258; juvenile, 244; preliminary hearings in, 36, 253; and provision of counsel, 205; and time lapse between arrest and trial, 223 (*see also* Time lapse)

Fielding, Henry, 85–86, 87

Fielding, Sir John, 85–86

Field interrogation, 45; defined, 501

Fine(s), 256; limitation on (and jurisdiction), 230, 255

Fingerprinting, 406, 407

Fiscal operations and funding, 428–429; British police, 85, 87;

correctional system, 285–286, 288, 293, 298, 302, 309, 313–323 *passim,* 326–331 *passim,* 354; and cost-benefit analysis of criminal justice system, 398–399; court system, 245; law enforcement, 150, 191, 203–204; legal aid, 192, 205–206 (*see also* Indigence); and parole costs, 354, 366, 372, 385; police, 90, 101, 103, 104, 137, 145, 354, 408, 412; and probation system costs, 328, 346, 352–353, 354, 356; research, 150–151, 357, 421–422; technological improvement, 412. *See also* Salaries; Taxation

Fixed sentence, 261; defined, 501. *See also* Sentencing

Florida: correctional workers, 323; court system streamlined, 246, 250; Crime Information Center, 409; Division of Corrections, 295; halfway house program, 287, 316; juvenile courts, 243

Florida State Police, 98

Food service function, correctional, 313–314

Ford, Gerald R., 364

Forensic: defined, 501. *See also* Laboratories, forensic

Fortescue, Sir John, 166

Fort Knox, Kentucky: provost marshal at, 139

Fosdick, Raymond B., 103

Foster homes, 287, 303, 304, 316, 346

Frank, Jerome, 225

Franklin v. *Shields,* 382

Frankpledge system, 83–84, 92

Fraternal Order of Police, 146, 453

Frisk, 45, 48; defined, 501

Funding, *see* Fiscal operations and funding

Gagon v. Scarpelli, 382, 497

Gantt chart, 116

Garfield, James A., 133

Gault, In re, 73, 74, 159, 245, 358, 497

General court-martial, 236; defined, 501. *See also* Military court system

General jurisdiction: defined, 501. *See also* Jurisdiction, court

General Services Administration, 410

Genghis Khan (Temujin), 85

George II, king of England, 85

Georgia: juvenile court system, 243; misdemeanor cases in, 255

Gettinger, Stephen, 331

Gideon v. *Wainwright,* 72, 190, 205, 496

Glades Correctional Institution (Florida), 293

Good cause, 66

"Good-time" laws, 367; defined, 501. *See also* Parole

Grand jury, 36, 253, 256; defined, 46, 61, 181, 271, 501; indictment by, 30, 48, 56, 59, 60–62, 181–182, 204, 270; origin of, 215; powers of, 182. *See also* Indictment, bill of; Jury

Greece, ancient: law and courts in, 12, 82, 166, 213

Griggs v. *Duke Power Company,* 138

Group homes, 284, 287, 303, 346

Guam district court, 235

Guidance, *see* Counseling; Prerelease guidance

Guilt: and guilty act (*actus reus*), 17; and guilty plea, *see* Plea(s). *See also* Probable cause; Proof (of guilt)

Habeas corpus, writ of, 70–71, 244, 255, 263; defined, 501

Habitual criminal statutes, 261

Halfway houses, 37, 262, 286–287, 288, 303–304, 309, 312, 318; for juveniles, 284, 316; opposition to, 327, 330

Hamilton v. *Alabama,* 190

Hammurabi, Code of, 82, 146–148

Hard Labour Act (England), 280

Harm: as element of crime, 18; social, crimes of, 20

Harrison Act (1914), 16

Harvard Law Review, 11

Harvard Law School, 218, 224

Hawes-Cooper Act (1934), 284

Health, Education and Welfare, Children's Bureau of the Department of, 241, 346

Hearing(s): adjudicatory, 73–74; detention, 73, 243; disciplinary (of prisoners), 312, 314; dispositional, 74, 243; evidentiary, 71; parole, 372–373, 382; preliminary, 30, 36, 52, 54, 55–56, 59, 180–181, 253, 255, 256, (defined) 46, 503; presentence, 70 (*see also* Investigation); probationers' revocation, 190, 348; sentence, (defined) 503, (factors in) 261–262

Hearsay evidence, 260; defined, 501. *See also* Evidence

Henry I, king of England, 13

Henry II, king of England, 13, 214

Henry V, king of England, 168

Henry VIII, king of England, 168

Higher courts: defined, 501. *See also* Court(s)

Highfields project (New Jersey), 287

Holmes, Oliver Wendell, Jr., 219, 224, 225, 232, 475

Home rule, *see* Autonomy

Homicide (manslaughter or murder), 18, 20, 53, 194

Hood, Roger, 353

Hoover, J. Edgar, 92

Howard, John, 281

How to Find the Law (Roalfe, ed.), 72

Hue and cry principle, 83, 84, 86

Hughes, Charles Evans, 232

Hung jury, 69; defined, 501. *See also* Jury

Husse, William, 168

Idaho parole system, 369

Illinois: court system, 67, 241; parole system, 383; probation laws, 341

Immigration and Naturalization Service, U.S. (Border Patrol), 92, 97, 447

Impeachment: of judge, 269–270; of Supreme Court justice, 231; of witness, 259

Imprisonment, *see* Custody and control, correctional; Prison(s); Prisoners

Indeterminate sentence: defined, 501. *See also* Sentencing

Index, traffic law enforcement, 120

Index crimes, *see Uniform Crime Reports (UCR)*

India, scriptures from, 366

Indiana: abolishes parole, 383

Indictment, bill of, 30, 48, 56, 59, 60–62, 181, 204, 270, 271; defined, 46, 182, 501; motion to dismiss, 66, 70, (defined) 502; or no bill, 61

Indigence: and appeal, 262; and bail, 193; and defense, 54, 190, 191, 193, 253, 256, 270; and fines, 256. *See also* Bail; Defense

Industrial Revolution, 86

Industry: and industrial psychology, 413; and industrial security (in fight against crime), 103; programs of, within correctional facilities, 314

Infamous and noninfamous crimes, 21

Inferior courts, *see* Lower courts; Trial Courts

Information (legal document), 46–47, 62, 181, 182, 253, 256; defined, 501

Information (supplied to police), 153, 182, 494–495; defense request for (pretrial discovery), 56, 256, 257–258; and protection of informer, 253, 272; on terrorism, 123–124

Information systems: police, 132, 409–410; statistical, 415; trial court, computerization of, 57, 59. *See also* Technology

Initial appearance, 52–53, 253, 255; defined, 46, 501

Injunction order: defined, 501

Innocence, presumption of, 63, 190, 197, 258. *See also* Adversary system

Innocent III (pope), 214, 215

Innovations, police department, *see* Police

Inputs (into correctional system), 400

Insanity, legal, 260

Intake (reception), correctional, 50, 72–73, 243, 312–313, 344–345

Intelligence (information), police, 123–124

Intent, *see* Criminal intent

Interlocutory decision: defined, 501

Intermediate appellate courts, 233, 238, 239; defined, 501. *See also* Appellate court(s)

Internal Revenue Service, 92, 97, 447

Internal Security Inspectors, 447

International Association of Chiefs of Police (IACP), 91, 102, 103, 136, 141, 145, 151, 451, 453

International City Management Association, 145, 453

Interrogation, field, 45; defined, 501. *See also* Investigation

Interstate Commerce Commission (ICC), 97

Intoxication: as defense, 194; and detoxification, 262, 302; and drunks in jail population, 325, 328; police as agency dealing with, 35, 439–440

Investigation: military, 236–237; police (at scene of crime), 121–123; prearrest, 45; presentence, 37, 44, 65, 70, 256, 261, 338, 347–348, 430; by prosecutor, 36, 55; Rand Corporation studies of, 123, 153; traffic accident, 119–120

Iowa regional prison system, 286

Iraq, early settlement in, 82

Irvine v. *California,* 493

Israel, court system in, 213

Jail(s), 37, 284–286, 288; county, 301–302, 330; defined, 47; future role of, 328–329; juvenile detention in, 243, 301, 328; lack of services and programs in, 315, 317, 318, 328; overcrowding of, 285, 302, 324, 330, 331; regional concept of, 302; security of, 311 (*see also* Security, prison); U.S. system of, 299, 301–302, 327. *See also* Prison(s)

James I, king of England, 215

Jay, John, 231

Jefferson, Thomas, 232

John, king of England, 214

John Jay College of Criminal Justice, 140

Johnson v. *Avery,* 497

Johnson v. *Zerbst,* 496

Jones v. *United States,* 494

Judge(s): administrative assistance for, 272–273; defined, 212, 501; education and training of, 268–269, 428, 430; federal, as "managers," 331, 392; impeachment of, 269–270; instructions and charge to jury, 67, 69, 260; military (U.S.), 236–237; number of, in state, appellate and trial courts, 28, 220–222, 238, 240; role of, 268, 269; royal, in England, 13; selection of, 269; sentencing by, 31, 70; and trial by bench, 67, 185, 258, 498. *See also* Sentencing

Judge-advocate general, 236, 237

Judicial branch (government), 473; defined, 501

Judicial circuits, *see* Court(s)

Judicial community, *see* Court system; Prosecution

Judicial ordeal, 32–33, 214

Judicial process, 257. *See also* Trial(s)

Judicial review, power of, 232, 473. *See also* Supreme Court, U.S.

Judiciary Act of 1789 (U.S.), 92, 168, 216, 225

"Judiciary clause" (of Constitution), 216

Jurisdiction, court, 21, 36, 52–53; appellate, 230, 233, 238, 239; challenge to, 264; concurrent, 239, 240, 499; defined, 230, 499, 501, 502; delinquency and dependency, 72, 241; federal, in states and territories, 72, 235; general, 36, 230, 239, 242, 256, 501; juvenile, 73, 242, 286, 344, 356; limited, 230, 233, 239, 240–241, 502; lower-court, 256; military, 235; mobility and, 142; and multijurisdictional process, 28; original, 230, 233, 235, 239, 244, 502; overlapping, 244–245, 255; special, 230, 240

Jurisdiction, police, 113; defined, 501

Jurisdictional structure of criminal justice operations (community level), 100, 300

Jury: arguments to, 67, 69, 260; challenges for cause and peremptory challenges to, 185, 194–195, 258–259, 502; deliberations, 67, 69, 260; examination (*voir dire*) and selection of, 67, 185, 194, 258; function, 268; hung, 69, 260; instructions and charge to, 67, 69, 260; petit, 214, 258–259, 271, (defined) 502; sentencing by, 31, 70, 260, 271; trial by, 67, 74, 185–186, 239, 258–260, 271; verdict of, 69, 260. *See also* Court system; Grand jury

Jury panel: defined, 501

Justice (presiding judge), 212; chief justice, 499; defined, 499, 501. *See also* Judge(s)

Justice (principle): administration of criminal, 44–74; "fighting system of," 31, 32; as goal of system, 401; and injustice in system, 438–442; military, 235, 236, 237; quality of, as measure of civilization, 213; social, 434–435

Justice, U.S. Department of, 97, 136, 142, 148, 169–170, 274, 293; and career opportunities, 446, 447, 453, 456

Justice board, 201

Justice(s) of the peace, 268; established in England, 85, 86

Justice of the peace courts, 36, 212, 217, 238, 240, 246; defined, 501

Justification as defense, 194

Juvenile courts, 71–74, 240, 241–244, 303; defined, 501; jurisdiction of, 73, 242, 286, 344, 346; origin of, 286, 341; power of, 74, 345

Juveniles: arrest proceedings against, 50, 71–74, 159–160, 241, 243, 245, 358, 497; detention centers for, 243, 284–288 *passim*, 301, 302–304, 316, 322, 325, 328, 345; foster and group homes for, 284, 287, 303, 304, 316, 346; houses of refuge for, 367; and juvenile delinquency, 72–74, 241–242, 302–303, 344–346 (*see also* Delinquency); parole for, 370; policy agencies responsible for, 295–296, 316; on probation, 243, 286, 287, 341, 342–343, 344–346; prosecution of (or refusal to)

charge), 202, 243; training schools and programs for, 37, 74, 242, 283–284, 294, 296, 297, 302, 311, 318, 322, 325, 370; youth service bureaus for, 242, 262, 286, 288, 302–303, (defined) 504

Kansas: juvenile court system, 243

Kansas City, Missouri, Police Department studies, 117n, 118, 145, 152, 399, 421, 422

Kennedy, John F., 92

Kentucky State Police, 100

Kent v. *United States,* 73, 159, 497

Ker v. *California,* 493

King's Court, 214

King's peace, 13, 168

Kinsey, Alfred, 438

"Labeling" theory, 287, 435–436

Labor: police division of (homogeneous asssignment), 109, 111; as punishment, *see* Punishment

Laboratories, forensic, 88, 122; technology in, 406–408. *See also* Technology

Labor unions, 284, 302; and police unions, 146, 156–157

Ladensky, Jack, 196

Larceny, 20, 21

Lateral entry (hiring policy), 424. *See also* Personnel, criminal justice system

Law(s): as cause of crime, 435, 437–438; changes in, 6; constitutional, 159 (*see also* Constitution, U.S.); and correctional organizations, 292; creation and accumulation of, 5–6, 10–11, 223, 237, 435, 437–438 (*see also* Congress, U.S.; Legislatures); defined, 4–5, 6, 502; divisions of, 9; of evidence, 259; ex post facto, 16; functions of, 6–8, 166; primitive, 5, 11–12; procedural, 9, 74, 159; as profession, development of, 166–167; rule of, 8–9, 16, (defined) 503; sociology of, 5–8, 38, 48–49; sources of, 10–11; substantive, 5, 9, 11, 21, 22, 159, (defined) 504. *See also* Criminal law; Legal profession

Law enforcement: alternative forms

of, 143–145, 439–440; and authority to act, 8–9, 35, 111, 174; "better," need for, 128; career opportunities in, 446–453; code of ethics, 99; community, 28, 29, 35, 38–39, 82, 83 (*see also* Correctional organizations; Court system; Police); contemporary issues in, 128–160; federal, 92, 93, 96–97, 103–104, 446–450; goals of, vs. correctional goals, 330 (*see also* Criminal justice system); history of, 82–93; local, county and municipal, 15, 98–101, 104, 451–453; police patrol and, 117 (*see also* Police); selective, 120; state, 89–92, 93, 97–98, 100–101, 104, 450–451; traffic, 98, 120; U.S., development of, 88–93; U.S., machinery of (1980), 16, 28, 96

Law Enforcement Assistance Administration (LEAA), *see* Office of Justice Assistance, Research and Statistics (OJARS)

Law enforcement officer: defined, 502

Lay witnesses, 260. *See also* Witness(es)

Leading questions, 259

Legal aid services, 192, 226, 457

Legal citation, 72

Legal codes, *see* Code(s)

Legality: of evidence, 123, 260; principle of, 16–17

Legal profession: career opportunities in, 456–458; development of, 166–167; minority groups in, 196. *See also* Counsel; Law(s)

Legis Acto Sacramenti, 33

Legislative branch (government), 473; defined, 502

Legislative courts, 230, 231

Legislatures: and responsibility for statutes and correctional standards, 10, 100, 138, 331, 370, 383, 438, 440

Leonard, V.A., 122

Lexis, 400

Liability, vicarious, 142. *See also* Responsibility

Limited jurisdiction: defined, 502. *See also* Jurisdiction, court

Litigation: against and by police, 141–142, 157

Lockup, 301–302, 308. *See also* Jail(s)

London Police Act (1839), 87. *See also* England

Los Angeles City Police, 143

Los Angeles County, 99, 101, 174

Louisiana courts, 217

Lower courts, 36, 230, 238, 240, 245, 255; abolishment of, 225, 241; defined, 502; duties of, 240; jurisdiction of, 256. *See also* Court(s); Trial courts

Lower federal courts, 233. *See also* Court system

McCray v. *Illinois,* 495

McKinley, William, 92

McNabb v. *United States,* 495

McNeil Island (Washington), 293–294

Magistrate(s), 30, 240; defined, 212, 502; United States, 235, (defined) 504. *See also* Judge(s)

Magistrate courts, 30, 36, 217, 230, 253; defined, 502. *See also* Court(s)

Magna Carta, 13, 214

Maine: juvenile training facilities in, 283; parole system, 383; sentencing, 441

Mala in se and *Mala prohibita* crimes, 21; defined, 502

Mallory v. *United States,* 495

Management, *see* Administration and management

Mandamus, writ of, 206

Mandatory release: defined, 502. *See also* Release (of prisoner)

Manslaughter, nonnegligent/voluntary, 20, 53, 194

Mapp v. *Ohio,* 493

Marbury v. *Madison,* 232, 473

Marshal(s): provost, (England) 85, (U.S.) 139; town (U.S.), 89, 90; United States (federal), 92, 93, 97, 235

Marshall, John, 232, 473

Marshall, Thurgood, 232 *illus.*

Martial law, 85

Marxism, 226

Maryland Parole Commission, 384

Massachusetts, 14; early prisons in, 281, 283, 367; juvenile court system and institutions, 243, 325; probation system, 339–341, 352; state law enforcement, 91

Massiah v. *United States,* 496

Maximum security, *see* Security, prison

Mayne, Sir Richard, 87

Media, *see* News media

Medical service, correctional, 314, 315, 323

Mempha v. *Rhay,* 348, 497

Mental state (*mens rea*), *see* Criminal intent

Merchant police, 85, 101

Mercian law, 12

Merit system, *see* Civil service system

Metropolitan courts, 217. *See also* Court(s)

Metropolitan Police (London), 87, 89, 92–111; and Police Act (1829), 86–87

Michigan State Police, 98

Military, the: correctional organizations, 294–295, 304; education and training of, in U.S., 140; and martial law, 85; and military police at Fort Knox, 139. *See also* Defense, U.S. Department of

Military Court of Appeals, U.S., 231, 237; defined, 504

Military court system, 231, 235–237, 304; courts martial defined, 501, 503, 504. *See also* Court system

Minnesota: group homes in, 287; probation system, 341, 357

Minority group(s): and "dirty work" of legal profession, 196; police behavior toward (ethnic groups), 157, 441; police recruitment of, 136–137, 138, 157, 423, 424–425; probation agencies and, 355

Miranda v. *Arizona,* 49, 74, 156, 190, 225, 252, 392, 496

Misdemeanor(s), 22, 47, 168; courts dealing with, 238; defined, 20–21; 238, 502; disposition of, 253, 255–256, 346; and disregard of

due process, 223, 255; and information (vs. indictment), 62, 253; and jurisdiction, 21, 53; and jury trial, 258; misdemeanant probation, 343, 346–347; and provision of counsel, 205

Missouri Plan (judicial selection), 269

Mistrial, 69. *See also* Trial(s)

Mobility: and jurisdictional limitations, 142–143; limited, and court system, 240; and social order, 417

Model Penal Code, 437

Model State Judicial Article, The, 246

Modus operandi, 52, 122; defined, 502

Morality and law, 15–16

Moral turpitude, crimes of, 21–22

Morrissey v. *Brewer,* 373, 382, 497

Motion(s): for bill of particulars, 66, 258, 502; for change of venue, 66, 257; for continuance, 66, 67, 258, 502; defense, 68, 257–258; defined, 66, 502; to dismiss, 66, 70, 502; filing, 66; pretrial, 66, 67, 70, 257–258; posttrial, 67, 260; to suppress evidence, 66, 70, 258

Municipal Corporations Act (England, 1835), 87

Municipal courts, *see* Court(s)

Municipal law enforcement, *see* Law enforcement

Municipal Yearbook, 453

Murder, 194; defined, 18, 20; and denial of bail, 53

Murphy, Patrick, 149

Mutual Agreement Programming (MAP), 374–375. *See also* Parole

Narcanon program, 287

Narcosis: as defense, 194. *See also* Drug addiction

National Academy (Quantico, Virginia), 140

National Advisory Commission on Civil Disorders, 442

National Advisory Commission on Criminal Justice Standards and Goals, 28–29, 103, 128, 246, 358; recommendations of, 203, 250, 262, 263, 274, 285, 410, 425–427, (on defense) 191, 192, 196, (on plea bargaining) 183, 257, (on police) 35, 152, (on probation) 344, 345, (on training programs) 204–205, 323

National Appeals Court (proposed), 232

National Center for State Courts, 217

National Commission on Productivity, 145

National Council of Juvenile Court Judges, 346

National Council on Crime and Delinquency (NCCD), 242, 329, 338, 346, 358, 425, 456

National Crime Commission, 35, 103, 104, 128, 245, 352, 353, 396; recommendations of, 129–132, 241, 242, 253, 257, 274, 344, 354, 420, 422, 424, 434; Standards for Parole (1967), 366, 380, 381, 383; Task Force for Corrections, 283, 286, 287, 302, 338, 354

National Crime Information Center (NCIC), 103, 142–143, 409, 410

National Crime Panel, 396

National Crime Prevention Institute (NCPI), 148

National Criminal Justice Information System (proposed), 410–411

National Employment Listing Service, 451, 453, 456

National Institute of Corrections (Federal Bureau of Prisons), 323

National Institute of Law Enforcement and Criminal Justice, 134, 150–151, 357

National Jail Census (1978), 284

National Labor Relations Board, 233

National Municipal League, 246

National Science Foundation, 143

National Security Agency, 449

National Training School for Boys, 294

National Volunteer Parole Aide Program (ABA), 384

National Workshop for Correctional and Parole Administrators, 364

Navy, U.S., 294–295, 304, 450. *See also* Military, the

Neutron activation analysis, 408

Nevada prison camps, 284

New Hampshire parole system, 369

New Jersey: probation laws, 341; special corrections programs, 287; state court system unified, 246, 270

New Jersey State Police, 92

New Mexico Police, 92

News media, 268, 274, 354, 396

New York City Police Department, 414; data communication system, 143; established (1844), 89, 93; women officers in, 139

New York (State): correctional workers, 323; Court of the Judiciary, 270; juvenile training facilities, 283; probation system, 352

Night watch: England, 84, 85; United States, 89

1984 (Orwell), 416

Nixon, Richard M., 364

No bill, 61. *See also* Indictment, bill of

Nolo contendere, see Plea(s)

Nol pros (nolle prosequi), 59–60, 173, 184; defined, 502

Non vult plea, 184. *See also* Plea(s)

Norman Conquest, *see* England

North Carolina state police organizations, 98

Northwestern University, 141

Not guilty plea, *see* Plea(s)

Nuclear Regulatory Commission (NRC), 97

Oath-taking, 33, 166, 271

Office of Justice Assistance, Research and Statistics (OJARS), 102, 104, 133, 136, 293, 304, 309, 357, 396, 408, 502; police study funded by, 128, 137, 150–151, 421–422; reform programs funded by, 288, 354, 428–429; state agencies funded by, 295, 299

Office of Law Enforcement Assistance (OLEA, later OJARS), 103, 133

Office of Naval Intelligence (ONI), U.S. Navy, 97

Office of Special Intelligency (OSI), U.S. Air Force, 97

Office of Special Projects, U.S. Navy, 116

Ogburn, William, 223

Ohio Peace Officer Training Academy, 136

Omission (failure to act), 17

Omnibus Crime Control Act (1968), 225, 358

Opinion: appellate court decisions, 263; expressed by witness, 260

Oregon v. Hass, 496

Original jurisdiction: defined, 502. *See also* Jurisdiction, court

Orozco v. Texas, 496

Orwell, George, 416

Ostrom, Elinor, 143, 144

Outputs (from correctional system), 400

"Overcriminalization," 16

Pardon, 364, 366, 368; defined, 500

Parens patriae, doctrine of, 73, 241–242; defined, 500, 502

Parishes, 85

Parker, A. E., 91

Parks, Robert B., 143

Parochial police, 85

Parole, 292, 327; abolition of, advocated, 283, 288, 317, 383; administration of, 338, 343, 368, 370, 383–384; board(s), 364, 367, 370, 371–373, 381–385; conditions of, 38, 374; contract, 374–375; cost of, 354, 366, 372, 385; defined, 39, 47, 364–365, 502; distinguished from probation, 364; eligibility and selection for, 261, 316, 365, 368, 370–373, 384, 438; history of, 366–368; increased use of, 37, 356, 372; juvenile, 370; period (length of), 373; personnel, *see* Personnel, criminal justice system; philosophy and objectives of, 365–366, 380, 383; problems, 380–383, 385, 392; process, 368–375; revocation of, defined, 502 (*see also* violation/revocation of, *below*); right to, and rights of parolees, 365–366, 372–373, 382, 385, 497; supervision, 38, 39, 365, 366–

Parole (*cont.*)

367, 368, 370, 373–374, 381, 383, 454; violation/revocation of, 47, 366, 370, 372–373, 374, 381, 382, 502

Parole, U.S. Board of, 373, 380, 384

PATRIC computer system, 409–410. *See also* Technology

Patrol, *see* Police

Patrol Administration: Managing by Objectives (Shanahan), 115

Peel, Sir Robert, 86, 89, 92, 111, 148

Penal codes, 9

Pendleton (civil service) Act (1883), 133

Penitentiary: development of, 280, 293. *See also* Prison(s)

Penn, William, 280–281

Pennsylvania: correctional workers, 323; county and municipal law enforcement, 100; court system, 237–238; early prison system, 281, 282, 288, 367; Emergency Service (Montgomery County), 439; probation system, 352, 357; State Police (formerly State Constabulary), 91–92, 93, 98, 139, 146

Penology, 4; "Golden Age of," 282

Peremptory challenge: defined, 502. *See also* Jury

Perjury, 271

Personnel, criminal justice system, 422–428; administrative, 268, 272–273; civilian (in law enforcement), 134–135; civil service, 133–134, 285; correctional workers, 28, 322–324, 326, 330, 454–455; judiciary, 28, 217, 218 (*see also* Judge[s]); lateral entry (hiring policy) of, 424; management, of correctional organizations, 309–310 (*see also* Administration and management); parole, 28, 38, 39, 343, 355, 365–374 *passim,* 381, 383–385, 454; police, 28, 85, 96, 109, 112–113, 129, 131–141, 144, 145; probation, 28, 37, 39, 73, 243, 342, 343, 354–357, 383, 414, 454; prosecution, 28, 203–205, 270, 427–428 (*see also* Prosecu-

tion); recruitment of, 131, 136–138, 157, 422–424; volunteer, 357, 367, 384, 414. *See also* Career opportunities in criminal justice system; Case load; Salaries; Working conditions

PERT (Program Evaluation and Review Technique), 116

Petit jury, 214, 258–259, 271; defined, 502. *See also* Jury

Philadelphia: alleged police brutality in, 142; early police in, 89

Pilot Study of Correctional Training and Manpower (1967), 355

Pinkerton Agency, 101

Plaintiff: defined, 502

Planning: correctional administration, 308–309, 326–327, 330, 358, 380–381; police administration, 114, 130, 143, 149–155. *See also* Administration and management; Research

Plato, 366

Platoon, police, 113

Plea(s): guilty, 62–63, 65, 66, 182–183, 184, 197, 245, 255, 256–257, 270, (defined) 503; *nolo contendere,* 62, 184, 256, 257, (defined) 503; *non vult,* 184; not guilty, 62–63, 66, 184, 256, (defined) 503

Plea bargaining, 47, 64–66, 154, 223, 255, 257, 261, 270; abolition of, recommended, 184, 257; defined, 502; as desirable skill, 197; as result of overburdened system, 173, 182–183, 192 (*see also* Case load)

Police: administration, 108–116, 123–124, 128–132, 135, 142, 148–157, 420; assessment of, 135–136; authority (unity and chain of command), 111–112; auxiliary, 101, 131; and auxiliary services, 109, 144; beat system, 88, 113, 119; and citizen-to-patrol officer ratio, 144; communications, *see* Communications, technological; in community (service to, and relations with), 34–35, 39, 108, 113, 119, 128–130, 152, 157–158, 435, 440; conflict of, with courts, 273, 392–393, 398; coordination and co-

operation, 103–104, 112, 129, 130, 132, 142–144, 149, 392, 408; counseling by, 414; county, 99–100; in criminal justice process, 29, 31, 34–35, 38–39, 44, 130, 200, 250, 451–453; departmental organization of, 109–116, 122, 129, 153, (and reorganization) 143–145; discipline (conduct), 151; discretion of, 49, 153–159, 201, 438, 440; as expert witnesses, 260; of future, 429; history of, 83–93; innovations and modernizations in U.S. departments, 90–91, 113–116; intelligence (information), 123–124; interrogations by, 45, 52, 501; jurisdiction/territory, 113, (defined) 501; lawsuits against and by, 141–142, 157; line and non-line functions of, 108–109, 117; military model for, 83; nongovernmental, 101–103; operations, 116–124, 129, 131; origin of word, 84; patrol, 108, 113, 115, 117–119, 121–123, 131, 144, 416, 422, (split force) 153; personnel, *see* Personnel, criminal justice system; planning and research, 130, 143, 149–155; productivity, 103, 123, 145; and prosecution, 36, 123, 200–201; recruitment, 131, 136–137, 138, 157; reform, 149; response time, 34, 152–153, 399–400, 421; role of, 128, 130, 133; salaries of, 85, 87, 101, 131, 135, 137, 423, 453; special, 101, 108; specialization among, 108, 121–123, 131, 153, 452–453; state, 28, 91–93, 98, 100, 101; as state's witness, 272; team policing, 119, 123, 130; training, *see* Education and training; unions, 146, 156–157; and vicarious liability, 142; women as, 88, 139, 423–424, 452. *See also* Self-policing

Police Acts (England, 1829, 1839, 1919, 1946), 86–88

Police chief(s): county, 100; duties and responsibilities of, 111, 299; election of, 89; executive training of, 139–141. *See also* International

Association of Chiefs of Police (IACP)

Police Chief (journal), 136

Police College (Bramshill, England), 88, 140

Police courts, 238

Police Crime Analysis Unit Handbook (Justice Department), 148

Police des moeurs, 84

Police Federation (England), 87

Police Foundation (U.S.), 145, 149, 422

Police Officers Standards and Training (POST), 104

Police Post-War Committee (England), 88

Policing Metropolitan America (Ostrom, Parks and Whitaker), 143

Politics: and parole, 372; prosecutors and, 186, 206

Polygraph tests, 154

Posse comitatus, 84

Post, police territorial, 113

Postal (Inspection) Service, U.S., 97, 448, 449

Postconviction remedies, 262–264; defined, 503. *See also* Appeal(s); *Habeas corpus,* writ of

Pound, Roscoe, 218–219, 225

Powell, Lewis F., 137, 232 *illus.*

Powell v. *Alabama,* 496

Prearrest, presentence investigation, *see* Investigation

Precedent, doctrine of (*stare decisis*), 10, 22, 215, 216, 244, 245; defined, 503, 504

Precinct, police territorial, 113

Predelinquents, *see* Delinquency

Prediction (probability of behavior), *see* Behavior

Preliminary hearing, *see* Hearing(s)

Premeditation, *see* Criminal intent

Prerelease guidance: centers for, 286–287, 288, 303–304, 311, 365; counseling, 318. *See also* Halfway houses

Presentence investigation, *see* Investigation

Presentence report: defined, 503

Presentment, 253. *See also* Initial appearance

President's Commission on Law Enforcement and Administration

of Justice, *see* National Crime Commission

Preston v. *United States,* 493

Pretrial procedures, 250–258, 324; negotiations, 182–184; and pretrial confinement/detention, 285–286, 299, 308, 328; pretrial discovery, 56, 256, 257–258; pretrial motions, 66, 67, 70, 257–258; pretrial release report, 54. *See also* Arraignment; Arrest; Bail; Hearing(s); Plea(s); Screening, pretrial

Prevention of crime, 19, 102, 114, 146–148, 438; and deterrence theory, 19, 31, 34, 123, 280, 292, 331; English Metropolitan Police and (1829), 86–87; police patrol and, 109, 117, 118, 153. *See also* Punishment

Preventive bail/detention, 254. *See also* Bail

Prima facie case, 55

Prison(s), 37, 39, 497; costs, 328; defined, 47; differentiated between adults and children, 241; of future, 430; organizations within (formal and informal), 297–299; overcrowding of, 283, 323–324, 328; U.S. system, 280–288, 293–294, 304, 328. *See also* Security, prison

Prison camps, 284

Prisoners: classification of, *see* Security, prison; numbers of (prison population), 285, 324–325; services for, 315–318, 497. *See also* Custody and control, correctional; Punishment; Rehabilitation; Release (of prisoner)

Prisons, U.S. Bureau of, 284, 292. *See also* Federal Bureau of Prisons

Private police agencies, 85, 101–103. *See also* Self-policing

Private Security Task Force, 102

Privileged communications, 193, 259; defined, 503

Privilegium clericale, 339

Probability (of behavior), *see* Behavior

Probable cause, 55, 56, 178, 256; defined, 45, 57, 503

Probation, 31, 292, 328, 497;

administration of, 338, 341, 342–343, 348, 355–356, 358, 368, 373; and auxiliary programs, 346; conditions, 342, 348; costs, 328, 346, 352–353, 354, 356; defined, 37, 39, 47, 70, 338, 364, 503; distinguished from parole, 364; eligibility for, 341, 342, 343–344, 346, 438; history of, 339–341, 343, 352; in hypothetical criminal incident, 64–66; increased use of, 325, 341, 353, 355, 356; juvenile, 243, 286, 287, 341, 342–343, 344–346; misdemeanant, 343, 346–347; personnel, *see* Personnel, criminal justice system; philosophy and objective of, 338–339, 341, 352–353; problems, 353–356; process, 342; and shock probation law, 64–65, 66; subsidy programs, 356–357; supervision, 39, 345–346, 355–356, 357, 454; violation/revocation of, 47, 190, 342, 348, 352, 354

Procedural law: civil, 72; criminal, 9, 32, 53, 57; defined, 503

Productivity, police, *see* Police

Program Evaluation and Review Technique (PERT), 116

Progressive movement, 225–226

Prohibition, 6, 8, 16, 437

Project on Standards for Criminal Justice (ABA), 338, 352

Project STAR (System and Training Analysis of Requirements for Criminal Justice Participants), 133, 137

PROMIS computer system, 400. *See also* Technology

Proof (of guilt), 256; beyond reasonable doubt, 33, 57, 63, 67, 74, 257, 258, (defined) 498, 503; burden of, 49, 55, 63, 68, 257. *See also* Probable cause

Prosecution, 28; alternatives to, 202–203; and burden of proof, 49, 55, 63, 68, 257; control of, 201–202, 206; defined, 167; discretion of (decision to charge and/or prosecute), 35–36, 59–60, 173, 178–180, 200–203, 206–207, 253, 260, 270, 272, 438; duties and responsibilities of, 35–36, 39,

Prosecution (*cont.*)
44, 55, 167–174, 186, 200–207, 256, 268, 270, 422; education of personnel, 427–428; history and development of (U.S.), 167–174; improvement of function of, 203–205; and influence and authority of contemporary prosecutor, 174, 186, 200, 206–207, 270; of juveniles, 202, 243; presentation of case by, 67–70, 154, 185–186, 259; and pretrial negotiations, 182–184, 256; and prosecutorial encounters in justice system, 179 *fig.*; two models of approach in (rigorous vs. laissez-faire), 173–174. *See also* Adversary system; Attorney(s) general; District attorney; *Nol pros*; Plea bargaining

Provost marshal: in England, 85; U.S. Army, 294

Psychiatrists: as court consultants, 348; as expert witnesses, 260, 272; as therapists, 262, 323

Psychology, industrial and experimental, 413–414. *See also* Behavior; Counseling

Public, the, *see* Society

Public administration, 412–413. *See also* Administration and management

Public defender, 191–193, 203–206, 207, 270–271; defined, 503. *See also* Defense

Puerto Rico: district court, 235; juvenile probation service, 346

Punishment: corporal, 14, (in juvenile reformatories) 283; discipline committees and, 297–298; hard labor as, 14, 280, 281, 282, 284; purpose of, 19–20, 280; regimentation as, 312, 313, 328; religious influence on, 14; and retribution, 19, 20, 37, 292, 354; treatment vs., *see* Rehabilitation

Quakers, early correctional systems of, 280–281, 288, 367

Quarter session courts: defined, 503. *See also* Court(s)

Quinney, Richard, 12

Rand Corporation studies, 153, 173–174, 193, 421; report, *The Criminal Investigation Process,* 123

Rape, 20, 21, 203; statutory, defined, 503–504

Rap sheet, 51, 410

Real evidence, 259. *See also* Evidence

Reasonable doubt, 33, 57, 63, 67, 74, 257, 258; defined, 498, 503. *See also* Proof (of guilt)

Reasonable suspicion, 48, 57, 178. *See also* Probable cause

Rebuttal, 67, 68, 185, 186, 259

Reception, *see* Intake (reception), correctional

Recidivism, 60, 203, 283, 298, 325, 327; defined, 503

Recreation, prisoner, 315, 317–318. *See also* Rehabilitation

Recruitment of correctional workers, *see* Personnel, criminal justice system

Reform: of court system, 218–219, 223, 225–226, 331; of criminal justice system, 420–430; of offender, 37, 280, 282; police, 149; prison, 280, 281, 282–283, 285–286, 288; societal, 434–435

Reformatories, *see* Elmira (New York) Reformatory; Juveniles; Women

Regimentation, *see* Punishment

Rehabilitation, 19, 20, 292, 400, 454; abandonment of concept of, 31, 283, 288, 322, 441; conflict between control/punishment and, 37–38, 308, 312, 323–324, 325, 341, 353–354, 381; early prison systems and, 281–282; of juveniles, 283, 287, 303; sentencing and, 44, 70, 261; short-term programs of, 316; and treatment (vs. punishment), 37, 60, 288, 310, 315–318, 325, 356. *See also* Community-based corrections; Diversion; Education and training; Halfway houses; Probation

Rehnquist, William H., 232 *illus.*

Reinier, G. Holbart, et al., 148

Release (of prisoner): at expiration of sentence, 364–365; mandatory, statutory or conditional, 364,

369–370, (defined) 502; temporary, 364, 365; work furlough or, 301, 317, 327, 384. *See also* Bail; Pardon; Parole; Prerelease guidance

Release-on-recognizance (ROR), 53, 54, 58, 254, 255. *See also* Bail

Religion: and law, 14, 15, 213–214, 215; and rehabilitation, 281. *See also* Roman Catholic Church

Research: correctional administration, 310, 326–327, 357, 398, 421; court-related, 225, 420–421, 422; on parole, 382, 383, 385; police administration, 149–155, 420, 422. *See also* Administration and management; Planning

Res gestae, 260

Responsibility: and accountability (individual), 116, 214, 325, 328; of correctional system, 400; in court systems, 243, 245, 246, 250, 258, 330–331; criminal, 18, (age of) 72, 242; delegation/delineation of, 83, 92, 111; government, (for corrections) 327, (for law enforcement) 97, (to prosecute) 201; legislative, 10, 100, 138, 331, 370, 383, 430, 440; of parolee, 384; police, and distribution of, 96, 108, 111, 117, 122; of prison warden/jailer, 297, 301; for probation, 342; public, 330; "state" (vs. community), 84; and vicarious liability, 142. *See also* Self-policing

Restraint, 19, 20. *See also* Custody and control, correctional

Retribution, *see* Punishment

Revenue Cutter Service, U.S., 92, 93

Reversal: of conviction, 70, 71; of probation order, 358. *See also* Appeal(s)

Rhode Island probation laws, 341

Right(s): of appeal, 44, 74, 239, 262–263; to clergy (*privilegium clericale*), 339; constitutional, 10, 44, 48–49, 52, 73–74, 253, 259, 260, 324, 352, 383–384, 473–491 (*see also* Constitution, U.S.); to counsel, 33, 49, 50, 52, 54, 159, 190, 270, 348, 358, 382, 496; to defense, 33, 44, 49; individual, law and, 5, 12, 28, 33–34, 63, 373, 374, 401, 411; of juveniles, 73–74, 159–160, 358; to parole, 365–366, 382; to parole hearings, 372–373, 382, 497; of police, to formulate policy, 156; to preliminary hearing, 52; to refrain from testifying, 49, 69, 193–194, 258, 260; to remain silent under questioning, 49, 50, 52, 245; to terminate interview, 49; violation of (and *habeas corpus*), 71

Robbery, 20; aggravated, 50–51

Rochester, New York, Police Department: CTP experiment by, 123

Rochin v. *California,* 492

Roman Catholic Church, 13, 213, 214, 280.
See also Religion

Rome, ancient: law and law enforcement in, 12, 33, 82–83, 166, 213, 214; Twelve Tables of, 12, 14, 33, 83

Roosevelt, Theodore, 224

ROR, *see* Release-on-recognizance (ROR)

Roselt, Arthur, 192

Route, police territorial, 113

Rowan, Sir Charles, 87

Royal Commission on the Police (England), 88

Rule of law, 8–9, 16; defined, 503

Russian courts, 216

Safe Streets Act (1968), 150, 428

Salaries, 422, 423; grand jury, 271; jail personnel, 285, 323; judges', 269; law enforcement, 448, 449, 451, 453, 455; legal profession, 457; police, 85, 87, 101, 131, 135, 137, 423, 453; prosecutors, 173, 203–204, 270, 423; public defender, 204, 205–206; Supreme Court justices, 231

Sanhedrin, Great, 213

Schmerber v. *California,* 493

Schneckloth v. *Bustamonte,* 71, 494

Schrag, Clarence, 354

Science, 415–416; behavioral, 412–415. *See also* Technology

Scopes trial, 195

Scotland: team policing in, 119

Scotland Yard, 87

Screening, pretrial, 50–51, 178, 344–345; defined, 180, 503. *See also* Discretion; Pretrial procedures

Search(es), 159; pat-down (frisk), 45, 48; and seizures, "reasonable"/unreasonable, 48, 252, 492–494

Search warrant, 15–48; defined, 55, 252, 503. *See also* Warrants

Secret Service, U.S., 92, 93, 97, 447, 449

Section (police unit): defined, 111

Sector, police territorial, 113

Securities and Exchange Commission, 233

Security, prison, 400, 454; classification of prisoners, 282, 297, 298, 310, 313, 326; defined, 310; maximum, 293, 297, 310; medium, 310–311; minimum, 91, 311–312

Security, private, *see* Private police agencies

Segregation of prisoners, *see* Solitary confinement

Selective enforcement: defined, 503. *See also* Discretion

Self-fulfilling prophecy, 436. *See also* Behavior

Self-incrimination: protection against (Fifth Amendment), 33, 49, 69, 73, 74, 260, 358. *See also* Confessions

Self-policing: of community, 82, 83, 84, 85, 89, 92; and private agencies, 85, 101–103

Senate, U.S.: and Supreme Court, 231

Sentence hearing: defined, 503; factors in, 261–262. *See also* Hearing(s)

Sentencing, 67, 257, 420; alternatives, 37, 262, 304, 342, 430, (defined) 503 (*see also* Diversion; Probation); case load and, 256; concurrent, consecutive, 261, 499; defined, 47, 261, 503; as deterrence of crime, 31; disparity in, 70, 262, 271, 284, 371, 438, 440; factors in, 261–262, 371,

440; indeterminate, 70, 261, 366, 367, 371, 383, 441, (defined) 501; by jury, 31, 70, 260, 271; length of sentence as distinguishing feature, (between felony and misdemeanor) 21, 47, (between infamous and noninfamous crime) 21; objectives of, 261; and parole, 371; and postconviction remedies, 262–264; presentence investigation and, *see* Investigation; reforms advocated, 283; and rehabilitative needs, 44, 70, 261; and shock probation, 64–66

Sergeants (English prosecutors), 168

Servitude (as punishment), 14

Shanahan, Donald T.: *Patrol Administration: Managing by Objectives,* 115

Shang Dynasty, 82

Sheppard, Sam, 274

Sheriff, 301; in county system, 99–100, 140, 285, 299; origin of, in England (as shire-reeve), 84, 85, 92; and team policing (in early U.S.), 119; U.S. adoption of office of, 88–89, 91, 93

Shift (time division): police, 112–113, 119, 453; prison supervision, 298, 455

Shire-reeve, *see* Sheriff

Shock probation law, *see* Sentencing

Smith v. *Illinois,* 495

Social class/disparity, 133, 439, 441

Social control, 5, 6, 7, 9, 11, 212–213, 216, 365, 435

Social Defense Section of the United Nations, 355

Social justice, 434–435, 439; defined, 503

Society: change in, 6, 8, 274–275, 365; expectations by, and demands of, 37, 141, 327, 374, 436; law in, 5–22, 28, 38; maintenance of order in, 7, 15, 82, 83–84, 274, 365 (see also Social control); primitive, 5, 11–12; and public attitude toward corrections, 330, 353, 354, 357, 365, 373, 381–385 *passim* (*see also* Parole); and public as court participant, 268, 273–

Society (*cont.*)
275; self-policing of, 82, 83, 84, 85, 89, 92; state (government) as representative of, 168. *See also* Community-based corrections; Culture(s)

Society (Quaker) for Alleviating the Miseries of Public Prison, 367

Sociology, 4–6, 218–219, 415, 454

Solitary confinement, 281, 282, 298, 315

Solon, 82

Southern Police Institute (University of Louisville), 140–141

Special court-martial, 236. *See also* Military court system

Specialization, police, *see* Police

Special jurisdiction, 230. *See also* Jurisdiction, court

Special sessions courts, 238. *See also* Court(s)

Spinelli v. *United States,* 495

Split-force patrol, *see* Police

Staff, *see* Personnel, criminal justice system

Standard Juvenile Court Act. 346

Standards: ABA Project on, 338, 352; court, 384; for defense, 191–192, 196; education (for correctional personnel), 323, 455; jail, 331; minimum, for police and police chiefs, 137–138, 140–141; parole, 366, 380, 383, 384, 385; probation and probation agency, 344, 355, 358; recruitment, for law-enforcement positions, 136, 424; social class and, 439

Standards and Goals, *see* National Advisory Commission on Criminal Justice Standards and Goals

Star Chamber (England), 215, 224

Stare decisis, see Precedent, doctrine of

State(s): attorney(s) general, 168, 170–172; constitutions, 225, 246; correctional organizations, 295–299, 304, 322, 327, 330; juvenile courts, 341; law enforcement, 89–92, 93, 97–98, 100–101, 104, 450–451; parole systems, 367–368, 373, 375, 383; power of, and safeguards against, 6, 15; prison systems, 304, 316; probation functions, 342–343, 348, 356–357

State, U.S. Department of, 449

State courts, 36; and criminal cases, 244; levels of, 238–241; reforms suggested, 226; reversal of decisions of, 71, 244; subordination of, to U.S., 216; system of, 237–241, 244; variations among, 217, 237–238, 240. *See also* Supreme courts, state

State police, 28; career opportunities with, 450–451; origin of, 91–92, 93; powers of, 98, 100; resident trooper, 101

Statistics, 415. *See also* Information systems; Technology

"Status offense," 242; defined, 503

Statute of limitations: defined, 504

Statute of Winchester, 84

Statutory law, 10, 22

Statutory rape: defined, 504. *See also* Rape

Statutory release, *see* Release (of prisoner)

Stead, John, 140

Stevens, John P., 232 *illus.*

Stewart, Potter, 232 *illus.*

Stoner v. *California,* 493

Substantive law, 5, 9, 11, 21, 22, 159; defined, 504. *See also* Law(s)

Summary court-martial, 236; defined, 504. *See also* Military court system

Summary procedure, 22

Superior courts, 230, 238. *See also* Court(s)

Supervision, *see* Parole; Probation

Supreme Court, U.S., 54, 138, 217, 224, 225, 263, 264, 348; in *Bakke* case, 137; case load of, 231, 232, 234, 235; as court of appeals, 233, 235, 237; defined, 504; and due process, 48, 65, 250; and federal *habeas corpus,* 71; and indigent offenders, 190, 256; and jurisdiction, 230, 233; and juvenile cases (*parens patriae*), 73–74, 241–242, 245, 358; and *Miranda* case, 49, 74, 190, 392; origin, composition and power of, 215, 216, 231–233; and parole, 373, 382; and plea bargaining, 64; and reversal of state court decisions, 71, 244, 274; and speedy trial, 67–68; and statutory law, 10

Supreme courts, state, 36, 246, 358

Sutherland, Edwin, 11

Synanon program, 287

Systems approach, 392–402; contributions and benefits, 397–400; limitations, 401–402

Tarlton v. *Clark,* 366

Task Force Report (National Crime Commission): *Corrections,* 347; *The Police,* 35

Taxation: for police protection, 85, 103, 133, 428; and tax limitation measures, 145, 429. *See also* Fiscal operations and funding

Team policing, 119, 130; and CTP, 123. *See also* Police

Technology, 223, 274, 416, 429, 438; communications, 408–409; computer, 57, 59, 143, 395, 397, 400, 409–411; laboratory, 406–408; weapons, 411–412. *See also* Communications, technological

Teeters, Nagley K., 364

Temporary release, *see* Release (of prisoner)

Temujin (Genghis Khan), 85

Territorial district courts: defined, 504. *See also* District courts

Territory: division into parishes, 85. *See also* Beat system; Jurisdiction, police

Terrorism, 123–124, 226

Testimony: of accused, 49, 69, 193–194, 258, 260; defined, 259, 504. *See also* Witness(es)

Texas, 245; Board/Department of Corrections, 292, 297; commission plan (judiciary), 270; correctional workers, 323; Dallas police reform, 149; Department of Public Safety, 139; juvenile court system, 243; prison programs, 296, 314, 318, 324, 353; state penal code definition of burglary, 17; state police powers, 98

Texas Rangers, 91, 93, 98

Theft, 20, 21

Thomas, D. J., 137

Ticket of leave, 366
Time: concurrence in (and criminal act), 18; of police response, 34, 152–153, 399–400, 421. *See also* Shift (time division)
Time lapse: in appeal, 263; between arrest and trial, 52, 223, 250, 251, 253, 257, 258, 324, 420, 429; between presentment and hearing, 256; and speedy trial, *see* Trial(s)
Time magazine, 383
Tithing system, 83–84, 86
Torts, 10, 11, 12, 168; defined, 504; and tort claims against U.S., 235
Townsend v. Sain, 71
Traffic: engineering, 120–121; law enforcement, 98, 120; specialized units for, 108, 119
Traffic courts, 217, 240, 255
Traffic Institute, 141
Training, training schools, *see* Education and training
Transportation: and jurisdictional boundaries, 142; police equipment, 90, 132
Transportation, U.S. Department of, 97
Treasury Department, U.S., 92, 447–448, 456; and Treasury Guard Force, 97
Treatment, *see* Rehabilitation
Trial(s): "by battle," 32–33; by bench (vs. jury), 67, 185, 258, 498; defined, 47, 502; disposition of misdemeanors as, 255; by jury, 67, 74, 185–186, 239, 258–260, 271; and mistrial, 69, 260; records of, 35, 230, 240–241, 255; "speedy," 49, 67–68, 196, 250, 255, 256, 324, 421; and trial process, 33, 39, 44, 67–71, 258–262, (goal of) 37, (sequence of events in) 67. *See also* Pretrial procedures
Trial courts: arraignment in, 62–66; in court system, 36, 212, 231, 234, 239, 241; information systems, 57, 59; judges and terms for, 220–222; of original and general jurisdictions (state), 239–240; and trial process, 67–71. *See also* Trial(s)
Trial *de novo,* 241; defined, 504

Tribunal(s), 212, 213; defined, 504. *See also* Court(s)
True bill, 61, 62. *See also* Indictment, bill of
Tuns (population groups), 83
Twelve Tables, *see* Rome, ancient

Uniform Code of Military Justice (UCMJ), 236, 237, 304
Uniform Crime Reports (*UCR*) (Federal Bureau of Investigation), 20, 103, 148, 152, 396, 415; defined, 504
UNI-GOV, 143
Unions, *see* Labor unions
United States: agencies, 97 (*see also* individual agencies, departments); colonial, postrevolutionary and contemporary, 13–16, 216–217, 225; court system development in, 214, 215, 216–218, 225; historical influence on law and court system of, 166, 214, 215, 216–217; police department organization in, 83; police development in, 88–93; population increase in (1900–1980), 223; prosecution process in (history and development of), 167–174. *See also* Adversary system; Constitution, U.S.; Court system; Federal correctional organizations; Law enforcement; Military, the; Supreme Court, U.S.
U.S. Abstracts, 217
United States v. Ventresca, 495
United States v. Wade, 190
Unity of command (police), 87, 111. *See also* Administration and management
University of Louisville, 140–141, 148
Urban Institute, 145
Urban planning, police and, 150
Ur-Nammu, 82
Utah special corrections programs, 287

Vale v. Louisiana, 494
Venire, 258. *See also* Jury
Venireman: defined, 504
Venue: change of, defined, 499;

concept of, defined, 230, 504; motion for change of, 66, 257
Verdict(s), 69, 185; defined, 504; directed, 78, 185; guilty, 256, 258, 260, (under courts martial) 237. *See also* Appeal(s)
Vermont, 437; prison system, 286, 296, 323; probation laws, 341
Vicarious liability, 142
Victimless crime, *see* Crime(s)
Vigilantes, 89, 274. *See also* Self-policing
Virginia: attorney general in, 168; probation and parole programs, 356, 383
Virgin Islands district court, 235
Voiceprinting, 407
Voir dire, see Jury
Vollmer, August, 90–91
Volstead Act (1919), 8, 16, 437
Volunteer (correctional) workers, *see* Personnel, criminal justice system

Wade decision, 190
Wardens, prison, 282, 297
Warden v. Hayden, 493
Warning (to suspect), 48, 50, 52, 74
Warrants: defined, 504. *See also* Arrest warrant; Bench warrant; Search warrant
Warren, Earl, 232, 392
Washington, George, 231
Washington, D.C.: trial delays protested, 257
Washington (State), 357, 369
Watch (police time division), *see* Shift
Webster case, 137
Weeks v. United States, 492
Wessex law, 12
Westlaw, 400
Whitaker, Gordon P., 143
White, Byron R., 232 *illus.*
White, E. B., 124
White House Police Force, 97
Wickersham Commission on Law Observance and Enforcement, 91, 103, 128, 241, 282, 283
Wilkins, Leslie T., 364
William, Duke of Normandy (William the Conqueror), 13, 84
William II, king of England, 13

Wilmington Police Department split-force patrol, 153
Wilson, O. W., 122
Winship, In re, 74, 497
Wisconsin Division of Corrections, 287
Witness(es), 268; cross-examination of, 33, 67, 68, 185, 259, 382; defined, 271–272; direct examination of, 67, 68, 185, 259; impeachment of, 259; lay/expert, 260, 272; right to cross-examine, 33; state's, police as, 272. *See also* Testimony
Wolf v. *Colorado,* 492
Wolff v. *McDonnell,* 497
Women: on police force, 88, 139, 423–424, 452; reformatories for, 283, 288, 294
Work camps, 284
Work furlough or release, *see* Release (of prisoner)
Workhouses, 280, 281, 285, 301
Working conditions: correctional personnel, 422–423, 455; law enforcement personnel, 451, 453; legal profession, 457
Workload, *see* Case load
Writ(s), 215; of *certiorari,* 263, 264; of *habeas corpus,* 70–71, 244, 255, 263; of mandamus, 206

Youth courts, 242. *See also* Juvenile courts
Youth services bureau: defined, 504. *See also* Juveniles

ABCDEFGHIJ-BP-8210/80